PASTORAL
LITURGY

Joseph A. Jungmann, S.J.

Christian Classics ✠ Notre Dame, Indiana

Originally published in German under the title *Liturgisches Erbe und Pastorale Gegenwart* by Tyrolia–Verlag, Innsbruck.

First published in English by Challoner Publications (Liturgy) Ltd., 1962.

Introduction © 2014 by John F. Baldovin, S.J.

Founded in 1865, Ave Maria Press is a ministry of the United States Province of Holy Cross.

www.christian-classics.com

Paperback ISBN-13 978-0-87061-287-9

Cover image © Erich Lessing / Art Resource, NY.

Cover and text design by David R. Scholtes.

Printed and bound in the United States of America.

CONTENTS

PART III
THE FUNDAMENTALS OF LITURGY AND KERYGMA

PREFACE

This collection of studies and lectures, made chiefly at the instigation of Verlag Tyrolia, brings together works from various and often slightly inaccessible places. They have been chosen because they ought to arouse some interest even beyond purely specialist circles, and quite apart from the often accidental circumstances of their origin. So as to avoid repetition the text has been shortened in many places. On the other hand, the references have been expanded and brought up to date as much as was necessary.

Simply by observing the external presentation of the various sections, we see that quite unlike things are being united within a single cover; historical studies with detailed source-references on the one hand, lectures and articles from periodicals with a purely practical purpose on the other. On closer examination, however, the reader will see that both types are concerned with the same field of enquiry—the questions of current liturgical revival on a foundation of well-founded Church tradition; and more than this, that along the whole way the same pastoral ideal is being kept in mind. What is dug out of the sources by laborious analysis becomes the standard according to which is finally constructed a tidy synthesis, touching the details of practical life. We may even dare to hope that the concern which underlies all of these essays may come fully into its own through this reciprocal development and illumination, and that the work of the kingdom of God today may thereby be advanced.

Joseph A. Jungmann, S.J.
Innsbruck,
Lent, 1960

INTRODUCTION TO THE NEW EDITION
BY JOHN F. BALDOVIN, S.J.

The fiftieth anniversary of Vatican II's Constitution on the Sacred Liturgy (Dec. 4, 2013), as well as the encouragement of the preconciliar Eucharist by Pope Benedict XVI (2007) and the introduction of a new English translation of the Roman Missal (2011), have all sparked debate about the liturgical reforms of the past half century. The republication of Joseph Jungmann's *Pastoral Liturgy*, which has been out of print for many years, provides a welcome opportunity to refresh our understanding of the motives for that reform.

Pastoral Liturgy was published in English in 1962 as the Council was getting its start. The book is made up of a collection of essays on historical and pastoral subjects, which Jungmann wrote in the 1940s and '50s. Clearly the most famous and influential of these is "The Defeat of Teutonic Arianism and the Revolution in Religious Culture in the Early Middle Ages." Originally published in the *Zeitschrift für katholische Theologie* in 1947 (and updated for the collection in the late 1950s), this essay is uncannily prophetic of the outcome of the Constitution on the Sacred Liturgy (*Sacrosanctum Concilium*). In fact, as Kathleen Hughes has argued, the essay demonstrates the significant influence that Jungmann had on the creation of the document.[1]

Jungmann was born in 1889 in the small village of Taufers, tucked away in the Pustertal in the Austrian South Tyrol.[2] He studied for the diocesan priesthood and was ordained in 1913. Four years later he entered the Austrian Province of the Society of Jesus. In 1923, he completed his first doctoral thesis on the subject of grace in the catechetical and homiletic texts of the first three centuries CE. Two years later he completed his second doctoral thesis, or *Habilitationschrift*, titled "The Place of Christ in Liturgical Prayer."[3] It was to the subject of that thesis that Jungmann returned in "The Defeat of Teutonic Arianism." Jungmann served as professor of practical theology and liturgy at the Jesuit faculty of theology at Innsbruck from 1926 until his retirement in 1963—with the exception of 1939–1945, when the Innsbruck faculty was closed down by the Nazis. Jungmann also served as editor of the important theological journal *Zeitschrift für katholische Theologie* until his retirement.[4]

Jungmann's greatest achievement was his magisterial history of the Roman liturgy of the Eucharist: *Missarum Sollemnia: The Mass of the Roman Rite: Its Origins and Development*.[5] There, with impressive scholarship (despite the lack of his library) he traced the development of the Roman liturgy as a whole, as well as each of its elements. This work was probably the single most important scholarly contribution that helped to prepare for Vatican II's *Sacrosanctum Concilium*. On the basis of his scholarship Jungmann became a member of the preparatory commission for this document and also served on the *Consilium* that implemented the Constitution after the Council's end. His only work that was published in English first, *The Early Liturgy: to the Time of Gregory the Great*,[6] was based on a series of lectures he gave at the University of Notre Dame summer school in the 1950s.

The present work, *Pastoral Liturgy*—whose full German title, *Liturgisches Erbe und Pastorale Gegenwart*, could be rendered literally in English as "Liturgical Inheritance and the Present Pastoral Situation"—appeared in German as the Council was in preparation. Here Jungmann deals with a number of historical issues, the pastoral implications of which the Council would have to face. The subjects range from some rather technical issues—like the relationship between the Bishop of Rome's Sunday celebration of the Eucharist and the celebrations in other churches in the city,[7] and the priest touching the gifts during the Eucharistic Prayer[8]— to more clearly pastoral issues like the reform of the Church's daily prayer[9] and the liturgy as a school of faith.[10] It should be stressed that *Pastoral Liturgy* is a fine translation for the book's title, since Jungmann himself always insisted that his first concern was the life of the Church and not simply historical research as such. In the introduction to the volume, which honored his life and work, he made it quite clear that his most prominent concern was always pastoral theology and the proclamation of the faith.[11]

A quarter of the book is taken up by the essay, "The Defeat of Teutonic Arianism." The remainder of my introduction will concentrate on this extremely important piece.[12] Jungmann's major concern from the outset is to understand the development of liturgy and piety in relation to the development of Christian doctrine. In terms of liturgical prayer, the crucial turning point comes with the Arian crisis of the fourth century and its insistence on the equal divinity of the Son with the Father. Of course, theologically speaking, there is no problem at all with this affirmation. But Jungmann does find the liturgical consequences somewhat problematic. The language of worship experiences a subtle shift—from the agency of Christ (to the Father *through* Christ) to an emphasis on the Trinity as such. The result is that the role of Christ as high priestly mediator in salvation history is downplayed, and the coherent picture of salvation history gives way to individual moments in that history. In Christian art, for example, the crucified Lord tends to replace images of the risen Christ.

There seem to be two processes at work here. In the first place, Catholic Christians in the West (over)emphasized the Trinity against the invading foreign tribes (Vandals, Visigoths, et al.) who had been evangelized by the Arians. Secondly, the Germanic (or Teutonic) mentality favored a rather subjective and reified imagination over the spiritual world of the ancients, which was often characterized as a Platonic worldview. The significance of the transformation of Christianity from the Late Antique world of the Mediterranean to the new Northern (Germanic or Teutonic) culture should not be underestimated. According to theologians like Alexander Gerken, it particularly affected the ability to understand symbol in tension with reality, which was an important characteristic of early Christian thinking with regard to the sacraments.[13]

Jungmann traces similar developments in the Greek East, of which he states: "This warfare [over Christological formulae] was essentially the defense of the Church's inheritance, but concentration of attention on the threatened points and the bitterness engendered by repulse of heresy recoiled in a change of religious outlook" (10). Byzantine prayers to Christ and to the Theotokos (Mary) are examples he gives of this shift. For Jungmann, liturgical prayer addressed to Christ began only in the late fifth century; but that view has been challenged recently by Albert Gerhards, who finds official Eucharistic prayer addressed to Christ through-

out the Greek Anaphora of St. Gregory Nazianzen and partially
in the Anaphora of Addai and Mari, which both predate the fifth
century.[14] More recently Jungmann's views on prayer to Christ
have been nuanced by Bryan Spinks, who argues that Jungmann
neglected a good deal of evidence from sources like apocryphal
prayer texts.[15]

Jungmann proceeds to outline the development of Christological (and Marian) piety in the West. He describes the difference
succinctly in the following passage:

> The distinction between primitive and medieval
> Christianity is . . . that for the Fathers, the hu-
> manity of Christ is the starting off place for the
> new humanity, the new creation now irradiated
> with divinity—as they are ever ready to declaim
> against heresy; whereas the Middle Ages sees the
> humanity of Christ primarily as it was in the days
> of His earthly life, in the form of a servant, in
> that form which—contrasting with all that faith
> knows of divine transcendence—it can alone ap-
> peal to sense and arouse feelings of compassion,
> of amazement, of thanksgiving and repentance in
> the hearts of the faithful. (57)

He then deals with the aspects of the liturgy that grow increasingly distant for the faithful in the course of the Middle Ages,
such as language and access to communion. He does not dispar-
age all of this development. He realizes that much of this piety
has led to true holiness, but at the same time he insists that the
clericalization of the liturgy as it was experienced on the eve of the
Reformation has also led to a certain hypertrophy.[16] He continues
to trace similar developments in the period of the Baroque.

Jungmann concludes his *tour de force* with a balanced and sober reflection on the relation between historical-liturgical study
and the pastoral needs of the present day. He clearly understands
that liturgical reform does not merely consist in an antiquarian
retrieval of the past but rather in the adaptation of a corporate
understanding of Christian worship to contemporary social and

cultural circumstances. Towards the end of the piece, he makes the plea that "[l]iturgy must become pastoral," (98) and continues with prescriptions regarding various aspects of the Church's liturgical life.

I began this introduction by claiming that Jungmann was prophetic with regard to the Vatican II reform of the liturgy. The reader can easily judge whether this claim is accurate from the following:

> The construction of the Mass ought to be made more obvious. The chief sections, *Proanaphora* [= Liturgy of the Word], Offertory, Canon, and Communion should be easily distinguished; and various details should be made more intelligible. For example, the symbolic handwashing could be brought forward to the beginning of the Offertory. Scripture reading ought to be enriched by the introduction of a cycle covering several years. Popular intercession which was supplied at the end of the last century by prayers after Mass ought now to come fully into its own through the revival of the prayer of the faithful as an organic part of the Mass immediately after the Scripture readings and sermon. Sunday prefaces should once more take up the note of Easter joy, and the thanksgiving after Communion could be re-fashioned so as to allude to the Communion of the people. (100)

In the current situation, where so much nostalgia and amnesia reign in many parts of the Church, these reprinted essays of a master historian, theologian, and pastoral strategist are a welcome contribution to the conversation.

Notes to the Introduction

1. Kathleen Hughes, "Jungmann's Influence on Vatican II," in Joanne Pierce and Michael Downey, eds., *Source and Summit: Commemorating Josef A. Jungmann. S.J.*, Collegeville: Liturgical Press, 2000, 21–32. All seventeen essays in this volume, prepared to acknowledge the fiftieth anniversary of Jungmann's death, constitute a commentary on this landmark essay, "The Defeat of Teutonic Arianism."

2. The whole of the Alto Adige and South Tyrol became Italian territory after World War I.

3. A translation of the second revised edition was published by Alba House in 1965 and reprinted by Liturgical Press in 1989.

4. For biographical details, see Hans Bernard Meyer, "Das theologische Profil von Josef Andres Jungmann, S.J. " (16.11.1889 bis 26.1.1975), *Liturgisches Jahrbuch* 39 (1989), 195–205; Robert Peiffer, "Josef Jungmann: Laying a Foundation of Vatican II," in Robert Tuzik, ed., *How Firm a Foundation: Leaders of the Liturgical Movement*, Chicago: Liturgy Training Publications, 1990, 58–62; Balthasar Fischer and Hans Bernard Meyer, eds., *J.A. Jungmann: Ein Leben für Liturgie und Kerygma*, Innsbruck: Tyrolia Verlag, 1975.

5. Translated by Francis Brunner, C.Ss.R., New York: Benziger Bros., 2 vols., 1951–1955. First published in German in Vienna in 1948.

6. Translated By Francis Brunner, Notre Dame: University of Notre Dame Press, 1959.

7. "Fermentum: A Symbol of Church Unity and its Observance in the Middle Ages," (287–295); see J. F. Baldovin, "The Fermentum in Fifth Century Rome, *Worship* 79 (2005), 38–53.

8. "Accepit Panem," (277–282); see J. F. Baldovin, "Accepit Panem: The Gestures of the Priest at the Institution Narrative of the Eucharist," in J. Baldovin and N. Mitchell, eds., *Rule of Prayer, Rule of Faith: Essays in Honor of Aidan Kavanagh, O.S.B.*, Collegeville: Pueblo, 1996, 123–139.

9. "Why was the Reform Breviary of Cardinal Quiñonez a Failure?" (200–213).

10. "The Liturgy—A School of Faith," (334–345).

11. J.A. Jungmann, "Um Liturgie und Kerygma," in Fischer and Meyer, 17; see Rudolf Pacik, "Josef Andreas Jungmann: Liturgiegeschtliche Forschung als Mittel religiöser Reform, *Liturgisches Jahrbuch* 43 (1993), 62–84; see also Jungmann's 1960 Preface to this book.

12. See also the fine commentary by Joanne Pierce, "'Christocentric' and 'Corporate': Heretical Reverberations and Living Reform of Western Liturgy," in Pierce and Downey, 7–20; in the same volume, J.F. Baldovin, "The Body of Christ in Celebration: On Eucharistic Liturgy, Theology, and Pastoral Practice," 49–62.

13. See Alexander Gerken, *Die Theologie der Eucharistie*, Munich: Kossel Verlag, 1977, esp. 101–111. See also the chapter "The Heirs: The Germanic Miracle World," in Arthur Mirgeler, *Mutations of Western Christianity*, translated by Edward Quinn, Notre Dame: University of Notre Dame Press, 1964, 44–65; and James Russell, *The Germanization of Medieval Christianity: A Sociohistorical Approach to Religious Transformation*, Oxford: Oxford University Press, 1994.

14. Albert Gerhards, "Prière addresé é Dieu ou au Christ? Relecture d'une these importante de J.A. Jungmann à la lumière de la rechetrche actuelle," in A.M. Triacca and A. Pistoia, eds., *Liturgie, Spiritualité, Culture: Conférences S. Serge XXIX*, Rome: Edizioni Liturgiche, 1983, 101–114; *idem., Die griechische Gregoriosanaphora. Ein Beitrag zur Geschichte des eucharistischen Hochgebets*, Münster: Aschendorff Verlag, 1984.

15. Bryan Spinks, "The Place of Christ in Liturgical Prayer: What Jungmann Omitted to Say," in *idem.*, ed., *The Place of Christ in Liturgical Prayer: Trinity, Christology, and Liturgical Theology*, Collegeville: Liturgical Press, 2008. 1–19.

16. Critics like John Bossy, *Christianity in the West: 1400–1700*, New York: Oxford University Press, 1985, do not always appreciate the nuance of liturgical scholars like Jungmann. See his critique at 37.

ABBREVIATIONS

Albers = Br. Albers, Consuetudines monasticae, 5 Vols. Stuttgart—Monte Cassino 1900/12.

Bäumer-Biron = S. Bäumer, Histoire du Bréviaire, trad. par R. Biron, Paris 1905; as against the German edition (Geschichte des Breviers, Freiburg 1895) it has a better index and additional material.

Baumstark, *Liturgie comparée* = A. Baumstark, *L.c.*, 3. *éd. revue par* B. Botte, Chevetogne 1953.

Baumstark, *Nocturna laus* = A. Baumstark, N.1, *Typen frühchris tlicher Vigilien feier*, ed. by O. Heiming, Münster 1957.

Bishop = E. Bishop, *Liturgica historica*, Oxford 1918.

Brightman = F. Brightman, *Liturgies Eastern and Western*, Oxford 1896.

CSEL = *Corpus Scriptorum ecclesiasticorum latinorum.*

DACL = *Dictionnaire d' archéologie chrétienne et de liturgie.*

DThC = *Dictionnaire de Théologie catholique.*

Dix = Gr. Dix, *The Treatise on the Apostolic Tradition* of St. Hippolytus of Rome, London 1937.

Eph. liturg. = *Ephemerides liturgicae.*

Franz = A. Franz, *Die Messe im deutschen Mittelalter*, Freiburg 1902.

HBS = Henry Bradshaw Society.

Jungmann, *Missarum Sollemnia* = references to 4th edition, Vienna 1958.

JL = *Jahrbuch für Liturgiewissenschaft.*

Klausner = Th. Klausner, *Das römische Capitulare evangeliorum* I, Münster 1935.

Künstle = K. Künstle, *Ikonographie der christlichen Kunst* I, Freiburg 1928.

Leroquais = V. Leroquais, *Les sacramentaire et les Missels manuscrits des bibliothèques publiques de France*, 4 Vols., Paris 1924.

L.ThK = *Lexikon für Theologie und Kirche* (unless stated otherwise, 1st edition 1930/38).

Mansi = J. D. Mansi, *Sacrorum Conciliorum nova et amplissima collectio.* Florence 1759 seq.

Martène = E. Martène, *De antiquis Ecclesiae ritibus*, 2nd edition, 4 vols., Antwerp, 1736/38.

MG = Monumenta Germaniae Historica.

PG = Patrologia Graeca.

PL = Patrologia Latina.

ZkTh = *Zeitschrift für katholische Theologie.*

PART I

THE OVER-ALL HISTORICAL PICTURE

THE DEFEAT OF TEUTONIC ARIANISM
AND THE REVOLUTION IN RELIGIOUS CULTURE
IN THE EARLY MIDDLE AGES

Pierre Pourat's four volume history of the spiritual life is a most instructive guide through changes in spiritual history which have often produced effects far beyond the sphere of ascetics.[1] The book is instructive, moreover, by what it does not present. Volume I concludes, for the West, with the death of Gregory the Great; Volume II, after a cursory glance at Cluny, begins with St. Bernard. These two periods are separated by exactly half a millenium—five hundred years during which no important compendium of spiritual teaching appears to have been written, although, without doubt, neither spiritual nor intellectual life was at a stand-still. Indeed, we may safely assert that in all the two thousand years of the Church's history, no period has ever seen a greater revolution in religious thought and institutions than that which took place in the five centuries between the close of the patristic age and the dawn of scholasticism. After the Christological battles had been fought out, the history of dogma ran into a placid phase interrupted by nothing greater than minor episodes such as the appearance of the Adoptionists and later, of Berengarius. And yet within the limits marked out by dogma there were taking place unobtrusively, certain shifts of accent and changes of viewpoint having consequences so wide that they have left their mark on all subsequent ages right down to our own times.

This book attempts to give some idea of the nature of the problem and of the main lines along which a solution is to be found. It is not a complete study but rather the broad outline of a theme which can be expounded only in a greater number of specialized essays.

The task is to illuminate, within the period mentioned, the history of the kerygma against the background of the history of

1. P. Pourrat, *La spiritualité chrétienne*, 4 volumes. Many editions have appeared since 1918. This reference is to Vols. I and II of 1926 and 1927 respectively.

dogma. To this end, apart from the field of liturgy and Christian art, the whole sphere of ecclesiastical literature belonging to the period would have to be examined, especially homiletic and spiritual writings, even including the fragments of correspondence. The present outline is designed to encourage younger men to undertake more detailed work, the aim of which would be to make the minutiae of historical study serve a higher theological purpose: the discernment of what is an essential possession in religious life, and what the passing fashion of an age.[2]

1. The contrast between early Christian and early medieval religious culture

Our theme concerns changes which have taken place somewhere behind the world of sensible appearances, but which are revealed both in cultural and artistic forms. The following facts—to mention only some of the points of contrast—are particularly obvious.

In the early Christian age the liturgy is essentially *corporate public worship* in which the people's Amen resounds, as St. Jerome tells us, like a peal of heavenly thunder; there is a close connection between altar and people, a fact constantly confirmed by greeting and response, address and assent, and acknowledged also in the verbal form of the prayers, above all by the use of the plural. This is all abundantly proved to us by liturgical forms which endure to this day. And, as our still current texts of all the liturgies again prove, the sacrificial meal of the congregation is regarded as the obvious consummation of the celebration. Five hundred years later the uniformly rich liturgical literature which begins with the Carolingian age shows us how the priest consciously detaches himself from the congregation when the sacrifice proper begins, while the people only follow from a distance the external and visible

2.   Recently published by specialist students: H. J. Schulz, *Die Höllenfahrt als Anastasis:* ZkTh 81 (1959) 1-66; H. B. Meyer, *Alkuin zwischen Antike unde Mittelalter:* ibid. 306-350; 405-454.

action of the celebration in terms of its symbolic meaning. The spiritual action in the Canon, was to remain hidden from the people; and this tendency was later to harden into an unambiguous prohibition of this being translated into the vernacular. In space too, the altar becomes withdrawn from the people and the Communion of the people becomes an exception, something reserved for special feast days.

In early Christian times the celebration is dominated by the *Easter motif*: for a long time Easter is the only universally celebrated festival. It is a Baptismal festival of great splendour with lengthy preparation; and it ends with the Pentecostal festival. From the very beginning this festival had its reflection in the weekly cycle;[1] for Friday and Sunday are, indeed, nothing other than Good Friday and Easter Sunday, stamped with the memory of the Passion and the Resurrection. It is true that in the early Middle Ages Easter and Sunday undergo further development, but, in the Gallican Church especially, Epiphany takes its place along with Easter as a Baptismal climax, preceded similarly by a complete Lenten season. The Christmas cycle enters into rivalry with the Easter cycle. Associated with the principal feasts, as their derivatives, are found—amongst others—the great Marian feasts, of which the Annunciation and the Purification (Candlemas) are also dated by their relation to Christmas. In its understanding of Sunday also, the old theme is overlaid with ideas culled from the Christmas mystery: for not only the Resurrection and the descent of the Holy Spirit, but also the Incarnation has to take place on a Sunday.[2] Thus Sunday is extended to become the day dedicated to the glorification of the Blessed Trinity; and a further consequence is that the weekly cycle is re-cast: Sunday becomes the first day of the week whose basic Trinitarian motif is to be continued throughout the subsequent days in the votive Masses *de Sapientia* and *de Spiritu Sancto*.[3]

The recession of the Easter motif is particularly apparent in the

1. Perhaps more accurately, its *prototype*: v. C. Callewaert, *Sacris erudiri*, Steenbrügge 1940, 300 seq.

2. John's, *liber de dormitione Mariae* (ed. C. Tischendorf, *Apocalypses apocryphae*, Leipzig 1866, 106 seq.); *Bobbio Missal* ed. Loew (HBS 58) 150. For more examples of Irish origin. v. H. Dumaine: DACL IV, 986 seq.

3. A. Franz, *Die Messe im deutschen Mittelalter*, Freiburg 1902, 136-149; cf. also, *Der liturgische Wochenzyklus*.

formulation of liturgical prayer. The ancient Roman tradition held fast, as its inviolable norm, the universal practice of the early Christian liturgy. According to this usage the official prayer which the Church offered at the altar was always addressed to the Father and presented 'through Christ'; and prayer was thus offered to God while the mind was directed to the glorified Redeemer, the transfigured Head of the Church. The Gallic-Carolingian Church departs from this rule. The practice of addressing Christ is more and more set on a par with that of addressing God the Father, and the latter practice, where it appears in newly formulated prayers, favours the form of address to the Blessed Trinity: *suspice, sandacta Trinitas.*

The field of Christian art also yields similar contrasting pictures, with the difference it is true, that the medieval counterpart of early Christian art required a considerably longer time than liturgical forms did before it could attain independence of the old models and win through to a complete disclosure of its own character. As is now everywhere recognized, the characteristic feature of early Christian art is its symbolic—or more exactly—its *eschatological quality.* Hope in the world to come, in the treasures of salvation unlocked by Christ, constitutes its basic theme,[4] as the discoveries of Dura-Europos compel even the sceptical to admit, without relying on the most important sources of these art-monuments—the catacombs and the sarcophagi.[5]

Free from the multiplicity of concrete detail which would be appropriate in a narrative picture, and abbreviated into mere symbols, we find both Old Testament types and New Testament portrayals, all pointing to that victory over death which is assured us through Christ's Resurrection (Noe, Jonas, the youths in the fiery furnace, Daniel in the lion's den, Susanna, the raising of Lazarus); to the water of eternal life (Moses striking the rock, the Samaritan woman at the well); to the heavenly marriage-feast (the miracle of the loaves, a picture of a meal, bread and fish); or Christ himself is depicted as Redeemer, the bringer of salvation, whether it be in the symbol or in the Christ monogram or in the guise of

4. H. Lother, *Realismus und Symbolismus in der altchristlichen Kunst,* Tübingen 1931: J. P. Kirsch, *Der Ide engehalt der ältesten sepulkralen Darstellungen in den römischen Katacomben: Rom. Quartalschrift* 36 (1928) 1-20. L. Hertling—E. Kirschbaum, take a middle position, *Die römischen Katakomben und Martyrer,* Vienna 1950, 229 seq. 247 seq.
5. O. Casel, *Älteste christliche und Christusmysterium:* JL 12 (1934) 1-86.

Orpheus or—most important of all—as the Good Shepherd. The Good Shepherd comes down from heaven to seek the lost sheep—mankind, whom He now brings back rejoicing to the flock, along the way which leads over the Cross.[6] And even in the art of the mighty basilicas where the great representational picture appears,[7] we find Christ in triumph, in heavenly glory, surrounded by the apostles or martyrs or the elders of the Apocalypse, by the saints who have already gone to glory. There is usually a supporting series of Old Testament pictures balanced by a similar series from the New Testament; and, without meaning to portray any exact juxtaposition of particular scenes, the great fact of the history of salvation is brought out, viz. that the Old Testament finds its fulfilment in the redemptive work of the New.[8]

In the Church art of the early Middle Ages the old themes are certainly still alive, as is also the formal style of their execution. This is true also of the old series of pictures. But in the examples we know of the latter from the 9th and 10th centuries, it repeatedly happens that only the New Testament series or only a single Old Testament series appears:[9] the historical perspective of salvation is reduced, while the particular story becomes independent.

We have glimpses of historical painting now also in productions which replace representational pictures. This is true in particular of portrayals of our crucified Lord. What is striking is not that our crucified Lord appears amongst the illustrations of a Bible manuscript or in the panel of a church door, but that He now appears where, according to the idiom of the earlier period, we should have expected to see the glorified Christ. From the 11th century it becomes customary to place a crucifix upon the altar,[10] and by the 12th century the picture of the crucifixion or the crucifixion group has already been installed as the dominant subject

6. Th. Kempf, *Christus, der Hirt. Ursprung und Deutung einer altchristlichen Symbolgestalt*, Rome, 1942, esp. 178. 188 seq. cf. also Th. Klauser, *Studien zur Entstehungsgeschichte christlicher Kunst I: Jahrb. f. Antike und Christentum I* (1958) 20-51.
7. We might rather call this, which occurs so frequently, the *symbol of faith*. On the wall above the altar we find a picture of that which forms the ideal, the belief of the congregation. The same thing is expressed in words in the Eucharist, and we know how close to one another are the most ancient Eucharistic formulae and the oldest confessions of faith.
8. cf. K. Künstle, *Ikonographie der christlichen Kunst I*, Freiburg 1928, 33-37.
9. Künstle I, 55-57.
10. J. Braun, *Das christliche Altargerät*, München 1932, 469 seq.

on the wall behind the altar.[11] Even before this, the picture of the crucifixion appears in isolation, and indeed, without any transfiguring idealization, in the sacramentary as an embellishment at the beginning of the Canon, at the *Te igitur*.[12] It is not long until this has become detached from the text and the representation of the Passion with its supporting figures becomes imbued with even starker realism.[13] In the sculptures of the Romanesque period the crucified Saviour continued at first to be surrounded by a faint radiance of the reigning Christ, which completely disappears only with the advent of Gothic. The reigning Christ himself, the *Maiestas Domini*, is amongst the favourite subjects of Romanesque sculpture.[14] But this supra-temporal expression of the subject— to some extent a secondary historical development—along with the representation of the Crucifixion, detached itself from the picture of the Last Judgment,[15] which appears neither in the place of the *Maiestas* in the apse,[16] nor—as was the usual consequence— above the west door of great cathedrals. And in the end, theological reflection produces the expansion of the theme: the representation of the Blessed Trinity appears on the scene in the form of the Throne of Grace.

And so there are to be seen in this sphere, as in the history of the liturgy, an increasing emphasis on the individual and upon what is subjective, and the beginnings of the break-up of the basic Easter motif. It is the same movement which in Gothic is carried

11.   J. Braun, *Der christliche Altar II*, München 1924, 291 seq. 455 and table on p. 199 seq.
12.   The earliest example is provided by the *Sacramentary of Gellone* (770): V. Leroquais, *Les sacramentaires et les missels manuscrits* IV, Paris 1924, Table II; ibid. Table XV, an example from the 9th century.
13.   *Sacramentary of St. Denis* (11th cent. op. cit. Table XXXI): Mary and John with expressions of pain. This is seen more strongly marked in other examples from the 11th and 12th centuries: Table XX. XLIV.
14.   This raises the question: Have we here the development of a western theme or are we dealing with the adoption of a Byzantine concept? The second view is that of R. Berger, *Die Darstellung des thronenden Christus in der romanischen Kunst*, Reutlingen 1926, 73 seq. cf. U. Rapp, *Das Mysterienbild*, Münsterschwarzach 1952, esp. 127 seq.
15.   Crucifixion group and the World Judgment appear one above the other in the west apse of the Church of St. George, Reichenau (9th-10th cent.); Künstle I, 535. The same juxtaposition, with even greater realism is seen in a later period, e.g. on the main door of Freiburg Münster (ibid. 544 seq.). The contrast between the early Christian parousia— picture which shows the 'transfiguration of the people of God,' 'the ultimate meaning of the present state, the earthly hiddenness, of the Church,' and the representation of the Judgment as a verdict upon the moral action of the individual member of the Church, is emphasized by Abbot I. Herwegen, *Antike, Germanentum und Christentum*, Salzburg 1932, 47 seq.
16   Examples supplied by Künstle I, 57.

farther in the fondness for childhood and Passion pictures, and for pictures of saints; and which has its parallels in corresponding developments in devotional life in general.

This briefly sketched contrast between early Christian and medieval devotional attitudes has been pointed out with special emphasis by Abbot Ildefons Herwegen. He makes the contrast appear even sharper, for, as antitype to the early period he adduces from medieval art and life, forms which have evolved even farther and which for the most part have been deliberately excluded from the preceding argument. [17] Abbot Herwegen defines the contrast thus: in the early period mystery predominates—the world of grace, what is objective and corporate: in the Middle Ages the emphasis is laid more and more upon human action and moral accomplishment, upon what is subjective and individual. [18] No appraisal is thereby intended—unless it be to this extent, that the ideal mean is seen in equilibrium, in the complementary fulfilment of both factors. [19]

Abbot Herwegen also undertakes an explanation of this most decisive change in the history of Christian culture, the beginning of which he places in the Carolingian period. A hint of this is already given in *Kirche und Seele* his first work; and in his second relevant work *Antike, Germanentum und Christentum* it is indicated even in the title. When, at the beginning of the Middle Ages, Christianity came to the young Teutonic peoples, these accepted it in terms of their own mode of thought, which was vastly opposed to that which until then had prevailed in the ancient world, especially where the comprehension of spiritual values was concerned. 'For the man of the ancient world, what is most spiritual is most real.' [20] 'The man of the ancient world rests in a being which is objective and universal yet filled with abundant life: the Teuton is restlessly caught up in the subjective, individual flux of becoming.' [21] Such an attitude—the spirit of the Gothic has been said to have the same significance [22]—left its

17. I. Herwegen. *Kirche und Seele. Die Seelenhaltung des Mysterienkultes und ihr Wandel in Mittelalter*, Münster 1926.
18. *Kirche und Seele* 4. 15 seq. 23 seq.; *Antike* 41 seq. 51 seq.
19. *Kirche und Seele* 4; *Antike* 68 seq.
20. *Antike* 26.
21. Ibid. 40.
22. Cf. A. L. Mayer-Pfannholz, *Liturgie und Laientum. Wiederbegegnung von Kirche und Kultur*, München 1927, 238.

mark upon the whole range of forms of religious thought and
life: and in the vision of the Christian mystery, in the way of
regarding Christ, the Church, sacraments and cultus, this led,
Herwegen explains, to the objective and permanent giving way
—as far as was possible within the limits safeguarded by ecclesiastical authority—to what was subjective, temporal, mutable and
historically transitory.

There can be no doubt that in this a really active factor of
evolution is being described. This fact had already been established,
at least of the later Middle Ages, by the history of art, although
perhaps not with such clarity. It is obvious in the Gothic period
that the feeling for what is concrete and particular and for subjective sympathy—in representations of the Passion, let us say—
determines the nature of the work. Devotional forms too, show
this same line of development. Romanticism, which begins
indeed even before the opening up of the cleavage now under
discussion, shows scarcely a trace of this attitude. It is always
characterized by well-proportioned order, by the factor of other-
wordly transfiguration, and thus, by kinship with the spirit of
the Roman liturgy.[23] But along with this we must take into
consideration the fact that the new cultural impetus which was
alive in the Teutonic communities was not able to find expression
so speedily in pictorial art as in the sphere of the word and of the
mind itself. Upon the soil of liturgical and religious life, manifestations which derive undoubtedly from the Teutonic spirit
are established at an appreciably earlier date.[24] To this belong the
composition of the Sequences, the first great exponent of which
is Notker Balbulus of St. Gallen (d. 912); the intermittent
tendency to poetize the liturgy;[25] and isolated practices in external
ceremonial arising from Teutonic juridical symbolism such as
folding hands at prayer, handing over the vessels at ordination,

23. The relationship between romanesque and liturgy is given special prominence by
H. Lützeler, Die christliche Kunst des Abendlandes 3, Bonn 1935, 39 seq. cf. also A. L. Mayer,
Altchristliche Liturgie und Germanentum: JL 5 (1925) 84–86.

24. Mayer, Altchristliche Liturgie 80–86.

25. Mayer 92 seq.

and certain isolated customs once but no longer attached to the solemnization of marriage.[26]

These things remain on the fringe of liturgical and religious culture. On the strength of them we can scarcely claim to derive the full extent of the altered view-point, seen in the Carolingian period, but showing itself even in the Gallican tradition, from the subjectivism and moralism of the Teutonic mind.[27]

2. *Greek Influences and Parallels*

Considering national factors alone, which went to form the religious-cultural stamp of the early Middle Ages, we are bound to take account of Greece, even if its influence was exerted only from afar. More precisely: we dare not overlook the cultural heritage of the Greek Orient which overflowed abundantly during this period into the West, into the Gallo-Frankish part of Europe in particular. It is well-known that from the 4th century the Gallican liturgy, i.e. the liturgy of the whole non-Roman West, presents numerous features which point to an Oriental origin: the pre-eminence of Epiphany, the system of weekly and yearly fast-days, the veneration of Saturday, the Trishagion in the Mass, the Offertory procession, the Kiss of Peace before the Consecration, the Epiclesis—to mention but a few obvious examples. From the 6th century the *Kyrie eleison*, and also the Litany as a prayer-form, spread to Rome and then over the whole of the West. Similarly, but somewhat later, the Oriental Marian feasts and various liturgical practices connected with Palm Sunday and Holy Week appeared in the West. The example *par excellence* of Oriental influence is the Nicene-Constantinapolitian Creed

26. Cf. Mayer 88 seq.—I. Herwegen. *Germanische Rechtssymbolik in der römischen Liturgie* (*Deutschrechtliche Beiträge* 8, 4) Heidelberg, 1913. Some of the customs mentioned here—the slap on the cheek at confirmation, for example—certainly have a Teutonic origin, but their adoption in the liturgy can be proved to have occurred only at a considerably later date.
27. Karl Adam, *Kirche und Seele: Theol. Quartalschrift* 106 (1925) 231-239 opposes Herwegen's Teutonic theory.

itself. For examples of Oriental influences in art we need only
point to the monuments in Ravenna and at S. Maria Antiqua in
Rome, or more particularly to the ikons of the Mother of God
whose present day reproductions still show the Greek inscription
Μ(ήτη)ρ Θ(εο)ῦ. Some historians of art—Josef Strzygowski
and Emil Mâle, for example—relying on such facts, would build
up a case for an even deeper influence of the East upon Christian
art in the early Middle Ages.[1]

The over-all type of religious culture in the early Middle Ages,
moving away as it does, from ancient Christian patterns of piety,
cannot be explained in terms of Greek and Oriental influences.
We are thinking merely of a great number of isolated forces. Had
it been otherwise, no such deep chasm could have widened
between the mind of the East and the mind of the West by the
year 1000. And even if it were possible to detect the decisive
focus in those influences, we would only be taking the problem a
stage further back to ask why and how the religious culture of
the East, of Byzantium that is, had departed so far from the spirit
of a more ancient Christianity.

From quite another angle this last question remains most
important; for it is in the significant development which took
place in the East that we are able to unearth the factor which is of
the utmost importance for the cultural history of the West also;
and it is this which governs our present argument. This factor is
the reverberation of the Christological disturbances which the
Greek Orient suffered. This warfare was essentially the defence
of the Church's inheritance, but concentration of attention on the
threatened points and the bitterness engendered by repulse of
heresy recoiled in a change of religious outlook. In this we must see
the chief factor which explains the difference between the Byzantine world and the Greek world of primitive Christianity. The
difference is obvious. Admittedly, other factors—national characteristics, political absolutism and above all caesaropapism—contributed to the total make-up of the Byzantine mind. But within

1. Cf. also, on the influence of Syrian monasticism in particular, the argument of
Am. v. Silva-Tarouca, Stilgesetze des frühen Abendlands, Mainz 1943, especially p. 304,
370 and Index p. 380 seq. On the part played by Syrian culture in general in Western
culture of that period, cf. H. Pirenne, Geburt des Abendlands, Amsterdam o. J. (1939)
78-80; also ibid. p. 59 seq. where Pirenne stresses the persistence of the Byzantine influence
in the western Mediterranean basin until the advance of Islam.

this whole picture the religious components stood out clearly in contrast to all others and have their own history of development —a development with far-reaching effects.

To understand the character of the piety of the Byzantine age we have only to submit ourselves to the effect of any prayer or office of this later period. Compare simply the series of Communion prayers attached to any Byzantine liturgy with the corresponding prayers of a Greek liturgy of the 4th century. We find there a moving expression of the sense of individual sinfulness and nothingness. Glancing through the Canonical Hours we are struck both by the rhythm and imagery of the void, from which it is so largely constructed, and by the theological principle to which almost everything is subject. The hymn of praise is always to 'Christ our God' and to the 'God-bearer.' Almost every hymn ends with a *Theotokion;* and a refrain of adoration of 'the most holy Trinity' recurs throughout. Here we detect the tremors from the disturbances of that age when the relation between Nature and Hypostasis in Christ and in God was defined, and the dogma of the ΘΕΟΤΟΚΟΣ was pronounced. From now on the God-bearer has an assured and honoured place in piety. We have already pointed out the series of Marian feasts which at that time were taken into the Church's calendar in the East. Now too, the ikon of the ΘΕΟΤΟΚΟΣ is given a place of honour. From the time of Justinian, in churches which had, as well as the altar-apse, a second focal point in the dome, she was granted the place above the altar, while Christ the Pantocrator was displayed in the dome.[2] Again, in homiletic literature a striking amount of space is devoted to meditations on Christology and sermons on the Marian theme, of which the most popular aspects are the Annunciation and the Assumption.[3] It is significant that in the extensive homiletic collections we have of the Fathers, the Fathers of the first three centuries are completely absent—clearly because they do not quite fit into the new pattern of thought.

The anti-heretical attitude of Greek piety is revealed most clearly in the doxologies, and here we are able to trace the

2. Künstle I, 40.
3. O. Bardenhewer, *Geschichte der altkirchlichen Literatur V*, Freiburg 1932, 142 seq. cf. 147, 153 seq. cf. A. Ehrhard in K. Krumbacher, *Geschichte der Byzantine Literature* 2, Munich 1897, 162.

development of the new formulations step by step to the conflict with heresy.

At Antioch, that explosive spot in the battle over the decision of Nicea, in the year 350 the current form of the doxology: Glory be to the Father through (διά) the Son (the older and less troublesome form had been through Christ) in (ἐν) the Holy Spirit, was opposed by the traditional Syrian form: Glory be to the Father and to the Son, and to the Holy Spirit.[4] Feeling ran so high that Flavian who was Patriarch at the time and who took up a conciliatory position banned the audible recitation of the doxology.

In Caesarea, to reach clarity from similar confusion, in 375 Basil published his treatise De Spiritu Sancto in which he clearly distinguished the Catholic sense of the old formula which had been misapplied stubbornly by the Arians, by his διά-ἐν; but at the same time justified the new form, which emphasised, in contrast to the heretics, the equality of being in the divine Persons with its: Glory be to the Father with (μετά) the Son along with (σύν) the Holy Spirit.[5] Chrysostom too, having used a conflated form for some time, uses only this one at the end of his homilies from 390 onwards.[6]

It is not only in the doxologies, where Basil turns into prayer what he had emphasized theoretically concerning the Trinity and Christology in his dispute with Arianism, that the influence of the defensive struggle upon his religious attitude is clearly shown. A new study[7] demonstrates how his doctrine of Redemption and of the redemptive sacrifice, his doctrine of grace and of sin, and his Mariology, even when he is not directly engaged in refuting heresy are strongly coloured by his concern to acclaim the divinity of the Redeemer and to instil into his hearers and readers a sentiment towards Christ of intense reverence, almost of trembling fear. Similar research on other Fathers of that period might well produce like results. It is worth noting, in particular, how fear was stressed at this time with regard to the Eucharist:

4. For this and what follows see for detail: J. A. Jungmann, Die Stellung Christi im liturgischen Gebet, Münster 1925, 151 seq.
5. Ibid. 155 seq.
6. Ibid. 164 seq.
7. M. J. Lubatschiwskyj, Des hl. Basilius liturgischer Kampf gegen den Arianismus: ZkTh 66 (1942) 20-38.

'the terrible Sacrifice'; 'the fearful table'; 'the hour of terror' are all expressions which appear in Chrysostom,[8] but which were known already to Basil,[9] and which later in their strongest forms become characteristic of those liturgies belonging to a Monophysite, that is to an extreme anti-Arian milieu.[10]

Zeal to emphasize the divinity of Christ with particular reference to the mystery of the Eucharist, is displayed in yet another way—in the way the concept of Christ as High Priest was used. The records of Christian prayer-life in the first three centuries show that very often prayer was addressed to God, 'through our High Priest Jesus Christ,' with a glance, as it were, up towards our Redeemer who as man is our Mediator and High Priest. In the later Greek texts the expression is now used as a predicate of the divinity in which He performs the Sacrament and carries out the Sacrifice: High Priest now becomes equated with Consecrator.[11]

There was no suggestion whatever of denying that Christ had a human nature or even of excluding the awareness of it from the life of devotion;[12] but in certain contexts it is no longer kept in mind. Such a context is found when a liturgical prayer requires solemn formulation. While the older manner of speech regularly called to mind the humanity of Christ through which we gain access to God, now our mind is turned towards His divinity. It is as though we were viewing the twin steeples of a cathedral from a point so close to one of them that the other is obscured. The humanity is lost sight of: we see only the divinity which unites Father and Son. Thus, adoration is given to Him along with the Father or the prayer is addressed directly and solely to Him. The striking thing is not that prayer is being made to Christ. From the beginning this was obviously the accepted thing. Less still are we surprised that He should be honoured with liturgical

8. E. Bishop, in R. H. Connolly, *The liturgical homilies of Narsai* (*Texts and Studies VIII, I*), Cambridge 1909, 92-97. Since then the question has been discussed by G. Fittkau, *Der Bigriff des Mysteriums bei Joh. Chrysostomus*, Bonn 1953, 122-155; cf. my argument in ZkTh 77 (1955) 485 f.
9. Lubatschiwskyj 35.
10. Jungmann. *Die Stellung Christi* 220 f.
11. Ibid. 211-215. This view of the change in meaning of the concept of the High Priest is contested by S. Salaville, *Studia orientalia*, Rome 1940, 8; but is defended by A. Raes, *Théologie, liturgie et piété orientales*: Orientalia christiana periodica 7 (1941) 270.
12. Cf. my elucidations in opposition to Salaville ZkTh 65 (1941) 232 seq. Also on same topic H. J. Schulz ZkTh 81 (1959) 46 seq.

hymns for that had always been the custom. The significant thing is that the solemn corporate prayer of the liturgy, in particular the prayer of the Eucharistic liturgy itself, is directed to Christ. This practice had been forbidden for the West at two African synods about the end of the 4th century,[13] showing that the tendency was creeping in there to adopt this mode of prayer in contrast to the traditional form. We find the prayer to Christ within the Mass first of all in the Syrian *Testamentum Domini*,[14] a treatise of supposed late 5th century, Monophisite, Syrian provenance.[15] At the same time there appeared in Syria for the first time in the Gregorian Anaphora a complete rite of the Mass which keeps up the address to Christ throughout.[16] On Monophysite soil, in the Ethiopian liturgy, the further step is now taken: a complete rite of the Mass is composed wherein prayer is addressed exclusively to the Mother of God.[17] Even here, orthodoxy is not in question: it is used by Uniate as well as schismatic Ethiopians. But quite obviously this sort of view of the faith is leading fast to a point where we are bound to topple over into heresy through an unbalanced emphasis on the divinity of Christ. This is, in fact, what has happened in thorough-going Monophysitism.

We see the same thing happening at other points too. When Monophysitism was branded as heresy and could no longer remain within the Church, the champions of the tendency which lurked behind it gathered together in Monothelitism, the doctrine which claims that although Christ's human nature may not exactly have been swamped by His divinity, yet His Will was totally absorbed in divinity so that in Him only the divine will remains. Once more, in the eyes of the simple, the preachers of such Christology must have appeared as guardians of the Redeemer's honour. The same tendency was at work when, because of a similar situation, zealots renewed their attempts to

13. Mansi III, 884. 922: *cum altari assistitur, semper ad Patrem dirigetur oratio.*
14. I. E. Rahmani; *Testamentum Domini Nostri Jesu Christi;* Mainz 1899, 43. The *Anamnesis* from the *Apostolic Traditions* of Hyppolitus is adapted thus: *Memores ergo mortis tuae et resurrectionis tuae offerimus tibi. . . .*
15. O. Bardenhewer, *Geschichte der altkirchlichen Literatur IV*, Freiburg 1924, 273 f.
16. E. Renaudot, *Liturgiarum orientalum collectio I*, Paris 1716, 90-126. New edition by E. Hammerschmidt *Die Koptische Gregoriosanaphora*, Berlin 1957. Hammerschmidt also upholds the Syrian and anti-Arian origin (between 350-400) 176 seq.
17. *Die äthiopische Anaphora unserer Herrin Maria*, published by S. Euringer: *Der Katholik* 95 (1916) I, 241-266.

enhance the glory of the ΘΕΟΤΟΚΟΣ.[18] But it is most under-standable that a Marian cult springing from such a root should have been met with suspicion in orthodox theological circles. This seems to have been what happened with Maximus Con-fessor the giant in the battle against Monothelitism. It is told of him that once as he passed through a certain place he was stopped and threatened as an enemy of our Lady who denied her the title ΘΕΟΤΟΚΟΣ. He was made to pronounce the anathema against all who would not call Mary 'God-bearer.'[19]

It became a veritable competition to see who could prove his Catholicity by the greatest measure of zeal for the honour of Mary. And so it becomes intelligible how in the liturgical prayer of the Byzantine liturgy, in the place where of old Christ stood as Mediator of self-offering to God, now Mary appears in such fashion that, commemorating her and all the saints, the congrega-tion lay themselves in Christ's hands.[20]

3. *Battle-grounds and Spheres of Influence in the West*

Influences like those at work in the East must have been active in the West also to cause that change in the structure of religious life of which we spoke earlier: but we do not look for a simple transference or for a straightforward reproduction of the same process. Had that happened there could not have been such a marked difference in the end products. The Christ-image of the East—the Παντοκράτωρ—does not coincide with that of the West which stresses much more the historical and human epiphany

18. Pourrat I, 477-482 cites the following as '*panégyristes de la Sainte Vierge*' in the early Byzantine Middle-Ages: Sergius, Andrew of Crete, Germanus and John Damascene, of whom the first was the founder of Monothelitism, the second of the same ilk '*d'une orthodoxie in peu douteuse.*'
19. *Acta Sanctorum*. Aug. III, Paris 1867, 107. Almost exactly the same case a thousand years later when the Jesuit missionaries came to Abyssinia. See A. Mendez, *Expeditionis Aethiopicae* lib. II (*Rer. aeth. Scriptores VIII*, Rome 1908, p. 206. 329): J. Ludalfus, *Ad suam historiam aethiopicam commentarius*, Frankfurt 1691, 361-363.
20. Jungmann, *Die Stellung Christi* 238 seq. *Constitutiones Apost. VIII* 6, 8 (Funk I, 480): Ἑαυτοὺς τῷ μόνῳ ἀγεννήτῳ Θεῷ διὰ τοῦ Χριστοῦ αὐτοῦ παράθεσθε. Against this we have in the *Chrysostom Liturgy* (Brightman, *Liturgies eastern and western* 363): Τῆς παναγίας . . . Μαρίας μετὰ πάντων τῶν ἁγίων μνημονεύσαντες ἑαυτούς . . . Χριστῷ τῷ Θεῷ παραθώμεθα

of our Lord and ends up with the dominant representation of the Crucified. The West lacks too, the strongly eschatological character of eastern piety, which indeed exceeded that of primitive Christianity by allowing this world to decline in darkness, always and only looking forward to the Resurrection and final glory.[1]

At quite decisive points, however, there is a whole series of phenomena which are of the same sort in both fields: Christ as Mediator becomes less important, the Trinity more so; the cult of Mary increases; thus we are compelled to consider the fight against Arianism as a chief factor in development in the West also.

From the start at Nicea, the West had played a regulative part in this struggle. From time to time western sees, among them no less a see than that of Milan, rad been overrun by Arians and had to be re-conquered. But the heal field of battle was always in the East. The repeated assaults on the Nicene Creed, the series of new rival statements of faith all proceeded from the East. Likewise, the East was the theatre of the final overthrow of heresy and of the subsequent attempts to provide a deliberately antithetical Christology which in the end made the ὁμοούσιος safe—but which in various ways slipped over into the opposite extreme, first into Nestorianism with its separation into two Persons so that the humanity in Christ became isolated, and then into Monophysitism with its tendency to fuse the two natures into one divine nature so that the humanity was threatened with annihilation.

Eventually the West, too, became a scene of combat. In the time of the Arian Emperor Valens, the Visigoths, the first of all the Teutonic peoples to become Christian, finally accepted Arianism. This form of Christianity spread amongst their brother races, and Arianism became the form of religion of the Teutons who ruled over northern Italy, southern France, Spain and North Africa from the 5th century. It may well be that the attachment of these lands to Catholicism at first hung very much in the balance: the Romans professed the Catholic Faith, the Teutons the Arian.[2]

1. Cf. M. Tarchnisvili, *Der eschatologische Zug orientalischer Frömmigkeitshaltung*: Krüger —Tyciak, *Morgenländisches Christentum*, Paderborn 1940, 333–348.
2. H. v. Schubert, *Geschichte der christlichen Kirche im Frühmittelalter*, Tübingen 1921, 28–31. The picture is made to appear much less peaceful by P. de Labriolle, *L'Eglise et les Barbares* (Fliche-Martin, *Histoire de l'Eglise IV*, Paris 1939) 367–385.

The Vandals were the first exception. In their plundering they spared neither churches nor the clergy whose influence they sought to eliminate.3 Their aim became steadily more obvious: to establish the universal tyranny of Arianism. In 484 King Hunerich tried to demonstrate the practical superiority of Arian teaching by means of a religious disputation; and forthwith he began to make good his doubtful victory by force. Once more a religious disputation was tried by King Thrasamund (d. 523) when the Catholic St. Fulgentius played a prominent part.4 In Spain the tension just below the surface issued occasionally in the attempt to force the Catholic population into the Arian state Church, in which attractive inducement and force both played a part. This happened especially after the Swabians under King Rekiar (448-456) became Catholic for the first time and broke the united front of Teutonic Arianism. Thereupon King Eurich tried to destroy the Catholic hierarchy by exiling the bishops and making new appointments to sees impossible.5 A similar situation arose when a hundred years later the Swabians came finally into the Church, and the influence of the Byzantines on the south-east coast on the one hand and the Catholic Franks in the north on the other, strengthened the Catholic position. King Leovigild instigated a fresh and yet more purposeful and merciless attack. He confiscated Church property and exiled bishops always supplementing force and threats with inducements in which gold played a part. Thus he even succeeded in drawing bishops into heresy.6 To make the transition easier, re-baptism, once the rule, was no longer required. All that was required was an imposition of hands and a profession of faith in the form: Glory be to the Father through the Son in the Holy Spirit.7 The end of strife came in 589 when King Rekkared and the whole nation of the Visigoths came into the Catholic Church.

The important fact in all this is, that alongside physical resistance to outward force there had to be *spiritual and intellectual resistance* as well. And this must have been going on all the time as a

3. Victor of Vita, *Historia persecutionis Africanae* (CSEL 7).
4. As a result of this occasion he composed two controversial treatises: *Contra Arianos* (PL 65, 205-224) and *Ad Thrasamundum* (PL 65, 223-304).
5. H. Leclercq, *L'Espagne chrétienne*, Paris 1906, 232-234.
6. Isidor of Seville, *Historia Gothorum* n. 50 (PL 83, 1071). Leclercq 259 seq.; cf. ibid. 254.
7. III Synod of Toledo (589) can. 16 (Mansi IX, 986).

tension in daily life of those who lived even where the leaders were not engaged in open strife. Caesarius of Arles, whose cathedral city was under the rule of East Gothic Arians during most of his episcopate, complains of the subtle and complicated problems by means of which the Arians disturbed simple Catholics, and he felt obliged to produce a little treatise in which he provided the faithful with a set of counter questions.[8] Open force and bloody persecution results in any age in a strengthening of faith amongst those who have courage: it is mental resistance, the need to oppose the alluring heretical thesis with its antithesis, which has power to modify the spiritual possession of the defenders. These very points of doctrine which are exposed to attack must be emphasised and more sharply defined: formulae which are misunderstood are neglected. This is what happened concerning the doctrines which led to schism at the Reformation in the 16th century. And we ourselves in times of racial discrimination and Jewish ostracism ceased using Old Testament names where we could do without them, and let our manner of thinking become attuned to national values.

An atmosphere of strife surrounded Church life for a specially long time in Spain—until the end of the 6th century. These centuries of strife were formative times for Spanish religious life and for the development of the style of the liturgy in particular. Anti-Arianism could not but affect these things and leave its mark on them. That this did indeed happen is shown most clearly in the Mozarabic liturgy, as we shall see more particularly later on.

Now, it was the Spanish Church of the Visigoth period which become the most influential tutor of the West, not directly, but indirectly through France, as we shall explain. It is not necessary to prove that the intellectual life of France from the Carolingian period onwards determined the cultural history of the Middle-Ages. As is well known, in Church life, in forms of worship, in canon law, in monastic life, and, not least, in theological science, from the 9th century it was the countries north of the Alps that took the lead, while Italy suffered a period of set-back. From the 10th century onwards, the cultural heritage which had accumu-

8. Caesarius of Arles, *De Mysterio s. Trinitas* n. 1 (ed. Mai, *Nova Patr. Bibliotheca* I, Rome 1952, 407).

lated in the Carolingian North, streamed in ever increasing volume into Italy and became the cultural standard in Rome itself. In the Cluniac reform we see one aspect of this cultural exchange, in the Roman features of the German Emperor, the other.[9] Ultimately it was from Rome that the new spirituality and new ways spread to the Church at large. What had been established in the Carolingian empire now became normative for all of the West. The structure of the liturgy is but the most outstanding example.

It is true that Spain was not the only place where the fight against Arianism had reacted upon the Church. In France too, there had been opportunity, for this to happen. Until 507 the Visigoths occupied the whole of southern Gaul, with Toulouse as their capital, and for thirty years longer, until 536, the East Goths ruled over large tracts in the south-east of the country. Amongst the Franks themselves and their rulers Arianism had taken firm hold until Chlodwig received Catholic baptism in 496. Until 517 Arianism had been the dominant religion of the Burgundians and we still possess fragments of the theological discussions which the last Arian king, Gundobald, had with Bishop Avitus of Vienne.[10] Even in later times the waves of conflict between the two beliefs surged ever and again into the Frankish lands.[11] And so in this sphere also we must take account from the start of a certain anti-Arian flavour in the style of religious life. But on Gallic soil the battle was not so long-drawn out, and apart from the South, was never so violent as in Spain: nor was intellectual life so intense here as in the Iberian Peninsula. We do not know of a single theological author of the Merovingian period. Venantius Fortunatus, who came from Italy in any case, was a poet; Gregory of Tours was content to write only history; but Spain during the same period can boast a whole series of eminent men, beginning with Leander of Seville. In the 7th

9. Th. Klauser, *Die Liturgischen Austauschbeziehungen zwischen der römischen und der fränkisch-deutschen Kirche vom 8, bis zum II. Jh: Hist Jahrbuch* 53 (1933) 169-189. That the German influence was strongly felt and acknowledged in Roman circles is shown by the expression used by Gregory VII to introduce a reference in the Canonical Hours to what seemed to him to be an unwelcome development: *a tempore quo Teutonicus concessum est regimen nostrae Ecclesiae* (189 Anm. 76).
10. Avitus, *Dialogi cum Gundobado rege* (MG *Auct. ant.* VI, 2, p. 1-15); v. Schubert 94.
11. We should note what Gregory of Tours (d. 594) says himself about his own life. *Hist. Franc. V.* 44 (PL 71, 358-361).

century a solitary figure stands out whom we can honour as one
of the Fathers of the Church—the Spanish Isidore of Seville.
We might expect, therefore, that the intellectual reaction to
Arianism would show itself in clearly defined forms principally
in Spain. The powerful influence exerted upon Gallic lands in
these times by the southern Mediterranean lands is proved by
the history of dogma in the 5th and 6th centuries, when the Council
of Orange (529) brought the Augustinian controversy about
grace to an end. The writings of Fulgentius and of other African
Fathers which we possess could only have come down to us by
being passed on through Spain and Gaul. It is not astonishing
that Spain should have exercised an influence on neighbouring
countries, especially while the kingdom of Toulouse remained
to form a bridge. In particular, Isidore of Seville exerted a powerful influence. The exposition of the Gallican Mass which belongs
to the 7th century and which used to be attributed to Germanus,
already shows dependence on Isidore.[12] His continuing influence
upon the Eucharistic doctrine is admitted.[13] The men who made
most impact on ecclesiastical life in France, men like Pirminius
(d. 753) and Theodulf of Orleans (d. 84), came from Spain. And
yet the main line of communication along which the Church in
Spain distributed its heritage to the Carolingian kingdom lay
through the British Isles. Although there is no kind of literary
account of this round-about influence, that is, of the effect of
Spain upon Scoto-Irish culture, it has nevertheless been proved
beyond doubt in exhaustive studies, first in the field of the history
of tradition and of palaeography by Ludwig Traube who coined
the phrase 'Spanish symptoms,' and second in the field of liturgical
study by Edmund Bishop.[15]

And here we come upon a group of significant facts. Part of a
Dyptich-formula from the Irish Stowe Missal (beginning of the

12. *Expositio antiquae liturgiae gallicanae* ed. J. Quasten (*Opuscula et Textus*. ser. liturg. 3).
Münster 1933, 230-238.
13. J. R. Geiselmann, *Die Abendmahlslehre an der Wende der christlichen Spätantike*,
Munich 1933, 230-238.
14. Concerning the origin of St. Pirminius, see G. Jecker, *Die Heimat des hl. Pirminius*,
Münster 1927, p. 184 refers to other leading Spaniards in France.
15. E. Bishop, *Liturgica historica*, Oxford 1918, 165-210. Important contributions are
found also in G. Manz, *Ausdrucksformen der lateinischen Liturgiesprache bis ins II. Jh.*,
Beuron 1941, esp. 23-42. On Spanish texts which may have come directly into French
sacramenteries, cf. i.a. L. Brou, *Encore des 'Spanish Symptoms' et leurs contre-partie: Hispania
sacra* 7 (1954, 467-485, 468-478).

9th century) takes us back to the old Spanish Mass,[16] as do the Preface of a Mass for the dead[17] and a collect of martyrs.[17a] The Bobbio Missal, from an Irish monastic community of the late 7th century, also has a Spanish flavour.[18] Again, a series of prayers for a deceased person which the Anglo-Saxon Alcuin appended to the *Sacramentarium Gregorianum* which came from Rome,[19] is likewise taken from a Spanish source. It has also been proved that Spanish influence had affected the form of consecration of a bishop in Ireland.[20] But in particular the 8th century English book of prayers known as the *Book of Cerne*[21] contains a number of formulae taken from the Mozarabic liturgy. Here there are several prayers for the dead, a prayer from the Mozarabic Holy Week liturgy and a prayer which the priest is supposed to pray *pro se ipso*.

Various indications all point to the conclusion that this transference must have been accomplished in essentials during the second half of the 7th century,[22] that is, in the period when the Spanish-Visigoth Church was in full bloom; and it must have come about by the passing on of Spanish texts first to Ireland, from whence they travelled on to the Anglo-Saxons who, once national antipathies had been overcome, were ready to learn from the *Scotti*. All know how powerfully then the culture of the Scoto-Irish monks passed on, both directly and via the Anglo-Saxons to France and so to the whole of Europe.

We can illustrate what has been said by the history of the use of the Nicene-Chalcedonian Creed at Mass.[23] This Creed is part

16. *The Stowe Missal* ed. Warner (HBS 32) 14.

17. Ibid. 23 cf. Elipandus of Toledo, EP. 4 (PL 96, 875).

17a. Manz 24 seq.

18. Detail in A. Wilmart, *Bobbio* (*Missel de*): DACL Z, 439–962, esp. 946 seq.

19. L. A. Muratori, *Liturgia Romana vetus* II, Venice174 8, 213–218. cf. Bishop 185 seq.; H. B. Meyer, *Alkuin* (above 4 Anm. 2) 322 seq.

20. E. Eichmann, *Königs—und Bischofsweihe: Sitzungberichte d. Bayr. Akad. d. Wiss., Philos-philol. u. hist.* K1. 1928, 6. Abh., 23 f.

21. Ed. A. B. Kuypers, Cambridge 1902, with appendix by E. Bishop, *Liturgica historica* 166–178.

22. Bishop *Liturgica historica* 170.

23. B. Capelle, *Alcuin et L'histoire de symbole de la Messe: Recherches de théol. ancienne et médiév.* 6 1934) 249–260. cf. Th. Klausner, JL 14 (1934) 453 f.

of the Roman Mass today, but in the West we find this Creed prescribed for the first time, for Spain, at the Council of Toledo (589). The Anglo-Saxon Alcuin must have brought the custom to the court of Charlemagne from his home in York. Its first appearance on Frankish soil was in the Emperor's Palatine Chapel at Aixe. This credal statement, whose Christology and doctrine of the Holy Spirit provides those safeguards of faith which the confessional strife of the 4th century had proved necessary, can be taken as a typical example of the way in which forms, designed to combat Arianism, spread throughout the Church. We cannot say with certainty that this creed was part of the Mass until 515 when it was included at Constantinople by a Patriarch with Monophysite leanings who wished thereby to show his zeal for orthodoxy. In Spain, Britain, and the Carolingian Empire, the Creed in the Mass came exactly half a millennium later, in 1014, in connection with the coronation visit of Emperor Henry II to Rome. From this date it became definitely a possession of the entire Church.

What does all this prove? It proves the possibility at least, that the explanation of the contrast between the religious culture of the rising Middle Ages and that of the Patristic age is to be found to some extent in the handing down and the spread of forms of devotion which were created in theatres of anti-Arian warfare. Our task now is to pin-point the chief elements which produce this sort of transformation, and to show that they did in fact produce the stated effect upon religious culture in the particular sphere. To achieve this end we will have to be clear about the most important points of controversy in the dispute with Teutonic Arianism. This dispute cannot have been merely a reproduction of the Eastern conflict of the 4th century. At the same time we do not expect to find any fresh theological views arising out of it.

4. *The Defensive Battle against Teutonic Arianism and its Immediate Reaction*

The Arianism of the Teutonic peoples was quite simply that which Wulfila and his Goths took over from Byzantium in the middle of the 4th century.[1] In essence it was the confession of the Synod of Seleucia-Rimini (359),[2] a confession which expressed its Christology in a series of Catholic phrases and then pointed out that the Son was only *like* the Father (ὅμοιος, similis), as Scripture said.[3] That the Son is less than the Father is the core of Arianism. This belief constantly recurs and is supported, for want of any sort of theological reasoning, by a series of Scripture texts which are supposed to prove it.[4] A similar relationship is maintained to exist between the Son and the Holy Spirit, there being no hesitation at all in describing the Holy Spirit as a creature, while there is a little uneasiness over applying such a concept to the Son. We end up with, not only three divine Persons, but three separate beings as well. The result is a doctrine of God, distinguished from Tritheism or Ditheism only by mechanical reliance upon Scriptural texts upholding Monotheism, without any regard for coherence or system.[5]

1. X. le Bachelet, *Arianisme IV. Arianisme chez les peuples germanique*: DThC I, 1849-1859. cf. v. Schubert 22 seq.
2. At the beginning of his religious dialogue with Augustine, the Arian bishop, Maximus, refers explicitly to the Synod of Rimini. See: *Augustini collatio cum Maximino* (PL 42, 710 seq.). Likewise King Hunerich in his edict of 483. Victor of Vita, *Historia persecutionis Afr.* III, 5 (CSEL 7, 73 seq.). The great Visigoth National Council of 589 produced a corresponding explicit denunciation of this synod, can. 17 (Mansi IX, 986).
3. A. Hahn *Bibliothek der Symbole*, Breslau 1897, 207 seq.
4. In this context we have the most instructive 73 articles of a comprehensive list of Arian arguments with their refutations, compiled by an unknown author: *Contra Varimadum* lib. I (PL 62, 351-400). With a few exceptions, this deals with Scriptural passages which seem to posit the subordination of the Son to the Father or the superiority of the Father over the Son. On question of authorship, see: O. Bardenhewer, *Geschichte der altkirchlichen Literatur* III, Freiburg 1912, 414. cf. IV (1924) 555 seq. For our purpose it is sufficient to know that it deals with Teutonic Arianism, as the name of the deacon Varimad, who is spreading Arianism around Naples, betrays. The letter of the Visigoth king Sisibut (612-621) to the King of Lombardy (PL 80, 376) contains a list of three Arian Biblical proofs of the same sort. Almost all are to be found in the *Contra Varimadum*, and possibly they give an even better idea of the current style of Arian argument. The emissary of King Leovigild who had to dispute with Gregory of Tour did not restrict himself so much to Biblical texts: *Hist. Franc. V*, 44 (PL 71, 358-360).
5. The judgment of L. A. Winterwyl is relevant: *Das christologische Dogma und der frühgermanische Arianismus*: Hochland 37 (1939) 140, 213-222, 221: 'In spite of any interrelation, Father and Son are two Gods in the Creed of Wulfilas whose Arianism stands midway between Christianity and Paganism.' In any case, the Creed of Wulfilas is preserved only in mutilated form. See: Hahn, *Bibliothek der Symbole*I3, 270 seq.

The Catholic defence took its cue from this procedure.[6] Various divine attributes were denied the Son of God by the Arians. We find Bishop Cerealis in 480 presenting the Arian Maximus with Sciptural texts proving that the Son is almighty and invisible.[7] Eternity, omniscience and impassibility are likewise contested.[8] Avitus of Vienne finds it necessary to prove to the Burgundian king, Gundobad, that the Son existed before His birth from the Virgin.[9] Besides using Scriptural texts which express or imply the subordination of the Son to the Father, without stating expressly that they have His humanity in mind, the Arians also pounced upon liturgical texts which seemed to support the same position. King Leovigild demanded of Catholics who had seceded to Arianism during the last attack upon the Church, the recitation of the following doxology as an Arian profession of faith: Gloria Patri per *Filium in Spiritu Sancto*,[10] a formula which followed the pattern of doxology universally current in the Church up to the middle of the 4th century and which was just as Catholic as the Scriptural texts adduced by the Arians. Neither in the doxology nor in the texts was it said that

6. Isidor of Seville, *Historia de regibus Gothorum* n. 8 (PL 83, 1060 seq.) describes the Arian belief of the Goths thus: *ut crederent Filium Patre maiestate esse minorem et aeternitate posteriorem.* . . . *Aliam quoque Patris sicut personam sic et naturam asserentes, aliam Filii, aliam denique Spiritus Sancti, ut iam non, secundum Sanctae Scripturae traditionem, unus Deus et Dominus coleretur, sed iuxta idololatriae superstitionem tres dii venerarentur.*—*Caesarius of Arles, Serm.* 123 n. 3 (ed. Morin 491) expresses the Arian doctrine in these words: *Pater maior est, Filius minor, Spiritus creatura,* and he adds the comment (n. 1; Morin 491): *Nolite Christum minorem facere Patre, nolite unitatem dividere, nolite unum Deum diversis gradibus divendo veluti idola gentium in vestris cordibus fabricare!* The Arian opponent of Vigilius of Thapsus (end of 5th cent.) *Contra Arianos I,* 24 seq. (PL 62, 196 seq.), openly declares, *tres usias id est tres substantias.* cf. Fulgentius, *Ep. VIII,* 12 (PL 65, 369 seq.). Similarly, Avitus of Vienne, *Dialogi cum Gundobado regi* n. 6 (MG *Auct. ant.* VI, 2, p. 4 Z, 14): *Si ut vultis tripartita est substantia maiestatis.* On the other hand, African Arians decline to use the phrase *Triusiani:* Fulgentius, *Contra Arianos,* 7 (PL 65, 219A). Describing the Catholic view, the Arian preacher Fastidiosus adopts the same attitude: *Homousianis asserentibus inseparabilem atque inviduam Trinitatem, nec Patri Filium fuisse minorem nec Patrem ingenitum Filii sui esse factorem.* In Fulgentius, *Ep.* 9 (PL 65, 375D) cf. Fulgentius, *Contra sermonen Fastidiosi* (PL 65, 507-528).

7. Cerealis, *Contra Maximum* c. 5, 16 (PL 58, 759 seq. 765). In 427-428, the Arian bishop Maximus had argued against St. Augustine that only the Father is almighty and invisible in the strict sense. v. *Augustini collatio cum Maximino* (PL 42, 715, 729 seq.). Stubbornly, he stresses the visibility of the Son: ibid. (PL 42, 728). Even in primitive Arianism this point of dispute had played a prominent part. cf. G. Morin, JL 8 (1928), 102 seq. This was related to the fact that hitherto people had been accustomed to attribute the theophanies of the Old Testament to the Son.

8. Cf. Council of Toledo III (589) can. 6, 7, 9 (Mansi IX, 985).

9. Avitus, *Ep.* 30. al. 28 (MG *Auct. ant.* VI, 2, p. 60-62).

10. Mansi IX, 986.

per Filium applied to the Son, only in respect of His divinity. Amongst the passages which Bishop Cerealis is said to have adduced against his Arian opponent occurs a phrase which was attached to every doxology: *ex Patre per Filium in Spiritu Sancto esse omnia.*[11] The *per Christum*, once universally used in the Catholic liturgy, was accorded great respect amongst the Arians as we can well understand. Sermons are frequently ended with it.[12] An unknown Arian polemicist points to the alleged inconsequence of Catholics who, he says, while condemning all who subject the Son of the Father, do the same themselves with their: *neque est alius per quem ad te aditum habere, precem facere, sacrificationem tibi offere possimus, nisi per quem tu nobis misisti,* and with their comment on the Sacrifice: *quod tibi offerimus stantes ante conspectum tuae divinae pietatis per Jesum Christum Dominum et Deum nostrum, per quem petimus et rogamus.*[13]

The central issue is and remains, the ὁμοούσιος. How can the ὁμοούσιος be proved from Scripture? This was the task set the Catholics by K. Hunerich when he summoned them to a religious disputation on February 1, 484 and called them 'stiff-necked ὁμοουσιανι.'[14] The corresponding counter-profession of the Catholics was: *Trinitatem unum Deum inviolabilem confitemur:* and they shouted this at their persecutors who had expelled them beyond the city walls.[15] A Roman virgin who was forcibly baptized by the Arian Vandals in Spain countered the *ut beatam scinderet Trinitatem,* which they demanded with her, *Patrem cum Filio ac Spiritum Sanctum unius credo esse substantiae essentiaque.*[16] Apologists too, who opposed Arianism from the Catholic side,

11. Cerealis, *Contra Maximinum* C17 (PL 58, 765). cf. on this formula: Jungmann, *Die Stellung Christi* 156 seq.

12. Sermon of the Arian Fastidiosus in Fulgentius, *Ep.* 9 (PL 65, 377A). *Homilien des Arianerbischofs Maximin,* ed. by B. Capelle: Revue Bénéd. 40 (1928) 56, 68, 70.

13. G. Mercati, *Antichi relique liturgiche (Studi e Testi* 7) Rome 1902, 52 seq. Printed also in PL 13, 611 seq. and in L. C. Mohlberg, *Sacramentarium Veronense,* Rome 1956, 201 seq. On the Arian misinterpretation of the formula, v. Fulgentius, *Ep.* 14 n. 37 (PL 65, 425): also his *Contra Fabianum fragm.* (PL 65, 815).

14. Victor of Vita, *Historia persecutionis Afr. II,* 39 (CSEL 7, 34); III, 4 seq. (ibid. 73). The attempt of the Vandals in North Africa to convert the subjugated peoples to Arianism led to the development of a theology. v. K. D. Schmidt, *Die Bekehrung der Germanen zum Christentum I,* Göttingen 1939, 368 seq.

15. Ibid. II, 28 (CSEL 7, 34).

16. Gregory of Tours, *Hist Franc.* II, 2 (PL 71, 192).

mostly start off from this point, the unity of the Godhead,[17] and they are most careful to stress and elucidate the unity between Father and Son and their equality in essence. Against the much vaunted *palmaris interrogatio* of the heretics, of which Fulgentius tells us, namely: Why do Catholics sacrifice to the Father alone? they explain that the sacrifice is in fact offered to the Trinity even if the prayers mention only the Father. Had not Abraham sacrificed to the One who appeared to Him: according to the assumption then made, to the Son.?[18]

On the other hand, they dared not obscure the Trinity of Persons. In Spain especially, from the 4th century onwards, there was a constant danger of Priscillianism, which added to the errors of the Manichaeans, those of Satellius who denied that there were three divine Persons, saying that the Son and the Spirit were only modes of the Father's operation (Modalism). This was the opposite extreme to Arianism, more conditioned by simplicity of mind and even farther removed from the revealed Word. Thus the well-known formulae of the Spanish synods evolve, with ever increasing sharpness and precision, defining and contrasting Trinity and Unity. Against Arianism they stress the unity of the divine Being: against Priscillianism, the Trinity of Persons.[19]

For nearly two centuries Church life in Spain stood under the shadow of this defensive warfare. The pattern of religious life in the Spanish Church could not but show enduring signs of this conflict. Looking through the Acts of the National Council of Toblo,[20] which took place in 589 after the conversion of the Visigoths to the Catholic Church, we are struck by the passion with which the heresy—*perfidia Ariana*—and its author—*rectae fidei pestis Arius*—are condemned.[21] A little later, King Rekkared wrote to Pope Gregory the Great and in his letter referred to the

17. The *confessio fidei* which was presented to King Hunerich in 484: Victor of Vita, op. cit. II, 56 seq. (CSEL 7, 46 seq.), Vigilius of Thapsus, *Contra Felicianum* C. 1, 2 (PL 58, 757 seq.).
18. Fulgentius, *Ad Monimum* II, 2-5 (PL 65, 179-184). It becomes obvious that from now on prayer will have to be addressed expressly to the Blessed Trinity, cf. 15 above.
19. Denzinger, *Enchiridion*, n. 15-40; 231-234; 275-287. K. Künstle, *Eine Bibliothek der Symbole*, Mainz 1900; also his *Antipriscilliana*, Freiburg 1905.
20. Mansi IX, 977-1005.
21. Mansi IX, 984D-980B.

nefanda Ariana haeresis.[22] Here is evidence of righteous indignation at the long separation, for purely political reasons, of a noble stem from the maternal lap of the Catholic Church and from the full truth of the Christian Faith. With all the zeal of the noble convert, men are not content now to adopt sober statements of faith, but seize on the sharpest antitheses to heresy, which have grown out of time of conflict.

The National Council of Toledo 583 already shows how these antitheses have become grafted into the liturgy and into devotional life. Until this time, in accordance with the decree of Leovigild, the form of the doxology: *Gloria Patri per Filium in Spiritu Sancto*, which had been interpreted as implying subordination of the Son to the Father, had been accepted. Now, not only is Leovigild's *libellus detestabilis* repudiated, but all who will not say: *Gloria et honor Patri et Filio et Spiritu Sancto*, are anathematized.[23] After the King and Queen had subscribed the confession of Faith, the loud acclamations included not only the *Gloria Deo Patri et Filio et Spiritu Sancto*, but also, *Gloria Deo nostro Jesu Christo*.[24] This brings vividly to mind the parallel antithesis of eastern piety contained in the form of address, 'Christ our God.' King Rekkared refers in his opening speech to our Lord's words: 'Where two or three are assembled in my name, there am I in the midst of them'; and then he continues: *Credo enim beatam sanctae Trinitatis divinitatem huic sancto interesse concilio.*[25] Attention is being concentrated on one end: to ensure that equal honour and adoration is given to all three Persons in the Trinity. Zeal in opposing the *minor Patre* in every possible way leads to the interchange of statement about the Trinity with statements which are only properly applicable to Christ.

It is no surprise to find this same spirit embodied in the old Spanish liturgy, later known as the Mozarabic liturgy.[26] This liturgy, was composed mainly in the century following the conversion, and the men most responsible for its formation were the

22. In Gregory the Great, *Ep.* IX, 61 (PL 77, 997 seq.).
23. Can. 14, 16 (Mansi IX, 986).
24. Mansi IX, 983.
25. Mansi IX, 979 seq.
26. Cf. Jungmann, *Die Stellung Christi* 85–93. As this context shows it is misleading to describe the old Spanish liturgy as Visigothic. Its older stratum has nothing at all to do with the Visigoths: its later stratum, however, is marked by the re-action to Visigothic Arianism.

great Bishops of Toledo, Eugenius, Ildefons and Julian.[27] An old stratum of the old Spanish liturgy reveals the same theological structure, particularly the same form of address in prayers, as is found in the Roman liturgy of ancient times as of the present day. Prayer is presented to almighty God, through Jesus Christ our Lord. In the sources we now have which display the old Spanish liturgy as it was at the time the invasions began,[28] about half of the Prefaces show this in their opening phrase at least. In some cases the offering of prayers through Christ is expressed with great emphasis, as in the formula of the *missa omnimoda: Dignum et iustum est nos tibi semper gratias agere, omnipotens Deus noster, per Jesum Christum Filium tuum Dominum nostrum, verum pontificem et solum sine peccati macula sacerdotem;* and then the prayer goes on with *per quem*, to ask that God may accept both sacrifice and praise.[29] This is the prayer-language of the early Church.

The majority of *Prefaces*, however, show the influence of the new viewpoint in what follows. If, in the development of the song of praise, in the petitions which as a general rule emerge from its conclusion, Christ is mentioned, the transition from this to the *Sanctus* is made through a set formula: *cui merito*, that is, *cui merito omnes angeli atque archangeli non cessant clamare ita dicentes: Sanctus.*[30] The *Sanctus* is thus seen as an adoration of Christ. The same thing is found taking place in the call to thanksgiving which in general is the same today in the Roman liturgy as in the ancient liturgies: Gratias agamus Domino (Deo nostro). In the sources we are considering, the call to thanksgiving runs: *Deo ac Domino nostro, Patri et Filio et Spiritui Sancto, dignas laudes et gratias referamus;*[31] a stage in anti-heretical development which

27. G. Mercati: *More 'Spanish Symptoms,'* in the *Journal of Theological Studies*, 1907, reprinted by Bishop in *Liturgica historica* 203-210. The same conclusion is drawn by D. de Bruyne: *De l'origine de quelques textes liturgiques mozarabes: Revue Bénéd* 30 (1913 421-436). He describes the period from 590-690 as the Golden Age of the Mozarabic liturgy.

28. Férotin: *Le Liber ordinum*, Paris 1904; and *Le Liber mozarabicus sacramentorum*, Paris 1912. The two collections preserve about 230 Mass formularies. Even the unchanging parts of the Mass are contained in the *missa omnimoda (Liber ordinum* 229-243).

29. Férotin: *Le Liber ordinum* 237. Similarly a Sunday Mass: Férotin: *Le Liber moz. sacr.* 632. Cf. Jungmann: *Die Stellung Christi* 90.

30. Férotin: *Le Liber moz. sacr.* 528. And in the 7th century mss. of the so-called Moneschen Masses (PL 138, 863-882) the *Sanctus* in about half the cases is dedicated to Christ, sometimes moreover, with the formula *cui merito.* Cf. Jungmann *Die Stellung Christi* 82.

31. Férotin: *Le Liber ordinum* 236.

is apparent also in the contemporary Byzantine liturgy.[32] Subsequently, however, the Mozarabic liturgy took a farther step and transferred Trinitarian statements to the Christological field. The so-called *Missale mixtum* (1500) prescribed by Cardinal Ximenes contains the expression: *Deo ac Domino nostro Jesu Christo Filio Dei, qui est in coelis, dignas laudes dignasque gratias referamus.*[33]

This transition from one form of address to another in prayer is characteristic of the Mozarabic liturgy. Amongst these prayers it is particularly in the *Prefaces* that this is found. An Advent *Preface* has this address after the *Dignum et iustum* est: *Domine Jesu Christe Deus noster;* in what follows: *clementissime Deus;* and near the end: *unita aequalis et indivisa Trinitas.*[34] In this rite of the Mass, this transition from one form to the other is a constantly recurring feature: and it occurs without conforming to any observable rule. The very arbitrariness with which address to God, to Christ, to the Blessed Trinity are found together or are interchanged, is what brings out so clearly the affirmation of the *aequalis gloria* which is to be attributed to all three Persons—especially to the Son—just as much as to the Father. The 13th canon of the Synod of Toledo almost makes this its whole platform: *Quicumque Filium Dei et Spiritum Sanctum cum Patre non crediderit esse glorificandos et honorandos a.s.*[35] This was not demanded as a consequence of the Being of the divine Persons, but was directly provoked by the contradicting attitude of the Arians and their criticism. One of the Arian arguments dealt with in the treatise against Varimad runs thus: *quia illi soli (sc. Patri) sacrificium immolatur;* another thus: *qua solus Pater afidelibus adoratur*[36] A reference to Psalm 71, 10, disposes of this: *et adorabunt eum omnes reges terrae, omnes gentes servient ei;* but the most effective and comprehensive reply lay in the Catholic liturgy itself, wherein prayer and even sacrifice were offered not solely to the Father. Most important of all was the addressing of prayer to Christ. They begin with the address: *Domine Jesu Christe* or *Christe Deus* or

---

32. Perhaps not in the invocation but in the response: 'It is meet and right to adore the Father, the Son, and the Holy Spirit, one in essence and inseparable in Trinity.' F. E. Brightman: *Liturgies eastern and western,* Oxford 1896, 384.
33. PL 85, 547.
34. Férotin: *Le Liber moz. sacr.* 17.
35. Mansi IX 986.
36. *Contra Varimadum* c. 51, 58 (PL 62, 386, 390).

some similar phrase. Their true nature is often disclosed only in the
sequel, for the address is frequently quite neutral (*Domine* or the
like) leaving us in doubt which address is presupposed; and likewise, the concluding phrases too, are neutral as a rule. In fact, these
are so expressed, that the address might equally well be made to
the Father or to the Son or to the Blessed Trinity.37 A favourite
form is: Sancta Trinitas or Trinitas Deus. Except in the Prefaces
already mentioned, the old *per Christum* has virtually disappeared.
Like an empty shell amongst the concluding phrases we find an
occasional *per;* and that, only in the context, *per te Christe* or *per te
Deus*, which only shows the more plainly how in these prayers
the mediation of Christ has been quite forgotten.

It seems amazing that liturgical compositions dating for the
most part from the 7th century should still reflect such a bellicose
attitude, when there was no longer any reason for it. But apart
from the fact that the type of prayer which had been forged
out of the heat of conflict had been able meanwhile to gain legal
sanction, the inner mentality, the structure of faith's awareness
had itself been formed in an atmosphere of violent debates.
Recent converts took up the very same attitude. We detect this
very clearly in a letter written by King Sisibut (612–631) to the
young Catholic King of Lombardy, Adalwald, who was hemmed
in on every side by Arians.38 The language of this letter never
departs from the tone which is apparent in the utterance of King
Rekkared, quoted above. The writer knows no language strong
enough to condemn the *exsecranda Ariana pernicies* and to warn
the young king against it. He even drags in the ignominious end
of the heresiarch. The religious phraseology, born of theological
warfare, can once more be recognized when Sisibut speaks of
the *indemutabilis, indivisibilis, increata, creatix omnium sempiterna
Trinitas*, who has brought salvation to His people; or when he
gives the assurance that all will go well *fautore Christo*.39

We find a similar way of speaking in the writings of Spanish
bishops of the 7th century. We are struck by the frequency with
which God is referred to as the Trinity and where Christ is named

---

37. Cf. Férotin's survey of the formulae in *Le Liber ordinum*, 534–541.
38. Sisibut: *Ep.* 8 (PL 80, 372–378).
39. Ibid. (372D, 373C, 374B).

where God is meant.[40] This was not the customary language of the early Fathers. The anti-heretical element was not uniformly strong. Anti-Arianism made little impact upon the theological essays of Isidore of Seville, the greatest Spanish Churchman of the 7th century, and in his more personal writings, like the *Synonima* or his letters, it is insignificant. Isidore's deeper knowledge of the Fathers and greater theological education made him more independent of the popular piety which surrounded him.

Outside the Spanish-Gallic sphere, that is in the realm of the Roman Church, almost all signs are lacking of the devotional attitude having been forged in the heat of credal wars. If we discount the above-mentioned 7th century Greek influence, the Roman sacramentaries show scarcely a trace of this. Even the works of Gregory the Great, written when the credal crisis in Spain was at its height are scarcely affected by it.[41] It would be a most attractive task to examine how influences mingle within the young Anglo-Saxon Church, how the Venerable Bede for example, still prefers Roman thought and prayers,[42] but how here, too, Irish-Spanish forces, more and more, mould the shape of religious life.[42a]

The records we have of the Gallican Church—mainly 6th-7th century records—show traces of a similar anti-heretical frame

40. A study which paid much more attention to finer expressions of the new religious attitude would be worth while. For example: in Braulio of Saragossa (d. 651), *Ep.* 3 (PL 80, 650 seq.), we read that Christ knows how much he begged the prayers of Isidore (to whom he was writing) that he, would be protected from the assault of temptations by *Trinitas sanctissima.* Again in *Ep.* 20 (PL 80, 667): *Commendarimus eum creatori Christo Domino.* We must note certainly, that similar expressions do occur occasionally elsewhere. Cf. K. Baus: *Das Nachwirken des Origenes in der Christus-frömmigkeit des hl. Ambrosius: Röm. Quartalschr.* 49 (1954, 21–55) 27, 47. There must be quite a number of these in our sphere.

41. Cf. J. A. Jungmann's sketch of Gregory's attitude to the *kerygma* in *Die Frohbotschaft und unsere Glaubensverkündigung,* Regensburg 1936, 45–52. In Gregory an anti-heretical shift of emphasis becomes obvious when we pay heed to the more personal language of his letters. C.f. the Innsbruck dissertation of H. Erharter: *Schwerpunkte in Glaubensbewusstsein Gregors des Grossen, dargestellt aus dem religiösen Gehalt seiner Briefe* (1959, unpublished).

42. Cf. J. Bach: *Die Dogmengeshichte des Mittelalters vom Christologischen Standpunkt I,* Vienna 1873, 86–93.

42a. E. Iserloh: *Die Kontinuität des Christentums beim Übergang von der Antike zum Mittelalter in Lichte der Glaubensverkündigung des hl. Bonifatius: Trierer theol. Zeitschr.* 63 (1954) 193–205 is relevant here; and also H. B. Meyer, S.J.: *Alkuin zwischen Antike und Mittelalter:* ZkTh 81 (1959) 306–350, 405–454. Both of these studies disclose a widespread weakening of the sense of grace and an advance of the moralistic outlook. Iserloh discovers that Boniface 'seems to know of nothing more than a moral bond between the Christian and Christ' (200). Meyer likewise affirms that Alcuin sees sinful man separated by 'a deep gulf' from Christ (453) who appears as God and Judge.

of mind; but they show it with less definition.[43] A certain indecision over form of address in prayer colours the Gallican liturgy, although the basic and predominant stratum still preserves the old, traditional form. The address *Salvator mundi* is characteristic of Gallican prayers to Christ. There is a notable arrangement of the Communion Hymn, made up of some three verses in a particular order and described as the *trecarum*. This is quoted explicitly as *signum catholicae fidei de Trinitatis credulitate procedens*.[44] In the Baptism Ordinal too, a preference for Trinitarian symbolism is revealed; as when the Creed is repeated thrice, *ut ipse numeras repetitionis in signo conveniat Trinitatis*.[45]

Now we can approach the problem of how the ferment of anti-Arian piety continued to affect later ages. We can ask: What sort of modifications and changes did it help to bring about in the form of medieval spirituality? We are concerned specially —as we already stated—with the Carolingian sphere, that crucible of medieval culture wherein indigenous Gallican traditions are now interacting on a religious culture from Spain, mediated through Anglo-Saxons, above all through Alcuin and his school; and where at the same time there is a fusion of elements derived from the Anglo-Saxons with elements coming in directly from Rome.

5. *Fides Trinitatis*

We have already taken note of how in the time when issues of belief were being fought out, the dogma of the Trinity came

43. Jungmann: *Die Stellung Christi*.
44. *Expositio antiquae liturgiae gallicanae*, ed. Quasten (*Opuscula et Textus, ser. liturg*. 3), Münster 1934, 23. Cf. Jungmann: *Missarum Sollemnia* II, 490 seq., 595.
45. *Missale gallicanum vetus* (ed. Mohlberg (1958) m. 64: cf. n. 27, 172). Also M. J. Metzger: *Zwei Karolingishe Pontifikalien vom Oberheim* (Freiburg 1914) 158 sees there a 'reflex from the Arian struggles.' At least it would appear that in Gaul at Baptism the usual Apostles' Creed was replaced frequently by the more anti-Arian Nicene—Constantinopolitan Creed. Cf. P. de Punie:: *Catechumenat:* DACL II, 2608 note 9; E. Bishop: *Journal of Theological Studies* 4 (1903) 586. In even later texts, this Symbol which newly ordained priests have to recite after ordination is described simply as *fides sanctae Trinitatis;* v. V. Leroquais: *Les pontificaux manuscrits*, Paris 1937, I, 112-132, 256; II, 18, 233, 310, 366. Cf. also the texts on the title Trinitas in Manz (above c.3 note 15) 497-499.

to dominate the religious scene. As long as Christianity was primarily intent on overcoming the world, as long as the light of Christianity stood opposed to heathen darkness, it presented the Christian idea as the *good news of salvation;* come alive for us in Christ. But now, when faith in the mysterious inter-relation of the divine Persons has become threatened, the true Faith is seen as *fides Trinitatis.* During the confessional struggle of the 4th and 5th centuries the τριαδικὴ πίστις had already become a slogan. The Egyptian Basilican Anaphora[2]—a Greek liturgy—contains the prayer, 'Keep us believing in the Holy Trinity until our life's end.' This battle-cry of the East resounds in Western Christendom, even in things which stand apart from confessional controversy.[3] And the sound becomes even louder after the West itself has passed through the struggle. In the older *Gelasian Sacramentary* in which the Roman liturgy with 7th century Gallican interpretations has come down to us, there is a *Hanc-igitur* formula which prays for religious, *laetantes instanter in sanctae Trinitatis fide catholica perseverent.*[4] According to a 9th century *Confiteor* from St. Gatien in Tours, the worshipper accuses himself thus: *Filiolos meos et filiolas, quos in baptismo Christi suscepi, et omnes mihi subiectos fidem sanctae Trinitatis non decui.*[5] In an *Ordo* from Bobbio we find Extreme Unction ending with the desire: *ut . . . salveris in fide sanctae Trinitatis.*[6] Today, in the office for Novem-

1. St. Hilary—*De Trinitate* II, 1 seq. (PL 10, 50 seq.) is already regretting that heresy has necessitated this meditative pre-occupation with the mystery of the Trinity: faith would have sufficed, but the heretics compel us *illicita agere, ardue scandere, ineffabilia eloqui.*
2. E. Renaudot, *Liturgiarum orientalium collectio* I, Paris 1716, 88. For more related oriental texts see Jungmann, *Die Stellung Christi* 193 note 17.
3. According to the letter of Paula of Eustochium written in 386 to Marcella—in Jerome *Ep.* 46 c. 3 (PL 22, 485)—the *Trinitatis fides* is alluded to by the three names of the Holy City: Jebus, Salem and Jerusalem. St. Patrick—to whom the symbol of the three-leaved clover is not attributed for nothing—desired, as he observes in his *Confessio* n. 6 al. n. 14 (PL 53, 804A), to preach the Christian message according to the measure of faith in the Trinity, in *mensura itaque fides Trinitatis.* The expression *fides Trinitatis* for the Christian faith is also found in Gregory the Great, *Moralia* 33, 18, 20 (PL 76, 683 seq.)—in this place occasioned certainly by the context: in order to be able to understand *funis* in the allegorical interpretation of Job 40, 20, as faith, the word is derived from *funiculus triplex,* and this leads on to the Trinity.
4. III, 50 (Wilson 264). Similarly ibid. I, 88 (133) in the second *oration* of the dedication of a church.
5. Sacramentary of St. Gatien-Tour: E. Martène, *De antiquis Ecclesiae ritibus* I, 6, 7, *Ordo* III (Antwerp 1736: I, 776). This witness corresponds no doubt to the provision of the Synod of Frankfurt 794, C. 30 (MG *Concilia* II, 1, 169): *Ut fides catholica sanctae Trinitatis et oratio dominica atque symbolum fidei omnibus praedicetur et tradatur.*
6. L. A. Muratori, *Antiquitates Italicae medii aevi* IV, Milan 1741, 845D.

ber 11 we still pray: Sanctae Trinitatis fidem Martinus confessus est—clearly a heritage from the Carolingian age.[7] The Mozarabic rite for Palm Sunday is of special significance concerning this dominant Trinitarian pre-occupation of the Gallican Church. This rite, includes the *traditio symboli* which invite us to review the content of faith.[8] The opening phrases of this so-called *missa* address themselves to this same task; they are nothing but a developed definition of Trinitarian dogma, put in high-sounding language. It begins: *Catholicam fidem, fratres carissimi cordis integritate servantes, Deum Patrem, Deum Filium, Deum fateamur et Spiritum Sanctum. Neque tamen Deos plures adfirmare gentiliter andeamus, sed in tribus unum Deum fiducialiter adoremus. Una quippe est Trinitas essentia, nec est altera creatrix aeterna substantia;* whereupon, the equality on power, rank and eternity and the unity of all divine activity in creation and redemption are emphasized.

What is new is not that the mystery of the Trinity is stressed in general, nor that people advert to it readily—shown sometimes even by the incidental use of the notion of *three-ness.* That had always been quite natural, and there are examples from the earliest times.[9] Nor is it that the substance of Faith is presented under three headings corresponding to the three Divine Persons. The Apostles' Creed had already displayed this and Novatian had entitled his exposition of Christian doctrine: *De Trinitate.* What is new is a manner of speech which seems to identify the substance of Faith with the doctrine of the Blessed Trinity,[9a] and to mention this holy mystery very frequently, calling it to mind in the most diverse connexions. In the pre-Frankish Roman

7. Cf. *Liber responsalis* (PL 78, 811D). From later times cf. Anselm of Canterbury, *De fide Trinitatis et incarnatione Verbi* (PL 158, 251-284).

8. Férotin, *Le Liber moz. sacr.* 223-226.

9. Such a thing is provided by the three daily hours of prayer with prayers at the third, sixth and ninth hours, already part of the Christian's rule of life in the 3rd century. Tertullian—*De oratione* C. 25 (CSEL 20, 197 seq.)—finds that these have been appointed in order to remind us that we are *debitores trium Patris es Filii es Spiritus Sancti.*—Cyprian—sixth and ninth hours, already part of the Christian's rule of life in the 3rd century *De dom. oratione* C. 34 (CSEL 3, 292), sees in the three hours and in the three hour interval between them a *sacramentum Trinitatis.* There was no need, therefore, of any Arian attack to make Isidore of Seville express similar thoughts—*De eccl. off.* I, 19 (PL 83, 757 seq.).

9a. We see such an identification on a large scale when Alcuin expounds the doctrines of the faith in his chief dogmatic work under its title *De fide s. Trinitas:* v. H. B. Meyer, loc. cit. (ZkTh 1959), 405 seq.

liturgy the three Persons are rarely mentioned explicitly,[10] and the word *Trinitas* is mentioned only twice;[11] but in the Carolingian age Trinitarian modes of thought began to spread through the Roman liturgy. Trinitarian Prefaces of non-Italian origin appear in the mid-8th century in the older Gelasian Sacramentary. By A.D. 800 the fully developed Trinitarian Mass which is normal today had appeared in sacramentary manuscripts.[12] This was inserted in these texts by Alcuin and allotted to the Sunday within the weekly cycle of votive Masses.[13] Alcuin may even have composed it himself. The Trinitarian motif becomes the mark of Sunday.[14] And then towards the close of the millennium a special feast in honour of the Blessed Trinity was observed amongst the Franks. It is significant that Alexander III (d. 1181) declined to observe this feast in Rome, considering it super-fluous.[15] From the 9th century on, the Roman-Frankish Missals have the type of Offertory prayers which begin *Suscipe, sancta Trinitas* and also the concluding prayer *Placeat, tibi sancta Trinitatis,*[16] and the form of address is that current in the Gallican liturgy. The *Kyrie* of the Mass, which in the Roman tradition as in the eastern was a simple appeal to Christ wherein *Kyrie* and *Christe* are interchangeable, is given a rigid Trinitarian meaning in the

10. Cf. A. Klaus, *Ursprung und Verbreitung der Dreifaltigkeitsmesse,* Werl 1938, 3-17; 28-31.
11. In a Preface of the *Leoniarum* (Mohlberg n. 354) which makes the twelve foundation-stones of the heavenly Jerusalem suggest that the mystery of the four-fold Gospel is based in the Trinity. This passage is related to Augustine, *Enarrationes in ps.* 86 n. 4 (PL 37, 1103 seq.).
12. Klaus 21 seq. The heart of the Mass of the Trinity, the Preface, certainly displays a set of formulations as they appear in a time of dogmatic strife in the Pentecost sermons of Leo the Great—hence Roman in origin, and 'not much after the end of the 5th century.' A. Chavasse, *Le Sacramentaire Gélasien,* Paris 1958, 254-260. This sequence may well be unnecessary; v. J. A. Jungmann, *Um die Herkunft der Dreifaltigkeitspräfation:* ZkTh 81 (1959), 461-465.
13. PL 101, 445 seq. Klaus 76-107; G. Ellard, *Master Alcuin liturgist,* Chicago 1956, 157-161.
14. Cf. above 6. The beginnings of such a conception of Sunday appear as early as the end of the 7th century in Ireland in the Bangor Antiphonary, in which a hymn in praise of the three Persons and their unity, in the form of a collect, follows the Sunday *Laudate pueri* and *Te Deum.* F. E. Warren, *The Antiphonary of Bangor* II (HBS 10) 32 (n. 123; cf. n. 125); cf. 81.
15. Klaus 108-121; P. Browe, *Zur Geschichte des Dreifaltigkeitsfestes:* Archiv f. Lw. 1 (1950) 65-81. The feast was prescribed for the universal Church in 1334 by John XXII; Klaus 127 seq.
16. Both, along with other formulae of the same sort, in the Sacramentary of Amiens; v. the Order of the Mass in the Sacramentaries, ed. by V. Leroquais (*Eph. liturg.* 1927) 441, 444.

Carolingian 9th century commentary of The Liturgy.[17] This interpretation, dictated by the triple triad of the *Kyrie*, has come down to the present day. From the 10th century, a special prayer honouring the Blessed Trinity is found to preface the various Hours in the monastic Office.[18] The widely circulated *Admonitio synodalis*, belonging to the same period, demands that when giving the blessing priests should hold their fingers so as to symbolize the Trinity: *strictis duobus digitis et pollice intus recluso, per quos Trinitas innuitur*.[19] To this day the three finger symbolism has persisted in the gesture accompanying an oath.[20] In the Carolingian period documents and manuscripts which begin 'in the Name of' the Trinity become more common.[21]

We discover a similarly strong emphasis on the mystery of the Trinity here and there in the sparse records we have from that time of the preaching of the Faith, in so far as this can be distinguished as a self-contained expression of the deposit of Faith. In the collection of fifteen short catechetical sermons—formerly attributed to Boniface, but now known to have been written some decades later[22]—in five places the preacher gives a concise exposition of Christian doctrine. Each time, however, the argument has to return to the confession of the three divine Persons

17. Amalar, *Liber off.* III, 6, 2 (Hanssens II, 253); cf. Jungmann, *Missarum Sollemnia* I, 439 seq.
18. L. Eisenhofer, *Handbuch der Katholischen Liturgik* II, Freiburg 1933, 504. Th. Symons *A note on trina oratio: Downside Review* 42 (1924) 67-83, following JL 4 (1924) 251.
19. The passage is not contained in all of the versions of the text—not yet critically examined—(v. H. Leclercq: DACL VI, 576-579), but occurs, amongst other places, in a version from a Neresheim ms. which can be traced back to St. Ulrich of Augsburg (PL 135, 1071 seq.). On the history of the gesture of blessing, v. Eisenhofer, *Handbuch* I (1932) 280 seq.
20. Express allusion to the three divine Persons first occurs in the Appenzeller handbuch of 1409. E. v. Künssberg, *Schwurgebärde und Schwurfingerdeutung (Das Rechtswahrzeichen 4)*, Freiburg 1941, 1 seq.
21. Isolated provisions of Charlemagne, e.g. those of 806 concerning the division of the kingdom begin with the words (MG *Leges* I, 140): *In nomine Patris et Filii et Spiritus Sancti;* also his encyclical of 812 concerning the liturgy of Baptism (ibid. I, 171). Similarly the Donation of Constantine, dated 816 and apparently originating in the Frankish court (C. Mirbt. *Quellen zur Geschichte des Papsttums*, Tübingen 1924, 107-112). From 833, solemn diplomas all begin: *In nomine sanctae et individuae Trinitatis;* J. Hösl: *Invokation:* L.ThK V (1933) 445 seq. Relevant, too, at this point is the Gelasian Sacramentary of Cod. 348 of St. Gallen (c. 800), the title-page of which begins with large illuminated lettering: *In nomine sancte Trinitatis incipit liber sacramentorum.* K. Mohlberg, *Das frankische Sacramentarium Gelasianum,*[2] Münster 1939, p. 1.
22. Ps—Boniface, *Sermones* I-XV (PL 89, 843-872). On the problem of origin cf. F. Flaskamp, *Die Missionsmethode des heiligen Bonifatius: Zeitschrift für Missionswissenschaft* 15 (1925) 48 seq.

as the token of true Faith. Thus we read, for example: *Hoc est verbum fidei, quod praedicamus, ut credamus in Deum Patrem omnipotentem, et in Jesum Christum Filium eius unicum Dominum nostrum, et credamus in Spiritum Sanctum, unum deum omnipotentem in unitate et Trinitate, trinum in personis et nominibus et unum in deitate maiestatis et potestatis.*[23]

The new formularies thus show themselves to be living germs which are to blossom out into even more elaborate forms in the future. At the turn of the 10th century the invocation of the three divine Persons and of the Blessed Trinity is attached to the beginning of the Litany. This was hardly ever known in the 9th and 10th centuries.[24] From the 13th century, the naming of the three divine Persons, attached to the administration of Baptism by our Lord Himself, soon entered into the normal form of the administration of other sacraments[25]—Confirmation and Penance—having first of all become the accepted form in blessings.[26] From about the same period it became customary to begin more and more prayers and pious works[27] with the Trinitarian formula, allied to the sign of the Cross, made preferably with three fingers.[28] And then, since the height of the Middle Ages it has been accepted in the Catechism as the shortest compendium of the Catholic Faith. In religious writings of the High Middle Ages, Trinitarian principles assumed an almost dispro-

23. Ps—Boniface, *Serm.* VI, 1 (PL 89, 855B); cf. ibid. I, 2; V, 1; VIII, 2; XV, 2. In these statements the doctrine of redemption is mentioned to the extent that, in the enumeration of the Persons, Jesus Christ, that is the God-man, is named in second place. Apart from this the story of redemption is told simply in another context. Cf. a similar summary in Pirminius, *Scarapsus* c. 286 (ed. Jecker: *Die Heimat des hl. Pirminius*, Münster 1927, 66). But with Pirminius the Trinitarian idea does not play such a big part. V. also the legendary *Vita* of St. Patrick, ed. Stokes: *The tripartite life of St. Patrick* (*Rerum brit. Scriptores*), London 1887, I, 100, quoted by W. Konen, *Die Heidenpredigt in der Germanenbekehrung*, Diss. Bonn 1909, 26 seq. In later times, Wolfram v. Eschenbach makes the priest recite a Creed which deals almost solely with the Trinity before the baptism of Feirefiz (*Parzival* XVI, ed. Lachmann6 817, V. 11 seq.).
24. For proofs v. Jungmann, *Missarum Sollemnia* I, 440 n. 49.
25. Thomas Aquinas is amongst early evidence: *Summa theol.* III, 72, 4; 84, 3 ad 3. At Confirmation the Trinitarian formula appears already in the *Ordo scrutinii* (7th cent.) and it recurs thereafter more frequently (Andrieu II, 446); e.g. in the *Ordo* of St. Amand (Andrieu III, 473) and in the Donation of Constantine (C. Mirbt, *Quellen zur Geschichte des Papsttums*, Tubingen 1924, 109 Z. 46).
26. Cf. Eisenhofer, *Handbuch* I, 278.
27. It appears at the beginning of the prayer at the altar steps not until the 14th century: thus in the Cistercian Missal: F. Schneider, *L'ancienne messe cistercienne*, Tilburg 1929, 131 seq.
28. Thus Innocent III: *De s. altaris mysterio* II, 45 (PL 217, 825).

portionately great importance. St. Bonaventure is the best known example of this. He finds indications of the Trinity everywhere and even his manner of presentation is permeated by the idea of the Trinity.[29]

Visual art too searched for ways of expressing the mystery. From the 11th century on, the Baptism of Jesus is 'treated in every New Testament scheme, and is represented oftener than any other New Testament scene' but not, as in more ancient art, in order to turn our attention to the Sacrament of Baptism, 'but because of the revelation of the Trinity associated with it.'[30] Towards the end of the Middle Ages this sort of picture became grouped along with others which show the Father (and often the Holy Spirit, too) in human form beside the Son—and a fresh development is on the way, expressed especially in the numerous pictures of the Coronation of Mary and in the various pictorial forms of the Throne of Grace.

We have already pointed out that we are no longer dealing with the direct recoil caused by the repulse of Arianism. But this is certain: it was the heightened interest in all things connected with the Trinity which the defensive struggle engendered that was the catalyst, setting this process in motion, making popular and giving ever new forms to these ideas.

6. 'Christ Our God'

The repercussion of the defensive war upon the conception of the Faith showed itself in an emphasis laid upon the mystery of the Trinity: even more directly, it was revealed in the concep-

29.   Cf. P. Pourrat, *La spiritualité chrétienne* II, Paris 1927, 266: 'In honour of the Blessed Trinity, every thought was divided into three parts, and every statement supported by three reasons.' On the number three and its application in church building v. J. Sauer, *Symbolie des Kirchengebäudes und seiner Ausstattung in der Auffassung des Mittelalters,* Freiburg 1902, 71 seq. In the *Theol. Revue* 41 (1942), 79 seq., G. Schreiber points out Trinitarian concepts in the medieval view of history and discusses Trinitarian ideas in various cultural spheres in the Middle Ages. Cf. especially A. Dempf, *Sacrum Imperium,* München 1929, 268–284.
30.   Künstle, *Ikonographie* I, 378.

tion and description of Christ Himself, around whose Person that warfare had been fought out.

The reply to most of these Bible texts with which the Arians confronted the Catholics, claiming that they proved the Son's Subordination to the Father, had to run something like this: these apply to the human nature in Christ, not to His Divinity. Thus, when they pointed to His praying, His submission to the Father's will, to His abasement in suffering and to His glorification by the Father, this was the reply. And the reply was repeated over and over again. It must, therefore, have filtered down to some extent into the popular mind; for King Sisibut, who represented the viewpoint in faith of the newly converted Visigoths rather than the science of the theologians, bemoans the fact, in a letter to the King of Lombardy, that the Arians constantly understood what was said of the human Nature to imply the subordination of the Son of God, whereas the Catholic Faith knew full well how to distinguish what concerns the human Nature and what the divine, and knew that Christ is under the Father only in the form of a servant—*forma servi*.[1] The treatise against Varimad,[2] too, supplies this solution in several places in long series of answers—but produces it without that robustness and tenacity which would have been appropriate. Often it is little more than a parry, as when the author counters the words: 'Father glorify the Son' with the observation that the Son, too, has glorified the Father;[3] or when in reply to the assertions that thanksgiving is offered to the Father through Christ (*per ipsum*) he can only say that Paul is already giving thanks to the Father without mentioning the Son,[4] or when he counters those passages which tell of the Son praying to the Father with those which show Him working miracles without prayer.[5]

Catholic apologetics show a certain nervousness when touching on the condition of the risen or glorified Christ and His sovereignty. Concerning this, they do not like speaking about subordination at all. Against the quotation of the names which the

1. Sisibut, *Ep.* 8 (PL 80, 376).
2. *Contra Varimadum* lib. I (PL 62, 351-400). Cf. above c. 4 n. 4.
3. Ibid. I, 17 (PL 62, 366).
4. Ibid. I, 45 (PL 62, 382 seq.); cf. I, 59 (390 seq.).
5. Ibid. I, 29 (PL 62, 372 seq.).

Father has given Christ, Avitus of Vienne[6] maintains the classic distinction: *non ei quem genuit, sed illi quem misit*.[7] But in other places we detect the tendency not to speak at all about the ruling of the God-man, Christ, in respect of which He remains subject to the Father; but to speak only of the common rule of the three divine Persons,[8] and even to minimize the Lord's office as our advocate with the Father (1 Jn. 2, 1: Rom. 8, 13). The same office of Paraclete is predicated of the Holy Spirit who likewise makes intercession for us.[9] Clearly, in such an atmosphere, the Easter-picture of the glorified God-man would have to grow somewhat pale, and the interest which had been distinctly apparent in the Gallican Church since the 5th century, would have to turn for satisfaction more and more to the Christmas and Epiphany themes, to the adoring worship of the Son of God appearing on earth, clothed in human flesh. In particular it now became quite natural to avoid where possible the old *per Christum* in liturgical prayer; and the attached phrase: *qui tecum vivit et regnat* had to be para-phrased or given a new interpretation at least, in line with current thought.[10] The *in unitate Spiritus Sancti* is changed to the clearer, and formerly much used, *cum Spiritu Sancti* in order to stress the

6. Phil. 2, 9. This and related passages, which speak of Christ's glorification by the Father, recur frequently in Arian polemics. Cf. e.g., Sisibut, *Ep.* 8 (PL 80, 376C).
7. Avitus, *Dialogi cum Gundobado rege* n. 29 (MG *Auct. ant.* VI, 2, p. 12 Z. 7).
8. The deacon Ferrandus proceeds from this idea in the letters of Fulgentius, *Ep.* 14, 35 (PL 65, 424): *Unum regnum Patris et Filii et Spiritus Sancti credimus et fatemur, simul eos dominari creaturis omnibus sentientes.* For this reason he objects to the style of the conclusion of prayers which run—even in Africa: *Per Jesum Christum Filium tuum Dominum nostrum, qui tecum vivit et regnat in unitate Spiritus Sancti*; but it never occurs to him (and even Fulgentius does not correct him) that here the *regnare* is applied to Christ in His human nature, and he is surprised only that the expression with reference to the Holy Spirit runs thus: *ut regnantes adunare, non simul regnare Spiritus Sanctus intimetur*. In similar state-ments, Fulgentius cites the same prayer-endings—*Ad Monimum* II, 5 (PL 65, 184)—to prove the equality of the three divine Persons: *Cuius (sc. precationis) consummatio, dum Filii et Spiritus Sancti complectitur nomen, ostendit nullum esse in Trinitate discrimen.* The *commune regnum Patris et Filii et Spiritus Sancti* is stressed also in the treatise *Contra Vari-madum* II, 62 (PL 62, 425 C). King Sisibut, *Ep.* 8 (PL 80, 378), likewise speaks in the same strain of the Holy Spirit, *qui cum Patre et Filio in unitate virtutis aequalis vivit et regnat.* Avitus of Vienne, *Dialogi cum Gundobado rege* n. 15 seq. (MG *Auct. ant.* VI, 2, p. 7), himself refuses to see any subordination in the passage 1 Cor. 15, 24: *cum tradiderit regnum Deo Patri*, because the Father has indeed handed over the Kingdom to the Son. It is only when he comes to 1 Cor. 15, 28 (*tunc etiam ipse Filius subiectus erit illi*) that he recognizes that it is the created nature which is under discussion.
9. *Contra Varimadum* II, 55 seq. (PL 62, 424). Cf. also the commentary on Nahum n. 45 (PL 96, 727), ascribed to Julian of Toledo, which sees Christ as *advocatus*, because He invites us to penance, grants righteousness and leads to glory.
10. Cf. the 134 items included in the index of Mozarabic doxologies and concluding formulae in Férotin, *Le Liber ordinum* 534-541.

equal power of the three Persons.[11] Besides this, by assuming a neutral form of address, directed now to the Father, now to the Son, and now to the Trinity, care is taken to attribute the *regnare* (of the new dominant phrase *qui vivis et regnas*, or *dominaris*) to the divine power.

There is certainly no question of denying in a monophysite way that Christ continues to live in His human nature since His glorification,[11a] but wherever possible, a separation of the divine and the human is avoided. They prefer to speak of the glorious life of the Trinity, of the eternal sovereignty of God; and if Christ is named we have the strong impression that it is His divine nature which predominates, very much as with prayers in Oriental liturgies which address 'Christ our God.' There is a Spanish inscription from the time of King Rekkared recounting the dedication of three Churches. It begins: *In nomine Dei nostri Jesu Christi consecrata est ecclesia.*[12] Frequently we feel that 'Christ' is used synonymously with 'God.' To this context belongs the much quoted introduction to the *Lex Salica: Vivat qui Francos diligit Christus, eorum regnum usque in sempiternum custodiat.*[13]

There is no doubt that with these and related manifestations from later times (and earlier times too) we are confronted with a popular simplification of the Christian message, accommodated to the primitive spirituality of these people and their less than sketchy instruction. But we cannot deny that even where it was possible for it to develop, the preaching of the Faith encountered

11. Ibid. n. 50 seq.
11a. Theodoret, *Eranistes* II (PG 83, 157 D).
11b. It is obvious that such an emphasis need not always be traced to anti-heretical roots. Cf. e.g., the expression, 'Jesus Christ our God' in Ignatius of Antioch (*Ad Rom.*, in the title) or *Christus Deus noster* in Aetheria, *Peregrinatio c.* 23. Similar expressions crop up frequently again in Gregory the Great.
12. H. Leclercq, *Espagne*: DACL V, 457 seq. The inscription runs: *Haec sancta tria tabernacula in gloriam Trinitatis indivisae . . . aedificata sunt.*
13. *Lex salica einendata* ed. Holder (1879) I seq. The ms. of Besancon-St. Gallen 731 (ed. Holder 1880, p. 1) concludes the blessing: *. . . dominantium Dominus Jesus pietatem concedat.* Cf. the judgment of H. v. Schubert in *Geschichte de christlichen Kirche im Frühmittelalter* 166 on Christ in the life of the Franks: 'He was like a national God to them.' And Ida Fr. Gorres, *Die siebenfache Flucht der Radegundis*, Salzburg 1937, 37, says about the Franks of the early Merovingian period, that for many of them Christ was merely a new God of battles—the one who gave victory. And a similar picture emerges of the remaining Teutonic tribes in H. Lother, *Die Christusauffassung der Germanen* (Gütersloh 1937), the conclusions of which are summed up by H. Wiedemann, *Theol. Revue* 36 (1937), 203: the Teutons were not converted to Christianity, but to Christ whom they recognized as a stronger deity.

many such notions. In his *Life of St. Willibrod*, Alcuin puts a missionary sermon into the mouth of this saint; and this equates Christ and God in a most decisive passage. The missionary preaches to the king: 'It is not God whom you worship, but the devil who holds you captive, O King, in the most deadly delusion, so that he may consign your soul to the eternal flames. There is no God but the One who created heaven and earth. . . . As His servant I testify to Him here and now so that you may forsake the mirage of ancient error which your fathers cherished, and become baptized into the Faith of Almighty God, our Lord Jesus Christ (credens in unum Deum omnipotentem Dominum nostrum Jesum Christum).[14] The editor of a collection of catechetical writings from St. Emmeram—taken to be a Carolingian mission catechism[15]—has already observed how little they contain of specifically Christian doctrine.[16] Of the five sections which make up the collection, four, deal with the Baptismal liturgy, and, in describing the Creed, mention the Passion and the Resurrection of the Redeemer, and then speak of receiving His body and blood; but the most comprehensive part, designed as systematic instruction—the *Ratio de catechizandis rudibus*—never touches any nearer upon the mystery of Christ but simply demands a renunciation of the devil in favour of Christ whose commandments must be kept, and then expounds wordily the substance of the commandments and the necessity of abandoning idolatry and of worshipping only the Creator of the world.[18]

14. Alcuin, *Vita Willibrordi* c. 11 (*Acta SS Nov.* III, 442). Cf. H. Wiedemann, *Die Sachsenbekehrung*, Hiltrup 1932, 55. Clearly the learned Alcuin distinguishes the concepts on other occasions, even when concerned with popular instruction, just as Charlemagne had done in the sermon guide of the *Admonitio generalis* of 789 (n. 81; MG *Leges* I, 66). Cf. chiefly Alcuin, *Ep.* 110 (MG *Ep. Karolini aevi* II, 159), where he draws up a sermon-plan for the mission to the Avars. First should come the immortality of the soul and eternal reward; then the *fides sanctae Trinitatis* is to be taught most carefully, and then the *adventus pro salute humani generis Filii Dei D. N. Jesu Christi* and the Passion and Resurrection of the Lord are to be expounded. On the other hand, Alcuin, too, definitely inclines to this simplified form of expression. Willibrod's train of thought recurs when we read in the explanation of the ceremonies of Baptism—*Ep.* 134 (loc. cit. 202 Z. 16)—*Exsufflatur etiam, ut fugato diabolo Christo Deo nostro paretur introitus*. Similarly in *Ep.* 137 (loc. cit. 214 Z. 23). Cf. *Ep.* 143 (loc. cit. 226 Z. 8): *in Christi Dei nostri tempora*. The expression *Deus Christus* also in *Ep.* 110 (loc. cit. 158 Z. 6); *Ep.* 138 (loc. cit. 216 Z. 28). Cf. the chapter *Christus unser Herr und Gott* in H. B. Meyer, *Alkuin zwischen Antike und Mittelalter* (ZkTh 1959) 317–324.
15. J. M. Heer, *Ein Karolingischer Missionskatechismus*, Freiburg 1911.
16. Heer, 32–40.
17. Heer, 94.
18. Heer 77–88.

The title and introduction of the work are, oddly enough, borrowed from St. Augustine who makes the history of salvation his central point. The impression is given that there is but one end in view: to persuade the candidate to be baptized and to keep the commandments—so different from St. Augustine's attitude. Anything more instructive, while in a sense included in principle, can, it seems, be left a bit vague. In particular the notions of God and of Christ may be allowed to some extent to coalesce.[19] The series of fifteen Carolingian model-catechisms, traditionally regarded as sermons of St. Boniface,[20] in more than one place contain a survey of the history of salvation, executed in part with reasonable expansion, set alongside appropriate moral exhortations. But, except when Scripture is being quoted—and sometimes then too—the choice of phrase is such that it seems to be God who was born of the virgin,[21] who has suffered insult and scorn, blows and scourging for us.[22] Almighty God has entered the world to turn away damnation from us,[23] God has so loved us that He died for us;[24] and we pray that He shall lead us to eternal joy, *qui nos creavit Jesu Christus Dominus noster.*[25]

No one is going to see dogmatic error in such phraseology. By virtue of the *communicatio idiomatum*, anything attributed to the Son of God can be attributed to the God-man, Jesus Christ, and *vice-versa.* It is another question, whether such speech is to

19. It is possible, as Heer assumes (34-36), that the author had in mind Alcuin's plan mentioned above in note 14, so that the doctrine of Christ and the Redemption were to have been treated later. Nevertheless it is significant that the actual traditional 'Mission Catechism' which, in any case, reflects missionary practice, leaves out the sections in question. In the mission work of St. Boniface too, we discover an emphasis on morality and discipline. V. E. Iserloh, *Die Kontinuität des Christentums beim Übergang von der Antike zum Mittelalter in Lichte der Glaubensverkündigung des hl. Bonifatius: Trierer Theolog. Zeitschrift* 63 (1954) 193-205. A missionary practice directed principally to the fulfilment of law and precept might consider verbal knowledge of the Creed and the frequenting of the feasts of our Lord after Baptism, as adequate knowledge of Christ and of God. St. Pirminius, too, strongly stresses the celebration of the principal Christian feasts. Besides this, he provides a detailed Christ-*kerygma*, in accordance with his faithfulness to tradition—*Scarapsus* c. 8-10 (Jecker 39-41; cf. 76, n. 8).
20. Ps—Boniface, *Sermones* (PL 89, 843-872). That these are model catechisms is shown by the introduction addressed to the clergy.
21. *Serm.* II, 2 (PL 89, 847 A).
22. *Serm.* X, 1 (PL 89, 862).
23. *Serm.* III, 1 (PL 89, 848 B).
24. *Serm.* XIV, 3 (PL 89, 869 D); *Serm.* II, 3 (PL 89, 847 B).
25. *Serm.* XIV, 3 (PL 89, 870 A); followed by a Trinitarian ending: *qui regnat cum Patre,* etc. Cf. the phrase *ministrare Christo Deo, Serm.* III, 4 (849 C); *Serm.* XII, 1 (865 A): we must preserve faith and Baptism *ante conspectum summi Dei et Salvatoris nostri Jesu Christi* (cf. Tit. 2, 13), *quia creati sumus ad laudem sui sancti nominis.*

be commended from a kerygmatic point of view; whether it should be made to serve only to emphasize the divine glory of Christ in individual cases, or be adopted as the norm of basic teaching. But here we are not concerned about the merits of this or that mode of preaching. We are dealing only with the question of how that suppression of Christ's humanity, which was brought about in the West as a result of the confessional strife of the 5th and 6th centuries, now continues to act and to contribute to the formation of the style of medieval piety.

An inevitable effect caused by the coalescence of the notion of God and Christ, by the neglect of the humanity of Christ, was this: Christ's mediation became more difficult to grasp. We have already seen how in the course of polemic the *per Christum* of liturgical prayer receded more and more. But during the time of confessional warfare it was not polemic alone which pressed the phrase into the background. In the new climate, the conditions for its living use were no longer present. The conditions were correspondingly all the more favourable for the development of the *veneration of the saints*. With great fervour, the devotion of the people was directed to the saints. The Church's rules for prayer stress all the while that they can be invoked only in the sense implied by the formulae *ora pro nobis*. At the same time, it is the saints who form the bridge to God.[26] The great surge of devotion to the saints is reflected, among other things, in the furnishing of churches. The image of Christ maintained, as of right, its old accustomed place. In the form of the crucifix it is set prominently, high up on the triumphal arch or some such place. Later it is placed on the altar between candles. It is worth noting, however, that the altar-pieces, which begin to have their vogue in the late Carolingian period, and their derivative altar-pieces with side-wings always have a picture of a saint as the dominant figure. To begin with this had usually been the martyr-saint whose relics reposed in the altar-stone. The zeal with which men

---

26. In the forms of the *Confiteor* which appear from the Carolingian period on, confession is made to *Deo et omnibus sanctis eius:* thus, for example, Udalrici, *Consuetudines Cluniac* II, 30 (PL 149, 716). St. Paul's order no longer appears (1 Tim. 5, 21), God—Christ—the elect angels, or as so often: God and Christ. But the abbreviation of which we speak had occurred even earlier. V. Benedict, *Regula* c. 58: the oblate promised obedience *coram Deo et sanctis eius* or—as C. Butler observes in his commentary on the Rule (1912 p. 102)—Cassian, *Institutiones* VII, 9: *coram Deo et angelis eius.*

hunted for relics of martyrs and built costly shrines to house them is amazing. These shrines appeared in their thousands and in ever new forms and styles, with ever new names and titles.[27] And all this was an endeavour to win the intercession of the saints. This could scarcely have gathered such momentum, had men been accustomed to view the Person of the Redeemer as much from the mediatorial and human side as from that of adoration of awesome divinity.

The development of this process moreover did not lead to any disappearance from the sight of the faithful of our Lord's earthly form. On the contrary, the Saviour walking this earth becomes simply the *epiphany of God*. While maintaining a basic, faithful profession of all that the Church taught, particularly about the two natures in Christ, this epiphany was regarded in such a way that all human will and feeling in Christ receded, and His earthly appearance was seen as but the point of God's operation.[28] This is the impression we gain on reading the descriptions in the *Heliand* in which the Teutonic hero-ideal at least helps to fashion the picture.[29] Christ is the All-powerful, the King of Heaven whose might is boundless. All human traits, especially any which reveal weakness and abasement, are obliterated by the bright rays of divinity. We find a similar picture in other early Teutonic poetry.[30]

This same careless interchangeability of *Christ* and *God* continues and is used even more clumsily in old French poetry. There

27. J. Braun, *Die Reliquiare des Christlichen Kultes und ihre Entwicklung*, Freiburg 1940.
28. Cf. the mark of Monophysite tendencies, which can be shown in many places even today, in K. Adam, *Jesus der Christ und wir Deutsche: Wissenschaft und Weisheit* 10 (1943) 75. Likewise in France and elsewhere, E. Masure, *Le sacrifice du chef*,6 Paris 1957, 113 n. 1; 115 seq.
29. The degree to which we must take account of the Teutonic hero-ideal is seen when we compare old Anglo-Saxon poetry which is much more in the Roman tradition and the foundation of which, as can be clearly seen, was scarcely touched by the anti-heretical movement. Cf. the analyses of J. Bach, *Die Dogmengeschichte des Mittelalters vom christologischen Standpunkt* 1, Vienna 1873, 81–85.
30. A number of proofs in H. Böhmer, *Das germanische Christentum: Theol. Studien und Kritiken* 86 (1913, 165–280) 214 seq. I cannot say whether we are at liberty to generalize the picture as Böhmer does, or whether the outlines of his sketch are not too rough and ready. The people: 'knew only that the Redeemer-Christ was the Redeemer-God, the God-king, the custodian of heaven, the almighty, the powerful, the sublime, the good, the kind Lord of all, the Father of the tribes, the God of glory, the eternal Lord and God . . . the omnipotent Creator and God of the great angels, of the human race and of all spirits, who is able to perform all things which He desires . . . and who also once clothed Himself in flesh, suffered, died, rose again.' Admittedly the 'Christ' of the monk Otfried of Weissenburg displays a different picture of the Redeemer—closer to men and more luminous. Cf. Bach I, 98–101.

46 PASTORAL LITURGY

is a specialist study of the theology of this literature which heads a relevant chapter with a refrain from this poetry which runs: 'Dear Father Jesus, Father of your mother.'[31] The author sees fit to ask in a subsequent chapter: 'Sabellius redivivus?'[32] We have here, indeed, a phraseology which could belong to the Modalist heretics of the 3rd century. Here we find thriving in happy profusion the late fruit of an anti-Arian polemical mind: formulae which had once been used in Spain by the very opposite of the Arians—the Priscillians. But they re-appear now with the very important difference, that by recognizing the Church's teaching authority they accept an implicit correction, a Catholic interpretation. We would discover a very similar picture, were we to study the theological and Christological attitude represented by German poetry of the same period.[34]

Some of the pre-scholastic sermon literature is itself on a par with this. Of German sermons in the 10th-11th centuries it has been said that they express 'the complete deification of Jesus, which delighted in applying the name "God" and "Creator" to

---

31. L. E. Wels, *Theologische Streifzüge durch die altfranzösische Literatur* I, Vechta 1937, 33-44. The idea of Christ as Creator of His mother already appears in isolated passages of Augustine. In the early Middle Ages it was on everyone's tongue—and in the printed form, Father of His mother. Vide A. L. Meyer, *Mater et filia. Ein Versuch zur stilgeschichtlichen Entwicklung eines Gebetsausdruckes:* JL 7 (1927) 60-82. Wels 36 seq. 40-42. Cases where, for no apparent reason, Christ is described as Father, occasionally appear even in earlier times. Examples in Wels 37 seq. Another case in Julian of Toledo, *Antikeimena* II, 11 (PL 96, 670 C). Benedict, *Regula* C. 2, 63 (Butler 12, 110) is apposite. Cf. (with numerous textual references) B. Steidle, *Abba Vater: Benediktin. Monatsschrift* 16 (1934) 89-101; M. Rothenhäusler, *Der Vatername Christi: Studien w. Mitt. 2. Geschichte des Benediktinerordens* 52 (1939), 178 seq.; Balth. Fischer, *Der Psalter als Christusgebet, Christliches Psalmenbeten nach Benedikt von Nursia: Trierer Theolog. Zeitschrift* 57 (1948), 321-334, esp. 330; ibid. on Benedict's interpretation of Romans 8, 15: *Colligere fragmenta* (Festschrift Dold), Beuron 1952, 124-126.
32. Wels 45-51. Cf. also the statement of H. Hatzfeld, *Liturgie und Frömmigkeit in den südromanischen Dichtersprachen:* JL 13 (1935), 76: 'The distinction in naming Christ and God the Father is seldom made in the romance poetry of the Middle Ages.' Wels, who sometimes champions the orthodoxy of these poets, believes (43 seq.) that their mode of expression must be explained as a protest against Arianizing false doctrine such as Abelard expounded in the 12th century. (In fact such doctrines were of interest only in theological circles.)
33. Cf. K. Künstle, *Antipriscilliana*, Freiburg 1905, 19-22. Priscillian taught a Docetist theology which left Christ with only an appearance of humanity, and, besides this, led to a purely nominal Trinity and ultimately to Patripassianism. Thus, for example, he says: *unus Deus trina potestate venerabilis omnia et in omnibus Christus est* (21).
34. There are repeated references to this phenomenon in H. Dittmar, *Das Christusbild in der deutschen Dichtung der Cluniacenserzeit*, Erlangen 1934, 13, 25, 41 seq., 59 seq., 76, 91. For a later period vide Wolfram von Eschenbach, *Parzival* IX (ed. Lachmann6 448, V. 2, 11 seq.).

Him even in respect of His human actions and sufferings.' Thus they spoke of *God* eating and drinking with the disciples, of *God's* feet, of *God's* Passion, and so on.[35] This language is common enough even in the late Middle Ages[36] and appears to have gone out of fashion only after preachers began to receive a more thorough theological education, in particular, after the Council of Trent.[37] We must again call to mind, therefore, that as well as the shift of accent, brought about by the reaction to Arianism at the beginning of the Middle Ages, we must also take into account the tendency to simplification and coarsening of the gospel message, a process which took place most of all where contact with the sources of the Faith had grown weak, and where intellectual analysis of the substance of Faith was neglected.[38]

Again, it is no accident that in the Christian art of the high Middle Ages God the Father is no longer portrayed symbolically as a hand raised out of the clouds, but is shown in human form.[39] This step had at least been made easier by the vagueness of the boundary between the notion of God and of Christ.

35. R. Cruel, *Geschichte der deutschen Predigt im Mittelalter*, Detmold 1879, 108 seq. The name Father is not infrequently used of Christ (ibid.). Examples of similar forms of speech in researches in 11th century mss. by A. Linsenmayer, *Geschichte der Predigt in Deutschland*, Munich 1886: the father of the household in Mt. 20, 1, is our Lord, the holy Christ, who 'rules over all He has created' (53 seq.); I believe in 'the three Persons, one true God . . ., that He was born and taken prisoner and martyred' (59).

36. 'God's corpse' was almost the regular term for the Eucharistic Body of our Lord, 'God's martyrdom' such a favourite expression for the Passion of Christ that proof is superfluous. A German version of the *Anima Christi* from the 14th century begins: 'God's soul save me, God's corpse . . .'; Balth. Fischer, *Das Trierer Anima Christi*: Trierer Theol. Zeitschrift 60 (1951) 192. 'The Lord God on the Cross' and 'the Lord God's corner' are examples of such modes of speech which have come to the present-day.

37. The *Manuale curatorum* of Fr. Joh. Mr. Surgant (in many editions since 1502) there still is a much used form of addressing the faithful: 'Devout children of Christ.' Cf. the summaries in *Katholik* 69 (1889) II, p. 181, 499, 510, 512 seq.

38. Cf. Karl Adam in his criticism of Herwegen's *Kirche und Seele*, Theol. Quartalschr. 106 (1925), 235: 'But the decisive reason (for the preference for ethics to enjoying the mystery in the Middle Ages) lies not in the peculiarity of the Teutonic spirit, but much more in the depth and sublimity of the message of redemption and grace, which can all too easily be misinterpreted by the average believer in a semi-Pelagian and moralistic sense when there is no zealous pastoral care imbued with a genuine Pauline spirit.' Phenomena like those under discussion here can be pointed out here and there in Christian antiquity, in that popular Christianity, that is, which we see in the New Testament Apocrypha. Certainly in this we must once more take account of that factor in the history of dogma which is supplied by the Gnostic background of much of this literature.

39. Cf Künstle, *Ikonographie* I, 233-235.

7. *Christus Secundum Carnem*

Quite clearly, Christian piety of whatever age, must centre round the Person of Christ. If, in the religious thought of the early Middle Ages, the ascended Christ recedes because His glory has become merged in that of the Trinity, then devotion to Christ has to find another sphere in which to operate. The *Christus secundum spiritum* to some extent disappears and the *Christus secundum carnem* is forced with all the more emphasis into the foreground. As the different development which took place in the East shows, this was not the only possible solution of the situation;[2] but it was the one into which the West was forced. And the fundamental mysteries of the work of salvation, the Incarnation and the Death on the Cross, become the introduction to and point of departure for further development.

The strife over the Person of Christ in due course moved on directly and unavoidably to the mystery of the Incarnation and the Virgin Birth. By the 4th century there had arisen isolated incidents of a clash between Arian and Catholic teachers over Marian dogma.[3] This too had to be defended, especially after the rise of Nestoranism with its belief that Mary had given birth to a purely human being. Thus the word Θεοτόκος had already become the badge of Catholicism by 431 at Ephesus. Now churches began to be dedicated to the Mother of God. Santa

1. II Cor. 5, 16. According to the penetrating examination of E. B. Allo, *Seconde epître aux Corinthiens*, Paris 1937, 167-169 and 179-182 this is the meaning of this not very evenly worked-out passage: if we apostles, especially those of us who knew the Lord in His earthly life, once knew Him in an earthly fashion (*secundum carnem*), we no longer know Him in such a way; and the decisive thing now is our spiritual relation to the Risen One.

2. By taking up again the Christological formula which originated with Cyril of Alexandria—μιά φύσις του Λόγου σεσαρκωμένη—the Byzantine Orient stressed the deification of the humanity in Christ; but at the same time it affirmed that this had been consummated in the Resurrection. Here too, then, in the re-action against Arianism, the Divinity of Christ has been over-stressed, but without doing any damage to the Easter thought-content. Cf. H. J. Schulz, *Die Höllenfahrt als Anastasis:* ZkTh 81 (1959) 1-66; and, *Der österliche Zug im Erscheinungsbild byzantischer Liturgie: Paschatis Sollemnia*, ed. by B. Fischer and J. Wagner, Freiburg 1959, 239-246. For the dogmatic-historical basis of this important study, v. *Das Konzil von Chalkedon*, ed. by A. Grillmeier and H. Bacht, Würzburg 1951/54.

3. The Arian origin of the attack on Catholic Mariology is abundantly clear in Helvidius, the pupil of the Arian Auxentius; G. Grutzmacher, *Helvidius: Protest. Real—Encyklop.* VII, 654 seq. The adherents of Bonosus, too, at a later date, are associated with Arians; cf. F. Loofs, *Bonosus:* ibid. III, 314-317. Cf. H. Rahner, *Die Marienkunde in der lateinischen Patristik (Kath. Marienkunde*, ed. by P. Straber, Paderborn 1952, 137-182) 146 seq., 166 seq.

Maria Maggiore is the best-known example showing an express connexion with the dogmatic decision of Ephesus. Feast days too, provided the newly assured dogmas with an appropriate expression. The rapid spread of Christmas celebration, even in the East, and of the keeping of Epiphany in the West was evidently encouraged by the fervour of the struggle for Catholic Christology.4 Soon the series of feasts of Mary, of which we have already spoken, were to follow.5 During the 7th century these found their way into the calendar everywhere in the West also.

A measure of the growing stress on the Christmas motif over against the previously dominant Easter motif is the fact that Dionysius Exiguus (d.c. 544), on fixing the new calendar, dates the year no longer from the death of the Saviour, but from *incarnatione Domini*. For all its brevity, the Apostles' Creed had firmly placed the appearance of the Saviour within history; but it dates it not from His birth but from His saving Passion: *passus sub Pontio Pilatio*.6 Thus far had the new fashion taken hold in Rome itself where Dionysius carried out his work. The popularity of the Christmas mystery gathered much greater momentum in the religious sentiment of the Gallic-Spanish Church than in Rome. Christmas and Epiphany in this region had already acquired a season of preparation by the 5th century, thus coming into line with Easter.7 Further, in the *Anamnesis* of the Mass, Incarnation and Passion began to be mentioned alongside the Passion and Resurrection.8

This impulse is manifested particularly well in Spain in veneration of the Mother of God. Ildefons of Toledo (d. 667) is the first author of a treatise specifically in her honour—the *libellus de virginitate perpetua sanctae Mariae*. We must assign the Twelve sermons on Mary to the same milieu: they are often transcribed along with his treatise.9 As early as the 7th century the vernacular

4. B. Botte, *Les origenes de la Noël et de l'Épiphanie*, Lowen 1932, 11 seq., 29 seq.
5. Above 5 seq.
6. Certainly, that the words *sub Pontio Pilato* have a temporal significance is not uncontested; v. F. Kattenbusch, *Das Apostolische Symbol* II, Leipzig 1900, 630-635.
7. Epiphanie became not merely a baptismal festival, but had a Lent prefixed to it also. Jungmann, *Gewordene Liturgie* 237-259 ('Advent' and 'pre-Advent'—ZkTh 1937, 345-362).
8. Proof in Jungmann, *Missarum Sollemnia* II, 276.
9. PL 96, 239-279. Cf. Bishop, *Liturgica Historia* 176 seq.

Burgundian *Missale Gothicum*[10] took over[11] several eulogystic phrases from the ninth of these sermons, and used them in the Preface of the Mass for the Feast of the Assumption.[12] About A.D. 700 a Bobbio manuscript[13] quotes the lyric verses from the seventh;[14] and these appear again a little later in the land of the Franks in the middle of a Christmas Preface of the *Gelasian Sacramentary*.[15] In these verses, the devout worshipper imagines himself transported to the crib at Bethlehem where he addresses these homely words to the mother of the divine Child: *Lacta mater cibum nostrum, lacta panem de coelo venientem, in praesepio positum velut piorum cibaria iumentorum. . . .*[16]

These words ring with a quality we are accustomed to hear during the height of the Middle Ages. They express a pious mediation which no longer sees the whole scheme of salvation only from the angle of its own consummation, from the per- spective of the exultation of Him who now sits at the Father's right hand; but which takes the contemplating soul back into the historical course of this story of salvation.[16a]

We should take note that in the West the veneration of Mary advanced most in those regions where the battle against Christo- logical heresy lasted longest; and it was in the same places that the strongly Marian poetry of the Syrian Church was translated

10. PL 96, 272. Cf. Bishop 177.
11. Ed. Bannister I (HBS 52) 31 seq.
12. The same Preface, somewhat shortened, also in the Bobbio Missal; variants, v. Bishop loc. cit. and *Missale Gothicum* II ed. Bannister (HBS 54) 27 seq. On Spanish origin cf. ibid. I (HBS 52) P. LXVIII, where south-west France and Rome are said to be sources of the *Libelli missae* of the *Missale Gothicum*. See also separate proofs of the con- flation with Spanish texts and the notes in Bannister II (HBS 54).
13. Bishop loc. cit.
14. PL 96, 268.
15. The older *Gelasianum* I, 9 (Wilson 9); *Gelasianum des Cod. Sang.* 34 B (Mohlberg n. 79).
16. The text goes back to Augustine. V. A. Chavasse, *Le sacramentaire gélasien*, Tournai 1958, 211 seq. Cf. E. Dumoutet, *Le Christ selon la chair et la vie liturgique au moyen-âge*, Paris 1932, 86. A fragment of a Marian prayer the separate sentences of which, once obviously linked with phrases from the Song of Songs, begin with *Veni;* published from an Irish palimpsest of the 7th century, Jh. A. Dold, Revue Bened. 38 (1926), 283; cf. 280, 285 seq. Examples of similar expressions of feeling in A. Dumon, *Grondleggers der Midde- leeuwse vroomheid: Sacri's eruditi* I (1948), 206–224. But here and there we find a related note in the early Christian period; v. Balth. Fischer, *Psalmenfrömmigkeit der Martyrerkirche*, Freiburg 1949, 11, 24 seq. Cf. further H. Weisweiler, *Das frühe Marienbild der Westkirche unter dem Einfluss des Dogmas von Chalcedon; Scholastik* 28 (1953; 321–360 and 504–525), 523 seq.
16a. Cf. also L. Scheffczyk, *Das Mariengeheimnis in Frömmigkeit und Lehre der Karo- lingerzeit*, Leipzig 1959, 126 seq.

and circulated.[17] The impulse carried on from here into the realm of the Frankish Church. From the time when St. Pirminius founded the monastery there, the veneration of the Mother of God had a great vogue in Reichenau. In this and other places, Churches built by him were principally dedicated to the Mother of God.[18] Alcuin, in his *Liber sacramentorum* provided two rites of the Mass for every day of the week. One of these is usually dedicated to one of the mysteries of salvation and the other to some special intention; but for Saturday, he makes both forms *de sancta Maria*.[19] And so within the weekly cycle, one day has already become dedicated solely to her. An indication of this setting apart of Saturday to her commemoration is provided by Peter Damian,[20] who already knows of a daily Office of our Lady which he is eager to popularize.[21]

Peter Damian (d. 1072), monk of Avellana and later a cardinal, belongs to the great reform movement of the 11th century. But the growing momentum of devotion to Mary was even stronger and more definite in that other, more important and older branch of this same movement—that of Cluny. Here we find the assertion: 'that the special service of Mary is a prominent mark of the Cluniac reform and of the reformers who are attached to it; that the most Blessed Virgin is, indeed the special patroness of the reformers.'[22] The mark is clearly displayed by the great 10th century abbots who are already praising Mary as *mater misercordiae*.[23] The new feature is also shown, among other ways, by the special Mary church or chapel which was a feature of all the reformed Cluniac monasteries of the 10th and 11th centuries. A procession was made to this chapel, morning and evening

17. Bishop, *Liturgica historica* 178 n. 3; cf. 161 seq.
18. V. the chapter *Sancta Maria Dei Genitrix* in A. Manser—K. Bayerle, *Aus dem liturgischen Leben der Reichenau: Die Kultur der Abtei Reichenau*, Munich 1925, 331 seq.
19. PL 101, 455 seq. Cf. G. Ellard, *Master Alcuin liturgist*, Chicago 1956, 144-173 esp. 168 seq.
20. Petrus Damiani, *Opusculum* 33, 4 (PL 145, 565 seq.).
21. Petrus Damiani, *De horis canonicis* c. 9 seq. (PL 145, 230): *horas beatae Dei Genitricis audire quotidie non gravetur.* In the lifetime of St. Ulrich (d. 973) we already find a sequence of prayers in honour of Mary added to the canonical Office: Ulrich prayed these daily and there is evidence of this in Bishop Berenger of Verdun (d. 962); v. Eisenhofer, *Handbuch* II, 559. Cf. Baumer-Biron I, 376; U. Berlière, *L'ascèse bénédictine*, Paris 1927, 49.
22. E. Tomek, *Studien zur Reform der deutschen Klöster im 11 Jh.*, Vienna 1910, 45; cf. 222 seq.
23. Tomek 222 seq., 44 seq.

every day, and special prayers were recited.[24] After Lauds and all the Hours, a Marian versicle (Post partum Virgo) with a corresponding prayer was said.[25] The Premonstratensians and the Cistercians[26] carried the development a stage further. In St. Bernard the movement reached its climax and full bloom. He was the great advocate in praise of the Virgin Mother, who in his homilies *super Missus* and in his sermons on the Assumption, never tired of praising the excellence of Mary.[27] From this time on we see the Marian theme playing an increasingly important part in the poetry, the art, and the popular devotion of the Middle Ages.[28]

But both in St. Bernard[29] and in pictorial art, this theme does not by any means appear in isolation. Quite plainly it is put at the service of the mystery of the Incarnation: Mary does not appear without her divine Child. As the records of the later Middle Ages in particular show, the theme is closely bound up with the whole story of the childhood and youth of our Redeemer. Above and as background to all other Marian feasts stands their origin —Christmas, which finds popular expression in the Nativity Plays and in other ways. The person of the Redeemer and the events of His life remain the chief point of interest.

In view of this it is somewhat surprising that scenes from the public life of Jesus play such a small part. They could have provided such a wide field for devout mediation on the Saviour's

24. Udalrici, *Consuetudines Cluniac.* I, 5 (PL 14b, 649 B). Here in the 11th century we already find the beginnings of the custom by reason of which the addition of the Marian antiphons to the end of the Hours became usual after the 13th century; cf. Eisenhofer, *Handbuch* II, 554 seq.; W. R. Bonniwell, *A History of the Dominican Liturgy*, New York 1944, 149–162; 209 seq.; 356–358.
26. G. Schreiber, *Prämonstratensische Frömmigkeit und die Anfange des Herz-Jesu-Gedankens:* ZkTh 69 (1940) 185.
27. Cf. Pourrat, *La spiritualité chrétienne* II, 76–89; Berlière, *L'ascèse bénédictine* 239–244.
28. St. Beissel, *Geschichte der Verehrung Marias in Deutschland während des Mittelalters*, Freiburg 1909, 195 seq. The increase in devotion to the Mother of God at this time is shown by Künstle, *Ikonographie* I, 92, who says concerning the models used for her in the art of the high Middle Ages: 'all of the older Marian types, especially those taken from Physiologus, (are) primarily Christologic.' Cf. also the important proofs in G. G. Meersseman, *Der Hymnos akathistos in Abendland*, Freiburg 1958. Popular Marian devotion did not always keep within proper bounds; cf. Beissel 268, 491 seq., 502 etc. For relevant phenomena in southern Romance poetry of the high Middle Ages, v. H. Hatzfeld, *Liturgie und Volksfrömmigkeit in den südromanischen Dichtersprachen des Mittelalters* I. *Das Marien thema:* JL 13 (1935) 66–74; esp. 69 seq.
29. Cf. Pourrat II, 60 seq.; J Ch. Didier, *La dévotion à l'humanité du Christ dans la spiritualité de s. Bernard: La vie spirituelle* 24 (1930) 1–19.

earthly life.[30] Even when interest is directed to the earthly life
of Jesus, the focal points still remain those connected with the
great events of salvation, those events which were kept alive in
the minds of the faithful both by the Creed and the liturgical
year. Thus, alongside 'conceived by the Holy Ghost, born of the
Virgin Mary,' the second theme is designated by the words,
'suffered under Pontius Pilate, was crucified, dead and buried.'

Christianity has always put the work of salvation at the heart
of its devotion. But it is significant that primitive Christianity
determined its weekly and yearly commemoration day, not with
reference to the pouring forth of the Saviour's blood during the
Passion, but with reference to His glorious exultation. To this day,
we celebrate Sunday every week—not Friday; and year by year
we celebrate Easter Sunday more particularly than the days of
the Holy Week. From the beginning, our Lord's Cross has received
supreme honour; but where it has been more than a mere aid to
memory and has been used as a figurative representation, then
it has always been seen as the Cross of Glory—not simply the
blood-stained ignominious wood, bearing the Saviour's broken
body. When representations of the Crucified Lord begin to be
made, usually it is the Victor, surrounded with the aura of His
risen glory, who is depicted: *regnavit a ligno Deus*.

In the Middle Ages, the new spirit ruling religious life showed
itself with special clarity in this very theme of the Passion. They
desired to follow the course of the Passion-story in all its detail,
and the favourite scenes were those calculated to evoke sympathy.
People no longer spoke, as does the Canon of the Roman Mass,
of the *tam beata passio*, that is, of the Passion seen in the light of the
glory of the Resurrection, but of our Lord's bitter sufferings
which arouse our compassion.

Such a tendency arose early on Syrian soil. Syrian religious
poetry and Aetheria's account of the Holy Week in Jerusalem
show it in evidence as early as the 4th century. It seems to have
been Syrian merchants who first introduced realistic representations of the Crucified Saviour into Gaul, arousing great amaze-

30. Cf. Künstle, *Ikonographie* I, 388: 'The high Middle Ages neglected the miracles of
the public life of our Lord in general, in a remarkable manner: all the more did they dwell
fervently upon His Passion.' Cf. the separate portrayals in Künstle I, 320-658.

ment.[31] We may reasonably assume that these objects were the product of popular devotion.

Similar tendencies appeared in the West in the 7th century when, in a tone mainly deprecatory, Bishop Braulio of Saragossa (d. 657) is found speaking of the people's desire to venerate relics of our Lord's Passion—especially of the Holy Blood—and of the wide-spread notion that such things ought to have a place in the cathedrals.[32] The same Bishop himself shows an interest in this historical approach to Passion—meditation, by trying to explain an omission from the Roman liturgy of one of the Good Friday Offices by saying that this no doubt was meant to express the apostles' confusion during these days.[33] At about the same time the *Missale Gallicanum vetus*[34] provides prayers for Good Friday which could have been composed by a late medieval mystic. As with the Christmas prayer mentioned earlier, we find here a going back into the very hour of the mystery, as when the worshipper begs in fervent words for the kiss of the Crucified, the beloved Bridegroom: Hac nunc tu (hora) noster dilecte sponse, osculare de cruce; at the same time saying, as if making excuse: licet post crucis tropheum.[35] Interest in all the details of our Lord's self-emptying is shown also in other Gallican sacramentaries where the Octave of Christmas, observed in Rome at first simply as the Octave is celebrated as the Circumcision and named accordingly.[36] Veneration of the Cross on Good Friday—witnessed by Aetheria in Jerusalem—first came to Rome during the 7th century, probably from Greece. But it was strictly contained within the rules of the Roman liturgy. On the other hand, we find the practice much more developed in northern lands from the 10th century onwards. Here to the accompaniment of singing, the rite had become expanded into a burial ceremony,

31. Gregory of Tour, *De gloria Martyrum* c. 23 (PL 71, 724 seq.). Cf. H. Leclercq, *Croix et crucifix:* DACL III, 3079.
32. Braulio of Saragossa, *Ep.* 42 (PL 80, 689 seq.). The writer stresses, in opposition to those, that the Church holds fast by the sacraments and Holy Scripture.
33. Braulio of Saragossa, *Ep.* 14 (PL 80, 661 B). On the veneration of relics of the Holy Cross and on the devotion to the Cross even in an earlier period, cf. M. Viller—K. Rahner, *Aszese und Mystik in der Väterzeit,* Freiburg 1939, 295-300.
34. Ed. Mohlberg (1958) n. 118.
35. Cf. the appraisal of this passage in A. Baumstark, *Vom geschichtlichen Werden der Liturgie,* Freiburg 1923, 91.
36. *Missale Gothicum* ed. Bannister (HBS 52) 16 seq.; Bobbio Missale ed. Lowe (HBS 58) 32 seq.

calculated to affect the senses and the feelings. Here is the Medieval Passion Play in embryo.[37] Mention is made in the Roman-German Pontificale, composed about A.D. 950 in Mainz, of special prayers for the veneration of the Cross to be made at the first, second and third genuflexion.[38] In monasteries, the Passion becomes a favourite subject for pious meditation. Literary records show that this was so at least from the 8th century, beginning with Alcuin[39] and the treatise De Passione Domini of Candidus of Fulda (c. 820) which meditatively follows the course of the Passion.[40] Here again St. Bernard is the first climax. It has been said of him that he saw the whole life-work of Christ from the point of view of the Passion.[41] In the poetry of the period too, in the picture of Christ the features of the victorious king, are augmented more and more by those of the patient sufferer.[42]

The Passion theme was forced into the foreground of pictorial art at about the same time as in devotional life. Preference was now given to scenes, formerly neglected, which are specially capable of arousing feeling. The scourging appears for the first time in the 10th century.[43] With ever increasing elaboration there now follow more pictures of the Way of the Cross, up to the taking down from the Cross. At first these are restrained, but realism slowly gains ground until we arrive at the naturalistic Passion pictures of Gothic art. The portrayals of the Resurrection and of the glorified Christ, which in many places were plentiful in the Byzantine art of the early Middle Ages,[44] are not absent in this period and later, it is true; but they are no longer at the centre

37. K. Young, The Drama of the Medieval Church I, Oxford 1933, 121 seq., 553.
38. M. Hittorp, De divinis cath. Ecclesiae officiis, Cologne 1568, 65 seq. (recte 67 seq.).
39. A corresponding prayer for Good Friday, but without the rubric, in the Pontificale of Pritiqus, which belongs to the 9th century; cf. A. Wilmart, JL 4 (1924) 67 seq. Cf. also the penetrating research of A. Wilmart, Auteurs spirituels et textes dévots du moyen-âge latin (Paris 1932) 138-146, into 'Les prières de s. Pierre Damien pour l'adoration de la croix,' and the same author's. Prieres médiévales pour l'adoration de la croix: Eph. liturg. 46 (1932) 22-65; further—Dumoutet, Le Christ selon la chair 18 seq.
39a. G. Ellard, Devotion to the Holy Cross: Theol. Studies 77 (1950), 333-355, esp. 344 seq.
40. PL 106, 57-104. Further proofs in Berlière, L'ascèse bénédictine 236-239; Dumoutet 19 seq.; Dumon (above note 16).
41. W. Kahles, Radbert und Bernhard. Zwei Ausprägungen christlicher Frömmigkeit, Emsdetten 1938, 25; cf. 44-50; 115 seq. v. also Pourrat II, 71-75.
42. H. Dittmar, Das Christusbild in der deutschen Dichtung der Cluniazenserzeit, Erlangen 1934, 87 seq., 95.
43. Künstle, Ikonographie I, 434 seq.
44. Künstle, Ikonographie I, 507 seq.

of interest.[45] They form rather, the final scene in the Passion drama; and so, because of this and perhaps also because representatives of redeemed humanity are depicted as well, they have lost their historic-redemptive significance. They bear more the character of vanquished suffering than of the beginning of glory.[46]

These manifestations we have just sketched, and which appear even more clearly and emphatically as the Middle Ages advance, are a sign of how the humanity of Christ has become the favourite subject of religious life, in contrast to primitive Christianity's emphasis on Christ's divinity.[47] Devotion to the humanity of Christ was the great medieval innovation.[48] To speak thus is not wholly accurate. Christ's divinity was never so strongly stressed as in medieval religious language which made the widest possible use of the *communicatio idiomatum*, as we have observed; and conversely, in the minds of the Fathers, Christ's humanity had always been to the fore-front. Take Augustine, for example. In his *Enarrationes in psalmos*, which reveals most directly, perhaps, the mind of the great Fathers of the Church, he continually speaks of Christ who has overcome Satan through His weakness upon the Cross, and who now is Head of the Church which along with

45. It is significant that devotion to the Way of the Cross—belonging to a later age—with its attached series of pictures, ends in the laying in the grave. When the Catholic missions in Japan were destroyed in the 17th century, those suspected of being Christians had to walk on a sheet of metal on which four pictures were portrayed: Mary with the Child; *Ecce Homo;* the Crucifix; the deposition; H. Preuss, *Das Bild Christi im Wandel der Zeit,* Leipzig 1915, 178 seq. Antiquity, too, had a summary in four pictures of the Christian mystery in the interpretation of the four living creatures of Ezechiel. In these, the Passion, and even more, the victory of the Redeemer, were emphasized. Cf. Künstle, *Ikonographie* I, 611 seq. Preuss, loc. sit. tells us of a totally different and tragic sort of truncation of the Christ-theme when he describes an exhibition of pictures of Christ in Berlin in 1898 at which not a single Crucifix appeared. Following Harnack's view, here we have Christ no longer living on in glory, no longer the God-man, bringing redemption, but Christ the ideal of manhood pure and simple.

46. This is expressed by St. Bernard, for example, when he makes the Ascension appear as an occasion for sorrow to the apostles and devout worshippers, because of the parting involved—a clear contradiction of the Gospel account (Lk. 24, 52). V Kahles 23, 115.

47. Thus, int. al.—in spite of the title of his book—Dumoutet, *Le Christ selon la chair* 8 seq.

48. Thus, int. al. F. Vernet, *La spiritualité médiévale,* Paris 1929, 77 seq., following P. Rousselot. It is significant that Vernet describes the ancient Christian antithesis more exactly by saying that in those days people paid more heed to the divinity of Christ, because this was threatened by the Christological heresies and by Pelagianism (79). But by the 4th-5th centuries we have already reached the point where the new style of piety is being introduced. But Vernet adds, rightly: inasmuch as people looked upon the God-man, it was not the crucified but the triumphant Christ whom they saw.

Him constitutes the *Christus totus*. Such a train of thought obviously is speaking about the humanity of Christ. The attitude of older witnesses who, developing Pauline theology, saw Christ as the second Adam, the Mediator, the High-Priest, through whom we offer prayer to God, is not substantially different—even if the idea of the Mediator, from the stand-point of the *Logos*-theology of the time, is often joined to the concept of the Word of the Father. The distinction between primitive and medieval Christianity is much more, that for the Fathers, the humanity of Christ is the starting off place for the new humanity, the new creation now irradiated with divinity—as they are ever ready to declaim against heresy; whereas the Middle Ages sees the humanity of Christ primarily as it was in the days of His earthly life, in the form of a servant, in that form which—contrasting with all that faith knows of divine transcendence—it can alone appeal to sense and arouse feelings of compassion, of amazement, of thanksgiving and repentance in the hearts of the faithful.49

Whatever the ultimate explanation may be of this evolution, of medieval devotion to Christ which has been called 'Jesus piety,' it certainly cannot derive directly from the reaction to Teutonic Arianism, which we have described. This is indicated clearly by the very different evolution in the East. Setting aside moral and racial factors, which played their part,50 the important thing was the different approach to anti-Arian Christology in the West. On a foundation of pure Chalcedonianism which sharply separated the two natures in Christ and then set them simply side by side, the temptation was always present to lay so much stress on the divine nature that the meaning of the human nature for redemption, especially in its Easter consummation, all too easily

49. Kahles, *Radbert und Bernhard*, pertinently points in this regard to the antithesis between the Patristic and the medieval form of contemplation. As the chapter titles themselves show, the question at issue is the 'pneumatic' image of Christ of the Fathers, on the one hand, as against the 'empirical-psychological' image of Bernard on the other; the 'objective-pneumatic' imitation of Christ of the former, contrasted with the 'individualistic-ethical' imitation of the latter.

50 Cf. above (c. 1 preceding note 17) the thesis of Abbot Herwegen. A. L. Mayer, *Altchristliche Liturgie und Germanentum:* JL 5 (1925) 80-96. Cf. also the other relevant studies of this author, esp. *Die Liturgie und der Geist der Gotik:* JL 6 (1926) 68-97. Kahles, *Radbert und Bernhard* 138 seq. attempts in particular to trace the original power, through which Bernard shaped the new spiritual attitude, back to the Teutonic factor of his Burgundian ancestry.

was lost to view.[51] But this was the form resistance to Arianism took in the West.

8. Christ, the Church and the Sacraments

Such a thorough-going change in the structure of basic Christian thought could not but make itself felt in other spheres of faith. This happened especially with the conception of Church and sacraments.

If the clouds which took the Lord away from His disciples up to heaven now, to some extent, hide the glorified God-man from the minds of the faithful, inasmuch as they have become accustomed to allowing His heavenly life to be swallowed up in the divine majesty in which He becomes one with the Father;[1] so too that light by which the Church is seen as the Body of Christ grows dim also. For Christ can only be described as Head of the Church in His glorified humanity. It is only of His humanity that the faithful can become members through Baptism, so that they form one Body with Him, that they corporately become, indeed, His Body. It is well-known how little the thought of the Church as the Body of Christ flourished in the Middle Ages.[2]

It is true that to the medieval Christian mind the Church remained a creation of divine origin, but its cohesion was seen to result principally from moral forces. This becomes particularly clear in the change which took place in the notion of the Church as the Mother of All the Faithful.[3] The early Church had been

51. Cf. H. J. Schulz, *Die Höllenfahrt als Anastasis* (ZkTh 1959) 53-57.
1. Above c. 6 at n. 9.
2. Cf. E. Mersch, *Le corps mystique du Christ II*, Löwen 1933, 132, 139, 278 seq.; Herwegen, *Antike Germanentum und Christentum* 48 seq. Cf. A. Mayer-Pfannholz, *Der Wandel des Kirchenbildes in der Geschichte: Theologie und Glaube* 33 (1941) 22-34. Certainly in Patristic times the notion of the Church as woman, as virgin and mother was more popular than that of the Body of Christ; cf. A. Wikenhauser, *Die Kirche als der mystische Leib Christi*, Münster 1937, 231.
3. A. Mayer-Pfannholz, *Das Bild der Mater Ecclesia im Wandel der Geschichte: Pastor bonus* 53 (1942), 33-47.

accustomed to interpret the image of mother primarily in the simple biological sense, as the well-known inscription on the Lateran Baptismal font shows: *Virgineo foetu genetrix Ecclesia natos, Quos spirante Deo concipit, amne parit.*

The Church is mother of her children because she gives them life in grace and feeds them for eternal life: She is the Bride of Christ, the second Eve, the Mother of the Living.4 In the Middle Ages even when they continue to use the title of 'Mother,' men see in the Church chiefly a sovereign. 'The mother and nourisher becomes more and more the leader and commander'.5 The title of 'Mother' becomes transferred even as early as Gregory VII, for preference, to the guiding authority of the Church: the *Sedes Apostolica* in Rome is the princeps et universalis mater omnium ecclesiarum et gentium.6 Whereas hitherto the *mater Ecclesia*, throned upon the church-building, had appeared on the *Exultet*-scrolls of Holy Saturday, from the 13th century there appears a bishop in the same place and attitude.7 It is now the temporal, organizational aspect of the Church which stands in the fore-ground. It was in this light that the singer of the *Heliand* had already seen the beginnings of the Church when he portrayed it as the confederacy of Christ's faithful ones, all bound to him chiefly by moral ties.8

A consequence of this stress on the temporal character of the Church and its juridical-hierarchial apparatus was the coming into prominence of the contrast between clergy and laity. Out-ward circumstances assisted this development. Only the clergy now understood the liturgical language. The Teutonic peoples were accustomed to having an upper stratum of society who possessed sole power to direct; and to this group all of the higher clergy belonged. New theological concepts, too, played their part. The Carolingian clergy begin to wonder how the *Canon*

4. Cf. the collection of texts by Hugo Rahner, *Mater Ecclesia. Lobpreis der Kirche aus dem 1. Jahrtausend christlicher Literatur*, Einsiedeln 1944.
5. Mayer-Pfannholz, *Das Bild der Mater Ecclesia* 40. There is plentiful evidence here.
6. Gregory VII, *Resgistrum* ed. Caspar 238, 343, 503; in Mayer-Pfannholz 41.
7. Cf. M. Avery, *The Exultet Rolls of South Italy*, Princeton 1936, Volume of tables, table CXL: The Ecclesia seated upon the church building, from the Exultet roll of St. Vincent of Volturno, painted 981-987; table CLVIII: Bishop seated upon the church building, from the Exultet roll of Salerno, 13th century (a reference of my colleague in religion, Fr. Hugo Rahner, S.J.).
8. Herwegen refers to this: *Antike, Germanentum und Christentum* 47.

60   PASTORAL LITURGY

of the Roman Mass is able to speak of the faithful: *qui tibi offerunt hoc sacrificium laudis*, and they add: *quo quibus tibi offerimus*,[9] if they do not in fact delete the former phrase.[10] Only the priest is permitted to enter the sanctuary to offer the sacrifice. He begins from now on to say the prayers of the Canon in a low voice and the altar becomes farther and farther removed from the people into the rear of the apse. In some measure, the idea of a holy people who are as close to God as the priest is, has become lost. The Church begins to be represented chiefly by the clergy. The corporate character of public worship, so meaningful for early Christianity, begins to crumble at the foundations.

We would not be far wrong, were we to take account of the overshadowing of the idea of the glorified God-man who is Head of the Church and the connected medieval thought of the Church as primarily a juridicial institution when we come to explain the new situation concerning the relation between Church and State in the course of the Middle Ages. The point of view we have described led first of all to the prominence of the temporal and institutional aspect of the Church and consequently of the social resemblances between the two entities, between the *civitas Dei* and the *civitas terrena* which St. Augustine had already contrasted in his historico-philosophical work; and thus the conception of the two spheres of jurisdiction became juxtaposed as though there had been a straightforward separation of these two jurisdictions, resulting from the blurring of the boundaries between the concept of God and of Christ.

If civil and ecclesiastical authority both come from the same Christ-God, the temptation becomes even stronger, to combine the two authorities in a single theocratic system, as though it were perfectly clear that the state derives from the social, human nature in God whereas the Church, as the realm of supernatural order, is based upon the work of the God-man and is held together by Him.[11] This temptation became operative all the

9. The expansion is traceable, probably, to Alcuin, certainly to his circle; more detailed documentation in Jungmann, *Missarum Sollemnia* II, 205 seq.
10. Examples in A. Ebner, *Quellen und Forschungen zur Geschichte und Kunstgeschichte des Missale Romanum*, Freiburg 1896, 404 seq.
11. This awareness permeates the entire letter which the Saxon priest Cathuulf wrote to Charlemagne in 775: *Memor esto ergo semper, rex mi, Dei regis tui cum timore et emore, quod tu es in vice illius super omnia membra eius . . . et episcopus est in secundo loco, in vice Christi tantum est.* MG Ep. IV, 503.

quicker because a series of other factors were pressing towards the same system. The distinction between Christ and God has already been abandoned when Abbot Smaragdus (d.c. 830) warns the king: *Fac quidquid potes pro persona quam gestas . . . pro vice Christi qua fungeris.*[12] The *Ordo* for the coronation of a king, according to the Roman-German Pontificale (c. 950) is on the same level when it expresses the wish that the King may reign for ever: *cum mundi salvatore, cuius typum geris in nomine,*[13] and here the anointing[14] which is now attached to the rite must have assisted the transition from *unctus* to *Christus.*[15] Since the 11th century, theological discussions had been going on which developed the theory of the two swords given by Christ to Peter (Lk. 22, 38). The attempt was made, it is true, to trace back the assignation of temporal power primarily to the Pope—*Papa habet utrumque gladium*—unambiguously to the positive intention of Christ; and also to fix limitations accordingly.[16] Other views, however, are remarkable for their inclination to absolutism. On the day of his coronation, September 8, 1024, King Conrad II was greeted thus by the Bishop of Mainz: 'You have attained the highest dignity, you are Christ's representative'.[17] In his notorious letter of 1076 to Hildebrand, Henry IV, grandson of Conrad, complains of the behaviour of Popes: 'As though royal power were not in God's hands, in the hands of our Lord Jesus Christ who has called us to rule.'[18] The *Saxon Mirror* (1220) explains the origin of supreme power and refers to the two swords: 'God left two swords upon the earth to protect Christendom.'[19] The

12. Smaragdus, *Via regia* c. 18 (PL 102, 958).
13. M. Hittorp, *De divinis catholicae Ecclesiae officiis ae ministriis,* Cologne 1568, 1346. Cf. M. Andrieu, *Le Pontifical Romain au moyen-âge,* Rome 1940, 383. Cf. W. Durig, *Der theologische Ausgangspunkt der mittelalterlichen liturgischen Auffassung vom Herrscher als vicarius Dei: Hist Jahrbuch* 77 (1958), 174-187, which had already discussed the texts mentioned—from a different point of view, admittedly.
14. C. A. Bouman, *Sacring and Crowning,* Groningen 1957, 107 seq.
15. Cf. the address of John VIII to Charles the Bald (877): Mansi XVII App. 172; Durig 184.
16. Cf. the study of J. Lecler, *L'argument des deux glaines: Recherches de science religieuse* 21 (1931) 299-339; 22 (1932) 157-177; 280-303.
17. Thus according to the account by Wipo, *Das Leben Kaiser Konrads* II. Pflüger und Wattenbach (*Die Geschichte der deutschen Vorzeit* 41) 25.
18. Bruno, *De bello saxonico* c. 67 (MG Scriptores V, 352): *quasi nos a te regnum acceperimus, quasi in tua et non in Dei manu sit regnum relimperium; qui Dominus noster Jesus Christus nos ad regnum, te autem non vocavit ad sacerdotium.*
19. I, 1 (ed. Müller 21). The Latin text which serves today as a translation, replaces God by Christ (ibid. 3).

Swabian Mirror hands this on with less finesse when it says that, 'When He went up into heaven' He (God) left two swords upon the earth for the protection of Christendom.[20] Such a way of thinking, even if typical only of the laity, did not make it easier to apportion mutual interests neatly.

The Spiritual nature of the Church was partly clouded over: understanding of the individual's life of grace suffered in consequence. They continued to receive the sacraments. They were an obligatory part of Christian life. Children were baptized, the faithful were blessed as of old, and, presumably, the number of Christians living at that time in a state of grace was no less than at other times. But it is remarkable how weak was the Christian's sense of sanctity. The prayer literature of the period shows this. A negative attitude dominates the scene from the 9th to the 11th century. Self-accusation, confession of personal unworthiness and sin recurs with endless monotony, even in our best known texts— those of prayers for monks and clergy.[21] Appreciation of Baptism —a sense of the objective sanctity which remakes the being of a Christian, which we receive as a share in Christ's holiness through Baptism and the other sacraments, which remains with us despite all the wretchedness of frail human nature so long as we avoid mortal sin—all this seems to have vanished. Men seem to be preoccupied with clinging to moral goodness, with attaining a moral heroism raising them well above the average.[22] The supernatural world has receded: this world is to the fore.

The attitude to the Eucharist is typical. Frequency of Communion becomes less and less, until people have to be urged to make their yearly Communion.[23] This is not to be explained simply by saying that the laity were luke-warm in those days. Too great a tension has been allowed to develop between the holiness and sublimity of what was received and the sinfulness and nothingness of him who received. Forms of a *Confiteor* appear in the 10th century wherein accusation is made of receiving

20. Preface (ed. Lassberg p. 4 seq.).
21. F. Cabrol, *Apologies*: DACL I, 2591-2601.
22. Cf. Herwegen, *Antike, Germanentum und Christentum*, 47 seq. The psychological transition to this obscuring of the sense of the supernatural in the Christian mind is more fully developed by K. Adam, *Christus Unser Bruder?* Regensburg 1930, 55-57; cf. also Jungmann, *Die Frohbotschaft* 83 seq.
23. P. Browe, *Die Pflichtkommunion im Mittelalter*, Münster 1940; P. Browe, *Die häufige Kommunion im Mittelalter*, Münster 1938.

Communion without first having made a confession.[24] This is obviously a product of the pastoral outlook. We are far away indeed from the early Christian conception of the Eucharist as the daily bread which the Christian as a citizen of the heavenly city is called upon to eat.

At the same time, men do not abandon the Blessed Sacrament. A new relationship to the Eucharist arises, coming fully into evidence only at the turn of the 12th century. From then on, however, we can speak of a formal Eucharistic movement, having as its object not the approach to the Blessed Sacrament but withdrawal from it.[25] The Sacrament which men dare not receive is at least to be contemplated from a distance and devoutly adored. From this derive various practices: the elevation of the Species at the *Consecration;* exposition of the Sacrament upon the altar; carrying the Sacrament in solemn procession; and other forms of devotion. The object is not the *use* of the Sacrament but its *cult;* for, as popular meditation loves to think; here, it is *God* whom man confronts in prayer. The resulting forms may, indeed, be on the whole quite legitimate—an enrichment of a Eucharistic piety derived from another source, and ultimately capable of integration with it;[26] but it still remains true, that until that integration was accomplished these forms represented a deviation from the original meaning of the Sacrament: and a major factor which set off this deviation was the state of Christological thought, still affected by defensive polemic and not yet having attained balanced expression.[27]

---

24. Ps.—Alcuin, *De psalmorum usu* II, 9 (PL 101, 499 C). More related proofs in P. Browe, *Die Kommunionsvorbereitung im Mittelalter:* ZkTh 56 (1932), 375-415, esp. 382 seq.

25. P. Browe, *Die Verehrung der Eucharistie im Mittelalter,* Munich 1933.

26. On restrictive measures by ecclesiastical authority about the end of the Middle Ages, v. Browe, *Die Verehrung* 166-173.

27. A significant development of this study from the point of view of the continuing evolution of this devotional life down to the present and of its pastoral breadth is offered by F. X. Arnold, *Das gott-menschliche Prinzip der Seelsorge und die Gestaltung der Christlichen Frömmigkeit: Das Konzil von Chalkedon,* Würzburg 1954, 287-340.

9.   *The State of Liturgical Life on the
Eve of the Reformation*

The dying Middle Ages were admittedly no longer a time of
blossoming in the life of the Church: it was a time of decline, of
decay, to be followed by an extensive collapse. What was the
liturgy like at that time?

The answer cannot be given briefly. Things were not so bad,
however, as we might think, judging from the general state of
the Church at that time. According to the traditional view of the
liturgy, there must have been an undoubted blooming of the
liturgy on the eve of the Reformation.

Everywhere, in town and country, the worship of God was
carried out with great splendour on Sundays and feast days. Work
ceased and rest from work was enforced by civil sanctions. As a
Synod of Salzburg(1456) insisted afresh, the city gates must be
closed on Sundays and feast days so that the peace be not disturbed
by travellers with their carts[1]. Feast days, which varied from state
to state, were numerous—about fifty in all. Thus, besides Sunday,
there was on average one holiday of obligation each week. The
days of the apostles and of commemoration of famous saints and
martyrs and virgin-martyrs were all observed by cessation of
labour. Then there were many local holidays. People took time
to worship God: inns were open as a rule not for profit, but for
necessary provisions, and most of the free time was devoted to
worship. The centre of liturgical life was, as of old, the cathedral
church with its canons and clergy.

But in the towns, and often in the country too, there were also
the parish churches with their parish services, as well as many
others: numerous monasteries belonging to the ancient enclosed
and mendicant orders; the collegiate churches with their comple-
ment of canons—usually a symbolic number, 6-12-24—whose
work was to sing the Divine Office. Not only on Sundays and
feast days but every day these had to celebrate solemn worship as
in the cathedrals and monasteries. All of the seven canonical Hours
were either said or sung publicly in choir, and each day the

X.   Address to the congress of the *Genootschaft voor Liturgiestudie* on liturgy and the ecu-
menical movement, in the abbey of Berne (Heeswijk, Holland) on February 2, 1958.
1.   L. A. Veit, *Volksfrommes Brauchtum und Kirche im deutschen Mittelalter*, Freiburg
1936, 83.

Solemn Mass was the climax.

It was a peaceful, comfortable life. To this day 'une vie de chanoine' is a proverb in France and there is one like it in Spain. They mean by it a comfortable life, free from care. But a beautiful idea lay behind all this: the thought that here and there groups should be set apart from the community to offer prayer. The highest of all human activities is to give glory to God and these groups of men in a sense represented all who were working, and made possible an incessant flow of divine praise. For there were endowments in these churches provided by the people, although mostly they came from the estates of the nobility; and that is why the places in these collegiate churches were often reserved for the nobility who provided for their posterity in this way.

The people at least were aware of this liturgical profusion: The day was divided up according to the bell which tolled the various canonical Hours. The Synod of Trier (1238) decreed that the parish church sound the canonical Hours.[2] For Tierce which preceded the conventual Mass there had to be a threefold signal—according to Durandus.[3] This was also a call to church for the faithful. The penetration of Sext into everyday life is revealed by the Spanish word for the midday rest—a word now universally used, Siesta (*Sexta*). In England we find None popularly emphasized. It is 'noon,' midday—hence 'forenoon,' 'afternoon.' This is the sense it has in the late Middle Ages when None was advanced from its proper time (3 p.m.) to noon.

The spiritual and didactic books of the late Middle Ages, the Christian's Looking Glass of the Franciscan Dietrich Kolde,[4] for example, show us that these chimes were no mere time signals, but even by those who did not go to Church, were regarded as a summons to prayer. Prayers were prescribed for each of these Hours.

The zeal of the faithful for divine worship is shown in the church buildings. Apart from modification or re-building in the Baroque period, most South German and Austrian churches date

2. J. Hartzheim, *Concilia Germaniae* III, 560.
3. Durandus, *Rationale* I, 4, 12.
4. *Der Christenspiegel des Dietrich Kolde*, ed. by Cl. Drees (Franziskanische Forschungen 9), Werl 1954, 194-202.

from the end of the Middle Ages. And even where such modification with its Baroque result has taken place, the pointed spire and arched structure betrays derivation from the earlier period. But in the towns Gothic cathedrals and minsters arose in all places where the burgesses offered their wealth and ability to erect and furnish the house of God with great magnificence. The very size of these buildings must fill us with amazement—Cologne Cathedral, St. Stephen's in Vienna, or Ulm Minster and St. Stephen's in Nimwegen. The towns were small, a town of 10,000 inhabitants was a city almost—and yet they had not one church but many in each town.

Viewed purely quantitatively, we see a high level of liturgical life at the end of the Middle Ages. Yes, we see the onset of liturgical hypertrophy. It was no longer healthy when, in some towns, the clergy numbered one in twenty of the population,[5] and we are not counting religious houses. For, to the corporations who maintain the solemn liturgy of the cathedrals and collegiate churches there belonged also a host of altar-priests whose only obligation was to offer a low Mass daily and say the Office. It is reported that in Breslau in the 15th century two churches had 236 such priests between them.

Even that was liturgical life, if in a mass-produced and decadent form.

Setting aside the principle of worship of Sunday and feast days, the people shared in this wealth of liturgical life by the endowments with which they supported the clergy and built and furnished the churches. But the liturgy itself was a clerical liturgy. This was so not merely in conventual churches where the intention had always been to provide a liturgy only for the religious, as with the Cistercian whose churches had small naves reserved for the lay-brothers, but it was true also of churches where the people were meant to worship.

A more or less broad gulf separated clergy and laity. Characteristic of Church life in general, as the Middle Ages drew to a close, was the tension between the laity and the clergy—certainly the higher clergy. The opening words of the Bull of Boniface VIII are well-known: *Clericis laicos semper infestos esse manifestum est.*

5. J. Lortz, *Die Reformation in Deutschland* I, Freiburg 1939, 86.

This could have been meant to apply to the political world. It was the investiture struggle which had started the whole thing off, but it reacted deep down into the spiritual realm too. An early symptom of this was that after the investiture struggle, where from ancient time, prayers had been offered in the Canon of the Mass for temporal rulers, neither emperor nor king is now mentioned. In Missals where they continue to be named, the passage is deleted. Towards the end of the Middle Ages the tension between clergy and the people in general was heightened by the immense wealth of the clergy. In Germany the Church owned one-third of the land.[6] The many jealously-guarded privileges of the clergy, too, aggravated the situation and led to that socialistic feeling which broke out in the Peasants' War.

The people were devout and came to worship: but even when they were present at worship, it was still clerical worship. This fact received very palpable expression towards the end of the Middle Ages in those places where rood-screens were built into churches. This was done where the clergy carried out the sung office and the solemn liturgy in the choir, that is, in collegiate churches but it was done also in many parish churches. The choir-stalls which had marked off the choir from the nave, were transformed into a wall or carved partition, hiding the choir completely from the people. Later, this transverse partition was elaborated into a sort of stage and called a *lectionarium*—a lectern. The choir could even take up its stance on this.

The chief service which took place behind the partition, and the high altar of the church was no longer for the people. And so a second altar was erected in front of the screen or lectern—the so-called people's altar or Crucifix altar on account of the Crucifix set above it. Here a special service for the people was carried out.

But even this service was not a people's service in the old sense. At it the people were not much more than spectators. This resulted largely from the strangeness of the language which was, and remained, Latin. Thus, the readings themselves were con- sciously thought of as symbolic indications of the preaching of the word of God. For the most part the reader did not even face the people—that was a settled tradition.

6. Ibid. 82.

And yet the Carolingian reform had urged the people to answer the Mass. That all joined in the *Sanctus* was taken for granted at that time and for a long time afterwards. In the 11th century we find Burchard of Worms, in his book on Confession, referring to someone who had accused himself of talking instead of answering the priest's greeting and beginning to pray.[7] Towards the end of the Middle Ages we hear no more of this: *the people have become dumb.*

The simple chants of the Ordinary—*Kyrie, Gloria, Sanctus,* etc.— have long since become a matter for the choir, the clergy in the choir-stalls. If they are 'choral' the word betrays the fact that a special clerical song has taken over from what should have been community singing—a *chorale.*

In many places we find a further step being taken. The *chorus clericorum* themselves sing no longer, or they do not sing on their own. Musically trained laity are taken into the choir. The singers, the church-choir appears, taking their place on the lectern, to begin with, and increasingly adopting polyphonic music. An enrichment of the liturgy: a growing estrangement from the people.

Even before there were any lecterns, these conditions were expressed in the architecture of the church, at least in the position of the altar. The principal altar, which in early Christian times had stood on a raised platform between the sanctuary and the nave, became pushed more and more into the back of the apse— away from the people. It is true that its place was taken by a multitude of side-altars, required for the numerous altar-chaplains. These side-altars did not always have their own chapel, nor were they always arranged round an ambulatory (as in many Gothic cathedrals), but were to be found all around, at pillars or in niches, or wherever a little space could be found. And these side-altars were a new obstacle in the way of a truly corporate divine worship.

On the whole, divine worship, including that which was offered for the people, was most solemn. Since Carolingian times it had always been accompanied by many dramatic elements, with things which people could grasp through eye or ear without

7. Burchard of Worms, *Poenitentiale Eccl. Germ.* n. 145 (PL 140, 970).

much need of understanding words. There were practically no low Masses for the people's Sunday worship. There was a *Missa Cantata* at least. An old law forbade the saying of low Mass on Sundays in public churches.[8] It was the mendicant orders who first partially broke through this law in the 13th century; but in many places, especially in country districts, it is still in force— Sunday worship is sung worship, *Missa Cantata*.

In the *Missa Cantata*, as much as possible is taken over from the solemn Mass—the double incensing, for example: the altar is kissed more frequently and the signs of the Cross are multiplied. The reading always has its special place, on the right, or on the left. The ceremonies at the Consecration too, are such as the people can understand. On great feasts and frequently on Sundays too, the service began with a procession in which the clergy carried what relics they possessed through the church. Everywhere, if the necessary clergy were available—and there was no lack of clergy —divine worship was performed with ceremony: it was supremely solemn, but in large part remote from the people. And so it had become an external activity, carried out according to pre-scribed rules. Indeed, we might well say that it had become a lifeless civil act.

But even at the end of the Middle Ages there remained a vestige of lay participation.[9] There was the sermon; and towards the end of the Middle Ages the sermon enjoyed a certain increase in importance through the activity of the mendicant orders. The priest would at least relate some instruction, a few remarks about the meaning of the current feasts or the lives of the saints who were being commemorated, to the lessons from the liturgy of the Sunday and the days following. Congregation singing in the vernacular appeared first in association with the sermon as the sermon in song.

And we know examples showing Sequences for the great feast days with German interpolations between the Latin stanzas. Such a song is the Easter 'Christ has arisen.' The stanzas of this were interpolated between those of the *Victimae Paschali* and sung to the same tune. But in particular, it was to the end of the Scripture

8. Cf. *Decretum Gratiani* III, 1, 52 (Friedberg I, 1308).
9. For more detailed evidence of the following references, v. the author of *Missarum Sollemnia*.

reading part of the service, to the sermon, that certain popular elements were attached. Most important were the *intercessions*. There still seems to have been a recollection that in the early times this was the place for the *prayer of the faithful*, for intercession for all the needs of Christendom. The priest announced a list of intentions of varying length, and after each one an *Ave Maria* was said. We have an example of this sort of thing from Austria, dated 1480. The list here comprises twenty-one items each with an *Ave*. In other places they said a *Pater* as well.

Another way in which the people took part was at the Offertory procession. This was still part of the liturgy on great festivals at the end of the Middle Ages. It was done chiefly at Christmas, Easter, Pentecost, often on the Assumption, on All Saints and the dedication of the Church. But it was at Nuptial and Requiem Masses that Offertory processions most frequently took place. The preachers of indulgences, too, made their financial gain chiefly through the Offertory procession. The people went up to the altar or walked round and paid their subscription. But we have to admit that an appreciation of the liturgical meaning of these processions was more and more being lost. It scarcely occurred to people, that through their offering they were sharing in the sacrifice of Christ; were expressing the surrender of their own hearts to God's will in the Spirit of Christ: their chief thought seems rather to have been that they could thus obtain a share in the fruits of the Mass on behalf of their deceased relatives or for some other intention. It is most significant that reception of Communion was very rare. Not through Communion but through a material gift did people seek to win a share in the fruits of the Mass.

There was another part of the Mass which people still appreciated at the end of the Middle Ages. That was the elevation of the Host at the *Consecration*. For the very reason that people did not want or did not dare to communicate—and the pastoral attitude put people off rather than encouraged them—they wanted all the more to look at the Host. By contemplating the sacred Host they hoped to gain a blessing on their earthly lives, and certainly profit for their eternal souls. It was this same longing for contemplation which found poetic expression in the Grail Legend. Whoever looked upon the Grail with faith would receive salvation, and health from it. This urge to contemplate made people want to see relics of the saints and demand their exposition on set days. The same urge to contemplate was directed to the sacred Host. We can speak of a formal Eucharistic movement in the Middle Ages, but its end was not participation in the Eucharist or more frequent Communion. It attempts only to advance the contemplation and veneration of the Blessed Sacrament. Now exposition of the Sacrament during the whole of Mass and the Holy Hour begins. Blessed Sacrament processions too, begin to take place. Confraternities spring up whose object is to venerate the Blessed Sacrament, and a start is made with all that can be called in general 'Corpus Christi devotion.'

Associated with the sound and noble heart of these pious practices there are, however, dangerous and superstitious ideas. At any rate, Cardinal Nicolas of Cusa when he travelled through Germany in 1450 as cardinal legate, objected in many places to the lengthy exposition of the Blessed Sacrament and to the carrying about of the Sacrament, uncovered, on any and every pretext: he also forbade any more foundations of Blessed Sacrament confraternities, pointing out that the Sacrament had been instituted as *food*, not as a show-piece.[10] The threatening evil was that men would indeed venerate the Sacrament, but would see in it first and foremost the source of temporal blessing. A sight of the sacred Host, especially at the Consecration, was supposed to produce beneficial effects described as *fructus missae* or *virtutes missae*. Whoever beheld the sacred Host in the morning would not become blind that day, would not die suddenly, would not go hungry, and so on.

The same sort of benefits were said to attach to hearing Mass. While a man was hearing Mass he did not age; the holy souls in purgatory did not suffer while a Mass was being said for them at each Mass one soul got out of purgatory; food taken after Mass was more nourishing, and so on.[11]

And so the notion gained acceptance: you only have to be present at Mass—devoutly present, of course. But its effects are automatic. Now the true notion of the *ex opere operato* effect of a sacrament was contained in this; but it is uncouth and much

10. P. Browe, *Die Verehrung der Eucharistie im Mittelalter* 1933, 170 seq.
11. A. Franz, *Die Messe im deutschen Mittelalter*, Freiburg 1902, 46 seq.

exaggerated. And with its one-sided view of the fruits of the Mass it has already taken a false direction. Whereas sacrifice, and above all the sacrifice of the Mass is meant to be a gift to God by which we pay Him homage, now men are thinking more of the gifts and benefits which we may receive through it from God. And the very gift which we are supposed to receive from the altar of sacrifice—Communion—is disregarded. Hearing Mass—and even more, giving Mass stipends or attending Offertory processions—degenerates into an external action by which, it is thought, one can obtain temporal and spiritual benefits without much trouble to oneself. If we consider this practice and that of indulgences and pilgrimages, we can understand to some extent the reproaches which Luther made and which thereafter were repeated a thousand times over: that under the Papacy people wanted to merit or to buy heaven with human works alone. And to some extent we can understand his radical conclusion, which made him assert with colossal exaggeration, that we are unable to give or to sacrifice anything at all to God, we can achieve nothing through the Mass, neither for the living nor the dead, and all prayers and practices connected with the idea of sacrifice are human additions to that which Christ has instituted.

In the late Middle Ages there was another way of regarding the Mass and the liturgy, and this presents a more cheering picture. But here too, the way does not lead to a deeper, sacramental Christianity. It is the allegorical intepretation of the ceremonies to provide meditation on the life of our Lord, especially on His Passion. The Mass, is indeed, sacrifice and memorial—unde et memores; and throughout the Middle Ages since the time of Amaler, the commentaries on the Mass and popular instruction always expressed this memorial character with great emphasis in their allegorical interpretation. But admittedly, as Kolping has expounded,[12] it is no longer the Anamnesis of the work of Redemption as such, of the mystery of salvation, which is in mind: a disintegration has taken place. A multiplicity of mysteries has arisen—a series of separate events in the story of the Redemption, called to mind by the various ceremonies. The priest in his

12.   A. Kolping, Amalar von Metz und Florus von Lyon, Zeugen eines Wandels im liturgischen Mysterienverständnis: ZkTh 73 (1951) 424-464.

chasuble represents Christ clothed in His robes of scorn. The movement to and fro at the altar is His going back and forth between the two judges. The *Lavabo* is Pilate washing his hands, and so on. By the ceremonies we are reminded of the events, of the separate 'mysteries.' Such a style of meditation was indeed to be justified as an irradiation from the fundamental mystery; but this fundamental mystery itself, the sacramental making present of the work of salvation, the Mysterium Christi which ought to enfold us, and into which we ought to enter deeper and deeper, is decidely too little grasped.

The same sort of thing can be said of the observance of the liturgical year. Observation of the Christian year is perhaps that part of Church life which remained most alive amongst the people as the Middle Ages declined. Christian festivals were celebrated with great fervour. Their meaning, and that of the great festivals were thoroughly taken to heart. Pictorial art demonstrates this. Its chief subjects, besides the painting of the various saints, patrons and benefactors, were the Christmas theme and the Easter theme. There are countless variations in late Gothic art on the Nativity scene, and on the whole story of Christ's infancy beginning with the Annunciation and ending with pictures of the Holy Family. Even more richly portrayed is the Lord's Passion in all its phases and forms, from the Agony in the garden to the laying in the sepulchre, and then the Resurrection and Ascension.

Of this too, it can be said that the transition to the sacramental, to that which is made present in the Church was mostly lacking. Compassionate meditation depicts the Passion of Christ down to the last detail, speaking of the bitter pains and even of the rose-red blood. The Resurrection too, is depicted; but it is here most particularly that we see the treatment differing from the treatment of the same subjects in early Christian art. In early Christian art the Resurrection—or rather the Risen One—had often been portrayed. It had been the first topic in the early iconologies. By it had been indicated all the Old Testament pictures dealing with deliverance, in which we were to see both Christ's and our own Resurrection.[12a] But when the Risen One is shown in late Gothic art it tells us only of a past event, of the mighty triumph

12a. Cf. above c. 1 par. 5 seq.

of the Redeemer and of the guards lying prostrate as though dead.

The extent to which the Christian mind, the popular sentiment, indeed, of the late Middle Ages, had none the less penetrated these themes belonging to the chief feasts of the Church is seen most clearly in the mystery plays, the Christmas plays, Shepherd plays, Three King plays, the Passion plays and the Easter plays. They experienced the holy mysteries as though present at them. This could only be a pseudo presence far removed from the presence of that which we call the *Mystery*.

The themes had certainly been extended, just as in the liturgical year great space had been given to saints' days. Mystery plays about various saints emerge—especially about the patron saints of church or town. At the end of the Middle Ages the mystery play about Anti-Christ, the *Ludus de Antichristo* in which Pope, bishop, emperor and king all appear, was acted with special gusto.

These plays were not performed by professionals. The whole town or village took part, as we find done to this day in Oberammergau, for example. Neither time nor number of players presented any problem. In 1498 there was a Passion Play in Frankfurt in which 250 people took part and which lasted four days. Plays were usually performed in the afternoon.[13]

Every teacher who has done dramatic work with his pupils knows how much the actors identify themselves with the parts they play upon the stage. This too, is the experience of the audience if they enter deeply into the play. For the players in the medieval mystery plays it was just the same, and there we find fresh evidence of how deeply the religious themes of these plays had imbued the spirit of the age: for many of the family names we know today must have arisen in this way. In Germany we find, for example, not only the name *Devil* and *Newdevil* (the old actor having died and a new one having taken his place) but also *Lord-God* and *Monk, Bishop, Pope, Emperor* and *King*—almost all characters we meet in the Antichrist Play alone. And this did not happen only in Germany. *Pope, King* and *Bishop* are common enough in England, and in France we can think of *Leroy*,

13. J. Janssen, *Geschichte des deutschen Volkes am Ausgang des Mittelalters* I, Freiburg 1878, 228 seq.

Lhermite, *Labbé* and *Lermoine;* and there must be others too, whose origin cannot easily be explained except on this theory of psychological identification with the characters in the mystery plays.

Here once more we see a few brighter colours in the medieval religious scene on the eve of the Reformation, for it was not only in the religious plays that liturgical themes became wedded to the life of the people. It happened in many other ways too.

There was the calendar of saints with its most diverse figures, which spoke to the soul of the people and had nurtured popular sentiment. It was in the height of the Middle Ages that the practice became established of naming children after saints and honouring the saints as patrons. The names of apostles were the favourites, and feast days of apostles were holidays of obligation; many family names, too, arose in the same way at the end of the Middle Ages. We need mention only St. John, whose name occurs all over the world in patronymics.

But it was not only individuals who received a saint's name at Baptism. The guilds played an important part in the economy of towns in those days; and each guild liked to have its patron saint. Each guild chose a heavenly patron because of some character which he possessed or with which legend endowed him, which seemed appropriate. The copper-smiths venerated St. Vitus who had been martyred in a boiler; the archers, St. Sebastian; the tailors, St. Martin because of his cloak; the fishermen, St. Peter, as did the key-smiths because of the keys; the mountain-dwellers, St. Barbara because she had been immured in a tower; the cart-wrights, St. Catherine because of her wheel.[14]

An image of the saint was put on the banner and on the coat of arms of the guild. On the patronal feast a special Mass was said for the guild when all members had to assist at the Offertory procession. The larger guilds had their own chapel or altar, at least, to which endowments were attached. At church processions, the guilds appeared as a body, carrying their banners and insignia before them, and observing a strictly planned order. In the procession in Munich in 1484, forty-three guilds took part,

14. Cf. A. Bruder, *Über Wappen und Schutzpatrone der alten Zünfte*, Innsbruck 1885; F. v. S. Doyé, *Heilige und Selige der römish-katholischsn Kirche* II, Leipzig 1929, 890-905.

walking past the Blessed Sacrament in a set order.[15] In their heyday the heads of the guilds insisted on all members fulfilling their religious duties and leading honest lives; and mutual assistance was an accepted responsibility of members.

Not only the guild but often a single house or business would have its own patron through whom temporal work was joined with eternal things. And so the inns bore, not just any name and sign to commend themselves to travellers, but for preference chose a Biblical term as we can see from today in many an old town or village.[16] The owners liked to use the name of one of the evangelists, all of whom were commemorated in the liturgy with special feast days, and whose symbols appeared so often in the religious art of the period. Thus we find such names as: *The Angel, The Ox, The Lion, The Eagle.* Or they chose a sign from some feature of the story of the Three Kings, the patrons of travellers: *The Star, The Crown, The Three Crowns, The Elephant, The Rose, The Moor,* or as is common in Switzerland even today, *The Three Kings.*

It was taken for granted that hospitals should be named after saints. From the 12th century onwards it had become increasingly the rule to place hospitals under the protection of the Holy Spirit. The more helpless the medicine of those days was to cure illness, the more did men look to heaven for help. The Holy Spirit was invoked in hymns as a healing power: *Lava quod est sordidum, riga quod est aridum, saxa quod est saucium!* Hospitals for lepers were named after Lazarus of the Biblical parable and we have the name still in *lazaret.*

Going through the streets in an old city like Vienna today, we are struck by the names above the chemists shops. Most of them have a religious significance: *Holy Trinity Pharmacy, Angel Pharmacy, Mary's Pharmacy, St. Martha Pharmacy, St. Leopold Pharmacy.*

Every need, every situation became associated with its appropriate patron. Expectant mothers turned to St. Anne whose cult and feast day became quite the rage. Each ailment had its special patron from amongst whom in the end the favourites were selected, becoming known as the *Fourteen Helpers* or the *Fourteen Saints.*

15. A. Mitterwieser, *Geschichte der Fronleichnamsprozession in Bayern,* Munich 1930.
16. K. Hoeber, *Der biblische Ursprung alter Wirtshausnamen,* Cologne 1934.

The peasant too, on the land, honoured the patrons of his station, principally Wendelin and Leonard the patrons of cattle, and also Anthony the hermit in whose temptations, according to late medieval painters, animal forms played such a large part.

Not only did the obscure village and town dweller place his life and work under heavenly protection, but the knight, the count, and the prince bowed before God, assuming office to the accompaniment of the Church's blessing, usually with a special liturgical celebration. When an aspirant reached the proper age and had proved himself proficient in handling his weapons, he was knighted with solemn ceremony. Because of the religious nature of this ceremony it was known as the *dedication of a knight*. The *Pontificale* of Durandos contains a special rite with which the Bishop instals the aspirant knight in his station. The act takes place within the Mass. Before the Gospel, the Bishop pauses and with quite a long prayer blesses the dagger which he then hands to the candidate who returns it to its sheath. Blessing the young knight, the Bishop then fastens the dagger about him; the knight draws the dagger and waves it thrice in the air. The new knight then receives the Kiss of Peace and—as in Confirmation—a light stroke of the cheek. This is nothing but the accolade of knighthood, once conferred by a temporal superior, now conferred by the Bishop.[17]

The highest political offices too, those of emperor and king, are now consecrated by the Church with liturgical blessing. Public opinion in the late Middle Ages demanded that the Emperor be crowned by the Pope; and the negotiations which took place after every accession were a most important affair of government. Coronation was a most elaborate business. As well as being crowned, the Emperor was installed as a canon of St. Peter's with the rank of deacon. Thus he received the privilege of singing the Gospel on Christmas Eve dressed in full regalia— a privilege which was indeed used.

The whole economic and political life of the people, society from peasant to king was framed within a supernatural order, an order richly expressed in liturgical forms. In spite of everything,

17. M. Andrieu, *Le Pontificale du Moyen-Âge* III, Rome 1940, 449-450; cf. E. Michael, *Geschichte des deutschen Volkes seit dem 13. Jahrhundert* I, Freiburg 1897, 231-240.

therefore, we may speak of liturgical life flowering on the eve of the Reformation, flowering even in respect of the people's participation. But it was the flowering of autumn. What Huizinga said about 'The Autumn of the Middle Ages' is very much to the point. It is no happy sprouting from the root, but the last branching out, the late consequences of ancient tradition—like the logic-chopping of the late scholastics, often mere empty play. There was a mighty facade, and behind it—a great emptiness.

The liturgy is no longer understood in its sacramental depth, and lies unused, in spite of the Eucharistic movement of the time, in spite of the tremendous regard for the Mass, in spite of the frequency with which Mass was celebrated—perhaps because of this frequency. No longer is the Christian mystery seen as something very much present, as the leaven which must constantly penetrate and transform Christianity—through the Sacrament. It is seen almost entirely as an event of the past upon which to meditate more and more deeply by means of some such laudable devotion as the Way of the Cross or the Rosary. It is significant, however, that meditation stops beside the sepulchre, or, if it does go on to the Resurrection as in the Glorious Mysteries of the Rosary, it scarcely ever reaches the mystery of the Church. Christ glorified, who lives on in His humanity as Redeemer, is hardly ever seen. It is as though, after His Ascension He had disappeared, become absorbed in Divinity, in the Blessed Trinity. Thus He is referred to simply as 'the Lord God,' and when His life in the Eucharist is mentioned men speak of 'God's corpse' as of 'God's torments,' 'God's Passion,' and 'God's pierced hands and feet.' He is no longer recognized as the living Head of the Church, who, through the Holy Spirit, gives life to the whole organism of the Church, and who goes on working through the mystery of the sacraments. Even amongst theologians, we will scarcely hear a mention of the Church as the Mystical Body of Christ. We in our own time must re-discover this fact. The Church in the late Middle Ages had become predominantly an earthly sociological entity. The actual form given in those days to the Church by those who were her representatives, with their lust for power, their avarice, their disedifying lives, contributed a great deal to this development. For this reason the Church no longer played much part in religious life.[18] This is obvious with regard to the German mystics. It applies also to the admirable *Devotio moderna*. In the Imitation of Christ the word 'Church' scarcely ever occurs. The one inexhaustible theme is God and the soul, and perfect surrender to God. Even in liturgical life the Church as Church—the community of the Faithful—keeps on receding. Subjectivism is on the ascendant.

Late Gothic Church-architecture had already revealed this. The house of God begins to be split up into a multitude of chapels in which the separate guilds, separate families even, have their own guild or family altar and their own worship. Even the public worship of Sundays and feast days at the third hour, hitherto so strictly a community service, is losing its hold. Perhaps the reason for this was the struggle of the new pastoral orders to have their own services fully accepted alongside the parish worship. But this is where the development began which reached its end in the principle that the individual has fulfilled his obligation by attending Mass on Sunday anywhere and at any time. Synods had fought long—from the 14th to the 16th century—against this. In the end Rome decided in favour of freedom. But it is significant that Rome's decision against the stress on the community of the Church expressed in community worship, was first given in the fateful year 1517.[19]

Again we are bound to lay bare a dissolution at the heart of ecclesiastical and liturgical life.[20] What remains firm is on the fringe. To begin with faith is not disturbed. But the things men are living by are fragments of faith, peripheral things. Veneration of the saints and their relics—genuine or fake—is often quite unrestrained. Protections and blessings are sought in ever new ways: the *rituals* become full of new benedictions. Confraternities are founded and new devotions spring up all around. Religious life becomes more and more complicated. A growing insecurity and many-sided discontent is apparent everywhere. It

18. Cf. J. Lortz, *Wie kam es zur Reformation?* Einsiedeln 1950. Here Lortz describes the development from as early as the 12th century as 'a separatist movement away from the Church.' This sort of analysis amounts to an all-embracing exposition of the causes of the Reformation.
19. Cf. Jungmann, *Missarum Sollemnia* I, 326.
20. Cf. also F. Vandenbroucke, *Aux origines du malaise liturgique: Questions liturg. et parviss.* 40 (1959) 252-270.

was very easy for Luther to strike a staggering blow at this system. And we have to recognize that, at least to begin with, it was genuine religious concern which moved him as it moved the other reforming currents which were already at work within the Church. Luther demanded a return to a simple Christianity. Greatly exaggerating, he preached: Away with all human works, with all priestcraft and sacrifices; away with convents and choirs, away with indulgences and cult of the saints: *sola fides, sola Scriptura*.

With this he had struck, unfortunately, not merely at all the peripheral accessories and the empty shell, but at the liturgy itself in its very heart. In this way the gulf has become so deep, the gulf we all lament.—

10. Liturgical Life in the Baroque Period.

Amongst the forces which led to the rise of Baroque culture we must mention first and foremost that religious revival which sprang from the Council of Trent. On debated points, doctrines of faith had been clarified; the life and activity of the clergy had been properly regulated; many rank growths within religious life had been pruned severely away, if not torn out by the roots. Pius V, following the spirit of the Council, had revised the Roman Breviary in 1568 and the Roman Missal in 1510 and prescribed these as obligatory. The Church's worship was now prevented from running wild, as it had threatened to do at the hands of ignorant priests, to the vexation of the faithful. The work was completed by succeeding Popes who added the new edition of the Roman *Pontificale* (1596) and of the Roman *Rituale* (1614). From then on the Congregation of Rites, founded by Sixtus V in 1588, kept a watchful eye on things to see that the set rules were obeyed. Now once more a feeling of security, of being on firm ground, could thrive. The appearance of great bishops like Charles Borromeo, the effective work of the new orders, the re-conquest of vast regions which had already fallen to innovation all contributed to the sense of triumph which found a medium of expression in Baroque.

It is reasonable to expect that this expression was realized above all in a new blossoming of liturgical life. This can be shown to have happened—if we are ready to recognize the guarantee of this life in conscientiously fulfilled precept and obediently followed standards. Precisely as a result of this standardization of form the liturgical life of the Baroque period entered a unique phase of historical neutrality such as no other period in the history of the liturgy has known, a phase of persistent uniformity such as we find to be the pre-requisite of all healthy life in the realm of nature.

It is true that under Urban VIII commissions are still called, on occasion, for the improvement of liturgical books. But pedantic improvement of classical metre, made by a few humanists, to the Office hymns can scarcely be counted as important events from the point of view of liturgical development. As little could we declare the Quartos and Folios in which men like Gavanti or Cavalieri casuistically elaborated the laws of liturgy to be genuine advances. Baroque liturgy is governed by the law of stability.

This is true admittedly only if we limit what we mean by liturgy to what was demanded of celebrating priests according to the newly prescribed and obligatory books of the Roman liturgy. Things are quite different the moment we take into consideration what was celebrated as legitimate public worship, sanctioned by the hierarchy within the domains of individual bishops. Here we meet the rich liturgical life of the Baroque period. Public worship is *festival*, and Baroque culture is primarily a culture of the festival, the assembling of all possible sensuous creation in the service of high ideals.

And so there was in Baroque culture an unmistakable resurgence of festival celebrations, particularly in the town churches. This was expressed chiefly in an enrichment of Church music. In the past, song had traditionally kept the form of the unison chorale, sung as a rule by a clerical choir or the choir of canons in a collegiate church, now there is an increase of part-singing and finally, true polyphony. For this a special choir is needed, and to meet this need the shape of the church itself is altered. For the choir and the organ—now almost perfected—choir and organ lofts are built, and these things find their way into the smallest village churches. Festivity is now the key-note of Church architecture and furnishing. But on this subject we need say no more.

If festivity becomes the chief characteristic of church worship, a festivity in which the bulk of the people do not take part, but rather have something presented to them, then this is but a reflexion of the feudal structure of society at that time. The peasant and the citizen are supposed to gaze and listen in rapt enjoyment, as do the aristocratic families from the vantage-point of their boxes—carefully built into the plan of the church. But all the same, the Baroque period understood how to engage the people actively in the service. This happened first of all, in emulation with Reformation practice, through a great increase in the popularity of congregational singing. The successors to the song before and after the sermon were the hymns in the vernacular which were related to the feasts of the Church—as the Synod of Salzburg (1568) emphasizes. These dare to enter the Eucharistic service—somewhat hesitantly. The Spiritual Hymns and Psalms of Johann Leisentritt (1567) mentions hymns at Offertory and Communion. The Mainz *Cantual* of 1605 encourages the singing of hymns in the vernacular at the Gradual, after the Consecration, at the *Agnus Dei* and the Communion and even during the Sung Office. But most of all, hymn-singing comes into its own at evening devotions, which are slowly becoming more important, and at pilgrimages. The distinctively Baroque hymn-book is now at hand with the Little Spiritual Psalter produced by the Cologne Jesuits in 1623, which has been widely distributed in many editions since 1637.[1] A host of new melodies appear, traceable in substance back to P. Fredrich von Spee.

If on the whole, worship ran along the assured lines of the old liturgical books, yet there was one occasion when the liturgical creativeness of the Baroque could express its urge to be festive: Corpus Christi. From the beginning the subject of this was the Eucharist. But it was not the Eucharist in its fulness as a sacrifice of thanksgiving. It was purely and simply the Eucharist as the

1. J. Gotzen, Art. *Kirchenlied:* L.ThK V (1933) 1011.

sacramental Presence of the Body of Christ, as the *nearness* of the Lord, that miracle to which those words of the Old Testament might be applied: 'No other people's gods are so close to them as our God is to us.' And here the celebration centred round the procession.

The Corpus Christi procession became a triumphal march with which the Christian people acclaimed their Lord and Shepherd. Earlier times, too, had known their processions: the solemn procession bearing relics to a shrine and on the anniversary of this event, the entry on Palm Sunday, and the Good Friday procession: but Corpus Christi, favoured by the early summer-time, assumed more and more the festive aspects of the procession and, as well as the content of the old meadow and town perambulations with their blessings on the weather, it assimilated to itself also the most important elements of the old mystery plays. Holy Thursday became a festival purely and simply, not only in Spain where the consummate art of a Calderon with his *Autos sacramentales* gave a final splendour to the feast, but in Germany as well, although in a different manner. Here too, the procession often included both tableaux and dramatic scenes with which the Blessed Sacrament was given honour.[2]

Because medieval tradition had accustomed people to thinking of the Sacrament as primarily a memorial of the Passion, the focus of these scenes was on the sufferings of Christ. To these were added scenes from the life of Jesus and also, going farther afield, Old Testament scenes usually beginning with the expulsion of our first parents from Paradise.[3] The whole history of salvation was to be made alive. The patrons of the chief stations in life and the allegorical symbols of parts of the world and of the ages had to be present; behind them could then follow the confraternities, the clergy, and beneath a canopy, the Blessed Sacrament.[4] The various groups with their dialogues and rhymes were apportioned amongst

2. Cf. also A. Mitterwieser, *Geschichte der Fronleichnameprozession in Bayern*, Munich 1930; A. Dörrer, *Tiroler Umgangspiele. Ordnungen und Sprechtexte der Bozner Fronleichname-spiele und verwandter Figuralprozessionen vom Ausgang des Mittelalters bis zum Abstieg des Aufgeklärten Absolutismus* (Schlernschriften 160), Innsbruck 1957; O. Sengspiel, *Die Bedeutung der Prozessionen für das geistliche Spiel des Mittelalters in Deutschland* (Germanistische Abhandlungen 66), Breslau 1932.
3. In the Munich procession, 26 of the 55 scenes were devoted to the Old Testament, as early as 1574; Senspiel 31 seq.
4. See the Bozen processional order from 1590-1714 in Dörrer 223-228 and 198-301.

the trades and guilds according to a well arranged scheme.[5] Or it might be that the guilds came in an ancient traditional sequence which was itself part of the symbolism. Thus the millers and bakers who made the bread might come last, that is, immediately in front of the Blessed Sacrament; or it could be, last but one, the goldsmiths being nearest the Sacrament.[6] Or the separate groups might represent symbolically the principal motifs of the order of Redemption (the Brazen Serpent, the Easter Lamb, and the like).[7] All that might add to the beauty and the splendour was used: music and thundering cannons and waving flags. Dignitaries appeared wearing their robes of office; the girls were allowed to wear garlands on their heads. Not for nothing was it known in some places as 'garland day,' in others as 'dressing-up day.'[8] In Swabia it was quite simply called 'The Lord's Day,'[9] and in France it is still called 'fête-Dieu.'[10]

What we see concentrated in this great feast of the Baroque period appears diffused on several other occasions. The procession is not confined to Corpus Christi but is repeated, if not on every day of the octave as in Salzburg in the 18th century,[11] at least on the Sunday within the octave. Some places even, had a Eucharistic procession every Thursday. And there were other forms of procession on various occasions: to mark a local feast, on the first Sunday of the month, as a festival of an important confraternity especially that of the Rosary, or as a community pilgrimage to

5. In Bozen it was not until the new edition of the order in 1719 that the much expanded libretto, now closely attached to the very secular 'dragon-killing' (St. George saved St. Margaret), was thrown into relief as an 'introduction to the afternoon activities,' and set in contrast to the 'forenoon processions,' prescribed in the old style; Dörrer 298-356. Cf. also the order for the procession at Mainz in the Baroque period—L. Vert-L. Lenhart, *Kirche und Volksfrömmigkeit im Zeit des Baroks*, Freiburg 1956, 84 seq.
6. Thus in Munich according to the order of 1563 and 1750/73; Mitterwieser 33 seq. 67; cf. 17. An illuminating fact, proving that here we have a widespread and much-loved custom, is this: in my own native parish of Taufer in Pustertal (S. Tyrol), the miller and the baker, bearing lighted torches ('Tarzen'), take this honoured place in the Corpus Christi procession to this day.
7. Thus in the Mainz procession mentioned by Veit-Lenhart 84 seq. The narrative themes from the history of Redemption re-appear noticeably in more recent times; cf. Mitterwieser 66 seq.
8. Dörrer 14 seq.
9. Its name in Freiburg as early as 1555; Sengspiel 24.
10. A. Thierbach, *Untersuchungen zur Benennung der Kirchenfeste in den romanischen Sprachen*, Berlin 1951, 105.
11. Each play setting out from a different church. A. L. Mayer quotes from the reports of the society for folk-lore in Salzburg: *Liturgie in Barok*: JL 15 (1941, 67-154) 129.

a shrine[12]—a common practice of congregations dedicated to Mary. For good reason the Baroque period has been called 'the age of processions.'[13] The principle of movement, so important in Baroque, seems to have animated Church festivals also.

Plays attached to the liturgy too, do not remain confined to Corpus Christi. Such Passion Plays as live on today or have been revived, are all a residue of what was created in the Baroque period. But plays were associated more with other feast days than with Corpus Christi. At Christmas, people wanted to rock the Child in His cradle. In the cathedral at Brixen after Compline on New Year, Epiphany and Candlemas, the Christ child was rocked by two pupils from the cathedral school while the rest sang In dulci jubilo; and a special peal of bells always ushered in the ceremony.[14] The celebration of the Resurrection on Holy Saturday had always been the popular climax of the Easter liturgy. When the strains of 'Christ has arisen' were taken up, the image of Christ resting in the tomb was hidden and above it appeared the statue of the Risen One bearing the banner of victory. Sometimes the whole framework round the altar was like a mighty sepulchre.[15] On the feast of the Ascension in many places there was a special celebration at midday when the statue of the risen Christ had to be hoisted to the ceiling surrounded by dancing angels; and on Pentecost, from the same opening in the ceiling, where the Lord had vanished from sight, the Holy Spirit in the form of a dove had to circle down as the sermon was beginning.[16]

For Baroque piety, the Blessed Sacrament, the central point of all the splendour of the Corpus Christi festivity remained in a central place throughout the whole year. In those days, practices

12. Cf. G. Schreiber, Wallfahrt und Volkstum, Düsseldorf 1934, 21-62 the chapter Im Barok.
13. A. L. Mayer, loc. cit. 129.
14. H. Mang, Der Domgottesdienst in Brixen um 1550: ZkTh 52 (1928, 540-549) 544. As Mang observes, the custom of rocking the Child endured in the Tirol until the beginning of this century.
15. Cf. int. al. the thorough description of Baroque Holy Sepulchres by N. Grass in the collection which he edited: Ostern in Tirol (Innsbruck 1957) 221-269.
16. I can vouch for the continuance of these last two celebrations beyond the Baroque period from my youthful memories. Cf. also M. Grass-Cornet, Von Palmeseln und tanzenden Engeln: Ostern in Tirol 155-180, esp. 164 seq. Balth. Fischer, Liturg. Jahrbuch 8 (1958) 62, observes correctly that the continuance of such customs into the climate of today, meets with some suspicion.

with which the dying Middle Ages had surrounded the sacred mystery, and which we see slowly vanishing today, enjoyed their full blossoming. To these belong exposition of the Blessed Sacrament, especially the Great Prayer[17] and the Forty Hours Devotion which was now so thoroughly established as an independent act of homage to the Blessed Sacrament, that people completely forgot its ancient origin in a commemoration of the forty hours which our Lord spent in the tomb. Another such devotion was the solemn ceremony *de Venerabili*. In many places this was observed every Thursday as a 'Pentecostal Office'; and often the celebrant blessed the people with the monstrance, not only at the beginning and at the end, but also during the Sequence, *Ecce panis angelorum*, when he held the monstrance towards the congregation the whole time.[18] The monstrance itself, most often in the form of the sun with golden rays streaming out on every side, now becomes the principal item in every liturgical inventory. Subsequent development provides a throne for the monstrance on the lower storey of the mighty Baroque superstructure of the altar. This is now the focal point, the tabernacle immediately above the *Mensa*, having previously become a fixture as the embodiment of the *tabernaculum Dei cum hominibus*.

Another focus of devotion which is characteristic of Baroque piety is Mary the Mother of God.[19] Accidental, but therefore all the more unaffected evidence for this are John Berchman's observations, as a Jesuit novice in Mechelu in 1616–1618, that he sees the two striking features in the lives of the saints of his time to be, veneration of the Blessed Sacrament and devotion to the Mother of God.[20] It is only in the period after the 16th century that we find numerous Marian pilgrimages coming into popularity at first in Germany.[21] Quite a number of new feasts of our Lady originated in the Baroque period: the Feast of the Holy Rosary (1571, for the universal Church 1716), the Name of Mary (1683), Maria de Mercede (1696), Maria de Monte Carmelo (1726), Mary Immaculate (1708). In 1727, the Feast of the Seven

17. Veit-Lenhart, loc. cit. 206 seq.
18. Cf. Jungmann, *Missarum Sollemnia* I, 161, 564.
19. St. Beissel, *Geschichte der Verehrung Marias im 16 and 17 Jh.*, Freiburg 1910.
20. V. Cepari, *Vita del 6. Giovanni Berchmans*, Prato 1882, 55 seq.
21. Cf. Schreiber, loc. cit. 36 seq.

Dolours was promoted to higher rank.[22] To this we must add a multitude of local feasts of our Lady. In this process many of the new Marian titles take on a kind of independence so that popular devotion at times almost forgets that they are all titles of one and the same Mother of our Lord. This is in contrast to the older manner of venerating Mary and of setting her feast-days in the context of the whole drama of salvation.

Eucharistic devotion and Marian devotion are the two things which become joined in a special way in the new forms of evening devotions. Once liturgical Vespers had gone out of the people's reach, a new evening service was formed out of these two elements. We need only look at the names which were given to these services: 'Salve-devotion,' arising from the *Salve Regina*,[23] and in France 'Salut.' Along with this it appears as Benediction because the almost indispensable conclusion is now the Eucharistic Blessing.[24] This can be taken as an indication of what was most important in fixing the style of Baroque liturgical life. Of course there are also the multiplicity of the lesser cults of favourite saints with their triduums and novenas which fill the many prayer-books which now pour out in a flood. We cannot possibly follow all these side-tracks. But veneration of the saints was not so important in the Baroque period as it had been at the end of the Middle Ages. The Blessed Sacrament and the monstrance have now taken the place of relics and reliquaries and much of the cult of saints has given way to devotion to Our Lady. So much of progress towards essentials we must concede to the Baroque period.

Finally the old traditional Roman liturgy became more widely and more often used. But now it is not the people only who are at a distance from the liturgy because it is in a foreign language, as though shut up in a stronghold: the clergy, too, show that they remain unmoved by the spirit which is embodied in its prayers and ceremonies and in its particular conception of the old great feast days. The liturgy is part of the legal ordinance which has to be observed, but not something which people really live. Martin of Cochem has many fine things to say in his Explanation of the

22. Cf. A. L. Mayer, loc. cit. 135 seq.
23. St. Beissel, loc. cit. 494-505: Salve devotions.
24. P. Browe, *Die Entstehung der Sakramentsandachten: JL* 7 (1927) 83-103.

Mass—Sweeter than Honey (1697): but what he is expounding in a variety of fresh and homely images is almost always nothing but the theology of the Eucharistic sacrifice as defined at Trent: the incomparable merit and the atoning power which is in the Mass and in every occasion when Mass is devoutly heard. There is no attempt to examine the thought-forms and manner of meditation which gave rise to the detailed structure of the liturgy. Not only the sermon but the people's Communion, too, becomes separated from the Mass and is built up into a tremendously solemn occasion in the form of the General Communion—an independent devotional act, now split off from its liturgical context. Within the Mass itself it is the actual moment of Consecration, the Real Presence of the Lord, which is treasured. As we have already noted, this became the dominant and formative centre of Catholic worship in the Baroque period.

Throughout the whole course of liturgical life, one curious peripheral feature stands out. Medieval developments continue,[25] but people do not look back to their origins. The altars with side wings, themselves a partial denial of the true altar—the *mensa Domini*, now become monstrously elaborated. The altar-picture which had long since departed from the ancient apse-picture showing the Redeemer and become devoted to the patron saint, now portrays the latter no longer in his heavenly glory, but concentrates on earthly scenes of his martyrdom. The chasuble completely loses the character of a garment and becomes an ostentatious picture-canvas. Correspondingly, in the Eucharist scarcely any attention is now paid to sacramental preparation for our Lord's sacrificial self-offering, a preparation effected through the interchange between priest and people, by readings, prayer, praise and thanksgiving, and which is designed to create unity amongst the *plebs sancta*. Instead, attention is concentrated exclusively on the Real Presence. This is the specific source of life for Baroque piety. The measure in which the sacramental Presence becomes central, is also the measure in which truly sacramental thinking fades out.[26] Men show a tremendous zeal for reproducing the facts of the history of Redemption in pious drama, thus

25. Cf. also G. Schreiber, *Der Barok und das Tridentinum: Das Weltkonzil von Trent* I, Freiburg 1951, 281-425, esp. 386 seq. 400 seq.
26. Cf. H. Kuhaupt, *Die Feier der Eucharistie* I, Münster 1950, 74 seq.

bringing these facts close to them. But this is a kind of substitute for the continuance of the story of Redemption in the action of the sacrament, for the immediate nearness of salvation in holy Church and in the baptized person who has been incorporated into Christ's Passion and Resurrection. All this has been partly forgotten.

It is true that there were isolated approaches to a proper understanding of the liturgy. During the Baroque period France enjoyed the learned scientific work of the Maurins and also the devotional movement of Cardinal Bérulle which led into the heart of corporate worship;[27] but these things touched only a limited circle.

Finally, it was quite some time before anything happened to force religious life right back to ultimate sources. And anyway, the human mind is too small to assimilate all at once the full richness of what revelation offers. Borne along by a mighty religious tradition, still alive in the whole people, the Baroque period itself preferred to draw from secondary channels and yet from these it nourished an amazingly rich life.

27. Cf. E. M. Lange, *Vergessene Liturgiker des 17. Jahrhunderts:* JL 11 (1931) 156-163.

11. Conservation and Change in the Liturgy

Ever since people have been interested in history, old buildings have always been preserved. Even while the occupants are still there, living very uncomfortably no doubt, some trust or department will be ready to take them over and see to it that no stone is dislodged, no contour altered, so that the building can remain as a witness to a time long past, able to mediate to us something of its mighty spirit.

During the last century the Church's liturgy too has received similar conservation. In the dreary decades of the Enlightenment attempts were made, insensitively, to make worship conform with ideas of rationality and utility. Thereafter it was not only Viollet-le-Duc who turned with a fresh enthusiasm towards the Middle Ages and ushered in a style of building, faithful to the models of that time. It was then that Prosper Guéranger declared war on all real or supposed distortion of the Roman liturgy in France, and founded a centre at Solesmes for the strict practice of this liturgy, especially of Gregorian chant. At this time too, pilgrimages to old and modern abbeys began to take place. Poets and artists begin to depict what had struck their senses with wonder as they sought for God in the twilight of the abbey churches.

Karl Joris Huysmans visited the Trappists at Igny and there steeped his soul in every phase of the liturgy, in every turn of the melody; and then he reproduced his experience with artistic sensitivity. Sometimes he sees the final syllable of the verse of the psalm as a drop of water falling and breaking upon the earth, at other times it seems to, 'ascend with a mighty effort and turn into the agony-cry of a departing soul who bows naked and in tears before the Divine Majesty.' At other times he feels himself, 'borne up on clouds of song which are illuminated by children's voices like lightning and shaken by the thunder of the organ.' (*En route*, 1895.)

At about the same time Johannes Jorgensen visited the monks of Beuron. He set down his experiences in a delightful chapter of His Beuron. This chapter was re-printed in a youth magazine and for many of us at the beginning of the century this was what first awoke us to the hidden glories of the liturgy. The liturgy appeared to us as a marvellous thing, full of mysteries ready to be disclosed, a holy thing coming from somewhere far off in the early Christian ages, inviolable and unchangeable as the Word of God itself.

Such a view of the liturgy was indeed the standard fifty years ago. It was a period, we might say, of liturgical antiquarianism. The liturgy was a precious vessel with even more precious contents, chiefly the treasures of grace which are the sacraments, entrusted to the Church by their divine author. It was a sacred heritage, not to be meddled with. And indeed, not for centuries had the liturgy been changed, apart from new feast days, which had to be made to fit exactly into the old pattern.

At the same time liturgy was not only a privilege of the clergy but their preserve as well. Following the rubrics exactly, they had to carry out the sacred action in all its mysterious complexity and strict dignity, while the faithful attended the holy mysteries at a respectful distance, making their private devotions with the aid, it might be, of a prayer book. Indeed, common prayer in the vernacular had made its appearance during the liturgy. People said the Rosary and made the Stations of the Cross in church: they sang Christmas hymns and celebrated the Resurrection. Many dioceses like those in the Rhineland had a wealth of such material in their prayer books and hymn books, especially for Sunday and feast-day evening services. But these had no connection with the liturgy: they were part of that peripheral sphere which was distinctly marked off from the esoteric sphere, from the temple-precincts and the liturgy. And whenever the forms belonging to this outer zone appeared to be infiltrating the hallowed world of the liturgy they were instantly thrust out again as 'unliturgical.' Anything which was not in Latin and uncontrolled by the traditional rubrics could not be liturgical.

Liturgy ran the risk of becoming a subject for rubrical antiquarianism, an aethestic show-piece. Historical studies of the liturgy seemed to be a matter for archaeologists. It is no accident—and in a way it is reasonable—that the great dictionary which was begun in 1907 by Cabrol and Leclercq and which was not completed until 1953, associates liturgy and Christian archaeology: *Dictionnaire d'Archéologie chrétienne et de Liturgie*. And what can happen in science can happen also in life. Even today we can still regard liturgy as something of merely archaeological interest. A person who is not well-versed in church matters might easily attend the pontifical liturgy and be quite fascinated by the precisely ordered patterns of movement, by the richness of the vestments and furnishings, by the dignity of the singing; and yet the whole thing could strike him as a work of art from the past. He might leave the house of God saying—ambiguously—'ancient culture.'

It is always necessary, therefore, to observe and recognize in liturgy, the law of continuity. And this not merely from psychological considerations, out of regard for those who will take part in nothing and count nothing valid which is not of long-standing custom. Of its nature, liturgy is conservative. Man is caught up in constant change, but God never changes and His revelation too, which is committed to the Church, and the scheme of Redemption, given in Christ, is always the same. Prayer and worship are a constant flowing back and home-coming of the souls of restless, wavering men, to the peace of God.

And so, even the forms through which God has been glorified in the past, take on a kind of sanctity. They are consecrated by God like a votive offering which must not be taken away from the sanctuary once it is given. Religious sentiment is very much disinclined to change liturgical forms except for very grave reasons.

But like every living organism, the liturgy has to adapt itself to the present conditions of life. As a rule this is achieved by silent growth: but there are times of almost complete standstill, and times of stormy advance. Of the thousands of medieval liturgical manuscripts which we still have, scarcely two agree completely. Every fresh sacramentary, every new *Liber ordinum*, as well as showing faithful adherence to tradition, also displays additions demanded, it would appear, by local custom and changed sense of form.

Towards the end of the Middle Ages this growth became a wild unhealthy profusion and so the Council of Trent and Pope St. Pius V called a halt. The Roman Breviary (1568) and the Roman Missal (1570) were published by authority of this Pope; use was made obligatory for the whole of the Western Church with a few exceptions, and a period of standstill was inaugurated. Now it was laid down, as the Bull introducing the Missal put it, that: 'nothing was to be added or taken away or changed' (nihil umquam addendum, detrahendum aut immutandum esse)—an order, not indeed to be binding for ever, and itself introducing a novelty which could only have been possible after the invention of printing.

For three and a half centuries things went on under this regime until Pius X—another saint—began to speak once more of reform and described his own important measures as the 'first step' in this direction. Certainly, after so long a pause an imperceptible growth could not suffice. A jerk—more than one jerk—was clearly necessary; and not only because of the three and a half centuries which had slipped past. It was now more than a thousand years since the Roman liturgy had been adopted in Northern lands, where it had been preserved, guarded and used, but never assimilated. As the method of interpreting the ceremonies allegorically, and as the development of the prayers and rites shows, people had gained but little insight into the meaning of the traditional forms and little understanding of their sober and practical style, little understanding, indeed, of their religious and theological background. The religious thought of the Fathers and that of an Amalar or a Bernard of Clairvaux, in spite of a community of faith, belong to two different worlds.

Concerning these things, a great change has taken place since last century. Thanks to the emergence of historical theology, and Christian archaeology, too, the world of the Fathers and that in which our liturgy found its origin has been brought near once more. The ancient Christian world has revived. Much knowledge has become available to us. The early patterns of various liturgies are coming to light with increasing definition, and we are astonished to see their shapes in the liturgical forms we know today. And so they invite us once more to enter more deeply into their meaning.

The religious situation of our time also demands forms of Church life such as will be found in a meaningful, corporately celebrated liturgy. Huge sections of the people are estranged from the Church; others are perplexed with doubt and have no secure traditions; naive, habitual piety has withered before the biting blast of a scientific age. Only substantial faith can hold its own. Of such stuff is the liturgy which represents essential prayer which the Church offers to God in unity with her Lord. On the other hand, people are educated in such a way that the mass of faithful, inasmuch as they are prepared to take active part in their religion, will no longer be satisfied with second-rate explanations or with a pious suggestion of reverence for a remote mystery, nor with substitute forms and little out-houses on the fringe of the sanctuary. Like its architecture, the thinking of our time has become practical.

About the end of last century we have witnessed, therefore, the attempt to open the liturgy to the people. Schott's Church Missal with neat and illuminating explanations was sold in hundreds of thousands. This first phase of following the liturgical text in print has been followed by that which requires joining in the words and actions. This is the day of the people's Mass which is gaining in popularity in parishes in the form of the Sunday 'prayer and song-Mass.' The 'we' of the liturgy has come to life: the distance between the people and the altar has lessened, sometimes shown in the outward structure of the church. The faithful are beginning to gain a sense of the holy priesthood, which the first Pope attributed to them, and of their being called, as Pope Pius XII pointed out, to present their own sacrifice along with the ordained priesthood. This revival goes hand in hand with that revival and deepening of the sense of the Church which has characterized the last decades.

The liturgical revival has already gone farther than this. It is reaching a third phase. Liturgical revival has to overflow into a renewal of the liturgy which Pius X had already envisaged. The numbed limbs must be thawed out: after centuries of almost complete inertia natural life must be resumed, must in many ways be made good. The liturgy itself is on the move. This does not please everyone. It is as though the walls of an ancient building were beginning to totter; as though an axe were being laid to a thousand year old oak.

At first it was only the outward appearance of the liturgy which changed somewhat, as much as was possible within the framework of existing regulations. The people began answering the priest—as the rubrics had always allowed. Communion was received during Mass—as had always been the correct procedure. Occasionally the priest stood behind the altar-table facing the people as had always been permissible according to the rubrics.

It was not the worst of people who were uneasy at such 'innovations.' No less a man than Paul Claudel,[1] a few weeks before his death, declared his violent objection to the new practice whereby the priest faced the people and said his Mass 'into the empty air' in the presence of 'a mob of curious spectators' oppo-

1. P. Claudel, *La Messe a l'envers: Figaro littéraire* Jan. 29, 1955.

site him, instead of having a reverent people behind him in whose name he offered sacrifice. But these 'innovations' were but the beginning, the first stirrings of a fresh will to life. In his encyclical of 1947 on the sacred Liturgy, Pius XII stressed the fact of the development of liturgical forms and gave signal recognition to the relevant liturgical studies, especially those going on in Benedictine monasteries.[2] During his pontificate substantial results were achieved, on the whole a following out of the course set by Pius X. There was the new translation of the Psalms, the facilities for evening Masses, the mitigation of the rules governing fasting before Communion, and above all the bold revival of the Easter Vigil and now the whole of Holy Week. Also, the scope for use of vernacular—already seen under Pius X as inseparable from the concept of the liturgy—has been greatly widened through permission for regional Rituals, in particular the German *Collectio rituum* (1950).

More than this: for years the Roman periodical *Ephemerides Liturgicae* had been making suggestions and printing articles on how to improve liturgical books, first of all the Breviary and the Martyrology; then in 1949 quite publicly under the eye of Rome there was a report in this paper of the result of an enquiry it had made amongst representative liturgical and pastoral scholars amongst the secular and religious clergy, attempting to discover their views on the possible reform first and the Breviary and then of the liturgy in general.[3] Since then, in liturgical and pastoral theological journals, in separate essays, at the international liturgical conferences which have been going on since 1951,[4] ideas have been sketched out, with more or less prudence and restraint, of the coming shape of the liturgy; difficult problems have been discussed, and historical support has been produced in favour of this or that solution.

In all this, one topic has been clearly to the fore—the question of the liturgical language. At least with regard to the Mass there seems to be an insurmountable obstacle here in the decision of the Council of Trent which protected the use of Latin and in opposing

2. *Acta Ap. Sed.* 39 (1947) 523, 529.
3. A. Bugnini, *Per una riforma liturgica generale: Eph. liturg.* 63 (1949) 166–184.
4. The series of international study conferences: 1951 Maria Laach; 1952 Odilienberg; 1953 Lugano; 1954 Mont-César; 1956 Assisi; 1958 Montserrat.

the Reformers laid a ban of excommunication on all 'who say that Mass may be celebrated only in the vernacular'.5 But Hermann Schmidt had demonstrated in a study of the transactions of the Council, that while insisting on the use of Latin, the Council consciously avoided giving theological reasons for its decision. This all harmonized with the situation of the times, when Latin was still the language not only of scholars but of all educated people.6

And so it was possible for Cardinal Lercaro, Archbishop of Bologna, to say at the international liturgical congress in Lugano in 1953 that he hoped that the Christian people whom Pius X had invited to receive the Bread of the Eucharist would be granted an effective share in the Word of God through the lessons being read out in the vernacular by the priest.7 Even earlier than this Rome had written to Cardinal Bertram in 1943 giving permission for the association of the German Mass chants with the Latin rite used by the priest, and also regularizing the German High Mass which had been going on for a long time in several dioceses.8 In the course of time the diocesan prayer books and hymn books have produced a wonderful store of hymns but these can only be regarded as a temporary solution.

At last the question of the use of the living language of the people in the liturgy is being seriously raised on all sides. It is interesting for us to take a look at how the question has been approached in the Eastern Churches, and to note what Rome's attitude to this has been. A very recent publication reveals some most valuable things.9

For the region where the Byzantine liturgy was in use, the Patriarch Balsamon (c. 1190) asserted this principle: Those who do

5. Denzinger n. 956.
6. H. Schmidt S.J. *Liturgie et langue vulgaire*, Rome 1950.
7. *Liturgisches Jahrbuch* 3 (1953) 174.
8. Ibid. 108-110. This explanation, with a few reservations (concerning the ordinary psalms of the Missa Cantata without assistants) is confirmed in a writ of the Holy Office to the prefects of the Congregation of Rites 29:4:55; v. *Liturgisches Jahrbuch* 6 (1956) 115. Cf. also the encyclical *Musicae sacrae*: ibid. 104 seq. *Acta Ap. Sed.* 48 (1956) 16. The legal situation remains unaltered by the instruction of 3:9:58: *Acta Ap. Sed.* 50 (1958) 631-663. This states (n. 13 c): *Exceptiones particulares, a lege linguae latinae in actionibus liturgicis unice adhibendae, a Sancta Sede concessae, vim suam retinet.* In the same spirit the letter from the Holy Office to Cardinal Frings 23:12:58; v. *Liturgisches Jahrbuch* 9 (1959) 119.
9. C. Korolevskij, *Liturgie en langue vivante* (*Lex orandi* 18), Paris 1955; in German: Klosterneuburg 1958.

not understand Greek are to celebrate the liturgy in their own language, but the usual prayers must be exactly translated from the Greek. Following the same principle, the Slavs had for long been celebrating the liturgy in Slavonic, in that dialect which came to be known as 'Church Slavonic,' and which can still be more or less understood by the various Slav groups.

According to the same principle, the one-time Greek populations of the coastal regions of the near-East, the Melkites, once they had become Arabianized, took over Arabic as the liturgical language; and the Rumanians likewise adopted Rumanian. When the matter of re-union arose after the 13th century with groups of staunch Melkites, and about 1700, with Rumanians, the liturgical language provided no special point of discussion. Likewise, Armenians, Copts, Chaldeans and Ethiopians all retained their traditional liturgical languages when united with Rome. In these cases, the languages were no longer living languages.

Formal approval by Rome was never mentioned right down to the 19th century. Within the Byzantine Rite on the orthodox side, the principle of Balsamon was and is applied to the communities of new peoples: in recent years it has been applied, for example, to Chinese and Japanese.

An analogous case was that of the Uniate Hungarian Ukrainians who adhered to the Byzantine Rite but had long since forgotten their Ukrainian mother-tongue. Since the 17th century isolated liturgical texts had been translated into Hungarian, and in the course of the 19th century, the entire liturgy was translated. Only in 1896 was the case brought before the Roman authorities, at a time, that is, when unlike today—as Korolevski affirms— Oriental study and a liturgical movement were unknown, and when people were unaware of the precise nature of what had been going on at Trent. And so Hungarian was forbidden as a liturgical language. A series of petitions resulted in 1912 in Hungarian being replaced by Greek as the liturgical language for Greek appeared to correspond to the Latin of the West: but it was a dead language, as strange to the Hungarian-Ukrainian clergy as was the Old or Church Slavonic. The decision turned out to be quite impracticable. The status quo was left undisturbed and Hungarian became silently tolerated as a liturgical language.

This century a similar thing happened in Esthonia where in the 19th century Orthodox Christians of the Byzantine Rite had given up Old Slavonic in favour of the vernacular, that is Esthonian. Pius XI formally sanctioned the use of the vernacular for the Uniate branch of this community of Christians in 1929.

Another case is that of the Christians of the Malabar coast who had been subjected for a long time to the Latinizing influence of the Portuguese, but who had in general held on to their Syrian liturgical language. Here too, a group of Jacobite Christians existed who used their Indian language—Malayalam—in the liturgy. In 1930 they were re-united with Rome under Mar Ivanios (d. 1953) when they retained their own rite and also the use of the vernacular in the liturgy. This was sanctioned by Rome.

The language of the liturgy is only one of the things, and that not the most important, which arises when changes in the liturgy are being considered. In 1927 the great liturgical scholar Anton Baumstark remarked in conversation: 'I shall not see the day when the liturgical movement reaches its goal.' He was referring to the admittedly controversial proposal to have unlimited use of the vernacular; and he indicated that only then would we come face to face with the much deeper problem of how to make palatable to modern man the religious modes of thought and manners of speech which were crystallized 1500 years ago.

The problem is very serious. The solution must come from two directions: on the one hand through a certain amount of clarification and enlivening of liturgical forms, and on the other through a preaching of the Faith which matches the spirit of the liturgy.

Liturgy must become pastoral. An increasing emphasis on pastoral concerns has been the mark of the liturgical movement in recent decades; and this emphasis is now reacting upon the liturgy itself. Above all we are interested in the worship of Sundays and holidays of obligation. The essential action of this should be so designed that it is intelligible to the Catholic Christian of average education, who should be able also to take an active part in it. The type of Christian who merely 'assists' at Mass in a bored fashion must disappear. But more than this must be achieved. Public Worship must become both an invitation and a help to real adoration 'in Spirit and in truth': it must become the support of a joyful awareness of Faith and of a Christian life in the harsh everyday world.

This is the goal set by liturgical effort within the considerable possibilities which today presents. It aims at re-forming and reviving the people's participation in the liturgy. Since the Middle Ages the regulations governing the liturgy had almost entirely neglected this participation, but at the same time had left scope for revival and re-fashioning. Already as we know, significant things have happened. Wherever pastoral care has kept pace with the times the people are no longer dumb witnesses at worship. Congregational singing has received a great stimulus. People have become aware that they constitute a genuine part of the Church's worship and that, in its text and melody they have a means, which is theirs by right, of coming much closer to the liturgy than they would ever have come by traditional hymn singing.

This development has already precipitated a crisis in the world of Church music. Church music has had a long and illustrious history. It is now becoming more and more obvious that at least some Christians feel themselves called to the task of rebuilding the edifice of Church music from the very foundations. A complete withdrawal from a painfully established empire may not be necessary, but some way must be found of enabling orderly congregational singing to co-exist with Church music.

Not only amongst the people but at the altar, within the liturgy in the narrowest sense, things require to be done. There is no lack of proposals which seek to do justice both to the spirit of tradition and to pastoral needs.[10] They aim at making the shape of the Mass as celebrated by the priest, more straightforward. Many accessories are to be reduced or must disappear altogether. Thus the Mass for the revived Easter Vigil has had parts omitted at the beginning and at the end: and in a similar mood the decree of March 23, 1955, has reduced the number of prayers at Sunday Masses.

The construction of the Mass ought to be made more obvious.

10. In essence they are laid down in the *Liturgisches Jahrbuch* (since 1951) and in the periodicals *La Maison-Dieu* (Ed. du Cerf) and *Questions liturgiques et paroissiales* (Mont-César).

The chief sections, Proanaphora, Offertory, Canon and Communion should be easily distinguished; and various details should be made more intelligible. For example, the symbolic handwashing could be brought forward to the beginning of the Offertory. Scripture reading ought to be enriched by the introduction of a cycle covering several years. Popular intercession which was supplied at the end of last century by prayers after Mass ought now to come fully into its own through the revival of the prayer of the faithful as an organic part of the Mass immediately after the Scripture readings and sermon. Sunday Prefaces should once more take up the note of Easter joy, and the thanksgiving after Communion could be re-fashioned so as to allude to the Communion of the people.

Reform of the Christian Year has already begun vigorously with the revival of the Easter Liturgy. The direction indicated by Pius X has been followed by the decree of March 23, 1955, and Lent has received fresh emphasis over against any saint's feast-day which happens to fall during that time. The octave of the Immaculate Conception does not disturb the season of Advent, nor does St. Joseph's feast interfere with the Paschal season.

Developments concerning the Divine Office are important and full of promise. While cautious attempts are being made to reform the clerical Breviary, in several countries lay Breviaries have appeared simultaneously,[11] used primarily by religious communities who, without undue waste of time, are able to have their daily devotions in the vernacular in addition to the traditional Office, without being limited to the fixed form of the Little Office of Our Lady or to other secondary forms of prayer.

On the other hand diocesan prayer books and hymn books show that liturgical principles are beginning to affect the structure of evening devotions in the course of the Christian Year. We see the service based upon a Scripture lesson, responsorial prayer in various forms, and the conclusion with an appropriate

11. A critical review of six widely used lay Breviaries and one Marian Office adapted to the Church's Year is given by H. Schmidt, Officium Parvum B.M.V. et *Breviaria Parva in religiosis tam Fratrum quam Sororum Congregationibus: Periodica de ne morali canonica liturgica* 43 (1959) 115-133. Cf. also J. M. Hum, *Les fidèles et L'Office divin: La Maison-Dieu* 34 (1953) 157-163. This came to Germany first in 1933, then appeared in an improved form by commission of the liturgical referendum of the Fulda episcopal congress in the edition: *Officium Divinum Parvum*, Fr. Hildebrand Fleischmann O.S.B. (8th ed. Freiburg 1958), in view of the fact that meanwhile it had spread widely in other languages.

prayer. The astonishingly violent contrast which had existed between popular devotions and liturgical Vespers, although both derived from the same basic nature of the Christian community, has become softened. The Church's liturgy and the prayer of the congregation assembled in the church have drawn closer together, just as Church and people too have drawn closer to each other. But before these developments whose beginnings we believe we are witnessing today, have achieved some degree of completion, many years will have to pass—even if God grants peaceful days and favourable progress to His Church.

As can. 1257 expressly states, even liturgical reforms cannot be accomplished from above without more ado by the mere exercise of the authority of the Apostolic See. Liturgical science, too, may well prepare the way for reforming, may advance proposals well-grounded in history and theology, but it cannot infuse life. Within the Christian people themselves must exist the proper atmosphere. Therefore, it is pastoral work which must prepare the way for a revival of the liturgy, using as its tools, teaching and preaching and all the other means which contribute to the formation of a full grasp of the Faith. Preaching the Faith and public worship should be related as statement to reply: the two would have to achieve complete congruence.

The redemptive powers which are found in the mighty sweep of the liturgy with its transparent Christocentricity and profound sense of corporate life must come alive in preaching as well, if these powers are to produce their full effect; for they are contained first of all in the heritage of belief out of which the liturgy has grown.

By happy coincidence, the inauguration of the new catechism occurred during the decade of the first great liturgical reform in Germany. The ideal expressed above was before the minds of its authors. That is, they aimed at leading people towards a grasp of the Faith which would be fully expressed in the liturgy of the Church. We must reach a situation where the *Ecclesia orans* is no longer a mere ideal of liturgical books, partially realized by the celebrating clergy. It is the whole believing people who make up the *Ecclesia* which approaches God in prayer through the liturgy.

PART II

SEPARATE HISTORICAL PROBLEMS

1. The Origin of Matins

WHEN we examine the origins of the Canonical Hours, especially of those assigned to the night, we are directed by historical analysis of the Breviary, as a rule, to the early Christian Vigil. In the first flush of enthusiasm Christians had kept night-watch not only year by year at Easter, but week by week in preparation for Sunday. They had spent the night in prayer, praise and Scripture-reading. Thus the weekly night-watch preceding Sunday became regarded from the very beginning or a little later either as a complete vigil (*Pannychis*)[1] or it was developed into Vespers, and the nocturnal and morning Hours.[2] In any case, the parent of our nocturnal Office, Matins, whose daily recitation certainly goes back to the first days of monastic life, is always traced to the middle section of a regular, weekly Sunday Vigil based on the pattern of the old all-night Easter Vigil,[3] fused however, with the nocturnal services of the times of persecution.[4]

Serious objections can be made to this derivation. Let us grant that the early Christians were full of zeal. Is it likely, however, that the rulers of the early Church would ask the faithful to set aside one night every week when sleep was to be replaced almost entirely by prayer? But even if we do not accept this, it is most unlikely that the form of the Canonical Hours developed so directly and simply as the above assumption suggests. A thorough re-examination of the question is required, and we may expect

1. H. Leclercq, *Bréviaire:* DACL II, 1267 seq.; P. Battifol, *Histoire du Bréviaire Romain,*3 Paris 1911, 1-3; C. Callewaert, *Sacris erudiri,* Steenbrugge 1940, 283 seq.; M. Righetti, *Manuale di storia liturgica* II2, Milan 1955, 633.

2. R. Stapper, *Katholische Liturgik,*5 Munster 1931, 154; Eisenhofer, *Handbuch* II, 485 seq.; similarly J. Baudot, *Le Bréviaire,* Paris 1929, 11. 16.

3. Thus A. Baumstark, *Vom Geschichtlichen Werden der Liturgie,* Freiburg 1923, 10; ibid, *Nocturna laus,* Münster 1957, 77. 81. 88; L. Duchesne, *Origines du culte chrétien,*5 Paris 1925, 242; J. Brinktoine, *Das römische Brevier,* Paderborn 1932, 22-24, places the origin of the Christian vigils even further back in a Jewish model.

4. Baumer-Biron, *Histoire du Bréviaire* I, 60.

some results, because we now possess much new knowledge supplied by recent liturgical-historical study.

Looking at the relevant early texts, we first have to decide whether the particular case before us has to do purely with prayers which Christians offered during the night in private, or with a corporate celebration which lasted the whole night through and culminated in the Eucharistic sacrifice. For we do find these three forms of nocturnal prayer in the slightly later phase of early Christianity; and they persist into later times— to the time, indeed, when the nocturnal Hours of our Breviary come into being.

It has been proved beyond doubt that within the scheme of prayer which Christians were supposed to follow, and which many certainly did follow, from the end of the 2nd century besides prayer at the third, sixth and ninth hours and the morning and evening prayer—too obvious to require mention—there was also the custom of prayer at midnight. Clement of Alexandria, Tertullian and Hippolytus of Rome are the first in a long line of unbiased witnesses.5 The line carries on into the 5th century and even further. This custom is so much accepted by Tertullian that he asks: 'What is a Christian woman who is married to a heathen to do? Can she hide the fact that she rises from bed at midnight to pray? At her side lies a slave of the Devil.'6 Hippolytus mentions, indeed, a double interruption of sleep for prayer: prayer at midnight and prayer at cock-crow.7

Again it is firmly established that from the 2nd century on, the Church of the martyrs was accustomed to celebrate the Eucharist on Sunday in the early morning, that is, before dawn. To begin with we can cite the famous passages from the 112 or so letters of the younger Pliny, governor of Bithynia. At the trial of the Christians whom he had arrested it was disclosed that they

5. J. Stadlhuber, *Das Stundengebet des Laien im Christlichen Altertum:* ZkTh 71 (1949) 129-183, esp. 133 seq.—For Tertullian cf. esp. E. Dekkers, *Tertullianus en de geschiedenis der liturgie,* Brussels 1947, 117-126.
6. Tertullian, *Ad uxorem* II, 5 (CSEL 70, 118); Stadlhuber 136. In any case, Tertullian was answered by Hippolytus, *Traditio Ap.* c. 36 (Dix 65): the believing partner is to go into another room and say his night prayers there.
7. Hippolytus, *Traditio Ap.* c. 36 (Dix 65-67); cf. Stadlhuber 148 seq. Cf. Jerome, *Ep.* 22 *ad Eustochium* n. 37 (CSEL 54, 201): *Noctibus bis terque surgendum . . . nec prius corpusculum requiescat quam anima pascatur.* More of this in the numerous passages in which Jerome speaks of night prayer; v. Stadlhuber 171 seq.

were in the habit of meeting *stato die ante lucem* to sing an antiphonal hymn to Christ as their God.[8] That this refers to the celebration of the Mass is slowly becoming the predominant view of scholars.[9] The phrase *coetus antelucani* is expressly used of the Mass by Tertullian.[10]: 'Although the Lord had instituted the Sacrament *tempore victus*, we celebrate at assemblies before dawn.'[11] Tertullian's well-known advice,[12] that anyone who had scruples about receiving Communion at Mass on fast days should take the Body of our Lord and keep it until the hour of the day when fasting was over, presupposes that Mass was normally celebrated in the morning. Tertullian mentions the *nocturnae convocationes* for which people must occasionally be prepared:[13] but the meaning of this remains somewhat obscure. It could refer to a celebration of the Sunday Mass at an earlier hour of the night during the time of persecution. An all-night vigil is certainly not what is in mind.[14] Other texts from the 2nd and 3rd centuries which speak of the celebration of the Eucharist without mentioning a definite hour, suggest that the time was early morning, or at least do not deny that this was so. Thus Novatian[15] mentions the Christian who came from worship still carrying the Eucharist and who ran straight off into the theatre. This could only have happened in the morning. There is not a single sure mention that the Eucharist was preceded every Sunday by an all-night vigil during the early centuries.[16]

8. *Ep.* 97; v. the text as in K. Kirch, *Enchiridium fontium hist. eccl.*5 Freiburg 1941, 22 seq.
9. These texts have at last been thoroughly examined by F. J. Dölger, *Sol salutis*,2 Münster 1925, 103-136; C. Mohlberg, *Carmen Christo quasi Deo: Rivista die Archeologia cristiana* 14 (1937) 92-123; v. esp. 103 seq. In the language and conception of the heathen the *carmen Christo quasi Deo* could well be the Eucharistic prayer, which began with the dialogue, reached its climax in the *Sanctus*, and ended with the Amen. Other interpretations: R. M. Grant, *Harvard Theol. Review* 41 (1948) 274.
10. Tertullian, *De corona* c. 3 (CSEL 70, 158).
11. On interpretation of the texts v. Dekkers 109-112. Cf. *Apol.* c. 2, 6 (CSEL 69, 5 seq.) where Tertullian speaks about Pliny's letter and infers that it could only prove *coetus antelucani*.
12. Tertullian, *De orat,* c. 19 (CSEL 20, 192).
13. Tertullian, *Ad uxorem* II, 4 (CSEL 70, 117).
14. Dekkers 113 seq.
15. Novatian, *De spectaculis* c. 5 (CSEL 3, 3, p. 8). Cf. E. Dekkers *L'église ancienne a-t-elle connu la messe du soir: Miscellanea* Mohlberg I, Rome 1948, 239 seq.
16. The same thought in C. Marcora, *La Vigilia nella liturgia*, Milan 1954, 63-69. And C. Callewaert's—*Sacris erudiri* 283 seq.—attempted proof rests only on a presumption that the early Christians were fervent.—Dölger, *Sol salutis*2 117-124 gives a series of evidences that in early times Christians celebrated Mass before sun-rise, for symbolic reasons.

But the evidence is unambiguous that on certain occasions there was an all-night vigil which culminated in the Eucharist. This happened above all at the early Christian Easter celebration. At the middle of the 2nd century this is mentioned in the apocryphal *Epistola Apostolorum*. The Lord who commissioned this *Epistola* and also the celebration itself, is told that the imprisoned apostle was miraculously liberated in order to be able to join in the Pasch: 'He will spend a night of vigil with you and stay with you until cock-crow.' And when the memorial—that is the Eucharist—is over he will return to prison.[17] Tertullian writes of the hard lot of a woman married to a heathen when Easter comes round: 'Will her husband put up with her absence the whole night through while she is attending Paschal celebrations (*sollemnibus paschae abnoctantem*)?'[18] A little later in the Apostolic Traditions of Hippolytus we find an impressive picture of the Easter Vigil celebrations. Throughout the whole night the candidates for baptism are to listen to readings and instruction: at cock-crow the baptismal water and the holy oil are blessed; and then, after abjuration of the Devil and anointing, comes the baptism itself and the laying on of the bishop's hands. At length the newly baptized enter the circle of the faithful and along with them celebrate their first Eucharist.[19] The Syrian *Didascalia* which is almost as old tells how the faithful: 'keep vigil the whole night with prayer and supplication, readings from the Prophets, the Gospels and the Psalms . . . until the third hour of the day after the Sabbath,' then the fast is over, gifts are offered for the sacrifice and Easter-joy prevails.[20] Everyone knows of the splendour with which Easter night was celebrated in later times—in the time of Constantine,[21] shall we say. Hence, the saying of St. Augustine

17. *Epistula Apostolorum* ed. Duensing (*Kleine Texte* 152), 13 seq. Contrary to Dekker's assumption—*L'église ancienne a-t-elle connu la messe du soir* 238—this Pasch must have been the yearly celebration, not the Sunday. This would explain better the longing of the apostles and the deliverance by a miracle.
18. Tertullian, *Ad uxorem* II, 4 (CSEL 70, 117).
19. Hippolytus, *Traditio Ap.* c. 21-23 (Dix 32-42).
20. *Didascalia* V, 19 seq. (Connolly 189 seq.; Funk 288 seq.). The dating is somewhat contradictory. Does it mean the third hour after midnight or is this the indication of the later practice of anticipation? Cf. O. Casel, *Art und Sinn der ältesten christlichen Osterfeier*: JL 14 (1938) 29 n. 56.
21. Eusebuis, *Vita Constantini* IV, 22 (PG 20, 1169). Cf. also Gregory Nazianzen, *Or.* 45, 2 *in Pascha* (PG 36, 624 seq.). On the celebration in the Lateran v. H. Grisar, *Geschichte Roms und der Päpste* I, Freiburg 1901, 800-808.

who described the Easter Vigil as the *mater omnium sanctorum vigiliarum*.[22]

St. Augustine is aware of other vigils as well. Amongst these are that of the second baptismal season—Pentecost,[23] and those at the graves of notable martyrs. The *Passio* of St. Cyprian provides us with the first hint of the custom of a martyr vigil in Africa. When Cyprian was arrested the Christians spent the night outside the prison. The author sees it as a very special favour of divine mercy which has so arranged *ut Dei populus etiam in sacerdotis passione vigilaret*.[24] This vigil persisted. From St. Augustine we learn that the Feast of St. Cyprian was marked in Carthage in his time by a vigil.[25] The same thing applies to the day commemorating the holy Bishop Saturninus of Toulouse (d.c. 250) as his Acts, which are almost as old as Augustine's witness, testify of his own and of other martyrs' days,:[26] *illos dies vigiliis, hymnis ac sacramentis etiam sollemnibus honoramus*. In St. Ambrose' time such a vigil was held in Milan on the Feast of SS. Peter and Paul,[27] the day of the translation of the bones of SS. Gervase and Protase, associated with the dedication of the Ambrosian Basilica, was ushered in by an all-night vigil[28]—a custom which has left its mark to this day in the rules of the Roman *Pontificale* which prescribe a vigil (*vigilias*) before the relics which are to be translated during the night before the dedication of a church. We can presume that there was a similar vigil custom in Rome. Certainly vigils were kept there at the graves of prominent martyrs.[29] We have clear evidence of such a vigil in honour of St. Laurence at the beginning of the 5th century.[30] The older Gelasian Sacramentary provides a host of prayers for this occasion, over and above those under the title *In vigilia*, which may well be attributed

22. Augustine, *Serm.* 219 (PL 38, 1088).
23. Augustine, *Serm.* 266 (PL 38, 1225).
24. Pontius the deacon, *De vita et passione Cypriani* c. 15 (PL 3, 1495).
25. Augustine, *Enarr. in psalm,* 32, II, 1, 5 (PL 36, 279); 85, 24 (PL 37, 1099); *Serm.* Denis 11, tit. et n. 7 (Morin 43, 49); cf. V. Monachiro, *La cura pastorale a Milano e Cartagine e Roma nel* p. IV, Rome 1947, 198.
26. Th. Ruinart, *Acta Martyrum,* Regensburg 1859, 177.
27. Ambrose, *De virginitate* 19, 124 seq. (PL 16, 299).
28. Ambrose, *Ep.* 22, 2 (PL 16, 1020).
29. Jerome, *Ep.* 107, 9 (CSEL 55, 300); *Contra Vigil.* c. 9 (PL 23, 347 seq.).
30. *Vita s. Melanie* c. 5 (*Analecta Bollandiana* 1889, 23): Melanie's parents refused her permission to take part; then she kept vigil throughout the night in the oratory at home.

to a nocturnal celebration,[31] while other Offices of martyrs merely
receive the specified introduction to a normal Mass.[32] At an early
date a private form of the martyr vigil broke away from the
main stream of the publicly celebrated kind. This private form
usually was unattended by clergy and included no celebration of
the Eucharist. The Synod of Elvira in Spain (A.D. 300) was already
regulating such private vigils. Women were to be excluded from
them.[33] These vigils must have been very popular. The memory
of these things continues in the legend which tells of how the
parents of St. Agnes zealously kept vigil at her tomb.[34] Besides
all this there was still a vigil in Rome at the conclusion of the
quarterly ember weeks, as we can tell from the well-known
proclamation of St. Gregory the Great and also from parallel
texts of Leo.[35]

The way in which the Easter and Pentecost Vigils were celebrated is plainly revealed by the rite used, a rite which is preserved
in main outline to this day in the Roman Missal in the liturgy of
Holy Thursday (and in the Vigil of Pentecost). The basis is made
up of a series of twelve lessons which are sometimes followed by a
responsorial hymn and always by the prayer of the people and the
priest's collect. The same Missal shows the same order in a much
shortened form in the vestigal quarterly ember vigil on the
Ember Saturday, the rite for which was transcribed into early
medieval texts: *Sabbato in XII lectionibus*, followed by a *Dominica
vacans*, many of the older features of which show that it has, in
fact, remained without a Proper of its own. In the course of
things, as early as the 7th century, the night-service had been
advanced, as a rule, well into the early evening so that the concluding Mass itself fell upon the Saturday. Hence, the sacra-

31. II, 42 (Wilson 189 seq.).
32. These are the commemoration days of Gervase and Protase, John the Baptist, John
and Paul, Peter and Paul, all the Apostles, Andrew.—Hadrian's Gregorianum still shows
Christmas midnight Mass, but has also the formulary for the preceding days, which are
described as vigils (Lietzmann n. 5 seq.). The Leonianum contains a series of *orationes
pridie Pentecosten*—designed perhaps for the Pentecost vigil—which end with the Mass
(Mohlberg, *Sacr. Ver.* n. 187-199).
33. Can. 35 (Mansi II, 11). Cf. Jerome, *Contra Vigil.* c. 9 (PL 23, 347 seq.); *Ep.* 107, 9
(CSEL 55, 300): Laeta is not to let her daughter an inch away from her side.
34. *Des. Agnete* n. 14 (Acta SS. Jan. II, 717): *Cum igitur parentes b. Agnetis assiduis per-
noctationibus vigilarent ad tumulum eius.*
35. Mohlberg, *Sacr. Ver.* n. 860: *sabbatorum die hic sacras acturi vigilias.* Cf. ibid. 905:
Sabbatorum die hic ipsum vigiliis sollemnibus expleamus.

mentaries and lectionaries provided a special Mass for the Sunday. The original rite for the vigil thus becomes attached to the Saturday.36 Even earlier than this, the public martyr vigils must have undergone the same sort of anticipation; for in the Leonine text, alongside the feast-day Mass for St. Laurence there is another which belongs to the previous day, as we learn from the phrase, *praevenientes natalem diem* of the Preface.37 These two forms—the anticipated night office on the preceding day, and the creation of a special vigil Mass also on the preceding day—display clearly the way in which the early Christian vigil evolved at a later date. It is quite plain that no way at all leads from the old all-night vigil to our nocturnal Offices of the Breviary.

Concerning the original early morning (*ante lucem*) celebration of the Sunday Mass, in general the normal hour for community worship, circumstances changed greatly with the era of peace for the Church ushered in by Constantine. Previously Christians had to choose a time when they could meet for worship which was out of working hours, for they were bound by the working arrangements of their environment. But now it rapidly became the rule that public worship was celebrated on Sunday at the third hour.38 We can set the change to this new arrangement in Constantine's reign. Eusebius records39 that Constantine released Christian soldiers on Sunday so that they could offer prayer in church to God. We may presume that they were released during the day when otherwise they would have been occupied in their service. Cassian expressly states that the Egyptian monks at the close of the 4th century used to assemble on Saturdays and Sundays at the third hour in order to receive Communion.40 Neither,

36. For the conclusion even of the Easter vigil in late evening (*sacratissimo paschali Sabbato*) cf. Gregory the Great, *Dial.* IV, 32 (PL 77, 372 seq.). This agrees with the fact that in the older Gelasianum (I, 53) Sunday in *alba* is still the octave day of the celebration of Baptism which must have extended into Easter Sunday, whereas the rite in the Gregorianum (Lietzmann n. 95; Mohlberg-Baumstark, p. 28) has already been superscribed: *Die dominico post albas*; i.e. the octave was already being concluded on the Saturday because Baptism belonged to Holy Saturday. Cf. Jungmann, *Die Vorverlegung der Ostervigil seit dem christlichen Altertum: Liturg. Jahrbuch* 1 (1951) 48–54.
37. Mohlberg, *Sacr. Ver.* n. 740. The case of the St. Andrew vigil is exactly the same; ibid. 1231.
38. Jungmann, *Missarum Sollemnia* I,3/4, 323 seq.
39. Eusebius, *Vita Constantini* IV, 18 (PG 20, 1165).
40. Cassian, *De inst. coenob.* III, 2 (CSEL 17, 34). Cf. also a little later, Sidonius Apollinaris, *Ep.* V, 17 (PL 58, 547 C).

then, is there a way from the early morning Sunday Mass of
the early centuries to what we know as the Matins of our Breviary.
All outward resemblance is lacking and furthermore, only arbitrary assumptions can explain the change over to daily observance.
We are left with only the private night prayers which were
part of the daily prayer routine of the individual Christian, and
which at the height of the early Christian period had reached
full bloom. Undoubtedly it was this non-liturgical prayer which
people practised at home. Nor was it a special service of prayer
carried out by the clergy who were saying an Office 'in the name
of the Church.' Each of the faithful was expected to perform this
and every other hour of prayer, even children were not exempt.[41]
The transformation is seen in full swing in Chrysostom. In
his day there was already prayer every night in church, just as
the hours of prayer during the day, Tierce, Sext, None, were
observed in church. The public observance, however, existed
alongside the private practice. In Antioch, Chrysostom was
admonishing the faithful not to spend the whole night in sleep,
but to pray, at least in their own homes. But his wish was—and
here he used Psalm 133, 2 to support him—that people should
come to the sanctuary.[42] In Constantinople he discovered that
night prayer was badly neglected and he tried to restore it—
as public prayer in church. The women might stay at home: they
could indulge in prayer by day when the men had no time for
it.[43] But in this attempt at reform he found himself at odds
with easy-going clergy who were accustomed to sleeping
throughout the night[44] and who therefore resisted change.
At the end of the 4th and beginning of the 5th century we find
public night prayer already fully developed in Jerusalem; and it is
here that we find the oldest representatives of the monks as the

41. Jerome, *Ep.* 107, 9 (CSEL 55, 300); Laeta is to accustom her daughter from earliest
childhood to keep the Hours of prayer: *assuescat exemplo ad orationes et psalmos nocte
consurgene, mane hymnos canere, tertia, sexta, nona hora quasi bellatricem Christe stare in
acie....* And Chrysostom too, *Acta Ap. hom.* 26 (PG 60, 203), demands that parents should
waken their children so that they may say at least some prayer or other, and then go
to sleep again.
42. Chrysostom, *In psalm.* 133 *expos.* (PG 55, 386). Cf. F. X. Pleithner, *Älteste Geschichte
des Breviergebetes*, Kempten 1887, 209 seq.
43. From this and other observations it is clear that the demand is not confined to
Sundays and feast days, as Chr. Baur assumes—*Chrysostomus und seine Zeit* II (Munich
1930), 67 seq.
44. Palladins, *Dialogus de vita Chrisostomi* c. 5 (PG 47, 20); Pleithner 210 seq.

special bearers of this tradition of community night prayer. Western pilgrims tell us[45] that every day before cock-crow[45a] the doors of the Church of the Resurrection are flung open and along come monks and virgins (*omnes monazontes et parthenae*) and any of the laity who care to join them. This is the first account we have which gives some idea of the content of such an hour of prayer. We are told that until the light begins to break, hymns and psalms are sung responsorially and antiphonally and after each section there is a collect said by one of the presbyters or deacons who is present. When day has come there follows a second act which is completely public in character. The bishop and clergy appear and the catechumens too are present.[46] The 'morning hymns'—Ps. 62 in particular, as we learn from parallel sources— are recited, followed by certain intercessions. The night Hour had displayed a semi-public character: but now in this second act we meet the first of those two completely public Hours, which become observed by clergy and people in the larger city churches from the 4th century onwards. This is the Morning Hour—Lauds, which is balanced in the evening by Vespers. The celebration of Mass does not enter into the week-day programme but is reserved for Sunday.

St. Ephraem (d. 373)[47] speaks emphatically of a nocturnal Office for which the monks rise from their beds day by day, and Basil (d. 379) confirms this.[48] Indeed, we now find this practised everywhere by monks as a corporate act, closely related to the other equally publicly observed hours, Tierce, Sext and None, which along with the nocturnal Hour of prayer had formerly been part of a private rule of prayer. In his account *De institutis coenobiorum*, Cassian deals first of all with the corporate night prayers of Eastern monks and then moves on immediately to the corporate prayer of the third, sixth and ninth hours.[49] In his obituary on Paula (d. 404) St. Jerome praises the virgins with whom she had passed her religious life at Bethlehem: *Mane, hora*

45. Aetheria, *Peregrinatio* c. 24, 1 (CSEL 39, 71).
45a. On the disputed nature of these Hours cf. J. Mateos, *Lelya-Sapra*, Rome 1959, 430 seq.
46. Ibid. c. 24 (CSEL 39, 71).
47. The text in Pleithner 172 seq.
48. Basil, *Regulae fusius tract.* c. 37, 5 (PG 31, 1016); Pleithner 167.
49. Cassian, *De inst. coenob.* 1, II: *De canonico nocturnarum orationum et psalmorum modo*; 1, iii: *De canonico diurnarum orationum et psalmorum modo* (CSEL 17, 16–45).

tertia, sexta, nona, vespera, noctis medio per ordinem psalterium cane-bant.[50] And Aetheria, too, tells of the similarly performed sixth and night Hours in the same breath as she mentions the night and morning worship of the ascetics (c. 24, 3 seq.): concerning the third Hour she confines her remarks to Lent (c. 27, 4). Of St. Euphrasia it is recorded, that in spite of her multifarious activities she never missed any of the psalmody, whether in the night (*in nocturna psalmodia*), at the third, sixth or ninth Hour or at Vespers.[51] In her convent, Melanie the younger established psalmody and reading *nocturnis temporibus* along with the morning and evening Hours and the hours of Tierce, Sext and None.[52]

In all these cases we are confronted by the old order of private hours of prayer, but with the significant innovation that now they are performed corporately—at least in convents for religious.

It is no wonder that the term *vigilia*, which does not necessarily denote an all-night watch but simply any sort of night watch, should be applied to the corporate nocturnal Hour which had thus arisen. This has already happened with Cassian who speaks of *cotidianae vigiliae*,[53] *nocturnae vigiliae*[54] and *canonicae vigiliae*.[55] St. Benedict, too, describes the daily nocturnal *hours* as *vigiliae* or *vigiliae nocturnae*.[56]

The changing of the private Hours into a corporate act of worship was only a part of the great process of liturgical re-organization which occurred in the 4th and 5th centuries. We need not be surprised if in the course of this change we find that Sunday became specially marked in the night Hours. From of old Sunday had enjoyed the privilege of being the day on which the Eucharist was celebrated by the whole congregation. Since the 2nd century this had been prefaced by a Scripture reading service: but now people were not going to be content with this.

50.   Jerome, *Ep.* 108, 20 (CSEL 55, 335). In other passages Jerome speaks of the private execution of this Hour of prayer.
51.   *Acta SS.*, March II, 265, n. 18.
52.   *Analecta Bollandiana* 8 (1889) 49.
53.   Cassian, *De inst. crenob.* II, 17; III, 4 (CSEL 17, 31Z. 17; 38Z. 24).
54.   Ibid. II, 3; III, 5, 6 (CSEL 17, 19Z. 3; 40Z. 22. 28).
55.   Ibid. II, 13 (CSEL 17, 29Z. 8).
56.   St. Benedict, *Regula* c. 8 seq. (Butler 39 seq.). Caesarius of Arles' expression is even further from the original sense. He calls the morning worship of the laity—our Lauds—*vigiliae*. Cf. below. . . . Admittedly, Sidonius Apollinaris (after 470) already calls a morning service *cultus vigiliarum; Ep.* V, 17 (PL 58).

We can observe the rise of a special Sunday 'Vigil' closely in Constantinople under Chrysostom, noting also the peculiarity that here, following a widespread Eastern custom, Saturday was also specially marked out and that the people and the clergy together observed the nocturnal worship. Chrysostom had already been encouraging the people to take part in the night services. The Arians provided the occasion for specially accentuating Saturday and Sunday. They used to sing psalms during both of these nights, and towards morning would march through the city singing offensive refrains. This moved Chrysostom to institute even more impressive celebrations on these two nights for the Catholic section of the populace. In the end the Arians suffered a painful defeat and had to abandon their processions. The Catholic ceremonies alone remained.[57] At least in their hey-day, these celebrations took up most of the night.[58]

The same sort of thing was happening at this time in the See of Bishop Nicetas (d. after 414) in Remensiana on the route connecting Constantinople and Belgrade. In this place likewise the bishop encouraged the people and we find the nocturnal celebration preceding Saturday and Sunday; and here, too, the practice seems to have been a recent innovation.[59] Nicetas did not propose an all-night vigil for his flock. It is only *portionem aliquam* of these nights which men may devote to the divine service, as people do with a secular piece of work.[60]

Aetheria provides the final typical case. The daily nocturnal Office in community arose as a special activity of religious: but on Sundays the people shared in this. Before cock-crow people assembled in the fore-court of the Church of the Resurrection. Until the doors were opened the time was spent in the accustomed way in psalmody which went on until cock-crow. Then the public worship began. Some priest or deacon and another of the clergy recited a psalm which everyone answered and then more

57. Sozomen, *Hist. eccl.* VIII, 7. 8 (PG 67, 1536 seq.); Socrates, *Hist. eccl.* VI, 8 (PG 67, 689). Cf. Baumer-Biron I, 133 note 3, where the author stubbornly refuses to speak of any but a Sunday celebration.
58. Socrates, loc. cit.
59. This is the impression we get from the treatise, *De vigiliis servorum Dei* (PL 68, 365-372). Thus, too, O. Bardenhewer, *Geschichte der altkirchlichen Literatur* III, Freiburg 1912, 603.
60. Ibid. (PL 68, 367A).

prayer followed. The climax came with the reading of the Gospel telling of the Passion and Resurrection of the Lord—the latter read by the bishop himself. A further assembly for worship takes place after dawn (*cum luce*) and is set apart for the celebration of the Mass.[61]

At several places in Christendom in the 4th and 5th centuries we find, therefore, something which looks like the early Christian all-night vigil such as was observed at Easter. But it is quite clear that this Saturday and Sunday Vigil does not derive from the Easter all-night Vigil, but is only a special case of the private midnight prayer of the Christian which had been raised to the status of a corporate celebration. It is true that many similarities with the Easter Vigil may have arisen. The great crowd of people which the pilgrim from the West saw at the night service, reminded her of Easter: *ac si per pascha.*[62] And the form of service too, has here and there developed similar features. Thus it appears that the series of twelve lessons with the Song of Moses interpolated after the sixth and the *Benedicite* after the twelfth has been used for the Sunday as it is for the Easter Vigil.

The East shows this development first, but in the West, too, the same sort of earlier order seems to form the background to the Sunday Office.[63]

The point in time when the night celebrations began leads us to make a distinction which can be fairly widely established. The Eastern vigil associated with feast days began everywhere in the evening, and the tendency to shortening encouraged the custom of concluding the vigil before midnight and of beginning earlier and earlier in the evening.[64] The Sunday night Office however betrays its different origin by the fact that at least in the West it never begins before midnight, just like the nocturnal monastic

61. Aetheria, *Peregrinatio* c. 24, 8–25, 4 (CSEL 39, 73–75). On the whole thing cf. A. Bludau, *Die Pilgerreise der Aetheria*, Paderborn 1927, 58–66.

62. Aetheria, *Peregrinatio* c. 24, 8 (CSEL 39, 73Z. 11).

63. A. Baumstark, *Liturgie comparée*, 3 Chevetogne 1953, 40. Bäumer-Biron I, 143, takes the Pensum of the Sunday night Hours in eastern monastic centres about the year 400 to be at least 18 psalms and 9 readings.

64. Jerome, *In Matth. comm.* IV, 25 (PL 26, 184 seq.): It is a tradition, *ut in die vigiliarum Paschae noctis dimidium populos dimittere non liceat.*

Office.[65] St. Benedict mentions the eighth hour of the night (about 2 a.m.) without making any difference between Sunday and weekdays (c. 8). And the daily vigils, too, which the bishop who had been consecrated in Rome according to the rite of the *Liber diurnus* had to observe, are mentioned without any further distinction as times of day: *a primo gallo usque mane*—which comes to the same thing.[66]

Here the attempt is evident to bring the nocturnal hours nearer morning and to join them on to the old Morning Hour at dawn so as to avoid disturbing sleep, a measure which commended itself to the humane mind of St. Benedict. The harsher Columba, however, relentlessly held on to the Hour *ad medium noctis*.[67] In this way, the nocturnal Hours begin to take on the outward appearance of an introduction to the Morning Hour, which we know as Lauds and which was formerly called *matutinum* until it gave up the name to the nocturnal Hours. We can understand how the elaboration of the nocturnal Hours which have been pushed on towards morning goes hand in hand with the development of the Morning Hour, how, indeed, they are now able to appear as nothing but a monastic introduction to this Morning Hour.[68]

The account of Aetheria, as we saw, had already shown that

65. The picture is quite different with the order in eastern monasteries described by Cassian. In these there is in fact a weekly full vigil, beginning in the evening, and, in the long winter nights mitigated only to the extent that the last two morning Hours were given to sleep; *De inst. coenob.* III, 8 (CSEL 17, 42 seq.). This has to do with the night of Friday-Saturday. It is never said that the same vigil was repeated on Saturday-Sunday, as Bäumer-Biron I, 141, assumes; and this is most unlikely to have happened. On the contrary the single full-vigil was regarded as an improved adaptation of the nocturnal Hours performed elsewhere in the Orient during the two nights. When Cassian asserts that the custom he has described is observed in the entire Orient *a tempore praedicationis evangelicae*, he can only mean that it was so performed in eastern monasteries towards the end of the 4th century. This temporal restriction appears also from the fact that the tendency of assimilating Saturday to Sunday is traceable in the East also only from the 4th century; Bludau, *Die Pilgerreise* 103. In the West Cassian sees nothing similar; hence his great solicitude.
66. *Liber diurnus* n. 74 (Sickel 77; PL 105, 71). That this is our Matins (9 lessons and 9 responsories on Sunday) which presupposes Vespers and Lauds, is shown by Callewaert, *Sacris erudiri* 98-100. We have to do with the same order which Justinian tightened up a bit a little earlier (528) in his well-known prescription: *ut . . . nocturnas et matutinas et vespertinas preces canant;* Bäumer-Biron I, 226.
67. Cf. J. M. Hanssens, *Nature et genèse de l'office des Matines,* Rome 1952, 88 seq.
68. Hanssens, loc. cit. 96 seq., sees in this a complete explanation of its origin. His thesis is acceptable in so far as we cannot regard the present form of Matins and Lauds in our Breviary as *'une iuxtaposition de deux offices préexistants a leur réunion'* (96). But that does not mean that the tradition of the midnight prayer is not preserved in this.

the nocturnal preamble to the morning service of Sunday em-
braced a much more ambitious programme than on week-days.
This arrangement affected further development in the West.
As far as we know, the usual week-day Office for Nocturns
according to the Roman use, contained in the 6th century,
twelve Psalms with readings attached. This counted as a single
Nocturn.[69] But on Sundays and feast days were added two more
made up of three Psalms each with appended readings. This
arrangement lasted until the time of Pius X. Even St. Benedict
in his Rule elevated the *Pensum* to three Nocturns only on
Sundays.[70] The same thing has been done in other monastic rules
in the West since the 6th century. The Rule of St. Caesarius
(d. 542) and that of St. Aurelian (d. 533) provide 18 Psalms for
ordinary days, but on Sundays both rules add another 18 Psalms.[71]

At this point the question arises: What is the significance of
the fact that Matins for Sundays and feast days are composed of
three Nocturns? Does it perhaps mean that at one time there had
been three separate hours of prayer during these particular nights,
and that we have here an actual approximation to, if not an
evolutionary relationship with the ancient all-night vigil?
Medieval liturgical scholars took this to be self-evident;[72] and
even in our own day the same assumption has been stated.[73] But
our sources provide no evidence pointing this way. It is simply a
matter of a subsequent, external breaking-up of a single Nocturn.
All that has happened is that after every third lesson a break has
been made—which may have been accentuated, no doubt, by a
short breathing-space.[74] That the Nocturn was still conceived as
a single entity is proved by the fact that, according to all the formal

69. Callewaert, *Sacris erudiri* 145 seq.
70. St. Benedict, *Regula* c. 11 (Butler 42 seq.). The expression *nocturni* itself occurs in the
Regula without any number attached, in the wider sense of *vigiliae, vigiliae noctae* (c. 15. 17).
71. Caesarius, *Regula ad monachos* n. 20 seq. (PL 67, 1102); Aurelian, Regula (PL 68,
393 seq. 403 seq.); cf. C. Callewaert, *De Breviarii Romani liturgia,* Brügge 1931, 158.
72. Durandus, *Rationale* V, 3, 17; the three Nocturns represented *primitivae Ecclesiae
tres interpolatas excubias,* because they rose thrice in the night to praise the Lord.
73. E. Vykoukal, *Nokturn:* LThK VII (1938) 609.
74. Cassian is most likely to be understood in this sense when he describes the above-
mentioned full vigils of Friday-Saturday. *De inst. ceonob.* III, 8 (CSEL 17, 42 seq.):
(*vigilias*) *tripartitis distinguunt officiis.* As a reason he informs us: *ut labor hac diversitate
divisus delectatione quadam defectionem corporis relevet.* That they should have gone to rest
between these two part-Offices to be roused once again from sleep is ruled out completely by Cassian's account. On the origin of these Nocturns cf. also Baumstark,
Nocturna laus (145 seq. 208), who points back to a Syrian model.

laws of the Roman liturgy, there must be a collect at the end. A collect does occur at the end of the whole of Matins, except, according to the oldest tradition, when Lauds follows immediately.[75]

There is, in fact, a direct and unbroken line of development from the private midnight prayer of the zealous early Christian of the 2nd century to the Nocturns of our Breviary—for Sundays as well as for week-days. At no point, however, does the parent stem of these hours run into the line of development which derives from the early Christian vigil.[76]

It is an open question still, whether this line of development goes back beyond the 2nd century to the primitive Church.

Tertullian described the three daily Hours of prayer as 'Apostolic Hours';[77] and when he comes to expound their significance in more detail,[78] he is able to cite an example for each from the New Testament. The descent of the Holy Spirit falls at the third hour. Peter's prayer at the sixth and the two apostles' entry into the Temple at the ninth. He does not mention the nocturnal Hours in this context, and where he does speak of them, no Scriptural model is given.[79] These Biblical models for the three Hours of prayer are, in fact, traceable to the tradition of prayer which goes back to apostolic times and ultimately to Judaism. And if we add to this the account of how Daniel offered his prayer thrice in the day (Dan. 6, 11), the tradition would appear to go even farther back. But we lack clear evidence that in New Testament times, a prayer at midnight was an obligation upon pious Jews.[80] The models of night prayer which we read about

75. Cf. above, the account of Aetheria. Similarly the prescription in St. Benedict's Rule C8 (Butler 39 seq.).
76. On the full vigil of Friday-Saturday of Cassian's eastern monks, v. above note 65.
77. Tertullian, De ieiun. C. 10 (CSEL 20, 287).
78. Tertullian, loc. cit. (CSEL 20, 286 seq.); De orat. c. 25 (CSEL 20, 197).
79. Later, Basil refers to the example of Paul and Silas, Regula fusius tract. c. 37, 5 (PG 31, 1016).
80. Nonetheless, there comes to mind a passage from the Rule of Qumran, unfortunately rather obscure: they pray as night begins, and during the course of the night (Burrows: at its circuit; Schubert: at its height). Cf. J. A. Jungmann, Altchristliche Gebetsordnungen im Lichte des Regelbuches von 'En Fescha: ZkTh 75 (1953, 215-219), 216. (This study was not included in this collection in the hope that some explanation might be forthcoming from this direction.) J. Brinktrine, Das römische Brevier, Paderborn 1932, 23 seq., for the origin of Matins refers to the Jewish custom of introducing great festival with a nocturnal celebration, and this seems to be supported by some Scripture passages (Is. 30, 29; I Chron. 9, 33; Ps. 133, 2); but this has nothing to do with private night prayer.

in the Acts of the Apostles do not permit the conclusion that there was any fixed custom.

The occasion when the brethren spent the whole night in prayer during Peter's spell in prison is amply accounted for by the circumstances (Acts 12, 5-12). Again, when Paul and Silas were languishing in prison in Philippi (Acts 16, 22-24) with their feet in stocks so that there was no question of sleeping, and they prayed aloud and praised God in the middle of the night, this does not presuppose a habit of praying in the middle of the night. Nor may we assert that in primitive Christian times the nocturnal Hour of prayer had been related to the three Hours of the day-time. The evening service in Troas is plainly of another sort (Acts 20, 7-12). This cannot be connected with individual private prayer at midnight, but must rather be associated with the Sunday Eucharist *ante lucem*—unless it should simply be explained by the extraordinary circumstance that Paul had to leave early next morning.

There are, nevertheless, a number of texts which give general support to the view that there was a custom of night prayer; and later authors do not contradict these. We could point to the words of the psalmist: *Media nocte surgebam ad confitendum tibi* (Ps. 118, 62) or *In noctibus exollite manus vestras in sancta* (Ps. 133, 2). Above all there is our Lord's exhortation to pray without ceasing (Lk. 18, 1)—which is repeated by His apostles (Eph. 6, 18; I Thess. 5, 17), as well as His saying that the elect cry to God 'day and night' (Mt. 24, 42; 25, 13), and finally His own example, 'He spent the whole night praying to God' (Lk. 6, 12). There is thus no lack of stimulus and starting-points for a habit of night prayer such as we find without doubt towards the end of the 2nd century. It would have been quite natural for the beginnings of this to have occurred early in the 1st century so that Paul and Silas were in fact following an existing custom. This explanation of the origin of the private midnight prayer of the Christian and consequently of our nocturnal Hours is not affected adversely by accounts of the origin of primitive Christian night worship which, failing to make necessary distinctions, would gather every-thing under one set of concepts, viz., those which undoubtedly had a controlling significance for the Easter and Sunday early morning Eucharist, and the Easter night vigil. The thoughts controlling the services are, of course, the Resurrection and the Parousia respectively.

If we trace the practice of midnight prayer in the primitive Church to the stimulus of the New Testament, we must begin to wonder why we—including many zealous priests—do not feel urged by the same Biblical example to practise the same midnight prayer. Indeed, such an item in the daily programme of a Christian living in the world seems unthinkable to us. But we must bear in mind that in those days when only primitive means of lighting were available, people lived much closer to a natural rhythm. There were few activities in the average household which could be carried out at night. In winter, nighttime covered more than twelve hours of the day. People would not sleep all the time therefore. And even when the few household duties which were possible by candle-light or an oil-lamp had been performed, there was still enough time left for sleep so that people could rise and give some time to prayer without doing themselves harm. This required, moreover, very little light.

This remained so even when night prayer expanded into the protracted nocturnal choral Office of a monastic community,[81] for the choir knew the psalms by heart and only the readings and hymns had to be taken from the appropriate book.[82] There are few monastic communities today who adhere with heroic steadfastness to the ancient tradition of a nocturnal Office. In most cases, the Nocturns are brought at least near enough to morning, as they were in Jerusalem[83] at the close of the 4th century and as the Rule of St. Benedict[84] and other ancient monastic rules[85] provide —so that the Morning Hour can be attached to them. Thus the

81.   After the reform of which Cassian tells us, the monks of Bethlehem were allowed to sleep *usque ad ortum solis*, with the reason that this was the point in time, *quo iam sine offensione vel lectio parari vel opus manuum posset adsumi.*
82.   It is clear that the length of the night was a contributory factor here from the fact that often the longer winter nights were provided with a more comprehensive programme; v. Callewaert, *Die Breviarii Romani liturgia* 159.
83.   v. above p. 115.
84.   v. above p. 117.
85.   Thus in the Rule of Caesarius and Aurelian; v. Callewaert, *Sacris erudiri* 59 with n. 28.

interruption of sleep is avoided. But the morning Office must therefore cover a wide scheme, especially as Prime follows without much pause. The scheme was once more enriched about the year 1000 when a new climax in the Conventual Office[86] began to assert itself—quite apart from the private Masses of priest-monks which had long since been customary. Finally, the last component in the consecration of the day appears. Since the 15th century this has rapidly gained prominence: it is the Morning Meditation which no earnest priest today will neglect.

Obviously it is difficult to carry out morning after morning, in all its detail, a rule of life based upon a contemplative ideal, not to mention the demands of a daily routine designed for pastoral service which a man must approach untired. And so the anticipation of the Nocturns has become the commonest way out of the difficulty. In the prevailing conditions this is a solution, not only condoned but regarded as most suitable. The solution may pass also because—apart from a few exceptions—Matins in the Roman Breviary, unlike Lauds, contains scarcely any clear allusion to night time, apart from the hymns for week-days.

2. *The Pre-Monastic Morning Hour in the Gallo-Spanish Region in the 6th century.*

One of the most important factors which has come to light as a result of recent study of the history of the Canonical Hours is that in this early period a sharp distinction must be made between cathedral and monastery, between the Office said by priests and that said by monks. Whereas older authors like Mabillon and even Bäumer scarcely pay any heed to this fact, in more modern works it assumes increasing importance. So it

---

86. When they were first founded, the Carthusians did not know of this. In early days, when the separate Hours had not yet become fixed 'canonical' entities, multiplication was avoided, as Cassian shows in his account *De inst. coenob.* III, 11 (CSEL 17, 44) where we learn that eastern monks observed only one Hour on Sunday before the *prandium* (*unam tantummodo missam*) which served both for Tierce and Sext.

is with A. Baumstark,[1] W. C. Bishop[2] and, especially, Abbot P. Salmon.[3]

Corresponding to this distinction is the further knowledge that our Roman Office belongs entirely to the monastic type.[4] This is particularly noticeable in what is provided for the nocturnal and morning Offices, which are made up of three Hours: Matins—usually made up of three Nocturns—Lauds and Prime.

The central question which remains is that about the origin and status of Matins. J. M. Hanssens has devoted a penetrating study to this[5] which takes account of all of the Eastern and Western liturgies and results in the thesis that Matins and Lauds were originally a single morning Office to which was prefixed—first in monastic circles—a fairly long set of psalms. Gradually, lessons were added in various numbers as special Hours became assigned to the later hours of the night and separated, possibly, from the original Hour. This thesis may not have found general acceptance[6]—amongst other things, the relation to early Christian midnight prayer remains obscure—but it has certainly greatly illuminated the Office of the morning Hours, especially that which we call Lauds. For centuries what we know as Lauds was called *Matutin* ('Matins'). As numerous accounts show, this was the same Morning Hour which had constituted the morning service at least in episcopal churches, both in East and West, since the 4th century. The evening service of Vespers was its counterpart. These were the two Hours in which the people took part in varying numbers. Other Hours played little part in public worship.

On the other hand, the reports and documents after the 6th century show our Lauds closely connected with our Matins

1. V. the chapter *Kathedrale und Kloster* in A. Baumstark, *Vom geschichtlichen Werden der Liturgie*, Freiburg 1923, 64-70; ibid., *Liturgie comparée*,[3] Chevetogne 1953, 123 seq.; again ibid., *Nocturna laus*, Münster 1957, esp. 124 seq., 206 seq.
2. V. esp. the study *The Breviary in Spain* by W. C. Bishop, *The Mozarabic and Ambrosian Rites (Alcuin Club tracts 15)*, London 1924, 55-97.
3. P. Salmon, *Aux origines du Bréviaire Romain: La Maison-Dieu*, n. 27 (1951) 114-136.
4. The statement of Bishop, loc. cit. 56, is correct therefore, that in the Roman Breviary we have before us the monastic Office of the basilica—monastery of Rome, the same, that is, as that of Monte Cassino.
5. J. M. Hanssens, *Nature et genèse de l'office des Matines (Analecta Gregoriana 57)*, Rome 1952.
6. Cf. B. Botte, *Questions liturgiques et parrissiales* 36 (1955) 275. Cf. also the restriction above Pt. II, c. 1, n. 68.

as one of the seven or eight Hours which are still current today. Thus they comprise a section of the choral Office which in the Roman basilicas was performed day by day in very much the same way as in the monastic congregations of St. Benedict. In the sources available to us there is almost no trace of any intermediate phase, of any transition—at least not as far as Roman or Italian regions are concerned.

By contrast Southern Gaul and Spain provide a relatively greater wealth of accounts and documents concerning just this critical period of transition. Only in this century have the bulk of these documents, especially those concerning Spain, become available; and even with these, the basic stratum already appears to be overlaid with more recent developments. But patient, comparative study promises to yield an attractive harvest. In Spain, too, the process ends in the *Breviarium Gothicum* of the reform of 1500, a composition which, as its name suggests, is already not unlike the *Breviarium Romanum*. And so, the light thrown on the Morning Hour of the Gallo-Spanish realm can be expected to illumine also the parallel evolution of the Roman Office.

First let us consider a document which came to light only very recently and which has become a decisive pointer in the studies we hope to pursue (I). Then we will examine the previously known extra-liturgical sources for the history of the Office in South Gaul and Spain, in order to find the elements of the Morning Hour which, as shall appear, was observed by both clergy and people (II). The study of the Morning Hour of the Mozarabic liturgy plus the facts we have already discussed will then make it possible for us to determine more precisely the outline of the pre-monastic Morning Hour in this region.

I. *Exortatio Matutina*

In the first number of the newly published series, *Palimpsest Studien,*[7] P. Alban Dold gives us the fruits of his work on the deleted text of *Cod. Sangallensis* 908. The remainder of this had been published four times between 1824 and 1879,[8] but despite

7. A. Dold, *Palimpsest-Studien* I (Texte u. Arbeiten I, 45), Beuron 1955.
8. C. E. Hammond, *The ancient Liturgy of Antioch and other liturgical fragments*, Oxford 1879, 53-56.

its great antiquity had received no further attention on account of its bad condition and the puzzles it presented.

As might be expected, P. Dold's diligence established the text in many places and substantially enlarged it, determined the sequence of the pieces, and gained more precise information concerning its provenance and age. On these last points earlier editors had said that it was Gallic and, from the results of palaeographic examination, of the 6th century. P. Dold accepts the 6th century as 'in the main possible' (9) but prefers a Spanish or at least a Visigoth setting (21, 30).

The contents comprise two series of texts. The present editor 'entitled the first series *orationes pro defunctis* and the second, following a title which occurs above five sections in the text itself, he describes as *exhortationes matutinales*. We are now concerned with this second series.9

The sections show ten rites of apparently the same construction (n. IV-n. XII). Each rite must have been made up of three formulae: the first bearing the title *exhortatio matutina* (contained in five cases); the second described as *collectio* (in four cases); the third entitled (in one case) *consummatio*.

Concerning the meaning of the texts P. Dold makes many worth-while contributions, but comes to no certain conclusions in the evaluation of our texts. He declines to accept the proposed interpretation of one of the first expositors, J. V. Arx, one-time librarian at St. Gallen, according to whom they are addresses of a bishop who, after the persecutions were over, gathered his people around him, encouraging them and praying with them. And any parallel to the prayers of the *Apostolic Constitutions* VIII, 38 seq. is out of the question. He inclines himself to the assumption that the title *exhortatio matutina* might mean the same as 'what elsewhere in the Spanish-Gallic rites is denoted by the superscription *praefatio missae*' (29). It might therefore 'very well have to do with morning Masses which—like *Lauds* later on—were held in the early morning at sunrise.'

Dold adds that the *orationes matutinales* of many sacramentaries 'point to some such interchangeability' (29).

9. Dold, p. 14-18 (Text); p. 28-33 (Commentary).

Clearly this shows that there is room for a new attempt at interpretation. The text makes it worth-while, and the foundations are there already.

So that the reader has the basis for understanding the arguments which follow, we shall quote first of all the most complete of the ten rites—the first (n. IV):

... nox corporum abscedat et mentium et quia benedictus est de die in diem ipse diem praebeat in corde qui rediret in tempore, per dnm nrm.

Collectio. Reple dne os nostrum laude tua, ut per vocis officium cordis nri in te dirigamus arcanum ac misericordiam tuam utroque inclinemus obsequio et confitendo pariter et credendo, per dnm nrm.

Consummatio. Ds qui post blandis operis indutias adque otium quiescendi reducto ac reddito die tempus renovas operandi, adque ita pondus vitae praesentis adtenuas, ut vices temporum salutifera ordinatione distribuas, Respice nos initia diei istius tuis laudibus consecrantes, ac practeritae noctis otio hoc redeunte die laboris suple commercium, ut cuius ortum sanctae meditationis ingredimur, eius tempora semeli legum tuarum observatione curramus, per dnm nrm.

Because even in this the introduction is missing, let us substitute that belonging to the eighth rite (n. XI) the content of which will serve:

Item exhortatio matutina. Dm aeternum et sine tempore f.k. omni laudemus in tempore, qui ad resurrectionis imaginem cotidiani operis discutet molem, ut dum post sepultas somno curas vitae officiis reparamur ac velut a mortis similitudine transacto noctis tempore discutimus, resurgendi spem cotidianis vitae defectibus ac recursibus teneamus et mutatione praesentium capiamus gaudia futurorum, Praecantes ut eodem ipso inluminante mentis nostrae diurno officio vigeant quo custodiente nocturno otio siluerunt adque ad cultum devotionis fideliter exhibendeum protegat a iaculo voluntatae (l. volitante?) ...

In these texts we are struck by the formal style and bold construction of the period, strictly controlled by the laws of the *cursus*. But these are characteristics of almost every text of both the Mozarabic and Gallican liturgy.

On the other hand it is by no means to be taken for granted that the text of a liturgical prayer of Gallic-Spanish provenance will still preserve the old form of address according to which prayer is offered to God the Father and is concluded with *Per*

Dominum. In these prayers, however, this happens in every case. The prayer is always addressed to God (*Domine, Deus*) and, in all ten cases where there is a conclusion, and even in the introductory invitations to prayer, this is expressed by the phrase *Per dnm nrm (ihm xpm)*.[10]

Here and there, even in our well-known Mozarabic liturgical texts, prayers appear which observe the rules of address belonging to the old tradition. They can be identified as constituents of an older stratum. But it is extremely unusual to find them concluding in a reference to the Mediator or even in the simple form *Per Dominum nostrum*.[11] There is no case at all of its being used consecutively as the invariable ending in a series of any length. By far the greater number of these Mozarabic Mass prayers are traced to Eugen, Ildefons and Julian, the great Bishops of Toledo in the second half of the 7th century.[12] The form of address in the Mozarabic prayers would fit this period well also. They are completely determined by the opposition to Arianism which the Visigoth rulers of the country had not given up until A.D. 589 The thought of Christ's mediation gives way to emphasis on His divinity, as is specially manifest in a multitude of addresses to Christ.[13] The rules of our palimpsest must, therefore, be older. In this we may well have our earliest old Spanish liturgical text. It must belong to the period before the fight against Arianism had led to a fundamental alteration in the attitude of prayer; and as this attitude must have been in the process of formation

10. The same told of the preceding *orationes pro defunctis*, but with an exception here. The formula II, 2 (p. 13), a collect, begins with *De vivorum* and ends: *quia tibi est gloria aput aet (enum) patrem*—presumes, that is, the form of addressing Christ. Because in our palimpsest we have a copy (cf. the frequent errors in transcription), these prayers for the dead could originate elsewhere than in the texts of the Morning Hour which we have in mind.

11. Cf., say, the index of 134 different concluding formulae and their most important source in M. Férotin, *Le Liber ordinum*, Paris 1904, 534-541; Jungmann, *Die Stellung Christi* 85-93.

12. Cf. D. de Bruyne, *De l'origine de quelques textes liturgiques mozarabes: Revue Bénéd.* 30 (1913) 421-436. M. Férotin too, stresses that almost all of the liturgical texts contained in the mss. of the 9th-11th century belong to the time before the Moorish invasions. *Le Liber mozarabicus sacramentorum*, Paris 1912.

13. Use of the few prayers which can with certainty be traced to a single author, in this case to Julian of Toledo (d. 690), is the Introit of the Mass *omnimoda*, and it is characteristic of the new attitude. It begins: *Accedam ad te Domine . . . fili David*, and ends: *Per te, Deus meus quivivis. . . .*; Férotin, *Le Liber ordinum* 230. The effect of the ancient mediatorial formula is shown in the all but meaningless *Per te*.

and establishment for some considerable time before A.D. 589—
otherwise it would have been given up once more after the happy
issue of events in that year—our prayers must belong to the
preceding period, to the beginning of the 6th century at the
latest.

Our first concern must be, however, to discover the *living
context* of these remarkable prayers. Were they Mass prayers?
Certainly they are not Sunday or feast-day prayers for public
worship at the third hour of the day. Quite clearly they are
designed for early morning on week-days; and more than that,
they are not designed for a week-day in a religious or a clerical
community, but for ordinary folk doing a secular job of work.

They are associated with early morning, as appears from the
phraseology of several of the formulae. The worshippers have
just risen from sleep: *nox corporum abscedat et mentium* (IV, 1) are
the first words which the fragment contains. After the refreshing
pause from work (*post blandas operis indutias*) and the hours of
rest, God has brought round the new day—the time to work
(IV, 3): 'and we dedicate the beginning of the day to Thy
praise' (ibid.). Moved by the approach of returning daylight to
supplicate for eternal light we present the service of our night-
watches (*vigilae*) to God (VII, 1).[14] As the morning hour returns
(*matutini tempus* [1. *temporis*] *circulo redeunte*) we ask God, who is
the Day of all days, to illumine our souls with the approach of
His brightness (n. IX, 1). Sorrows having been buried in sleep,
we are once more prepared for the business of life (n. XI). We
are roused from the image of death (sleep) and we are to lay
firm hold on hope in the Resurrection (ibid.).[15]

We can feel that this is not devised for choir-monks or a group
of prebendaries. The prayers are spoken on behalf of men whose
day is filled with wearisome work. The *blandae operis indutiae* of
nightly rest is followed once more by the *tempus operandi*—the

14. *Ad officium supplicationis officio temporis revocati et ad exorationem luminis aeterni serie
redituiae lucis adfusi Deo nostro, f(ilii) k(arissimi), a quo vigilandi munus accipimus, vigiliarum
nostrarum ministerium deferamus oratione humili, voce flebili, confessione laudabili, spiritu
contribulato, corpore prostrato . . .*; Dold 15.
15. Associating rising in the morning with the memory of Christ's Resurrection or
with thoughts of the Resurrection, was part of the scheme of the early Christian order of
prayer. Cf. the review of J. Stadlhuber, *Das Stundengebet des Laien im Christlichen Altertum*:
ZkTh 71 (1949) 129-183, esp. 148 seq. 170, 177 seq.

pondus vitae praesentis presses on (n. IV, 3). The sorrows of life having been buried for a brief spell in sleep, men face again the activities of life (n. XI). God will accept the fruit of His people's faith both in its confession and in *operum consummatione perfecta* (X)

We are dealing, therefore, with a service of worship for lay people on a working day. People went early to bed in those days when little work could be done by light of the simple types of lamps which were available. No one could sleep twelve hours a day on average—or more in the long winter nights. It seemed obvious, therefore, at least after the Church had gained its freedom, to institute a daily early morning service—for those at any rate who lived nearby and who were willing to come.

The first clear indication we have which shows that such a thing happened is provided, as far as the West is concerned by the *Traditio Apostolica* of Hippolytus of Rome—roughly a century before the Edict of Constantine.[16] The writings on Canon Law which derive from the *Traditio* enable us to trace the line farther into the East.[17] For Jerusalem, we can use the detailed account of the pilgrim Aetheria.[18] In the West there are only isolated traces which can be verified—outside the Gallican-Spanish milieu, which interests us most of all and to which we now turn.

II. *Evidence from extra-liturgical sources concerning the Morning Hour in South Gaul and Spain.*

There are several indications that both in Gaul and in Spain a regular church service, attended by the faithful in greater or lesser numbers, took place early in the morning. In the principal churches it must have been an established custom. There is an early mention of this in the Commentary on the Psalms by Hilary of Poitiers who says that one of the greatest signs of God's grace lies in the fact that the Church assembles for the *matuti-*

16. Hippolytus, *Traditio Ap.* c. 33 (Dix 60): the deacons and presbyters were to assemble daily at the place appointed by the bishop . . . and when all were present they were to instruct the assembled company, and having prayed, each was to go off to his own work.

17. *Koptische Überlieferung der Ägyptischen Kirchenordnung* (Funk, *Didascalia et Constitutiones Apostolorum* II, 115, 116 seq.); *Constitutiones Apostolorum* VIII, 32, 18 (Funk I, 538); *Canones Hippolyti* c. 21 (Riedel 214).

18. Aetheria, *Peregrinatio* c. 24.

*norum et vespertinorum hymnorum delectationes.*¹⁹ When John Cassian makes Abbot Theonas say that the custom of consecrating the first-fruit of the day is practised by the laity (*saeculares*) as well, who hurry to Church *ante lucem vel diluculo*, we may take this as evidence not merely of what happened in Egypt, but of what happened in Gaul.²⁰

Then there are the Gallic Synods which are clearly alluding in various pronouncements to the Morning Hour (and to Vespers also as a rule). The Synod of Vannes in Brittany (405) threatens priests with punishment if they are absent from the morning praise (*a matutinis hymnis*) without the excuse of illness.²¹ At the same time we see the attempt being made to institute a unified rule for psalmody: *ut vel intra provinciam nostram sacrorum ordo et psallendi una sit consuetudo.*²²

If in this case only a limited region is involved, it is otherwise with the great Synod of Agde (506), presided over by St. Caesarius of Arles who was described as 'the first head of the Church in the kingdom of the Visigoths' (v. Schubert) whose influence then extended far into the north of Gaul. Amongst other things it was resolved here: *Hymni matutini vel vespertini diebus omnibus decantetur,* and to achieve this a series of more detailed instructions is laid down to which we must pay attention. The foundation is contained in this: *quia convenit ordinem Ecclesiae ab omnibus aequaliter custodiri.*²³ It is probably more or less the same regulation which was laid down a few years later by the Synod of Gerona (517) and promulgated from Tarragona. (After the defeat of the Visigoths in 507, their kingdom still included Navarre in Gaul but not the city of Arles.) The regulation from Tarragona runs: *ut quomodo in Metrapolitana Ecclesia fuerit, ita in Dei nomine in omni Tarraconensi provincia tam ipsius Missae ordo*

19. Hilary, *In ps.* 64, 12 (CSEL 22, 244). The phrase is dictated by the verse of the psalm: *exitus matutini et vespere delectabis.* Later, Rouen, too, was renowned for its zeal in psalmody: *cotidiano sapienter psallentium per frequentes ecclesias et monasteria secreta concentu.* Because such worship took place *continua diebus ac noctibus Christi Domini praedicatione,* a Morning Hour must be included. Paulinus, *Ep.* 18, 5 (CSEL 29, 132).
20. Cassian, *Coll.* 21, 26 (CSEL 13, 2, 602). That Cassian's conversations of the desert Fathers are not to be taken as verbatim reports from their own lips. S. O. Bardenhewer, *Geschichte der altkirchlichen Literatur* IV, 561 seq.
21. Can. 14 (Mansi VII, 955).
22. Can. 15 (ibid.).
23. Can. 30 (Mansi VIII, 329 seq.).

quam psallendi vel ministrandi consuetudo servetur.²⁴ Our assumption is all the more likely because Pope Symmachus had expressly delegated to Bishop Caesarius of Arles supervision over the Church in Gaul and Spain in the year A.D. 514.²⁵ After this, the demand for a unified ritual crops up repeatedly; and at the second Synod of Vaison (529),²⁶ and at the Synod of Braga for the Swabian Kingdom (503),²⁷ express reference is made moreover, to the Morning Hour (and to Vespers).

At the fourth Synod of Toledo in 633 a unified order for the Morning Hour was demanded for the whole of the Visigoth empire—Spain and southern Gaul.²⁸ The same demand was repeated at the eleventh Synod in the year 675.²⁹

The repetition of this resolution certainly shows that uniformity was never fully realized and that individual sees assumed considerable autonomy in liturgical matters.³⁰ But at least these Spanish synods prove that, from Spain's southern tip to the banks of the Rhone, not only were Morning Hour and Vespers regular church services, but that they had a set form of ritual which was recognized as legitimate. And if it can be proved that the outline of this form in Spain was no other than that which is to be found farther afield at Arles, the old metropolis which still took the lead in the 6th century, then the assumption is justified that the same sort of Morning Hour was the rule in the wider Gallican sphere.

These synods provide considerable information about the structure of the Morning Hour. It is a daily service. This had been stressed, long since, in 506 at Agde and in 517 in Gerona;³¹ and it had been laid down clearly in the Canons of Martin of

---

24. Can. 1 (Mansi VIII, 549). Only seven bishops took part in this synod. John of Tarragona presided.
25. Jaffe n. 769. Cf. G. Baader, *Arles*: LThK I² (1957) 865.
26. Can. 1 (Mansi IX, 777): *unus atque idem psallendi ordo in matutinis vel vespertinis officiis teneatur.*
28. Can. 2 (Mansi X, 616): *per omnem Hispaniam atque Galliam conservetur unus modus in Missarum sollemnitatibus, unus in vespertinis matutinisque officiis.*
29. Can. 3 (Mansi XI, 138): *uniuscuiusque provinciae pontifices rectoresque ecclesiarum unum eundemque in psallendo teneant modum.* Then *vespera, matutinum* and Mass also are expressly mentioned.
30. Strongly stressed by P. Salmon, *Aux origines du Bréviaire Romain: Le Maison-Dieu* n. 27 (1957) 114-136, esp. 130.
31. Above p. 130.

Braga (d. 580).³² It was the daily morning service of the period which lasted until the end of the first millenium, during which the celebration of Mass was generally reserved for Sundays, feastdays and holy seasons,³³ and when the celebration of Mass on these days did not take place until the third hour of the day, Matins being associated with the dawn.³⁴ The Morning Hour was a public service, led by the clergy who, as a rule, were obliged to attend.³⁵ But it was principally intended for the laity. In Merida in the 7th century it was announced by a bell.³⁶ At the grave of St. Martin of Tours a bell was sounded for Matins in the time of Gregory of Tours.³⁷ The same Gregory tells how in the time of the Huns someone was locked in the Church overnight and was realeased *convenientibus ad matutinos Hymnos populis*.³⁸ That attendance at Matins at least on Sundays was a practice in Gaul in the 7th century, even amongst very lukewarm Christians, is shown by the case of the Merovingian majordomo Ebroin who was a notorious murderer. He was himself

32. Can. 63 (Mansi IX, 857): the clergy who live near the church must come *ad quotidianum psallendi sacrificium matutinis vel vespertinis horis ad ecllesiam.*
33. This appears from the monastic order of divine service, amongst which that of Cluny was the first to have the daily conventual Mass. Cf. Jungmann, *Missarum Sollemnia* I, 269 n. 59 seq. Direct evidence on the material under discussion is provided by Caesarius, *Serm.* 73, 1 (Morin 293): Mass took place only *aut in die dominico aut in aliis maioribus festivitatibus.* This agrees with what is to be found in Mozarabic liturgical sources. F. Cabrol's conjecture—DACL XII, 445—that the original Mozarabic Morning Office was identical with the *missa catechumenorum* is untenable. Admittedly there were private Masses and Mass celebrated in small groups as votive Masses and Requiem Masses especially, outside monasteries indeed. A pertinent reference is Gregory of Tours, *De gloria conf. c. 65* (PL 71, 875 seq.) who tells of a woman who had Mass offered daily throughout a whole year for her deceased husband, and who occasionally received Communion also. North Africa at the close of the early Christian period seems to have proved an exception to the absence of any custom of having public Masses on ordinary weekdays; v. Jungmann, *Missarum Sollemnia* I, 322; cf. also V. Monachino, *La cura pastorale a Milano Cartagine e Roma* (*Analecta Gregoriana* 41), Rome 1947, 192, who rightly stresses that here it was Masses of a more private nature which were meant, taking place in cemetery chapels and private houses.
34. There is an early example of this last case in Sidonius Apollinaris (d. 479), *Ep. lib.* V, 17 (MGH *Auct. ant.* 8, 90): There was a service before daybreak (*processio antelucana*) at the grave of St. Justus, attended by a great number of people, *cultu peracto vigiliarum, quas alternante mulcedine monachi clericique psalmicines concelebraverant, quisque in diversa secessimus, non procul tamen, utpote ad Tertiam praesto futuri, cum sacerdotibus res divina facienda.*
35. Cf. above n. 32.
36. Paul of Merida, *Vita Patrum Emerit. c.* 8 (PL 80, 135 C., 136 A). There is a mention of the *matutinum officium* in this work also c. 1, 3 (ibid. 119, 127).
37. Gregory of Tours. *De miraculis s. Martini* I, 33 (PL 71, 936 C): *Mane autem facto signo ad matutinum commoto.*
38. Gregory of Tours, *Historia Franconim* II, 7 (PL 71, 201).

murdered one Sunday as he entered church for Matins.[39] It was also possible that there might have been a rota according to which the clergy of a particular church took turns at conducting the service;[40] and if they defaulted they could be deposed.[41]

Morning Hour and Vespers were not a feature of the big city churches alone.[42] If a church or chapel had been consecrated by the depositing of sacred relics, then it had to be honoured through *psallendi frequentia*. And so, no church should be dedicated with the depositing of relics if there were no clergy in the vicinity who could carry out this service.[43]

Matins and Vespers are the only Hours of the day which are constantly mentioned in synods[44] and which are for ever being mentioned in records. The all-night vigil on specified days is the only other thing which is considered. By some bishops this was practised with great zeal and was made a weekly custom in the various churches.[45] But it had nothing to do with the daily ritual.[46] At the same time in Gaul and in Spain there were thriving convents everywhere in which a highly developed Office of the Hours was observed. All the Hours which we know today, and some others besides, were accounted for. But the ritual belonging to this was distinct from that designed for the clergy and people. The provincial Synod of Braga (561) makes an express distinction between the two sorts of ritual,[47] and the *Rituale antiquissimum*, which is preserved in an 11th century manuscript

39. *Vita S. Leodegarii* (d. 679) c. 16 (PL 96, 368). As late as the *Nibelungenlied* we hear of how Kriemhilde, when she found the dead Siegfried at her door, wanted to go straight off 'to Matins before day dawned.' It was her daily custom ('which the pious Kriemhilde seldom neglected'); *Der Nibelunge Not*, Str. 945 (Lachmann).
40. Synod of Tarragona (516) can. 6 (Mansi VIII, 542): In country churches the presbyters or deacons took turns at a full week's service; but it had to be ensured, *ut omnibus diebus vesperas et matutinas celebrent*. Only on Sundays did all have to be present.
41. II Synod of Orlean (533) can. 14 (Mansi VIII, 837).
42. V above n. 40.
43. Synod of Epaon (517) can. 25 (MG Conc. I, 25): . . . *nisi forsitan clericus cuiuscunque parochiae vicinus esse contingat qui sacris cineribus psallendi frequentia famulentur*.
44. Only the 2nd Synod of Tours (567), which mentions Sext as well (and Duodecima in place of Vespers), makes an exception; can. 18 (Mansi IX, 796 seq.). This already displays a strong monastic influence, but it bears the signatures of only nine bishops from northern France.
45. Cf. Salmon, *Aux origines du Bréviaire Romain* (above n. 30) 122 seq.
46. When a daily full vigil was arranged in the cathedral at Auxerre in the 6th-7th century (Salmon 123), this was clearly a peculiar exception.
47. Can. 1 (Mansi IX, 777): *unus atque idem psallendi ordo in matutinis vel vespertinis officiis teneatur; et non diversae ac privatae neque monasteriorum consuetudines cum ecclesiastica regula sint permixtae*.

of Silos, distinguished the obligatory prayer of monks, *monachi*, from *cathedralis ordo quod est Matutini et Vespertini sive Completi officium.*48

Over and above these general facts, our extra-liturgical sources indicate also some of the detailed contents of the Morning Hour. Gregory of Tours tells of the death of his uncle, Bishop Gallus of the Auvergne (d. 551). At dawn on the day of his death he heard psalm-singing coming from the church and was told that they were singing the *benedictio*. Then he himself recited in turn after Psalm 50, the *benedictio*, the *Allelujaticum cum capitello* and finished off (*consummavit*) the Morning Hour.49 As our study proceeds we will show that Th. Ruinaert is correct when he identifies the *benedictio* with the *Song of the Three Children* and the *Allelujaticum* with Psalms 148-150. *Capitellum* can only be what we mean by *preces*, and we meet the *consummatio* in the palimpsest we have already mentioned.50

Some other details come to light from the Canons of the Council of Agde (506)—already quoted.51 They are already speaking of forms known as *antiphonae*,52 which are always to be followed by a collect. The *hymni matutini* which we have already encountered and which seem to constitute the fixed core of the Hour can only be the Alleluja—psalms—Psalms 148-150,53 which

48. Férotin, *Le Liber mozarabicus sacramentorum* 770; cf. same author, *Le Liber ordinum*, p. XXIX seq.
49. Gregory of Tours, *Vitae Patrum* c. 7 (PL 71, 1034): *At ille psalmo L et benedictione decantata et Alleliyatico cum capitello expleto consummavit matutinos.*
50. Above p. 125.
51. Can. 30 (Mansi VIII, 329 seq.): *quia convenit ordinem ecclesiae ab omnibus aequaliter custodiri, studendum est, ut sicut ubique fit, et post antiphonas collectiones per ordinem ab episcopis vel presbyteris dicantur; et hymni matutini vel vespertini diebus omnibus decantentur; et in conclusione matutinarum vel vespertinarum missarum, post hymnos capitella de psalmis dicantur; et plebs collecta oratione ad vesperam ab episcopo cum benedictione dimittatur.*
52. F. Cabrol, *Agde*: DACL I, 875, believes that here we are dealing with psalms sung by two choirs. On the much disputed idea of the antiphon in early times, v. H. Hucke, *Die Entwicklung des christlichen Kultgesangs zum Gregorianischen Gesang*, Röm. Quartal-schrift 48 (1953) 147-194 esp., 160 seq.; ibid. *Zu einigen Probleme der Choralforschung: Die Musikforschung* 11 (1958) 385-414, esp. 336 seq.; A. Baumstark, *Nocturna laus*, Münster 1957, 124-126. Cf. also n. 66 below.
53. Against H. G. J. Beck, *The Pastoral Care of Souls in South-East France during the sixth century*, Rome 1950, 119. For a long time the psalms were described as ὕμνοι, *hymni*; examples up to the 4th century in J. Kroll, *Die christliche Hymnodie bis zu Klemens von Alexandria*, Konigsberg 1921, 6. But even as late as Egbert's Pontificale in the 10th century, the last psalms in the Psalter (145-150) and some others, were described as *hymni* (ed. Greenwell 118).

were everywhere part of the morning Office,[54] and which we
will meet in the same place once again when we come to examine
the Mozarabic liturgy. After the psalms we have the lines of the
preces once more, now described more exactly as *capitella de
psalmis*. A collect is supposed to provide the ending. The bishop's
blessing must have ended Vespers alone.

From the Synod of Braga (563) we learn that hymns in the
narrower sense did not yet form part of the normal Office. Half
a century later than Agde, this synod still sets itself against hymns;
nihil poetice compositum in Ecclesia psallatur.[55]

The Synod of Vaison (529)—an assembly presided over, as was
that of Agde, by Caesarius—tells us of a custom which prevails
in the East and in Rome and Italy, and which is now to be introduced into their own territory. It is the custom of singing the
Kyrie eleison as a repeated cry of great fervour *ad Matutinos* and
also during Mass and Vespers.[56]

And finally, shortly before, in 517, the Synod of Gerona had
provided that at the close of the *Matutinae* and of Vespers the
priest should recite the Lord's Prayer.[57]

In the Morning Hour of the Mozarabic liturgy we will find
the clues which enable us to piece together these several elements.
But first of all we must learn all we can from another source which
runs at a different level, but which is specially useful as a commentary able to fill out and illumine the facts we have so far
discovered. This is the *Homilies* of Caesarius, the bishop under
whose chairmanship both the councils took place which have
provided most of our conclusions about the origin of our Morning
Hour.

These homilies are addressed to simple people: peasants,
artisans, merchants; and the preacher is always showing that he
expects the faithful to attend the *vigiliae* regularly—even on
working days. The context shows that by this he means the

54. Arnobius the younger, *In ps.* 148 (PL 53, 566 C), says that they sing this *per totum
mundum* at *aurora*.
55. Can.12 (Mansi IX, 778).
56. Can. 3 (Mansi VIII, 727): *Et quiatam in sede apostolica quam etiam per totas orientales atque
Italiae provincias dulcis et nimium salutaris consuetudo est intromissa, ut Kyrie eleison frequentius
cum grandi affectu et compunctione dicatur, ad Matutinum et ad Missas et ad Vesperam Deo
propitio intromittatur.*
57. Can. 10 (Mansi VIII, 550): *ut omnibus diebus post Matutinas et Vespertinas oratio
dominica a sacerdote proferatur.*

Morning Hour.[58] If not prevented by illness, the faithful are to come *ante lucem ad ecclesiam*, especially when the nights are long.[59] The duration must have been barely half an hour. To ensure that poor people would not be hindered in their work, special care was taken to end the service at the customary time, even if it included a sermon.[60] Above all, the faithful were to hear the lessons on these occasions. But it was expected that in the long winter nights they would arrive earlier.[61] And this was specially so in Lent: *ut ad vigilias maturius surgere studeatis*.[62] Then they were supposed to apply themselves also to the *orare vel psallere*, and not to wordly chat which would, moreover, disturb others during the *psallere aut lectiones divinas audire*.[63] On the whole the preacher is able to praise the faithful for coming zealously *per totum annum* to hear the divine lessons.[64]

From his *Vita*,[65] too, we learn how Caesarius expended much effort to bring his people out to share in the psalmody. There is a clear mention of hymn-singing along with psalms which was not to be left to the clergy alone. (Hymns in the narrower sense must be meant here because they are mentioned along with psalms.) This is in harmony with the observation made at one point in the Homilies, that the faithful have no difficulty at all in remembering and in singing devilish love songs and so they should be

58. On the designation of the Morning Hour as *vigilia* and on its relation to the full vigil in Gaul at that time cf. Beck (above n. 52) 109-111.

59. *Serm.* 72, 1 (Morin 290).

60. *Serm.* 76, 3; 118, 1 (M. 303, 470).

61. *Serm.* 72 (M. 290).

62. *Serm.* 86, 5 (M. 341); cf. 196, 2; 198, 5 (M. 750, 759). Similarly for Advent: *Serm.* 188, 6 (M. 729). Usually the nuns were invited: *Serm.* 156, 4 (M. 603). But the mothers, too, with their children who were to be baptized at Easter, were to attend the *vigilas* throughout Lent. *Serm.* 84, 6 (M. 333).

63. *Serm.* 72, 1 (M. 290). There are also individuals *qui et tardius ad vigilias veniunt et ubi verbum Dei recitari coeperit, cito decedunt*; *Serm.* 76, 3 (M. 303).

64. *Serm.* 196, 4 (M. 751).

65. *Vita Caesarii* I, 19 (MG *Scr. Merov.* III, 463 seq.): *Adiecit etiam atque compulit ut laicorum populari tas psalmos et hymnos pararet altaque et modulata voce instar clericorum alii Graece alii Latine prosas antiphonasque cantavent, ut non haberent spatium in ecclesia fabulis occupari.* As the editor observes loc. cit., *Graece* must mean the *Aius* (= °Αγιος, Trisagion) which we know as part of the Gallican liturgy, as in the Roman liturgy of Good Friday, Greek and Latin are sung. Another view in Beck 116 n. 90.

able to learn and to use *aliquas antiphonas*[66] and one or other of the
psalms—he mentions Ps. 50 and Ps. 90.[67] Caesarius also refers to
Psalm 50 as a fixed component of the Morning Hour. On days
when a sermon follows the lesson he permits the psalm to be
recited earlier.[68] Otherwise the psalm obviously was recited after
the lesson. In similar cases the *psalmi matutinales* were finished
earlier[69] so that all could leave the church at the usual time. Here
it is clearly the Alleluja—psalms—148-150—which are meant,
during which the faithful were as a rule supposed to be present.

Morning service thus began with *orare et psallere*. This does
not mean that the *orare* preceded the *psallere*. Elsewhere Caesarius
stresses the fact that the *psallere* is always followed by *supplicare*
when people must genuflect or bow down. Whoever omits the
orare after the psalmody is like the farmer who sowed seed in the
field but did not cover it so that the birds came and devoured it.[70]

For Caesarius, the heart of the Morning Hour is the lesson,
during which even the less zealous attend—Caesarius lays great
store by the lesson. Not only in church but at home the faithful
should apply themselves to *lectio divina*.[71] The usual subject is
holy scripture, but in church this is often read along with other
lectiones longiores and *passiones prolixae*, so that Caesarius permits
those who find standing too tiring, to sit upon the floor.[72] Apart
from the above mention of the *supplicare* which generally concluded the psalmody, nothing in particular is said about any
prayer at the conclusion of the Morning Hour. Certainly it was
not very long and therefore the faithful did not have to be specially
admonished about it. But it was already taken for granted that the

66. As Caesarius speaks of *antiphonae minores* in his Epistle to Nuns n. 66 (ed. Morin 23),
and these were often added to the separate psalms, he obviously means here spiritual songs
of some magnitude which would be viewed as an antidote to secular songs. Gregory of
Tours speaks of *antiphonae* which belonged to *matutinae* and were more or less independent
songs, being followed by a *responsorius psalmus* sung by a deacon. *Vitae Patrum* VIII,
4 (PL 71, 1043 seq.).
67. *Serm.* 6, 3 (M. 33 seq.).
68. *Serm.* 76, 3 (M. 303).
69. *Serm.* 116, 1 (M. 470).
70. *Serm.* 76, 1 (M. 302 seq.).
71. This told especially of the long winter nights: in *Serm.* 6, 2 (M. 33), Caesarius asks:
*Quando noctes longiores sunt, quis erit qui tantum possit dormire, ut lectionem divinam vel tribus
horis non possit aut ipse legere aut alios legentes audire?* And Ambrose, too, in a similar strain:
In ps. 118, *Serm.* 7, 30 seq. (PL 15, 1291 seq.): *Non dormiamus ergo totis noctibus, sed maximam
partem earum lectioni et orationibus deputemus.*
72. *Serm.* 78, 1 (M. 309). This must have had the full vigil primarily in mind.

reading should be followed by prayer and this is presupposed by Caesarius even when he is dealing with reading in private.[73]

To sum up, we can say that the more definite features of the Morning Hour are to be seen principally in the region of Arles. These apply to the first half of the 6th century. There are still difficulties, however, in the way of attributing them to a rigidly completed system. On the other hand we detect a noticeably vigorous attempt being made in the region influenced and led by Arles up to the time of Braga and Toledo, to establish a unified ritual for this Morning Hour. If a similar arrangement of the Morning Hour turns up in liturgical documents after the 7th century on Spanish soil, and we find once more the elements we have already discovered, now fully integrated, then we have a right to conclude that the Morning Hour in the early 6th has shown a corresponding structure there.

III. *Matins in the Mozarabic Liturgy*

The manuscripts which make known to us the Mozarabic liturgy and its Office[74] almost all come from a late phase—from the 10th and 11th centuries. This is the period just before the re-conquest of the old ecclesiastical capital of Toledo (1085) which is connected with the replacement of the Mozarabic by the Roman rite.[75] The experts agree, however, that the material contained in these manuscripts can be traced back to the time before the Moorish invasions (711).[76] Over and above this there are exceptions of early origin which confirm the judgment that the Mozarabic sacramentary, which was recently brought to light by the Milan palimpsest codex, and the contents of which coincide at the relevant points with the essentials of the later

73. *Serm.* 7, 3 (M. 41); 100, 4 (M. 392).
74. Amongst more recent relevant studies we name: L. Bron, *Bulletin de liturgie mozarabe: Hispania sacra* 2 (1949), 459-484; W. S. Porter, *Monasticismo espanol primitivo. El oficio hispano-visigotici:* ibid. 10 (1957), 385-427.
75. This point of time does not represent the complete submergence of the Mozarabic liturgy as is shown from the fact that in the Toledo ms. 35, 1 (10th cent.) there prove to be 14th century rubrical insertions concerning the arrangement of singing; Férotin, *Le Liber mozarabicus sacramentorum* 687. The same thing is true of *Cod. Tol.* 35, 4 and *Cod. Tol.* 35, 7 (ibid. 709, 758; cf. 721).
76. Cf. Férotin (hereafter the author's name alone stands for *Le Liber mozarabicus sacramentorum*) 754.

manuscripts, belongs to the period about A.D. 700.[77] And for the Hours, we have a document, one of the manuscripts of which is assigned to the same period. This is the *Orationale* of Tarragona.[78] Admittedly this only shows the *orationes* and notes the prefatory antiphons where they occur. But whenever there is a correspondence it agrees completely with the later documents, especially over the arrangement of rites; and this permits us to relate their structure to the Hours of the 7th century. Particularly surprising is the concurrence of the *Orationale* with the much later manuscript of the *Antiphonale*.[79] A word of warning is called for at this point. The rite of the Hours of prayer, as displayed in the majority of relevant manuscripts, may be far removed from the almost incredible stuff which the saintly Fructuosus of Braga (d.c. 665) seems to have provided day by day for his monks, yet the normal Office of these manuscripts is so richly devised that it can no longer be regarded as a service for the people, but as something solely for a clerical or monastic choir. True, there are only isolated references to Nocturns as well as daytime Hours. Almost all present us with but one *ordo* for Matins and Vespers for the various feasts and solemnities of the Christian year. This is seen most impressively in the long set of rites contained in the *Antiphonarium* and the *Orationale*. And the only Hours indicated are those mentioned in the decrees of the synods of the Gallican and Spanish region. But even these two Hours, as they appear in the manuscripts, reveal a greatly widened programme wherein, with many modifications, hymns and prayers follow one another in endless sequence. The *Orationale* has 29 prayers at Matins on the feast of St. Eulalia. On Christmas there are 35.[80] The hymns usually described as antiphons, and which are often furnished with neums, display, for the most part, the form of the Roman responsories: a refrain follows the first and the second verse of the psalm and also follows the *Gloria Patri* if this occurs. The text, however, is liable to be changed every time. The other songs likewise, called

77. A. Dold, *Das Sacramentar im Schabcodex* M. 12 *sup, der Bibliotheca Ambrosiana* (Texte u. Arbeiten I, 43), Beuron 1952, 14.

78. Critical edition by J. Vives, *Oracional Visigotico*, Barcelona, 1946.

79. V. A.W. S. Porter, *Studies in the Mozarabic Office, Journal of Theol. Studies* 35 (1934), 266-286 esp., 269 seq., 283.

80. V. survey by Vives, p. XXI.

variously, according to their position within the Office, *Lauda*, *Sonus*, *Psallendum*, reveal the same structure. Quite apart from musical considerations, only a well-trained choir could possibly have mastered these songs.[81] There are only a few elements such as the *Kyrie* and the *Pater noster* of the concluding prayers, and the two or three much-repeated psalms, which were suitable for public worship in which the people could be expected to take any part at all. Such participation is not mentioned expressly in the bulk of the manuscripts.

Nor, as a rule, is there any more talk of a reading: but there are exceptions. There is, for example, the manuscript of a Martyrology from the Benedictine abbey of Cardeña near Burgos, dated 919. At three places within the text of a festival Mass of a martyr an incidental remark to the people is interpolated. They are addressed thus: *Fatres carissimi*. For the feast of St. Cecilia and her companions the remark runs: *Omnes gloriosissimos Martyrum triumphos Matutinis horis, qui adfuerunt audierunt. Nunc vero quod residuum est de eorum gestis auribus intimabo vestris.*[82] Because the Spanish Passionary reproduced in the script of Cardeña is traced to the 8th century,[83] it would appear that a reading during Matins designed for the faithful was not unheard of even as late as the 8th century—perhaps later; and consequently active participation of the faithful at Matins was not unknown at that time. This participation can be assumed with greater confidence to have been a custom in the 6th and 7th centuries—the period in which we are specially interested. Beneath a certain definable overgrowth which we see in the manuscripts we can expect to find once more that Morning Hour observed by clergy and people alike, and which the synods of the 6th century were at such pains to regulate.

We do well to take as our starting point the scheme of a Mozarabic rite of Matins as worked out by one of the first students in this field—M. Férotin. He distinguished between a *Matutinum*

81. This position of the songs is arrived at from the description in a preface to the *Antiphonarium mozarabicum* (ed. Silos p. XXX): *Antiphone modos reciprocatos canunt uni incipientes et alii subpsalmantes, tertio post Gloriam pariter cantates.* Cf. ibid. XXXI.
82. Férotin 938; cf. 939 seq.
83. B. de Gaiffier, *La lecture des Actes des Martyres dans la prière liturgique en Occident: Analecta Boll.* 72 (1954), 134-166; esp. 163.

festivale and a *Matutinum dominicale* which is associated with days lacking a festival character.[84]

The two schemes are compared below. To ensure greater clarity, the essential elements in the structure are given Roman numerals. The elements which are obviously secondary are left unnumbered. Parts often omitted are enclosed in brackets:

MATUTINUM FESTIVALE	MATUTINUM DOMINICALE
	(Hymns)
I. Ps. 3 with antiphon.	I. Pss. 3, 50, 56 all with antiphon.
II. 'Antiphona' (Resp.)—Oration, 'antiphona' (Resp.)—Oration, 'antiphona' (Resp.)—Oration. Responsorium—Oration. On greater feasts the same pattern but with more repetition and with music. Ps. 50 with antiphon.	II. 'Antiphona' (Resp.)—Oration, 'antiphona' (Resp.)—Oration, 'antiphona' (Resp.)—Oration. Responsorium—Oration.
III. Canticum with antiphon. 'Benedictiones' (Dan. 3) with antiphon. 'Sono' (Resp.).	III. Canticum with antiphon. 'Benedictiones' (Dan. 3) with antiphon. 'Sono' [Resp.].
IV.	IV. 'Laudes.'
V. Hymnus. Versicle.	V. Lectio. Hymnus.
VI. Completoria.	VI. Completoria.
VII. Benedictio. (Psallendum [Resp.])	VII. Benedictio. (Psallendum (Resp.).)

From a superficial examination we learn that we may look for the old parent stem of the Morning Hour in the two second halves (IV–VII). The preliminary part (I) contains psalmody made up of one or three psalms. By old tradition, the three psalms are 3, 50 and 56, described also as *psalmi canonica*.[85]

84. Férotin p. LXIV-LXVI. H. Jenner, *Mozarabic in Catholic Encyclopoedia* X, 617 seq. gives an instructive introduction to the remaining outlines of the Mozarabic Office, so difficult to trace on account of its many changes; also W. C. Bishop, *The Mozarabic and Ambrosian Rites (Alcuin Club Tracts* 15), London 1924, 55-97—for Matins esp. 75 seq.
85. Thus in *Cod. Tol.* 35, 4 and *Cod. Tol.* 35, 7 (Férotin 708-719; 758). Isidore, *Reg. mon.* c. 6, 4 (PL 83, 876) speaks about *tres psalmi canonici*, having their position at the beginning of the daily *officia vigilarum* (here distinguished from Matins). *Ps.* 3 is regarded as the morning psalm. The connexion between Pss. 50 and 60 seems to be a thing of the Gallican penitential liturgy; cf. J. A. Jungmann, *Die lateinischen Bussriten*, Innsbruck 1932, 96 seq.

In section II the Morning Hour becomes expanded most of all. Here, too, it must originally have been concerned with true psalmody, in these very places, indeed, where the manuscripts note four responsories around four variable psalms which were sung responsorially.[86] But the responsorially sung psalms have turned into responsories of the type known to the Roman liturgy. The terminology is striking in this connection. Only the fourth of the responsories is actually called by the name: the first and second regularly receive the name 'antiphona': the third likewise, if it is not entitled *allelujaticum*. The responsories do not appear under separate titles.

These four responsories, each accompanied by its own *Oration*, which as a rule was related to the text of the responsory, form a strict unity in the Mozarabic liturgy, a 'unit of prayer,' a 'prayer-phrase,'[87] and occasionally this is called a *missa*.[88] As indicated already, on greater feast-days, seven or more such 'phrases' might follow one another.

Psalm 50 (Miserere) of the feast-day ritual, which the Synod of Barcelona (c. 540) had already ordered to be recited at this place, *ante canticum*,[89] is part of the festive contents of the Mozarabic as of many other liturgies. This, too, is usually accompanied by an *Oration*. Not only can it appear, as we have seen, amongst the *psalmi canonica* (I), but can be put in later. A rubric in the London manuscript of the Mozarabic Psalter gives it a place *post hymnum*[90] —i.e. at the end of section V. This may be its original position. We have heard how Caesarius said that only when there was a

86. W. C. Bishop 82; Pinell 412-419. As Pinell emphasizes 423, the monastic model must have taken a hand in this.
87. *Orationale* ed. Vives n. 1144 (Z. 21).
88. As we know, the word appears in a similar phrase in the monastic Rule of Caesarius and Aurelian (indicating a group of three lessons each with collect); v. the material in J. Bona, *Rerum liturgicarum libri duo* I, 2, 3; cf. Pinell 403 seq. It is certainly wrong of many expositors—C. Gindele for example—to interpret the dismissal (*missa*) in the orders of the monastic Offices: *Bened. Monatsschrift* 32 (1956) 212-214, as though *missa=dimissio*, in the basic sense that after his lesson, the individual reader was dismissed. It is very easy to start from the basic meaning of *mittere*: what is 'set down' below someone, so that *missa* becomes a related form to *missus* (cf. French 'mets'). This explanation which I advance in ZkTh 78 (1956) 323 is, however, untenable, as Frau Prof. Chr. Mohrmann proves to me in a letter dated 9th November, 1958. It would seem rather that the meaning of 'a unit of prayer' which we have here, has arisen out of an earlier meaning 'concluding prayer of a prayer-unit.' Cf. also Chr. Mohrmann, *Missa: Vigiliae christ.* 12 (1958, 67-92) 84 seq.
89. Mansi IX, 109; cf. Pinell 386, 423 seq.
90. The Mozarabic Psalter ed. J. P. Gilson (HBS vol. 30), London 1905, 297.

sermon was Ps. 50 to be said earlier—i.e. not as on other occasions
when it did not come until after the reading and sermon. Here
we seem to have a practice which occurs elsewhere as well. In the
Italian churches too, according to Cassian's account, the psalm
followed the morning psalms (i.e. Pss. 148-150),91 and for Basil
likewise, this psalm forms the end of the nocturnal prayer at
dawn.92 The psalmody section of responsories, with or without
Ps. 50, is followed by a further section of a like sort—that of the
Cantica (III). There are two Cantica, both accompanied by an
antiphon, one of these changing according to the office,93 the
other, the Song of the Three Children (Dan. 3) appearing in
several different shortened forms. A responsory called the 'Sono'
is added to this.

With Laudes, section (IV) we come to the kernel of the Morning
Hour.

In Férotin's synopsis this title appears only in the form for
Sunday, and there supplemented by 'Antiphona.' And indeed, in
his description of the manuscripts he never speaks definitely of
any psalms belonging to this. But here as elsewhere we must
take note, that the manuscripts only indicate the peculiarities of
the several daily offices, pre-supposing knowledge of what we
would call the ordinarium. From other sources it is clear, however,
that it is Pss. 148-150 which are meant here. These form the
principal part of the Morning Hour in the Mozarabic as in other
liturgies.94 This is shown by the practice dictated by the printed

91. Cassian, De coenob. inst. III, 6 (CSEL 17, 41): per Italiam hodieque consummatis matutinis,
hymnis quinquagesimus psalmus in universis ecclesiis canitur. Cf. J. M. Hanssens, Nature et
genèse de l'office des matines 83. In the Milan Office, too, Ps. 50 is placed between the
canticle Benedictus and the psalms of Lauds (in our table between sections III and IV).
92. Basil, Ep. 207, 3 (PG 32, 764). Cf. Baumstark, Liturgie comparée,3 Chevetogne 1953,
45 n. 2.
93. The Mozarabic liturgy does not simply draw upon the resources of the two traditional collections of nine and fourteen Biblical canticles respectively, the origin and
development of which have been clarified by H. Schneider—four essays in Biblica 30
(1949). The concept has been expanded. In his article Cantique, DACL II, 1975-1994,
written in 1910, F. Cabiol comes upon a list of 84 Biblical canticles (1987 seq.) in the
Mozarabic liturgy. The Mozarabic Psalter of the London ms. alone, edited by Gilson,
shows a set of 77 canticles (HBS vol. 30, 149-185). A complete synopsis with 122 canticles,
which must have existed in essence in the 7th century, is given by A. W. S. Porter,
Cantica Mozarabica officii: Eph. liturg. 49 (1935) 126-149.
94. A. Baumstark reiterates in his Liturgie comparée (43), not without bitterness, his
previous assertion, that until the Breviary reform of Pius X in 1911 nothing had been so
common to Eastern and Western liturgical usage as the use of these three psalms in setting
the tone of the morning Office: they had been so used in the worship of the synagogue
itself.

Breviarium Gothicum of Cardinal Ximenes with its rule that on Sundays all three of the psalms mentioned be used, on week-days only one.[95] There are isolated notes in the manuscripts which demonstrate this also.[96] There is an Office of the dead in the *Liber ordinum* which expressly inserts Psalm 149 in this place in Matins;[97] and the Antiphonary of Leo in many rites notes the beginning now of Ps. 148, now of Ps. 150,[98] while at other times they contain the less definite descriptions: *Laudes, Alleluja.*[99] The similarly constructed Morning Hour of the Milan liturgy provides parallels which point in the same direction.[100]

Finally it is significant that in the 5th century Cassian states that Pss. 148-150 are a part of the Morning Hour *in hac regione.*[101] And because he describes them in the same breath as *hymni,* and shortly before (c. 5) as *matutini hymni* it is obvious that the expression *matutini hymni,* which is familiar to us from the synodal decrees of Vannes (465) and Agde (506)[102] applies to our psalms—the so-called Alleluja psalms which Gregory of Tours mentions as the *Allelujaticum.*

The reading, too, must belong to the old elements of the Mozarabic Morning Hour (V), Férotin, however, indicates this only in the festive form of the Hour. In fact, for other reasons it may have become omitted early on from the liturgical practice of many churches—following a psychological law which we see operating even today. It is common experience that it is the prescribed lesson which is the first thing to disappear from evening devotions set down in diocesan prayer books.

95.   PL 86, 55 seq., 61 and passim. It is well-known that the re-vitalization of the Mozarabic rite by Cardinal Ximenes had to rely principally on mss. The facts mentioned above in n. 74 show that living practice had not died out with the 11th century. In using the *Breviarium Gothicum* to reconstruct the old Spanish rite we must always proceed with caution.
96.   Thus in *Cod.* 7 of Silos (Férotin 844 seq.); for example, there is a note within Matins at this place: *Laudes: Laudate.* Similarly *Cod. Tol.* 35, 5 (ibid. 724, 727); *Ordo psallendi de primitis* (ibid. 661); *Orationale* (ed. Vives) n. 915, 918 (Apparatus); *Mozarabischer Psalter* (ed. Gilson 347). Admittedly it may more often be abbreviated psalms which are meant. But cf. *Orationale* n. 523: *post explicitas Laudes quas psallendo vadunt . . .,* i.e. in the course of Matins they sang, on their way in the neighbouring churches, the psalms of Lauds which they knew by heart.
97.   Férotin, *Le Liber ordinum* 401; cf. 404.
98.   *Antiphonarium mozarabicum* (ed. Silos 1928) 19, 21, 33, 38, 50, 55, etc.
99.   Ibid. 2, 11, 13, 95, etc.
100.   V. P. Bonelli in M. Righetti, *Manuale di Storia liturgica* II,2 Milan 1955, 695.
101.   Cassian, *De coenob. inst.* III, 6 (CSEL 17, 40 seq.).
102.   Above p. 130. Cf. also Gregory of Tours, *Hist. Francorum* II, 7 (PL 71, 201; above p. 132).

In reality, the reading is not always absent even from the festive form of Matins in the Mozarabic manuscripts. *Cod. Toled* 35, 5, indicates a non-Gospel Scripture reading for feast days as well.[103] It is almost never absent from the *Breviarium Gothicum*.[104] It is specially clearly indicated in some of the martyr feast days in the Passionary of Cardeña.[105]

The hymnus provides a decorative addition. This follows the reading and, moreover, on certain days it falls at the climax of Matins. From the Synod of Braga we have learnt that it still was meeting opposition in the 6th century.[106] At this place, after the lesson, in many cases we find the *Te Deum*[107] or, more regularly, one of the metrical hymns of which the Mozarabic Church possessed such a store.[108]

In many places we find an indication that there was a 'versus' at the end of the hymn.[109] In this we see that element which the decree of the Synod of Agde (506) had in mind when it says that *post hymnos capitella de psalmis* is to be recited.[110] Certainly *hymni* does not mean a metrical hymn but, as already explained, the preceding psalms of *Laudes*.

According to a law of style governing all liturgies, a canonical Hour is always rounded off with an *Oration* said by the officiating cleric. In the Mozarabic documents this bears the special title: *Completoria* or *Completuria* (Section VI). The importance attached to this *Oration* is shown by the expression used of it in the Vespers and Matins of the *Breviarium Gothicum*.[111] Here it bears the appropriate title of *Supplicatio* and it begins with an invitation to prayer followed by a threefold *Kyrie eleison*. Then comes the *Completoria* itself,[112] which carries on into a *Pater noster*, the separate petitions

103. Férotin 724.
104. V. for example the days of Christmas: PL 86, 122 seq., 126 seq., 131, etc.
105. Above p. 140. On the original circumstances of the lessons cf. also W. C. Bishop 85; and yet Caesarius should be mentioned even before Aurelian; v. above p. 137.
106. Above p. 135.
107. Cf. the enumeration of examples in the index of Férotin 1045.
108. After the canticles, the London ms. indicates a long appendix of metrical hymns (Gilson 185-291). Research has provided knowledge of 210 hymns: Cl. Blume, *Die mozarabischen Hymnen* (*Analecta Hymnica* 27), Leipzig 1897.
109. Thus almost uniformly in the hymn-appendix of the Mozarabic Psalter (Gilson 186 seq., 190, 192 seq., etc.); and frequently also in Férotin's mss.
110. Above n. 51.
111. PL 86, 49, 57 seq.
112. The title *capitula*, as Bishop 82 affirms, is but a mistaken corruption of the contraction in the ms.

of which are answered by the well-known *Amen, Quia Deus es,* and finally by *Sed libera nos a malo.* The officiating cleric then adds the *embolismus: Liberati a malo.*

We find only accidental traces in the old manuscripts that there are fixed forms for this framework of the closing prayer. They are sufficient, however, to show that the same arrangement may be pre-supposed for A.D. 1500 as for A.D. 700.

Neither in the *Orationale* of Tarragona nor in the great bulk of excerpts which Férotin gives from the manuscripts, nor anywhere else, do we find an example of the invitation to prayer before the *Completoria* of Matins—although similar formulae are well attested in other contexts,[113] above all the first formula (*missa*) of the Mass rites which turn up frequently. At an early date the invitation to prayer at this place became a fixed formula which it was superfluous to quote. The *Breviarium Gothicum,* too, amongst all its wealth of formulae, displays but few expressions of this invitation to prayer; and those it does display are endlessly repeated without changing.

Even for Férotin, however, there is one document which provides an exception to this silence. This is the *Rituale antiquissimum* of Silos, the first manuscript of which dates certainly not from earlier than the 11th century, but which possesses a striking antiquity—as the name given to this codex underlines. It supplies us with an Office of the dead, and another for deceased bishops and priests. Clearly it does not purport to be a monastic ritual. Both of these offices consist of only Vespers and Matins. In both a form of invitation to prayer before *Completoria* at Vespers is quoted. The second runs: *Oremus Redemptorem . . . ut spiritus et animas famulorum suorum omnium fidelium defunctorum episcoporum abbatorum presbyterorum . . . inter agmina beatorum propitius conlocare dignetur.*[114] The invitation to prayer can certainly be accounted and old tradition. There is a further point of interest for us, however, at this part of the old *Rituale:* both times the formula we have mentioned is followed immediately by *Kirie, Kirie, Kirie.* This harmonises with the *Kyrie eleison* found at the same place in the printed breviary and confirms it as traditional; and it allows us to fix the position of the *Kyrie eleison* mentioned at the Synod of Vaison (529).[115] We are advanced a step farther by a note for Easter Monday at Matins from the *Codex Toled* 35, 5 (10th century).[116] Between the indication of the hymn and *Completoria* there is the rubric: *Non dicitur Kyrie eleison usque ad sanctum Pentecostem.* Thus, the *Kyrie* was part of the content of Matins at this place throughout the year. It means also that the *Kyrie*—perhaps not a mere threefold *Kyrie* either,[117] was uttered kneeling; for during Pentecost what was avoided was praying in a kneeling position. At this point a passage in our 6th century palimpsest forces itself upon our attention (VII, 1). It speaks in the *Exhortatio* of the prayer about to be offered. This is not to be offered simply *oratione humili* but *corpore prostrato.*[118]

Evidence of the *Pater noster* as a continuation of the *Oration* is found also in some places in the *Orationale of Tarragona*—that is to say, by about A.D. 700. Thus, the *Completoria* of *Matutinum* ends at least twice with a reference to Christ and to the words which follow: *quo cubente dicimus.*[119] On other occasions the word *Pater* is specially noted in the same place.[120] In the *Ordo psallendi de primitus* the *Completoria* of *Matutinum* ends: *Nos quoque clara voce poscentes ad te petimus its dicentes: Pater.*[121] The decree of the Synod of Gerona concerning the Lord's Prayer at the end of the Morning Hour is realized here.[122]

115. Cf. above n. 56.
116. Férotin 736.
117. Cf. the *miserationes* (frequently *Miserere Domine* followed by litany-verses, all answered by a *Kyrie eleison*) before the collect in an Office—Gilson, The *mozarabic psalter* p. 305 seq., cf. 298.
118. Cf. above n. 14.
119. Vives nn. 444, 872. The same ending even more frequently in the *Completoria* of Vespers: nn. 507, 542, 872.
120. Vives nn. 342, 1015; thus in the Verona ms. In the London ms., which is certainly later, this is so in many cases, as the apparatus in Vives shows—nn. 312, 356, 377, 384. Even more frequently is it the case in the parallel form for Vespers. Likewise the text for the canonical Hours, added to the Mozarabic Psalter, displays the annotation *Pater* in many places after the formulary described as *Completoria;* Gilson 305, 312, 315, 317, etc. The same thing applies to the Office of the Dead in the *Liber ordinum* ed. Férotin 401, 404.
121. Férotin 661; cf. 654, 658, 827.
122. Above n. 57. This explanation makes sense of the decree of the 6th Council of Toledo (633) also, can. 10 (Mansi X, 621), which blames those priests who want to say the Lord's Prayer only on Sunday and not every day. The assumption of P. Sejourne, *Saint Isidore de Seville,* Paris 1929, 187, that the *Pater noster* by itself formed the conclusion of the Hours is improbable.

The situation with regard to the *Benedictio* (VII) is unambiguous. Along with the *Completoria* it belongs to those elements which recur in every rite of Matins and of Vespers. We find the direction that the bishop is to give the blessing at the close of Vespers being given at the Synod of Agde (506).[123] At that time no provision had yet been made for an episcopal blessing at the Morning Hour. Perhaps they did not want to make attendance at daily Matins óbligatory for the bishop.[124] But a priest had no right, according to a strict decree of this synod, to impart blessing at a service of public worship.[125] This limitation was beginning to be broken frequently towards the end of the 6th century.[126] And so, the words of blessing soon became added to the Morning Hour.[127]

And now, if we examine the outline of the cathedral Morning Hour in the Visigoth Church of the 6th-7th century more closely in the light of the knowledge we have gained, we can come to the following conclusions. Two strands are clearly separable. There is an old strand which corresponds to the descriptions of the synods and the references of Caesarius and which keeps its popular character (IV-VII in the synopsis below). To this older strand belonged the Alleluja psalms (148-150) described sometimes as *hymni matutini*, sometimes as *Allelujaticum*. To it there belonged also a lesson which, however, often seems to have been omitted; and finally, the concluding *Oration* which was prefaced by the *Kyrie* of the people and which moved on to the *Pater noster* at which the laity joined in by answering the separate petitions. The whole thing ended with a prayer of blessing.

The later strand, bearing the mark of artistic psalmody (I-III), and intended essentially for execution by a choir or by clerics, had for its basic part once more some few psalms—the *psalmi canonica*—plus a Biblical canticle, principally that contained in Daniel 3. This has been greatly elaborated, however, to embrace a great number of psalms and canticles. But the psalms do not

123. Above n. 51.
124. In two passages of the *Vita Caesari* (I, 43; II, 16), it is said that Caesarius gave the blessing at the end of the Office, but in both cases this was at Vespers; cf. Beck, *The Pastoral Care of Souls* 114.
125. Can. 44 (Mansi VIII, 332): *Benedictionem supra plebem in ecclesia fundere . . . presbytero penitus non licebit.*
126. More detailed references in Jungmann, *Missarum Sollemnia* II, 545 seq.
127. This is already demanded by the Synod of Barcelona (540) can. 2 (Mansi IX, 109).

follow one another simply in their Biblical sequence as was customary in monastic Offices at quite an early date.[128] How this applies to the principal canticle of the Three Children in the Fiery Furnace, judged by the Biblical form, becomes revealed more exactly through the responsorial form of singing. (From Dan. 3, 52 or 3, 57 onwards the constant refrain verse is indicated.) Very quickly progress in music led to the responsory form in which the refrain becomes the dominant feature while the psalm or canticle survive only in vestigial form. The unit of psalmody—the *missa*, consisting of four responsories and the corresponding collect, then becomes the new basis which can be repeated *ad lib* and varied according to the rank and kind of the feast.

Thus, in the sphere influenced by the Gallican-Spanish Church of the early Middle Ages, we can see as the forerunners of the developed monastic office, the outlines of a pre-monastic Morning Hour for clergy and, even before this, a Morning Hour designed as public worship.[129]

MOZARABIC MATUTINUM	AGDE—VAISON—GERONA
I. Psalmi canonica 3 (50, 56).	
II. Three 'antiphonae' and a responsory each with an Oration; all called 'missa' and allowing repetition.	II. 'antiphonae' each with its collectio.
III. Cantica. Sonus.	
IV. Pss. 148-150.	IV. Hymni matutini.
V. (a) Lesson. (b) Hymnus. (c) Versus.	V. (c) Capitella de psalmis.
VI. (a) Invitation to prayer. (b) Kyrie. (c) Completoria. (d) Pater noster with embolismus.	VI. (b) Kyrie. (c) Oration. (d) Pater noster.

128. The only exception is Matins in Lent and on Rogation days. During Lent the whole Psalter is gone straight through twice, but with some omissions, e.g., the *psalmi canonici* and the *psalmi matutinales*; v. A. W. S. Porter, *Studies in the Mozarabic Office: Journal of Theol. Studies* 35 (1934), 226-286, esp. 280 seq.

129. Cf. also Pinell 423.

VII. Benedictio.   VII. Benedictio.
      Caesarius   Gregory of Tours
                                 I. Ps. 50.
II. 'Antiphonae' orare et psallere.
                               III. 'Benedictio' (Dan. 3).
IV. Psalmi matutinalis.   IV. Allelujaticum.
V. (a) Lesson (sermo).   V.
    (b) Prosae.
    (c) Ps. 50.   (c) Capitellum.
                             VII. Consumm (avit).
                  Palimpsest
      VI. (a) Exhortatio matutina.
          (b) (Corpore prostrato).
          (c) Collectio.
      VII. Consummatio.

It is interesting to notice how the monastic office develops from the order of the Morning Hour designed for the clergy. This can be seen in the *Regula monachorum* of St. Isidore of Seville. In this we see along with *Matutinum* (called *vigiliae* by Isidore) and Vespers, an Hour corresponding to Prime (following Hanssens), and also the Hours of Tierce, Sext and None, as well as Compline. The following structure for the rite of the *vigiliae* of the monastic Office is described by Isidore.[130] First, the three *psalmi canonica* (already known to us), *deinde tres missae psalmorum*, i.e. 3 × 4 = 12 psalms; here it is still the complete psalms which are presupposed, not only selected verses; *quarta (sc. missa) Canticorum*, i.e. a section made up of *cantica*; *quinta matutinorum officiorum*; this can only mean what the synods describe as *officia matutina* or *hymni matutina*—the morning service designed to include the people, having the three Alleluja psalms as its core. We are then told that on feast days because of the solemnity *singulae missae* are to be added.

In this we see to some extent how the scale of the Office grows in its monastic version. The Morning Hour for the people contained only a single *missa*—the *officia matutina*—the clerical office, three of those (apart from the section comprising four responsories and that comprising the *cantica*); but in the monastic morning Office of Isidore we find five *missae* as the normal content. And this is but one of seven Hours: for clergy and people only the

130. Isidore, *Regula monachorum* c. 4, 6 (PL 83, 876).

two Hours—Matins and Vespers—had been envisaged. According to isolated later sources, Compline also appeared. But even so the monastic Office still displays a moderate programme. A decree from Egypt prescribes 110 psalms for the daily day and night Office.[131] Gregory of Tours (*De cursu stellorum*) speaks of a Morning Hour which by itself ran to 30 psalms in winter. At that time there were churches in the West in which relays of monks kept up continuous psalmody day and night as was the custom of the Akoimets in the East.[132] For the purpose of this extended Office the common monastic practice was not to select certain psalms, but simply to pray right through the Psalter. Praying through the psalms in their Biblical sequence without any regard to theme—*currente psalterio*—as the *Reguli Magistri* puts it, is a basic feature of the monastic Office.[132a]

IV. *The Morning Hour in the Roman Liturgy*

Now we must ask whether we can transfer the picture we have been able to form in Gaul and Spain, at least in broad outline—to Italy and North Africa, to that region which gave rise to our Office and eventually to the *Breviarium Romanum*. The scarcity of sources does not allow us to expect many more signs either for or against this. The signs we have seem to support the idea that we can transfer our picture.

First of all, here also in the 5th and 6th centuries the fact comes to light at several points that besides Vespers there was also a Morning Hour and, moreover, a Morning Hour which the people attended. This is obvious of Milan in the time of St. Ambrose. He invites his hearers to come to church—*ad ecclesiam*—in the morning before going to work and to start the day *ab hymnis et canticis* and *a Beatudinibus* (*In ps.* 118 serm. 19, 32). The same is found in Augustine. He compares the zealous Christian with the ant who makes provision for winter: *Vide formicam Dei surgit quotidie currit ad Ecclesiam Dei* (so there must be a daily service in church), *orat, audit lectionem, hymnum cantat, ruminat quod audi-*

131. Hanssens, *Nature et genèse de l'office des Matines* 68.
132. Ph. Schmitz, *Geschichte des Benediktenerordens* II, Einsiedeln 1949, 328; J. Pargoire, *Acemetes:* DACL I, 307-321.
132a. Cf. Baumstark, *Nocturna laus* 156-166.

vivit. (In. ps. 66, 3). Lesson and 'Hymnus' are the essential things. There is no mention of the Mass here, although it is in North Africa that we have the clearest indications that a daily Mass was celebrated. Here it is almost certainly our Morning Hour for the people that is being mentioned. And Paulinus of Nola, too, gives various hints which suggest that with his clergy he held a *matu-tinum officium* and also Vespers in which the faithful joined.

We know that there was a service at which a lesson was read to the people in Ravenna about A.D. 600 from the famous letter of Gregory the Great,[133] in which he tells the bishop not to allow his *Moralia in Job* to be read to the people because this had not been written with the people in mind at all. (It is certain that here it is not lessons during Mass which are under discussion.) This letter also shows that such a reading for the people was known at Rome.

We conclude then, that there had been a daily Office in the Latin Church at the close of early Christian times. This was more or less designed for clergy and people in common and consisted of a Morning Hour and an evening Vespers. (Meanwhile the place of the former has been taken by daily Mass, and the place of the latter, in northern lands, by an evening devotion on some days, quite separate from the clerical Office.)[134]

If now we turn aside from the participation of the people and think rather, of an Office which the clergy at least had to perform, then we find clear evidence of this within the Roman liturgy—in the Roman sacramentaries. The *Gregorianum* contains, apart from Mass rites, a series of eight *Orationes* entitled: *Orationes matutinales.* These are suitable for the Morning Hour: all speak of the light or of the contrast between night and day. There follow another 37 formulae, called *Orationes vespertinales seu matutinales,* and bearing on the whole a more neutral character.[135] In the Gelasian Sacramentary, too, we meet a few of the *Orationes,* of those indeed specified for the Morning Hour. Two occur in the *Leonine Sacramentary.* The two series named are alone stipulated thus as belonging to the canonical Hours. In this we have a pointer to the fact that it was only the Morning Hour and Vespers which was an

133. Gregory the Great, *Reg. ep.* XII, 24 (MG Ep. II, 1, p. 352).
134. Cf. Th. Schnitzler, *Stundengebet und Volksandacht: Brevierstudien,* Trier 1958, 71-84.
135. *Sacramentarium Gregorianum* ed. Lietzmann, Münster 1921, n. 203 seq.

Office obligatory on the clergy. In both cases the Office was concluded with one of these *Orationes*, recited by a priest.

We learn more about detail from the *Liber Diurnus*, the ritual book of the Papal Chancellory. In a section, which the editor Sickel dates as 7th century—others, with good reason, put it in the 6th century—there is a formula 'Cautio episcopi,'[136] a contract in which the bishops consecrated in Rome had to promise that he would keep the Vigil in church with his clergy *a primo galle usque mane*, would *vigilias celebrare* (we have already seen that *vigilia* means no more than 'Morning Hour'); and which prescribes that during the shorter nights of summer *tres lectiones et tres antiphonae atque tres responsori* be sung. In winter there were to be four of each and on Sundays always nine. From the point of view of extent, and if by *antiphona* we understand antiphonally sung psalms, that would be like the *Pensum* as in our Easter Matins:- three psalms, three lessons, three responsories. It is taken for granted that this morning Office will be concluded with at least the three Alleluja psalms—148-150—and an appropriate *Oration*, i.e. with what formed the basis of Lauds, and which did not require special mention, just as it seemed superfluous to mention Vespers. That is, we have here a Morning Hour certainly, but a Morning Hour already feeling the influence of monasticism and being expanded to some extent by that influence. The Morning Hour has acquired a preamble which we now call Matins.[137]

Looking more closely at this preamble we see that it includes not only psalmody but lessons also. These lessons obviously have been taken over from Lauds and then freshly arranged. In all this the ruling principle must have been that *Matutin* was to be over by day-break; for with dawn, *incipiente luce*, according to Benedict, Lauds had to start (*Regula* C. 8). Now the psalms of Matins, too, were fixed and could be neither increased nor decreased in number. On the other hand the length of lessons might be shortened or lengthened as required. This may have been a reason for transferring the lessons to Matins. We cannot but admire the

136. *Liber diurnus Romanorum Pontificum* ed. Th. Sickel, Vienna 1889, 77 seq.

137. This explanation of the origin of our Matins is upheld by J. M. Hanssens, *Nature et genèse de l'Office des Matines*, esp. 96 seq.

form which Matins has now acquired: it is made up of Nocturns,[138] each Nocturn an agreeable alternation of psalmody and lesson, the psalmody always ending with a *Pater noster* which here fulfils the function of an *Oration;* and this *Pater noster* for its part rounded off with a kind of *embolismus* as in the Mass—the so-called *absolutio.*

The expansion of the Morning Hour, of which we have been speaking should be traced to the monastic influence.[139] In Rome monasticism early exercised a powerful influence on worship. As early as the mid-5th century under Xystus and Leo the Great, basilica-convents were beginning to be built in Rome, convents whose monks had the duty of singing the Office in its full monastic cycle in the neighbouring basilica. And so a full monastic office was possible in these churches long before St. Benedict's time. Later on, the number of these basilica-convents increased. There were four of them in St. Peters in the 8th century; that of St. Martin's provided the arch-cantor for the basilica. At that time it was a rule that every basilica should have a choir of monks. Various Popes favoured monks, as a result of unfortunate experience with secular clergy, and transferred more and more duties to them. This was done especially by Gregory the Great. This led, understandably to tension between the clergy and the monks. A settlement seems to have been reached by the secular clergy carrying out the Morning Hour (besides celebrating Mass on set days) and possibly Vespers, while the monks were left to see to the rest of the Hours. This is the assumption, at any rate, which has most to commend it. Gradually this Morning Hour belonging

---

138. The arrangement of Matins into Nocturns is described in the Milan liturgy too, as a subsequent addition ('artificiale'); v. P. Borelli in M. Righetti, *Storia liturgica* II,2 Milan 1955, 687.

139. P. Borelli, *Brevario e cura d'anime,* reveals a similar sort of development in Milan. *Contributo del Rito Ambrosiano alla solutione del problema dell' antica Vigilia Mattutina: Ambrosius* 1957, 36-49. According to this the Milan clergy before the 7th century knew of a nocturnal Office probably only before Saturday and Sunday, and besides the readings and psalmody this contained only three psalms or canticles. The same thing can be proved for a series of other churches also. The saying of the whole Psalter, which took two weeks—Monday to Friday—to get through in Milan, is traced back to monastic influence here also. Alongside this we can establish the existence of a monastic practice of reciting all the 150 psalms in the nocturnal Office before certain feast-days (and in the Office of the Dead), and on these occasions the psalms were divided into three 'columns'; cf. O. Heiming, *Die altmailandische Heiligenvigil: Heilige Überlieferung (Herwegen-Fest-schrift)* 1938, 174-192 esp., 185 seq.

to the secular clergy acquired the larger preamble which we learn about from the 'Cautio episcopi' of the *Liber diurnus*. But in any case we are still centuries away from any demand being made upon the secular clergy to say the whole Office as known to monks, in the form, in particular, wherein the whole psalter was prayed right through—*currente psalterio*—although at that time the seculars were not overburdened with work.

On the other hand, there are indications that gradually the demand was being made upon those clergy who did not participate in a public choir Office to perform a private *Pensum* of prayer,[140] similar to the choir Office. The Synod of Chalons in 650 laid an obligation upon the clergy who lived in the castles of the nobility: *divinum officum implex et sacra libamina consecrare*, i.e., to say the Breviary and celebrate Mass.

If we want to make a guess at what the Morning Hour of the clergy in the Roman liturgical sphere was like before it received its monastic expansion, we might say something like this. Concerning the Morning Hour—and likewise for Vespers—the difference from the Gallican-Spanish practice could not have been very great. At the Synod of Vaison we hear indeed, that in introducing the *Kyrie eleison* into the Office, they had a Roman-Italian pattern in mind (the *preces*, too, always were part of the Roman Morning Office, at least outside feast-days). With reference to the *Miserere* psalm an express kinship is proved between the Roman and Gallican Office. Cassian mentions this saying that in all Italian churches *consummatis matutinis hymnis* is sung. (The place which this psalm came to occupy was variable in the Spanish Office. In the Roman liturgy until the time of Pius X, this psalm came at the beginning of Lauds in the daily Office, *de feria*. Today it is confined to the little-used second scheme of this.) Above all, the three Alleluja psalms were part of the fixed programme of the Roman Morning Hour (and remained so until the reform of Pius X); and from these the Hour received the name Lauds. And those Alleluja psalms which were, indeed, sung

140. Cf. the historical research of P. Salmon, *Die Verpflichtung zum kirchlichen Stundengebet: Brevierstudien*, Trier 1958, 86-116. The obligation upon all clergy, even those holding no benefice, is first mentioned by isolated theologians and canonists in the 13th century; ibid. 102 seq. The obligation to say the Breviary was first formulated as a universal law of the Church in Codex J. C (can. 135).

the world over, must have formed the basis of the Morning Hour, that part in which the people took part.

And if today the psalms of Lauds are followed only by the Little Chapter, here is the place where once stood a serious reading; for precisely in this place—after the *psalmi matutini*—did we find Caesarius and the Mozarabic sources putting the lesson. Once again, as in the last section, and as with our Office today, the conclusion came with the *Oration* which could be represented by the *Pater noster*. Regularly, however, the popular preamble to this must have been provided by the *preces* to which was attached a multiple *Kyrie eleison*.

In our Lauds as in the Mozarabic Morning Hour, this basic material underwent an expansion by way of prefix: first the *Canticum* (above all the *Benedicite* as in the Gallican-Spanish sources), then one or two psalms appropriate to the Morning Hour, featuring at least the word *mane* or *lux;* finally at the climax, if the *Miserere* were not there, the introductory psalm of Lauds took its place—*Dominus regnavit.*[141] So far, only a selection of psalms was used, psalms which corresponded to a set theme. Only with the monastic Office do we arrive at a protracted preamble which we know as Matins whose psalmody follows the Biblical sequence of the psalms.[142] In St. Benedict's Rule there are twelve psalms; in the Roman Breviary before Pius X there were eighteen on Sundays. The lessons, too, became attached to this psalmody. At Lauds the lessons could become left out or limited to the *Capitulum.*

What has been said is enough to show what has to be done by a reform which would return to the clerical Office and so build upon tradition. Such a reform would obviously have to base the Office for the Morning Hour upon Lauds. It would have to do without the psalms of Matins—the Office of a greater feast with

141. J. Pascher, *Das Psalterium des römischen Breviers: Brevierstudien,* Trier 1958, 9-20, esp. p. 13, where the author comes to a strikingly similar conclusion by quite a different way. Sometime before Benedict, the Roman Lauds must have consisted of a group of three psalms which was then expanded by the canticle and the morning-psalm.

142. Cf. Baumstark, *Nocturna laus* 117 seq., and my own observations ZkTh 79 (1957) 350 seq. and those of J. M. Hanssens in *Gregorianum* 39 (1958) 747-756, esp. 752 seq.

its careful selection of psalms at Matins is a separate problem[143]—but it would have to salvage the lessons at all costs in some form or other, whether they are put into Lauds or collected separately elsewhere so that they can be used to cultivate the spiritual life of the priest.

3. Essays in the Structure of the Canonical Hours

1. Psalmody as the Introduction to the Hours

In our present scheme, the large first part of the day Offices and the first half of the Nocturns are made up of psalmody. A second selection beginning with a lesson always follows, but it appears as a secondary adjunct. Is this the impression which ought to be given?

We are thinking of antiphonal psalmody—psalms sung by two choirs. The origin of this style of execution is well-known. However antiphony may have been performed originally, it first appears along with the beginnings of the monastic movement. It began in Antioch about the middle of the 4th century.

The fact is equally evident that responsorial psalmody was a practice in the Church even earlier. It was, in fact, an inheritance which could be taken over from the worship in the synagogue, a style of singing wherein one voice sang the psalm while the whole congregation 'answered' each verse or section by singing a fixed refrain. It was a favourite practice to attach such a responsorially sung psalm—a 'responsory'—to a lesson. This is still customary today, although the psalm is reduced to a single verse with the *Gloria patri* in Matins, and with a like abbreviation in the little

143. As appears from the researches of J. Pascher (loc. cit. 15), the Roman order for Matins on a feast-day with its special selection of psalms and their attached antiphons, must go back to the period before Benedict. That early period, which as yet knew of no confession of devotion, and hence did not make so many demands upon the clergy at feast-days—the matter did not arise for the monastic Office—marked the feast-days with a lengthened Office. The same was true of Sundays; cf. above.

Hours, and also, but with much repetition, in the preamble to Mass on the quarterly Ember Saturdays which have evolved from the ancient Christian vigil.

Lauds and Vespers at least were known in the Church before the middle of the 4th century, and the other Hours had already spread throughout monastic circles; and so it is most likely that the first liturgical form of these Hours of prayer had already been fashioned before antiphonal psalmody had become established. This assumption is supported by various documents from both eastern and western monastic sources.[1]

This leads to the further supposition that in the separate hours, according to Roman and Benedictine Office, the section beginning with the *capitulum* i.e. the lesson (of Matins) followed by a vestige of responsorially sung psalmody is the older part and represents the true basis of these Hours; and that the preliminary antiphonal psalmody is the later, supplementary section, and consequently secondary element. Can this supposition be strengthened by definite evidence?

It is quite certain that the first section of the various hours represents the monastic component. It is significant that in this section, apart from the few original feast days, the psalms are sung in the order in which they come in the psalter. The whole psalter is designed to be prayed through within a set time. This is the way in which the monks and hermits used the psalter in earliest times. In contrast to the ordinary people who were usually able only to repeat a refrain, these had leisure and opportunity to commit the whole psalter to memory and pray it by heart, privately or corporately in choir. Indeed, it was regarded as a great and worthy accomplishment to be able to go through the whole psalter every day.[2] The same ideal became a fundamental principle of liturgical psalmody in monastic houses, especially in the East. The two monks who visited the monastery on Sinai in the 6th century

1. The 'twelve prayers' or the 'three prayers' of the separate Hours which are spoken of by Pachomius or in the *Historia Lausiaca*, clearly belong to this ancient order. Cassian's description—*De inst. coenob.* II, 7-12 (CSEL 17, 23-28)—points also to an older style of psalmody.
2. Many proofs in Baumstark, *Nocturna laus* 156-166: *Das Durchbeten des Psalters.*—The use of the daily Psalter in private devotions was widespread amongst the Irish monks; v. L. Gougaud, *Christianity in Celtic Lands*, London 1932, 90 seq.

affirm that in this place the whole psalter was prayed through in the course of the night.3 St. Benedict, too, says that the holy Fathers used to perform in one day what he, with greater leniency, set as the *Pensum* for the whole week.4 At an even later date Coptic and Nestorian monasteries were still keeping up the practice of praying through the entire psalter each day.5

The Office in cathedrals and parish churches, by contrast, used the psalms much more sparingly—at least to begin with. When we first begin to hear about details only isolated psalms are named as in the *Apostolic Constitutions*, which shows that at Vespers, the evening psalm (Ps. 140) and at Lauds, the morning psalm (Ps. 62), was prayed.6 A *Typicon* from the Constantinopolitan patriarchal rite, disentangled from later sources by Anton Baumstark and attributed to the 9th century, shows no sign in Lauds and Vespers of the recitation of the psalms in their Biblical sequence, a custom which later spread throughout this region too.7 In the West also, the tidier form of the cathedral liturgy was only gradually supplanted by the richer monastic order.8

At the moment, however, we are only interested in the relative importance of the antiphonal psalmody which introduced the various Hours, as it in fact exists. Did people see in this psalmody, as we tend to do today, the basic material of the Hours, so that what follows was a mere appendage, a coda, or was it the other way round? Was the psalmodic section seen, rather, as the preamble to the real substance? In what follows we shall merely indicate a few signs which favour the latter view.

Aetheria's description of the Sunday night Office in Jerusalem reveals a sharp division into two parts. The Office proper began at cock-crow: only then were the doors of the Church of the Resurrection opened. But for fear of being late, many came earlier and took up their places. 'Hymns and antiphons' were sung, each with the interpolation of appropriate prayers. It was not until cock-crow however, that the bishop came down and went into the grotto beside the *anastasis*. All the doors were flung open and the

3. The account first published by J. B. Pitra, in a summary by Bäumer-Biron 182-185.
4. *Benedicti Regula* c. 18.
5. Baumstark, loc. cit. 157 seq. .
6. *Const. Apost.* VIII, 35, 2; 38, 1 (Funk I, 544 seq.).
7. A. Baumstark, *Das Typikon der Patmos-Handschrift* 266: JL 6 (1926) 98 seq. esp. 101.
8. On the distinction between monastic and cathedral liturgy v. above p. 122.

160   PASTORAL LITURGY

people poured into the brightly lit basilica. Now there followed
three times over a psalm, sung responsorially and answered by the
people, and having an *oration* attached. Incense was brought and
the bishop himself read the Gospel of the Resurrection of the
Lord.9 Bludau makes the pertinent observation on the psalmody
which preceded the arrival of the bishop: it seems 'to have had no
other purpose than to occupy the faithful who were waiting for
the doors to open and the morning service to begin'. 10It is this
section of the nocturnal service in which, at least on weekdays the
monastic circles (*monazones et parthenae*) primarily take part. The
stress is on the second part which reaches its climax in the reading
of the Gospel.

It is no accident that to this day the same division into two parts
can be seen at the same place, but even more clearly, in the
Byzantine liturgy. In the Vespers for a feast day there is a first
section which contains, besides the introductory psalm with its
attached petitions, genuine psalmody (*stichologie*), which here, at
any rate, is made up of selected psalms (Pss. 140, 141, 129, 116).
Not until after this come the entry of the clergy and the Office
proper, which has all the characteristics of the most ancient tradition. During this the φῶς ἱλαρίον, known as early as the 4th
century, is sung. Lessons from the Old and New Testament follow
and these clearly form the heart of the Hour. They are concluded
with solemn prayer.11

Particularly instructive is a regulation found in the *Canones
Basilii* originally a Greek collection of laws, handed down in

9. *Aetheriae Peregrinatio c.* 24, 8-10 (CSEL 39, 73 seq.).
10. A. Bludau, *Die Pilgerreise der Aetheria*, Paderborn 1927, 60.
11. Now most conveniently presented by F. Mercenier—F. Paris, *La Priere des Eglises de
rite byzantin* I, Amay 1937, 3-27. The rite is more exactly described in the Διάταξις τῆς
ἀγρυπνίας (the name betrays the connexion with the older service), which was written
down by the Patriarch Pilotheus (d. 1379), and which today still forms the opening of the
Εὐχολόγιον τὸ μέγα (Athens 1902, 5 seq.). This entry is led by two candle-bearers and the
deacon with the censer. The same structure is found in Vespers of other eastern rites. The
east Syrian rite expressly shows an entry after the first psalmody; and there are traces of
it in the Armenian; v. A. Raes, *Introductio in Liturgiam orientalem*, Rome 1947, 192, 197,
and in the synopsis p. 202 seq.—The principle that the first section of the nocturnal service
did not require the presence of the bishop and his clergy is confirmed by St. Augustine.
Admittedly this has to do with the special case of Easter Eve. In one of his addresses
Augustine uses the phrase: *Siaut ergo nunc, qui in nomine Domini ad vos ipse veni, vigilantes
vos in nomine eius inveni . . . Serm.* Wilmart 4, 3 (*Sermones post Maurinos reperti*, ed. Morin
p. 685). Scripture readings with expository homilies attached formed the core of the
celebration conducted by the bishop in full vigils as well. Cf. also V. Monachino, *La cura
pastorale a Milano, Cartagine e Roma nel secolo IV*, Rome 1947, 198 seq.

Egyptian Arabic. Canon 97 gives the admonition[12]: if people are celebrating the mysteries on Sunday, they should not 'celebrate impatiently, but wait until the whole congregation has assembled: while they are still arriving they should read psalms.' The psalms, therefore, were used to fill in the time usefully until the real beginning of worship. The same function is fulfilled today in many parish churches by the Rosary—the 'Gathering Rosary'—said by all the faithful together before the official start of worship.

The same sort of thing seems to be shown by a remark of Gregory of Nyssa in his description of the life of his sister Makrina. When travelling to the Synod of Antioch he visited her in her monastic hermitage but found her ill. He would have liked to talk with her later into the evening—'but the voice of psalmody was heard calling to Vesper thanksgiving (πρὸς τὰς ἐπιλουχνίους εὐχαριστίας) and so she let me go off to church.'[13] Clearly, the bishop, as honoured guest, had to lead the principal part of the celebration.

The examples we have adduced all belong to the East it is true. But in respect of the earliest composition of the Office the West took its pattern from the East. In that great monastic mediator between East and West, John Cassian, we may perhaps find a trace that the opening psalmody was regarded as a preparation for the real substance of the various Hours. Little stress seems to have been laid upon the monks all being present at the start of the psalmody. (Today this is the custom and the monks assemble and enter all together.) The rule said merely: At Tierce, Sext and None, any who are still absent at the end of the first psalm may not enter the oratory thereafter and must perform a penance. For the night Office, this dispensation was extended up to the end of the second psalm.[14] There is a similar regulation in the Rule of St. Benedict.[15]

The fact that psalmody, which constitutes the first section of the Hours and Nocturns, was not so highly esteemed as the second sections which begins with the lessons is expressed, indeed, by the

12. W. Riedel, *Die Kirchenrechtsquellen des Patriarchats Alexandrien*, Leipzig, 1900, 273.
13. Gregory of Nyssa, *De vita s. Macrinae* (PG 46, 981C).
14. Cassian, *De inst. coenob.* III, 7 (CSEL 17, 41).
15. c. 43. In Butler's edition there is a reference to Pachomius as well as to Cassian in the same sense.

custom much followed today of simply reciting the psalms at
Lauds and Vespers, except on occasions which demand the solemn
rite, and only beginning to sing *a capitulo*, thus marking off the
latter section in contrast to the first.

2. *The Scope of the Lessons in the Office*

As publications advocating a reform of the Breviary increase, the
emphasis is being laid more and more upon the lessons, especially
upon the Scripture lessons. Matins at least—so it is proposed1—
should be devoted basically to readings.

In many places the thought may arise that this would destroy
the whole character of the Breviary which people are accustomed
to see as the uninterrupted praise of God by the Church and
which occasionally in official ecclesiastical language even becomes
identified with the psalms.2 The question might be asked: Will
not the instructive aspect become unduly emphasized at the
expense of the devotional aspect, and does the history of the
canonical Hours itself not provide objections?

There are many records scattered about in various descriptions
of the history of the Breviary which show the space granted within
the canonical Hours to the lessons.3 It might be useful to collect
these records, to fill them out where possible, and to show the line
of development.

No proof is needed that the lesson was part of the basic material
of extra-Eucharistic worship. It is sufficient to call to mind the
structure of the liturgical celebrations which go back to the most
ancient times: to the Saturday vigils of Holy Week and to the
quarterly Ember Saturdays; to the records in the *Peregrinatio*

1. Th. Klausner, *De ratione reformandi Breviarium Romanum: Eph. liturg.* 63 (1949) 406-411, esq. 407 seq.
2. Z.B. in *Cod. I. C.* can. 413, 2.
3. The most important of them are summarized shortly in passing by P. Parsch, *Breviererklärung im Geiste der liturgischen Erneuerung*, Klosterneuburg 1940, 104 seq.; then by J. Leclercq, *L' office divin et la lecture divine: Maison-Dieu* n. 21 (1950) 62-54.—Important statements in E. Martène, *De antiquis Monachorum ritibus* I, 2, 59-61 (= *De antiquis Ecclesiae ritibus*, Antwerp 1736-38, IV, 31 seq.).

Aetheriae[4] and in the old Armenian lectionary;[5] to the analogous tradition of oriental church communities;[6] to the first accounts, indeed, of an extra-Eucharistic service.[7]

It is certainly true that there was a form of canonical prayer built up essentially of psalms, the sequence of which was broken only by interpolated *orationes*. Cassian speaks of this as a custom observed in Egyptian monasteries;[8] and here it was only Vespers and the night Hours which were each provided with a reading from the Old and the New Testaments.[9] Even in parish churches the tendency seems to have grown up of doing this sort of thing. This appears from the exhortation of the Council of Laodicea (4th century) that during worship (ἐν ταῖς συνάξεσιν) the psalms should not be strung together, but that each one should have a lesson attached to it.[10]

In general, great stress must have been laid upon the lessons in the parish churches—in the East as in the West. Socrates tells us that on Wednesday and Friday the holy Scriptures were read and expounded apart from the Eucharistic service in the Alexandrian Church. In Cappadocia and Cyprus this took place at Vespers on Saturday and Sunday.[11] The biographer of St. Stephen the younger (d. 767) tells us that as a boy his mother frequently took him to the vigils at the shrines of martyrs. During the reading of the lessons he used to stand in front of the shrine watching the reader, and simply by listening he was able to repeat afterwards all that had been read, were it a passion narrative, a life-story, or

4. In as far as it is not concerned with the monastic weekday Office; v. esp. the description of the Morning Hour on Sunday, c. 24, 10 seq. (CSEL 39, 74), the statements on Good Friday c. 31 seq. (CSEL 39, 83 seq.), also the account on the way the pilgrim arranged her devotions along with her travelling companions at the places of pilgrimage (4, 3 seq.; 10, 7 (CSEL 39, 41 seq. 51 seq.).
5. F. C. Conybeare, *Rituale Armenorum*, Oxford 1905, 516–527.
6. A. Baumstark, *Liturgie comparée*[3] 39 seq. 128. In particular, several oriental rites display one or more readings at Vespers; v. J. Caspar, *Les heures canoniales dans les rites orientaux: Maison-Dieu* n. 21 (1950) 95–99; cf. Raes 202 seq.
7. Hippolytus of Rome, *Traditio Ap.* c. 33 (Dix 60).
8. Cassian, *De inst. coenob.* II, 7 (CSEL 17, 23 seq.).
9. Ibid. II, 6 (CSEL 17, 22 seq.). In the weekly vigil (cf. above Pt. II. c. l. n. 65) the monks, too, added three lessons to each of the three sections of psalmody. Ibid. III, 8 (CSEL 17, 43).
10. can. 17 (Mansi II, 567). The idea of Bäumer-Biron I, 123, that it could not have to do with the Hours of Prayer, is acceptable only to this extent, that it does not mean the Hours of the monks. On extra-Eucharistic public worship we may compare the above-mentioned passages from Aetheria—n. 4—, excepting the full vigils.
11. Sokrates, *Hist. eccl.* V, 22 (PG 67, 636, 640).

a sermon of one of the Father's—even one of Chrysostom's. 12In
the West, St. Augustine speaks of the reading which people
attended in Church every morning.13 St. Caesarius powerfully
exhorts the faithful to attend diligently to the lesson of the
'vigil',14 and at home, too, they ought, he says, to practise *lectio
divina*, especially during the winter nights when they should either
read themselves or have something read aloud to them.15 The
letter of St. Gregory the Great to the Bishop of Ravenna, which
has been mentioned already, shows how in his time it was the
custom to incorporate lengthy readings in the Hours which the
people attended.16

But even in monastic circles, where such emphasis was laid on
psalmody, a liturgical lesson had in many places grown to considerable dimensions and had become a fixed component of
canonical prayer. The monks of Sinai, who got through the whole
psalter every night, were able to put in one of the Catholic
Epistles (Js. I. Pet. I Jn.) after every fifty psalms; and they urged
their guests to permit them to read the books of the New Testament also after the office.17

We find more detailed information for the West from the
monasteries of southern Gaul in the 5th and 6th centuries in the
monastic rules of Caesarius and Aurelian. If we confine our attention to the rather clearer descriptions of the Rule of Aurelian
(d. 549),18 we discover the following arrangement. The night
Hours always contain two lessons. In winter, however, the scheme

12. *Vita S. Stephani jun.* (PG 100, 1081 C).
13. Above p. 151. Cf. also Augustine *Confessiones* V. 9 (PL 32, 714), where he tells us
that his mother went daily to church *mane et vespere, ut te audiret in tuis sermonibus*, and
to pray. The morning visit could have been associated with the daily *oblatio ad altare*
mentioned earlier. On another occasion *Ep.* 64, 3 (PL 33, 233), Augustine exhorts that
care be taken not to read out unsuitable or heretical books to the faithful. But it is not
clear if he has the Hours of Prayer in mind in this place.
14. Above p. 137.
15. Ibid. n. 71.
16. Above p. 152. A late example, from Rome indeed, that the intention was to serve
the laity by having readings within the Office is provided by the *Ordo officiorum Ecclesiae
Lateranensis* (ed. Fischer 45) of 1145, which ordains that in the Matins of mourning on
Good Friday, after the Lamentations the other six lessons should be taken from the
sermons of St. Augustine for the appropriate day: and there is this observation also:
*Hoc idem facimus in Parascere et in Sabbato, quia populus magis laetatur et aedificatur de
sermonum lectionibus, quas intelligit, quam de psalmorum expositione vel epistolis Pauli, quarum
intellectus est difficilis.*
17. Bäumer-Biron I, 184 seq.
18. The chapter on liturgy in C. Blume, *Der Cursus s. Benedicti*, Leipzig 1908, 39-44.

is duplicated and the number is thus stepped up to four. Besides this, in the long winter nights to fill up the time until Lauds, i.e. until dawn, three *missae* are added. The term *missa* is not used always in the same sense in the Gallican liturgical sources, not even when applied to the prayer liturgy. In the Rule of Aurelian the idea behind the word is defined more precisely: When the Nocturns are over, *quando noctes crescunt, cotidie ad librum facite missas tres. Unus frater legat paginas aut tres aut quattuor, quomodo mensura fuerit libri: si minute fuerit scriptus aut maiori forma, tres paginas, si minor, quattuor; et fiat oratio. Iterum legat tantum; fiat alia oratio. Tertio legat idem tantum; et surgite, dicite antiphonam de psalmis in ordine; postea responsum, deinde antiphonam. Iterum legat alius frater.*19 The second and—so we may expand it—the third brother, too, are to stick to the same arrangement. This makes the number of lessons as $3 \times 3 = 9$, extending to 27-36 pages. 20 Tierce, Sext, None and Duodecima (i.e. the second part of Vespers) all contain one lesson apiece on ordinary days and Prime has two;21 on Sundays and feast days the scheme is somewhat more elaborate.22 On winter week-days that makes ten lessons, more than twice the number already mentioned, i.e. 60-70 pages every day. We must not however, reckon a page as the equivalent of what we would print today on an octavo sheet.23 More precisely, on ordinary days the books of the Old and the New Testaments were

19. Blume 42.
20. That this is the correct meaning of *missa* appears from the parallel passage in Caesarius' rule for nuns (Blume 36 seq.; Morin, *Floril. Patr.* 34, 23): in summer after Vespers there are to be *sex missae, . . . hoc est lectiones decem et octo memoriter dicendae sunt; et post psalmi decem et octo . . .* But after the Nocturns there should be *missae tres ad librum fieri debent usque ad lucem.* The length of from three to four pages, specified by Aurelian, clearly refers to the readings *ad librum*; those recited by heart were naturally somewhat shorter; cf. below p.169. The structure of the *missa* seems to be the same in both cases. From autumn onwards, Caesarius demands *missae quattuor* (Blume 37; Morin 24, Z. 13); Caesarius seems to have anticipated the related psalms and collects.—In winter we hear once again of three *missae* (Blume 38; Morin 25, Z. 6). The extent of the readings is again specified—this time it is less: for each collect (*per singulas orationes*) 2-3 pages; if there was not enough time to get through these then one page would suffice—and the abbess would give a sign to the sister who was reading. The assumption made by C. Callewaert, *De Breviarii Romani Liturgia,* Brügge 1931, 43, and others, that here *missa* denotes a single reading, is thus untenable.
21. Blume 42 seq. Besides this, the time between Prime and Tierce is devoted to private reading (42).
22. Blume 40 seq.
23. Cf. the *Passio s. Julian,* about to be mentioned, where 39 leaves, i.e., almost 79 pages of the ms. are equivalent to 28 pages of the printed edition (in great octavo). With Caesarius the individual readings are a bit shorter: he was content with maybe 1-3 pages. V. above n. 20.

166   PASTORAL LITURGY

read *ordine suo*.24 On feasts of martyrs the readings of one or two
of the *missae* were taken from their passion-stories.25 On such days
in particular the lessons seem sometimes to have been most
extensive. Caesarius speaks of *passiones prolixae* which were often
read out.26 The lectionary of Luxeuil27 which was composed
about 700 A.D. provides an example of such really lengthy reading. In this, the *Passio* of St. Julian, appointed for Jan. 5, runs to
39 pages of the manuscript.28 The same lectionary appoints a
complete book of holy Scripture as lesson on the three rogation
days at Tierce, Sext and None—and this is for congregational
worship. On the first day it is James, I Peter and Tobias; on the
second, II Peter, I John and Judith; on the third, II and III John,
Judas and Esther.29 And as well as this, a shorter passage from the
Gospels is attached to each of the nine lessons.

St. Benedict wished to avoid overburdening either the *Pensum*
of Psalmody or the lessons. Longish lessons are provided only for
the 'vigils'—i.e. for our Matins. In this place the books of the New
and Old Testaments as well as the recognized writings of the
orthodox Fathers were to be read (c. 9). This rule, obviously, was
meant to be understood in the way it came to be more precisely
defined since the 7th century in the lectionary of St. Peter30—a
lectionary which gained ground increasingly, and finally predominated in monasteries and cathedrals. The readings here began
in Advent with Isaias.31 The reading was always taken up where
it had been left off; and in the course of the year, skilfully arranging things so as to harmonize with the great festival seasons, the
whole of Scripture was read. Thus, if Scripture contains 1184
chapters—excluding the psalms—this would mean that for each
day there was a *Pensum* of rather more than three chapters: or if

24. *Regula s. Casearii* (Blume 38; Morin 25, Z. 5).
25. *Regula s. Aureliani* (Blume 44).
26. Caesarius, *Serm.* 78 (Morin 309).
27. P. Salmon, *Le Lectionnaire de Luxeuil*, Rome 9144.
28. Printed by Salmon, p. 27-56. The lection is for the nocturnal vigil on the commemoration day of the saint. The last section of the *Passio*, as the editor remarks, may have
served as a reading at Mass.
29. Salmon 140-168.
30. As *Ordo* XIV in Andrieu, *Les Ordines* III, 25-41. To the oldest test of this (*Cod. Vat.
Pal.* 277) cf. C. Silva-Tarruca, *Giovanni Archicantor di S. Petro a Roma e l'Ordo Romanus da
lui composto* (*Atti della pont. Academia Romana die Archeologia, Memorie* I, 1), Rome 1923,
173-178.
31. Andrieu III, 40.

we discount the 89 chapters of the Gospels and the 100 of the Epistles of St. Paul which were prescribed by the said order to be read in other places,[32] there would be something less than three chapters per day in the regular *Scriptura occurrens*. But we must not imagine that the division was absolutely regular. The winter nights accounted for the greater part.[33] In fact, according to the lectionary of St. Peter (old edition) during the few months from the beginning of December until Easter, all of the Prophets and the Pentateuch were read. That makes 490 chapters—almost half of the whole scheme.

The picture is confirmed and illumined by the descriptions which Ulrich of Cluny gave during his tour of Germany in 1080 to his friend Wilhelm von Hirsau.[34] According to his account, at Cluny the whole of Genesis (50 chapters) was read in the six weekdays between Septuagesima and Sexagesima (there was a special order for Sunday); the other books of the Octoteuch, were finished by the beginning of Lent, much of them admittedly being read in refectory. In the time which remained until Passion Sunday, St. Augustine's *Enarrationes in Psalmos* were fitted in. Jeremias was read in the nine days from Passion Sunday until Wednesday of Holy Week. By contrast, Scripture-reading during summer was cut down to a minimum. Because of the shortness of the night it was almost all transferred to the refectory. As autumn advanced, the lessons in the vigil became longer. The whole of

32. Ibid. (*Cod. Vat. Pal.* 277); *psalmi omni tempore, Evangelium et Apostolum similiter.* The slightly later *Instructio eccl. ordinis* (Andrieu, *Les Ordines* III, 147) speaks rather of the reading from St. Paul which was apportioned to the third Nocturn of the Sunday order: *Epistolae Pauli apostoli omni tempore in posterioribus tribus lectionibus tam in die dominico ad vigiliis quam et in missarum sollemnis leguntur.* Anyway, the whole Gospel of the day was still read in the Office as well, right down to the 11th century; cf. Bäumer-Biron I, 386 seq. In yet another Roman lectionary of the beginning of the 8th century (*Ordo* XIII B, Andrieu II, 502; Bäumer-Biron II, 450 seq.), which had also found its way into later mss. of the *Decretum Gratiani* I, 15, 3 (Friedberg 40 seq.) and which corresponds almost exactly to the present-day lectionary, the reading from St. Paul has been transposed from the third Nocturn, where the reading of the homily now becomes increasingly popular, (v. Baumstark, *Liturgie comparée³* 131 seq.), to the customary *Scriptura occurrens* of the first Nocturn in the season after Christmas. This change may be connected with the adoption of the Gallican conception of Advent: in the same document (Andrieu III, 500; ibid. 485) the readings from the Prophets, formerly fixed for after Christmas, are begun at the beginning of November, corresponding to Advent which, according to the Gallican liturgical tradition, began in November. Cf. Jungmann, *Gewordene Liturgie* 277 seq.
33. Cf. the observation above p.121. Later, the cold of winter is also accepted as a reason for the shortening of the readings. V. an opinion from 1117 in Bäumer-Biron II, 50.
34. *Udalrici Consuetudines Cluniacenses* I, 1 (PL 149, 643-645).

168   PASTORAL LITURGY

Ezechiel which started off the Prophetic readings,35 now advanced to November, was read in the first ten days of that month. Daniel and the Minor Prophets were not sufficient to fill up the three weeks which remained: Gregory's Homilies on Ezechiel were added. The whole of Isaias with its 66 chapters was read in six nights; and the rest of Advent was filled up by readings from the Fathers. The readings from St. Paul, now transferred to Christmas-tide, were completed between Sunday in the octave of Christmas and Septuagesima; and possibly Chrysostom was added to this. Sometimes, for example, Romans was read in two nights. Similar accounts come from other sources. Under Abbot Johannes von Gorze (d. 976) the lessons from the Prophets which fell in November were all read in two weeks. Daniel was read through in a single night Office.36

It is obvious that the writings of the Fathers too, were incorporated in this order of lessons. A lesson would usually comprise a whole sermon of one of the Fathers.37 The feast days—gradually increasing in number—also began to have lessons from the Lives and Passions of the saints and martyrs. Fundamentally the reading would consist of a complete work. In many places it was the custom to divide this up into nine (or twelve in the monastic order) lessons to fit the lessons of the nine or twelve Offices on the appropriate day. For this reason many lectionaries since the 9th century have numbers from I-VI or from I-XII in the text or in the margin, and these indicate the divisions of the lesson. If a passage was too long altogether we might well find a note in the margin: *in refectorio*.38 In the older monastic rules (Pachomius, Aurelian) there was even provision made for the monks doing some light manual work during the long readings, to prevent them from falling asleep.39

As well as the principal lessons of the night Office and those for the refectory—often associated with them—according to the Roman-Benedictine order a special lesson was introduced before

35. V. above n. 32.
36. E. Martène, *De antiquis monachorum ritibus* I, 2, 59 (loc. cit. 32).
37. Ibid.
38. V. Leroquais, *Les Bréviaires manuscrits des Bibliotheques publiques de France* I, Paris 1934, p. LI seq. Cf. E. Mundig, *Das Verzeichnis der St. Galler Heiligenleben und ihrer Handschriften in Cod. Sangall. 566 (Texte u. Arbeiten 3-4)*, Beuron 1918. The marginal numbers here run from I-VI.
39. Martène, *De antiquis monachorum ritibus* I, 2, 61 (loc. cit. 32).

Compline. According to St. Benedict (c. 42) four or five pages from the *Collationes* or from the *Vitae Patrum* were supposed to be read. At Lauds the appropriate reading is introduced by Benedict as one which is to be executed *ex corde* (c. 12) *memoriter* (c. 13). At Vespers he speaks in the same strain of the *lectio recitanda* (c. 17). At Prime too he says that after the psalms: *recitetur lectio una;* and the same goes for Tierce, Sext and None (ibid).

In this we meet the ancient monastic custom of learning and reciting by heart lengthy passages of holy Scripture.40 In the Egyptian monasteries it was already customary to recite passages from Scripture other than the psalms during the Offices; and these too were recited by heart. It was said that Anthony and Hilarion knew the Scriptures by heart.41 This must often have led to confusion. As the result of some diversion, a monk who had committed fourteen books of the Bible to memory might be unable to recall a single verse at the critical moment.42 In our view, the *capitula* of the Hours, too, must have been lessons of normal length.

Coming closer to detail, it was for the superiors to decide the choice and length of the readings, especially of the non-Scriptural books, always within the limits set by the traditional norms.43 When they had got to the end of the Scriptural material, even in the night Offices, readings from the Fathers could take their place —as we saw proved of Cluny. And on feast-days with their nine (or twelve) lessons, in the late Middle Ages even, the *Passio* of the relevant martyrs could provide the material for the public reading.44 In making his choice, the superior was simply guided by what the monastic library had to offer, and by his own idea of what would make the most suitable spiritual reading for his community.45 For it is obvious that the reading was thought of not as an external performance but as spiritual nourishment, above all as the enlivening of prayer which otherwise might so easily

40. D. Gorce, *La lectio divina des origines du cénobitisme a S. Benoit et Cassiodore* I, Wépion 1925, 73 seq. 157 seq.
41. Gorce 64, 68.
42. Gorce 74.
43. Bäumer-Biron I, 398; II, 49. On the sign which indicates the end of the reading, cf. Callewaert; *Tu autem Domine miserere nobis: Sacris erudiri,* Steenbrugge 1940, 185-190.
44. Bäumer-Biron II, 50 seq.
45. Added to the common liturgical reading there was also the private and predominantly meditative reading, the *lectio divina* in the narrower sense. On 'this, v. the work of Gorce named in n. 40 above; and, for the later period, U. Berliere, *L'ascèse bénédictine,* Paris 1927, 169-185.

become benumbed—as Isidore so pertinently describes: *Si quidem oratio fit pinguior, dum mens, recenti lectioni saginata, per divinarum rerum quas nuper audivit imagines currit.*46 Thus the liturgical reading and the reading at meals formed a unity.47 What could not be finished in choir was finished at table.48 With the Franciscans as late as the 13th century the evening reading at table still had its place between the blessing which opens Compline, as we know it, and the words of Peter, *Fratres sobrii estote*, which are now attached to it.49

In the course of time the lesson was shortened for two reasons. First, there was a desire for a fixed order which would then have to be moderate in its demands. After the 8th century, within the Roman liturgy, lectionaries appeared for non-Scriptural readings in the canonical Hours, and the texts were clearly defined.50 Elsewhere, free choice of the *Passio* or Life of the saint and the length of the passage lasted longer; but the Biblical as well as the Patristic texts began to be more exactly determined. As we learn from comparison of manuscripts, this process must have been going on in Rome and in the region of Monte Cassino in the 11th century.51 We may conclude from this that a reform must have been taking place under Gregory VII, without going so far as to say that there was any intention of establishing a universally obligatory standard.52 In all this, the shortening was on a modest scale to begin with.53

The present state of the short lessons, in which samples, only, of many books of Scripture are read, was arrived at in the 13th century when the *Breviarum Romanae Curiae* came into being. This was designed, bearing in mind the demands of travel and business which were made upon the Papal court; and it was taken

46. Isidore, *De eccl. off.* I, 10, 3 (PL 83, 745).
47. Cf. the *Ordo officiorum Ecclesiae Lateranensis* ed. Fischer: many passages in index under Refectory reading (*Tischlesung*).
48. Z.B. loc. cit. 127, Z.2.
49. P. A. Caron, *L'office divin chez les Freres Mineurs au XIII siecle*, Paris 1928, 23.
50. c. 730—the lectionary of Agimundus, ed. by J. Low: *Röm. Quartalschrift* 37 (1929) 15-39; the sermon-book of Alanus of Faifa ed. by E. Hosp; *Ephem. liturg.* 50 (1936) 375-383; 51 (1937) 210-214; principally that of Paul Warnefried (c. 790, and others in Migne PL 95, 1159 seq.), which forms the basis of our modern Patristic readings.
51. Bäumer-Biron II, 39 seq.
52. Ibid. II, 12 seq. 42 seq.
53. Bäumer-Biron adduce as example the readings from Lamentations during Holy Week. These already had the triple shape they have today.

up and spread widely by the Franciscan Order which likewise was
much given to travelling about.54 This brings us to the second
factor through which the transition to full abbreviation was accomplished. Consideration had to be given to those who could
not pray the Office corporately in choir. With this in mind,
Monte Cassino had, as well as its normal lengthly lessons, an
Office containing short selections for the use of travelling monks.55
Formerly brethren who were travelling were only required to say
the parts they knew by heart, but from the 10th century on, they
begin to take with them a book which could conveniently be
carried, and which contained the essentials. This was the *Breviarium*. In many cases only the first words were given of those psalms
and hymns which all knew by heart; and now lessons were given
which very often, indeed, were shortened to but a few lines.56 In
1270 the General Chapter of the Dominican Order ruled that on
certain feast days at the Office in choir the unabridged homilies
should be read as of old: *extra choram*, however, the shortened
lessons might be used, and on saints' days they were to take lessons
de communi in the *breviaria*.57

From what has been said it is clear that for centuries the lesson
occupied a large space in the canonical Hours, and during the
nocturnal Hour, in spite of the considerable *Pensum* of psalmody,
it still carried the emphasis. Furthermore, it was not there for
decoration or variety but as spiritual reading to support and
strengthen spiritual life. Before the time of printing every book
was a thing of great value: thus it is obvious that most of this reading was a public affair, composed mainly of holy Scripture, but
including also the reading of such recognized religious literature
as was available.

The conditions are quite different today. Books can be bought
fairly cheaply. There is a wide selection of spiritual reading in all
languages. On the other hand, the majority of those who say the

54. Bäumer-Biron II, 24 seq. 29.
55. Martene loc. cit.
56. Leroquais loc. cit. LIII seq. And yet in the oldest known example (A. Dold, *Lehrreiche
Basler Brevier-Fragmente*, Beuron 1954; turn of 10th century) Biblical readings can be
traced, having the five-fold arrangement of modern Breviary lessons. Cf. Zk Th 77
(1955) 121.
57. Bäumer-Biron II, 108. In 1557 John de Aize took up a different attitude, and this
played a big part in the decision to suspend Quinenez' Breviary, in which abbreviations
in other places gave more space to New Testament reading. Cf. below   .

Breviary and who are occupied in exacting pastoral work are not called to lead a contemplative life dedicated wholly to prayer. All the more then, do they require the spiritual nourishment of the lessons. The desire is therefore justified that it should be made possible for them to set apart, following the ancient model, a considerable part of the time they are obliged to give to canonical prayer, to the *lectio divina;* and within the framework of this to read above all, through the whole of Scripture in the course of a few years.[58]

3. *Genuflexion between Psalm and Oration*

Since the canonical Hours were designed as a corporate possession, in the early centuries of the Middle Ages a connecting link was almost always tucked in to form a transition from the lesson or psalm to the summing-up prayer. At this point the whole assembly prayed before the superior offered the prayer to God in the *oration;* and this prayer of community was regularly said kneeling, if the mood of the day did not forbid it.

In the description which Cassian has left us of the canonical prayer of the Egyptian monks [1] we learn of the following custom. At the end of each of the twelve psalms of the night and day Offices, all rose from their seats and raised their arms in silent prayer. Then they prostrated themselves upon the floor, but rose again immediately along with the leader of the hour of prayer—usually a priest[2]—who, after another brief silence, said the collects (*orationem collecturus est; precem colligit*).

Cassian mentions along with this a second custom, existing in Gaul, deviating somewhat from the first, and which he would like

58. Important proposals have been made by Hugo Rahner, *Die Vaterlesungen des Breviers: Brevierstudien,* Trier 1958 (Report of the study-conference at Assisi), 42-56. He develops the idea of a 'Breviary of instruction' (besides the prayer-book), in which a selection of the best spiritual literature, arranged according to main themes, would be provided, only the length of time spent on reading being specified. Cardinal Lercaro had similar ideas in mind when he addressed the congress at Assisi on 'The simplification of the rubrics and the reform of the Breviary': *Erneuerung der Liturgie aus dem Geiste der Seelsorge (Akten des I. Internationalen Pastoralliturgischen Kongresses,* ed. by J. Wagner, Trier 1957) 314-338. He stressed particularly the need to bring the demands of can. 125, 2 concerning the devotional life of the clergy into harmony with the obligation to say the Breviary; the lessons of the Breviary, at any rate, should provide material for meditation (329).
1. Cassian, *De inst. coenob.* II, 7 (CSEL 17, 23 seq.); cf. ibid. c. 5 10 seq. (CSEL 17, 22. 25 seq.).
2. Ibid. c. 10 (CSEL 17, 25).

to suppress. The custom was to kneel, not for a moment (*puncto brevissimo*), but immediately after the psalm ended and to remain thus for some considerable time. Cassian attributes this second custom to the desire for comfort. But even this austere monastic Father had to admit that this fashion represented an acknowledged ecclesiastical usage; for community prayer in a kneeling posture, whether signalled by a *Flectamus genua* or not, whether with a litany or merely with silent prayer, was widely practised as the transition to the concluding oration.3 In the Roman liturgy this style became the norm.

But in the context of the prayer liturgy of ascetic and monastic groups we find that it is, in fact, the custom which Cassian preferred which is mostly confirmed—even before Cassian's time.

The treatise *De virginitate*—very likely the work of St. Athanasius—commends the nuns, whether praying in group or privately, to recite as many psalms as they were able to recite, standing, and after each psalm to say a prayer and to genuflect.4 In the slightly later histories of the monks, which Palladius tells, such a manner of praying is occasionally mentioned.5 Theodoret of Cyrus tells how the Abbot Julian of Saba instructed his disciples to go out into the desert in pairs during the Morning Hour. One was to stand and sing fifteen psalms while the other knelt; then they were to change places and thus continue their prayer until towards evening.6 There is no mention at all here of the *oration*.

This style of prayer had spread through the West as well. Isidore of Seville decreed that his monks should throw themselves down on the ground in adoration after each psalm; then they had to rise at once and proceed with the next psalm. They were to act thus *per singula officia*.7 The Irish monks had a similar custom. According to the *Regula coenobialis* of St. Columba (d. 615) all

3. Cf. Jungmann, *Missarum Sollemnia* I, 471 seq.
4. *De virginitate* c. 20 (PG 28, 276).
5. Palladius, *Historia Lausica* c. 36 (BKV² 5, 392): after having prayed in a standing position, a monk named Posidonius drove out a devil 'after the second genuflexion'. In other passages which mention 100 or even 300 prayers, genuflexion is not explicitly mentioned. On the other hand, praying while standing all the time, the whole night through 'without ever bending the knee' is cited as 'an ascetic practice'; ibid. c. 19. 31 (BKV² 5, 361. 380).
6. Theodoret, *Hist. religiosa* c. 2 (PG 82, 1309).
7. Isidore, *Regula monach.* c. 6, 1 (PL 83, 876). When P. Pourrat, *La spiritualité chrétienne* I², Paris 1926, 413, says of this genuflexion, '*sans doute en prononçant le Gloria Patri*', his interpretation clearly mistakes the meaning of this gesture.

were supposed to bow down before God at the end of every psalm;[8] and we must take this to mean, that on ordinary days they all knelt down together as they recited thrice in a low voice *Deus in adiutorium meum intende, Domine adiuvandum me festina*, words which, no doubt, served also as a timing signal. Only during Easter-time and on Sundays would this be supplemented by a slight bowing (*moderate se humiliantes*) [9]The rule of St. Ailbe of Em y (d. 540) also, knows of the *Deus in adiutorium* along with the kneeling at the end of each psalm.[10]

We find Columba's directions repeated on the continent by one of his pupils, Bishop Donatus of Besançon (d. 656), in the rule for nuns in a convent which he founded. There is this difference: Donatus makes the kneeling last throughout only a single *Deus in adiutorium*.[11]

To this extent the ancient practice was kept up in the corporate prayer of monastic choirs. The primitive custom, however, then gave way to a new order of psalmody in which the *oration* no longer followed each separate psalm, but followed the whole series of psalms to form the conclusion of the Hour; and in which now the kneeling came only once, before the *oration*, corresponding to present-day Roman usage in the appropriate ferial Offices. On the other hand, the association between psalm and kneeling was kept up for centuries, in private prayer and in penitential practice. It is worth while looking at this development.

In the 18th century *Vita tertia* of St. Patrick we read that the saint's custom was to pray 100 psalms during the first part of the night and to make 200 genuflexions;[12] i.e. he made two genuflexions at each psalm. We can say that this was a custom in the

8. Columbanus, *Reg. coenob.* c. 10 (ed. Seebass: *Zeitschr. f. Kirchengesch.* 1897, 221; PL 80, 216 seq.): *humiliatio in Ecclesia post finem cuiuscumque psalmi.* Cf. J. Ryan, *Irish Monasticism*, Dublin 1931, 343 seq., where, however, no reason is given for this genuflexion towards the altar.
9. Ibid. c. 10 (Seebass 228; PL 80, 220 seq.): *. . . in fine omnium psalmorum genua in oratione, si non infirmitas corporis officerit, flectere aequo animo debent, sub silentio dicentes: Deus in adiutorium.*
10. Quoted by L. Gougaud, *Christiantiy in Celtic Lands*, London 1932, 331 seq., previously *Eire*, III (1907) 92-115.
11. Donatus, *Regula* c. 34 (PL 87, 284 seq.); cf. c. 26 (PL 87, 283). In place of Columbanus' *aequo animo*, Donatus has: *aequo moderamine*, which would also be a correct interpretation of Columbanus' text—'regularly'.
12. P. Grosjean, *Patriciana: Analecta Bollandiana* 43 (1925) 253. The association of psalmody and genuflexion was praised by the Council of Cloveshoe (747) can. 27 (Hadden-Stubbs III, 373).

8th century at least. Later legends of St. Patrick speak of 300 genuflexions per day. Two hundred of these are accounted for by the above *Pensum:* 100 more must have been attached by St. Patrick or the other 50 psalms said in the second part of the night.₁₃ It is well-known that the Irish divided the Psalter into three 'Fifties.'₁₄

Kneeling allied to the psalms figures largely in the penances of the penitential writings, especially as a discharge of the penitential fast, which receives the most consideration. In the so-called *Canones Hibernensis* which was already current in the middle of the 7th century,₁₅ there is a chapter entitled *De arreis* (arra=substitute). Here as a substitute for *a superpositio* (i.e. a double fast-day) 100 *psalmi et* 100 *flectiones genuum* is indicated (c. 1). Amongst other things, the substitute for a triduum of fasting (c. 2) was 12 *flectiones in unaquaque hora*, which is reminiscent of the twelve psalms of the principal Hours. And as penance for a year (c. 4) is appointed, along with other things *canticum psalmorum cum canticis et oratione horarum et in eis 12 geniculationes.* ₁₆

Concerning these so-called 'redemptions' the original draft of the *Poenitentiale Cummeani* of the mid-7th century is very reticent.₁₇ But in a 9th century redaction, the so-called *Excarpsus Cummeani*, a prescription appears which was common property of the penitential books₁₈ of the time.₁₉ The penitent had to: *pro unoquoque die cantet psalmos 50 flectendo genua, et* (alternatively) *sine genua flectendo cantet 70, et pro hebdomada una 300 psalmos per*

---

13. Thus according to the Life of Joscelin of Furness (c. 1210) c. 18 (*Acta SS Mart.* II, 574), whose statement has been adopted by our Breviary lesson for 17th March.
14. In the hymn, 'Genair Patraic' (8th century) the Psalter is simply called 'the three fifties'. Bernard-Atkinson, *The Irish Liber hymnorum* II (HBS 14), London 1898, 33. In the prayer-brotherhood of St. Gallen-Reichenau in 800, 50 psalms counted as a substitute for one priest's Mass, 150 psalms for three; M. Gerbert, *Vetus liturgia Alemannica* I, St. Blasien 1776, 369.
15. They had already been adopted in a shortened form in the genuine *Poenitentiale Cummeani* ed. Zettinger: *Archiv. f. kath. Kirchenrecht* 82 (1902) 517; cf. ibid. 537.
16. F. W. H. Wasserschleben, *Die Bussordnungen der abendländischen Kirche*, Halle 1851, 139.—Cf. also ibid. c. 8-10, where 40 psalms and as many *flectiones* and then 60 psalms and *flectiones* are discussed.
17. Zettlinger, loc. cit.
18. On the discussion of the difficult material of penitential books we have also the article *Bussbücher*, by C. Vogel in L Th K² II (1958) 802-805.
19. Cf. the general survey of the specification of redemptions in the four penitential books of this period by W. Hormann, *Bussbücherstudien: Zeitschr. d. Savignystiftung f. Rechtsgesch.*, Karon, Abt. 4 (1914) 482; besides the critical edition by Hormann of the *Poenitentiale Martenianum*: ibid. 477.

176 PASTORAL LITURGY

*ordinem flectendo genua psallat, aut si flectere genua non potest, cantet 420 psalmos.*20 It is clear that by *flectendo genua* we are still to understand here separate kneeling after each psalm, because occasionally the expression *venia* is used of this, and in medieval terminology this signified a single genuflexion.21

But *flectendo genua* begins to take on the sense of continuous kneeling: the required psalms are prayed while kneeling. As early as Regino of Prüm (d. 915) we find the 50 psalms which were substituted for a day's fast being prayed, kneeling.22 The penance book, the socalled Corrector, contained in the *Decretum* of Burchard of Worms (d. 1025), displays the same idea as part of its tradition: *genibus flexis;* moreover it adds a mitigating explanation which leaves nothing in doubt: *Si autem talis est, quod tamdiu in genibus iacere non potest . . .*23

Along with this we find genuflexion mentioned repeatedly, but detached from recitation of the psalms, as a favourite penitential exercise. Again, Ireland seems to have been the home of this practice. A 7th century legend of St. Patrick24 tells of how the saint had fasted three days and three nights *cum centenis oraculis flectenisque assiduis.* These reports are expanded in later legends.25 It is told of other Irish saints that they had performed 300 genuflexions every night and as many every day.26 The Irish *Liber hymnorum* recounts that St. Columba made 1200 genuflexions daily except on feast days so that his ribs had become visible through his habit.27 At any rate, in the 9th century such practices must have been very popular amongst the Irish. Walafried Strabo, Abbot of Reichenau, a monastery which saw the coming and going of many Irish monks, tells of how the *Scotorum natio*

20. H. J. Schnitz, *Die Bussbücher und das kanonische Bussverfahren,* Düsseldorf 1898, 603.
21. A Vienna ms. of the 10th century repeats this requirement: *cum veniam psalm. L et sine veniam LXX,* Schmitz 353.
22. Regino, *De synod. causis* II, 452, al. 444 (ed. Wasserschleben 391; PL 132, 369 seq). Cf. the similar regulations for other amounts of penance, ibid. c. 447-454, or 439-446.
23. c. 12 seq. following mss. of 11th-13th centuries. Schmitz 458. Besides this, the same tradition has, however, the further rule (c. 14): *Qui in ecclesia genua centies flexerit, id est si centies veniam petierit . . . instissimum est;* Schmitz 458.
24. The *Vita,* written by Tirechan, ed. W. Stokes, *Tripartite Life,* London 1887, 312; quoted by H. Leclercq, *Genuflexions:* DACL VI, 1020. *Oracula* could always mean the psalms too.
25. Cf. above p.174-5.
26. Leclercq 1021.
27. Bernard-Atkinson, *The Irish Liber hymnorum* II, 63. The text of the hymn to Columba is ascribed to the 9th century; ibid. 224 n. 1.

practised genuflexion with great fervour, always keeping to definite numbers.28

The practise of genuflexion by itself, detached from the psalms comes into penitential practice, then, from the 9th century.

In Regino's list of 'redemptions' which concludes his manual for episcopal visitations29 under the heading, *Ex dictis sancti Bonifacii episcopi*, the discharge of a day's fast is described thus: the psalm *Beati immaculati*, thrice, and six times the psalm *Miserere mei Deus et* 70 (*vices*) *prosternat se in terram et* (*per*) *singulas Pater noster dicat*. Whoever did not know the psalm—this must mostly have been the case—prostrated himself a hundred times instead, saying: *Miserere mei Deus* and *Dimitte Domine peccata mea*.30 In the law code of Edgar of England (d. 975) there is mention of 60 genuflexions along with prostration upon the ground: this was counted the equivalent of one day's fasting.31

On the other hand the original association of genuflexion with prayer is preserved, in a modified form at least, when, in the example already cited from Regino, we find a 70 times repeated *Pater noster* in place of psalms allied to as many genuflexions.32 Frequently the *Pater noster* is the obvious substitute for a psalm, especially when the number 50-150 or multiples thereof appear. Regino's rule of 'redemption' (according to which those who did not know the psalms could prostrate themselves repeatedly upon the ground instead, saying, *Miserere mei Deus* etc.), appears in

28. Walafried Strabo, *De exord. et incrementis* c. 25 (PL 114, 952 seq.).
29. Like c. 46: in the Beda-Egbert *Excarpsus* (Schmitz 699; cf. ibid. 460. 462. 672 seq.), also from 9th century. The derivation from Boniface is denied by Wasserschleben (loc. cit.).
30. c. 454 or 446 (Wasserschleben 392; PL 132, 370).—In c. 44 of the Beda-Egbert *Excarpsus* (Schmitz 699) 200 *genuflexus* is given as a possible substitute for one day of penance. As well as this, as equivalent of a month's penance is given: the Psalter once (variant, 1000 psalms) and 200 *genuflexa*; c. 42 (Schmitz 698).
31. *Leges Edgaris, De satisf.* n. 18 (Hardruin VI, 673 A): *Pro unius diei genuflectat homo ille, ad terram se inclinet* 60 *vicibus dicens Pater noster.*—This bowing towards the ground seems to be an accepted practice alongside genuflexion proper. There may be some connexion with the *palmata* mentioned in other regulations for penance and penance-substitutions. Cf. B. Poschmann, *Die abendländische Kirchenbusse im Mittelalter*, Breslau 1930, 148 note. According to this, the *palmata* consisted in the penitent 'prostrating himself on the ground and striking the floor with the palms of his hands'. The *palmata* often accompanied the prescribed psalms—in double the number—; e.g. in Burchard, *Decretum* XIX, 25 (Schmitz 462): a certain fast can be replaced by the threefold recitation of the Psalter *cum palmatis* 300 *per singula psalteria*. In the same chapter, however, we find as the substitute for a three-day fast: 25 psalms *cum totidem veniis per noctem et cum palmatis* 300.
32. Above p. 177.

178   PASTORAL LITURGY

Burchard of Worms in the expression: *per singulas genuflexiones
Pater noster dicat.*33 About 1220 in Sienna the imprisonment of a
murderer was associated with a ritual in the course of which the
arch-priest announced his penance: all through Lent except on
Sundays he must fast on bread and water, *et* 100 *genuflexions faciat
et* 100 *Pater noster dicat in die et* 100 *in nocte.* 34

For long, similar penances were common in the Icelandic
Church. According to the rules for penance prescribed by Bishop
Thorlak (d. 1193) part of a nine year penance for certain sins of
unchastity was genuflexion and the *Pater noster* 100 times on every
fast day.35 For another type of sin 100 and 50 genuflexions on
alternate days during Lent were prescribed, plus the same number
of *Paters.*36 More recent Icelandic penitential regulations speak of
50 or 30 genuflexions with the same number of *Paters.*37 An Icelandic code of penance composed before 1330 required a *Pater-
noster-psalter* in several cases, and with every *Pater noster* there was
a genuflexion.38

We see here how the form of the Rosary, of the Mary-psalter,
is beginning to appear. In fact, from the 12th century onwards the
Marian element emerges showing the same imitation of the
Biblical psalter and and the same connexion with genuflexion.
The monk Aybert who died in Hennegau in 1140 and who prayed
the whole psalter every day, bowed down 100 times a day and
prostrated himself on the ground 50 times, at every *flectio* (i.e. 150
times) saying the *Ave Maria.*39 It is told of St. Maria of Oigny

33. Burchard, *Decretum* XIX, 24 (Schmitz 462).
34. L. A. Muratori, *Antiquitates Medii aevi* V, Milan 1741, 768; Schmitz 53 n. 12.
35. Schmitz 708.
36. Schmitz 710.
37. Schmitz 714. Ibid 715—the association of 7 *Pater noster* and *Ave* with 7 genuflexions.
38. Schmitz 717 seq. That is clearly the meaning of the Icelandic expression which the
translator, Finnus Johannacus (in his *Kirchengesch. Islands* II, 188 of 1775), whom Schmitz
copies, reproduces in the meaningless words: *quavis nocte Pater noster et psalterium ad
quodvis Pater noster in genua recumbentes recitanto* (Schmitz 717) i.e. *toties psalterium, Pater
noster cum genuflexione recitetur* (Schmitz 718; the exression recurs twice in a like manner
p. 718 seq.); i.e. the *et* or comma (if we are not to read it as *ex*) between *Pater noster* and
psalterium is to be deleted. We are dealing with an Our Father Psalter, pre-cursor of the
Marian Psalter, as becomes quite clear from the fact that in the same context we find
special rules for penance for penitents who can read and know how to serve at Mass
(718). The average Icelandic adulterer (this is the type of sinner under consideration in the
phrase in the second passage mentioned) was not able to pray the Biblical Psalter.
39. *Acta SS* Apr. I (1865) 674, n. 14; cf. *Acta SS* Aug. I (1867) 434, n. 404. St. Beissel,
Geschichte der Verehrung Marias in Deutschland während des Mittelalters, Freiburg 1909,
234 n. 5.

(d. 1213) that she prayed the whole psalter daily whilst standing, and also that: *per singulos psalmos flexis genibus beatae Virginis salutationem angelicam offerebat.*40 About the same time, in the newly founded Dominican order a practice was observed of attaching to the end of Matins a devotion introduced by a monk called Josbert. This devotion consisted of five psalms, the first letters of which spelt out the name Mary. The devotion was spread more widely in the following way by the general of the order, Jordan of Saxony (d. 1237). It began with an *Ave Maris stella;* after each of the five psalms there was a *Gloria Patri*, a genuflexion and an *Ave Maria*, the genuflexion being associated with the angelic salutation.41 At the same time, however, we find genuflexion along with the *Ave Maria* apart from the psalter altogether. Again from the early days of the Dominican order there is the account of how the brethren performed 100 or even 200 genuflexions in the morning, saying the *Ave Maria* as they did so.42 Caesarius of Heisterbach (d. 1240) tells of a devout lady who every day prayed 50 *Ave Maria cum totidem veniis.*43 It is reported of a Cistercian nun, Ida, that in the year 1226 she performed 1100 genuflexions daily which she accompanied with the salutation to the Blessed Virgin.44 This almost impossible performance becomes credible if we remember those records which describe Maria of Oigny, whom we have mentioned. For the above-mentioned prayer-practice of the 150 psalms stood within the framework of a greater plan which the mystics made to embrace a 40-day cycle. First of all it contained 600 genuflexions, then the psalter as described with 150 genuflexions, the 300 genuflexions with scourging, and finally 50 simple genuflexions.45 In the chosen number we can see how clearly the Biblical psalter—i.e. the 'fifties' of the third part of the psalter—stands out as the norm: $4 \times 150 + 150 + 2 \times 150 + 50 = 1100$.

The same thing can be said of the appearance of the rhyming psalter. These are poems in praise of Jesus or His mother, made up of 'Quinquages' (50 stanzas each); and the oldest of these even

40. James of Vitry, *Vita* III, 29: *Acta SS* Jun. V (1867) 553.
41. M. Gorce, O.P., *Le rosaire et ses antécédents historiques,* Paris 1931, 23 seq.
42. Gorce 26, following the chronicler of the order—Galvagur.
43. Caesarius of Heisterbach, *Dial. mirac.* VII, 49; Beissel 234 n. 3.
44. A. Manriquinus, *Annal. Cistere.* IV, ann. 1226, c. 4, 8; Beissel 234 n. 2.
45. loc. cit.

take the title for the separate stanzas from the corresponding
psalm.46 Of special interest to us, however, are the German Mary-
psalters of the 18th century, which show just this structure, but at
the same time contain the direction that the worshipper should
make a genuflexion (*venia*) at each of the 150 stanzas. Only during
the last fifty stanzas is prayer with outstretched arms ('Golgotha')47
to occur, and this after every ninth stanza (with genuflexion) i.e.
at the tenth—in honour of the Crucified.

Besides this, we find the original rite, still in palpable form, in a
13th century penitential *ordo* for Ash Wednesday contained in the
Ordinarium of Bayeux. The rites of penance begin with the seven
penitential psalms following an address by the bishop. Each has a
genuflexion at the end: *septem psalmos poenitentiales cum prostratione
et Gloria Patri in fine cuiuslibet psalmi.*48

If later tradition does not mention genuflexion at each psalm or
at each prayer in a series of prayers, before the concluding *oration*
of every *hour*, we still read in our Roman Breviary the rubric
concerning the *preces feriales*, viz. that on those few days when
they now apply (because of the dominance of Sundays and feast-
days), they are to be said, *flexis genibus*. This may remind us at
least, that a reverent bowing before God, a humble petition by the
congregation before the chief prayer is said by the officiating
cleric, when the joy of a feast-day does not predominate, is very
much part of the ancient traditional plan of Christian prayer.

4.   *The Kyrie Eleison of the Preces*
   Much has been written about the Kyrie of the Mass: but it is no
less ancient in the liturgy of prayer. In 400 A.D. the pilgrim
Aetheria heard it daily in Jerusalem at Vespers from the lips of a
band of children, who used to answer the separate invocations of

46.   Eighteen such poems of the latei Middle Ages have been published in Latin by G. M.
Dieves, *Gereimte Psalterien des Mittelalters (Analectica hymnica* 35), Leipzig 1905. There is
no mention here of genuflexion.
47.   Beissel 244. One example of such a Marian Psalter, published in the *Zeitschr. f.
deutsches Altertum* VIII 274-298, is cited by R. Stroppel, *Liturgie und geistliche Dichtung
zwischen* 1050 *und* 1200, Frankfurt 1927, 144.
48.   U. Chevalier, *Ordinarie et Coutumier de L'eglise cathédral de Bayeux*, Paris 1902, 102.
The said Ordo also in E. Martène, *De ant. Eccl. ritibus* IV, 17, Ordo VI (Antwerp 1737:
III, 148). That the words *in fine cuiuslibet* (*psalmi*) also refer to the *prostratio*, here to be
understood as a genuflexion each time, is seen from the fact that it is not until the sequel
that continuous kneeling is ordered: *Prostrato episcopo . . .*

the litany.₁ Here we do not intend to give a complete account of
the history of the *Kyrie eleison* in the *preces* or even a history of the
preces itself. Balthasar Fischer has already given an excellent sketch
of the outlines of the latter.₂ The following points deserve
emphasis.

The *preces* are not interpolations appropriate to penitential days,
but rather the normal preliminary in common prayer to the
summing-up *oration*. In the liturgy of the city of Rome their
original form is the simple *Kyrie* litany, with an announcement of
intentions and the response *Kyrie eleison*. From the time of
Columba and his Irish monks onwards, a new style spread abroad
of answering the announcement of intentions. Verses of psalms
were used, for example: (*Oremus*) *pro fratribus nostris absentibus.
R: Salvos fac servos tuos, Deus meus, sperantes in te.* A Gallican form
of using the psalms in the *preces* was added to this Irish way. In
this, psalm verses, divided into versicle and response, were simply
strung along one after the other without any announcement of
intentions. On Gallican soil, both forms became fused with the
(oriental)—Roman style of the simple *Kyrie*-litany. Thus arose
our current form of *preces*, and in the process the Roman form
suffered much shortening.

Here we shall clarify a few points of detail concerning the beginning of the *preces*.

In our Roman order the *preces* regularly begins—even apart
from the canonical Hours, e.g. at a funeral, at grace for meals—
with *Kyrie eleison, Christe eleison, Kyrie eleison* and *Pater noster*.
How did this combination arise? What does it signify?

We meet with this connexion between the *Kyrie* and the *Pater
noster* as the early Christian period draws to a close—and we find
it in the East. At the night Hours of prayer, which the two monks
John and Sophronius got to know for themselves when they
visited the Sinai monastery at the turn of the 6th century,₃ the Our
Father with the *Kyrie eleison* followed thrice at the end of a series
of psalms or hymns; and the conclusion to the whole thing was
made up of Our Father once again, plus a 12 or 30 (or 300) times

1. *Aetheriae Peregrinatio* c. 24, 5 (CSEL 39, 72).
2. B. Fischer, *Litania ad Laudes et Vesperes. Ein Vorschlag zur Neugestaltung der Ferialpreces:
Liturg. Jahrbuch* 1 (1951) 53-74.
3. V. Bäumer-Biron I, 182-185.

repeated *Kyrie eleison*. A little earlier, the *Pater noster* joined with the *Kyrie eleison* is found in the Rule of St. Benedict:—*litania et oratio dominica* were expressly cited as the ending of Vespers (c. 17). A similar stipulation applies to *Lauds* (c. 13). In both cases we must take the *litania* to mean the complete *Kyrie*-litany with an announcement of intentions and responses. In contrast, for the night Hours and the little *hours* we have to take the description *Kyrie eleison et missae sunt* (c. 17; cf. c. 9) to denote—following Callewaert[4]—an abbreviated form of the *Kyrie*-litany, followed, no doubt, by the *Pater noster*. The meaning of this *Kyrie* is disclosed more precisely when the Abbot of Sinai adds this prayer to the multiple invocations of the *Kyrie*, by way of comment: 'Son and Word of God have mercy on us, send us the help of thy grace and save our souls.'[5] This is a humble cry of supplication which is meant to strengthen the chief prayer—the Our Father, which in this context takes the place of the collect.

We find a similar idea in Amalar when in discussing the second part of Prime he mentions the *Kyrie* and says that this precedes the Lord's Prayer—*saepissime*.[6] And God is, indeed, propitiated thereby, *ut cum sua miseratione et dignatione possimus congruentur illum invocare Patrem nostrum et intendere verbis orationis*. This is no chance idea of an inventive writer; for he expresses almost the same thought when he deals with the *Kyrie* of the Mass which precedes the *oration*. Here he formulates the universal principle: *Ante omnem orationem specialem sacredotum necesse est praecedere miserocordiam Domini*—which he then explains more fully.[7] Just as in the Mass the *Pater noster* is preceded by the invocation of the Saviour's words and the *audemus dicere*, so elsewhere it is preceded by the *Kyrie* invocation.

We might ask whether for Amalar the Lord's Prayer after the *Kyrie* still had as much weight as an independent *oration*. Quite clearly this is so for Benedict and the monks of Sinai. We find the same value put upon it in the conclusion of various Hours of the

4. Callewaert, *Les étapes de l'histoire du Kyrie: Revue d'Hist. ecd.* 38 (1942) 20-25, esp. 31 seq.
5. Bäumer-Biron I, 183.
6. Amalar, *Liber officialis* IV, 2, 22 (Hanssens II, 412). Cf. ibid. III, 6, 5 (284); IV, 4, 1 (421).
7. Ibid. III, 6, 4 (Hanssens II, 284). He affirms the actuality of the sequence (*Kyrie ac deinceps orationem*) ibid. III, 9, 5 (289).

old Spanish Office where the Lord's Prayer simply forms the continuation of the *oration* introduced by the *Kyrie*8 or where it
follows this immediately as in the Morning Hour of an 11th
century *rituale* from Silos in Spain.9 We can also prove that the
Pater noster introduced by the *Kyrie eleison* still had the full worth
of a concluding *oration* in Rome as late as the 12th century, and
had it even when, according to ancient tradition, it was said *sotto
voce*, except for the last phrase.10 With Alamar, however—i.e. on
Gallican-Spanish soil in the Carolingian period—a change was
already taking place. Amalar himself, with his theoretical cherish-
ing of the *Pater noster* after the *Kyrie*, is still clearly in the older
tradition. But the order of prayer upon which he comments
already knows a special concluding *oration* over and above the
Lord's Prayer.11 And every time, this concluding *oration* is separated from the Lord's prayer, not simply by a few versicles, but the
whole psalm, *Miserere*, precedes the versicle at Prime, so that
Amalar sees the *Kyrie* and *Pater noster* as a first unit and the following versicle, *Miserere* and *oration* as a separate, second unit.12

   Elsewhere in the same period, we find this change, this assimilation of the *Pater noster* into the *preces*, fully accomplished. The
stringing together of verses of psalms within the *preces* in Gallican
fashion—and the almost silent recitation of the *Pater noster* would
have assisted the process. An order for the Sacrament of Penance
is laid down in the *Poenitentiale Vallicellanum I* (end of 8th century).
This has three psalms which are to be said before confession. After
each of these is an *oration* which is introduced by *Kyrie eleison*,

8.   Above p. 145. Pinell (above p. 138) 401 seq.
9.   M. Fero in, *Le Liber mozarabicus sacramentorum*, Paris 1912, 771. The same arrangement
is repeated in the interim Hour between Tierce and Sext (*Ordo quarte et quinte coniuncte*).
The text of the *embolismus* is given here (775): *Erue a malo, confirma in bono, Deus noster,
qui vivis et regnas in saecula saeculorum*. On the peculiarity of this Gallican *embolismus*
J. A. Jungmann, *Die lateinische Bussriten*, Innsbruck 1932, 207 n. 171. In both cases
mentioned, the *embolismus* is followed by a nine-fold *Deus miserere nobis* and a series of
further supplicatory ejaculations.
10.   *Ordo officiorum eccl. Lateranensis* ed. L. Fischer, p. 1. Cf. also below n. 23 at the end.
V. also the account of John the deacon (c. 1260) in J. Mabillon, *Museum Italicum* II, 566
(PL 78, 1385). Further references are supplied by H. Chirat, *La Maison-Dieu* 20 (1949)
29 seq.
11.   Thus in the Little Hours. Amalar, *Liber officialis* IV, 2, 26 (Hanssens 413); IV, 4, 10
(425).
12.   Amalar, *Liber officialis* IV, 2, 23 seq.; 4, 1–9 (Hanssens 412 seq. 423-5).

184   PASTORAL LITURGY

Christe eleison, Pater noster and a few versicles.13 There is a similar order for after confession, before the prayer of absolution.14 The same arrangement occurs in the *Poenitentiale* of Bishop Halitgar of Cambrai (c. 829).15 The same combination of *Kyrie* invocation plus the Lord's Prayer, to which versicles have become attached, used as a transition to the *oration*, is met in the litany of the prayer book of Charles the Bald, written in 870,16 and also with striking regularity at the end of the litany preceding Extreme Unction in the *ordines* for confessing the sick from the turn of the 9th century.17 The order appears about the middle of the 10th century in the 'Ordo qualiter agatur concilium provinciale' of the Roman-German *Pontificale*: On each of the three prescribed days a lesson from the *Gospels* will first be read; then after the psalmody (only alluded to in first place) comes the: *Kyrie eleison et Pater noster cum precibus istis*, whereupon a number of psalm verses lead into the *oration*. This sequence of prayer is repeated a second time and recurs thrice on the second day (prayer for those taking part, for the royal house, for the sick), and twice on the third day (for the dead, and for the enemies of religion).18 According to the same *Pontificale*, after the absolution on Holy Thursday, the bishop is to say the *Pater noster* after the *Kyrie eleison* at the end of the Litany of the Saints; and once more this is followed by *preces* and *oration*.19

In all this we must remember, that at this time the Litany of the Saints, whose history begins in the West at the close of the 7th century did not regularly have this ending until much later, apart from its use during Extreme Unction.20 It is seen, however, in the

13. H. J. Schmitz, *Die Bussbücher und die Bussdisziplin der Kirche*, Mainz 1883, 239 seq. The *Christe eleison* betrays the Roman component in this Frankish penitential book. The dating in the close of the 8th century is confirmed by W. u. Hormann, *Bussbücherstudien: Zeitschr. d. Savignystiftung f. Rechtsgeschichte*, Kan. Abt. 2 (1912) 151 n. 1.
14. loc. cit. 341.
15. H. J. Schmitz, *Die Bussbücher und das Kanonische Bussverfahren*, Dusseldorf 1898, 271. 273.
16. ed. Felizian Ninguaida, Ingolstadt 1583, 96.
17. V. the examples up to the 12th century in E. Martène, *De antiquis Ecclesiae ritibus* I, 7, Ordines VI. XIII. XIV. XV. XVII. XXV (Antwerp 1736: I, 859-943).
18. M. Hittorp, *De divinis Ecclesiae catholicae officiis ac ministeriis*, Cologne 1568, 152-155.
19. Ibid. 52.—Cf. M. Andrieu, *Le Pontifical Romain* I, 216.
20. The most important old litany texts are listed by M. Coens, *Anciennes litanies des Saints: Anal. Boll.* 54 (1936) 6 seq. Ibid. 11 seq. copy of some more texts of litanies. Litanies in the order for Anointing the Sick have been listed above n. 16. The early history of the litanies has been clarified by E. Bishop, *Liturgica Historica*, Oxford 1918, 137-164. The above assertions and following statements are supported by the comparative study of about 45 printed litany texts of the 8th-11th centuries.

Litany of the *Officia per ferias*, attributed to Alcuin,[21] and in a similar Office from Corbie about 900, which we learn about from Hugo Menard.[22] A veritable blossoming of this combination seems, however, to have begun in the 12th century. It occurs over and over again in the *Consuetudines of Farfa* which belongs to this period.[23] In the Rhineland Mass *ordo* which emerged in the 10th century, the *Kyrie* and *Pater noster* as a preamble to the *oration* has been interpolated in a whole series of places after the 11th century.[24] Until today they have been retained in the *Praeparatio ad Missam* and in the *Gratiarum actio post Missam*. Elsewhere, too, since that time, this *Kyrie eleison* plus the Lord's Prayer either alone (as in the *Benedictio mensae ante prandium*) or, more commonly at the head of a series of versicles, has formed, on many occasions, the prelude to an *oration*, which somehow or other receives emphasis.

It is a separate question, whether this *Kyrie* invocation possessed from the start the form in which we now have it: *Kyrie eleison, Christe eleison, Kyrie eleison*. Callewaert assumes that St. Benedict knew this form.[25] On the face of it this is very unlikely. Admittedly Gregory the Great gives evidence of the *Christe eleison* beside the *Kyrie eleison* in the Mass, but not showing the alteration which we now use, where *Christe eleison* is the middle member in a group of three. With him one phrase was said as often as the other. And the First Roman *Ordo* speaks merely of an idefinitely repeated singing of the *Kyrie eleison*. Similarly, the *Capitulare ecclesiastici ordinis* of the second half of the 8th century speaks of a nine times repeated, i.e. a thrice-repeated triple, invocation; but it speaks exclusively of *Kyrie eleison*.[26] In the *Ordo* of St. Amand, in

21. PL 101, 524.
22. PL 78, 358.
23. B. Albers, *Consuetudinis monasticae* I (1900) 31. 50. 53. 69, etc.
24. In the *Praeparatio ad Missam* (Jungmann, *Missarum Sollemnia* I²⁻⁴, 336; between the Lavabo and the collect which was associated with it at an earlier period (II, 101); between the psalms, which were said as response to the *Orate fratres*, and the attached collect (II, 176 n. 9); between the prayers and the words of Scripture following the Communion, and the Post Communion (II, 502); between the *Benedictus* with its attached psalm and the collect *Deus qui tribus pueris*, of which again there is earlier evidence (II, 572). Again in connexion with limited local usage (v. ibid. I, 624 n. 43 seq.; II, 87 n. 152; 457). The *Kyrie eleison* and *Pater noster* merit emphasis. The Pontificale of the Bibliotheca Casanatensis (11th-12th centuries) and, later, the English Missals introduce these after the psalm *Judica* (I, 385 seq.), because a collect is missing here, and the *Pater noster* serves as a collect.
25. Callewaerts, loc. cit. (above n. 4) 32 seq.
26. Andrieu, *Les Ordines Romani* III, 98. 121.

which a Frankish cleric re-edited the First *Ordo* towards the end of
the 8th century, we find for the first time two choirs each singing
the *Kyrie eleison* and the *Christe eleison* thrice, and then the *Kyrie
eleison* again.27

Examining the endings of the litanies, leaving Extreme Unction
out of account to begin with, we find that there are, amongst
some 20 parallel texts belonging to the 8th-11th centuries and
containing a *Kyrie* ending, two which display our present-day
alternating form as in the Mass, i.e. having each of the three invocations repeated thrice.28 The simple *Kyrie eleison, Christe eleison,
Kyrie eleison* is found in the Litany of the Freiburg *Pontificale*
(c. 850),29 and in that of the rite for the consecration of a church
in the Roman-German *Pontificale* (c. 950)30—and fairly regularly
in the *ordo* for the sick as well.31

But we are in a position to determine more nearly when our
present-day threefold form of the invocation appeared. In the
Capituli movitiarum, a list of decrees concerning monastic reform,
dated at 816, shortly before the reform decisions of Aachen were
put into effect, there appears—apparently as an innovation—the
insistence that at the *Kyrie eleison* the text *Kyrie eleison, Christe
eleison, Kyrie eleison* must always be used.32 In describing *Prime* in
the fourth book of his *Liber officialis*, which was completed about
830,33 Amalar already takes this text for granted.34 In the ending
of the litanies, however, the old fashion lingered on for a long
time: the single *Kyrie eleison* was followed by a single *Christe*

27. Ibid. 159.
28. The above-mentioned litany of Corbie and the northern French litany of an Amberg ms. of the 9th-10th century in A. Beck, *Kirchliche Studien und Quellen*, Amberg 1903, 387.—Each of the three invocations are twice recorded in a Holy Saturday litany of the 11th century: in Tommasi-Vezzosi, *Opp. V*, 94.
29. M. J. Mitzger, *Zwei karolingische Pontifikalien vom Oberrhein*, Freiburg 1914, 68.
30. Hittorp 109.
31. In one like this from Fleury (9th century): Martène 3, 15, *Ordo* I (II, 1066); in another from Tours (8th-10th centuries): ibid. 1, 7, VI (I, 863) and in three later orders: ibid. 1, 7, XV. XVII. XXV (898-913. 943).
32. Albers III (1907) 98.
33. J. M. Hanssens, *Amalarii episcopi opera liturgica omnia* I, Citta del Vaticano 1948, 135.
34. Amalar, *Liber officialis* IV, 2, 18 seq. (Hanssens 410-412). The same text about 829 in Halitgar also; v. Schmitz (above n. 14).

eleison,35 or a triple *Kyrie* was followed by a triple *Christe;*36 but
by far the most wide-spread form in the older texts is the simple
or triple *Kyrie eleison* without anything else added. 37

As a beginning to the litany, too, the universal rule is the triple
or simple *Kyrie eleison*, by itself or followed by the *Christe eleison*
an equal number of times.38 Our current form: *Kyrie eleison,
Christe eleison, Kyrie eleison* is a rare exception in the older texts of
the litany.39

From this we conclude, that this structure of the *Kyrie* invocation was first fashioned in connexion with its Trinitarian significance, which appeared in the 9th century and slowly spread
everywhere,40 because people had forgotten that from time immemorial the word *Kyrie* in the litany had meant *Christ*,41 and
they began to be anxious about giving separate honour to the
three Divine Persons. The same development led to the three
Divine Persons being named at the beginning of the litany.42 And
this is a late repercussion of that disturbance which the vindication
of Christological and Trinitarian dogma against Teutonic Arianism had created in the Gallo-Spanish sphere.43 In St. Benedict's
time, such a way of regarding the threefold invocation was still
centuries away. On the other hand it is obvious, that the accepted

35. On the simple alternation of *Kyrie eleison* and *Christe eleison* cf.—as early as the
4th century—Victorinus Afer, *Hymn.* II (PL 8, 1142). Cf. also above.
36. The latter in the litany from Regensburg (9th century) ed. Coens (*Anal. Boll.* 1936)
20.
37. The threefold *Kyrie*, for example, in the Sacramentary of Gellone, written about
780: Martène I, 1, 18, *Ordo VI* (I, 189). Likewise in the *Ordo* of St. Amand of the same
period: Andrieu, *Les Ordines* III, 249.
38. In the *Consuetudines Cluniacensis* of the monk Ulrich, written about 1080 (I, 5;
PL 149, 650), the litany begins *Kyrie eleison, Christe eleison, Christe audi nos.*
39. It is found (amongst more than 40 litany texts showing a beginning) in a Cologne
litany of the beginning of the 9th century (*Anal. Boll.* 1936, 11; in the Freiburg
Pontificale (mid 9th century): Metzger 68; in the Sacramentary of St. Denis (mid 9th
century): L. Delisle, *Memoire sur d'anciens sacramentaires,* Paris 1886, 360; in a litany from
Benevant from the 12th century, in F. Cabiol, *Litanies:* DACL IX, 1556.
40. Jungmann, *Missarum Sollemnia* I, 439 seq., cf. ibid. 106.
41. It is significant that Amalar, *Liber officialis* IV, 2, 18 (Hanssens II, 411), shows
hesitation in interpreting the said three-fold style of the invocation in a Trinitarian sense.
He would like to apply the first invocation to the Trinity, thinking that that is why it is
said thrice: *ac ideo merito ter dicimus Kyrie eleison;* but he adds: *sine semel propter unam
substantiam.* For the second and third invocations he preserves the reference to Christ.
For the *Kyrie* of the Mass he shifts to the Trinitarian interpretation in the third edition of
the *Liber officialis* (after 831) III, 6, 2 (Hanssens II, 283; cf. 548 seq.).
42. Invocations beginning *Pater de coelis Deus* etc., not found before 11th century.
Martène I, 4, *Ordo XII* (I, 571).
43. Cf. above 1 seq.

188 PASTORAL LITURGY

form can and should be thought of as a threefold invocation of Christ, as, in a sense, an anticipation of the *per Christum* of the ending of the collect.

At first, the *Kyrie* had been put in front of the *Pater noster* because the latter still took the place of a collect. Thus it had a function like that of the genuflexion—as we showed earlier. It was a humble, supplicating gesture of the community, preparatory to the priest's prayer. It comes as no surprise, therefore, when the parallel with genuflexion shows itself in other ways. In the Apostolic Constitutions one kneels before the *oration*, saying the *Kyrie* as response to the deacon's litany of petitions. In the Roman liturgy, thereafter, both elements persist, but separately. The genuine Roman form which was first used in the liturgy consisted of kneeling down at the *Flectamus genua*—signal, and praying a while in silence before the *oration*. The *litania* with *Kyrie*—invocation must not have been introduced until later from the East— as the language suggests—and its use was limited to specified occasions. But both *Kyrie* and genuflexion or even kneeling appear again, now in a new relationship.

We hear about an important rite of this sort[44] in a letter dated 774 which Pope Hadrian sent to Charlemagne congratulating him on his victory over the Saxons, and assuring him of the prayers of the Romans. It is said that since the day the king left Rome (after his visit during the siege of Pavia early in 774), priest and monks and the people of the titular churches and in the poor-houses have never ceased to pray for the King day by day and hour by hour, crying out to God with loud voice in the *Kyrie eleison*, 300 times repeated, and entreating God's mercy for him on bended knee (*flexis genibus*).[45] The *Kyrie* is also associated with kneeling and it

44. In an appendix to the first Roman *Ordo*, which fixes the services on the weekdays of Lent, there is the note: *Nam sabbato tempore Adriani institutem est, ut flecteretur pro Carolo rege, antea vero non fuit consuetudo*; Andrieu, *Les Ordines Romani* III, 260 seq. Here too, the reference could be to a specially appropriate rite, as I have assumed in Zk Th 73 (1951) 90. In any case, the *flecteretur* can scarcely be retained on grounds of textual criticism. V. J. A. Jungmann, *Flectere per Carolo rege: Mélanges en l'honneur de Msgr.* M. Andrieu, Strassburg 1956, 219-228.

45. MG *Epp. Merowing. et Carolini aevi* I, 570; *cotidie momentaneis etiam atque sedulis horis omnes nostri sacerdotes sen etiam religiosi Dei famuli, monachi, per universa nostra monasteria simulque et reliquus populus tam per titulos quam per diaconos trecentos 'Kyrie leyson' extensis vocibus pro vobis Deo nostro adclamandum non cessant flexisque genibus eundem misericordissimum dominum Deum nostrum exorantes . . .*

shows that same tendency to multiplication, which affected genuflexion—as we have already proved.46

We first find the *Kyrie eleison* being repeated a considerable
number of times in the Eastern Church. The Byzantine liturgy has
in several places a twelve-fold and even a forty-fold *Kyrie eleison*.47
In the liturgy of the west-Syrian Jacobites, *Vespers* on week-days
during penitential seasons was ended with the *Kyrie* repeated 60
times.48 This usage went back a very long way in the East. When
the imperial capital of Constantinople was dedicated in 328, the
priest, standing before the statue of the emperor, recited a prayer
in litany form and all present joined in the κύριε ἐλέησον 100
times.49 And, as we have seen, the account of the Hours of prayer
practised by the monks of Sinai in the 6th century tells of a 300-
fold *Kyrie*.

It is not astonishing that after a long period of constant influx
from the East, in the course of which a series of orientals occupied
the Papal chair itself, many eastern fashions appeared in the
Roman liturgy in the 8th century, and that one of these should be
the 300-fold *Kyrie*. Nor is this the only place where this can be
indicated in the West. As well as speaking of moderate repetition,50 an account of the procession in Rome on the eve of the
Feast of the Assumption in the time of Otto III (d. 1002) tells us
how a statue was set up on the steps of St. Mary Minor and how
all of the people, *omnis chorus virorum ac mulierum* repeated their
rhythmic cry on bended knee—300 times. *Genibus humiliter ante
eam (iconem) flexis, pugnis etiam pectora caedentes, una voce per
numerum dicunt centies Kyrie eleison, centies Christe eleison, item
centies Kyrie eleison.*51 The parallel with genuflexion also runs to
the 300 times, even if in this case the result clearly is not arrived at
through the number of the psalms.

<hr/>

46. Above p. 175.
47. V. the enumeration in Fr. J. Dolger, *Sol salutis*², Munster 1925, 64 n. 2.
48. A. Baumstark, *Festbrevier und Kirchenjahr der syrischen Jakobiten*, Paderborn 1910, 218.
49. Following the account of the παραστάσεις σύντομα χρονικαί (8th century) in Dölger 70, where light is thrown on the ancient belief that 100 is a lucky number.
50. As in the Rule of St. Aurelian, according to which, in every Hour, at the beginning after the psalms, and at the end there was a three-fold *Kyrie*; and at the end of the Morning Hour, a twelve-fold *Kyrie*. Cf. Blume, *Der Cursus s. Benedicti*, Leipzig, 1908, 40. 42.
51. J. Mabillon, *Museum Italicum* II, p. XXIV seq. (=PL 87, 868).

From this time on, a multiple *Kyrie* becomes, in the main, accepted usage in the Roman liturgy, in the Mass in fact. There is no mention, however, of a fixed number. The triple *Kyrie* at the beginning of the *preces* is but the stylized form of the multiple invocation. From this at least we learn the proper way to say it: not with the choir answering the precentor each time, but taken up by the whole choir, the precentor merely announcing it—a rule seldom followed today.

The above examples already show traces of the *Kyrie eleison* possibly being regarded as a formal penitential rite. The parallel genuflexions would fit in with this idea. We could quote can. 20 of the Council of Nicea (325) which excluded genuflexion on Sundays and during Pentecost.52 When in Rome in 831, Amalar asserted that in Rome the *Kyrie eleison* followed by the collect was recited in the canonical Office on Sundays too, whereas in other places—his Frankish homeland obviously—only the collect was said. He then gives a plain reason for this; As we omit genuflexion while we think of our resurrection, so on those nights we omit the *preces flebiles* which is associated with genuflexion.53 The practice seems, nevertheless, to have been still new to some extent in the land of the Franks at that time; for the monastic reform decrees which we have already mentioned have to stress that the *Kyrie eleison* should always be said kneeling on both knees, except in refectory.54 On the other hand we have evidence of a similar but perhaps independent tradition in a document of the Mozarabic liturgy which, in the 10th century, notes at Lauds of the Easter festival, that throughout the whole Pentecostal cycle the *Kyrie* should be ommitted.55 Neither concerning the Roman nor any other liturgy has anyone ever dared to use the same argument concerning the *Kyrie* of the Mass for Sundays or feast-days. In the monastic ritual it has been preserved in the Breviary for everyday and at all the Hours. In the Roman Breviary this is the case at least in the *Officum capituli* of Prime: before the *oration* at Prime and Compline on ordinary Sundays and simple feast-days, it first

52. Mansi II, 677.
53. Amalar, *Liber officialis* IV, 7, 28 seq. (Hanssens II, 438).
54. Albers, *Consuetidines monasticae* III, 98; cf. 96 seq.
55. M. Férotin, *Le Liber mozarabicus sacramentorum*, Paris, 1912, 736.

became eliminated only with the rubrical reform of 1955, which
showed little understanding of the *preces*.

5. *The Lord's Prayer in the Roman Breviary*

In the Roman liturgy as in all others, the Lord's Prayer has
always appeared in the Mass in all its dignity and importance. In
the canonical Office, too, down the years until 1955 it has appeared
and been richly employed, but in this setting has never carried the
same weight. This was not always so.

In every Hour, as we know, St. Benedict in his Rule (c. 13),
made the Lord's Prayer serve as a collect;[1] and in doing this he
does not speak as though he wanted to introduce something new.
At the close of Lauds, and Vespers he has it said aloud in full, in
the rest of the Hours corresponding to the Arkan-discipline,[2] the
last phrase is audible. This rule is observed to this day in the
monastic office. The Synod of Gerona, too, decreed: *ut omnibus
diebus post Matutinas et Vespertinas oratio dominica a sacerdote proferatur.*[3] A similar usage must have been kept in Rome and must
have lasted there for a long time. In the 12th century we are still
hearing that in the Lateran Basilica the customary ending of an
Hour was the Lord's Prayer, prefaced by the nine-fold *Kyrie*, and
said by all in a bowed position, silently, until the last phrase: *Et
ne nos*, which was said aloud by the hebdomadary who was
answered aloud by the choir—on Easter Sunday just the same as
on week-days.[4] But there were occasions on which a special
oration was added. This happened when the Pope or one of the
seven cardinals—bishops was present, and this person said the
collect.[5]

The same sort of thing can be deduced for the intervening
period, from what we read in Amalar. According to him, each

1. Cf. p. 181.—On what follows v. Callewaert, *Sacris erudiri*, Steenbrugge 1940,
84–88.
2. Callewaert 86.
3. c. 10 (Mansi VIII, 550). The rule is taken up later in the *Decretum Gratiani, De cons.
dist.* 5 (Friedberg I, 1415). Cf. the decree of the 4th Council of Toledo (633) can. 10
(Mansi X, 621): no cleric was permitted to omit this prayer *aut in publico aut in privato
officio.* An example from 11th century Spain is adduced above.
4. *Ordo off. Eccl. Lateranensis* ed. Fischer p. 1; cf. 46. 48. 77.
5. Ibid. 1 seq. A corroborating account from the same period in John the deacon, *Liber
de eccl. Lateran. c.* 7 (PL 78, 1385 A).

Hour was concluded with the *Pater noster* and—although not invariably—a special collect. Indeed, he says of the *oration* that with
various Hours it follows *omni tempore*, but he explains his expression at once: *id est paschali, pentecostes, dominicis diebus et festis.*6
Here, then, the special concluding *oration* was a privilege of the
solemn Office for feast-days: it was missed on ordinary weekdays.7

What we deduce from Amalar is fully attested by explicit
directions from a few decades later in the Freiburg *Pontificale*. In a
section devoted to the concluding prayers of the Hours, this makes
a distinction between ordinary days (*privatis diebus*) and feast-days
(*diebus festis*). On the former, the Lord's Prayer at the various
Hours is followed by a number of versicles and then the psalm
Miserere: but on feast-days, we are told: *post histos versiculos
dicatur versum: Domine exaudi orationem meam, deinde collecta,* and
then as an example, no doubt, the concluding prayer of Prime is
quoted: *Oremus, Dirigene dignare.*8

What we learn here about the versicles which are attached to
the *Pater noster* is also instructive. Their original function was that
of a kind of seal to the mighty words of the Lord's Prayer. Even
today we are still accustomed very often to add some sort of
prayer—phrase to a concluding *oration*—a *Benedicamus Domino* or
Divinum auxilium or *Fidelium animae*. Amalar, too, gives evidence
of such versicles being joined to the Lord's Prayer. In part, these
versicles which he mentions, coincide with those of the *Pontificale*.
(He quotes only four verbatim. The *Pontificale* has ten.) Both
contain the versicles, *Ego dixi Domine miserere* and *Convertere
Domine usquequo*. The versicle, *Domine salvum fac regem,* corresponds to Amalar's relevant observation.9 Thus, if the *Pater noster*
was followed by an increasing number of versicles, which must
have been felt to be a picking up once more of the preceding
Kyrie invocation, and if now the collect more regularly succeeded
this, the danger obviously became greater that the Lord's Prayer,
especially if not said aloud in its entirety, would appear more and

6. Amalar, Liber officialis IV, 4, 10 (Hanssens II, 425).
7. Thus in P. Batifiol, *Histoire du Breviaire Roman*³, Paris 1911, 114 n. 1.
8. M. J. Melzger, *Zwei karolingische Pontifikalien vom Oberrhein,* Freiburg 1914, 64.
9. Melzger, loc. cit.; Amalar, *Liber off.* IV. 4, 6-8 (Hanssens II, 424 seq.). From a later
period v. examples in E. Martene, *De aut. Monachorum ritibus* I, 3, 15 (De aut. Eccl. rit.
IV, Antwerp 1738, 40 seq.).

more as part of the series of versicles and would eventually disappear along with them from the regular Office.

The *Pater noster* thus lost its former position in the process of enrichment and making more solemn, the worship of God, as appears in various other places. Just as, until the rubrical reform of 1955, we had become so accustomed to the normal daily Matins having three Nocturns, that we were unaware of the fact that it was a Sunday form we were using, which had gradually slipped into every-day use:10 so the conclusion of the Hours as on Sundays and feast-days, had become the daily form. But the process had gone a step farther with the *Pater noster*. In our Office, there would no longer have been any day or Hour which stuck to the old week-day order—but for one exception: that is the ending of the psalmody section of the Nocturn, of all three Nocturns indeed. In this, the officiating cleric and the choir all together say the Lord's Prayer only. They say this standing and with all the formality of a concluding prayer, strongly enunciating the first and last phrases—as St. Benedict had wanted it done at the conclusion of the customary Hours.11

The result indicated, was reached only in many stages. In the first stage we find the *Pater noster* still there, but on certain days another *oration* follows the attached versicle, at first during the chief Hours of Lauds and Vespers. The formula used is at first one of these formulae, a whole collection of which are contained in the older sacramentaries.12 After 1000 A.D. the collect of the Mass for the day began gradually to be preferred. 13 This stage, which we have just seen in Amalar, has been met earlier in the liturgy of penance.14 also dating from the 8th century onwards. This is the phase, which has persisted to this day in the monastic Office: every Hour has preserved, even on Sundays and feast-days, *Kyrie eleison, Christe eleison, Kyrie eleison*, at the end. There follows them, after the greeting,15 the appropriate oration. Something very similar

10. Cf. above p.118.
11. Only the first word, *Pater* was said softly in those days; Callewaert 86 n. 101.
12. Cf. e.g. in the *Sacramentarium Gregorianum* ed. Lietzmann n. 203 seq. under the title *Orationes matutinales* or *Orationes vespertinales seu matutinales*.
13. Thus already in two Collectars from the 11th century edited by E. S. Dewick and W. H. Frere, *The Leofric Collectar* (IBS 45. 56), London 1914-21.
14. Above p. 183-4.
15. The versicles which were formerly attached to the *Pater noster* have been deleted in the revision of 1608 and 1612. Callewaert 84 n. 97.

happens today in the formal grace at meals. Following the *Pater noster*, which is preceded by the *Kyrie*, comes the *oration: Oremus, Benedic Domine,*16 and the same sort of thing happens on other occasions for which the *Rituale* supplies the rules.

Thus the notion is validated, that the sequence of prayer: *Kyrie —Pater noster*—versicle, is nothing but a form of *preces* leading up to the *oration*. The way was already being prepared for this conception in Amalar's time when, it would seem, not only the *Kyrie* with its succeeding versicles, but also the intervening *Pater noster* was said kneeling.17 As development proceeds, however, the feeling is revealed that an Office designed for a feast-day will not tolerate *preces*. Even Amalar knew of churches which as was the— custom in Rome—abandoned these, *preces flebiles praesentis vitae quas solemus cum genuflexione promere,*18 elsewhere, at least in Vespers for Sunday. He notes the same thing for the Easter octave.19

With Durandus (d. 1296) the principle has gone even farther. Here we meet the *oration* again in all of the Hours: the *preces*, too is a regular component of an Hour, but rather of days which are not feast-days, of the majority, that is—the *dies profesti*.20 When Durandus lists the normal contents of an Hour, he mentions as the last two in a set of seven or eight: *preces* and *oratio*.21 And at the same time it is clear that the *Preces* including the *Pater noster* was said kneeling.22 It would be logical, therefore, if both of these together were to disappear on Sundays and feast-days.23 And yet, Durandus knows of churches where the *Pater noster* is still said at every Office, and moreover, as he expressly mentions, said standing.24 Clearly, we see the ancient regard for the Lord's Prayer still alive here.

A stage farther reached in the development of the Office as the new Franciscan Order practised it in connexion with the *Officium*

16. The above exposition of the historical context should bring out the difficulty to which H. Chirat, *La Maison-Dieu* n. 20 (1949, IV) 31 n. 34, has referred.
17. Amalar, *Liber off.* IV, 2, 18 seq.; 3, 3; 4, 10 (Hanssens 410 seq.—415 seq.).—Cf. above.
18. Ibid. IV, 7, 28 (Hanssens II, 438).
19. Ibid. IV, 23, 24 (Hanssens II, 479).
20. Durandus, *Rationale div. off.* V, 5, 14 seq.; V, 9, 9.
21. Ibid. V, 10, 8.
22. Ibid. V, 14 seq.; V, 6, 2.
23. Ibid. V, 5, 16.
24. Ibid. V, 5, 17.

secondum consuetudinem Curiae Romanae in the 13th century. The *preces* and with it, the *Pater noster* has disappeared from all feast-days, even in those having but three lessons. Only in Prime and Compline do they appear, and here, only on days with nine lessons, apparently those feasts which correspond to our Doubles, like the Feast of St. Jerome on September 30th.[25] They are present too, and in an extensive form, on simple week-days of a non-festive kind, without these having to be—as today they must be—days of penitence and fasting.[26]

Another move was completed with the Breviary of Pius V (1568). At Prime and Compline the *preces* is now allowed only on semi-doubles, and still appears in all of the Hours only during Advent, Lent, on Ember days and vigils. Even this meagre residue almost all fell victim to the reform of 1955; for the *preces* is only kept now in the ferial Office of Lauds and Vespers in Advent, Lent and on Ember days.[27] The *Pater noster* introduced by *Kyrie* is returned, apart from this, for occasions like grace at meals,[28] burial services etc., where the *Pater noster* is still felt to be the solid core of the various prayer structures.

In this gradual disappearance of the *Pater noster* from the final act of the canonical Hours we have a typical case of that law of suppression to which our attention has been drawn by P. Erhard Drinkwelder O.S.B.[29] A large A has a small b attached to it; this grows into B; AB then turns into a B; and in the case before us now, not even B remains in the end. Here it is indeed, the Lord's Prayer, which has fallen victim to such a process.

25. P. A. Le Caron, *L'office divin chez les Freres Mineurs au* XIII *siecle*, Paris 1928, 10 seq., 16 seq. 40.
26. Le Caron, 20 seq. 29, 30 seq., 34.
27. *Acta Ap. Sed.* 47 (1955) 223. In this the tone was set not by a glimpse into the history of a worthier arrangement, but by the attempt to accommodate the clergy who were clamouring for abbreviation. Cf. the opinions collected before the reform by A. Bugnini: *Eph. liturg.* 63 (1949) 179. Balth. Fischer had already referred to the under-valuing of the *Presces* discussed here in *Das Anliegen des Volkes im Kirchlichen Stundengebet: Brevierstudien*, Trier 1958, 62 seq.
28.   On the whole, the oldest versions of our formal grace at meals do not contain the *Pater noster*; v. the 8th century *Ordo convivi* (Andrieu, *Les Ordinales* III, 218-221), the 9th century Freiburg Pontificale (ed. Metzger 62). And in the *Praeparatio ad Missam* in the *Gratiarum actio post Missam* in the old text the *Kyrie eleison* along with the *Pater noster* was tucked in before the collects only after the 11th century. V. Jungmann, *Missarum Sollemnia* I, 356; II, 572.
29.   E. Drinkwelder, *Die Grundfunktion der Gesänge im Amt: Heiliger Dienst* 2 (Salzburg) 143 seq.

By contrast, the Lord's Prayer has fared better in the Eastern
Church with the exception of the Armenian liturgy, it is common
property as part of the ending to all of the Hours, preceded
solemnly by the *Trishagion*.30 And even those rare vestiges, preserved in the Roman liturgy and showing the ancient position of
the Lord's Prayer in the *preces*, reveal the great esteem in which it
was held.31 The *Kyrie eleison* always forms the preamble, the prelude to it, just as, elsewhere since the 4th century, the *Kyrie* or
litany had provided the prelude to the *oration*—in the Mass, for
example. Finally we may be permitted to recognize a parallel to
the preamble to the *Pater noster* as used in the Mass. Here the
Lord's command is appealed to in justification of the boldness
(παρρησία cf. *Eph.* 312) with which we presume to turn to God
as our Father: so in the former place, the Lord Himself is invoked
because it is He alone who can lead us to the Father.

Such a preparation for the Lord's Prayer is balanced by the
appearance in other places of its echo. The versicles attached to it
in older canonical prayer were already an example of such accre-
tion, which seemed to develop according to a kind of law. Indeed,
the attached collect itself was probably felt at first to be a kind of
echo of the Lord's Prayer; but in the end this echo itself became
the dominant sound.

The oldest form of this echo of the Our Father is the Doxology.
At the end this takes up once again the theme of the first sentence
—the praise of God: 'For thine is the kingdom and the glory and
the power, world without end.'32 Most of the Eastern liturgies
end the Lord's Prayer of the Mass with a doxology like this.33 The
Western liturgies do not have the doxology, but in the *embolismus*
they retain the idea of a final petition. In the Gallican liturgy this
is contained in a form which almost always changes with the rite
of the Mass. The basic text can be put roughly thus: *Libera nos a*

---

30. For Vespers first of all, v. the summary by A. Raes, *Introductio in liturgiam orientalem*,
Rome 1947, 204 seq. In the Byzantine rite at least the Lord's Prayer appears in the Little
Hours in the same fashion, after the 'Ὁμολόγιον τὸ μέγα.
31. In fact, J. Brinktrine describes this *Pater noster* of the *Preces* as the 'climax of the Hour'.
Das römische Brevier, Paderborn 1932, 64.
32. Thus already as interpolation in Scripture mss. of Mt. 6, 13. Cf. *Didache* c. 8.
33. Jungmann, *Missarum Sollemnia* II, 354 n. 49.

malo, omnipotens Deus, custodi nos in bono nobis aeterna concede.34 The Roman form never changes: *Libera nos quaesumus Domine* . . . ending also with the *Per Dominum nostrum*, which is only partly true of the Gallican texts. This matches the Eastern liturgies which sometimes, in the Mass, take up first one of the concluding petitions, expand it, and then add the Doxology.

Over and above this, there is another case extant in the vestiges of the old adaptations of the Our Father in the canonical Offices, which shows an echoing of the prayer in the sense already described. The request for a blessing which follows the Our Father in the various Nocturns must be understood in this sense; and it is, in fact, described as *absolutio*, i.e. as a concluding formula.35 Certainly, these formulae were not at first just designed as conclusions for the *Pater noster*—at least not in Rome, where, according to Amalar's evidence,36 there was no *Pater noster* attached to the Nocturns, but only a 'capitulum', of which he gives an example: *Intercedente beato principe apostolorum Petre salvet et custodiat nos Dominus*. At almost the very same time, however—about the middle of the 9th century—the Freiburg *Pontificale* supplies ten formulae of the same sort under the title: *Versus ad nocturnas post orationem dominicam*.37 In any case, at least in the Roman-Frankish liturgy these formulae actually followed the *Pater noster*. All speak of the intercession of saints who are able to mediate God's help to us. In their own way they correspond to the *embolismus* of the Roman Mass which asks to be delivered from all evils *per Dominum nostrum Jesum Christum*—a style of prayer to which men had to some extent become unaccustomed as a result of the sharp reaction against the Arian misrepresentation of

34. Cf. *Missale Gothicum* ed. Bannister (HBS 52, 2. 6 etc.). In Rituales of the passing Middle Ages this prayer is found modified to become a formula of blessing attached to the *Pater noster* and other formulae in the administration of the Anointing of the Sick: *Liberet te ab omni malo, conservet te in omni opere bono et perducat te . . . ad gloriam sempiternam*; v. J. A. Jungmann, *Die lateinische Bussriten*, Innsbruck 1932, 207 seq.
35. The recension with 'absolution' presented by Eisenhofer, *Handbuch* II, 511, rests exclusively on the text of the third formula in use today *Avinculis . . .* and has already been rejected by J. Grancolas, *Commentarius historicus in Romanum Breviarum*, Antwerp 1734, 94. Cf. also the expression *ad absolutionem Capituli* in the rubric at the end of Prime. Baumer-Biron I, 387 cites (presumably following Tommasi-Vezzosi IV, 573—though not to be found there—) a superscription (apparently from the 12th century): *benedictiones ante lectionem post absolutos nocturnos*.
36. Amalar, *De ordine antiphonarii*, prol. 6 (Hanssens III, 14).
37. Metzger 62.

Christ's mediation, preferring to put in its place the intercession of the saints. This sort of thing still appears in the *absolutio* in the *officium sanctae Mariae in sabbato: Precibus et meritas beatae Mariae semper virginis*—already to be found in the Freiburg *Pontificale* but with a different ending. Of the remaining three formulae commonly used in the Office, the first and second are prayers invoking Christ (*Exaude Domine Jesu Christe; Ipsius pietas*) i.e. a definite counterpart after the Lord's Prayer to the *Kyrie eleison* before it. Apart from this, many of the formulae in the old sources cannot be distinguished from the blessing formulae which have been handed down along with them, and with which the following lesson was begun, after the reader's *Jube domne benedicere*.38

If only a slight residue remains in our canonical prayer of the old traditional use of the *Pater noster*, at the same time this has transferred itself to other places of the same canonical prayer and re-appeared afresh, if only, indeed, as a kind of preface at the beginning of the Hours and as a coda at their ends. In this use we see an importation from the private prayers of the faithful. Here we find the Lord's Prayer first of all in connexion with the Apostles' Creed. Since the days of St. Augustine this very practice had been imposed upon all the faithful at baptism when they were instructed that they should begin and end every day by reciting the Creed and the Lord's Prayer. In the same way we find the two sacred formulae attached to the monastic Office in the same position. St. Benedict of Aniane (d. 821) taught his disciples to say them daily before Matins and before Prime (of old they rose from bed twice), and again in the evening after Compline.39 It is this usage which we find closely connected with the Breviary from that time onwards.40

The regulation that the *Pater noster* be said before and after each Hour, with the *Ave* attached before the hour as well, is of much later date. This addition to the Hours in this precise form can first be traced to shortly before the appearance of the Breviary of 1568.

38. On formulae of this kind since the 10th century v. Bäumer-Biron I, 386 seq. In the collection of *Benedictiones lectionum officii* from Montserrat about 1500, edited by A. M. Olivar: *Eph. liturg.* 63 (1949) 47-56, the list is headed by some formulae designated *deprecatio*, which are to be regarded as absolutions (45 seq.).
39. Vita s. *Benedicti Anianensis* c. 52 (PL 103, 379).
40. Cf. Jungmann, *Gewordene Liturgie* 165-172 (= *Zeitschr. f. Aszese u. Mystik* 1934, 259-265): *Pater noster und Credo im Breviergebet eine altchristliche Tauferinnerung*.

The Our Father was certainly ordered to be said at the end of the
Hours by the canonist Huguccio (d. 1210).41 This practice appears
clearly related to the following modification in the custom of
prayer. Outside the canonical Hours of prayer the material of
vocal prayer was no longer found in the Old Testament psalms,
but in the great and simple prayer texts of the New Testament,
the Our Father which now became repeated—one Our Father to
each psalm42—and the *Ave Maria* which then began more and
more to take over this function, while on the other hand it became
bound up with the Our Father in an external and almost in-
destructible unity, because of the easy way in which the texts
could be run together.43

It was right, therefore, that the reform of 1955 should clear up
this flooded land44 which existed both before and after the various
hours, even if in the process *Pater noster* and *Credo* both vanished
from the end of the daily Office.45 This was the fruit of a new
appraisal of the value and dignity of the Lord's Prayer. The same
return to the former veneration of the chief prayer of the Christian
life is taking place outside the Office as well. The all-German
Rituale, approved in Rome in 1950, gives the Our Father back its
place before the *Ecce Agnus Dei* as Communion prayer in the
order for Communion of the sick. It is introduced by the simple

41. More details of this circumstance, now obliterated, thanks to the reform of 1955, in
the first publication of contemporary studies: Zk Th 73 (1951) 353 seq.
42. Ibid. 354 seq. Cf. also above p. 177 seq.
43. On attempts at a deep justification of the connexion between the two formulae
v. Zk Th 73 (1957) 356 seq. In many places we can sense that the consecutive repetition of
the formula is a substitute for another more appropriate prayer-text (especially where the
repetition occurs without that arrangement and enrichment such as it has in, for example,
the Rosary). Cf. above 9. 177. We have an early example in the *Consuetudines of Farfa*
(11th century) according to which one was supposed to pray 50 psalms for deceased
relatives of a monk—or at least the *Miserere* psalm 50 times, or the *Pater noster* the same
number of times, but, *qui tam insciolus est*—; Br. Albers, *Consuetudines monasticae* I,
Stuttgart 1900, 200. An example from today: on the balustrade which surrounds the
Confession above the tomb of St. Peter there were—a few years ago anyway—little
tablets containing specially indulgenced prayers; but the condition was attached that the
faithful, if need be, could substitute for them ten *Paters* and ten *Aves, si illas legere nesciverint
vel nequirenint*. In other cases no attention has been paid to this substitutional nature of the
repetitive use of the basic prayers, e.g., in the new arrangements for the *Totus-quoties*-
indulgence in the decree of the Penitentiary of 10:VII:1924: *Acta Ap. Sed.* 16 (1924) 347,
where, in place of the former unspecified prayer, six *Paters, Ave* and *Glorias* are now
universally prescribed.
44. *Decretum generale de Rubricis ad simplicionem formam redigendis: Acta Ap. Sed.* 47 (1955,
218-224) 222.
45. As the commentary of A. Bugini—J. Bellocchio, *De Rubricis ad simpliciorum formam
redigendis*, Rome 1955, p. 42 seq., shows, this tradition was not heeded on this point.

words: 'Let us pray, dear brethren, as the Lord taught us to pray'. And it is rounded off with a kind of *embolismus*, serving as an echo and having at the same time a bearing on the situation: 'We beseech thee, O Lord, graciously to deliver thy servant from all evil and to strengthen him with the Bread of Life, the Body of our Lord Jesus Christ, who liveth and reigneth with thee for ever and ever'.[46] The very same application of the Lord's Prayer occurs in the *Ordo Sabbati Sancti*, decreed on 9.2.1951 as the conclusion to the ceremony of renewal of Baptismal vows,[47] with the only difference that here the Lord's Prayer serves also the purpose of a concluding collect—in the spirit of the most ancient tradition: *Nunc autem una simul Deum precemur, sicut Dominus noster Jesus Christus orare nos docuit: Pater . . . Et Deus omnipotens, Pater Domini nostri Jesu Christi, qui nos regeneravit ex aqua et Spiritu Sancto quique nobis dedit remissionem omnium peccatorum, ipse nos custodiat gratia sua in eodem Christo Jesu Domino nostro in vitam aeternam.* The most recent invitation to the laity to join with the priest on Good Friday and in the *Missa lecta* in saying the Lord's Prayer as a Communion prayer, is but a farther step along the same road.

4. *Why was Cardinal Quinonez' Reformed Breviary a Failure?*

As the middle ages drew to a close, the need for a reform of the Breviary began to be felt in many places. Of all the attempts at reform arising from humanist motives or from a desire to clean up the chaotic, late medieval, rank growth, the most significant was that of Cardinal Francis Quiñonez, undertaken at the behest of Pope Clement VII. Assisted by his chaplains, he began in 1529 and laid the completed work before the Pope in 1534.

In 1535 it appeared, accompanied by a Brief of Paul III, and with the title: *Breviarium Romanum ex sacra potissimum Scriptura et*

46. *Collectio Rituum ad instar appendicis Ritualis Romani pro omnibus Germaniae diocesibus,* Regensburg 1950, 34.
47. *Acta Ap. Sed.* 43 (1951) 136.

probatis Sanctorum historiis collectum et concinnatum.[1] The eagerness with which men were looking for such a revision of the Breviary, is revealed by the fact that the Cardinal's work, called the 'Cross Breviary' after his titular church of S. Cruce, was printed eleven times within a year in various places (Rome, Venice, Paris, Lyon, Antwerp, Cologne).

At the same time it met with severe opposition in the Sorbonne at Paris. Thereupon the Cardinal put out a second edition in the following year, 1536. This had some alterations and again it was introduced by a Papal Brief, which gave permission to all secular priests to use this Breviary if they so wished. The most important changes were that the antiphons, completely left out in the first edition, were re-introduced in some places. The second edition[2] was received with the same enthusiasm, and in the 32 years which elapsed before it was proscribed, on the publication of the Breviary of Pius V, it was printed more than a hundred times.[3] But antagonistic voices were not lacking who in the end decided the fate of the work.

What was new in this Breviary? And what were the objections raised against the revisions?

The innovation consisted in part in the elimination of certain recent accretions, in part in a series of measures which led on to a far-reaching reorganization of the Office. The removal of the accretions—attached to the Office mainly through the fervour of the Cluniac monks—was greeted almost universally as an obvious thing to be done. The Breviary of Pius V did not re-introduce them. It was a question of the daily obligatory observance (apart from feast-days) of the Office of the Dead, the Little Office of our Lady, the Penitential Psalms and the Psalms of Degrees. It was only the Marian Office which some critics missed—especially those in the Sorbonne—who took the view that the hitherto

1. In 1888 a reprint of the first edition of this Breviary was brought out by J. Wickham Legg at the Cambridge University Press.
2. It has been reprinted as Vol. 35 in the collection by the H. Bradshaw Society: the second recension of the Quignon Breviary, prepared and edited by J. Wickham Legg, I. text, London, 1908. This edition of the text was followed, as Vol. 42 of the same collection, by a commentary by the same editor: II. *Liturgical Introduction, with Life of Quignon, appendices, notes, and indices*, London 1912. The separate citations in the following exposition refer to this edition.
3. The list of editions made by J. W. Legg (I, p. XIII-XIX) contains 100 complete editions and three of the *Diurnale*.

accepted order of the Breviary should not be disturbed.4 The measures for reorganization aimed at a basic shortening of the Office. Over and above this, as the preface to the second edition put it, three chief advantages were to be sought: 1. More stress was to be laid on the Scriptures of the Old and New Testaments. 2. The wearisome and time-wasting conglomeration of diverse sections should be done away by having a simpler construction. 3. The stories of the lives of the saints should be better expressed.

Above all, while retaining the traditional Hours, abbreviation would be achieved by giving each of the Hours only three psalms, at Lauds, the last psalm being replaced by one of the traditional *Cantica*. In spite of abbreviation, whole psalms were used. In the previous arrangement (more or less as in the period between Pius V and Pius X) the psalms had stressed chiefly the *Commune Sanctorum* and so had been confined to a small number which were constantly repeated: now all 150 psalms were divided out between the Hours of the separate days of the week in a more or less arbitrary fashion, not even according to their Biblical sequence.5 Only on Friday and Sunday was any heed paid to the traditional theme appropriate to the day. The governing point of view seems in the main to have been that the longer psalms should be assigned to Matins. In all this it was the rule that no feast-day could interrupt the sequence of the psalms—not even Christmas.

In respect of the lessons, the new order went just as far in favouring the holy Scriptures. There were only three lessons after the three psalms in Matins of every Office, but these were much more extensive than in the previous Breviary. The first was taken from the Old Testament, the second, and often the third, from the New Testament. (In penitential seasons a homily from one of the Fathers, and on a saint's day the life of the saint might have to be read as one lesson.) Provision was made that the whole of the New Testament with the exception of a few passages from the Apocalypse would be read. From the Old Testament the entire books of Genesis and Kings were read. A selection was made of the rest. Copious use was made of the Wisdom Literature. In apportioning

4. J. W. Legg II, 108. 111. Also Dominicus Soto and John de Arze demanded the retention of the Marian Office; ibid. 132 seq. 143 seq.
5. In the new Gallican Breviary of Langres, 1731, which was based upon Quinonez, the Biblical sequence of the psalms was reintroduced; J. W. Legg II, 39.

the Old Testament through the Christian Year, Quiñonez stuck fairly closely to tradition: in Advent, the Prophets; from Septuagesima on, Genesis, interrupted on Passion Sunday and continued after Easter; in autumn, the Books of Kings.

The simplification of the structure was a bolder stroke. The cardinal's Breviary was designed for secular priests who would say it in private, not in choir.6 Quiñonez faced the consequences of this presupposition. He swept away practically all that had to do with a structure suited to prayer in choir. Most of the responsories, most of the antiphons, went, as did the *absolutio* after the *Pater noster* at Matins. And the *capitula* of the separate Hours, now little more than token readings, were likewise removed. Even the *preces* was sacrificed.

The three psalms (at Lauds, Vespers, and Compline still with the traditional New Testament canticle attached—*Benedictus, Magnificat, Nunc Dimittis*) were followed immediately by the *oration*, introduced however, by *Domine exaudi:* On the other hand, every day, except on feast-days, two *commemorationes* with antiphon, versicle and collect were added to the *oration* at Lauds and Vespers. These were then concluded with *Benedicamus Domino* and *Fidelium animae*. The *Pater* and the *Ave* are there at the beginning of every Hour, and then, as of old, (*Domine labia*) and *Deus in adiutorum*. The hymn, too, is retained; but it comes before the psalms, not only in the little Hours and at Matins, but also at Vespers and Compline. This usage is found also in the Milan liturgy. There is no hymn at Lauds, and this is taken along with Matins as a single Hour.7

The calendar, too, is essentially simplified. Before Pius V's time, the principle that the Breviary should be perfectly in line with the Missal, was unknown. In this Quiñonez was given a free hand which he used to good purpose. Octaves were severely cut down. In the first draft of 1535 they were confined to the highest feast-days and, moreover, they affected the daily Office but little. In the

6. This was indicated in the Brief of Paul III which was designed *omnibus et singulis clericis ac presbyteris duntaxat saecularibus*; J. W. Legg I, p. III. Quinonez always keeps in mind the case when two or three will be praying together; he gives appropriate directions for such a case at the *Confiteor*, which he appoints for the start of Matins, and at the Invitatory, which is said only at the beginning of the psalm, but which, in cases where there are several people, is to be repeated once immediately, and then again at the end of the psalm, by the rest of the worshippers. J. W. Legg I, 32 seq.
7. J. W. Legg I, 37.

second edition of 1536 they are slightly increased in number.8 The
saints who remain in, belonged predominately to early times. Very
few names from the Middle Ages appear—in the second edition
rather more than in the first.9 In the lessons belonging to these
saints' days, Quiñonez looked for elegance of style and, where
possible, historical reliability. Lives of Popes he took from the
humanist, Platina.

As can be seen, the new Breviary made an attack at several
levels. It contained solutions which even today no one would
want to defend. One of these is the unconditional preservation in
principle of the 150 psalms as a weekly performance which
allowed of no exception—not even if Corpus Christi or All Saints
or Christmas fell within the week.

Nor is there any doubt that the lectionary, which after Easter
Sunday could unconcernedly pick up the thread again with Gen.
25, 19 seq., was a bit rigid. There was a rooted objection, too, to
the idea that the psalms for Compline, instead of being chosen at
random, should be chosen from psalms which seemed suited to
the mood of evening prayer. And yet these failings could easily
have been made good without any denial of principle. They were
aesthetic errors of little weight.

The spread of this Breviary shows how widely and with what
enthusiasm it was received, first of all by those for whom it was
intended. It was designed for the clergy who were occupied in
pastoral work or in study. With certain reservations the famous
canonist, Martin de Azpilcueta—called Navarrus (d. 1586) commended it as suitable for this purpose.10 It is mentioned amongst
the Jesuits as the Breviary commonly (ordinarie) used.11 In 1546
St. Ignatius received from Paul III the general privilege for the
members of his order to use this Breviary.12 Peter Canisius—as he
tells St. Ignatius in a letter written from Ingoldstadt in 1550—

8. Cf. J. W. Legg II, 35.
9. Ibid. II, 33.
10. M. de Azpilcueta, Commentarius de oratione, horis canonicis atque aliis divinis officiis.
The remarks concerning the new Breviary which are scattered throughout this work
(c. 3. 10. 11. 18. 20.), are reprinted by Legg II, 122-130. In the edition of Azpilcueta before
me, Opp. omnia IV, Venice 1702, p. 22 seq. 86. 96. 151 seq. 214-217. As against the 1560
(or earlier) edition, this one, like that of 1597, quoted by Legg, contains additions in the
style of the Breviary of Pius V.
11. Responsorio P. Manaraei ad P. Lancicii postulata 23 (Monumenta Ignatiana IV, 1, Madrid
1904, 518); J. W. Legg II, 23 seq.
12. O. Braunsberger, B. Petri Canisii Epistolae et Acta (1896 seq.), I, 196 n. 2.

applied for permission for several clergy at the legation to use it;13 and in 1561 he was granted authority through General Lainez to permit its use.14 Francis Xavier, who used the old Breviary himself, applied from Lisbon for permission for six priests to use the new Breviary and for the authority for himself to grant this permission to his six fellow-travellers to India.15

Soon, however, the new Breviary was affecting a wider sphere than that of individual prayer. Permission to use it, at first obtainable only through the Papal seal, was soon obtainable from nuncios and legates, and finally, as the letter just quoted shows, more easily still. After this Spanish dioceses took up the new Breviary straight away or refashioned their own on the model of the Cross Breviary.16 In this way the new Breviary got into the choirs of the cathedrals.

Understandably, this evoked hostility to the scheme. The Spanish conciliar theologian, canonist in the dioceses of Palencia, John de Arze, who in 1557 at the Council of Trent had submitted a mighty memorandum entitled: *De novo Breviario Romano tollendo consultatio*,17 became the mouthpiece of the opposition. This memorandum pulls the new Breviary to pieces. In his capacity as *officium Consultoris* (138)—the author was an ambassador of Charles V—de Arze demanded the immediate withdrawal of the book by the same authority which had introduced it. Apart from Easter and Pentecost, according to the author, this basic pattern of three psalms has not only been condemned already by Gregory VII, but runs contrary to apostolic tradition (c. 1). The received arrangement of psalms and Nocturns must not be disturbed (c. 2). In this century of innovation especially, nothing should be altered (c. 3). In the new Breviary, veneration of the Mother of God and aid to the faithful departed has been unlawfully reduced (c. 4 seq). This Breviary is Bible-reading rather than prayer (c. 5). The Church has committed to her privileged

13. Ibid. I, 346.
14. Ibid. III, 70; cf. II, 702.—On the other hand, the use of the new Breviary was explicitly prohibited by the Emperor for a projected Imperially endowed canonry at Innsbruck, because the canons were to be obliged to attend in choir; ibid. II, 881.
15. G. Schurhammer—J. Wicki, *Epistolae s. Francisci Xaverii* I, Rome 1944, 68; cf. ibid. 143.—Legg II, 21.
16. Legg II, 72 seq.
17. It is edited by Legg II, 134-212; and also the notes p. 276-282. On John de Arze cf. the the statements of C. Gutierrez, *Espanoles en Trento*, Valladolid 1951, 574-581.

206 PASTORAL LITURGY

servants (*potioribus ministris*) the task of studying Scripture: to the *rudiores clerici* on the other hand, the Office of psalmody. The task of the latter is very different from the task of the former (*ab officio doctorum, interpretum, et magistrorum*). Random Bible-reading is harmful to the *idiota clericus, qui nihil interdum praeter latinam grammaticam novit*, to the *vulgus clericorum* (c. 6). In particular, it is worthless for them to read much in St. Paul's Epistles. The right sort of arrangement is to be found in the hitherto accepted Breviary (c. 7). The new Breviary leads to the decline of choir-prayer, and the youth of the day are at fault in this already. It encourages discontent, and annoys the people (c. 8).[18] Because its use will not be confined to those who are busy, but will be granted to all, it will encourage laziness and make men strangers to the Church's prayer (c. 9).

Rebellion against the Church's arrangement of the vigils and psalmody originates amongst the heretics, beginning with Vigilantius and ending with Luther (c. 10). Today it is attacking cathedral chapters and creeping into the Missal (c. 11).

According to de Arze, the traditional Office in its totality (three nocturns, number of the lessons and of the psalms etc.) is a thing of divine right. Biblical support was sought for the three Nocturns, from *Esdr* 9, 3, for example (in a Vulgate reading).[19] With Lauds they form the four night-watches of Scripture (c. 12). The antiphons were revealed to Ignatius of Antioch by angels; and the same sort of things hold of the rest of the order. Deviation from tradition has always been taboo in the Church (c. 14), and it must not be tolerated here either. The people will take offence if the clergy augment their income and diminish their service (c. 15). If there are faults to be removed from the accepted Breviary, they must be dealt with in another way (c. 16). The spirit of innovation must not be tolerated (c. 17).

18. At this point de Arze quotes the case of Saragossa, which had acquired a certain notoriety amongst the authors; he adverts to this again in c. 15: *Dissidium Caesaraugustanum inter clerum et populam occasione diminuti officii, quod vocant Tenebrarum, noverunt Hispani omnes, et quam infremuerit populus in clerum, et eo relicto confugerint omnes ad Monachos;* J. W. Legg II, 186; cf. 156. A reference also in Dominicus Soto, ibid. 131.

19. This has to do with a style of reading (*quater in die et quater in nocte*), which is noted in many mss. of the Vulgate after the 8th century; v. *Biblio sacra iuxta Latinam Vulgatam Versionem et Codicum fidem: Libri Ezrae, Tobiae, Judith* (Rome 1950) 115.

Then he goes on to discredit the alleged advantages of the new Breviary. He even refuses to recognize the improvement in the Lives of the Saints, censuring, among other things, as a bad blunder, the annotation to the reading for July 22, which observed that in St. Mary Magdalen we may perhaps be able to distinguish three separate women (c. 18). Finally, with a reminder of the judgement of God, the fathers of the council are implored to tear this evil up by the roots.

We can assume that the fathers of the council did not take every word of this *consultatio*—which should have been called, it has been said, a *declamatio*—as gospel truth. It must, nevertheless, have strongly influenced the mood of the council, and, indeed, the mood of the decisive elements in it; for in its earlier phase the council had shown itself inclined towards the cardinal's Breviary.20 The council itself did not in fact come to any ruling on the matter, but a canon which was to have rid the world of the Cross Breviary was already drafted in three forms.22 According to this, all innovations made in the last 50 years (first form: 30 years in second and third forms) were to be rescinded, unless the Holy See or a provincial council should decide otherwise. All priests who were attached to a particular church must continue to follow its Office. In the second and third versions the Breviary system having only three psalms and three lessons was attacked.

It is true that none of these proposals became law, but when the Roman Breviary was prescribed in 1568 by Pius V, their objects were achieved, and that, without the condition of possible modification by a provincial council. In the introductory Bull '*Quod a nobis*' which is still printed at the beginning of every Breviary, amongst the inconveniences which must be removed, the Breviary of cardinal Quiñonez is mentioned in the opening sentences. Each and every Breviary which has not a 200-year-old tradition behind it, is ruled right out of court.

It is very easy to assume that this shows the effect of de Arze's

20. Cf. a statement at the Council in 1546; *Concilium Tridentinum* ed. Goerres I, 504 (= V, 25); Legg II, 22.

21. Sessio XXV. (Concluding session of 4. XII. 1563.)

22. Legg II, 213-215.

memorandum.23 Bäumer thinks that de Arze's opinion decided the minds of the fathers of the council,24 and it may well have counted in the final solution which was arrived at through Pius V.25 In the conditions of these times, various arguments, which the Spanish conciliar theologian threw into the scales, must, in fact, have carried great weight. Great as was the cry for reform, as little was the time opportune in face of spreading heresy, for risking experiments, especially measures which might bring disunity amongst the clergy and confusion in public worship. Permission to use a shortened Breviary like that of Quiñonez might have caused just such confusion.

In every cathedral and collegiate church, in many a parish church, too, in those days, the Office was still said in choir. This took several hours each day. The idea that such a Breviary, through which busy clergy could fulfil their obligations, could be taken over into the choir, was one which might well appeal to easy-going canons. In those days when cathedral and collegiate chapters were still accustomed to considerable liturgical autonomy, there was little to prevent such a thing happening. But the struggle between ancient observance and new custom would have immediately set in.

On the other hand, in an age when the chief occupation of the majority of canons was the choral Office, there was little reason for its being shortened. (Obviously, the secularisation of church properly since the 18th century has fundamentally altered the situation.) If then, the office had to be the same for all the clergy, then the most welcome solution was to keep a middle course with regard to size. It would be enough to drop the above mentioned additional Offices—as Pius V did.

23. The introductory sentences of the Bull makes striking observations: the style of the Roman Breviary is said to have been formed by Pope Gelasius and Pope Gregory I and reinstated by Pope Gregory VII (cf. de Arze, c. 2. 13); it is said, too, that many bishops had departed from the Roman order and fashioned new styles of Breviaries (cf. ibid. c. 16). *Hinc illa tam multis in locis divini cullus perturbatio, hinc summa in Clero ignorantio caeremoniarum ac rituum ecclesiasticorum*, errors which could not remain *sine magna piorum offensione* (cf. ibid. c. 8).

24. S. Bäumer, *Geschichte des Breviers*, Freiburg 1895, 403 (= Bäumer-Biron II, 141).

25. In a secret consistory of 8. VIII. 1558, Paul IV had already rejected the cardinal's Breviary; *Concilium Tridentinum* ed. Goerres II, 325. This decision of the Pope was most probably based on personal opinion; v. Legg II, 12 seq. 26. His successor Pius IV permitted a wider use of the Breviary; ibid. II, 26.

The argument from history must have made some impression at that time in favour of the old traditional Office, especially as the Sorbonne had based their opinion on the principle, that arrangements which originated in the ancient Church may not be changed. That Matins was built up of three Nocturns was taken as a case in point, the fact being overlooked that in the 6th century this was so only on Sundays.26 But, as was constantly quoted,27 by rejecting an Office having only three psalms and three lessons at Matins,28 Gregory VII had vindicated the traditional arrangement of the psalms against attempts at innovation. Likewise, the antiphons were not to be kept out if Ignatius of Antioch had learned them from the lips of angels. Again it was overlooked, that the evidence for this is found only in the 5th century, and the antiphons, moreover, are not what we mean by the word, but antiphonal singing by two choirs.29

To show that each hour must have its *capitula*, they cited the canon of the Synod of Agde in 506 A.D. But again on closer examination, the word is seen to mean not the short lesson of these Hours, but the *capitella de psalmis*, i.e. the responsorially spoken versicles which were selected from the psalms.30 And yet for this they could have cited the ancient monastic use of short readings said by heart, as witnessed, although under different titles, by the Rule of St. Benedict31 and in the oldest monastic literature.32

From what has been said it is apparent that all of these arguments carried weight only because of the state of things at that time and because of lack of knowledge of history. There was one exception to this. One consideration which might still be valid

26. Cf. above p. 118.
27. Besides de Arze (in many passages) D. Soto also (Legg II, 132).
28. G. Morin, *Etudes, textes, decouvertes* I. Maredsous 1913, 459 seq.—As the Pope complains, this custom had spread in Rome also, *maxime a tempore quo Teutonicis concessum est regimen nostrae Ecclesiae.*—In the 16th century the test was known from the *Decretum Gratianum* III, 5, 15 (Friedberg 1416).
29. The legend is first reported by Socrates, Hist. eccl. VI, 8.
30. F. Cabrol, Hyde: DACL I, 876.
31. c. 12: *ex corde*, c. 13: *memoriter*, c. 17: *lectio recitanda.*—It appears that in the 16th century they no longer regarded the *Capitulum* as a reading, but as a decorative adjunct like antiphon and responsory.
32. D. Gorce, *La lectio divina des origines du cénobitisme a S. Benoit et Cassiodore* I Wépion 1925, 64. 68. 73 seq., 157 seq.

against a Breviary—project in the style of Quiñonez is that stressed by Dominicus Soto, himself a conciliar theologian at Trent.[33] He objected thus to the cardinal's Breviary: *quod finis orandi non est psalmos addiscere, aut sacrarum Scripturarum studium, ut illic habetur, sed laudes Deo dicere precesque fundere.*

If we must concede that the cardinal was not concerned with Scripture study, it still remains true, that he had striven for the undisturbed utilization of the entire psalter and for protracted Scripture reading.[34] Without any doubt, the praise of God and prayer on behalf of the whole Church was the primary purpose of the Office. If we conclude from this that the lessons should diminish, then we would also have to conclude that with the psalms we should not strive so much to have the whole sequence of psalms in the Office, but for a selection of those which the worshipper could say in adoration and with supplication: but the principle, which the monks of old had in mind when they took as their ideal the daily recitation of the entire psalter in its Biblical sequence, is still being maintained. It is this: all the psalms as they stand in the Bible are the holy word of God. Reciting them, quite apart from understanding them,[35] must, therefore, always be pleasing to God. Few would defend this principle today. On this view of the praise of God, the traditional accessories, too, such as the antiphons and responsories which gave a special sense of the history of redemption to the praise of God, have a claim to retention—at least in the Office for feast-days.

On the other hand, if we want to emphasize the aspect of prayer, greater stress would have to be laid upon the *preces*, which, along with the concluding *oration*, contains the actual intercession for all the needs of Christendom, and which have been almost

33. Legg II, 131-133 provides the relevant sections from D. Soto's *De justitia et jure* I, 5, 4 (Antwerp ed. 1568).

34. Soto, likewise, finds fault (loc. cit.) with the restriction to three psalms and the too scant attention paid to feast-days; and he, too, stresses the danger of encroachment upon the choir and the debt owed to tradition, especially in an age of threatening heresy. He also supports the retention of the daily Marian Office and the Office of the dead.

35. Cf. the sympathetic remarks on the use of the psalms by ancient Christian ascetics, with which H. Thurston S. J. begins his study of the Rosary as a Marian Psalter: 'They chanted the psalms not because they liked to say them, but because they thought that God liked to hear them, and had put them there to be said.' *The Month* 96 (1900) 407.

completely ousted from the daily Office by the inroads of saints' feast-days.36

But this question of the right relationship, between prayer and readings in the Breviary cannot be settled until we have first settled a wider question, the question, that is, whether in the daily office the primary thing which is being demanded of clerics is the performance of a definite *pensum* of prayer to be offered in the name of the Church.37 Should it be a *pensum*, that is, of vocal prayer which, if properly said, certainly does affect him spiritually in some degree, or should it be rather, first and foremost, a nourishment by which he keeps his own spiritual life healthy? If the second view is correct, then Scripture reading or spiritual reading in general, along with genuine prayer, will assume greater importance.

Finally, at this point historical considerations are able to shed some light. Until the height of the Middle Ages, spiritual reading within the Office was counted much more important than it ever has been since. Even in the monasteries of the Cluniac observance it was seen to, that every year the whole of Scripture was read— not simply a selection from Old and New Testaments, as with Quiñonez. To this was added a considerable amount of reading from the available spiritual literature—from what was in the monastery library, that is: commentaries on Scripture, sermons of the Fathers, martyrologies, lives of the saints.38 As long as all books had to be written by hand and books, therefore, remained luxuries, reading took the form of reading aloud during the public choir Office. When, after the 11th and 12th centuries, private canonical

36. And the decree of the Congregation of Rites dated 23.III.1955: *AAS* 47 (1955) 218-224, to achieve shortening, provided for further limitation of the *Preces* (223). Cf. for historical illumination and for an evaluation of this part of the Office, Balth. Fischer, *Litania ad Laudes et Vesperus: Liturg.Jahrbuch* 1 (1951) 55-74, esp. 56 seq.; ibid. *Die Anliegen des Volkes im kirchlichen Stundengebet: Brevierstudien*, Trier 1958, 57-70.
37. The idea that in the Office the worshipper prays *not* merely for the Church but *nomine Ecclesiae* (cf. *CIC* can. 1256), is adumbrated in Peter Damian's *Dominus vobiscum* (PL 145, 221-252), which tries to prove that even the hermit praying alone can use the priests' greeting *Dominus vobiscum*, because he represents the unity of the Church. We have a pointer to the date at which this idea took hold in the *Consecratio Virginum* of the Roman Pontificale of 1497, which is the first to show the consecrated virgin receiving the Breviary from the bishop who says: *Accipe potestam legendi Officium et incipiendi Horas in Ecclesia*; R. Metz, *La consecration des Vierges*, Paris 1954, 333; cf. 454. As Metz observes, the formula is modelled upon that used on entrusting the reading of the Gospel to a deacon.
38. Cf. above p. 163.

prayer developed more and more out of the choir Office, and the
Breviary, was composed and printed in a compendius volume, the
contents of the many choir-books had to be reduced, and under-
standibly, it was the scope of the lessons which was cut down.

It is significant that this Breviary for private devotion very soon
ousted choir-books, at least where the lessons were concerned: so
much so, that in the 16th century, Quiñonez' attempt to give a
more important place once more to Scripture reading, was seen as
an attack upon hallowed tradition. On the other hand, in those
days it was only natural that spiritual reading should occasionally
be emphasized,39 because, with the production of printed books,
such reading apart from the Office could not be expected of the
secular clergy. The practice of spiritual reading apart from the
Office had always been common in monasteries.40

In the age of the printed book, and of literature in the vernacular, the direct consequence would be this: the Breviary outside the
choir would become quite relieved of lessons except, perhaps, for
a token residue in the *capitula* of the Hours; and in each nation,
along with a set order of lessons, the bishops would fix, and from
time to time extend, a canon of spiritual reading which was suitable as Breviary material.41 It would not be regarded as any dis-
advantage, that everyone was not reading the same thing.

After 1568, Quiñonez' Breviary did not altogether disappear.
Whether taken from Quiñonez or from the sources he used,42 the
improved hagiographies appear in the Breviary of Pius V. The
majority of Quiñonez' alterations are still present in the English
Book of Common Prayer.43 The new Gallican *Brévière* of the
18th-19th century were also influenced by Quiñonez,44 and the

39. U. Berliere, *L'ascese bénédictine*, Paris 1927, 169-185.
40. So by M. de Azpilcueta, *De oratione* (above n. 10) c. 20, n. 210 (*Opp.* IV, 216; Legg II, 127). He thinks that clergy who have received permission to use the shortened Breviary of the cardinal, although they are not over-busy, ought to be asked to fulfil some additional obligation of hearing or reading *ex Sacra Scriptura vel alia materia spirituali aliqua*, roughly corresponding to the separate Hours. Pius X strongly recommends spiritual reading to priests. *Exhortatio ad Clerum catholicum: Acta Ap. Sed.* 41 (1908) 569-571.
41. It would come to the same thing obviously if a meditation of a certain duration were appointed. In the previous order a distinction between choir and individual is admitted in the way the Martyrology is treated.
42. Legg II, 68 seq. inclines to the second assumption.
43. Legg II, 75-79.
44. Ibid. 83.

cardinal's Breviary persists in the Lay Breviary45 and in the Breviary used by non-priestly communities.46 In the diocese of Cologne the question of a revision of their own particular Breviary came up after 1821. On this occasion, one of the proposals was to introduce the Breviary of Quiñonez. They were not at all sure if Rome would approve.47 In Trier also, which until that time had been permitted to retain its own Breviary, a draft of a Breviary was put forward in 1864 by the provost of the cathedral, M. Schu; and this was based on Quiñonez.48

The idea of having a Breviary designed for private use—and possibly for parochial worship—after the fashion of cardinal Quiñonez—was put forward in the 18th century by another member of the Sacred College, cardinal J. M. Tommasi (d. 1713), who is venerated as a saint.49 Tommasi, a student of Church history, was able to turn to the *pristina norma* with decisively greater right than critics of Quiñonez had been able to claim, to support his design to stress the lessons along with the psalms, to do without antiphons and responsaries, and to propose the *Pater noster* as the concluding prayer of the Hours.50 It is true that a reform which not only corresponds to the fundamentally changed conditions of the clergy—certainly no longer threatened by idleness, and enjoying an education totally different from that which de Arze saw—but also builds upon an understanding of the historical process, is scarcely possible, with relevant scholarship being in the state it is at the moment. We are only beginning to be fully aware of the distinction between the monastic Office and

45. In this sense Azpilcueta had commended it, loc. cit. c. 18 n. 51 (*Opp.* IV, 152).— The Breviary which J. B. Colbert, the well-known French minister of Louis XIV, had printed for himself in 1675 is, contrary to a much repeated statement, related to that of Quinonez only in the basic outline of its structure. It has been reprinted by T. R. Gambier-Parry (HBS 43-44), London 1912-13. On its relation to Quinonez v. I, p. VIII seq.
46. A version of Quinonez' Breviary was reprinted in Milan in 1751 for the female branch of the *Humiliates*: Bäumer-Biron II, 148.
47. Bäumer-Biron II, 342.
48. Ibid. 344; Legg II, 81.
49. J. M. Thomasius, *De privato Ecclesiasticorum Breviario extra Chorum* (*Opp.* ed. Vezzosi VII, Rome 1754, 62-68). This seems to have in mind a *Votum* intended for the Congregation of Rites. Cf. Legg II, 83 seq. Cf. also the annotated special edition of the text by Legg, *The Reformed Breviary of Cardinal Tommasi* (The Church Historical Society 80), London 1904. The tabulated synopsis on pp. 45-59 of the apportioning of the psalms in 15 new Gallican Brevaries from 1679-1750 is worthy of note.
50. It was not only Quinonez in his Preface who appealed to the ideal of antiquity. Paul III emphasized in his Breve that the norm to be followed was the *reterum sanctorum Patrum Conciliorumque instituta*; Legg I, p. XXX; cf. p. XXIII.

that of the cathedral or parish. We are not yet entirely clear about the origin of Matins.[51] And furthermore, a balance between history and expedience will not be accomplished all at one go.

In the various discussions about a possible reform of the Breviary, which have taken place in recent years with the encouragement of Rome,[52] those voices deserve special attention, which not only recognize that a thorough-going reform is urgently required, but also emphasize, that our own time will not be able to produce the perfected article.[53]

In the meantime we can be thankful for the beginnings of a provisional reform in the decree of the Sacred Congregation of Rites of March 23, 1955.

.

5. *The Extended Celebration of Epiphany in the Roman Missal*

Looking at the notes on the Masses for the Sundays after Epiphany in contemporary standard commentaries on the Mass or in English editions of the Missal, we find those Sundays described as their name 'Sundays after Epiphany' suggests, partly as an extension or echo of Christmas: but any more detailed comment, if attempted at all, shows a considerable departure from this theme. In particular, with the Gospel for the third Sunday no sort of close connexion with the festival is brought out, apart from those connexions which can always be seen.

These Sundays, in fact—certainly from the second Sunday on—present a completely neutral appearance. In contrast to Easter the Preface of the feast is said only until the octave day (since 1955: commemoration of the Circumcision): on Sundays the common

51. For some new insights produced by A. Baumstark in his book *Nocturna laus* (Münster 1957), cf. above p. 156.
52. Cf. int. al. Balth. Fischer, *Brevierreform: Trierer Theol. Zeitschr.* 59 (1950) 14-26.
53. P. Salmon, *Presupposti storici di una riforma del Breviario: Eph. liturg.* 63 (1949) 412-418; P. M. Gy, *Projets de reforme du Bréviaire: La Maison-Dieu* 31 (1950) 110-127; cf. his comments on J. M. Hanssens, *Nature et genese de l'office des Matines* (Rome 1952), in the *Revue des Sciences phil. et théol.* 38 (1954) 597 seq.; and those of A. G. Martimort on the Decree of March 23, 1955, *La réforme des rubriques: La Maison-Dieu* 42 (1955) 5-28, esq. 13. 27 seq.

Preface, *de ss. Trinitate*, reappears. Green is the colour on the frontal: and the season is regarded as *tempus per annum*. And so, if Easter and hence Lent, falls early, the Sunday rituals can be transposed after the other *dominica per annum* at the end of the year.

As we know, the Preface, *de ss. Trinitate*, only became the usual Sunday Preface after 1759. Our present rule about colours was made by Pius V, and its origins lie no farther back than the 12th century. Nor was there any occasion to transpose the Sundays—at least in our present fashion—as long as separate books occupied the place of the complete Missal, which only came into use in the 12th-13th centuries. These sacramentaries and lectionaries interpolated the extra Sundays, demanded by an early Easter, into the period between Pentecost and the feast of SS. Peter and Paul, choosing the material chiefly from a special supply which was there for that purpose.₁ We see the medieval conception of the liturgy finding its first expression in this assimilation to the *dominicae per annum*.₂ It is possible, that behind this outward appearance, similar, as we shall see, to what happens with the period before Advent,₃ there lies a more basic stratum, in which these Sundays reveal an even more distinct character. A few points suffice to establish the truth of this.

1. In most sets of Gospels, between the octave of Pentecost and June 29, there were available 5-6 Sunday lections. This allowed for Easter falling on the earliest possible date (March 22—Pentecost octave, May 17). V. St. Beissel, *Entstehung der Perikopen des Römischen Messbuches*, Freiburg 1907, 164. At the other end, in case of a late Easter and consequently a late Septuagesima, up to ten pericopes were provided for the season after Epiphany; ibid. 172, cf. 133 n. 1. The same phenomenon in the oldest collection of Gospels in Klausner (below n. 10). Because between Septuagesima and Epiphany there could not be more than six Sundays, the last mentioned phenomenon takes us back to a stage in the evolution of the Church's Year in which the pre-Fast period had not yet been formed—i.e. back into the 6th century.

2. Certainly, what Amalar of Metz, *De ordine antiph.* c. 27 (PL 105, 1280), sees in the weeks from 'Theophania' until Septuagesima, is the *ministerium praedicatorum* portrayed in the activity of the Church. According to Bernold of Constance, *Micrologus* c. 30 (PL 151, 1005), between Candlemas and Septuagesima we ought to read and sing *de infantia Christi*. Durandus, *Rationale* VI, 30, 8, has the time between Epiphany and Candlemas dedicated to joy *de apparitione divinitatis* (just as the time between Christmas and Epiphany is dedicated to joy *de apparitione humanitatis*); but his individual expositions are only very slightly affected by this idea. And yet the Middle Ages, up to the 13th century, possessed a set of six special Prefaces for this period; four of these had a strong Christmas flavour; v. J. Lemarié, *Les préfaces des dimanches apres l'Epiphanie dans les sacramentaires gélasiens du VIIIe siecle: Eph. liturg.* 73 (1959) 393-401.

3. In the study, *Advent und Voradvent:* Zk Th 61 (1937) 341-390 (= *Gewordene Liturgie* 232-294).

First of all we are struck by the fact that a Proper is provided only for the second and third Sundays.4 The Sundays which follow merely repeat the text of the third Sunday. And when the Sunday ritual is transposed to the end of the year, these Propers are not transposed. Instead, they are replaced by Proper chants of the twenty-third Sunday after Pentecost—likewise used on several Sundays and bearing a pre-Advent character.

Contemporary commentaries mostly affirm that these chants have an Epiphany character, at least in the Introit, which comes from Psalm 96: *Adorate Deum, omnes Angeli eius: audivit et laetata est Sion: et exsultaverunt filiae Judae. Dominus regnavit exsultet terra: laetentur insulae multae.*

As is well known, early Christian exegesis applied the *Dominus regnavit* of this and other psalms to Christ.4a In this sense, our Lauds for Sunday likewise opens with a *Dominus regnavit* (Ps. 92). And so the Epiphany motif is readily made to fit: Christ the King has appeared; along with the angels of heaven, the Church on earth should offer Him homage.5 The same *Dominus regnavit* then occurs in the Alleluja—hymn; and the gradual (Ps. 101, 16 seq.), *Timebunt gentes nomen tuum, Domine, et omnes reges terrae gloriam tuam*, is but an expression of the same thought: princes and peoples are to bow before Him. In contrast, an Epiphany—thought is not so apparent in the Offertory or Communion. But we must return to that later.

As all the commentators stress, the chants for both Sundays are determined by the same mood of obeisance before Christ: the Introit, *Omnis terra adoret te* with the Psalm *Jubilate Deo*, the beginning of which is taken up once more in the Offertory: likewise the Alleluja—verse, *Laudate Dominum omnes Angeli eius;* and the Communion, which picks up a text from the Gospel.

4. The very same, partly with notation for the psalm verses of the Offertory and Communion, for the same Sundays in the oldest evidence of the Roman Mass Antiphonary. R.-J. Hesbert, *Antiphonale Missarum sextuplex*, Brussels 1935, n. 21. 26. The Roman original of the antiphonary ms. printed by Hesbert, is placed in the year 635 by Th. Klausner, JL 15 (1941) 469. It is placed not before 700 by A. Chavasse, *Les plus anciens types du lectionnaire et de l'antiphonaire romains de la messe: Revue Bénéd.* 62 (1952, 3-94) 28; but in the mere presence of Proper chants only up to the third Sunday he detects a sign that this section is more ancient; ibid. 21.
4a. Cf. Balth. Fischer, *Die Psalmenfrömmigkeit der Martyrerkirche*, Freiburg 1949, 11-16.
5. Cf. the pleasing liturgical exposition of Psalm 96 by P. Parsch, *Das Jahr des Heiles*[1], I, Klosterneuburg 1937, 381 seq.

Apart from those chants, after the second Sunday, when the Gospel passage tells of the miracle at Cana—already mentioned on the feast of the Epiphany—the commentators find no further continuation of the thoughts of the Christmas cycle,6 except perhaps in a very remote way in the lessons.7

The lessons now deserve much closer examination. The Epistles reveal a striking feature. From the first to the fourth Sunday, all are taken from the Epistle to Romans; and they form a *lectio continua*.8 They are, indeed, passages devoted entirely to the Christian's moral life, but passages from that same Epistle which described in a mighty sweep the renewal of humanity in the new Adam, and which was read therefore, in the Christmas Mass and in the canonical Office at Christmas-time.9 Anyway, the idea of a continuous lesson may have been stronger than the desire to produce passages appropriate to the extension of the Epiphany celebration.

Against this, in the Gospels, it is perfectly clear, if we look at older schemes of passages—especially as they have been made available by Theodor Klausner—that we have before us a scheme dictated by the festival. The oldest Roman system of Scripture

6. Parsch, *Das Jahr des Heiles*11, I, 353: '. . . a period lacking any festive character. In content and in history, only the first two Sundays carry on the Christmas thought—the rest not at all.'

7. U. Bomm, A Latin-German Missal published at Einsiedeln 1937, p. 98. The Sundays after Epiphany are called the 'Time of Finale', and they should show us 'the majesty of the Kingdom' founded by Christ, and 'the Church's dispensation of grace as the Body of Christ upon earth (readings) and at the same time as the transfiguration in the eternal joy of the heavenly hosts (songs).'

8. Rom. 12, 1-5; 12, 6-16; 12, 16-21; 13, 8-10. The same passages, applied in the same way, in *Comes* of Murbach (8th century), and in *Comes* of Würzburg (7th century); v. the tables in Godu, *Epitres*: DACL V, 335 seq. With slightly different divisions, the same four passages are to be found also in the list of Epistles from Capua (before 546-547), contained in the well-known Codex Fuldensis of the Vulgate; Godu, loc. cit. 298, n. 32. 16. 22. 33.—The Epistle for the fifth Sunday after Epiphany, Col. 3, 12-17, is to be found in the same place in the *Comes* of Murbach. As the sequence of the Pauline readings in the *Comes* of Würzburg shows (Godu 314, n. 241), it belongs to the continuation of the sequence of Pauline Sunday readings in the canonical order, which today ends on the 22nd Sunday after Pentecost with Phil. 1, 6-11. From there it has been taken over for the occasional completion of the sequence. Finally, the Epistle of the 6th Sunday, I Thess. 1, 2-10, does not appear in the old sources; nor does the special Gospel for this day (cf. below n. 12). This first appears to have been appointed in the Missal of Pius V, perhaps simply attached to the preceding Epistle to the Colossians of the canonical sequence.

9. The reading of St. Paul's Epistles after Christmas was already specified for the Office in the *Ordo librorum catholicorum* (first half of 8th century): Andrieu, *Les Ordines* II, 448.

portions which has come down complete, belongs to the period about 645, and it indicates seventeen portions between the second Sunday after Epiphany and the sixth inclusive. That is, there were portions for the favourite week-days—the old station days—as well as for Sundays.[10]

15. 2. Sunday after Epiphany Jn. 2, 1-11 (Cana).
16. 'Item' Lk. 4, 14-22 (Nazareth: 'all were amazed').
17. Wednesday Mk. 1, 40-44 (The leper 'he began to publish it everywhere . . .').
18. Friday Mk. 6, 1-5 (Nazareth 'They were amazed . . .').
19. Saturday Lk. 4, 38-43 (The miracle in Capharnaum).
21.[11] 3. Sunday after Epiphany Mt. 8, 1-13 (The leper; the centurion's servant).
22. Wednesday Mk. 3, 1-5 (The withered hand).
23. Friday Lk. 5, 12-15 (The leper. 'News about him . . .').
24. Saturday Mk. 4, 1-9 ('He taught them much through parables'. The Sower).
27.[11] 4. Sunday after Epiphany. Mt. 8, 23-27 (Storm on the lake. 'They were filled with wonder').
29.[11] Wednesday Mt. 18-26 (Woman with issue of blood. Jairus' daughter. 'News of this . . .').
30. Friday Mt. 4, 24-34 (Two parables. 'With many such parables . . .').
31. Saturday Lk. 14, 7-15 ('With parables'. At table).
32. 5. Sunday after Epiph. Mt. 13, 24-30 (Parable of Cockle).
35.[11] Friday Mk. 5, 1-19 (The Possessed. The Gadarene Swine).
36. Saturday Lk. 7, 11-16 (The widow's son of Naim. 'Fear seized them all . . .').
37. 6. Sunday after Epiph. Mk. 6, 47-56 (Walking upon the water. 'All who touched him . . .').

All of the portions belonging to this period fall into two groups: those which tell of the Lord's miracles, and those which tell of the power of His words.

10. Th. Klausner, *Das römische Capitulare evangelorum* I, Munster 1935, 14-17. In the list which follows the separate pericopes are given Klausner's numbering.
11. The numbering breaks down because at the point indicated, feasts of martyrs were interpolated. That Wednesday is missing before n. 35, has probably some connexion with the day being taken up by a martyr-feast. In the third type of Roman *Capitulare evangelorum* (c. 755), which agrees in general with the type reproduced above, in the place for this Wednesday is inserted: *Item alia*: Mk. 5, 21-34 (the woman with the issue of blood). Klausner p. 105, n. 34.

To the group telling of the power of His words being, 16, 18, 24, 30, 31, 32. Of these, 24 and 30 emphasize the fact that the Lord taught the people in parables. The parables in these portions and in 31 and 32, are given only as examples of this mighty and mysterious teaching activity. The particular content is not the first concern of this selection. In our present-day Missal, for the sixth Sunday after Epiphany the portion Mt. 13, 31-35, is added to the examples given. In this the portion for the fifth Sunday is carried on in the parable of the mustard seed and the parable of the leaven.12

At the head of this whole group stands the passage Lk. 4, 14-22. (n. 16). In the older Roman capitularies this has no specific assignation. It is labelled only 'item' and is put in after the second Sunday. In the later Roman-Frankish type of capitulary (c. 750) it is assigned to the third Sunday;13 in later lists of passages it is absent.14 Then there is the parallel account in Mk. 6, 1-5 (N. 18). Both of these tell in impressive language of the amazement of the Nazarenes at the didactic skill of their supposedly well-known co-citizen. Now the meaning of the Communion—verse, which is repeated from the third Sunday onwards, becomes quite plain, and this appears in the same form in the oldest Mass antiphonaries:15 *Mirabantur omnes de his quae procedebant de ore Dei.* In the context of the liturgy this amazement is directed not merely to the 'mighty Son of God' who Himself is the 'Word of God's own mouth', as modern comment no doubt would have it; but to the World of Christ Himself—more exactly, to the divine Wisdom which was revealed in His word. Thus the Biblical text of Lk. 4, 22: *quae procedebant de ore ipsius,* is altered to *de ore Dei.*16 This

12. This pericope seems to appear first in the Missal of Pius V. In the medieval sources given by Beissel, loc. cit., it does not appear. Even the *Missale Romanum* of 1474 does not contain it, because there is no provision there for a sixth Sunday after Epiphany; v. the reprint of this, ed. by R. Lippe (HBS 17; London 1899) 40, and the commentary (ibid. Vol. 33; London 1907) p. 29. Cf. the corresponding case of the Epistle, above n. 8.
13. Klausner p. 142, n. 20. In this type the subsequent notation of the pericopes suffers as a result of a transposition.
14. Beissel 172. The pericope appears both in the Gallican and the Mozarabic tradition, on the first or second Sunday after Epiphany, what is more. Beissel loc. cit.
15. Hesbert n. 26.
16. In general, in the Roman-Frankish type of Capitular mentioned above (n. 13), the concluding phrase of the pericope itself is annotated by this text: usq. 'procedebant de ore Dei'. Klausner p. 142, n. 20. At the Alleluja-verse of the second Sunday the analogous variant of the text of the Antiphonary of Compiegne (Hesbert n. 21): *Laudate Deum,* in place of *Laudate Dominum,* has not survived.

underlines the thought of Epiphany, that is, the feast is given the later meaning which arose in the Roman liturgy after the differentiation from Christmas had developed, and which forms the basic theme of the rest of the chants in the Epiphany rituals. The theme is: the manifestation of divinity in Him who has come to us in the flesh.[17] For this reason, in the rest of the portions of Scripture, too, the subject matter is not just any addresses of our Lord, but those in which the element of wonder appears, or mystery, which the crowd cannot fathom at all—as in the parables.

This theme of the Wisdom of God appearing in Christ is devoted to the Gospels of the two last Sundays—the fifth and sixth. All the other passages contain records of our Lord's miracles.

This is true not only of the rest of the rituals for the second, third and fourth Sundays in our present-day order, but, as the above lists show, it is true also of all the other portions in the Roman lectionary of the 7th century.[18] On the feast day itself in the antiphon to the Benedictus the miracle at Cana is mentioned as something closely connected with the subject of the feast, along with the manifestation of the incarnate One to the wise men from the East and the Baptism in Jordan. These are the most important ἐπιφάνεια of the Son of God. While the Gospel—lessons within the week of the feast have to do with revelation through the Spirit in the farther manifestation of the twelve-year-old Christ at Jerusalem (Lk. 2, 42-52) and in the testimony of the Baptist (Jn. 1, 29-34),[19] all the portions which follow, excluding the six which refer to the wisdom in teaching, develop the theme of Jesus'

---

17.   The oldest prayers do not yet show this differentiation: *in substantia nostrae mortalitatis apparuit* (Preface); *in veritate carris nostra:e visibiliter corporalis apparuit* (Communion).
18.   This is all the more striking because after the sixth Sunday after Epiphany, for which there is always room before Septuagesima, fresh themes immediately become introduced; thus on the following Friday Lk. 7, 36-47 (the woman with the oil of spikenard), on Saturday Mk. 2, 13-17 (call of Matthew). Klausner p. 17, n. 38. 39.
19.   Thus in a type from 695 (Klausner p. 14, n. 11. 13). The pericope appointed today for the Octave day, there bears the title, *feria IV. post theophania*. In the second, purely Roman type (c. 740) there are two more pericopes besides these within the Octave: Mk 1, 4-11 and Mt. 3, 1-17 with the account of the Baptism of Jesus (Klausner p. 59, n. 12. 14). In a third type—Roman also—(c. 755) these are once more omitted (ibid. 103). In a fourth, Roman-Frankish type (after 750) beside the pericope Mt. 3, 13-17, there appears in addition Mt. 4, 12-17 about the beginning of Messianic activity in Galilee (ibid. 141, n. 17).

miracles. The second Sunday has the miracle of Cana itself, with which the Lord began His series of miracles and 'manifested His glory'. And the rest of the passages all favour those stories which describe how the people marvel at what they see (n. 27, 36) and begin to raise a tumult of excitement, or in which repeated miracles appear (n. 19, 21, 35, 37).

This second group of Gospels of revelation which follow in Epiphany, the miracle-passages,[20] explain the last puzzling text of the Communion verse of the Mass, the verse which is used from the third Sunday on. *Dextera Domini fecit virtutem, dextera Domini extultavit me: non moriar, sed vivam, et narrato opera Domini:* It is the miracle-working hand of the Redeemer which is being praised—praised out of the mouths of those who have been blessed and who are unable to keep silence as they were bidden. This may also be linked with the fact that the favourite passages from amongst all of the miracles-stories are clearly those in which the hand of the Lord is prominently at work (n. 17, 19, 21, 23, 29). The story of the healing of the man possessed by an evil spirit appears in all three synoptic versions; and each stresses the outstretched hand and the touching of the sick person.

On the third Sunday when we still read Luke's account of this deed and when the *dextera Domini* is extolled for the first time, the *oration,* too, strikes a not altogether accidental note . . . *dexteram tuae maiestatis extende.* This strengthens the presumption, that the *oration* of the fourth Sunday as well has the Gospel-scene in mind —the calming of the storm at sea. *Deus, qui nos, in tantis periculis constitutos, pro humana scis fragilitate non posse subsistere; da . . . ut . . . vincamus.* In the Gelasian tradition, beginning with the Sacramentary of Prague, the two *orationes* belong to the third and fourth Sundays after Epiphany,[21] Sundays which in Rome at the same time had the same Gospel passages which we know today. Admittedly, the rest of the *orationes* on our Sundays, too, keep to the usual general pattern, i.e. to the scheme of ideas dictated by the offering of gifts and Communion: the Epiphany motif affects them no farther.

20. In other places too, the theme of Jesus' miracles was occasionally associated with Epiphany. Examples from the West in A. Bludau, *Die Pilgerreise der Aetheria,* Paderborn 1927, 87 seq.
21. P. Bruylantes, *Les oraisons du Missal Romain* II, Löwen 1952, nn. 406. 765.

At the same time we must look at the chants, which certainly go back to this early period. It is not only the *dextera Domini* of the Offertory for the third Sunday onwards which is to be understood in the light of the miracle passages: The Offertory for the second Sunday also, is illuminated by this; for it begins as a call to pay homage to the Lord who has manifested Himself: *Jubilate Deo, universa terra* ... (Ps. 65, 1.2); then it jumps on to a verse in which we seem to hear the thanksgiving of one who has been miraculously healed (Ps. 65, 16): *venite et audite meae.*[22] The Gradual for this second Sunday, too, takes up the same strain: *Misit Dominus vertum suum et sanavit eos et eripuit eos de interitu errum* ... (Ps. 106, 20 seq.).[23]

We can sum up by saying that the Epiphany-thought in the Roman liturgical year takes on a much more distinct character when seen in terms of its extension understood in its original light. It is concerned not with a certain appearance of Christ; but, in contrast to Christmas and to the original Eastern feast of Epiphany, both of which have for their subject, the Incarnation or the coming of the Redeemer,[24] with the manifestation of divinity in Him who has come to us in the form of a man. The power and the Wisdom of God have appeared in Christ. For this reason most of the records of the older Roman liturgy favour the expression *theophania.*[25] It is therefore, not a particular event which is being celebrated, but a concept of faith;[26] at any rate, a concept which is visibly expressed in a whole series of events and which never appears in abstract isolation.

And so it becomes clearer, that the Christmas cycle is devoted

22. In the oldest mss. in Hesbert n. 21, two verses formed from Ps. 65, 13 are added to this antiphon (in the present text).
23. The same idea in Hesbert n. 21. In the six mss. printed by Hesbert, that from Mont-Blandin contains a few more chants for a *dominica IV. post theophania*; again these represent cries for mercy, apart from the Offertory (Dan. 3, 40) and the Communion (Ps. 30, 3).
24. B. Bothe, *Les origines de la Noel et de l'Epiphanie,* Löwen 1932, 77 seq.
25. Thus in the Gelasian Sacramentaries, in the Mass Antiphonary, in the Gospel Capitulary. Instances of Θεοφάνεια, Θεοφάνια in the Greek Fathers, v. H. Stephanus, *Thesaurus Graecae linguae* IV (1841) 315. The Byzantine liturgy uses the appellation τὰ ἅγια θεοφάνεια.
26. A similar assertion about the original feasts of Christmas and Epiphany in A. Baumstark, *Liturgie comparée,* Chevetogne 1953, 174 seq. On the possibility of a 'fete d'idee' cf. below p.395. As ground-motif of Christmas, Baumstark takes the ὁμοούσιος: at Epiphany is added the idea of Christ's marriage with the Church, corresponding to the ancient idea of the ἱερὸς γάμος (175 seq.). The extent to which the Cana miracle can be made to fit in with this is discussed by Botte, loc. cit. 72 seq., who refers primarily to the ancient water-rituals in this connexion.

to the mystery of Christ the God-man, whom we must approach with humble homage; just as Easter is concerned with His action, the grace of which we must receive with thanks and seek more and more to obtain.

6. The Forty Hours Devotion and the Holy Sepulchre

Modern piety knows the Forty Hours as a period of forty hours' prayer before the Blessed Sacrament, exposed, on various occasions.

A whole list of essays has been produced on the origins of this Forty Hours of prayer.[1] According to these, the devotion first appeared in 1527 when Gian Antonio Belotti, preaching in Lent in the Church of the Holy Sepulchre in Milan, asked the faithful to remain forty-hours before the Blessed Sacrament, to obtain the help of God in time of war. This was to have been four times a year: at Easter, Pentecost, the Assumption and at Christmas. In 1529 the custom was then taken up in Milan cathedral. In the succeeding years the greatest advocates of the devotion were St. Antonius Maria Zaccaria and the Capuchin Joseph of Ferno. In Milan by 1537, the devotion already had assumed the form according to which the various churches took up the devotion in turn throughout the year so that there was a continuous chain of adoration—before the Blessed Sacrament, exposed, indeed. In other places the practice was kept up only during the whole of Lent. In 1550 St. Philip Neri took up the devotion; from 1553 the Jesuits adopted it, developed it and made out of it, amongst other things, the great reparation—devotion during the days of the carnival.

When we first hear of the devotion, the forty hours of our Lord's resting in the tomb are cited as the reason for that particular

1. The most important are: H. Thurston, *Lent and Holy Week*, London 1904, 110–148; P. Norbert, *Zur Geschichte des Vierzigstundigen Gebetes: Der Katholik* 78 (1898) II, 151–158; P. Tacchi-Venturi, *Storia della Compagnia di Gesu in Halia* I, Rome 1910, 199–206; F. Beringer, *Die Ablasse*[14] I, Paderborn 1921 seq. 316seq.; Eisenhofer, *Handbuch der katholischen Liturgik* II, 237 seq.

span of time.² The fact that the devotion started in a church dedicated to the Holy Sepulchre is relevant. Awareness of this, however, can never have been definite; or, at least, it must very quickly have faded into the background; for Pius IV, in his Bull granting permission for the devotion on November 17, 1560, points to our Lord's forty days and fasting in justification of the Forty Hours.³ Today, all thought that such is the foundation of the Forty Hours Prayer, has completely vanished.

On the other hand, in the first place Thurston points to a trace of this devotion existing as early as the 13th century,⁴ and adverting again to the resting of our Lord in the tomb. In 1214 the brotherhood of the Verberati in Zara received a legacy of ten pounds to defray the expenses of the Forty Hours' Prayer *in diebus passionis Jesu Christi*. There was another legacy for the same purpose in the same place in 1270. From Zara again, we have an account in the year 1380 telling that the *publica supplicatio XL horam* was held; and was held, in fact, from Holy Thursday until *distributa per horas et personas usque ad sabbatum Gloriae hora Meridiana*.⁵ The Blessed Sacrament is not mentioned, however, in connexion with this Forty Hours Prayer. From these accounts, Thurston concludes that the Forty Hours was originally nothing other than 'a special name for the pious vigil before the Easter grave'.⁶ In what follows we shall support this assertion with a few observations, and try to throw some more light on the development.

It was not the high Middle Ages which first had the idea of keeping vigil for forty hours by the grave of our Lord, even if it did receive an impetus during the time of the crusades. Behind the veneration of the forty hours of our Lord's resting in the grave lay a tradition reaching right back to the 2nd century. In a letter to Pope Victor, Irenaeus speaks of the custom of fasting before

2. Tacchi-Venturi I, 200.
3. Magnum Bullarium Romanum II, Luxemburg 1742, 34.
4. Thurston 123-126.
5. Ibid. 125. In the 14th century the *Gloria* of the Easter Mass, which in previous centuries might be begun only when the first stars appeared, could not be sung at midday. This is related to the fact that the evening of Holy Thursday is said to be the start of the Forty Hours Prayer: in *sero Coenae Domini*.
6. Ibid. 125.

Easter: some consider it proper 'to fast for one day, others for two, others for longer still; others, again, reckon their day as forty hours—a day and a night.'[7] That by forty hours was meant the time our Lord spent in the grave or more exactly, the time during which He was under the sway of death, is clearly apparent from Augustine:[8] *Ab hora ergo mortis usque ad diluculum resurrectionis horae sunt quadraginta.* Somehow, the number forty had already become a traditional holy number. It was arrived at by a rough estimate of the number of hours which was not exactly known.[9]

The single fast day of which Irenaeu speaks, might have been Good Friday, because Friday throughout the year was a fast day. But if forty hours was observed—allowing for the higher rough estimate—adding the time of entombment on to Good Friday, then we have two fast days in succession. Thus the wavering between one and two fast days, indicated by Irenaeus, is explained. Tertullian, too, gives evidence of Holy Saturday being a fast day along with Good Friday; and elsewhere he disapproves of the Saturday fast observed in the Roman Church, saying that Easter-Eve is a fast day *quamquam vos etiam sabbatum, si quando, continuatis, nunquam nisi in Pascha ieiunandum.*[10] At the beginning of the 3rd century Hyppolitus of Rome speaks of the rule to fast on two days; but he adds that expectant mothers and sick people who cannot fast for two days should fast on the Saturday.[11]

It was thought to be specially worth while to honour with fasting the time during which our Lord suffered His deepest humiliation: the time of His Passion, His death, and the time He spent in the grave, the prize of death. In the clear and penetrating remark of Tertullian, these days are *dies quibus ablatus est sponsus*

7. In Eusebius, *Hist. eccl.* V, 24, 12. Cf. O. Casel, *Art und Sinn der altchristlichen Osterfeier:* JL 14 (1934) 1–78, esp. 11. 16. 31.

8. Augustine, *De Trin.* IV, 6 (PL 42, 894 seq.).

9. Augustine, loc. cit. puts the question whether the time ought to be reckoned from the *hora tertia* (Mk. 15, 25) or from the *hora sexta* (Jn. 19, 14) when the Lord was crucified, or from the *hora nona* (Mt. 27, 46). From the hour of laying in the grave until the *diluculum resurrectionis* he reckons 36 hours, i.e., two whole nights and one whole day; but amongst other things, the perfection of the factors 4 × 10 commends the number 40 to him.

10. Tertullian, *De ieiun.* c. 14 (CSEL 20, 293).

11. Hippolytus, *Traditio Ap.* c. 29 (Dix 56).

(Lk. 3, 35).¹² Whenever possible, people were expected to spend these days without taking any food.¹³

To fasting, prayer was added. The pilgrim Aetheria, who celebrated Easter in Jerusalem about the turn of the 4th century, was able to describe how it was usual, after the strenuous exercises of Good Friday, to keep watch in the Church of the Resurrection. 'Those of the people who wish to, or rather, who are able, keep watch . . . The priests—the stronger and younger—keep watch there. All night through until the morning, hymns and antiphons are sung. A great multitude keep watch throughout the night, some from evening, others from midnight, as they are able.'¹⁴ And the synod of Toull (692)¹⁵ ordered 'Fastings, prayers, and acts of contrition' to be carried out until midnight on Easter Sunday.

The tradition of honouring Holy Saturday by fasting has endured to this day. The *Codex Juris canonici* in can. 1252 still orders full fasting and abstinence on the Fridays and Saturdays of Lent; the stressing of Saturdays applied especially to Holy Saturday. When, after the first World War fasting became limited by indult to but a few days, it was Holy Saturday which, along with Good Friday and Ash Wednesday was the first to be retained as a fast in the full sense.¹⁶ The limitation of the Holy Saturday fast to the first half of the day has been eliminated by the new regulations of 1955.

There is, on the other hand, scarcely any mention nowadays of any additional devotions on Holy Saturday. We feel no urge towards them. And as for fasting on Holy Saturday, we think of it rather as the day when Lent ends, just as Ash Wednesday is the

---

12. Tertullian, *De ieiun.* c. 2. 13 (CSEL 20, 275. 291). Such a fast is indicated even in the Gospel of the Hebrews (mid 2nd century) when this writing makes the Apostle James vow that he will eat no more bread until he has 'seen the Lord rise from amongst them that sleep'. E. Hennecke, *Neutestamentliche Apokryphen,*² Tubingen 1924, 55; cf. 49. Later, Augustine speaks about the Roman church, in contrast to that of Africa, observing the day every week as a fast-day, *quo die caro Christi in monumento requierit.* Ep. 36, 13, 31 (CSEL 34, 2, p. 60). Further references v. Jungmann, *Gewordene Liturgie* 227 seq. (=Zk Th 1931, 619 seq.).
13. The Syrian Didascatia V, 18, expressly commands it (Funk I, 228): 'On the Parascere and on the Sabbath fast completely, tasting nothing.' Cf. ibid. 19, 9; 20, 9. Cf. also Dionysius of Alexandria, *Ep. ad Basilidem* c. 1 (PG 10, 1277A).
14. Aetheriae Peregrinatio c. 37 (CSEL 39, 90).
15. c. 89 (Mansi XI, 982).
16. E.g., the induct of the Apostolic Administrator of Innsbruck-Feldkirchen 1 (1926) 14, names Ash Wednesday, and the Fridays in Lent, as days of fasting and abstinence, and also Holy Thursday until noon.

day when it begins. Today, the devout Christian, who has been
following the drama of Christ's Passion during the Holy Week,
feels the moment of Christ's death more as a release from the
tension which absolves us from any farther religious observances
until the moment of the Resurrection. The early Christian mind
did not think like this. That the Lord not only suffered but died;
that He not only died but was able to lie in the grave as a spoil of
death—for three days no less—was the subject of pious amazement
at so much voluntary humiliation. For this reason the phrase 'and
buried' expressly occurs in the otherwise laconic Apostles' Creed.17
Fasting was one way of expressing this amazement: the other way
was to persevere in prayer.

Traces of this spiritual need to honour those hours, not only
with traditional fasting, but through the practice of voluntary
penitential mourning, are still to be found in the *Instructio
ecclesiastici*, composed by a Frankish monk after the middle of the
8th century. After mentioning Vespers of Good Friday he gives
the following instructions—in barbarous Latin: *et ipsa nocte
abstentes se ab omni dilicia corporali, id est preter tantum pane et aquam
cum aceto mixtam non sumentes (cibum); cui autem Dominus virtutem
dederit, pertranseunt sine cybo usque in vigilia Pasche. Hoc autem apud
religiosus et venerabilis vivos observantur.18*

In the 10th century in the Teutonic North, the celebration of
Holy Week shows the first emergence of that desire for outward
expression and symbolization which later on was to display itself
in the whole range of Church culture, especially in Gothic Church
art. These were the expressions in the centre of which stood the
representation of Christ's tomb.19 The English *Regularis Concordia*,

17.   Cf. F. Kattenbusch, *Das Apostolische Symbol* II, Leipzig 1900, 639–641.

18.   Andrieu, *Les Ordines* III, 152. The same directions are repeated in the somewhat
more recent *Breviarium eccl. ordinis* (ibid. III, 189). On the other hand, the *Regula magistri*
c. 53 (PL 88, 1015 D) desires that no food at all be taken on Good Friday. Likewise the
Chapter of Aachen 817 A.D. c. 47 (Mansi XIV *App.* 397C) prescribe for Good Friday only:
non aliud nisi panis et aqua sumatur. There are similar regulations in the *Consuetudines* of
subsequent centuries.

19.   The relevant material has been sifted, carefully collected and made available mainly
by two Anglo-Saxon scholars: N. C. Brooks, *The Sepulchre of Christ in Art and Liturgy*,
Urbana (Illinois) 1921; K. Young, *The Drama of the Medieval Church*, 2 vols., Oxford
1933.—The work of C. Lange, *Die lateinischen Osterfeier*, Munich 1887, only deals with
the dramatic play on Easter morning and indicates the development of this from rich
liturgical sources.

which was composed between 965 and 975[20] and based on customs prevailing in continental monasteries (e.g. Fleury and Ghent), gives definite shape to the thought of our Lord's resting in the grave, in the first place, by having a symbolic grave erected in which the crucifix was laid after the veneration of the Cross on Good Friday. At the same time this document makes greater concessions to realism. The crucifix is wrapped in a cloth and is 'buried' while appropriate antiphons are sung: *In pace, in idipsum, Sepulto Domino* etc. Such texts are to be found over and over again in numerous sources all through the Middle Ages, and in the same context. The crucifix was then removed from the grave without ceremony before Easter Matins began. But at the end of Matin a cleric representing an angel is sitting by the empty tomb, dressed in an alb with a palm in his hand. Three others come, seeking, and are asked by him: *Quem quaertisi?* At his announcement of the Resurrection; the three turn towards the altar and cry: *Alleluia, resurrexit Dominus.* In the empty grave they discover only the clothes and they show these to the clergy. Matins is then finished off with the Te Deum.[21] In excuse the editor points to other monasteries and to the needs of the uneducated people: *usum quorumdam religiosorum imitabilem ad finem indocti vulgi ac neophytorum corroborandum aequiparando sequi . . . decrevimus.* In this we see the rite, the basic idea of which continues to this day on the one hand in the burial ceremony of south Germany and Austria,[22] which is attached to the Good Friday liturgy, and on the other, in the Resurrection celebration of Holy Saturday evening which is popularly regarded as the real transition to the Easter festival. In particular, the outlines of the later Easter plays can already be

20. V. Young I, 582 seq.

21. PL 137, 493-495; Young I, 249 seq. 581 seq.

22. In the later Middle Ages this was often performed most realistically. The figure of Christ was taken down from the beam of the Cross (in Prüfening in 1500, and elsewhere), wrapped in cloths and laid in the sepulchre; Brooks 38 seq. 105. Or an (altar) stone was laid nearby, or under the head of the Crucified, and the sealing was indicated by a special covering up, while they sang: *Sepulto Domino signatum* est. Thus in Moosburg; Brooks 104. In Seckau in the 16th century a strip of wax was run round the sepulchre, stamped with the great seal of the Chapter; B. Roth, *Die Seckauer und Vorauer Osterliturgie im Mittelalter*, Seckau 1935, 30. 61. In Rouen in the 13th century, to commemorate the piercing with a lance and the flowing of blood and water, the figure of the Crucified was first of all washed with water and wine which was drunk; Young I, 135. The same custom in England, ibid. I, 164.

discerned here.[23] On the other hand, the Resurrection celebrations grew out of the exaltation of the Cross (or the elevation of the Sacrament), which regularly took place before Matins, only later to be deferred to the place of the Easter play which followed Matins. Even in our own day these take place in large churches at the end of Matins.

The most important thing, however, is this: here, too, we find a continuation of that tradition which wanted to honour the hour of our Lord's resting in the grave, the tradition of watching and praying by the grave. At the end of the burial ceremony the *Regularis Concordia* says: *In eodem loco sancta crux cum omni reverentia custodiatur usque Dominicam noctem resurrectionis. Nocte vero ordinentur duo fratres aut tres aut plures, si tanta fuerit congregatio, qui ibidem psalmos decantando excubias fideles exerceant.*[24]

It is true that there are monastic regulations for Holy Week belonging to the following centuries, e.g. the whole group of the Cluniac observance, in which there is apparently no trace of such a devotion during the hours of the resting in the tomb. Strict fasting alone is stressed; and this means fasting on bread and water on Good Friday.[25] The additional tradition of watching and prayer seems to have been maintained only in those places where it was reinforced by symbolic representation of the holy sepulchre and the related customs.

An explicit description of this is to be found, in fact, in the section of these representations which tell of the liturgical structure of the burial and the Resurrection celebration; and this is found in various places from northern Italy to England, but especially in Germany. In 1453 Bishop Peter of Augsburg settled an endowment[11] for stipends for students who will pray the psalter continuously beside the grave from Good Friday until

23. The *Quem-quaeritis* dialogue which has already made its appearance, was originally (i.e., since the beginning of the 10th century) linked as a *Tropus* with the Introit which began with the word *Resurrexi*; Cf. Blume, *Tropen des Missale im Mittelalter* II (Analectica hymnica 49), Leipzig 1906, 9 seq. Joined to Matins, it became the starting point of the play, known, in many versions, as *visitatio sepulchri*. In many versions the hymn *Victimae paschali* is divided up to form a dialogue. The news of the Resurrection is announced by Mary Magdalen.

24. loc. cit. (PL 137, 494).

25. Cf. e.g., the five volumes of B. Albers, *Consuetudines monasticae* (1900-12), esq. II, 51. 99; III, 130; IV, 63 etc.

Easter in honour of our Lord's Passion and death.26 The same
thing is found in Biberach. At each side of the grave sat school-
children with huge psalters in front of them 'from which they sang
the psalms antiphonally day and night without ceasing.'27 In
Aquileia, too, the printed order for Good Friday, 1575, reads:
*Finitem autem Vesperis scholares secondum morem patriae incipiunt
legere psalterium.*28 In Halle it was eight priests in *capis nigris* who
sang the psalter day and night, when there was no public service
going on in the church. *Pauperes* had always to be present as well.
Each received a stipend.29 In the 17th century this tradition was
still alive in Salzburg. The *Rituale* of 1686 states that on Good
Friday and Holy Saturday: *Ad sepulchrum . . . adhibendi sunt nocte
ac die testes quidem et custodes, nec deesse debent qui secundum ritum
antiquum psallant.*30 In Moosburg in Bavaria, the *Brevarium
ecclesiae Mosburgensis* mentions the participation of the faithful
about the turn of the 15th century. Here it is stated—and this must
apply to other places as well31—that when the crucifix was raised
out of the grave, before Matins in the middle of the night, the
laity were supposed to be excluded; but this was impracticable.
Nam nobiscum viri et mulieres in ecclesia sacras vigilias observant; then
the people who were keeping vigil by the grave could not be put
out of the church without annoyance.32 This must have been a
widespread custom, not confined to a few isolated places. Evidence
of this is given by the polemical poem 'Regnum papisticum' of
the Protestant pastor Thomas Naogeorgus (1553) who describes
Good Friday customs as he knows them from his experience in

26. Pl. Braun, *Geschichte der Bischöfe von Augsburg* III, Augsburg 1814, 61; Brooks 43.
A similar endowment was made to St. Peter's in Vienna in 1412; H. Leutze, *Das Seelgerät
im mittelalterlichen Wien*: Zeitschr. d. *Savigny-Stiftung f. Rechtsgeschichte, Kan. Abt.* 75
(1958, 35-103) 67; cf. 102 seq.
27. Account from Biberach in 1535, ed. by A. Schilling in the archives of the Diocese
of Freiburg 19 (1887) 127 seq.; the section also in Brooks 95 seq.
28. Young I, 144.
29. Brooks 101.
30. Quoted in the decree of the Cong. of Rites 11. XII. 1896: *Decreta auth.* SRC IV,
Rome 1900, 430. Agrees with Salzburg *Rituale* of 1640, p. 343. The rubric has the same
meaning today in the common *Rituale* of Salzburg and Innsbruck-Feldkirchen; but it is
added, that where *pii custodes et devote psallentes* are not to be found, as in country churches,
the pious over-night exercise can be interrupted; v. *Collectio rituum in usum cleri
Administraturae Apostolicae Oenipontanae-Feldkirchensis*, Innsbruck 1951, 444.
31. Brooks 42; Young I, 124. A reason for the exclusion of the laity was the superstition
attached to this custom; cf. Young I, 553.
32. Brooks 42, 104; Young I, 141. This uninterrupted watching and praying is still
provided for in the current *Rituale* of Linz. V. below n. 35.

central Germany. He tells how the wooden figure of Christ along with the Mystical Bread covered with a transparent veil are laid in the sepulchre, to the accompaniment of singing; how the people bring in candles and flowers to adorn the grave, praying night and day (*noctemque diemque*) on bended knee. Provision is also made for psalm-singing; *Irdsunt conducti quoque qui psalteria cantent.*33 Similar customs prevailed in England. The sacristan, at least, had to keep watch all night. At other places in England there is evidence of continuous psalmody.34 Even today the memory of such customs has not completely died out.35 It is probably in connexion with this psalmody in honour of the Holy Sepulchre that we find the custom in various monasteries in the 10th and 11th centuries of praying the whole psalter on Good Friday.36

From this devotion at the Holy Sepulchre, in many places there was, at first, no other devotional object available, except the crucifix which was laid in the sepulchre on Good Friday. This was the case with the *Regularis Concordia* in England. The same was true of Moosburg37 about 1500, and in many other churches.38 Thus the Resurrection was symbolized only by the raising up of the crucifix, as, for example, at the end of the Middle Ages in Brussels39 and in Lübeck.40 Evidence of the way, too, in which the

33. *Regnum papisticum* (1553) 148 seq. A longer passage from this is reprinted in Young II, 525-531.
34. Brooks 87. Again, in other places they were content to incense the sepulchre for a while after the laying in the tomb, and for the rest, to light candles which burned until Easter morning. Thus in Durham according to a report of 1593; *Rites of Durham*, ed. Fowler (Surtees Society 107; 1903) 11 seq.; Young I, 138.
35. In the *Collectio rituum* of the Diocese of Linz (1929) 459 we read, concerning the laying of the Body of Christ in the Holy Sepulchre: *Parochus curet, ut ad recolendum Corpus Dominicum in Sepulcro die noctuque adsint adoratores,* a request, which then becomes a prescription, but limited to the hours of day time. Cf. also the Salzburg tradition, above n. 30. But the practice of uninterrupted prayer at the Holy Sepulchre is by no means dead; it was still taken for granted in Schingiswalde in the Upper Lausitz in 1938 (as S. Hübner informs me).
36. Albers, *Consuetudines* I, 51 (Farfa); IV, 64 (Fruttuara); E. Martène, *De antiquis monachorum ritibus, app.* (= *De ant. Eccl. rit.* IV, Antwerp 1738, 852D) (Verdun).
37. V. above p.230; Young I, 140 seq.
38. Brooks 33-36 arranges all the sources in which the Holy Sepulchre is mentioned, according to the way in which the laying down in the sepulchre is carried out: the Cross only; the sacred Host only; Cross and Host. The sources which mention the Cross alone are the most numerous by far. As I have learned from Münster, Trier, Luxemburg, and Frankfurt, according to north German custom, to this day it is only a picture of the Holy Body which is laid in the tomb on Good Friday. In that place, surrounded by flowers and candles, it is venerated, and raised up on Holy Saturday.
39. Brooks 97.
40. Brooks 34 n. 15.

Blessed Sacrament was put away and then elevated on Easter morning, is given by St. Ulrich of Augsburg (d. 973). On Good Friday he gave Communion to the people; and after he had buried what was left over (*quod remanserat sepulto*), according to custom, he prayed the psalter, as he did also on Holy Saturday. After *Prime* on Easter morning he celebrated the Mass in the same church, that is, in the church *ubi die Parascere corpus Christi super-posito lapide collocavit*. From there he then went *secum portato corpore Christi et evangelio et cereis et incenso et cum congrua salutatione versuum a pueris decantata* back to the Church of St. John the Baptist.[41] The Blessed Sacrament, therefore, had been reserved in the grave; and on Easter morning the Blessed Sacrament was carried in procession—not unlike that which takes place today, a thousand years later, often in connexion with the celebration of the Resurrection.[42]

But the use of the Blessed Sacrament alone, which was the end of the process, seems to have been exceptional before the 15th century.[43] It was much more common for the crucifix, or the figure detached from it (later a special sculptured figure), to be laid in the holy sepulchre, the Blessed Sacrament being laid there only in association with this.[44] In Churches in England they used a carved image of the Saviour which carried the Blessed Sacrament in its breast.[45]

In other places people tried to obstruct this development. The *Breviarium* of Zürich of 1260 gives reasons for its objections: *Nam contra omnem rationem est, quod in quibusdam ecclesiis eucharistia in huiusmodi arca sepulcrum repraesentate pone consuevit et claudi. Ibi enim eucharistia, quae est verum et vivum corpus Christi, ipsum Christi corpus mortuum repraesentat, quod est indecens penitus et absurdum.*[46]

41. *Vita s. Udalrici auctore Gerardo* (PL 133, 1020 seq.).
42. In Austrian dioceses like Vienna and St. Polten, according to former tradition, the Resurrection procession took place in the open-air, often taking a wide sweep round the whole village.
43. As Brooks 40 shows, besides the case mentioned there are only two or three others of which we have evidence.
44. According to 13th century usage, in Bayeux the bishop laid the Cross in the Holy Sepulchre upon a cushion, then alongside it, the pyx with the Blessed Sacrament, a paten, and an empty chalice; Martène, *De ant. Eccl. rit.* 4, 23, 27 (III, 369 seq.). On Easter morning the bishop carried the pyx back to the altar, then the chalice and paten, finally the Cross, whereupon Resurrection hymns were sung and the blessing was given with the pyx; ibid. 4, 25, 7 (III, 481 seq.).
45. Brooks 38.
46. Young 154.

Thus towards the end of the Middle Ages, the predominant form of the custom was to lay only the image of the Saviour in the grave. This occurred either immediately after the veneration of the Cross or after the Mass of the Pre-sanctified or not until after Vespers. For the celebration of the Resurrection, they turned to the Blessed Sacrament. Before worship proper began with Matins they brought in the Blessed Sacrament without any farther ceremony;47 or, as in Trier, the Blessed Sacrament was not brought from the altar until the celebration of the Resurrection when it was carried round the church in solemn procession.48 While this was happening, Easter hymns were sung, among them, no doubt since the 13th century, the 'Christ is risen';49 and then Matins was concluded with the *Te Deum*. In Strassbourg, where the Sacrament was still carried in a pyx (following the *ordinarium* of 1364), the sacred Host was elevated thrice before the people *sicut solet levari in missa.*50

Since the 16th century the final phase in the development has come about in this way. The image of the dead Redeemer lies in the grave, it is true, surrounded by flowers and candles; but above the grave, the Blessed Sacrament is exposed in a lightly veiled monstrance—not as a representation of the sacred corpse, but as the living object of devotion. The first evidence of this concluding phase is given by the Jesuits in Munich in 1580;51 and since then it has become the custom all over southern Germany and Austria. It has been more precisely regulated in various diocesan Rituals, as has been its culminating act, the celebration of the Resurrection.52 The rubrics say that the mood of mourning, appropriate to these last days of Holy Week should not be contradicted by too festive a style of the Exposition. This rubric is obeyed by having the surrounding candles dimmed by coloured Easter-globes, an ele-

47. Brooks 40 quotes examples from northern France. Cf. Young I, 303 seq. 620 seq.
48. Brooks 40, 107 seq.
49. Young I, 322 seq. 636.
50. Brooks 44.
51. F. J. Lipowski, *Geschichte der Jesuiten in Bayern* I, Munich 1816, 200; Brooks 66. Cf. on the same time in Grau, Young I, 124 seq.
52. E.g. in the *Collectio rituum* of the Diocese of Linz (1929) p. 454-459; *Processio pro deponendo ss. Corpore Christi in Sepulcro* (459), and p. 466-469: *Processio quae fit ad recolendam resurrectionem Jesu Christi vespere Sabbati Sancti*, with the attached rubric (468), that in larger churches the *Te Deum* and sacramental Blessing should follow Matins of the Easter feast. Similarly in the Salzburg tradition, which persists in the modern *Rituale* of Salzburg and Innsbruck-Feldkirchen; *Collectio rituum* (above n. 30) 441-444; 453-456.

ment in the furnishings of the Holy Sepulchre which is a concession to popular feeling with its sensitivity to atmosphere.

But now, since the *Missale Romanum* (1570) has been introduced
and made obligatory, a certain contrast to those rules has arisen,
for these seem to have scarcely any room for such customs in Holy
Week: and strict rubricists have always been speaking of the
'non-liturgical' character of the rites in question. And yet, after
many answers which tended rather to reject the notion, the Congregation of Rites, in their decree of 17; XII: 1896, finally decided
in favour of the idea that the devout watching on Holy Thursday
and on Good Friday can be centred not merely on the institution
of the Blessed Sacrament, but also on the *sepulta Domini*.53

Looking over our former conclusions, which are intended to
throw light on the connexion between the fasting for forty hours
in the 2nd century and the Forty Hours Prayer of the 10th century,
so much at least has become plain: the Forty Hours corresponded
to the time which our Lord spent in the grave, and the early
Christians honoured this time, not only with fasting, but with
watching and prayer as well—and, what is more, beside the
sepulchre. This watching and praying at the sepulchre persisted in
many places right down to modern times. Since the 10th century,
in isolated places, the Blessed Sacrament, too, has been laid in the
grave, and people have prayed and kept watch before it.54 As the
example from Aquileia shows, this tradition was alive not so very
far from Milan, both as regards the continuous psalmody and the
veneration of the Blessed Sacrament in the grave. The last feature
is specially worthy of note. For while in Germany, laying the
Blessed Sacrament in the grave on Good Friday is the exception,
in Brook's *Statistics* all three examples of a depositing in the grave
which endured into the 16th century in northern Italy55 show that
the phase has been reached where the Sacrament is laid in the
grave, either separately as in Parma56 and after the fashion of

---

53. *Utrumque, Decreta auth.* SRC III, 323 seq.
54. Above p.231-2.
55. Brooks 35 seq. A fourth instance (p. 35) originates in the *Rituale* of Venice 1736 and
hence cannot be considered as evidence of Medieval tradition.
56. The text of the rubrics from the year 1417 in Young I, 125.

Venice57, or along with the crucifix as in the *agenda* of Aquileia, 1575.58.

The evidence for a period of exactly forty hours prayer at the Holy Sepulchre at Zara remains, however, an isolated instance. It was almost inevitable that the idea would become lost as the Easter Vigil was advanced more and more into Holy Saturday. The Easter Mass could begin as soon as the first stars appeared: that meant, in the time of the Easter equinox, about 6 p.m. If the Good Friday liturgy began at None, then only $3+24=27$ hours were left. Anyway, we find the symbolic representation of the moment of the Resurrection associated, in the setting of the Resurrection celebrations, of which the vigil at the Holy Sepulchre was a part, not with the beginning of the Easter Mass or the Easter Vigil, but with the beginning of Matins; and on Easter Sunday, following Jerome's statement that the people should not be allowed to go from this vigil before midnight,59 Matins were scheduled for midnight. We thus arrive at a period of $9+24=33$ hours. It was hardly appropriate, therefore, to appeal any longer to the sacred period of 44 hours.

Nonetheless, are the forty hours of the *supplicatio XL horarum* at Zara so unique after all ? In 1380 these forty hours in Zara terminated with the *Gloria* of the Easter Mass; and, according to the state of development in the 14th century, that would fall at midday on Holy Saturday. Consequently, the beginning of this period of prayer fell *sero Coena Domini*. Putting this at 8 p.m., we arrive at forty hours exactly: $4+24+12=40$. Can we point to any tradition which shows these limits for the veneration of the Holy Sepulchre? There is, indeed, an unexpected case of this. The Milan liturgy still contains a Resurrection celebration which is connected with the beginning of the Easter Vigil.60 According to the Missal of 1560 and present day custom also, this economic yet impressive rite is as follows: after kissing the altar at the beginning of the Mass, the priest takes the chalice and paten and cries out thrice: *Christus*

57. The *Sacerdotale* of A. Castellani printed in 1523, which describes a solemn entombment procession (*lugubris processio*), wherein the Bl. Sacrament was carried on a bier covered with a black cloth, speaks of a *mos Venetus*. Young I, 126–129.
58. Text in Young I, 143 seq.
59. *In Matth.* 1. IV, 25 (PL 26, 184 seq.). The saying is quoted in the Breviary of Moosburg; Brooks 104.
60. G. Borgonovo, *Nuovo manuale di Liturgia Ambrosiana*, Varese 1937, 520 seq. The rite is also given in the Missal itself—in, e.g., the *Missale Ambrosianum* of 1831.

Dominus resurrexit, and the choir responds *Deo gratias* each time. The first time, the priest stands at the right side of the altar; the second time, behind the altar; finally, at the left side.[61]

But as well as this, the time indicated in Zara as the starting point of the veneration of the Holy Sepulchre, that is, Holy Thursday, is supported in many and striking ways in Italy—right up to the present day. This is seen most clearly from the relevant decrees of the Congregation of Rites. Here it is presupposed and acknowledged, if with undisguised disapproval, that the place in which the Blessed Sacrament for the Mass of the Pre-sanctified is kept on Holy Thursday, is called *sepulcrum.*[62] These decrees cite many things which are rejected as abuses: the inquiry from Narni on 7:XII:1844 asking whether it was permissible to cover the Blessed Sacrament with a cloth suspended from a high cross; that from Alba on 8:VIII:1835 asking permission to cover the Blessed Sacrament with a cloth hung from a high cross; the question from Lodi on 21:I:1662 asking whether black material might be used to adorn the grave. Other enquiries, which likewise presuppose that there is a sepulchre, but which receive more favourable replies, come from Otranto and Aversa—Italian dioceses.

The topic is raised once more in the decree of the Congregation of Rites dated 15:XII:1896 which applies to Rome itself. The indulgent decision of this decree was given on account of the affirmative reply of the assessors to the preliminary question: *Num altare in quo feria quinta in Coena Domini SS. sacramentum asservatur S. Sepulchri dici possit.* But in contrast to the divergent language of

61.   Martène, *De ant. Eccl. rit.* 4, 25 (III, 477). Similarly in the Missal of 1669, according to which the organ and the bells are to sound immediately (ibid.). The threefold cry which the bishop begins from his throne, however, in the 12th century in the *Ordo* of Beroldus ed. Magistretti (Milan 1894) 114. The same procedure in general in the Rite of Gerona in Spain (15th century); only in this the priest holds the lighted Easter candle in his hands and calls out the good news after the *Kyrie eleison,* while ascending the altar—at the lower, middle, and top step; J. B. Ferreres, *Historia del Misal Romano,* Barcelona 1929, 290: cf. ibid. XXIV. A threefold *Surrexit Dominus de sepulchro* (with response: *Qui pro nobis pependit in ligno, Alleluja*) is also to be found in the Papal service in Mabillon's *Ordo Rom.* XII (composed by the later Honorius III., d. 1227) c. 14, 32 (PL 78, 1077 C), and somewhat later in the more detailed description of Mabillon's *Ordo Rom.* XIV c. 95 (PL 78, 1219); in this the Pope kissed the feet of the image on the Cross. The ceremony took place, however, on Easter Sunday after Prime in the Sancta Sanctorum Chapel. There can hardly be a direct connexion with the Milan ceremony.

62.   The systematically arranged collection of P. Martinucci, *Manuale decretorum* SRC. 3. Regensburg Edition 1873, supplies free relevant decrees for Holy Thursday, under the heading *De s. Sepulchro in quo ss. Eucharistia respondenda et servanda est,* n. 1019-1023. The term 'Holy Sepulchre' for the altar on Holy Thursday, is not by any means unknown in Germany also.

the liturgical books, the assessors' opinion, published along with the decree[63], seeks justification only in the old, traditional, allegorical sense of the chalice as grave.

A second question to the assessors concerned the *locus repositionis* and the *repositio* of the Sacrament itself. In expressing their opinion they cited as examples, pictures containing scenes from Christ's Passion or the Roman soldiers such as are found in Spain and elsewhere; or the setting up in the church on Good Friday of a *Pieta* draped in a black veil, as in Bergamo. Here too, the reply inclines to toleration, for meditation on Christ's Passion is not, indeed, alien to the Holy Thursday liturgy.

Furthermore, in the *Missale Romanum* there is still a rite (removed, it is true, in 1955) which can only be explained by the idea of the Lord being laid in the tomb on this day. The sacred Host for the *Missa praesanctificatorum* is not kept in a pyx but in a chalice; and according to allegorical interpretation, the chalice represents a grave. This chalice is covered with the paten: this is the tomb-stone; and the common practice of lacing up the cloth over the chalice symbolizes the sealing of the grave.[64]

In the above-mentioned Italian dioceses the attempt was made to introduce those elements which were connected with the end of the Holy Thursday Mass into the 'reposition' of the Blessed Sacrament which followed. We are justified in thinking that reference to the allegorical significance of the chalice does not provide a very thorough explanation of why on Holy Thursday and in Italy principally, the place where the Eucharist was kept was thought of as a grave. On the contrary, this idea is perfectly explicable if here, as in Zara, which was under Venician influence from the 11th century and under Venician rule since 1202, the celebration of the sepulchre had to last forty hours and therefore had to begin along with the traditional exposition on Holy Thursday.[65]

63. *Decreto auth.* SRC IV, 419-421; cf. III, 323 seq.
64. J. Kettel, *Zur Liturgie des Gründonnerstags: Liturg. Jahrbuch* 3 (1953, 60-74) 65 seq.
65. The tendency towards beginning at that time already appears in Sicard of Cremona, *Mitrale* VI, 13 (PL 213, 319 seq.). He defends the advancing of commemoration of the Passion to Holy Thursday, because the Lord offered Himself in the Sacrament on this day, and because on the other hand Holy Saturday is already being illuminated with the joy of Easter; therefore the triduum is transposed (*transponitur*) from the days in which our Lord was killed by the Jews, to the period when He sacrificed Himself (*quod ipse manibus est oblatus*).

We need not be surprised to find that the number forty is not expressly mentioned in the random references which are all we have been able to evaluate here. That it did in fact persist, in Italy, too, is shown by Sicard of Cremona (d.1215).[66] Honorius of Augustodunum[67] and Durandus[68] mention it as the length of time our Lord was dead or lay in the tomb. The latter explains the custom in many places of holding another Requiem for the deceased forty days after their death by reference to the forty hours which our Lord spent in the tomb.[69]

A systematic research into the printed and unprinted material from the period at the turn of the Middle Ages might contribute much to all this. At least so much may have been made plain in what has been said: The ancient Christian devotion of the Forty Hours has had an uninterrupted tradition right down to the present-day. There have been two lines of development. There has been devotion at the Holy Sepulchre between the deposition in the grave and the celebration of the Resurrection, either disregarding the integrity of the whole original period or advancing the beginning of the devotion to the evening of Holy Thursday. And secondly, there has been the Forty Hours' Devotion which, since 1527, has been separated from its living source and become rather a form of the cult of the Blessed Sacrament. It would be wrong of anyone to reject or to ignore either form. But both forms would be greatly helped by our meditating on the concept which is their ultimate raison d'etre, by our entering into the mystery of Redemption at its deepest point—the voluntary humiliation of the God-man.

7. *The Octave of Pentecost and Public Penance in the Roman Liturgy*

Everyone knows that Pentecost was not originally a third major festival alongside Easter and Christmas, but was the concluding

66. *Mitrale* VI, 15 (PL 213, 341).
67. *Gemma an.* III, 98 (PL 172, 668).
68. Durandus, *Rationale* VI, 78, 3.
69. Ibid. VII, 35, 10.

day of Easter—Pentecost. For this reason, in the Roman liturgy, the octave day of Pentecost is a secondary structure—secondary, too, in that it lacks that unifying character which we meet in the Mass rituals of Easter week. The latter is based upon two sets of basic ideas: the Resurrection of Christ and its reflexion in the life of the newly baptized. But the twin thoughts of the pouring out of the Holy Spirit upon the infant Church and the gifts of grace to the newly baptized by no means suffice to explain the rituals of Pentecost week. Certainly, the chants still belong to this twofold set of ideas; for not only do the strains of sheer praise of God, which resound frequently without precise classification, and joy over the law of God (Offertory for Wednesday; cf. the expression of the idea of Baptism in the phrase: *Dominus leget dat*) correspond to the motif of the feast, but also the thanksgiving for the Bread of heaven (Introit for Monday: Offertory for Tuesday) belongs to the family of Baptism ideas and is met with likewise in Easter week (Offertory for Wednesday). The prayers, too, are in harmony with Pentecost week: they do not depart from the motif of the feast any farther than is usual in similar circumstances. With the lessons—and with the whole structure of the Wednesday and Saturday rituals—we must take into account the Ember days, which are already connected with this week in the earliest liturgical sources. But the Epistles, which up to Friday are all taken from the Acts of the Apostles and describe the first activities of the apostles, are entirely in keeping with the plan of a Pentecost celebration. And the last of the pre-evangelical lessons in the vigil Mass of Saturday deal with the outpouring of the Holy Spirit. Only the Friday lesson from Joel, and the 2nd-5th pre-evangelical lessons of the vigil, telling of harvest and first-fruit offerings, of which the last always forms the introduction to the Song of the Three Children on an Ember day, have an overtly Ember character.

Part of the Gospels bears a much stronger mark of the Ember day. Turn first to these days which are regarded as Ember days. The passage on Wednesday is taken from the Eucharistic commission address (Jn. 6, 44-52). It opens with the thought that only he can attain everlasting life who, led by the Father, is instructed, and proceeds to take the Bread of heaven. As we have indicated already, a reference to the Bread of heaven could be suggested by Baptism, and the mystery of Pentecost could be the cause of the portion of Scripture beginning with our Lord's words about the operation of inward grace.1 On the other hand, the Gospel about the paralytic, appointed for Friday, is clearly chosen to suit the Ember day: for the passage occurs also in the oldest lists of passages for Friday of the autumn Ember days.2 The same event (according to Mt. 9, 1-8) turns up again today on the Friday Ember day in autumn,3 and used to turn up in part on the Sunday after Pentecost.4 As can be recognized in the scene frequently portrayed in early Christian art, and plainly connected with the idea of Baptism,5 the interest is shifted primarily onto the forgiveness of sins, which the Lord grants the sick man: a theme belonging to other Ember day passages—dominating them, indeed, apart from the Advent Ember days, which have a theme of their own. The theme of the forgiveness of sins is plainly on the surface in the passage about the sinful woman in Lk. 7, 36-50, read on the Friday Ember day in autumn—at least in more recent times.6 But the rest of the Ember passages, too, deal with the conquest of sin, either directly: in the speech on strife, Mt. 12, 38-50, on Wednesday of the Lenten Ember week; in the description of the expulsion of the unclean spirit, Mk. 9, 10-28 on Wednesday of the autumn Ember week; or symbolically, in the form of healing of disease: in the story of the thirty-eight years old man, Jn, 5, 1-15, on Friday in the Lenten Ember week (with the warning: *iam noli peccare*) and in the story of the cripple woman Lk. 13, 10-17,7 on Saturday in the autumn Ember week.

This last example occurs also in the Pentecost Ember week which interests us at present. This occurs, indeed, in our contem-

1. St. Beissel, *Entstehung der Perikopen des römischen Messbuches*, Freiburg 1907, 166 takes a different view. He considers the pericope about the 'heavenly bread' to be occasioned by the quarterly Ember fast.
2. Th. Klausner, *Das römische Capitulare evangeliorum* I, Munster 1935, 39. 85. 124. 164; Beissel 139-152.—Only since the 9th century does the pericope of the sinful woman (Lk. 7, 36-50) appear in place of this one. V. Beissel 165 (n. 36; cf. p. 158. 160).
3. The earliest evidence of this v. Beissel 139. 149. 152 seq.
4. Cologne mss. since the 9th century; v. Beissel 165 ('I, 39').
5. Kunstle, *Ikonographie der christlichen Kunst* I, 19 seq.; cf. 33.
6. Above, n. 3.
7. The pericope in this version in the lists of pericopes of the 7-8th centuries, in Klausner 39. 85. 124. 164.—The application to the preceding parable of the barren fig tree, Lk. 13, 6-9, as in the division of pericopes we know today, could only have come about because the symbolism of the healing of the sick was no longer understood.

porary Missal which in this shows the Frankish tradition in using
Lk. 4, 38-44 with its account of the great healing of sick and
expulsion of unclean spirits in Capharnaum,8 as well as the original
Roman tradition in which Mt. 20, 29-34, with the healing of two
blind men at Jericho, was traditional.9 The Gospel passages for
Friday and Saturday thus can be fully explained as Ember
passages.

The Thursday passage about the mission of the apostles, in Lk.
9, 1-6, need not occupy us any further in our search for the
original structure of Pentecost week. It is missing in the older
types of Gospel capitualry, brought to light by Theodore Klausner,
and it makes its first appearance in the Roman-Frankish type
which appeared after 750.10 It is completely in harmony with the
Pentecostal motif, especially as expressed in the Epistle lessons
from Monday to Thursday. A rite for Thursday is lacking also in
the older material of the Mass antiphonary11 and in the older
sacramentaries—even in Hadrian's *Gregorianum*,12 which already
provides Thurdsay rites for Lent.

From this we learn two things: that as late as the end of the 8th
century the week of Pentecost still did not have the character of a
whole week dominated by Pentecost, and that from Wednesday
on it was virtually an Ember week, but with a feeling of Pentecost
about it. This need not surprise us: the winter Ember week, too,
since being re-fashioned in the 6th century, has preserved a
thoroughly Christmas liturgy.13

We are left with the Gospel lessons of Monday and Tuesday to
explain. Now the real puzzle begins. The very same lessons from
part of the oldest Roman tradition,14 just as the rest of the rite of
the Mass for these two days, represents ancient traditional Roman
material,15 taking us back, as concerns the sacramentary, at least to
the 6th century.

8. Beissel 164 (n. 10).
9. Klausner 28. 74. 115. 154; Beissel 164 (n. 11).
10. Klausner 154.
11. R.-J. Hesbert, *Antiphonare Missarum sextuplex*, Brussels 1935, n. 109-110.
12. Lietzmann p. 73.
13. Jungmann, *Gewordene Liturgie* 264 seq. (=Zk Th 137, 366).
14. Klausner 28. 74. 115. 154.
15. For the formulae of the sacramentary v. in K. Mohlberg, *Das frankische Sacramentarium Gelasianum*,¹ Münster 1939, p. 316, concordance table by G. Manz n. 107-111.

How does Pentecost Monday come to have the Gospel passage, Jn. 3, 16-41, with its statement that men will bring judgement upon themselves if they decline to believe in the Son of God whom the Father's love has sent? A certain despair can be detected in the attempted explanations of the commentators. It is true that the passage speaks of 'eternal life' and 'light', 16 both 'effects of the Holy Spirit'.17 But that is not the theme of the passage. It is true that in the light of the Biblical passages the sin which is denounced here can be described as a sin against the Holy Spirit,18 but there is no hint of this description in the text itself. And why does this passage limit itself—not only in our Missal but equally in the most ancient orders of lessons—to those very verses which are preceded a few sentences earlier and in the same narrative by the account of the nocturnal conversation with Nicodemus when the talk was about re-birth through water and the Spirit (Jn. 3, 5 seq.)?19 Does it not look as if the composer of this arrangement of lessons had deliberately avoided the thought of Pentecost? At any rate, the pronouncement of judgement was more important for him.

There is not much difference with the Gospel for Pentecost Tuesday, Jn. 10, 1-10, where the Lord describes Himself as the door to the sheep, through which only the rightful shepherd enters to whom the sheep listen. Admittedly the reference to 'eternal life', which Christ will give to His sheep, stressed by many, comes at the end of this passage too: but it is so remote from the mystery of the feast that other commentators do not even mention it.20 It would be easier to point to the parallel with the passage about the Good Shepherd on the second Sunday after

16.   Schott, *Das Messbuch der heiligen Kirche*,11 Freiburg 1934, 518 seq.; and also in later editions.
17.   The last phrase is a paraphrase on the content of the Gospel by Beissel 157 n. 3. Similarly E. Ranke, *Das kirchliche Pericopensystem*, Berlin 1847, 362. Beissel seems to consider the problem to be solved by this remark: that these pericopes, like those of the Vigil of Pentecost and of Pentecost Sunday, have to do 'with the Holy Spirit'. (166).
18.   I. Schuster, *Liber Sacramentorum* IV, Turin 1926, 162 seq.
19.   In a later, Roman lectionary, dated c. 755, the pericope Jn. 3, 1-15 appears on the Octave day of Pentecost; Klausner 115.
20.   Schott, loc. cit. 522, stresses rather the words 'door of the sheep'. Similarly Beissel 166. Cardinal Schuster (loc. cit.) refuses to bring in a relationship with Pentecost. He interprets the pericope as a warning against schisms. The lack of a relation to Pentecost is affirmed by H. Grisar also, *Das Missale im Lichte römischer Stadtsgeschichte*, Freiburg 1925, 83. Grisar suggests that some monumental gate or other in the vicinity of the stational church had suggested the 'door' of the parable.

Easter.21 But in the latter case we are dealing not with the same passage but with that which follows it immediately, Jn. 3, 11-16, and which with its statement about the Good Shepherd who gives His life for the sheep, bears a much closer relationship to the basic Easter theme, Redemption, than obtains between the passage for Pentecost Tuesday and either the Easter theme or the Pentecost theme. In both passages we would have to lay the emphasis on the increase in the numbers of sheep through Baptism.22 But even with this we reach a thought which is, at most, only on the fringe of the theme. And so, Pius Parsch provides the solution by saying that the image of the Good Shepherd—so dear to the early Church —was but the ordinary indication that a new division of time was beginning. It certainly occurrs—as it does here on the second day of the old Lent—on the first Sunday after the Easter octave and then once more on the third Sunday after Pentecost.23

The parallel to the first day of the old Lent—the Monday following the first Sunday in the penitential season—is worth careful examination. The commentator we have mentioned made another observation about the rite of the Mass for Pentecost Tuesday, which causes him to speak of two means by which, according to these rites, the Holy Spirit grants to His Church 'purification and protection' (cf. the collect: *expurget—tueatur*): the Church's penitential discipline and the Eucharist; for the Post-Communion for this day contains a petition for the gracious operation of the Holy Spirit, with the striking reason: *quia ipse est remissio omnium peccatorum*.24 How did the thought of penance get into the rite for the highly festive Pentecost Tuesday?

On the Monday following the first Sunday in the penitential season the readings centre round the theme of the shepherd and the flock. This thought dominates not the Gospel only (Mt. 25, 21-46; the shepherd divides the sheep from the goats), but the Epistle also (Ezech. 34, 11-16: God himself will tend His flock). And here the regulating fact is, that for a very long time it was on

21. Thus Beissel 166.
22. Beissel 166.
23. P. Parsch, *Das Jahr des Heiles* II¹⁴, Klosterneuburg 1952, 554 seq. And yet, Parsch does not seem to be entirely satisfied with this idea, which he puts forward only tentatively. He ends with the suggestion that in the case before us the Holy Spirit is in the end being represented as our Good Shepherd.
24. Parsch loc. cit.

244   PASTORAL LITURGY

this day—the first week-day of Lent as it then was—that public penance began.²⁵

On that day the sheep were indeed divided from the goats: the penitents were shown to the penitential part of the church and given the hair garments of penance which, according to St. Augustine, were a reminder of sin *propter hoedos ad sinistram futuros.* The Shepherd thus was coming to judge and divide His flock; but this time it was a gracious coming as Ezechiel had described it. Might the same sort of thing not be behind the passage for Pentecost Tuesday: an exercise of ecclesiastical authority for the benefit of those sheep who had fallen a prey to thieves and robbers and who were to be brought back by the crook of the only just Shepherd?

But the parallel to the first penitential week runs even deeper. We were surprised to discover that the Gospel passage for Pentecost Monday is inspired by the thought of judgement. The puzzle is solved if this day plays a part in the judgement of public penance. In the early Church the sacrament of Penance was recognized as a judgement, not merely in its essence: the process of penance was to a great extent, especially in its early phase, modelled upon the juridical process. It began with the accusation which came by no means from the sinner himself. Then followed the allotting and performance of the penance; only after which reconciliation was pronounced and the words of this same Scripture passage were fulfilled: God had not sent His Son into the world to condemn the world, but that through Him the world might be saved. It would appear, therefore, that not only the second but also the first day after Pentecost was already imbued with the thought of penance. The Monday and Tuesday following the completion of the Easter Pentecost cycle must once have been very important days in the Roman discipline of public penance.

What already seems highly probable becomes a certainty once we have taken into account another factor, as yet scarcely heeded by anyone. To this day, the same *statio* is set in the Missal for Pentecost Monday and Tuesday as is set for the Monday and

25.   V. the proof in Jungmann, *Die lateinische Bussriten in ihrer geschichtlichen Entwicklung,* Innsbruck 1932, 48–51.

Tuesday of the first penitential season:26 *ad S. Petrum ad vincula* and *ad. S. Anastasiam*. These were two churches especially equipped for penitential disciplinary proceedings.

The first of these churches was described in the 5th century as *titulus Apostolorum* and stood close to the city prefecture where the Roman court still sat. The reminiscence of justice which this provided27 was reinforced in a Christian way by the old shrine which was connected with the titular church and which was dedicated to the imprisonment of St. Peter in Jerusalem, and by the iron chain —kept here since the 5th century—with which he had been bound.28 The name which appeared at the same time: *S. Petrus ad vincula*, might also have been a reminder of the power of binding and loosing which the apostles had received.

This connexion, however, was not necessary for the church to recommend itself as suitable for penitential purposes. As a church of an apostle is was already set apart for this; for on Friday of each of the four Ember weeks, on which—except in Advent—the Gospel spoke of penance and forgiveness, the stational worship had been appointed from time immemorial to take place in the second of the churches dedicated to the apostles, *ad. SS. XII Apostolos*—a coincidence from which Hartmann Grisar has assumed that this basilica must have been 'the Church of Penance, i.e. the Place of Reconciliation'.29 Thus, St. Peter in Chains was not accidentally chosen for the opening of penance at the beginning of Lent; and it was no more accidental on Pentecost Monday either that it appeared as the stational church—and these two are the only cases.

The titular church of St. Anastasia, too, apart from the commemoration day of the saint in the second Christmas Mass, served as a stational church only on Tuesday of the first penitential season and on Pentecost Tuesday. As soon as the character of the preceding ritual is seen, we can no longer overlook the fact that the Mass ritual for the Tuesday of the first season is closely allied to that for the Monday and like this is strongly characterized by the tone of

26. As far as I know, it is only G. Morin who has drawn attention to this coincidence in *La Part des papes du VI siecle dans le developpement de l'année liturgique: Revue Bénéd.* 52 (1940) 3-14; but he declines to attempt an explanation.
27. Grisar, *Das Missale* 2. 26 seq.
28. J. P. Kirsch, *Die Stationskirchen des Missale Romanum*, Freiburg 1926, 92 seq.
29. Grisar, *Das Missale* 60 seq.

246 PASTORAL LITURGY

penitential discipline, especially in both of its lessons. The lesson
from Isaias is a sheer call to penance. And the purification of the
temple from commerce—Mt. 21, 10-17—is but a symbol of what
was happening as penance began.[30] That the church was filled up
with the trappings of penance is shown by the fact that when the
opening of penance was advanced to Ash Wednesday, the first
preparatory act, the *collecta* at least but in all probability the opening ceremony of penance itself, was transferred to St. Anastasia's.[31]
There can scarcely be any doubt that the choice of St. Anastasia's
as stational church on Pentecost Tuesday was connected with its
being furnished to facilitate penitential discipline.

Reviewing the facts just listed, the circumstances should
astonish us no longer. As everyone knows, public and solemn
opening of penance used to be the custom on Ash Wednesday.
But such an opening on Ash Wednesday only became possible
after Lent was extended to include Ash Wednesday, so providing
a period of full forty days fasting. This could scarcely have
happened before the 7th century.[32] Behind this was a more
ancient arrangement according to which Lent was calculated on
the basis, not of forty fasting days, but of forty days simply, beginning with Quadragesima Sunday and ending with Holy
Thursday; and within this, public penance had to begin on the
first week-day—that is, Monday in the first week of the fast. This
arrangement must have come in about the middle of the 5th
century and been standard practice in the 6th century. Its form
became fixed with the re-constitution of the nature of the stations,
traceable in all probability back to the time of Pope Hilary
(461-468).[33]

30. For the rest, the theme of the inauguration of penance is echoed in the readings of
the following days, in so far as these do not derive from the number 40 of Lent which had
just begun. On Wednesday the penance of the Ninivites is mentioned. On Thursday
appears the incident with the Canaanite woman whom the Lord 'called to repentance'
(first responsory of the day)—she operated in the region of Tyre and Sidon—cf. the saying
(Mt. 11, 21): 'If these signs had been done in Tyre and Sidon. . . .'
31. Lietzmann, n. 35: *Collecta ad S. Anastasiam*. Cf. Jungmann, *Die lateinische Bussriten*
50. n. 177.
32. The Monday in question must have assumed its liturgical significance before this,
as is shown by Sermon 42 of Leo the Great (PL 54, 281 D): v. A. Chavasse, *Le structure
du Careme et les lectures des Messes quadragésimales: La Maison-Dieu* 31 (1952, 76-119)
84 seq.—Certainly, very early—perhaps by the 5th century—Wednesday and Friday after
Quinquagesima had come to possess their stational services, but they were not counted in
the 40 days. C. Callewaert, *Sacris erudiri*, Steenbrugge 1940, 486. 580 n. 75.
33. Callewaert, *Sacris erudiri* 500-503.

An older, third stratum is perceptible even farther back than this. In it, the opening of public penance was not yet associated with the start of Lent at all. This stratum would fit into the early 5th century. From Innocent I (402-417) we learn[34] that it was customary in the Roman Church for penitents who had to do penance for greater or lesser sins to receive forgiveness on Holy Thursday, *quinta feria ante Pascha*. He says nothing about a set time for the beginning of penance. And in fact there was no such need to set an anterior limit as there was to set one for the time of reconciliation which in general would be a more public and more solemn act. Enlisting in the ranks of the penitents—as the individual usually had to do—could be done at any time.[35] One thing only was fixed: during the Easter-Pentecost cycle just as on Sundays all external penitential acts were suspended, particularly fasting and praying in a kneeling posture.[36] If for this reason they had declined in Rome to inaugurate Lenten penance on Sunday, the same reason must have led them not to start public penance once again during Pentecost.[37] Penance would have to be resumed, therefore, when the fifty days of holy joy were past. And so it came about automatically that not only was the customary stational fast put into operation once more during the first week after Pentecost, but the quarterly Ember week, which was due, was placed at the beginning of this period. Leo the Great takes it for granted that this was a standard custom in his own time.[38] It was obvious that public penance, too, would be resumed, and that this would be the first point, if anywhere, at which a form of inauguration of public penance would have to appear. And this is the very thing which our discoveries show.

More support for our thesis comes from a palimpsest from

34. Innocent I., *Ep.* 25, 7 (PL 20, 559).
35. Cf. Jungmann, *Die lateinische Bussriten* 44 seq. The earliest evidence of the opening of penance is given by the older Gelasianum—i.e. at the earliest, 6th century; ibid. 45 seq.
36. Tertullian, *De cor.* c. 3 (PL 2, 79 seq.) maintains that it is wrong (*nefas*), to fast or to kneel at prayer on Sundays or during Pentecost. Similarly Hilary, *In pss. c.* 12 (PL 9, 239); Jerome, *Dial. c. Lucif.* n. 8 (PL 23, 164); Augustine, *Ep.* 55, 15, 28 (CSEL 34, 202. Z. 9).
37. In Africa at least, the practice on this point was different. Augustine shows surprise at the large number of *poenitentes* who appeared on an Easter Tuesday. *Serm.* 232, 7 (PL 38, 1111).
38. See the instance in L. Fischer, *Die kirchlichen Quatember*, Munich 1914, 147 seq. Only after the 7th century are major variations in the beginning of the Pentecost Ember week to be found. These last until the 13th century; Fischer 149-161.

Bobbio dated at the beginning of the 7th century, in which, in connexion with passages from St. Paul there follows immediately after Pentecost Sunday the title: *In indul(gentia)*.39

In this way, the riddle about how Monday and Tuesday after Pentecost come to have special Mass rituals becomes solved; for as indicated the limits of the penitential season must already have been present in the 5th century, long before anyone ever thought of giving Pentecost a full octave on the model of the Easter octave.40

It was not only in Rome that the resumption of penitential practices after Pentecost received particular emphasis. In the East it had developed into a liturgical celebration of considerable dimensions. This was the *office* of γονυκλισία which took place in the Byzantine liturgy on Pentecost Sunday evening at the end of Vespers. It was made up of three series of long prayers of sup-

39. A. Dold, *Zwei Bobbienser Palimpseste* (Texte u. Arbeiten 19-20), Beuron 1931, 60. The author, who was able to decipher these, did not risk asserting that there was a connexion with Pentecost in his explanation (p. 71), but only because G. Morin had assured him that in liturgical history such an appellation for Pentecost would represent something totally new. The list of pericopes shows Roman as well as Gallican elements.

40. The thought of a full Pentecost octave is first apparent in the Roman Epistle-*Comes* (v. the traditional revision in G. Godu, *Epitre*: DACL V, 304. 313. 318), and even in the *Comes* of Würzburg, i.e., evidence from the second half of the 6th century. Whereas all other sources of the 6th-8th centuries—sacramentaries, Mass-antiphonaries, Gospel-capitularies—make the Ember days follow immediately on Pentecost Monday and Tuesday, thus containing no formula for Thursday, the Epistle-*Comes* first of all supplies pericopes for all the rest of the days of the week from Wednesday till Saturday and for Sunday, and only then makes the Ember days follow on. That this scheme of a Pentecost octave is more recent than that which provides Pentecost Monday and Tuesday with Mass formulae, is clear from the fact that here, too, both of these days are assigned to stational churches—*Ad vincula* and *Ad S. Anastasiam*; Revue Bénéd. 27 (1910) 57. For want of a better explanation, G. Morin, *La part des papes* (v. above n. 26) 10 seq., can only suggest as the reason for the choice of these stational churches, the special prestige of these shrines in the 6th century—the same attitude which led to the choice of the other stational churches of this octave (St. Mary Major, SS. John and Paul, St. Stephen) (ibid. 11 seq.). As Morin himself points out in *Revue Bénéd.* 26 (1910) 58 seq. on the first publication of the Würzburg *Comes*, the independent Pentecost octave of the *Comes* may only be an ephemeral order which was later set aside—perhaps by Gregory the Great. That the Mass formulae of Monday and Tuesday represent an older stratum is shown by the Leonianum, where all three prayers of our Pentecost Tuesday follow Pentecost, and then come the Ember prayers—and, indeed, the Tuesday Post Communion with the addition, mentioned above: *quia ipse est omnium remissio peccatorum*, which refers to penance (Mohlberg, Sacr. Ver. n. 223).—For the rest, in the prayers of these intermediate days we have the petition to be protected from our enemies, even more strongly stressed than is the case in our present-day formulae for Monday and Tuesday. Morin, *La part des papes*, 9 seq. recalls the threat to Rome by the East Goths (535-553) and suggests that this proves similar circumstances of origin as for the Sundays before the fast. And yet the prayers could just as easily have originated in the 5th century when hostile attacks upon Rome were common enough after 408.

plication and penance, during which great stress was laid upon kneeling,[41] which had been absent all through Pentecost. Such a kneeling Office on the evening of Pentecost was customary elsewhere in the East as well,[42] in the western Syrian and in the eastern Syrian rite,[43] and also amongst the Copts.[44]

The further question claims our attention: what closer relationship, if any, obtains between the two penitential days designated by the Mass rituals at the beginning of Pentecost week—clearly concerned with primarily public penance—and the quarterly Ember days which immediately follow them? Is the sequence and proximity purely external, and is the inner connexion provided simply by their both having a penitential character, and both reappearing at the earliest opportunity after the close of Easter festivity? Or is there a common scheme underlying both? To put it another way: Should the Ember days along with the first two days after Pentecost be regarded as components of the Roman public penitential discipline of the 5th century?

We may recall that from early days in the Roman Church solemn reconciliation was appointed to take place on Holy Thursday, but that in the 5th century, it was stressed that for reasons of particular penitential zeal or in special circumstances—apart from illness—reconciliation did not have to be limited to these days.[45] In these cicumstances the final day for such extraordinary penitential reconciliation must primarily have been the quarterly Ember Friday, with its station at *SS. XII Apostolos*, and having set Scripture passages which were appropriate to repent-

41. In Slav and in German by A. Maltzew, *Die Nachtwache oder Abend und Morgengottesdienst der Orthodox—Katholischen Kirche*, Berlin 1892, 657–697.

42. The assumption of Baumstark, *Liturgie comparée*² 156 seq. that this Office can be traced to the Pentecost celebration on Pentecost Sunday afternoon in Jerusalem, described in the Peregrinatio of Aetheria c. 43 (CSEL 39, 94 seq.) is obviously untenable. It is much more important to notice in this connexion, that the pilgrim then remarks with some emphasis, that regular fasting began again on the following day, c. 44 (ibid. 95): N. Nilles also stresses the penitential character of the Office said kneeling—*Kalendarium manuale* II², Innsbruck 1897, 405 seq., which entitles this: *De vespertino reconciliationis officio.*

43. Baumstark, *Festbrevier und Kirchenjahr der syrischen Jakobiten* 1910, 255 seq. From older Syrian mss., Baumstark records Jn. 4, 13-24 (our Lord reveals the sins of the Samaritan woman) as the original pericope belonging to this.

44. According to a 14th century ms. ed. by O. H. E. Burmester, *The Office of genuflection on Whitsunday*: Museon 47 (1934) 205-257. Cf. JL 13 (1935) 339.

45. Innocent I., *Ep.* 25, 7 (PL 20, 559). Similarly Leo the Great, *Ep.* 108, 4 (PL 54, 1012 seq.).

ance and forgiveness of sins.[46] (Both passages are not suited exclusively to the Pentecost Ember Friday.) It is plain that from the end of the 5th century onwards[47] the general fast was likewise made the occasion of transferring ordinations to the quarterly Ember vigil.

We might ask further if the penitential arrangements of the Ember days which had been assimilated into public worship—not unlike the penitential activities of Lent—might not have had a sacramental significance, a kind of absolution—value for those in the congregation who were in need of penance, but who did not fall into the class of penitents in the strict sense; and if, therefore, the Ember days, and Pentecost week in particular had not taken on a more all-embracing pastoral significance than it has with us. It is the idea of general purification from sin and guilt, contracted in the foregoing period, by means of the exercises of the Ember days which Leo the Great emphasizes in numerous sermons which he delivered at the start of these weeks,[48] and which are in tune with his Lenten sermons. Admittedly he speaks on these occasions only of fasting and alms-giving as means of striving for such purification and does not mention at all any definite ecclesiastical mediation through some special rite: in this connexion, the only thing he cites is the public vigil in St. Peter's. But apart from this we can scarcely discover any closer description of the details of ritual in his sermons, and the festive tone of his speech does not lead us to expect it.[49]

There can hardly be any doubt, that by the 5th century, at the end of the Papal liturgy there was regularly a blessing of penitents,

46. I expressed this conjecture in 1932 in *Die lateinischen Bussriten* 310, n. 265. It was made earlier by H. Grisar, *Das Missale*, 60 seq.; cf. above n. 29.
47. Gelasius, *Ep.* 14, 11 (Thiel 368 seq.). Cf. Callewaert, *Sacris erudiri*, 568 seq.
48. Cf. *Die Charakteristik des Quatembers nach Leo dem Grossen* by L. Fischer, *Die kirchlichen Quatember* 128 seq.
49. That we must pre-suppose that in the time of Leo the Great there was a form of ecclesiastical penance which was distinguished from another sort of public penance and which was repeatable, is a notion finding special support from French scholars like P. Batiffol and J. Tixeront. P. de Puniet also, in *Le sacramentaire romain de Gellone: Eph. liturg.* 48 (1934) 362, supports the idea of an opportunity for penance which recurred from time to time, perhaps yearly, in the time of Leo. In particular, certain passages in Leo's sermons give substance to the idea, e.g. *Serm.* 43, 2 seq.; 49, 1 seq.; 50, 1 seq. E. Goller thinks that this is most probable, *Papsttum und Bussgewalt in spätrömischer und frühmittelalterlicher Zeit: Röm. Quartalschrift* 39 (1931) 71-267. P. 119-153 examines Leo's doctrine of penance thoroughly; v. esp. p. 142 seq. 153. Cf. ibid., *Archiv f. kath. Kirchenrecht* 113 (1933) 318, where he once more formulates his objections—by the way.

somehow connected with the blessing of the people.50 Then such a penitential rite with imposition of hands and episcopal *supplicatio* must have become attached primarily to the quarterly Ember days. Whether or not this had a sacramental significance depended upon the condition of the penitent and the intention of the one who gave the blessing. But such questions lead us into the thorny tangle of the history of penance in later antiquity; and we do not wish to follow this line at present.

8. *The Weekly Cycle in the Liturgy*

By the reform decree of the Congregation of Rites, dated March 23, 1955, what were formerly single feasts have been reduced to a mere *memoria*, and a number of octaves and vigils have been done away with: as a result much more scope has been opened up for the *office de feria*. The calendar now appoints as the proper rite for such days, the Mass of the previous Sunday— leaving freedom, too, to choose another. Only on Saturday is the Mass and Office of the week-day governed by a special theme: *S. Maria in Sabbato*. It has already been worked out, how much more frequently this Office will appear according to the new regulations.1 Besides this, on the other days of the week there is freedom to choose from the whole series of votive Masses. In the *Missale Romanum* of 1570 these were related to individual days of the week by a common rubric; since 1920 they were assigned to particular days through express titles; and as well as this they have been somewhat enriched, as they already had been in part, in the editions of the Missal after the reform of Clement VIII in 1604. The following scheme shows us the picture:

Monday: de ss. Trinitate.

50. The thesis whch bears upon this, which I have already put forward in *Die lateinische Bussriten*, I have defined more clearly and established on surer foundations in the essay: *Oratio super populum und altchristliche Bussersegnung: Eph. liturg.* 52 (1938) 77-96. Cf. also *Missarum Sollemnia* II,2-1 533 seq.
1. J. Low, *Sulla frequentia dell'officium s. Mariae in Sabbato secondo il vecchio e il nuovo stato delle rubriche: Eph. liturg.* 69 (1955) 336-346.

Tuesday: de Angelis.
Wednesday: de Apostolis; since 1920 also: de s. Joseph and de ss.
             Petro et Paulo.
Thursday: de Spiritu Sancto; since 1604 also: de ss. Eucharistiae
             sacramento; since 1935 also: de N.H.I.C. summo et
             aeterno sacerdote.
Friday: de Cruce; since 1604 also: de passione Domini.
Saturday: de S. Maria.

No one could say that this scheme is clear or even convincing. Some reflexion on its origin and on the elements of its constitution might not be out of place; all the more because in a reform of the liturgy, great significance obviously lies in the weekly cycle, not only for the rite of the Mass, but for the Office as well. For now, in the hymns of the ferial Vespers which occur much more frequently, the cycle of the seven days of creation comes fully into its own, a thing of which hitherto the user of the Breviary was scarcely aware. If then, giving up the idea of working through the whole psalter every week—suggested from authoritative quarters as an imminent programme for reform—we envisage a new distribution of the psalms, the question can hardly be avoided: Is there not a strong case for apportioning the psalms to days of the week to a certain extent according to themes—as we already partly find it in Prime—which would then come to characterize the various days of the week?

1. *Easter Week in Early Times*

Since the days of the primitive Church, Christianity has made Sunday the basis of the weekly schedule. Sunday is the day of the Resurrection: more precisely, the day on which, through His Resurrection, our Lord completed, and set the seal upon the work of Redemption; and thus it is the day upon which from time immemorial the whole Church has kept the memory of 'the blessed Passion, Resurrection from the dead, and glorious Ascension into heaven' through the celebration of the Eucharist. Very early on, Friday, as day of the death upon the Cross, was added to Sunday. In the *Didache* (c. 8, 1) it is described, along with Wednesday, as a fast-day. Tertullian indicates that both Wednesday and Friday were days devoted to the sorrowful commemoration of the Passion of Christ.₁ The same thing is plainly stated in the slightly later document, the Syrian *Didascalia*;₂ for on Wednesday, as is frequently repeated from this time onwards, Jesus was betrayed to the high council by Judas and on Friday He died on the Cross.₃ Innocent I founded the Roman custom of the Saturday fast too, upon the circumstances of the Passion narrative: the apostles mourned and hid themselves on both Friday and Saturday, thus it is fitting to fast upon these two days.₄

Such a manner of thinking gave a Christian stamp to the week. Just as Sunday represented a weekly Easter, so the whole week appeared to be a faint copy of Holy Week. The great facts of the story of Redemption were to be set before the eyes of people, not only once a year, but in the course of the lesser weekly cycle as well. Thus the week came to be conceived, not as the Jews liked to see it and as at first the Christians accepted it, numbering from Sunday and going on with *feria secunda* and so on until it ended on the Sabbath, but as having Sunday for climax and conclusion, and beginning, therefore, on Monday. In compromise between the new conception and the fixed numbering of days, Sunday became known from an early date as the eighth day; the rest of the days of the week thus retained their corresponding enumeration, but Sunday was transposed from the beginning to the end.₅ The strength of this new conception of the week is seen from the way in which the young peoples on the eastern fringe of central Europe, Slavs, Hungarians, Latvians and Lithuanians, who became Christian only in the course of the Middle Ages, used terms to describe the days of the week which, while being derived from numbers, took Monday as the first day and not Sunday any longer.₆ Monday was clearly the beginning of the week and Sunday the end.

1. Tertullian, *De ieiunio* c. 10 (CSEL 20, 287).
2. *Didascalia* V, 14, 4 seq. (Funk I, 272 seq.).
3. Besides the *Didascalia*, v. also Augustine, *Ep.* 36, 13, 30 (CSEL 34, 2, p. 59 seq.). Wednesday and Friday are still the favourite week-days, quite apart from the quarterly Ember weeks, locally at least throughout the entire Middle Ages and later. V. G. Schreiber, *Gemeinschaften des Mittelalters*, Munster 1948, 286; Jungmann, *Missarum Sollemnia* I, 512-514.
4. Innocent I., *Ep.* 25, 4 (PL 20, 555).
5. J. A. Jungmann, *Beginnt die christliche Woche mit Sonntag?*: Zk Th 55 (1931) 605-621 (=J., *Gewordene Liturgie* 206-231).
6. Ibid. 614 seq. (219-221).

To some extent, it is striking that, at the close of the early Christian period, the cycle of the Christian Year experienced a substantial expansion by the new great feasts of the Christmas cycle and the older Marian feasts, but no similar thing can be shown to have affected the weekly cycle. This can be partly explained by the fact that the separate week-days outside of Lent and the Ember days received no liturgical pattern in the sense of a public celebration of Mass. (Within the seasons mentioned, this *had* been the case with the traditionally favoured days—Wednesday, Friday and Saturday.) The Office, too, in its early days had known a daily cycle wherein the events of our Lord's Passion were set at the proper hour,7 and in the course of centuries certain vestiges of this8 were preserved: but in the composition of its weekly cycle, carried out in a monastic setting where the weekly performance of the entire psalter was the basis, no inclination was shown to associate the separate days of the week with particular mysteries of the Redemption. At first, too, the cathedral order had devised only one morning Hour in which they were content to express, in a variable form, praise to God and greeting of the morning light (*mane, lux tua*) in psalms chosen for this purpose— and hymns likewise—and one Vespers, which made use of the concluding section of the Biblical psalter—Psalm 109 onwards9— and, in the week-day hymns already mentioned, praised the seven-day work of the Creator. Only on Sunday are the opening psalms of Lauds and Vespers (*Dominus regnavit; Dixit Dominus*) plainly dedicated to the Resurrection theme. This applies to Prime as well, which on Sunday had always begun with the Easter Psalm 117 (*Confitemini*).10

2. Alcuin's Week-day Masses

The place of the week-days as a fixed sequence was first acknowledged by Alcuin. It was with Alcuin's assistance that Charlemagne finally spread the Roman liturgy throughout his

7. J. Stadlhuber, *Das Stundengebet der Laien im christlichen Altertum: Zk Th* 71 (1949) 129-183.
8. J. Stadlhuber, *Das Laienstundengebet vom Leiden Christi in seinum mittelalterlichen Fortleben: Zk Th* 72 (1950) 282-325.
9. Cf. C. Callewaert, *Sacris erudiri*, Steenbrugge 1940, 67 seq. 76. 108 seq.
10. Callewaerts 125.

realms and so created a uniform liturgical order; but it was Alcuin likewise who composed a whole set of Mass rituals over and above the Roman liturgy and with notable deviation from its spirit. From that time onwards, seven of these frequently recur as Masses for week-days. As the most recent exponent of his liturgical life's work affirms, of all his measures in the liturgical field, this series of votive Masses seems to have been the cause nearest his heart.[1] We have two of Alcuin's letters which were sent as covering notes along with his votive Masses. One is to the Abbot of St. Vedastus in Arras and one to a monk of Fulda. With strong recommendation he is sending them his *cartula missalis, missas aliquas de nostro missale*, so that they can make use of the various intentions and desires on the appropriate days.[2] The titles which Alcuin mentions in both letters—he seems to have selected only single examples—do not entirely coincide with the series of Masses, traditionally regarded as his work under the name *Liber sacramentorum*.[3]

The two series of rituals below can count as authentic material from this *Liber sacramentorum*.

Sunday:	de s. Trinitate	de gratia S. Spiritus postulanda.
Monday:	pro peccatis	pro petitione lacrimarum.
Tuesday:	ad postulande angelica	pro tentationibus cogitationum.
Wednesday:	de s. sapientia	ad postulandam humilitatem.
Thursday:	de caritate	contra tentationes carnis.
Friday:	de s. Cruce	de tribulatione.
Saturday:	de s. Maria	in commemoratione s. Mariae.

There follows another nine common rituals in honour of apostles, martyrs, saints, and finally a ritual for each of the follow-

1. G. Ellard, *Master Alcuin Liturgist*, Chicago 1956, 226.
2. MG *Ep. Karol. aevi* II, 404-406. 454 seq.
3. In Migne, PL 101, 445-461 (Reprint of the edition by Frobenius, 1777), first of all seven Mass formulae for the separate days of the week are printed thrice; and of these, each time the first (usually the only one which continues throughout the Masses of the week) formula is dedicated to a motif bearing on the order of Redemption, the second to some great ascetic interest, and the third—entitled *missa s. Augustini*—is certainly not genuine; Ellard 152 seq.—Manuscript tradition of the Masses does not extend farther back than the 10th century; Ellard 156 n. 29.

ing: *pro inimicis, pro confitente peccata sua, pro salute vivorum et requie mortuorum.* We cannot be absolutely certain that the assignment to the separate days is Alcuin's own doing, but it is very likely; for this appears once more with the first series, which is of most interest to us, in the tradition of the Milan liturgy, in features of it, indeed, which take us back to the 9th century.4

Were we to try to describe this series, it would strike us that the idea of redemptive history being portrayed in the week, comes out most definitely on Friday which has been given the rite *de S. Cruce.* On the other hand, Sunday has lost its Easter character. This is perfectly in keeping with that recession of the thought of the risen God-man now living eternally in heaven, which was a characteristic effect, in the Gallican liturgical milieu in the early Middle Ages, of the struggle against Teutonic Arianism.5 In order not to minimise belief in Christ's divinity, they scarcely dared any longer to speak of the mediatorial position of the living Redeemer or to direct prayer to the Father *through* Him. He has become simply the second Person in the Trinity. If liturgical prayer is not addressed to Him directly, the preference is to address it to the Blessed Trinity: *Suscipe s. Trinitas, Placeat tibi s. Trintitas,* formulae which still belong to our rite of the Mass, an inheritance from that phase of liturgical history. And Sunday more and more becomes the day of the Blessed Trinity6—a development which did not fully permeate the Roman liturgy until quite late.7 A contributory cause of this may have been the fact that in predominantly apocryphal but widely influential literature, ever-increasing *benedictiones* were ascribed to Sunday: besides the Resurrection of Christ, not only the descent of the Holy Spirit and the creation of the world, the crossing of the Red Sea and the Last Judgement, but also the Incarnation of Christ, His birth, His baptism in Jordan, and the miracle of the loaves.8 In this, the

4. O. Heiming, *Die mailändischen sieben Votivmessen: Miscellanea liturgica,* Mohlberg II, Rome 1959, 317-339.
5. Cf. above p. 38; Fr. X. Arnold, *Seelsorge aus der Mitte der Heilsgeschichte,* Freiburg 1956, 37-44.
6. It is an exception when, in the 11th century, in the Missal of Robert of Jumieges, ed. Wilson (HBS 11) p. 241, the *Missa de s. Trinitate,* corresponding to the Sunday, is followed by another: *in memoriam Salvatoris Domini nostri.*
7. Cf. above p. 34; A. Klaus, *Ursprung und Verbreitung der Dreifaltigkeitsmesse,* Werl 1938.—On a similar penetration by the Trinitarian motif into the Byzantine liturgy, v. J. H. Dalmais, *Le dimanche dans la liturgie byzantine:* La Maison-Dieu 46 (1956) 65 seq.
8. V. the survey by H. Dumaine, *Dimanche* VII: DACL IV, 985-990.

connexion of the Incarnation or the Annunciation with Sunday can be traced back to a very old tradition. The first witness of it is Victorinus of Pettau (d. 303)9 and the Bobbio Missal10 has a whole series of Sunday *benedictiones* including our Lord's birth and baptism which are worked into one of its Sunday Prefaces. It is not surprising therefore, that in the course of such re-interpretation Sunday should once more have become placed at the beginning of the week—a process assisted by certain practical considerations—and that its new principal theme should have begun to influence the following week-days.

Alcuin himself does not reveal this last step. The Mass *de gratia S. Spiritus postulanda* is assigned to Sunday and not to one of the following days. The titles *de sancta sapientia, de caritate* have no Trinitarian significance at all, but describe the heavenly gifts for which men ask: it is only in passing that the rituals in question call to mind the uncreated Wisdom and the Infinite Love. The meaning indicated for the titles is shown specially clearly in the appointed lessons, in the Milan tradition, in fact. The *sapientia*—Mass uses Js. I, 3-6 (*si quid autem vestrum indiget sapientia . . .*) and Mt. 11, 25 seq. (*abscondisti haec a sapientibus . . .*), and the Milan tradition prescribes Jn. 17, 1-3 (*Haec est autem vita aeterna ut cognoscant te . . .*). The *caritas*—Mass uses I. Cor. 13, 4-8 (*caritas patiens est . . .*) and Jn. 13, 33-35 (*mandatum novum do vobis . . .*). Looked at from this angle, it is less surprising that Monday with its Mass *pro peccatis* should take up the preamble to this gradual progress in spiritual life:—a purification from sins. A heightened sense of sin is characteristic of the early Middle Ages, and especially of Alcuin's writings.11 (We recall the apologies within the liturgy). Sin, indeed, is the theme which dominates Alcuin's second series of votive Masses.

By contrast, however, the reaction which set in in religious life shortly after the year 1000—not merely as a result of the new way of administering the sacrament of penance: absolution immediately after confession, and great frequency—is seen in the way in

9. Victorinus, *De fabrica mundi* (PL 5, 312 seq.). The authenticity of this is uncertain.

10. Fifth Sunday Mass; ed. Lowe (HBS 58) 150 seq.

11. Cf. Ellard 162. 207 seq. H. B. Meyer, *Alkuin zwischen Antike und Mittelalter*: Zk Th 81 (1959, 306-350; 405-454) 430 seq.

which the Mass *pro peccatis* seldom appears any more[12] in the
weekly series which in other aspects was faithfully handed down
from Alcuin. It is mostly omitted. To fill in the resulting gap,
Alcuin's second Sunday Mass, *de gratia S. Spiritus postulanda* was
inserted, not on Monday but (because of the anticipation of the
superceded Mass or possibly of the preceding Mass) sometimes on
Tuesday,[13] sometimes on Wednesday[14] or even on Thursday.[15]

3. The Trinitarian Scheme and Veneration of Saints

In contrast to this pre-occupation with the human subject the
first daily phrases of Alcuin's set of Masses is handed on in the
Micrologus of Bernold of Constance (c. 1085) where they appear
expanded so that the Trinitarian motif no longer dominates
Sunday alone, but the two following week-days also. Here it is
plain to see that as Tuesday is dedicated to the Holy Spirit (with
the Mass *de Spiritu Sancto* i.e. Alcuin's second Mass for Sunday) so
Monday is dedicated to uncreated Wisdom. The honour given to
the Blessed Trinity on Sunday is thus taken as being applied to the
Father.[1] This series, Sunday: The Trinity; Monday: Eternal
Wisdom; Tuesday: the Holy Spirit, asserts itself now and lasts
throughout the entire Middle Ages.

It is to be found unanimously in the sacramentaries of the 10th,
11th and 12th centuries in south-west Germany.[2] It appears again

12. It appears again in the 11th century in the Sacramentaries of Moissac (Leroquais,
Les sacramentaires I, 102), of St. Méen (ibid. 113) and Udine (Ebner 271), in the Missal
of Robert of Jumieges (ed. Wilson; HBS 11, 242), in Clm. 10077 in Rhein-Pfalz in the
12th century (A. Franz, *Die Messe im deutschen Mittelalter*, Freiburg 1902, 140); in a striking
way again in the Missale Romanorum of 1558 (in the notation for the *Missale Romanum*
of 1474 ed. Lippe; HBS 33, 275). Transposed to Tuesday, as done in part in the cases
named, it is again mentioned by Durandus, *Rationale* IV, 1, 30.
13. 10th century Sacramentary of St. Maximin in Trier (Leroquais I, 85) and 11th
century Sacramentary from Reichenau and Echternach (ibid. 115. 124).
14. Two 11th century Sacramentaries from Luttich and Brittany (Leroquais I, 101.
109).
15. Missal of Monte Avellana (13th-14th century; PL 151, 938 seq.).—The start on
Monday is an isolated example in an 11th century Sacramentary from Florence, a document which shows unusual transporitions in other places too. (Ebner 34.)
1. Bernold of Constance, *Micrologus* c. 60 (PL 151, 1020). The Mass *de caritate* followed
on Wednesday, on Thursday that of angels.
2. Only with the transposition in the sequel (cf. previous note): Wednesday—of angels;
Thursday—*de caritate*; M. Gerbert, *Monumenta liturgiae alemannicae* I, St. Blasien 1777,
259-264; Franz, *Die Messe im deutschen Mittelalter* 140.

in the *Hortulus Animae* which St. Peter Cansius edited in 1563.₃
We find a unique use of it in the 'Liturgy for the Week' which
Alban Dold has brought to light from m.s. 18 of St. Gall. In this,
orationes are prescribed for the seven Hours of the individual days
of the week, and these always centre round the declared theme.
The Sunday *orationes* celebrate the Trinity; those of Monday concern Wisdom, sometimes in the objective, Trinitarian sense,
sometimes in the subjective, ascetic sense; those of Tuesday speak
of the Holy Spirit as uncreated Gift.₄ It is significant that from
roughly the same time—about 1000 A.D.—the separate invocations of the three divine Persons become more common at the
beginning of the litanies.

But in Bernold a development has begun which proceeds yet
another step. Honouring the divine Persons, thought of more or
less in separation from one another, leads on to giving honour to
the great princes of heaven. From the time of Charlemagne a
letter has been preserved from the otherwise unknown Catulfus
to the emperor in which it is proposed that he should institute a
yearly feast day *in honore sanctae Trinitatis et unitatis et Angelorum
et omnium Sanctorum.*₅

If here we find the Trinity, the angels, and the saints all gathered
together in a single festival, this throws some light on a phenomenon in the contemporary week-day Masses of Alcuin which has
not yet been mentioned, viz., that on Tuesday, separated from the
Trinity Mass only by the Mass for sins, we find the formula *ad
postulanda Angelica suffragia.*

3. In this there follow for the other days of the week the Offices of all Saints, of the
Bl. Sacrament, of the Passion of Christ and of Mary; St. Beissel, *Zur Geschichte der
Gebetbücher: Stimmen aus Maria-Laach* 77 (1909, II, 28-41; 160-185; 274-289; 397-411)
286. In an edition of 1592, on Monday the place of eternal Wisdom is taken by the Dead;
A. Schrott, *Das Gebetbuch in der Zeit d. Kath. Restauration*: Zk Th 61 (1937, 1-28; 211-257)
216. The full series indicated above appears, however, in an edition of the *Serta honoris et
exultationis* of Peter Michael in 1589; v. Schrott 217 seq. The same picture is presented by
the Book of Hours of the *Cod. Vat.* 3769 (c. 1500), an account of the contents of which
appears in Beissel loc. cit. 177 seq.; but in this on Wednesday it is not the Office of all
Saints but one concerning the mercy of God which appears, accompanied by a picture
of the *Ecce homo.* The old motif of the *de caritate* is thus being carried on.
4. A. Dold, *Liturgische Texte aus Cod. Sang.* 18: JL 7 (1927) 37-51. The dating is uncertain.
The ms. is 13th-15th century. As the themes indicated by Bernold appear for Wednesday
and Thursday (but with a transposition): angels, (faith, hope and) love, we must place its
origin in Bernold's circle.
5. PL 96, 1366.

But this line is soon to be attended with much more serious consequences. The sacramentary of St. Thierry which was composed towards the end of the 9th century contains the following distribution of week-day Masses: Sunday: the Mass of the day, de Trinitate, de Sapientia et de sancta Maria; Monday: Michael; Tuesday: John; Wednesday: Peter; Thursday: Stephen; Friday: the Holy Cross; Saturday: Theodoric (patron) and Theodulf.6 Here the week's theme has thus become God and His saints.7

Most likely it was a theological point of view that decided against providing the Roman Missal of 1570 with these more or less clearly separate devotions to the divine Persons and to the attached list of names of outstanding saints. It could so easily be mis-read as tritheism.8 Expressed in this form it is not so frequently found in the later Middle Ages. Devotion to the Blessed Trinity is confined to Sunday and to the Sunday Trinity Mass until this, too, is pushed on to Monday.

In the space left open, devotion to the saints was now able to spread all the more. The traditional order for the week seems to have supplied a starting-off place by placing the Angelica suffragia the beginning of the week following the day of the Trinity. A Breslau Missal of 1483 and one printed in Basel in 1519, agree in starting the sequence of week-day Masses thus: de Trinitate, de Angelis, de S. Johanne Baptista,9 an order, moreover, which is notably to be found in the Byzantine liturgy as well.10 A 14th century sacramentary from Lucon has the sequence: Monday: the

6. Martène, De antiquis Ecclesiae ritibus I, 4, 12, Ordo IX (I, 546).
7. We encounter a related scheme as motif for the day. The chronicler Hariulf, Chronicon Centulense IV, 26 (PL 174, 1345), tells of abbot Gervin of St. Riquier-Centula (d.1075) that he said daily (nocturnalem et diurnalem canonem) an Office de s. Trinitate, tum de Spiritu Sancto, post hoc de resurrectione Domini atque de s. Genetrice Maria, post haec de Angelis, postque des. Petro vel monibus Apostolis sine omnibus Sanctis. Cf. U. Berlière, L'ascèse bénédictine, Paris 1927, 235.
8. This tendency is clearly revealed in representations of the Trinity by three human forms, united in some way or other, which appear here and there in the corresponding period between the 10th and 16th centuries, and which were formally banned by Benedict XV. Künstle, Ikonographie der christlichen Kunst I, 222 seq.
9. Franz, Die Messe im deutschen Mittelalter 142 with note 1.
10. For the Trinity v. above n. 7. For the connexion: Monday—angels, Tuesday—John the Baptist, v. A. Stoclen, L'année liturgique byzantine: Irénikon—Collection IV (1928) 311 seq. Wednesday is given to the commemoration of the betrayal by Judas. Thursday is set aside for honouring the saints (apostles, wonder-workers, bishops, Nicolas) and Saturday likewise (confessors, martyrs, all Saints); ibid. cf. G. Schreiber, Die Wochentage, Cologne 1959, 35 seq.

angels; Tuesday: John the Baptist; Wednesday: Hilary.¹¹ A 14th century Munich manuscript (Clm. 831) specifies the Mass *de annunciatione b. Mariae* for Monday and *de omnibus Sanctis*¹² for Tuesday. Veneration of the saints begins to spread out over the whole week.¹³ But because, with few exceptions, Friday had always been set apart for the commemoration of the holy Cross, and Saturday to the memory of the Mother of God, if Monday was then given to the angels, only Tuesday, Wednesday, and within certain limits, Thursday¹⁴ remained at the disposal of prominent saints.

At the end of the Middle Ages it was very common to set apart Tuesday for the veneration of St. Anne or St. Anthony of Padua or the patron of the church or order (Benedict, Dominic).¹⁵ All Saints, too, was assigned to Tuesday.¹⁶ Elsewhere, Wednesday was given the Mass *pro patronis*.¹⁷ In the French little Books of the Hours very often one or other of these two days was set apart for All Saints.¹⁸. It would appear that it was not until the time of Pius V onwards that Wednesday is found associated with the

11. Leroquais, *Les sacramentaire* II, 376 seq.
12. Franz 141.
13. A more highly developed system of veneration of saints appointed for one of the week-days is shown in the Breviary of the Premonstratensians. In the Roman Breviary (until Pius X) the ferial Office of Lauds and Vespers remains the same on all days, and there appears the commemorations *de s. Maria, de Apostalis, de Patrono*; but that of the Premonstratensions has the following rubric at the end of the Psalter: *Fer. II de s. Patre Norberto. Fer. III de s. Johanne Bapt. Fer. IV de s. Patre Augustino. Fer. V de Patrono vel Titulari Ecclesiae. Fer. VI de s. Cruce. Sabb. de s. Joseph. Breviarium Praemonstratense* (1889), *pars hiem.* (Westmalle 1892) 162 seq.
14. Thursday is taken up in the early period by the Mass *de caritate*, later mostly by that of the Bl. Sacrament. The attempt to link Thursday with the memory of the Ascension, of which Durandus speaks in *Rationale* IV, 6, 21, has not yet succeeded. The *Regula Magistri* (6th century) always refused to countenance fasting on Thursday, because this was the day of the Ascension; c. 28 (PL 88, 998 seq.).
15. Separate proofs in G. Schreiber, *Die Wochentage. Abendländische und morgenländische Entwicklungen: Archiv f. mittelrheinische Kirchengeschichte* I (1949) 331-345, esp. 337 seq. (This author's studies of the week-days, quoted here, are collected and developed in the volume, *Die Wochentage*, Cologne 1959—Schreiber.) B. Danzer, *Die Wochentage in ihrer liturgischen Bedeutung: Theol.-prakt. Quartalschr.* 91 (1938) 637-654, esp. 642 seq. According to the currently valid *Enchiridion indulgentiarum* (Rome 1950), the devotions, appointed for Tuesday, to Ann, Antony of Padua, and Dominic, are provided with indulgences (p. 637: *Tertia feria*). The commemoration of St. Ann on Tuesday is expanded to devotion to Joachim and Ann in *The Heavenly Palm Garden* of William Nakatenus (1751, p. 122).
16. Thus a 15th century rhymed sequence *de omnibus Sanctis* is provided for Tuesday; *Analecta Hymnica Medil Aevi* Vol. 46, 227. On the whole, medieval hymns are seldom attached to particular days of the week.
17. 14th century Missal from Fritzlar; Franz 141.
18. V. Leroquais, *Les livres d'heures manuscrits* I, Paris 1927, p. XXVIII.

apostles.[19] In later prayer books Wednesday appears as a day on which St. Ignatius and St. Francis Xavier[20] were commemorated. Much later St. Joseph is assigned to this day. Not until 1920 was Wednesday set apart for him in the series of votive Masses,[21] and not until 1914 was the third Wednesday after Easter appointed in place of Sunday for his *Sollemnitas*. The attaching of indulgences to devotions to the saint on Wednesday appears at various times in the 19th century, however;[22] and as a practice in a French Benedictine monastery (Chalon), there is evidence of the weekly dedication of Wednesday to the special veneration of St. Joseph as early as the first third of the 17th century.[23] On Thursday, wherever the old tradition of having the Mass *de caritate* had fallen out, it comes about that, amongst other things, this day is assigned to St. Peter,[24] to St. Barbara,[25] or to All Saints,[26] or even to the Mother of God.[27] From the 13th century it had been more and more becoming the day of the Blessed Sacrament.[28] In the later Middle Ages with the growing devotion to the Passion of Christ the commemoration of our Lord's agony in Gethsemani became increasingly prominent as a characteristic of Thursday. This did not take the form of a special Mass ritual because it had to do with evening. It gave rise to an evening Gethsemani devotion[29] and to the sounding of the great bell after the ringing of the Angelus[30]— still done in many places.

19. Cf. above p. 251. Since Wednesday has been given to veneration of St. Joseph, the apostles (not in the Missal however) has been moved to Tuesday. Thus in the decorative head-pieces used towards the end of the 19th century for the beginning of the week-days in the Pustet publication of the Breviary (M. Schmalzl, C.SS.R., d. 1930).
20. So in Nakatenus, *Heavenly Palm Garden* (above n. 41) 122.
21. V. above p. 251.
22. F. Beringer, *Die Ablässe,*[11] Paderborn 1921-22, I, 233. 367; II, 250 seq.
23. Thus O. Pfulf, *Die Verehrung des hl. Joseph in der Geschichte: Stimmen aus Maria Laach* 38 (1890) 293, who appeals to P. Lucot, *S. Joseph* (Paris 1875).
24. Missal of Worms, before 1500; Franz 140 seq.
25. Nakatenus loc. cit. (above n. 41). Cf. Schreiber, *Die Wochentage* (1949) 343; *Die Wochentage* (1959) 25. 162 seq.
26. A 14th century Munich ms. (Clm. 831); Franz 141.
27. 11th century Florentine Sacramentary; Ebner 34. Here the *Mass ad postulanda Angelica suffragia* is appointed for Saturday.
28. An example of the Thursday Mass *de Corpore Christi* from the 13th century, mentioned by Franz 141. Endowments in the 14th century named by P. Browe, *Die Verehrung der Eucharistie im Mittelalter* 1933, 141 seq. Today the weekly Pentecost Office before the Bl. Sacrament exposed, is common in, for example, parishes in Brixen diocese. References to similar custom in Spain—Schreiber, *Die Wochentage* (1949) 342.
29. Schreiber, *Die Wochentage* (1959) 161 seq.
30. Relevant endowments in Bavaria since 1512—mentioned by Schreiber (1959) 161.

Monday still demands special examination. It never was seriously regarded as a day for the veneration of the saints. After originally having been taken up by the Mass *pro peccatis* and then by the Mass *de sapientia*, as we have seen, it was given to the veneration of the angels. But after the 11th century a new theme for this day appears, and it becomes the dominant theme: intercession for the departed. In Peter Damian (d. 1072) this intention first emerges as the theme of the Mass for Monday; but it still seems to be the Mass *ad poscenda Angelica suffragia* which we have —understood in this new sense.[31] The *Consuetudines of Vallombrosa*[32] which were composed about 1100 already contain a Mass of the Dead for Monday.[33] The preference for Monday as a day for this intention is connected with the belief that the souls in purgatory—in hell, too, according to ancient belief—were granted rest on Sunday, but on Monday had to go back once again to their pains.[34] And so, on this day they specially needed our help.

As we have said, the Mass *ad poscenda Angelica suffragia* seems to have taken on this significance and so kept its place on Monday. On this basis it appears on Monday along with the Mass of the Dead in John Beleth[35] and in Durandus.[36] The same connexion is clearly to be seen when St. Michael is named in the same place.[37] From of old, St. Michael had been associated at the offertory with the liberation of the holy souls. In the Roman liturgy, as is well-known, the special application of Monday to the commemoration of the dead is preserved in this fashion: on every Monday when the Office is *de feria*, the Mass must contain the *oration* for the dead.

These different systems of arranging the week-days did not only exist successively, but in the later Middle Ages existed concurrent-

31. Peter Damian, *Opusc.* 33, 3 (PL 145, 565).
32. B. Albers, *Consuetudines monasticae* IV, Monte Cassino 1911, 227.
33. 12th century endowments of Requiem Masses for every Monday, mentioned by Schreiber, *Totendienst am Montag: Rheinischwestfälische Zeitschr. f. Volkskunde* 5 (1958) 28–47. Cf. Schreiber, *Die Wochentage* (1959) 58 seq. 89–98.
34. Peter Damian, *Opusc.* 19, 3 (PL 145, 427 seq.) already tells of this opinion. Other sources in Franz 145–148.
35. John Beleth, *Divinorum officiorum explicatio* c. 51 (attached to edition of Durandus, Naples 1859, 782).
36. Durandus, *Rationale* IV, 1, 29.
37. *Consuetudines* of Vallombrosa (Albers IV, 227); *sine s. Michaelis.* Cf. Roman Missal of 1558 (in the notation of the Roman Missal of 1474 ed. Lippe, HBS 33, p. 275).—The week-day of the holy angels (now Tuesday or Wednesday) receives a new interpretation in the 17th century *Little Book of Hours*. It has become the day of the Guardian Angels. Examples in Schrott (above n. 29) 21. 232. 234.

ly, especially those affecting the first days of the week. This led, therefore, to various mixed forms.38 This led, as we can well understand, to considerable uncertainty, and even to confusion. Added to this there were the effects also of isolated new ideas. Gradually the Sunday Masses of the Missal spread to Sunday— even for private Sunday Masses.39 As a result, Monday had to take over the Mass *de ss. Trinitate* as well.40 Frequently now the Mass of angels was shifted to Tuesday;41 and both of these arrangements have been found in our Missal since the time of Pius V. Commemoration of the various saints became compressed into Wednesday as seen most clearly in our post-1920 Missal. And this day is also used to commemorate St. Joseph. The Mass of the Holy Spirit, which took the second place on Sunday with Alcuin, and which then moved to various days in the earlier part of the week, since Pius V has finally settled on Thursday.42 On the other hand, since the 13th century, Thursday has more and more become the day of the Blessed Sacrament.

The general impression remains that in the course of the Middle Ages in this way the beginning and the end of the week received more or less fixed assignations, while the middle days showed no such definite stamp. Peter Damian observes that in his monastery there were, apart from Sunday, only three days on which set Masses were customary: Monday, the Mass of angels; Friday, of the Cross; and Saturday, of the Mother of God.43 The same sort of thing is true of the *Consuetudines of Vallombrosa* (C. 1100) according to which there is also a Holy Trinity Mass prescribed for Wednesday (Monday has a Mass of the Dead); and in this

38. Thus, for example, a Canon Eynolf of Fritzlar (d. 1439) arranges Masses in the following order: Sunday, of the Bl. Trinity; Monday, for the dead; Tuesday, of the Holy Spirit; Wednesday, of the patron. Franz, *Die Messe im deutschen Mittelalter* 141.
39. The Synod of Mainz 1549, c. 61, shows that the Mass *de Trinitate* was used in public services too. (Hartzheim VI, 579): Because the singers often cannot cope with the Proper chants, the *officia de Trinitate et de Spiritu Sancto aut, quod decentissimum erat, dè resurrectione Domini* is to be tolerated. For private Masses only the daily formula was required at this time, as long as it was not a Sunday or holiday of obligation; Roman Missal of 1560 and 1561 (Lippe 273 seq.).
40. Thus the directions in the Missal of Pius V (above p. 251), but also as early as the Roman Missal of 1558 (Lippe 274).
41. Thus the Roman Missal of 1558 (Lippe 274). Danzer 642.
42. Also in Roman Missal of 1558; Lippe 277.
43. Peter Damian, *Opusc.* 33, 3 seq. (PL 145, 564 seq.). About the same time Berrold of Constance says—*Micrologus* c. 60 (PL 151, 1020 B)—that *pene usquequaque* on Friday *de cruce* is chosen, and *de s. Maria* of Saturday.

source the remaining days—Tuesday and Thursday—have the Mass of the preceding Sunday.44 Durandus, too, who mentions a specific Mass for every day of the week, observes only of Tuesday, Wednesday and Thursday that when no feast-day occurs, the Mass of the Sunday could be repeated.45 On Monday, Friday and Saturday this is not so. Repetition of the Sunday Mass is regarded as a way out on those days for which no prescribed Mass of the week-day is available, or on which no saint's day falls.46 These circumstances are to some extent confirmed from the canonical side too: for in the later Middle Ages married people were encouraged to abstain from marital intercourse not only on Sunday but also on Monday for the sake of the holy souls in purgatory, on Thursday because of Christ's arrest, on Friday because of His Passion and on Saturday in honour of the Mother of God.47 In this too, these days show a stricter regulation and more stringent obligation with this difference, that Thursday is added to their number.

4. Late Attempts at a Solution

In view of the lack of clarity in the outcome of this development it does not surprise us to find that since the height of the Middle Ages attempts have been made here and there to establish a more lucid weekly order. Of necessity these attempts remained on the fringe of the liturgy because this appeared to be something unalterable so that more thorough-going interference could not be risked. As a result they have been all the more consistently nourished by their original thought-framework. Above all we must mention Honorius Augustodunensis1—as early as the 12th century. In his notes on the psalms of the Nocturns he always

---

44. Albers, *Consuetudines monasticae* IV, 227.
45. Durandus, *Rationale* IV, 1, 30.
46. The week-day Masses were often chosen for Saint's days also. James of Bitry (d. 1240), *Historia occidentalis*, c. 15, tells of oppositions which had arisen between priests and lay-brothers in the Order of Grandmont. The former wished to have the daily Masses, the brothers demanded the Masses *de s. Maria* or *de Spiritu Sancto* or *pro defunctis*. Schreiber, *Die Wochentage* (1949) 340. Here too is evidence of the growing popularity of the Mass of the Holy Spirit. This may be connected with the fact that in those days hospitals for the sick were closely associated with the Holy Spirit (. . . *sana quod est saucium*).
47. D. Linder, *Der usus matrimonii*, Munich 1929, 160 n. 46.
1. Honorius Augustodunencis, *Gemma animae* II c. 67 seq. (PL 172, 640-642).

finds somewhere or other in the individual days of the week reference to specific events in the New Testament history of Redemption. These combine to form a well-arranged cycle, and in spite of the different order of the psalms in the Roman and in the monastic Office, it is the same in both. That such an agreement was possible is not in the end surprising, if we remember that a considerable number of psalms was available for use each day. In this, Sunday was not merely the beginning but also the end of the week. In detail, this is the scheme which he found:[2]

Sunday:	Incarnation	(Ego hodie genuite; Ante luci-ferum genui te).
Monday:	Baptism of Christ	(Dominus illuminatio mea; Vox Domini).
Tuesday:	Birth of Christ	(Ecce venio)
Wednesday:	Betrayal by Judas	(Dixit insipiens; Tu vero homo unanimis).
Thursday:	Eucharist	(Panem angelorum).
	Arrest	(comprehenditi eum).
Friday:	Death on the Cross	(homo sine adiutorio[3]).
Saturday:	Burial	(sicut foenum arui).
Sunday:	Resurrection	(dormivi et resurrexi).

Here we do not merely find—as with Alcuin—Friday kept strictly as the day of the death upon the Cross. In the last days of the week there again appears the ancient Christian *tridium cruxifixi, sepulti, suscitati* (Augustine). Wednesday, too, is once more drawn into the commemoration of the Passion, in the spirit of ancient Christian tradition; and between these, in organic continuity, Thursday has allotted to it the two-fold mystery of the institution of the Blessed Sacrament and the arrest of Jesus. At the beginning of the week, too, the parallel is made good to the Christian year, as it had meanwhile developed through the elaboration of the Christmas cycle. At the start of the week the Christmas motif appears. Conception, birth and baptism correspond to the three Christmas feast-days which grew up at the decline of the Middle Ages: the Annunciation (nine months before Christmas); Christmas itself, and Epiphany. The only striking thing is that the

2. One of other of the psalm-passages from the Roman Office, quoted by Honorius, in brackets.
3. Psalm 21 had not yet been specified for Prime; v. below c. 5, note 4.

baptism and birth of Christ have changed the places which would have been appropriate to chronological order. The cause of this may well have been the psalm verse for Monday which too obviously corresponded to the baptism (see above). On the other hand, John Beleth—also a 12th century figure—mentions in passing that Jesus was baptized on a Tuesday and began His fast on a Wednesday.4 A conception of the week must then have been current, according to which the chronological order was observed in this place, i.e. on Monday, the birth and on Tuesday the baptism of Jesus was commemorated—even if the reverse, represented by Honorius' placing the birth of Christ on Tuesday, is confirmed in the weekly scheme of Abbot Barbo which we shall mention now.

Honorius wanted his weekly order, as an element of the liturgy, to be understood as a more precise determination of the content of the nocturnal psalmody. This corresponds to the way in which its contents are directed to objective circumstances, to the facts of redemptive history. Towards the end of the Middle Ages we again come across attempts at refashioning the weekly order, but now more with a view to assisting the life of private devotion, and for this reason, dominated by the idea of personal appropriation of salvation. Thus, the subjective factor is now given more scope.

In this connexion the most important person who must be cited is Ludwig Barbo, a precursor of the *Devotio moderna*, who in 1408 when Abbot of a Benedictine monastery in Padua, published his *Modus meditandi et orandi*. First of all, the relationship to the choral Office and hence to the liturgy operates here too. Barbo, in fact, shows how the psalmody could be associated with meditation on particular motifs of faith; but at the same time, unlike Honorius, the author makes no attempt to base these motifs in any way upon the text of the psalms.

Barbo develops his thought, not in short catch-words, but in an expansive and edifying discourse. On Sundays we are to meditate on the goodness of God and so attain to love of God. On Monday we are to call to mind the Fall of our first parents and think on our own sins and so encourage longing for the Redeemer. On Tuesday

4. John Beleth, *Diurnorum officiorum Explicatio* (c. 89).

268   PASTORAL LITURGY

the object of meditation is to be the birth of Christ, on Wednesday, the flight into Egypt and also the public ministry of Jesus; on Thursday it is the persecution our Lord suffered at the hands of His enemies, and the institution of the Blessed Sacrament. Friday is kept as the day dedicated to the Passion of Christ. In conclusion, the descent into hell, the Resurrection and Ascension were to be appointed for Saturday.5

Here too, therefore, in the second half of the week the ancient Christian tradition has come into its own, even if the Sunday motif has been given to Saturday. And in the early part of the week too, the Christmas motif, corresponding to the Christian year, is again found in the foreground, but in such a way that we start off with the calamity of sin—which is a thought for Advent in any case—and so that Wednesday forms the connecting link between the birth and the beginning of the Passion sequence.

Clearly, the week forms the framework which guides meditation. It was a universal characteristic of the *Devotio moderna* of the 15th century that the foundation of its direction for mediation was not laid in the Christian year as was commonly done later, but in the week. However, the weekly cycle was very loosely interpreted. In the end it became usual to produce a series of seven meditation-outlines which fitted the days of the week only externally H. Watrigant speaks of a formal 'litterature des septaines hebdomadaires de meditation.'6 From the full flowering of the *Devotio moderna* we have the *Formula spiritualium exercitiorum* which was composed by an anonymous member of the Windesheim congregation. This contains six such Septenaries of which the first has for subject, the goodness of God; the second, the seven joys and the seven sorrows, of the Mother of God; the third, the Passion of Christ; the fourth, the life of Jesus; the fifth, the Last Things; the sixth, the angels and the saints.7 The last mentioned Septenary with its sequence: angels, patriarchs, apostles, martyrs, confessors,

5. H. Watrigant, *Quelques promoteur de la méditation méthodique au XVe siecle (Collection de la Bibliotheque des Exercices* 59), and J. (Tournai 1919), 16-28 (ed. of the text; the text is also found as an appendix to the Cisnero edition, Regensburg 1856, 288-303). Cf. also St. Hilpisch, *Chorgebet und Frömmigkeit im Spätmittelalter: Heilige Überlieferung,* Münster 1938, 263-284, esq. 276.
6. Watrigant 11.
7. H. Watrigant, *Le meditation methodique et l'école des Freres de la vie commune: Revue d'Ascèse et de Mystique* 3 (1922) 134-155.

virgins, all saints,[8] is reminiscent of that conception of the week which we have already met.[9]

This free application of the weekly scheme, which in an even freer style forms the groundwork of St. Ignatius' Exercises, will be met with more and more frequently in subsequent centuries.[10] We find it in the *Exercitatorium spirituale*[11] of Abbot Garcia Cisneros of Montserrat (published in 1500), but only when he is dealing with the *via illuminativa*[12] and the *via unitiva*.[13] At the first step, on the other hand, in discussing the *via purgativa*, he presents a weekly scheme which combines traditional elements with a new design. Where he gives hints on how meditation should end, he refers to saints to whom one should turn, and introduces a sequence which remains in line with the weekly sequence we have just mentioned.[14]. Most important, however; at this first step he indicates themes of meditation for the seven days of the week which keep to the thought of redemptive history at least for Friday and Saturday, and in general, keeps the mind on the Last Things. But in his Sunday motif about heaven, too, his eschatological series merges with tradition.[15] His weekly scheme runs: Monday: sin; Tuesday: death; Wednesday: hell; Thursday: judgement; Friday: Passion of Christ; Saturday: Maria (*dolorosa*); Sunday: heaven.

This weekly scheme is not purely and simply a new creation of Abbot Cisneros. The sequence of motifs seems first to appear—

8. loc. cit. 146 seq.
9. Above p. 260.
10. Examples of this from 16th-18th centuries in Schrott, *Das Gebetbuch* (above n. 29) 15 seq. 20. 223. 235. 236. 239. Meditations on the Passion of Christ, divided out amongst the days of the week, seem to have been specially popular. A set of such meditations in J. Perellius, *Thesaurus piarum et christianarum institutionem*, Dillingen 1583, 121-144; repeated in Fr. Coster, *Libettus sodalitatis*, Ingoldstadt 1597 (New editions in 18th century) 141-167. A weekly series on the purpose of life, sin and Hell, and one on the Passion in Hiphonsus of Liguori, *Meditazioni sopra le massime eterne e la Passione di Giesu Cristo per ciascun giorno della settimana*, Rome 1792.
11. I use the Regensburg edition of 1856. A German edition ('The School of the Spiritual Life') appeared in Freiburg 1923—with introduction and notes.
12. c. 23 (p. 74 seq.): The set of meditations beginning with Monday: Creation, Grace, Election, Justification, Gifts, Guidance, Glory, recurs in the *Cimeros Directorium horarum canonicarum* c. 5 (p. 253 seq.). It has been taken out of Mauburnus; v. the previous note —the German ed. of Cisneros p. 254.
13. c. 27 (p. 97 seq.).
14. c. 12 (p. 46 seq.) Monday: angels; Tuesday: patriarchs, prophets, apostles, disciples; Wednesday: martyrs; Thursday: confessors; Friday: Passion of Christ; Saturday: Mary and virgins; Sunday: Trinity.
15. c. 12 (p. 35 seq.).

270   PASTORAL LITURGY

though unrelated to the days of the week—in Gerard of Zutphen
(d. 1398), who, in a chapter entitled *de modo meditandi* enumerates
the subjects which he chiefly recommends for meditation:
*memoria peccatorum, memoria mortis, extremi iudicii, poenarum
infernalium, memoria coelestis gloriae, beneficiorum Dei et passionis
Dominicae, et si quae huiusmodi.*16 In John Vos of Heusden (d. 1424),
Gerard's motifs are already adapted to the days of the week, and
in such a way that the Passion of Christ falls on Friday and heaven
on Sunday.17 A further adaptation is found in Dietrich of Herxen
(d. 1459) who places death on the traditional day of the dead—on
Monday,18 thus establishing the sequence in which these motifs
for the week also recur in many editions of that favourite prayer
book of the 16th century—the Garden of the Soul.19 Cisneros,
who did not know of this assignment for Monday, by avoiding the
motif of the goodness of God, kept Saturday free for the honour
of Mary. With the resulting sequence for the last days of the
week—Passion of Christ, Mary, heaven—the series, which was in
the main centred round the Last Things, reappears in the Heavenly
Palm Garden, of William Nakatenus, first printed in 1660 and
having a vogue almost until our own day—a book which has been
said to be the most widely circulated of all Jesuit prayer books.20

16. Gerhard of Zutphen, *Tractatus de spiritualibus ascensionibus* c. 45 (Inkunabel-press,
Venice 1490; *Bibliothek des Jesuiten kollegs*, Innsbruck), unpaged, location, f l v.
17. Watrigant, *La méditation méthodique* 142. Vos presents this sequence—beginning
with Monday: Judgement, God's goodness, Death, Hell, Passion of Christ, Sin, Heaven.
18. Watrigant, *La meditation* 143.
19. St. Beissel, *Zur Geschichte der Gebetbücher: Stimmen aus Maria-Laach* 77 (1909, II)
185. The sequence here begins with Sunday: Heaven, Death, God's goodness, Judgement,
Hell, Passion, Sin.—On the history of the 'Garden of the Soul' cf. J. M. B. Clauss,
Hortulus animae: L ThK V (1933) 149.
20. It was republished in 1891, and again in 1893 in a Latin edition. I am using the
Cologne edition of 1751 (p. 743-761). Nakatenus rejects the Sin-motif and from Monday
to Thursday has the series: Death, Judgement, Hell, the Goodness of God; and under
the Goodness of God he treats chiefly the Blessed Sacrament, thus bringing Thursday
somehow into the redemptive-historic sequence.—It is worth noting that with Nikatenus
a duplicated scheme for the daily sections appears alongside the weekly scheme for
meditation (p. 122). This reproduces old tradition, but reveals the colouring of the century.
The first scheme specifies: Sunday: Trinity; Monday: Holy Spirit; Tuesday: the sweet
Name of Jesus; Wednesday: the Guardian Angel; Thursday: Blessed Sacrament; Friday:
the Cross; Saturday: Immaculate Conception of Mary. This same order (but with St.
Joseph on Saturday) had already appeared in 1625 in the 'Aureum thuribilum' (Schrotta
loc. cit. 21). Cf. also the weekly order of the *Micrologus* (above p. 258). The second weekly
scheme specified: Sunday All Saints; Monday: the Dead; Tuesday: Joachim and Anna;
Wednesday: Ignatius and Francis Xavier; Thursday: Barbara; Friday: the Seven Dolours
of Mary; Saturday: St. Joseph. The appearance of St. Barbara on Thursday is to be explained through her relationship to the Blessed Sacrament; Künstle, *Ikonographie der
christlichen Kunst* II, *Ikonographie der Heiligen* 113.

Once again, the attempt to turn the week into a fixed cycle of the Christian order of redemption is made in the new Gallican Breviaries. These brevaries, the first of which was the Paris Breviary of 1680,[21] are spoilt, it is true, by an autocratic initiative which led to bitter declaration of war by Abbot Prosper Guéranger and to its ultimate suppression in the middle of the 19th century; but the reforming ideas, which are realized in it and in which the resumed study of the Fathers bore fruit, can be distinguished very little from those which are re-emerging today and which have already led to the Roman reforms of 1955. All the new Gallican breviaries do not treat the week in the same way.[22] Nevertheless those which appear in the breviary of the Benedictines of Lorraine can be taken as typical.[23] In the psalter which is divided out amongst the week-days, every day bears a title-theme. These titles are:

Sunday:	Christus resurgens, Dei et divinae legis amor.
Monday:	Benigna Dei erga homines caritas et beneficentia.
Tuesday:	Amor proximi.
Wednesday:	Spes in Deo.
Thursday:	Fides.
Friday:	Christus patiens adiutor in tribulationibus.
Saturday:	Merces iustis promissa.

Apparently in this the tradition is preserved only for Sunday and Friday—for Sunday at least in the sense of more ancient tradition—and in general attention is directed to subjective appropriation of the heritage of faith. Without being aware of it, no doubt, men had set foot upon a track very like that one which Alcuin had trod a thousand years earlier. What appeared then as purification from sin, and as wisdom, and love, how appear as faith, hope, and

21. Cf. Bäumer-Biron, Histoire de Bréviaire II, 330-336.
22. In that of the Premonstratensians of 1786-87 (Copy in Wilten convent) all marking of the days is lacking. The Paris Breviary of 1680, which was a model for many others, differed from the breviary of the Lorraine Benedictines, discussed below, in this way: it specified Sunday as the Day of Thanksgiving Vide the Table of Contents in Katholik N.F. (Mainz 1856) 218.
23. By the kindness of Abbot P. Salmon I was able to use in Rome the copy belonging to the Abbey of San Gerolamo: Breviarium monasticum iuxta Regulam s. Benedicti, Nancy 1777. An edition of the Maurin-Breviary of 1787 is used by St. Hilpisch, Chorgebet und Frömmigkeit in Spätmittelalter: Heilige Überlieferung, Münster 1938, 283. The week-day motifs announced there are the same as those in the Breviary of 1777. But in contrast to this the Maurin-Breviary has altered the apportioning of the psalms correspondingly. (Ref. by P. Angelus Haussling, Maria Laach.)

love. Once the point of view is shifted from the subject, then orientation upon the theological virtues is a decided advance. From the subjective angle, the Saturday motif itself yields the consummation which forms the transition to the Sunday thought.24

5. *Conclusions and Prospects*

A general review of the development yields the following overall picture: The instruction of the weekly cycle runs parallel to that of the yearly cycle, but at some slight remove from it. In the early period, when the Easter cycle alone was elaborated within the whole year, attention was paid during the week only to those days connected with the commemoration of the Redemption: Wednesday, Friday, (Saturday), Sunday. The obvious expectation might well be that subsequent development of the week would follow that of the year, full scope being given to the commemoration of the sacred events of Christmas. But in Alciun, not only do we find no definite development in this direction, but even with the Easter cycle of ideas, only Friday is retained as the day commemorating the Passion. The space granted according to the old scheme to the climax of the Easter work of redemption, Saturday and Sunday, is occupied, however, by two themes which bear a certain relation to the early medieval emphasis on Christmas, i.e. to the stress, for apologetic reasons, on Christ's divinity. These themes are the Trinity and Mary.1 For the rest, the themes are dictated by interest in personal salvation: purification from

24. A similar project, but with its own special stamp, which prefers to see both Friday and Sunday in the light of tradition while taking a subjective line othewise, appears in connexion with Wilhelm Löhe (d. 1872) and the Evangelical Christianity of the Berneuch circle. The following order was there taken as the foundation of a re-casting of the Office: Sunday: the Day of Light, and the Resurrection of the Lord; Monday: beginning of labour; Tuesday: the spiritual warfare, because on this day Jesus uttered His last diatribes in Holy Week; Wednesday: Jesus is betrayed by His disciples, petition for the preservation of human society—families, parishes and nations; Thursday: because of Holy Thursday and the Ascension, petition for the unity of the Church and the extension of Christ's rule over all the world; Friday: the Cross of the Lord and our own cross; Saturday: a glimpse onto the decline of the week, at the end of life, the Day of Judgement, and the life of the world to come. H. Goltzen, *Der tägliche Gottesdienst: Leiturgia III* (Cassel 1956) 218 n. 373. J. Pinsk, *Liturgisches Leben* 4 (1937) 74 seq. tells of an earlier scheme from the same circle, not having, however, the stress on the redemptive-historical reference of Tuesday, Wednesday and Thursday.

1. Cf. above p. 32 seq. and p. 49 seq.

sin, the acquisition of wisdom and love. From this originated the development which then proceeded along several lines, elaboration of the Trinitarian theme, veneration of the saints, helping the souls of the departed. In the main, the great sweep of the yearly cycle is no longer to be found. Nevertheless it is possible to detect significant attempts to restore what had been neglected, even if their defects did not go very far. In Honorius Augustodunensis we can see a weekly order which not only fully reinstates the Redemption motif with due honour in the last days of the week, but also assigns Christmas motifs to the first days—clearly relying on the liturgy of the Christmas cycle. It is significant that a very similar order recurs 300 years later with Ludwig Barbo.

Since the Middle Ages, attempts along the same lines can be seen in other ascestics. But their new themes are concerned less with the history of Redemption than with the order of Redemption including its negative aspects. The editors of the new Gallican brevaries, too, saw their task in this light. They also retained the basic Easter motif for the end of the week, but, for the rest, they kept in mind more the desire for salvation, and to this end made use of the scheme of the theological virtues.

There can be no doubt which of the two solutions is to be preferred, as far, at any rate, as we have in mind the construction of the liturgical weekly order. It is most fitting that our spirit should constantly have set before it the mighty sweep of the Christmas—Easter Redemption history,[2] not only for the sake of describing our New Testament relationship to God (faith, hope, love) but in order to establish and enliven it.

Concerning the Easter motif cycle covering the Passion and Resurrection of Christ, we see isolated elaborations in recent times; and these should be mentioned. Leaving Wednesday out of account, in early times commemoration of the Redemptive events began on Friday: now this begins unanimously on Thursday, and this extension could even spread to the Breviary in an important

2. As far as the weekly arrangement of the Breviary, at least of the Breviary as used by the individual, is concerned, we may ask whether the concluding thoughts of the history of Redemption: the Church, the kingdom of God, eternal bliss, ought not to provide an extension of the Sunday motif—perhaps on Monday. All the more so because a great number of psalms, preserved for us, it would appear, by the Old Testament People of God, only find their full resonance in the world of this New Testament motif.—Cf. also the motif of the unity of the Church in the Evangelical project of Goltzen, loc. cit. (above n. 24).

way. For since Pius V—and only since his time—at Prime not only is Psalm 21, the Passion psalm, appointed for Friday, but Psalm 22, which, with its well furnished table and overflowing chalice,3 refers to the Eucharist,4 is appointed for Thursday. This association has been further strengthened since 1935 by the theme of Christ the High Priest for Thursday, which has a Mass ritual of its own.5 This is supported by evening devotions, not only by the holding of death-agony chimes, as in many churches, but by the holding of a Holy Hour on the first Thursday of the month.6

Friday, too, has acquired new and more decisive features. Corresponding to the death-agony chimes of Thursday there is the ringing of the great bell on Friday 'at the ninth hour', a widespread custom since the close of the Middle Ages. And as well as this, the devotion to the Sacred Heart of Jesus, which is connected liturgically with the first Friday of the month, firmly directs attention to the interior aspect of the mystery of the Passion.

It is not so easy to understand how the present-day dedication of Saturday to Mary fits into the scheme based on Redemptive history. As we saw, the connexion between Saturday and Mary was asserted by Alcuin. On the other hand Amalar, who is about one generation more recent knows nothing of this connexion; on Saturday, because it is the seventh day, he finds simply a reference to the holy Spirit and His seven gifts.7 At a still later date we find Saturday occasionally dedicated to St. Joseph.8 Conversely, Mary is commemorated on other days of the week as well. We have already mentioned a case where this falls on Thursday.9 In St. Denis there are two sacramentaries from the 9th and 10th centuries

3. Psalm 22, 5 in the as yet normative text of the Vulgate makes a literal contact with the words of institution: *et hunc praeclarum calicem.*
4. The five psalms—Pss 21-25—seem originally to have formed the conclusion of Sunday Matins. Very early, however, they were apportioned to Prime from Monday to Friday, not according to numerical sequence, but, for the two days mentioned, with deliberate choice. C. Callewaert, *De Breviarii Romani liturgia* (*Liturgicae Institutiones* II), Brugge 1931, 88 seq.; Bäumer-Biron I, 363-365. The corresponding Psalm for Sunday Prime is the one which was always proper to this time.
5. *Acta Ap. Sed.* 28 (1936) 54-56.
6. Increasingly furnished with indulgences since 1815. For the history of this v. F. Beringer, *Die Ablässe,*14 Paderborn 1921-22, I, 319 seq.; II, 135 seq.
7. Amalar, *Liber officialis* IV, 37, 12 (Hanssens II, 521 seq.).
8. Thus in the 'Auriem thuribulum' of 1626 (Schrott 21), in Nakatenus (since 1660; cf. above note 20) and again in the present-day rite of the Premonstratensians (above n. 39).
9. Above c. 3, n. 27.

which give evidence of three days each week when Mary was commemorated, Tuesday, Thursday and Saturday.[10]

In the end, however, Saturday came to be Mary's day. But neither in Alcuin's Mass ritual and the Milan liturgy nor in the rituals de s. Maria in sabbato of our present-day Roman Missal can he find a reason why Saturday should have been chosen. From the 12th century onwards, however, the idea emerges amongst theologians which does in fact give Saturday a Marian significance; and this is done indeed, in connexion with the motif in the history of Redemption which belongs to the adjacent days of Friday and Saturday. On Holy Saturday, when the apostles had fled, Mary was the only person who kept faith.[11] In the later Middle Ages, loving sympathy with the sorrow of the Mother of God after her Son's death was a favourite theme of piety. In art this theme found its chief expression in the Pieta. From this time onwards Mary's compassion with the sorrows of her divine Son are frequently found in the Little Books of Hours as a theme for Saturday.[12] Today the liturgy of Braga still has only two formularies for votive Masses on Saturday: one is De planctu Virginis Mariae, the other De pietate Dominae nostrae.[13] Here we find the thought of the Passion appropriate to the end of the week, coming out in Marian material.

From another angle, too, Saturday begins to attach itself to the scheme of the adjacent days, when the Mass of the High Priesthood of Christ; already mentioned, becomes attached to the first

10. Leroquais, Les sacramentaires I, 20, 67. In the more than 1000 special Marian feasts which, throughout the world and in the course of the centuries, have come to be celebrated, many have been fixed for particular days of the week. Thus all seven days have appeared as Marian days, with a preference—Saturday and Sunday apart—for Monday and Friday ; v. the summary by F. G. Holweck, Calendarium liturgicam festorum Dei et Matris Mariae, Philadelphia 1925, 425-448.
11. St. Beissel, Geschichte der Verehrung Marias in Deutschland, Freiburg 1909 307-310. The idea is first pointed out in Alanus of Lille, In Cant. Cant. (c. 1178) c. 1 (PL 210, 58 seq.) by Y. Congar, Incidence ecclésiologique d'un theme de dévotion mariale: Mélanges de Science theol. (Lille 1950) 277-292.—In his Rationale IV, 1, 31-35, that great collector Durandus gives this reason as the second of five reasons. In the first place he mentions an obscure miracle; in the third: Mary is the gate of heaven which is depicted on Sunday; the fourth: the celebration of the mother should precede that of the Son (which along with the first could most easily become regarded as the true reason); the fifth: God had rested on this day.
12. Thus in the above-mentioned (c. 3, n. 3) Little Book of Hours of Cod Vat. 3769 cited by Beissel (p. 178). He describes the accompanying illustration: Mary, pierced by a sword, with the seven colours in seven scenes.
13. Missale Bracarense (1924) (82)-(85).

Saturday of the month.14 Until today, Saturday has remained linked with Friday even in the rules for fasting and abstinence in Lent, which, according to can. 1252 § 2 should only be observed on Friday and Saturday.

Concerning Sunday we notice a progressive recession of the Trinitarian-apologetic feature, at least if we look at the use of the Athanasian creed. This creed, which in Alcuin's time very often occurred even in the daily Office,15 and which was generally said after that time in Prime only on a few Saturdays after Pentecost, in the rubrical reform of Pius XII (1955) is kept for Trinity Sunday. But the Preface which is related to it through content and origin still determines the character of the Sunday Mass.16 That Sunday is the day commemorating the Resurrection and so our Redemption is acknowledged in our present-day order only on the fringe of the liturgy and to some extent in the catechisms. And yet Sunday and Friday would have to be the main pillars of a re-formed weekly cycle (the still current obligation to abstain on Friday requires a conscious foundation in the memory of the Passion).

If we discount Saturday, the Christmas theme is lacking in our weekly order. The attempts which have been evident since the 12th century, to make a place for it during the first half of the week, have come to nothing in our liturgy, unless we want to see a beginning of it in the isolated connexion of a Monday with the Mass of the Annunciation17 or in the more frequent allocation of Tuesday to John the Baptist18 or of Wednesday to St. Joseph.

It is also striking that of all the themes represented in the liturgy only that of Saturday has claimed the privilege of determining the ritual of Office and Mass in place of the Sunday ritual, when there

14. Acta Sed. Ap. 28 (1936) 140 seq. In the Enchiridion indulgentiarum, (Rome 1950) 507 n. 657, this Saturday is referred to under the title of dies Cleri sanctificationi sacer.The connexion of Saturday with this thought may well be a result of the fact that in many Ember Saturdays it was customary to pray for good priests.
15. Bäumer-Biron I, 365 seq.
16. By a decree of the Cong. of Rites March 2, 1955, the Preface for Trinity has been extended to the Sundays after Corpus Christi and the Sacred Heart of Jesus also. Acta Ap. Sed. 47 (1955) 418 seq.
17. Above p. 261.
18. The latter linking can be proved to occur in the Byzantine liturgy also; v. p. 260, note 10. This seems, too, to have preserved the ancient idea of Wednesday as the day when our Lord was betrayed. Thus we have here a picture of a curious limitation, whereby Wednesday, Friday, and Sunday are plainly tied up with the mystery of Christ, while the days between are dedicated to the commemoration of saints.

is no other Proper for the day. In the high Middle Ages the same
privilege at least where the Mass was concerned, was given to the
theme for Monday (the angels and the departed), and certainly
always to that of Friday (the holy Cross).19

9. Accepit Panem

According to the text of the narrative of institution in our
Roman Mass, our Lord's action in taking the bread in His hands
is described in the language of intense reverence: *accepit panem in
sanctas ac venerabiles manus suas;* but a special significance for this
action is never expressed.

It is quite different in one section of the Mass rituals of the East
which describe the proceedings no less reverently, but then go on
to describe the taking of the bread with some ceremony. Thus in
the Liturgy of St. Basil: λαβὼν ἄρτον ἐπὶ τῶν ἁγίων αὐτοῦ
καὶ ἀχράντων χειρῶν καὶ ἀναδείξας σοὶ τῷ Θεῷ καὶ
Πατρί.1 The Lord takes the bread in His holy hands and holds it up
demonstratively, offering it to the heavenly Father. The same text
occurs also in the old Cappadocian tradition of the rite of St.
Basil2 which preserves for us the core, at least, of the Canon of the
text which must have been in use even earlier than Basil's time
(d. 379) in Caesarea and which, it would seem, he only revised.3
The same gesture as in this ritual is described in the same words in
the Mass ritual of Jerusalem, contained in the James Anaphora, in
the oldest original text, no less, as far at least as it can be made out
for the first half of the 5th century.4 And if the borrowing comes

19. Above p. 264 seq. We can trace that Saturday is primarily being given over to Mary
even earlier than the Missal of Pius V. The Synod of Avignon (1326) expressly decreed
that on Saturdays when there was no feast with nine lessons, the Mass *de beata Maria* was
to be used; can. 1 (Mansi XXV, 743).

1. F. E. Brightman, *Liturgies Eastern and Wetern,* Oxford 1896, 327.

2. Critical text in F. Hamm, *Die liturgischen Einsetzungsberichte im Sinne vergleichender
Liturgieforschungen untersucht,* Munster 1928, 25.

3. Cf. H. Engberdging, *Das eucharistische Hochgebet der Basiliusliturgie. Textgeschichtliche
Untersuchungen und kritische Ausgabe,* Munster 1931, p. LXXXIV seq.

4. Hamm 21; cf. 95. The later text—Brightman 51 seq.—already shows expansion and
also repeats the ἀναδείξας with the chalice.

278   PASTORAL LITURGY

from the Basilian side, then this would take us back another century.
The Biblical narratives contain nothing about this gesture. They
do not mention the hands at all but simply say: λαβὼν (ὁ
Ἰησοῦς) ἄρτον (Mk. 26, 26; Lk. 22, 19), ἔλαβεν ἄρτον
(I. Cor. 11, 23). However, in Cappadocia and Jerusalem in the
4th and 5th centuries this was how they imagined the action. Nor
can there be any doubt that the celebrating priest or the bishop
himself, from an early date if not from the very beginning,
enacted the gesture which was coming to be expressed in these
words, as he still does in all the oriental liturgies, except the
Byzantine.5 In the west Syrian Liturgy of St. James the rite
described as the ἀναδείξας is still demanded.6

The gesture is clearly one of offering. According to this
description, our Lord was offering the gift to God the Father
before sharing it out amongst the apostles, and now the priest is
doing the same. At this point the sacrificial character of the
Eucharist is being expressed, sacrificial in the sense in which it is
expressed elsewhere in various liturgies and specially clearly in the
Roman liturgy: the sense, that is, that even the material gifts are
presented to God before their consecration, so that they share in
that movement towards God which ultimately is appropriate to
the consecrated gifts, the Body and Blood of the Lord. The word
ἀναδεικνύναι which is used here occurs in classical Greek also
as a term for sacrifice.7 Sacrifice is essentially this: to offer a gift to
God in token of homage. Men cannot place a gift in the hand of
the invisible God; they can only give something away, accompanying this giving with words or signs, which assert that the gift
belongs to God alone. The signs employed may be various—a
depositing or libation at a holy place, a slaughtering or burning or
simply a raising up towards the place where God 'dwells'. This
last finds expression in the ἀναδεικνύναι.

5.   On the secondary character of this exception, v. J. M. Hanssens, *Institutiones liturgicae
de ritibus orientalibus* III, Rome 1932, p. 446.
6.   Hanssens III, 422: Saying the appropriate words, the priest with his right hand lays a
host upon the palm of his left hand, and makes the Sign of the Cross upon it.
7.   E. Paterson, *Die Bedeutung von* ἀναδείκνυμι *in den griechischen* Liturgien: Festgabe
fur Adolf Deissmann (Tübingen 1927) 320-326, refers to the expression from Greek sacral
language to the ἀ. τῷ Διὶ Ταυρον i.e. to the dedicating of a bullock to Zeus. Peterson's
further references from this source aimed at explaining the ἀναδεικνύναι of the *Epiclesis*
meet well-founded contradiction—v. O. Cassel, JL 7 (1927) 273 seq., and A. Baumstark,
ibid. 357.

The thought that at the Last Supper Christ, too, through an outward gesture offered the gifts to the heavenly Father, made its passing appearance in the West also. Although the text of the Roman Canon has never contained any more than the present words: *accepit panem in sanctas ac venerabiles manus suas*, about 820 Amalar is already speaking of an elevation of the host at this place:—*hic eam (oblatam) elevat.*[8] About 1068 the monk Bernard in his record of the Cluniac usage describes the elevation of the host thus: *Dum dicit 'accipit panem' ac:ipit hostiam . . . etusque contra pectus levat*, whereupon the host is once more laid down: *et dicto 'gratias agens' ponit.*[9] In many churches the host was held up in the left hand and blessed with the right.[10] In others the words of consecration were spoken over the host held on high and likewise with the chalice. Evidence of this is given by the poet-bishop, Hildebert of Tour (d. 1133), who, moreover, gives a very clear description of the rite: *sumptum (panem) tollit utraque manu.*[11] With Radylphus Ardens (d. 1101) the elevation is so expressed that he sees it as a portrayal of our Lord's being raised on the Cross.[12] Honorius Augustodunensis (d. 1152) an influential preacher, saw the elevation plainly as an offering[13]: *Examplo Domini accipit sacerdos oblatum sicut sacrificium Abel . . .* About this time the elevation of the gift at the Offertory, in the sense of an oblation, is already current;[14] and so, elsewhere, this further elevation would be taken in the same sense.

Subsequently the idea became blurred, for about the turn of the 12th century, apparently in Paris to begin with, a modification of the ceremony came about. This was the beginning of Gothic art and culture which tended towards what was realistic and moving, towards display and impression and which allowed this longing

8. Amalar, *Liber officialis* III, 24, 8 (Hanssens II, 339, Z.28).
9. M. Herrgott, *Disciplina monastica vetus*, Paris 1726, 264.—Similarly Bernold of Constance, *Micrologus* c. 15 (PL 151, 987).—Cf. also on what follows, P. Browe, *Die Verehrung der Eucharistie im Mittelalter*, Munich 1933, 29 seq.
10. *Speculum de mysteriis Ecclesiae* (PL 177, 370). The same rite also in the *Life* of Bishop Hugh of Lincoln (d. 1200), wirrten by his chaplain; v. Browe 30.
11. Hildebert of Tours, *Versus de myst. missae* (PL 171, 1186). The saying of the words of Consecration over the elevated offerings also in Stephen of Autun, *De sacr. altaris* c. 13 (PL 172, 1292 seq.); v. Browe 30.
12. Radulphus Sedens, *Hom.* 47 (PL 155, 1836): *Quando enim sacerdos elevat hostiam et ei imprimit crucis signum, elevationem Christi in cruce repraesentat.*
13. Honorius Augustodunensis, *Sacramentarium* c. 88 (PL 172, 793 D).
14. So for example, about 1030 in the *Missa Illyrica*: E. Martène, *De antiquis Ecclesiae ritibus* I, 4, Ordo IV (Antwerp 1736: I, 508 E; cf. 510 E).

280   PASTORAL LITURGY

for display to extend to the Blessed Sacrament.[15] The faithful would crowd round while the priest took the host in his hand and held it up at the *accepit panem;* to catch a glimpse of it at this moment they regarded as a joy and a grace. It was but logical that a Bishop of Paris should direct that priests should not elevate the host until after the words of consecration had been spoken, and then should elevate it high enough for all to see. Various synods, after this, re-iterated this rule. The reason given was: that the faithful might not adore a creature in place of the Creator.[16] And so, by an almost negligible displacement, the older ceremony of elevating the host took on a completely new meaning: it became the showing of the sacred host to the adoring people. In the *Missale Romanum* the same meaning for the elevation is still basically preserved in the rubric: *ostendit populo.* At the *accepit* only the taking has remained, but with the chalice this represents, nevertheless, a definite raising up.

If the Middle Ages evolved a ceremony of oblation at the *accepit panem,* this was but the late unfolding of what had been implicit in the nature of the thing from the start. Can the same be said of the Cappadocian—Palestinian parallel appearance in the early Christian period? As we learn from the *Penegrinatio Aetheriae,* in Jerusalem in the 4th century there was a lively interest in the external imitation of events from the New Testament story of Redemption. In particular, the celebration of Good Friday and Easter with their processional routes which, relying on Biblical reference, and local memory, followed out our Lord's last journey, provided a whole set of examples of this.[17] The ever-growing infusion of Jewish or 'Syrian' population,[18] which had led, since the 5th century, to the formation of a special Christian literature in a Palestinian dialect, allows the possibility that table-customs from the time of our Lord persisted, and that it was these which led to the ἀναδείξας of the liturgy.

Certainly, in the light of this ἀναδείξας, accounts which take us back to table-ritual in the time of our Lord, assume increased

15. Cf. E. Doumutet, *Le désir de voir l'Hostie et les origines de la dévotion au S. Sacrament,* Paris 1926.
16. Browe 37 seq.
17. *Peregrinatio Aetheriae* c. 29 seq.; A. Bludau, *Die Pilgerreise der Aetheria,* Paderborn 1927, 116 seq.
18. Bludau 182.

significance. What is told us on this subject in the Apostolic Traditions of Hyppolytus of Rome (c. 215) is most striking. From this we learn about an order for the *Agape*, which derives obviously from the ritual of the Jewish meal.19 In this we can see that the blessing of the table is connected with an offering. This appears most clearly with the cup: before drinking, each person takes his cup and 'gives thanks'.20 In the order of the solemn ritual meal of the Sabbath and the Chabura, as we know them more or less directly from Jewish sources in New Testament times, and also as it applies to the more elaborate rite of the Paschal meal,21 an act of praise is provided in which it is not the prayer, as far as we know it, but the accompanying gesture which displays the character of an offering. At the breaking of the bread at the start of the meal only a short word of praise is uttered but, the real prayer at table follows at the end of the meal as a solemn act of praise. While saying this, the head of the family or the host had to take the filled cup and hold it a hand's breadth above the table.22 This raising up is certainly intended to be a raising up to God—an oblation; and it is this same oblation which appears in Hippolytus.23 According to the universal assumption of the exegetes the cup at the end of the meal is that with which the Lord μετὰ τὸ δειπνῆσαι (I. Cor. 11. 25) offered His blood to the disciples.

It is not arbitrary, therefore, to see more in the ἀναδείξας of the Cappadocian—Palestinian liturgy of ancient Christian times than a true and expansive interpretation of the data of the Biblical

19. Lietzmann, *Messe und Herrenmahl*, Bonn 1926, 202-210.
20. *Traditio Ap.* c. 26 (Dix 45 seq.). Cf. the reconstruction of the text given here—standard, no doubt—by E. Hennecke, *Neutestamentliche Apokryphen,*¹ Tübingen 1924, 581 seq.—And the 'Blessing' from Feldkirchen, too, becomes an 'Offertory' in the same document. We hear of a prayer, in fact, which the bishop was supposed to say over the first-fruits of the earth; and this is regulated in a rubric which follows immediately: benedicuntur quidem fructus. The prayer which is preserved in Greek also, begins, however, thus: Εὐχαριστοῦμεν σοι, Κύριε ὁ Θεὸς καὶ προσφέρομεν ἀρχὴν καρπῶν.
21. Billerbeck, *Kommentar zum Neuen Testament aus Talmud und Midrasch* IV, 1828, 41-76.
22. Billerbeck IV, 72.
23. Perhaps Psalm 115, 4 belongs here too: *Calicem salutaris accipiam.* The redeemed one promises: 'I will take the cup of salvation' (Henne). The Hebrew period of the *accipiam* indeed affirms a raising. Thus we are dealing with a raising of the chalice associated with a sacrifice of thanksgiving.—The idea of this raising up of food and drink in offering is confirmed again by the ancient Israelite tradition that every slaughtering should be carried out in a spirit of sacrifice: v. J. Sint, *Schlachten und Opfern: ZkTh* 78 (1956) 194-205.

text. At least it is most likely that at the Last Supper our Lord Himself raised the cup in oblation. There seems to be no direct proof that there was a similar rite with the bread. But because the liturgies have no plain statement concerning the chalice the representation of the *accepit panem* as an oblation has all the more value as independent evidence, not having been suggested first by literary accounts, such as we have mentioned, of the oblation of the chalice.

10. *The Basic Shape of the Mass*

Every Catholic Christian has always understood quite plainly that in the holy Mass a sacrifice is offered: but it is quite another matter how we are to describe the formal nature of the actual liturgy. If we detach the liturgical action from the stylized framework in which we are accustomed to see it, what remains before us is, in fact, the outline of a meal: there is a table, there are bread and wine; and when the act of consecration has been performed, both are consumed. In other words, little or nothing is there, which reminds us of the forms of sacrifice which we know in religious history: no blood flows, nothing is burnt, nothing poured out.

A historical line of thought leads us to the same place: to begin with there was that episode which we call simply the Last Supper; and in the first generation of the disciples of Christ the institution of that evening lived on as a genuine meal, at least it was connected with a meal as its visible framework—or, more exactly, as the substance of the framework—and it was itself called the 'breaking of bread'.[1]

It might appear, then, that sacrifice had not entered into the perceptible shape of the Mass at all, or that it is only faintly indicated in it; for the eyes which have come to see by faith always see

1. We must remember, however, that in Justin's time it was more a matter of a 'symbolic form of meal', which is, moreover, a 'truncated' form of meal; thus H. Schurmann, *Die Gestalt der urchristlichen Eucharistiefeier: Münchener Theol. Zeitschrift* 6 (1955, 107-131) 131.

the separated species which speak of body and blood and so the sacrifice of Calvary. But it is as though what happened that day is to be hidden beneath the happy picture of a family table; it is indeed too gruesome in its outward circumstances to meet our immediate gaze, and again it is too sacred and too mighty in the spiritual substance of its merciful, redemptive love, for us to dare speak out about it all the time.

The tendency to accentuate the meal in the outward image of the Mass has appeared variously in the liturgical movement, and is expressed in a series of new publications. This tendency is characteristic of Joseph Pascher's thoughtful and stimulating book.[2] It is apparent even in the titles. What we are accustomed to call the Mass of sacrifice in contrast to the fore-Mass, he calls 'the sacred meal'. This theme is developed under the headings: the 'preparation' of the Eucharistic table: the 'Eucharistic table-prayer'; and the 'eating'. The more detailed explanation shows that in all this, Pascher in no way unsettles the idea of the Mass as a sacrifice: he emphasizes it even more strongly, and emphasizes also, in a thorough study, the co-sacrifice of the faithful (118 ff. 270 ff.). Moreover, he sees outward signs of the sacrificial nature. This is expressed in the two-fold species and in the words referring to them. But 'the sacrifice of the Easter lamb (is) symbolically transposed to the celebration of the meal' (225). 'The shape of the holy Mass is that of a meal' (31).

This symbolism of the meal, and more particularly, that of the table fellowship is fully developed by Pascher and pointed out in places where at first it does not force itself upon our notice. The service of the Word of God, more deeply understood, reveals itself to be a Eucharistic meal, because in it the Logos take upon Himself, not flesh and blood, it is true, but the accents of human speech—a thought which a reference to the Eucharistic commission address of Jn. 6 is able effectively to support. In the Kyrie according to Pascher, the entrance of the newly-baptized, accompanied by the reciting of the litany, is concealed—the newly-baptized who are about to be accepted into the fellowship of the sacred meal (384). The Dominus vobiscum, which can be regarded as a simplified kiss of peace (157), constitutes the fellowship be-

2. J. Pascher, Eucharistia und Vollzug.[2] Münster 1953. This edition is greatly altered in individual expositions compared with the first edition of 1947.

tween priest and people, and so is a living symbol of the Christ—
Church mystery which is repeated several times during the course
of the Mass (80 f. 302f); and the *Orate fratres* too, is understood in
the same way. In both cases the accompanying gestures reinforce
this impression and the simultaneous turning towards the congregation corresponds to the table-fellowship which will be fully
realized in the dispensing of Communion (305). These are insights, the correctness of which cannot be contested without more
ado; and we may wish that the attitudes and ideas they contain
may increasingly gain ground. It is indeed a beautiful idea if the
whole Church is seen in the end as a great table-fellowship
(374 ff), such as it was in the time of Ignatius of Antioch.

It is quite another question whether or not it is necessary or even
correct to regard the meal symbolism as the decisive and fundamental thing in the outward transaction of the Mass. If the Mass
is a sacrifice then this must find appropriate expression in the outward picture too; for sacrifice is essentially a demonstrative action,
the symbolic representation of inward readiness to give oneself.
In doing this the outward representation need by no means
exhaust the whole content of the reality behind it. Even Baptism
does not do this. Washing says nothing, for example, about in-
corporation as a member in the Church; and yet it is part of
baptism. But the outward, sensibly perceptible representation of
sacrifice cannot be wholly absent.

It is admitted on all sides today that the institution of the
Eucharist as presented in the New Testament accounts contains
the separation of the species. Further, the meal which predominated in the Eucharistic celebration of the primitive Church, was
admittedly regarded as a *sacred* meal, having some kind of dedication of a gift to God as a pre-requisite and which thereby represented the oblation which was set out to be enjoyed as holy food.

It is true that this would be a vague way of speaking, especially
if the sanctifying of the sacred meal never came into view.

There is reason to ask, therefore: Are there really no more signs
of sacrifice-symbolism? The answer must be very distinct. If we
look only for an expression of Christ's sacrifice, which constitutes
the inner core of the celebration, we will not find much sensibly
perceptible content. But if we concentrate our attention on the

fact that the Mass is not purely and simply a making-present of
the sacrifice of Calvary, but is the sacrifice of Christ, the worship-
ful sacrifice of the community of the redeemed who for ever
gather round this central point in order there to enter into the
dying and living of their Head, in His obedience to the Father,
then at once we see a sacrifice-symbolism which has not been
added to the essential happening in the course of time, but which
was given along with it and which we cannot ignore. For in the
moment when the Eucharist left our Lord's hands and was taken
up into the hands of His Church, and the Church presented the
Body and Blood of Christ upon the Eucharistic table, with thanksgiving, that is, looking up to God, consecration and self-offering
to God had begun to assume a visible form. It is no small thing
that in all known liturgies without exception the basis of the celebration is made up of thanksgiving to God, a thanksgiving from
which the oblation emerges: we give Thee thanks, and therefore
we offer unto Thee. Christ's sacrificial oblation remains veiled but
the veil is composed of those very forms in which the self-offering
of the co-sacrificing Church is expressed. This expression is given
first of all in words which belong of their nature to the sensibly
perceptible world. Then it is given, with increasing definition, in
visible signs and gestures also. To this belongs not only the elevation of chalice and host at the end of the Canon—so-called little
elevation—but also the preparatory raising of the bread upon the
paten and of the chalice at the Offertory, a gesture which every
child can understand. With this are associated also the deep bowing and the prayer to be accepted, the glance of entreaty to God,
the signing of the offerings with the sign of the Cross—not merely
for the sake of the sign of the Cross, but principally as an indicative
gesture—the out-spreading of the hands over the offerings, and,
finally—if we accept the obvious re-interpretation which is
founded in the origin of the thing—the elevation at the actual
consecration. In short, this includes everything which expresses
giving and offering the gifts to God. For if we wish to approach
in homage the mighty God who is present everywhere yet no-
where perceptible by us, we are able only to symbolize our giving
—even giving something away, libations, destruction all are but
symbols of our desire to give.

In this sense quite clearly the shape of the whole ritual between the service of the Word and the Communion consists not merely in the confraternity of a table-fellowship, but—with this as background—in the rising movement towards God, prepared for in the fore-Mass, and reaching its satisfying goal in the Communion-section. The ritual setting in which all of this occurs is not the result of a later secondary development, but was already present in the institution of Jesus in the primitive Church. At the turn of the first century we already find the celebration being called a *Eucharistia*, a thanksgiving. In all the liturgies the thanksgiving determines the structure of the chief prayer, as the universal invitation brings to our notice: *Gratias agamus Domino Deo nostro!* The first full text of a Mass which emerges into the light of history about 215 A.D. already contains, at a decisive place, the *offerimus*, growing out of the thanksgiving and carrying it on—the same as we do today after the consecration.

Very soon, however, the beginnings of visible symbolism are added to the audible representation of the desire to make an offering; and these can soon be proved. In that oldest of Mass rituals which we have just mentioned, the *Eucharistia* of Hippolytus of Rome, it is prescribed that at the beginning of the prayer of thanksgiving the bishop should spread out his hands over the offerings. Indeed it is at least highly probable that in the time of Christ Himself an offertory gesture was required in the ritual of a solemn meal, both at the inaugural breaking of bread and at the concluding prayer of thanksgiving which the head of the household had to utter while raising the cup—a rite such as the Lord Himself observed.[3]

Today there is a strong inclination to emphasize as the basic shape of the celebration of the Mass the community-symbolism and, more precisely, the meal-symbolism. In this we see a justifiable reaction to the long continued neglect of this important aspect of the Mass, a reaction which leads us to recognize that the notion of sacrifice alone cannot fully exhaust the meaning of the spiritual transaction, especially if we think solely of the sacrifice of

3. For a more thorough-going proof see the essay *Accepit Panem*—previous chapter. On the state of present discussion of the basic shape of the Mass cf. also *Missarum Sollemnia*[*] (1958) I, 27 seq.; II, 577 seq.

Christ. First of all it was the Reformation controversy which led to the question of the sacrifice of Christ moving exclusively into the centre of interest, and finally, to the thought of Christ's sacrifice becoming merged in the highly abstract concept of sacrifice in general. The medieval mind paid much more heed to the sacrifice of the Church; and they were much more vividly aware of our Lord's life and Passion alongside His sacrifice, than we are accustomed to be, and they found this portrayed in the symbolism of the ceremonies.

11. *Fermentum: A Symbol of Church Unity and its Observance in the Middle Ages*

We still call the reception of the Eucharist, 'Communion'. It is significant, however, that the meaning of this word in contemporary religious writing and even in the catechism is regularly defined as 'union', i.e. union of the individual with Christ. The original and precise meaning of the word has faded out of consciousness. The original meaning of the word *communio* was community —the community of faithful who are bound together through the common possession of the heritage of Redemption, especially of the Sacrament of the Eucharist which gathers all within itself, so that the *sacra communio* is at once the living foundation of and also manifestation of the *communio sanctorum*.

In ancient Christian times men were vividly aware of the community associations of the Eucharist. In particular, the Eucharist for long played a large part in community relationships in the special sense. The community, which the Catholic Church in its spacial extension over the world had to embrace, was assured if the pastors of the separate congregations remained united with their superiors, the bishops, and if these remained united amongst each other. At times people had not hesitated to express the community between bishop and bishop by an interchange of the

Eucharist.₁ This practice, then indulged in at Easter, was first forbidden in the 4th century at the Council of Laodicea.₂

This was practised even more within the bounds of a diocese.₃
In the time of Pope Boniface II (530–532), when the fundamental
stratum of the *Liber pontificalis* came into being, the custom was at
its height. The anonymous author was able to tell us of Pope
Melchiades: *Hic fecit, ut oblationes consecratae per ecclesias ex conse-
cratu episcopi dirigerentur, quod declaratur fermentum,*₄ and of Pope
Siricius: *Hic constituit, ut nullus presbyter missas celebraret per omnem
hebdomadam, nisi consecratum loci designati susciperet declaratum, quod
nominatur fermentum.*₅

The letter of Pope Innocent I to Decentius of Gobbio in 416₆
gives a complete description of the custom which also associates
the word *fermentum* with it.₇ *De fermento vero, quod dic dominica per
titulos mittimus, superflue nos consulere voluisti, cum omnes ecclesiae
nostrae intra civitatem sint constitutae. Quarum presbyteri, quia die ipsa
propter plebem sibi creditam nobiscum convenire non possunt, idcirco
fermentum a nobis confectum per acolythos accipiunt, ut se a nostra
communione, maxime illa die, non indicent separatos. Quod per
paroecias*₈ *fieri debere non puto, quia nec longe portanda sunt sacra-
menta, nec nos per cemeteria diversa constitutis presbyteris destinamus.*
The significance of the custom is obvious. As they hold the public
service of worship on Sundays, in their titular churches, the
Roman presbyters are to be conscious that they are in communion
(*communio*) with their bishop. To this end, they receive from him

---

1. Cf. Eusebius, *Hist. eccl.* V, 27; v. on this F. J. Dölger, *Ichthys* II, Münster 1922, 535 n. 3.
2. can 14 (Mansi II, 566).
3. The most important accounts up to the 9th century in F. Cabrol, *Fermentum*: DACL V
(1922) 1371–74; Eisenhofer, *Handbuch der katholischen Liturgik* II, 201 seq.
4. *Liber pont.* ed. Duchesne I, 169.
5. Ibid. II, 216.
6. Innocent I., *Ep.* 25, 5, 8 (PL 20, 556 seq.).
7. The appellation is difficult to explain in by saying that the Eucharist ought to permeate
the Church as leaven does the lump of bread (thus Eisenhofer II, 202; Du Cange-Favre,
Glossarium III, 440 seq.); the particle should rather be described as an 'addition' which is
added to the Eucharistic of one's own Mass at the appropriate rite of mixing.
8. *Paroecia* here no longer means 'diocese' as παροικία does in the canon of Laodicea,
but 'region' (belonging to a diocese), out of which soon arose the meaning 'parish',
V. P. de Labriolle, *La vie chrétienne en Occident* (Fliche-Martin, *Histoire de l'Eglise* IV,
Paris 1939) 577–580.

a particle of the Sacrament which is sent to them by an acolyte. Clearly out of reverence for the Sacrament—the reason also for the regulation of Laodicea—the custom did not allow of distribution to a greater distance.

For centuries the custom maintained itself vigourously in Rome: but the incidence of its practice gradually diminished. Some three centuries after Innocent's time the *fermentum* was no longer sent every Sunday to the priests in the titular churches, but only on greater feast days: Holy Thursday, Holy Saturday, Easter Sunday, Pentecost and Christmas.9 The service on Holy Saturday evening is specially emphasized in this connexion. On this day, so it says in the relevant document, no priest is to give anyone holy Communion until he has received the holy Particle from the Pope.10 This day is again mentioned at the turn of the 8th century in the *Ordo* of Saint Amand. On this day every Roman priest sends his *mansionarius* to the Latern Basilica. Here the messengers wait at the Papal service until the fraction of the Bread. When the fraction has been performed each receives a holy Particle on a corporal from the *subdiaconus oblationarius*. This is called a *sancta*,11 and he straightway takes it back to his own priest. The priest makes the sign of the Cross with it over the chalice and slips it into the chalice saying the *Pax Domini*.12

There are other accounts as well which agree that the *fermentum* at this time was always sent to the stational services if the Pope was not able to conduct these himself. In these cases great importance was laid upon clearly expressing the Pope's moral presence. And so it was the papal *subdiaconus oblationarius* who handed over

9. These cases (besides another case of a stational service conducted by a representative of the Pope) are mentioned in an undated text of which John Mabillon speaks in his commentary on the Roman *Ordines* VI, 2 (PL 78, 870 seq.), *ex vetusissimo codice*—from Regensburg. Cf. Cabrol, *Fermentum* 1371 seq. From internal evidence, the text has to be assigned to the time indicated.

10. Loc. cit.: *Tamen sabbato sancto Paschae nullus presbyter per ecclesias baptismales neminem communicat, antequam mittatur ei de ipsa sancta, quam obtulit dominus papa.*

11. Cabrol, loc. cit. 1372, takes this phrase to indicate an exchange; but this is unfounded. It is never stated that only the particle from the previous Papal Mass mentioned in the *Ordo Romanus* I (Andrieu II, 82. 98) is called *sancta*. Cf. also the previous note.

12. Andrieu, *Les Ordines Romani* III, 474. The existing text makes the priest say Dominus v obiscum, it is true, but clearly what is meant is the *Pax Domini*, indicated frequently in other places. Cf. Andrieu II, 60–64.

the holy Particle. At the *Pax Domini* the celebrant united this with his own oblation.13

The custom must still have been going on in Rome in the 9th century. A Roman *Ordo*14 makes this express observation on the rite of the Papal Mass: *Dum vero Dominus papa dicit: Pax Domini sit semper vobiscum, non mittit partem de sancta in calicem, sicut ceteris sacerdotibus mos est.*15. Obviously the *ceteri sacerdotes* kept up the practice on occasion at this time.

According to the evidence quoted so far, we must expect to find the continuance of this custom chiefly on those days which usher in the celebration of Easter. And here we come across a remarkable notice which has been interpolated in Roman lists of the Gospel pericopes. The two types of these lists whose origin is put at about 740 and 755, the more recent of which was in use until the influx of Franco-German liturgical ordinances, i.e. until about 1000 A.D. more or less, contain the same sort of annotation for Saturday before Palm Sunday: *Sabbato datur fermentum in consistorio Lateranensi*.16 In this Roman source this can be none other than our *fermentum* which we find described by this name in other Roman sources also; and *consistorium*, too, obviously means the same thing as we denote by the same word today: the assembly of the Roman curia around the Pope, in particular the *presbyteri cardinales* who are nothing but the titular priests of an earlier day.17 On this day, then, they were handed the *fermentum* for the coming celebrations, probably for the sequence of Easter *fermentum*-days which began with Holy Thursday.

13. The Mass *Ordo* of St. Amand: Andrieu II, 169.—Supplement (8th century) to the *Ordo Romanus I* (Andrieu II, 115): *Quando dici debet: Pax Domini sit semper vobiscum, deportatur a subdiacono oblationario particula fermenti, quod ab apostolico consecratum est, et datur archdiacono; ille vero porrigit episcopo. At ille consignando tribus vicibus et dicendo: Pax Domini sit semper vobiscum, mittit in calicem.*—Similarly in the Regensburg Codex of Mabillon loc. cit. (PL 78, 870 seq.).
14. *Ordo qualiter quaedam orationes et cruces in Te igitur agendae sunt*; Andrieu II, 251-305.
15. Loc cit. 304 seq. The rubric has become the basis of the present-day order of the Mass in the Mass *Ordo* of the Rhine. In part of the tradition this rubric has ceased to be understood and has been mutilated in various ways. The only thing which is maintained is that the *ceteri sacerdotes* should put a particle in the chalice at the *Pax Domini*, prescribing, however, that it should be a particle from the same Mass—for now the *fermentum* was no longer customary. The present-day practice of mixing the species at the *Pax Domini* (instead of immediately before the Communion), a practice which had come about quite early on, in the end became established.
16. Th. Klausner, *Das römische Capitulare evangeliorum* I, Münster 1935, p. 69. 110.
17. Cf. Du Cange-Favre II, 517 seq.

With this, however, we meet the transition to a new form of the custom, not yet brought into association with the *fermentum*, a form in which the element consecrated by the bishop is not designed merely for a series of days devoted to such a celebration, The *Ordo de gradibus Romanae*, composed about the turn of the 9th century contains, attached to the end of the liturgy for the ordination of priests, the regulation: *Tollit vero pontifex oblatas integras et dat singulis novitiis presbyteris, et inde communicantur usque dies VIII*.[18] Everyone of the newly-ordained priests, then received a complete consecrated host from the Pope; and he was to communicate from this for eight days, clearly by mingling a particle with the Communion at each of his Masses. In this way the inauguration of his priestly sacrificial activity was to be firmly bound up with the priestly action of his bishop. This custom is confirmed by the slightly older Ordo of Saint-Amand which we have mentioned; the only difference being that this prescribes Communion over a period of forty days, and the consecrated bread is described as *firmanta oblata*.[19] The word *firmata* like the later *formata* (*oblata*) can only be an etymological modification of the no longer understood *fermentum*[20] We find this forty-day *fermentum* transferred about the same time to the consecration of a bishop—as is seen in the 8th century Roman *Ordo* for ordinations.[21]

Roman liturgical books spread throughout northern lands from Charlemagne's time on; and people faithfully tried to bring these books to life to the very letter. We would not be surprised, therefore, were we to meet the custom of which we have been speaking

18. Andrieu LV, 199.
19. Andrieu IV, 285: *Deinde (after consecration) offerunt pontifici ante omnes presbyteros et communicant similiter eodem die ante omnes. Et accipit unusquisque a pontifice firmata oblata de altare, unde et communicat XL diebus.*
20. At that stage in the development of language—as Prof. Jos. Bruch (of Innsbruck University) kindly confirmed for me—the two forms had been very closely allied: *fermento* on the one hand, and *fermato* on the other. The form *formatum* exists in a 10th century text from Ravenna. The tendency to take over from litarary use a similar sounding word into every-day speech, is shown in a second case from this very *Ordo* of St. Amand, when it repeats *psallit* in the sense of 'he ascends' (Andrieu II, 159 seq.). The scribe clearly had *salire* before him, which developed this sense in Italian (salit=psallit, with the p silent). Cf. Andrieu II, 138 note 3.
21. Andrieu III, 613: *Dum vero venerit ad communicandum, domnus apostolicus porrigit ei formatum atque sacratum oblationem; et eam suscipiens ipse episcopus ex ea communicat super altare, et ceterum ex ea sibi reservat ad communicandum usque ad dies quadraginta.* The meaning taken by Andrieu III, 587: *formata=certificat d'ordination* hardly fitting our context. Cf Du Cange-Favre III, 565, and also A. Dold, 'Forma' and 'Formata': *Sacris erudiri* 2 (1951) 214-221, where Dold's own explanation of *forma* (Bread species) is not acceptable.

in northern lands too. Amalar wrote a letter to Abbot Hilduin of Saint-Denis which shows us that interest has at least been aroused in the enigmatic custom of sending the *fermentum* to the titular churches, about which they had been reading in Roman sources and which they tried to explain.[22] But the custom as it appeared in this form could not take root in the North because for long there were no large cities which could contain a multiplicity of parish churches. *Fermentum*-Communion may well have become a practice, however, at ordinations.

There is a letter of the famous Bishop of Chartres, Fulbert, dated 1006,[23] in which he gives an explanation to a newly ordained priest who had made an enquiry 'concerning the host which you recently received from the hand of the bishop at your ordination to the priesthood, why, in particular, it has to be used up by daily reception over a period of forty days'. Fulbert discloses in this that he sees it as a custom in common use, in particular by all the bishops in his province.[24] He recounts an incident also which reveals several other things to us and which gives him an opportunity to expound the meaning of this custom. One day when a newly ordained priest was clearing up the altar after his Mass he lost the sacred host which he had received from the bishop and which he kept in a parchment cover. (It must have been a wafer of unleavened bread at this time.) The following day when he celebrated once more, and, following the prescription, wanted to take a piece of this along with the customary Communion (*instante hora communicandi*), all searching was in vain. On this occasion Fulbert had enjoined the bishop to restrict Communion from the ordination-host to two or three days from henceforth. This bishop, however, had declined to do so, with the explanation, which Fulbert now hands on to his enquirer: the Sacrament which the bishop gives for Communion is meant to remind us of the forty days during which our Lord appeared to His disciples after His Resurrection, strengthening them for their task with heavenly nourishment; it is supposed to be in some sense (*quodammodo*) the Body which is risen and never more dies, whereas the priest's own consecration represents the Body as it dies for us daily, rises daily,

22. MG *Ep. Karolini aevi* III, 256 seq.
23. Fulbert, *Ep.* 3 (PL 141, 192-195).
24. Loc. cit. (193 C).

appears to us and is consumed.²⁵ The custom would seem to have a firm hold still, but its roots, the ancient symbolism of community, have already died. The custom itself would soon die away therefore. By the 13th century all traces are lost.²⁶

The old custom lasted longer in association with the consecration of a bishop. The monk of St. Alban's at Mainz, who composed the so-called Roman-German *Pontificale* about 950, keeps the relevant regulation in his ritual for the consecration of a bishop as he found it in its Roman source.²⁷ This ensured for the custom a further field for expansion and a longer observance. The rubric in question did not live now on German soil alone;²⁸ it is still found in the same text at the beginning of the 13th century in a *Pontificale* of Cuenca in Spain and in a crusaders' *Pontificale* of Constantinople.²⁹ In particular, it found its way into the 12th century Roman *Pontificale* and again in the new edition of this under Innocent III, a number of manuscripts of which still show

25. Loc. cit. (194 seq.). This is probably the essential content of the somewhat detailed but not very clear exposition. The thought that the daily Mass represented a daily dying and rising again of Christ came about as a result of the Mass allegories which flourished at the time, and according to which, the Canon, the *Commixtio* and Kiss of Peace, signified the Resurrection and manifesting of our Lord.

26. The custom appears even in the *Pontificale* of Soissons (c. 1100), given in Martène, *De antiquis Ecclesiae ritibus* I, 8, 9, n. 20 (Antwerp 1736: II, 68 B); likewise in the *Pontificale* of Chalon-s-M at the end of the 13th century, given in V. Leroquais, *Les pontificaux manuscrits*, Paris 1937, I, p. 123. In the rubric, which means the same thing in both documents, the foundation is seen to lie in the forty days between our Lord's Resurrection and His Ascension. A final echo of this is heard when, in 1400, a *Pontificale* of Bayeux the newly ordained is commanded to continue for forty days after his first Mass—obviously with celebration of the Mass. Leroquais I, 71.

27. M. Hittorp, *De divinis catholicae Ecclesiae officiis*, Köln 1568, 102: *Cum autem venerit ad communicandum, dominus pontifex porrigit ei formatam atque sacratum oblationem integram. Suscipiensque eam episcopus ipse ex ea communicet super altare, quod vero residuum fuerit, sivi reservet denuo ad communicandum unoquoque die usque quadraginta dies expletos.* This is the essence of the text of the Romanrite of Ordination from the 8th century; v. above note 21. A. Dold has published the text of our rubric from a sheet of parchment from the 11th century in the study mentioned in note 21. He gives the variant *forma* instead of *formata*.

28. The *Pontificale* of Bishop Christian I of Mainz (1167-83) provides the regulation, but in a modified and restricted form which shows little understanding of the usage: *electus communicabit de manu episcopi accipiens hostiam integram. Si quid residuum fuerit, servabit sibi ad communicandum cottidie per XXX dies.* Leroquais II, 24 (cf. ibid. 25 the correction of Maretène's dating).

29. Martène, loc. cit. I, 8, 10, n. 21 (II, 82). Then rubric from the *Pontificale* of Cuenca is also in Leroquais II, 362.

the rubric in the 14th century.30 There are several versions of it in French *Pontificales* too.31

Much more striking is the transference of the practice of the *fermuntum*—Communion during eight days to the rite of consecration of virgins. This is connected with the fact that, unlike the profession of monks, the conscration of virgins had always been a pontifical ceremony.32 The rubric in question then re-appears in various *Pontificales* until the late Middle Ages.33 With the Cistercian sisters of Port Royal, the bishop broke a large host in eight pieces, gave one piece to the nun for Communion, and put the other seven pieces in her right hand which was covered with a white napkin.34 The shift away from the original meaning of the practice is specially apparent here. The Sacrament from the bishop's altar is no longer intended to be a priestly celebration of the Eucharist in communion with that of the bishop, but represents simply sacramental strengthening for the new station in life, to which the bishop has granted entrance, a station which is certainly not a sacerdotal one; and the number of days for which

30. M. Andrieu, *Le Pontifical Romain au moyen-age* II (*Studi e Testi* 87), Vatican City 1940, 366.—According to J. Pascher, *Bischof und Presbyterium in der Feier der Eucharistie:* Munich *Theol. Zeitschr.* 9 (1958, 1610170) 167 seq., the custom of observing the *fermentum* at consecration of bishops and ordination of priests had been replaced by concelebration at the ordination Mass since the 12th century. No matter how much we are able to see in the older concelebration a new expression of the original idea of the *fermentum*, we must still take note, that inderlying the ordination concelebration there is a different meaning from that beneath the later *fermentum*-rite (first exercise of the newly received order).

31. Amongst the mss. which Leroquais describes it is recorded in the *Pontificale* of Reims (11th century), of Grenoble (12th, I, 156), of Poitiers (13th, II, 260), of Avignon (first half 14th, I, 61).

32. *Pontificale* of Angers (Leroquais I, 30): *communicet et reservet de ispa communione, unde usque in diem octavum communicet.* The same idea is expressed in evidence from Tours at the same period: Martène, loc. cit. II, 6, *Ordo* III (II 532 A).—Cf. also R. Metz, *La consecration des vierges*, Paris 1954, 214-217.

33. In Leroquais examples are reproduced out of *Pontificales* from Salzburg and Séez (11th century, I, 297), Montpellier (13th century, I, 237), Paris-Sens (13th century I, 227). There is an evidence of the Salzburg usage in M. Gerbert, *Monumenta veteris liturgiae Alemannicae I*, St. Blasien 17779, 97. Martène, loc. cit. II, 6, n. 15 (II, 524 C) names further examples from Reims, Avranches, Noyon, Paris (last case about 1400). Evidence from Milan and Amiens in P. Browe, *Zum Kommunionempfang des Mittelalters:* JL 12 (1934) 163. In a watered-down form it again appears in a *Pontificale* of Lucon at the end of the 14th century (Leroquais II, 152), where the rubric runs: *reservet de ipsa communione usque in diem octavum, ut in die octavo communicet.*

34. From an undated ms. in de Moléon, *Voyages liturgiques*, Paris 1718, 235.

this Communion is to last is much more important than the fact that it was received from the hand of the bishop.35

The appearance of the practice in the 9th century in association with the consecration of nuns is itself a proof that the new interpretation resulted from the transplanting of the practice onto Frankish soil. This corresponds to the general phenomenon that in the region belonging to the Frankish Church, even after it had adopted the Roman liturgy, the conception of the Eucharist which derived from Isidore and the Gallican liturgy predominated. According to this conception all attention is focused on the presence of Christ's Body and the symbolism of community, so powerfully stressed in the Roman-African milieu, progressively receded.36

12. *From Patrocinium to the Act of Consecration*

During the last hundred years, the act of consecration has assumed great importance in the devotional life of the Church. This is specially true of consecration to the Sacred Heart of Jesus and to the Immaculate Heart of Mary. In the end these acts of consecration have been furnished in individual cases with all the public formality and solemnity which mark liturgical activity. Apart from the fact that they have the privilege of using the vernacular and are not contained in books of the Roman liturgy, they do indeed stand in greater isolation within the total scheme of the Church's liturgy than did the old *Missa praesanctificatorum* of Good Friday; and this is not only because of the sentiment which marks their form of expression, which reminds us strongly of the apologies of the early Middle Ages, but also because of the

35. And so in the final phases of development it is rather the Communion which lasts throughout a specified number of days. For this the number may be eight—v. Browe 164, where reference is to the rule which came into existence about 1150 (PL 162, 1086 : pernovem dies); or there may be a return to three—v. a *Pontificale* of Aix (c. 1300) in Martène, loc. cit. II, 6, Ordo VIII, nota (II, 541 D), and the reference to the more recent *Pontificales* of Cambrai, Arles, Mende: ibid. II, 6, n. 15 (II, 524 C). Cf. also above note 33.
36. Cf. J. Geiselmann, *Die Eucharistielehre der Vorscholastik*, Paderborn 1926, 1-56; same author, *Die Abendmahlslehre an der Wende der christlichen Spätantike zum Frühmittelalter*, Munich 1933, esq. p. 174 seq. 259.

religious perspective which is preferred in them and which has the symbol of the heart as its central point. It is no wonder, therefore, that often quite a cry is made about examining the origin and meaning of these acts.1

It would be quite sensible for us, therefore, to examine the lines of development which have led to these forms. In what follows, however, we only aim at giving a rough sketch which at various points will require more exact historical research. This much will, nevertheless, come out, that the development has been reached mainly in two stages: the immediate precursors of the dedicatory formulae will turn out to be those in which the Marian congregations of early modern times, with a characteristic note of loyalty, began to express their devotion to their heavenly mistress. This will turn our attention further back into the cultural world of the Middle Ages in which, linking up with the ideas of the *patrocinium* the concept of loyalty and devotion made a place for itself in religious life. Our research may begin with this more remote preliminary stage and thus try to give, at the same time, a passing description of the course of the development.

Patronus and *clientela* are notions from Roman juridicial life which were applied as early as the 4th century to the relation between a much-venerated martyr and the community who cared for his tomb. In Milan, Ambrose named Gervase and Protase *patroni* of his church.2 In Rome, Leo the Great used the same term of Peter and Paul.3 But soon, cities and places having no tomb of any martyr were looking for a patron of the same sort. They chose a patron and assured themselves of his *patrocinium* by placing relics of their saint—at least his *brandeum*—in the church or chapel4. For centuries these relics were known as *patrocinia sanctorum*.5

Then the idea took hold that every church, even old established churches for public congregational worship—parish churches—

1.   V. for example, E. Walter, *Zur Verkündigung über Maria an die Jugend: Katechet. Blätter* 77 (1952) 181-191 esp. 186 seq.—For questions and suspicions from the Protestant side on the occasion of the consecration of Germany to the Heart of Mary at the Katholikentag in Fulda in 1954, cf. H. Asmussen, *Dem Unbefleckten Herzen Mariä geweiht?: Gloria Dei* 9 (1954) 202-210.
2.   *Ep.* 22, 11 (PL 16, 1023).
3.   *Serm.* 82, 7 (PL 54, 428).
4.   H. Leclercq, *Patron:* DACL XIII, 2515.
5.   Du Cange-Favre, *Glossarium* VI, 219. G. Cagov, *Il culto delle reliquie nell' antichtà riflesso nei due termini 'patrocinia' e 'pignora': Miscellanea Fransescana* 58 (1958) 484-512, esq. 495 seq.

should have relics of a saint in every altar, as is prescribed to this very day (can. 1198 § 4); and that this saint should be regarded as the patron of the church. Ultimately, in case of necessity a *patrocinium* could be founded apart from these conditions, as in Ravenna when in 545 a church was dedicated to the archangel Gabriel,6 and as in several places in both East and West, where churches are erected in honour of the Mother of God.7

The saint, the patron, to whom the church or convent was dedicated was seen as a person with legal rights. The church and its property belonged to him. To him, St. Peter, St. George or St. Emmeram, gifts and endowments were made; the priests and people attached to the church were his *familia*. He was expected and asked to protect his own. Phrases like *quorum nos fecisti patroniis adiuvari* or *eius apud te patrocinia sentiamus*, are very common in Roman sacramentaries.8 Like the Mass rituals themselves, they are primarily meant to be said at the grave of the saint in question.

The idea of the patron9 then became extended to cover a wider field, geographical and social. From the early Middle Ages St. Martin was looked upon as the protector of the Frankish kings and people.10 King Stephen the saint placed Hungary under the patronage of the Mother of God.11 Since the height of the Middle Ages, and especially after the flourishing of the guilds and corporations, the various classes and trades each chose a patron.12 In this case the choice was made by the individual groups, who had an emblem or banner fashioned by some artist; and so it happened that in different places different patrons were chosen by the same guild: but more recently it came about that very often the patron of a class or trade was decided by Papal order: Aloysius for young

6. Leclercq 2516.
7. St. Beissel, *Geschichte der Verehrung Marias in Deutschland während des Mittlelalters*, Freiburg 1909, 19-42.
8. Vide, for example, P. Braylantes, *Concordance verbale du Sacramentaire Leonien*, Löwen o. J. (1948), 424 seq., and the index in Lietzmann, *Das Sacramentarium Gregorianum*, Munster 1921, 159.
9. J. B. Lehner, *Patron*: LThK VI, 1-5.
10. Cf. J. Uttenweiler, *Martin*: LThK VI, 985
11. *Acta Ap. Sed.* Sept. I, 527. 531. 568.
12. A Bruder, *Über Wappen und Schutzpatrone der alten Zünfte*, Munich 1884, lists the patrons of 58 trades in alphabetical order, beginning with physicians (Cosmas and Damian) and painters (Antony the hermit) down to joiners (St. Joseph) and tin-smiths (Charlemagne).

students, Camillus of Lellis for the sick and those who attend them
etc.13 Pius XI in 1870 declared St. Joseph to be the patron of the
Church itself. Since the later Middle Ages each individual
Christian has received for his patron the saint whose name he was
given at baptism.14

Thus in the religious sphere the idea of patrons and patronage
assumes a certain breadth. It is applied to cases where the idea of
a protective relationship is present only in vague outline. It is
obvious that the ecclesiastical act of designating a patron can
become fruitful only in its religious fulfilment by the protege.

But since the early Middle Ages, and especially since Teutonic
notions of law became allied to ecclesiastical affairs, a whole
sphere of meaning has marked itself out in which the idea of
patronage again received a weighty emphasis. In secular life this is
the province of feudal law. The economically or socially weaker
put themselves under the protection of someone stronger. In this
way he put his hands in the enfolding hands of the master,15 just
as is done today by the newly ordained priest when he promises
honour and obedience to his bishop at the end of the ordination
Mass. The act is also called commendation: *se commendare, se
tradere, in manus* or *manibus se commendare* (*tradere*), and also
patrocinio se commendare (*tradere*). From the side of the overlord
there was the corresponding *suscipere, recipere, manus suscipere* and
the like.16 The overlord (*dominus, senior, patronus*, in the Church
sphere *advocatus*) accepted the duty of supporting his new vassal;
he took him into his *defensio* and *tuitio*.

There were legal relationships of this sort even in pre-Teutonic
times. They are implied in the nature of patronage. Even the
ceremony of the hands which to some extent were offered to be
bound by him who sought protection was known in antiquity.17
The new element associated with the Teutonic commendation
was this: no surrender to slavery without further rights was being
made; nor was it merely that obligation was being accepted to

13. The most recent provision of several patrons (Cassian for stenographers etc.) v.
Acta Ap. Sed. 46 (1954) 72.
14. Eisenhofer, *Handbuch der Katholischen Liturgik* II, 240-243.
15. H. Mitteis, *Lehnrecht und Staatsgewalt*, Weimar 1933, 30 seq. 480.
16. Examples, chiefly from the 8th and 9th centuries in V. Ehrenberg, *Commendation
und Huldigung*, Weimar 1877, 12 seq.
17. Mitteis 31.

perform certain practical services. A personal relation based upon faithfulness was being established: a faithful, life-long relationship in which the new servant put his powers at the service of the over-lord while the overlord granted him full protection. This found expression from the middle of the 8th century onwards by the vassal giving his overlord for life not only the *commendation* but also an oath of fidelity (homage).[18] It is characteristic of this that it no longer lays down specified services but is predominantly negative, requiring only the refraining from anything which might be harmful to the overlord.[19] Often the new relationship of faithfulness was strengthened by the 'feudal kiss'.[20]

These forms and concepts from the relationships obtaining in life now became transposed into the sphere of religion. A clear case is presented by the Confession *Ordo* of Arezzo, deriving from the milieu of Burchard of Worms and dated in the beginning of the 11th century. After the confession, the priest's intercession and the provisional absolution of the penitent, the priest says to him: *Fili, modo commenda te Deo et huic signo crucis Domini Nostri Jesu Christi.* The penitent responds to this invitation: *Tunc iunctis manibus offerat se ad pedes Crucifixi.*[21] This is exactly the procedure at the *commendation*, the terminology of which reappears here.

In other cases the relationship is applied to the service of Mary. The 12th century saw the flowering of the Cistercian and Pre-monstratensian orders, both of which cultivated a spiritual rela-tionship to the Mother of God. All Cistercian churches were dedicated to Mary. Her picture dominated the seal of the order. In all this, forms and descriptions were used which were taken

18. Mitteis 43 seq. 481; Ehrenberg 131 seq.
19. Mitteis 48 seq. Ibid. 53 as an éxample of the instruction which Charlemagne gave to his *missi* on the substance of the oath of fidelity (*Capitulare missorum generale* c. 2-9; MG *Capitularia* I, 92 seq.); there we read: *ne aliquem inimicum in suum regnum causa inimicitia inducat, ... ut beneficium domni imperatoris desertare nemo audeat.* The same negative formulation can be demonstrated for a later period in examples from the 12th century; Mitteis 481 seq.
20. Mitteis 497-500.
21. H. J. Schmitz, *Die Bussbucher und das kanonische Bussverfahren,* Düsseldorf 1898, 407. In a later ms. the rubric runs: *vinctisque manibus offerat se* Crucifixo: H. J. Schmitz, *Die Bussbücher und die Bussdisziplin der Kirche,* Mainz 1883, 778. In another Confession *Ordo* from the 11th century, edited by C. Lambot, the formal commendation is replaced by a prayer which begins: *Commendamus tibi Domine.* Cf. J. A. Jungmann, *Die lateinischen Bussriten,* Innsbruck 1932, 190-194; 195 n. 114.

from the forms of the feudal system. Above the monastery gate at Citeaux are the lines:

Ad nos flecte oculos, dulcissima Virgo Maria,
Et defende tuam, divina Patrona, domum.[22]

The emblem of Citeaux was the image of the Mother of God with the abbots and abbesses of the order kneeling under her mantle.[23] Caesarius of Heisterbach (d. 1240) also knew this motif as he shows in his description of a Cistercian monk in heaven, looking about in vain for his brothers until Mary opens out her wide mantle and discloses a countless number of brothers and nuns.[24] In the later Middle Ages especially, the motif of the protective mantle is wide-spread, commonly as an expression of protection being sought or hoped for, chiefly in connexion with the image of the Mother of God. There are isolated cases where Christ or some of the saints (Ursula, Barbara, etc.) are depicted with the protective mantle.[25] This image, too, is borrowed from the secular culture of the Middle Ages. If you took someone under your mantle this was a sign of giving protection.[26] Primarily, however, it was religious commenities who used this image to depict the heavenly aid which they sought or in which they trusted.

The Arch-Confraternity of Gonfalone, founded in 1264 at S. Maria Maggiore as the Compagnia de' Raccomandati di Madonna S. Maria,[27] one of the oldest of all brotherhoods and still in existence in Rome, in its title demonstrates the mental link with the medieval idea of *commendation.* It is written about by Baronius in 1267 under the Latin title *confraternitas commendatorum Virgini* and he describes its banner: *in cuius Collegii insignibus Deiparae pallio suo legentis effigies expressa erat.* It is, in fact, the

22. St. Beissel, *Die Verehrung Marias in Deutschland während des Mittelalters,* Freiburg 1909, 195 seq.
23. St. Beissel, loc. cit.
24. St. Beissel 209.
25. E. K. Stahl, *Schutzmantelbilder:* LThK IX (1937) 360-361.
26. For this, the passage from the *Willehalm* of Wolfram of Eschenbach is cited (291, 1-5): 'The lad stood before her . . . she bade him be seated . . . she wrapped part of her mantle around him . . .' Cf. Beissel 352. On the mantle as a sign of assured protection, v. G. Jungbauer, Mantel: *Handwörterbuch des deutschen Aberglaubens* V (1932-33) 1578-91, esp. 1588 seq. Here also is a reference to the custom of the mother legitimizing her child born before marriage, by taking it under her cloak at the wedding (the mantel-child).
27. R. Hindringer, Gonfalonieri: LThK IV (1932) 574 seq.

Madonna of the protective mantle.[28] The Rosicrucian brotherhood also put themselves under Mary's protective mantle; and this association is demonstrated of one of the oldest Rosicrucian brotherhoods, that which was founded in Cologne in 1474.[29]

Reception into the society and so into the protection and shelter of the patroness was effected in the Rosicrucian brotherhood of Cologne simply by enlisting.[30]

In religious orders it was effected through taking the vows of the order. In the old orders at least these preserved their ancient form as laid down in the Rule of St. Benedict (c. 58). This was the form of *professio super altare*. In this it was laid down that at profession the candidate promise to fulfil the duties of the order *coram Deo et Sanctis eius* and address the appropriate supplication *ad nomen Sanctorum quorum reliquiae ibi sunt, et abbatis praesentis*—a declaration which he laid in writing upon the altar.[31] This rule is more precisely defined in the profession rituals of the canonists from the 9th to the 11th century. In these the candidate says: *Ego fr. N. offerens trado me ipsum Deo et Ecclesiae s.N. et . . .* Then he lays his head upon his arms which are crossed upon the altar.[32] This rite which was added to the Offertory of the Mass gives striking expression to the *oblatio super altare*, and in a form, moreover, which has evolved 'in reliance upon ancient traditional ceremony'.[33]

The liturgy of profession which appears in several new orders after the start of the 12th century (in the Dominican Order for example) is clearly modelled upon Frankish feudal law. In the Dominican form the novice kneels in front of the prior who takes his hands in his, whereupon the novice says: *Ego fr. N. facio professionem et promitto oboedientum Deo et B. Mariae et b. Dominico et tibi N., magistro Ordinus.*[34] This is the *professio in manus*.[35] The vows, as we still commonly put it, are laid in the superior's hands.

28. Baronius-Raynaldus, *Annales, ad annum* 1267, n. 84 (III Lucca 1748, 232).
29. Beissel 354 seq. 544.
30. Beissel 544.
31. St. Benedict, *Regula monachorum*, ed. Butler, Freiburg 1912, 102.
32. I. Zeiger, *Professio in manus: Acta Congressus Iuridici Internationalis* (1934) III, Rome 1934, 187-202, esp. 192.
33. Zeiger 192.
34. L. Holstenius, *Codex Regularum IV*, Augsburg 1759, 46. 215 seq.
35. Zeiger 193 seq.

It is easy to understand how these forms from medieval feudal juridicial life were taken over into the foundations of the religious orders from the turn of the 11th century until the 12th century if, with Ivo Zeiger, we take note concerning the first of the orders in question that 'their founders and first law-givers, such as Hugo, Norbert and Gilbert, were partly Teutonic in nationality and knew about Frankish medieval feudal law because of their descent from noble families'.36

Even Ignatius of Loyola was still living amongst notions of chivalry. His nightly knight's vigil before the altar of our Lady of Montserrat, when he hung up his dagger and sword,37 and the idiom of the most important meditations of his Exercises make this quite evident. The meditations on the Kingdom of Christ, the foundation of which is the battle-cry of the King whom every knight must follow, issues into a prayer addressed to Christ: *O aeterne Domine rerum omnium, ego facio meam oblationem* . . . and concluding: *si Maiestas tua sanctissima voluerit me eligere ac recipere ad talem vitam et statum.*38

Traditions of chivalry with their religious adaptations persist also in the Congregation of Students, founded in 1503 in the Roman College of the Society of Jesus by Fr. John Leunis. At that time it was predominantly aristrocratic youth who could attend schools of higher education. Like other religious societies or confraternities, this one, too, chose a patroness and placed itself under her patronage, without, in the main, essentially modifying its own programme, which, striving for perfection and religious and apostolic zeal, was dedicated to Catholic youth. They placed themselves under the patronage of the Virgin-Mother, placing her image or monogram in their shrines or upon their emblems, and giving her a fitting place in their common prayer and personal devotions.39

Very soon, a prayer text appeared—in some sense a formula of homage—with which the individual members of the society kept alive and confirmed this relationship of patronage. This exists in two versions, which are still sometimes chosen for use as

36. Zeiger 196.
37. The thought came to him when he recalled that he had read in novels about chivalry; *Ignatius of Loyola, Lebenserinnerungen*, ed. by A. Feder, Regensburg 1922, 35.
38. Ignatius of Loyola, *Exercitia spiritualia*, ed. Roothaan, Regensburg, 1911, 130 seq.
39. J. Miller, *Die Marianischen Kongregationen im 16. und 17. Jh.*: ZKTh 58 (1934) 83-109.

'consecration rituals' at reception into the congregation.40
One of these comes to light in the *Libellus sodalitatis* of Fr. Franz
Coster S.J. This book appeared first—at least under that title—in
1586 in Antwerp.41 As yet the ritual is not described as an act of
consecration, but carries the straightforward superscription:
Oratio sodalitatis in admissione a singulis recitanda, and it runs42:
*Sancta Maria, mater Dei et Virgo, ego N. te hodie in Dominam,
Patronam et Advocatam eligo, firmiterque statuo ac propono, me
nunquam te derelicturum neque contra te aliquid unquam dicturum aut
facturum, neque permissurum, ut a meis subditis aliquid contra tuum
honorem unquam agatur. Obsecro te igitur, suscipe me in servum
perpetuum, adsis mihi in actionibus omnibus meis, nec me deseras in
hora mortis, Amen.*
It is almost certain that this formula goes back to Fr. Coster
himself who must have used it at the reception of the first members
into the newly founded congregation of Cologne in 1576.43 Not
only do the old chivalrous reminiscences come out in the threefold
title *domina, patrona et advocata,* but also the negative formulation
of the obligations accepted remind us of the oath of fidelity of the
feudal relationship.44 In a wordier and somewhat less clearly
defined form the same thoughts reappear—with the choice of the
Mother of God as *patrona, domina ac mater*—in the second, more
recent formula for reception into the sodality, which first comes
to us through Fr. Spinelli.45

40. E. Mullan, *Die Marianische Kongregationen dargestellt nach den Dokumenten*⁴ Vienna
1913, 543. Both formulae are here entitled *actus consecrationis.*
41. de Bakker-Sommervogel, *Bibliotheque de la Compagnie de Jésus* II (1891) 1511.
42. In the Antwerp edition of 1593 (between the index to contents and p. 1). Almost
without change, it remains the custom today. Cf. Mullan 543.
43. E. Villaret, *Les Congrégations Mariales* I, Paris 1947, 63 seq. 354 seq.
44. Cf. above at note 19. This negative formula occurs more frequently, and it has often
been criticized too. But this manner of speech and the aggressive tone of the formula
corresponds perfectly to the relationship of the vassal, who, according to the principle
of fidelity, fought for his master's cause, and in particular to the situation in Cologne,
where the threat of innovation made defence of the Catholic faith and the honour of
Mary a real issue. Cf. Villaret 357.
45. Petrus Antonius Spinelli S.J., *Maria Deipara thronus Dei,* Naples 1613, 513. In its
detail the formula has been modelled on the scholastics' vows of the Society of Jesus,
where Mary and not God is addressed. The formula bears the superscription: *Formula
offerendi se beatissimae Virgini Deiparie.* Spinelli underlines the idea of *oblatio,* in the
chivalrous sense indeed, using an illustrative story from Caesarius of Heisterbach (*Dialogus
miraculorum* VII, 39), about a nobleman who was so filled with devotion to Mary, *ut in
quadam paupere ecclesia in eus (sc. Mariae) honore dedicata . . . fune collo suo iniecto servum
glebae se illi super altare offeret,* from which he then redeemed himself by a corresponding
yearly payment to the church.

The distinguishing feature which here emerges in comparison with other religious societies is that the individual sodalist professes his allegiance to his patroness in a more or less solemn act and wishes to understand his adherence to the newly beheld ideal as his faithfulness to her.

Both formulae, although not at first officially introduced and long since unknown in the Roman parent congregation, must have spread rapidly46—far beyond the limits of the congregation. In 1622, both appeared in the *Hortulus Marianus* of Fr. Franz de La Croix S.J. There the formula of Fr. Spinelli is described as *primus modus sese peculiari culti B. Virgini consecrandi, communis omnibus cuiusque status.* Fr. Coster's formula appears under the title: *Secundus modus devovendi se B. Virgini, Sodalitati partheniae nomen dando.*47

It is here that the word *consecrare* (consecrate), first appears, the title for the act which from now on is to become the climax of religious devotion throughout the world. Here the word is taken to be synonymous with *devovere;* and it appears first of all applied to the lesser formula of Fr. Spinelli which was designed for a wider circle. From of old, the word *consecrare* had found a variety of applications in the liturgy, but until this time it had always had the sense that in consecration, God, through a sacrament, or the Church, through a sacramental, was placing a person in a higher religious state (bishop, priest, acolyte, monk, nun, even king and emperor according to the sacral notions of the Middle Ages), or was setting apart a thing to an exclusively religious use (church-building, altar-furnishings, liturgical vestments), or (as with oil, bread and wine) was changing them into a sacramentally significant condition.48 In all cases it was intended to signify at least what now is known as a *benedictio constitutiva.* From now on the word becomes used also for a religious act which takes place without the mediatorial intervention of the consecrating power of the Church and which thus is unable to alter the given status and con-

46. The *Libellus sodalitatis* of P. Coster went into five Dutch and nine French editions besides the thirty Latin ones during the following decades. V. de Bakker-Sommervogel II, 1510-14. I have come across the formula in question in the *Manuale Sodalitis* printed in Cologne in 1601 (p. 49). Spinelli's work, too, especially in adaptations, went into several editions in the 17th century. de Bakker-Sommervogel VII (1896) 1443 seq.
47. Villaret 358 seq.
48. Cf. say, the index in Andrieu, *Le Pontifical Romain au Moyen-Age* IV, Rome 1941, 178-180.

dition. In this age, when humanism still flourished, the classical sense of the Latin word, *consecrare* may have contributed to its extended connotation, so that we had in fact a new word before us with the old meaning as in (*se*) *offerre*,49 *tradere, commendare, devovere.*

By Fr. de La Croix' presenting one of the formulae to a wider circle a stimulus was given to extend such a *modus sese consecrandi* beyond the limits of the religious orders in which it had originated. The stimulus must quickly have taken effect, judging by the immediate spread of his *Hortulus Marianus;* for in the first ten years up to 1632 six Latin editions had already appeared as well as three French, two Dutch, one German and one Czech translation.50 This little book would not have been the only carrier of this idea.

In fact we immediately come across accounts of this sort of act of consecration visibly connected, indeed, in some cases with the Marian devotions practised in the congregations. At the command of King Philip IV of Spain, in 1643 the South American Spanish colonies were dedicated to Mary through a 'solemn consecration'.51 In 1664 the same thing was done for Portugal and all her colonies at the instigation of King John IV.52 This king was himself a Marian sodalist, and at that time congregations flourished in Lisbon.53 Something similar happened in Austria in the following year at the order of Emperor Ferdinand III, likewise a sodalist and great promoter of the congregations.54 At Mass on Easter day 1674 the missionary to the Indians, Jacob Marquette S.J., solemnly consecrated the new mission on the Mississippi along with his

49. The very formula which La Croix designates as *modus sese consecrandi*, in Spinelli, bears the superscription *formula offerendii*. V. above n. 45.
50. de Bakker-Sommervogel II, 1688-90.
51. A Freitag, *Maria und das Missionswerk (Katholische Marienkunde*, ed. by P. Strater, III. Vol., Paderborn 1951, 106-184) 159.—Most of the sources given by Freitag and cited in what follows were unfortunately inaccessable to me. Freitag's own style of expression is not always exact, as when he designates as a consecration to Mary, the taking possession of new lands by discoverers 'in the name of God and of Mary'. (156.)
52. Freitag 160. Today we still find commemorative tablets in Latin and in Portuguese in various places in former Portuguese colonies. Ibid 165.
53. Villaret 330 seq.
54. Cf. Villaret 225. 347. When the memorial hall of the Immaculate Conception in the palace square at Vienna was consecrated on May 18, 1647, Kaiser Ferdinand III made a vow concerning the Feast day in December, and he declares Mary to be 'the special Mistress and Patroness of this archdukedom'. But in this case there was no question of a formal consecration. E. Tomek, *Kirchengeschichte Oesterreichs* II, Innsbruck 1949, 546.

Indians to the Immaculata.55 He too came, all the more because of his student years at Pont-a-Mousson, from a region where the life of the congregations flourished. Later, the movement spread further. In 1844 when being refounded by the Vicar Apostolic Theodore August Forcade, the Japanese mission was consecrated to the Blessed Virgin.56 In 1914 the consecration of Uganda to Mary took place with great solemnity,57 and that of China on the occasion of the national council in 1924.58 Other missionary lands followed.59

The examples mentioned concerned lands for which a responsible authority chose Mary as patroness: but the notion of consecration to Mary has taken hold also on communities in which consecration, as in the Marian congregations, signifies the agreement of the member to accept a high religious and moral ideal for life. With the consent of St. Vincent de Paul, St. Louise of Marillac performed the consecration of the Congregation of the Sisters of Charity to the Blessed Virgin on December 8, 1658,60 an act which has been repeated every year since then. In 1662 the Lazarists took the same step after having consulted and learned that already a great many communities had placed themselves under the protection of our Blessed Lady, and that to perform a similar act for their own group would be well-founded for as yet they had no heavenly patron whose aid they could invoke.61

The act of consecration as practised by the student youth of the Marian congregation was not exclusively directed towards Mary. Although the Roman parent congregation had chosen Mary for patroness—under the title 'Mary proclaimed'—congregations might become completely affiliated to them even if they had placed themselves under a different heavenly patron. Sixtus V

55. Freitag 162.—The well-known prayer of consecration *O Domina, o mater mea*, likewise belongs to this period; it seems to have been first contained in a devotional book by P. Nicolas Zuchi S.J., which appeared in 1663. V. de Bakker-Sommervogel VIII (1898) 1525.
56. Freitag 167.
57. Freitag 170.
58. Freitag 163.
59. Freitag 159. 163. 166. 171.
60. The consecration formula contains the phrase: *Nous vous supplions tres humblement d'agréer l'oblation irrévocable de nos ames et de nos personnes que nous dédions et consacrons, en cette fete, a votre service et a votre amour . . . vous prenant pour notre Dame et maîtresse, pour notre Patronne et Avocate.* E. Crapez. *La Dévotion Mariale chez s. Vincent de Paul et les Lazaristes: Maria,* ed. by H. du Manoir, III. Vol., Paris 1954, 105 seq.
61. Crapez 106 seq.

HISTORICAL PROBLEMS 307

made this quite clear in a Bull of 1587. There was in fact, a Congregation of St. Barbara in Vienna which was distinguished from others only by its patronage. On reception, the sodalists used exactly the same words as members of other congregations—only the name was different: *Sancta Barbara, virgo et martyr, ego . . . te hodie in Dominam, Patronam et Advocatam eligo . . . .*[62]

No one will find anything strange in this when, as here, we are concerned with a clearly defined religious community: faithfulness to the Virgin or to St. Barbara implies nothing more than adherence to the high ideals of life of the community. To acknowledge the banner of the congregation was to swear loyalty.

If the possibility of choosing the patron was left open in this way, even when a special act of consecration was desired, then the seeker would look more and more to the greatest power and holiness the more the dedication, the act of consecration was stressed, and the less a fixed ideal for life was already set out by the society to which he belonged, the ideal only being confirmed by uttering the formula. Towards the end of the 17th century consecration to the Sacred Heart of Jesus appears. It begins at Paray-le-Monial. Did the commission, which St. Margaret Alacoque felt obliged to discharge, come to her suddenly? This does not seem likely.

The cue for a consecration was already being given in France at this time. We have met it already in the Society of St. Vincent de Paul. And the *Hortulus Marianus* of Fr. de La Croix had already appeared in three French editions by 1629.[63] St. Frances de Sales, too, founder of the Visitation Order must also have been exercising an influence in the same direction. In his youth, Frances de Sales had been a member of a Marian Sodality,[64] and he was so familiar with Fr. Coster's consecration ritual that it got into the edition of his spiritual writings,[65] and the second version, deriving from Fr. Spinelli, is still named after the saint.[66]

Frances de Sales now used the word and the idea of consecration more freely and, basically, more in the original sense. In the celebrated Introduction to the Devout Life he instructs his

62. Miller (above n. 39) 95 seq.
63. de Bakker-Sommervogel II, 217.
64. Villaret 91 seq.
65. Villaret 355.
66. Mullan 543.

Philothea about a 'protestation authentique' in which she is consciously to renew her baptisal vows, renounce Satan and resolve to turn towards God, 'lui donnant à ces fins, dédiant et consacrant mon esprit avec toutes ses facultés, mon ame avec tout ses puissances, mon coeur avec toutes ses affectiones', and through which she is to repel in advance all possible unfaithfulness67 'cette mienne resolution et consécration'; and he instructs her to ask God's blessing at morning prayer 'par le mérite de la passion de votre Fils, à l'honneur duquel je consacre cette journée'.68

Obviously this writing of the saintly founder was in everyone's hand in the convent of the Visitation. The transition to the idea of consecration to the Sacred Heart was thereby almost completely accomplished; for the contemplation of the Sacred Heart, even if in a special form, also played a prominent part in the saint's devotional life.69 Anyway, devotion to the Sacred Heart of Jesus had more and more become a favourite devotion in the Order of the Visitation between the life-time of the founder (d. 1622) and that of St. Margaret Mary, quite apart from the activity meanwhile of St. John Eudes. It was being said that the Order of the Visitation had been founded for the sole purpose of 'giving honour to the most adorable Heart of Jesus',70 and that its members should be regarded as 'filles du Coeur de Jésus'.71

After the great visions of St. Margaret Mary in the years from 1673 to 1675, to begin with, we hear the saint speaking only in a general way about prayers of devotion to the Heart of Jesus. The word 'consecration' does not yet occur in her own reports of this period, nor does it appear in the statements of her spiritual director Claudius de la Colombière (d. 1682).72 By 1678, however, it does occur in the writing of her superior.73 It would seem that after 1684 it is used by the saint herself in the sense of a complete

67. I, c. 20 (Œuvres choisies de S. Francois de Sales, ed. Perrodil, I, Paris 1843, 35 seq.).
68. II, c. 10 (loc. cit. 53).
69. A. Hamon, Histoire de la Dévotion au Sacré Coeur (5 Vols., Paris 1923-40) I, 128-131.
70. The word originated with the visionary Anna Margareta Clément (1593 to 1661),—Hamon III, 259.
71. Hamon III, 260.
72. Reports of the great exercises of the year 1677 contain repeated reference to an 'offrande' to the Sacred heart of Jesus, using the expression 'je vous offre'; Claude de la Colombiere, Œuvres completes VI, Grenoble 1901, 124-127.
73. As 'notary' of the saints, she had to write down the 'testament', by which these signed away their whole spiritual estate to the Heart of Jesus. Hamon I, 237: 'J'offre, dédie et consacre....'.

surrender of all feeling and desires to be in accord with God's will.74 After this time she speaks of the promise to all those 'qui se consacreront et dévoueront à lui'.75

In this the proceedings concerned persons consecrated to God and who by such 'consecration' were only re-affirming the obligation to strive for Christian perfection which their vows of religion imposed, and perhaps also strengthening their resolutions for the future, in this case renewing the *consecratio virginum.* But with Margaret Mary Alacoque a further step had also been taken: the consecration, the dedication to the Sacred Heart of Jesus was represented and commended as something on its own, quite independent of any relationship to the community, in circumstances, moreover in which—apart from the cultic act itself—it can scarcely signify more than an assurance of faithfulness to the common duties of the Christian life. In 1689 she published in a letter our Lord's wish that the King of France, Louis XIV, should assure himself of grace and salvation 'par la consécration qu'il fera de lui-même à mon Coeur', that He desired to see His image set upon his banners so that they would be made victorious over all his enemies.76

From now on the 'consecration', dedication to the Sacred Heart, which clearly according to the wish of its promoters was to be an expression of complete surrender to faithful service and also a token of mighty protection, had gone far beyond the confines of the little communities in which it had arisen. As early as 1692 the Carthusian sisters had adopted the consecration to the Sacred Heart.77 In 1720, in time of plague, the bishop and magistrates of Marseilles co-operated in carrying out the consecration.78 In 1777 in response to her request, Pius permitted Queen Maria Francisca

74. On November 3, 1684 she wrote to a nun with whom she was friendly, saying that on the first Friday of the month she could make 'this offering of herself' to the divine Heart, after Communion, '*vous consacrant toute a lui*'. As novice-mistress, before the Friday which later became the Feast of the Sacred heart, she set her novices the task: '*en vous éveillant, vous entrerez dans le Sacré-Coeur, et lui consacrerez votre corps, et votre ame, votre coeur . . .*' Hamon I, 331. 348.

75. Hamon I, 380 seq.

76. Text of the letter in Hamon I, 416 seq. Concerning French attempts at the time of the 200-year remembrance and during the First World War to make good the fulfilment of that wish, which could not be accomplished by Louis, v. Hamon V. 178 seq. 329.

77. J. Bainvel, *Coeur Sacré de Jésus*: DThC III, 336.

78. Hamon III, 439 seq. 446 seq.

of Portugal to consecrate her land to the Sacred Heart of Jesus.79
A similar consecration took place for Belgium in 1868 and for
Ireland in 1873 through their respective bishops.80 There is the
celebrated case of the consecration of Equador to the Sacred Heart
in 1873 by the president Gracia Moreno by public decree.81
Other consecrations of countries took place with at least official
participation of the governments, in Colombia in 1900, Mexico
in 1914, Spain in 1919, Belgium in 1919.82 Nowadays as a rule
territorial consecrations are carried out purely at the ecclesiastical
level. Between 1848 and 1852, 52 dioceses in France carried out
the consecration to the Sacred Heart.83 In 1873-74 a fresh wave of
diocesan consecration swept across North America.84 The movement reached something of a finale in the consecration of the
whole human race which Pope Leo XIII ordered in an encyclical
of May 15, 1899, and which had been pleaded for for several
decades, finally by that gifted nun, Maria of Droste-Vischering.85

A striking phenomenon is this: that meanwhile, consecration to
Mary had been assuming the form of a consecration to the Heart
of Mary. This change can be traced back to St. John Eudes
(d. 1680) who, since leaving the oratory of Cardinal Bérulle,
(1643) had represented the cult of the Sacred Heart in such a way
as to link it with the veneration of the Heart of Mary. In this he
was only elaborating what he learned from the cardinal to this
extent, that he tried to express the Incarnation motif, with the
ideas of absolute service to God which it implied, predominantly
from the Marian side. It was Mary's Heart which was said to be a

79. Hamon IV, 280 seq.—When Hamon, IV, 322 and elsewhere, speaks about the Tyrol
consecrating itself to the Sacred heart in 1796 and in 1809, this can be taken only in the
extended sense. The relevant texts speak only of a 'promise' or 'vow' to celebrate the
feast of the Sacred Heart solemnly on the second Sunday after Corpus Christi, in order
to obtain, it is true, divine protection against the misery of war. V. the text in N. Nilles,
De rationibus festorum sacratissimi Cordis Jesu et purissimi Cordis Mariae, Innsbruck 1885, I,
239-241.
80. Hamon V, 330.
81. Hanon V, 335 seq.; Nilles I, 196 seq.
82. Hamon V, 336 seq.
83. Hamon IV, 355.—For details and for the text of the act of consecration in the various
ecclesiastical provinces, v. Nilles II, 316-326. A certain climax was reached when Cardinal
Gilbert solemnly consecrated the country on the Mont-Martre in 1875. Hamon V, 80 seq.
84. Nilles I, 198-200; II, 326 seq.
85. Hamon V, 178-188. The meaning of consecration to the Sacred heart of Jesus is
thoroughly discussed by Bernard Leeming S.J. in Consecration to the Sacred Heart: Cor
Jesu I, Rome 1959, 595-655.

model of preoccupation with what was in the mind of Christ.86 In a sense, indeed, He was at the centre of her heart.87 Eudes liked to link the two hearts together as in the form of prayer which he already used the word *consecrare: Ave Cor amantissimum Jesu et Mariae . . . Tibi cor nosfrum offerimus, donamus, consecramus, immolamus.*88 He could not, it is true, maintain such a fusion in face of the opposition which rose up against it; but the linking together of the two hearts remained. The saint also gathered a following. In his Book of the Sacred Heart, which appeared in 1726, Fr. Joseph de Gallifet S.J. raised the cry: We do not want to separate devotion to the heart of Mary from devotion to the Sacred Heart of Jesus, *utrique nos totos tradamus et consecremus.*89 When, in the middle of the 19th century, a large number of French dioceses carried out the consecration to the Sacred Heart, in many cases consecration to Mary's heart was linked with it.90 So it was arranged at the proceedings of the provincial council of Albi (1850), when the reason given for it was that they desired to approach the Sacred Heart of Jesus *mediante Deipara Virgine.*91

86. Bérulle himself made great use of this idea; A. Rayez, *La Dévotion Mariale chez Bérulle et ses premiers disciples: Maria* (above n. 60) III, 31-72, esp. 56 seq. He finds already that in general one ought to offer oneself to Maria *'en qualité d'esclave'* (60). In some sense Bérulle anticipates the *Perfect Devotion* to Mary of St. Grignion de Montfort (d. 1717), which we find in the *'esclavage de la Sainte Vierge'*. Anyway, the existence of this style of piety can be shown in 16th century Spain. Ibid. 60, n. 84. The expression 'consecration' does not seem to appear in Bérulle; but Grignion knows it well enough. He had used it as a sodalist of Mary in the dedicatory formula in Rennes. Cf. J. M. Huppers, *S. Louis-Marie de Montfort et sa spiritualité mariale.*
87. Cf. Nilles I, 543-545.
88. Hamon III, 194. The origin of the prayer of St. Mechthild of Hackeborn—noted by Hamon—only touches the fringe. In the passage in question, the words of Eudes, which are cited (*Revelationes Gertrudiana et Mechtildiana* II, Paris 1877, 217), correspond simply to the expression: *offero tibi (Christi) cor meum.*
89. J. de Gallifet, *De cultu ss. Cordis Dei as Domini nostri Jesu Christi*, Rome 1726, 161. Cf. in the *Exercitium ad Cor Mariae*, which he prescribed (Ibid. 172) *cor meum . . . tibi oblatum et dicatum.* The edition of the book just cited is decorated characteristically with two engravings on the title pages: the Heart of Jesus, separated from His Body, and opposite, the Heart of Mary similarly portrayed.
90. Toward the end of the century a movement began to take shape which asked for the consecration of families to the Holy Family. J. Schmidlin, *Papstgeschichte der neuesten Zeit* II, Munich 1934, 559 seq. Cf. F. Beringer, *Die Ablässe* II,11 Paderborn 1922, 146-153. This movement was finally eclipsed by that of the enthronement of the Sacred Heart in the family, and absorbed by it. Hamon V, 297-304.
91. Nilles II, 318. This formula, however, does not reappear in other places. If it can be given a good meaning, and if a similar phrase appears in the *oration* of the feast of the Mediatrix which is celebrated in many places, then we must affirm that we do not require mediation primarily with regard to Christ, whose members we are in the closest possible way.

The same sort of thing took place in the ecclesiastical provinces of Bourges, Aix and Sens.92

About the time of the Vatican Council a movement was taking shape which encouraged the consecration to the heart of Mary not only of families, parishes and diocese, but desired also that the whole world be thus consecrated. The movement gained a mighty impetus as a result of the events of Fatima in 1917. On October 31, 1942, Pope Pius XII carried out the consecration of the world to the Immaculate Heart of Mary: 'As the Church and the whole human race were consecrated to the Heart of Thy Jesus . . . so we consecrate ourselves in like manner to thee, to thy Immaculate Heart for ever.'93

If we review the way in which the idea of consecration has arisen we are able to show that patronage stands at its origin. In the Marian congregations of the 16th and 17th centuries this was applied in a special form. In this the consecration signified assent to a high ideal which the congregation intended to pursue, under the banner of the Virgin-Mother, and in pursuing which they sought her assistance. Detached from this foundation and transferred simply to the Christian people or country, consecration to Mary remained as a solemn supplication for aid and protection;94 its performance, however, could only be a cultic act which perpetuated itself in further cultic acts, becoming perhaps a means of renewing, in deeper spirituality, the acceptance of general Christian obligations. In as much as the factor of the *consecratio* in particular, that is, the absolute surrender of the person with the love of his whole heart is emphasized, so this can only be carried out with reference to God or to Christ,95 or to another heavenly person 'in so far as . . . the consecrational oblation is made to him as accessory to the supreme surrender to God'.96 This can be seen most clearly with respect to Mary, Mother of God and Mother of the faithful.

92. Nilles II, 320–325.
93. *Acta Ap. Sedis* 34 (1942) 346.
94. It is only this aspect which could be realized when on July 7, 1952, in an apostolic encyclical, Pius XII consecrated Russia to the Immaculate Heart of Mary. Acta Ap. Sedis 44 (1952) 511.
95. Cf. C. Feckes, *Die Weihe der Kirche und der Welt an Maria: Katholische Marienkunde* (above n. 51) III, 328.
96. Ibid. Cf. Karl Rahner, *Von der Not und dem Segen des Gebets,³* Innsbruck o.J. (1949), 95–117: *Weihebegete*; esp. 115 seq.

The occasion for choosing just those last forms of renewed devotion to God and His law may well have been that the already popular Marian veneration seemed to provide a particularly favourable point of contact. But it was in harmony with the mood of such a consecrational oblation that since the 17th century it should have been directed increasingly to Christ whose kingly prerogatives were to be recognized as is stressed above everything else in Leo XIII's formula of consecration.

It was the influence of the mystics which led to the predominance and retention of the symbol of the heart and to its application to Marian devotion as well; for this symbol was what had led them on to the highest flights of the love of God. In many cases it must have been through the transference of this symbol to the general bulk of the Christian people that the individual simple Christian more easily grasped the notion, that such a 'consecration' could only be a word connected with the deepest love, something 'from heart to heart', which must not be allowed to die ineffective. In other cases the danger will not have been excluded that forms once incandescent in the fire of mystical grace, will become mere empty husks, and that, besides the outward act, the only things which are grasped are the promises with their attached expectations, which will not always correspond to the guarantee, truly given.

Consecration, as complete self-offering, can only have one meaning for the Christian: a fresh, more conscious, and where possible, more resolute confirmation of that relationship in which he stands in any case. For, in Baptism, the Christian is fundamentally consecrated to God and offered to Christ. And he confirms this consecration and oblation every Sunday at least in the holy Sacrifice, as often as he assists at it seriously and with understanding.[97] For this reason, in the early days of such acts of consecration, Frances de Sales linked the preamble to Baptism, and phrased the consecration as a renewed renunciation of Satan and a renewed surrender to God—a way followed by Gringion de Montfort himself.[98] And thus we found also that in the pre-

97. Cf. C. Vagaggini, *Il senso teologica della liturgia*, Rome 1957, 62: '*Ogni atto liturgico in cui l'uomo riceve la santificazione e rende il suo culto a Dio, implica dunque un impegno . . . unimplicito giouramento.*'
98. Hupperts (above n. 86) 256. The complete text of his consecration-formula is given by E. Campana, *Maria nel culto cattolico* II, Turin 1933, 307 seq.

liminary stages of the act of consecration, the profession of religious vows took place for a long time as *professio super altare*, being incorporated in the Offertory of the Mass.

And finally in our own times we are witnessing how the various acts of consecration, always intrinsically valuable wherever genuinely performed, begin to re-unite with a classical form and with their sacramenetal basis, when the Christian people solemnly renew their Baptismal vows in Easter night.

13.   *The Fundamental Idea of Sacred Heart Devotion in the Context of the Church's Prayer*

On the face of it, it is unlikely that in earlier times, at least in the dawn of its history, the Church as the Bride of Christ had less understanding of the love of its Bridegroom and less responsive devotion to that love than we attribute to those centuries in which devotion to the Sacred Heart of Jesus has spread throughout Christendom like a living breath. We need only read a few sentences from St. Paul, the beginning of Hebrews, say, or point to the blood of so many martyrs and to the Fathers' enthusiasm for Christ, which led them not only to sing the praise of the divine-human mystery of love, made plain in Christ, in their commentaries on the Song of Songs, but to find allegories of the same inexhaustible theme in almost every chapter of the Old Testament. And those were the very days during which that treasury of prayer was being fashioned, the liturgy of the Church which day by day and year by year nourishes our spiritual life.

It is perfectly obvious that there is a marked contrast between the form of expression of those early days and those which have been preferred in recent centuries, especially the devotion to the Sacred Heart of Jesus. The early period consistently regarded and portrayed the mystery in its redemptive-historical development. St. Paul's interpretation of the mystery of godliness in I Timothy (3, 16) is like a programme of this portrayal '. . . manifested in the flesh, was justified in the spirit, appeared unto angels, hath been preached unto the Gentiles, is believed in the world, is taken up in glory'; and it is the same with St. John in the Gospel-passage for the feast of the Sacred Heart where he tells of the soldier piercing our Lord's side with a lance, and then thinks not only of the nations who will look up to Him whom they pierced, recognizing in the blood and water the continuing sacramental fruits of the redeeming death, but also the prefigurative adumbration, the Lamb, not a bone of whom was permitted to be broken.

The whole of Patristic literature with very minor exceptions consists of commentary on holy Scripture, and so is tied to this the redemptive-historic outlook. The scholastics were the first to systematize the elements of the order of salvation which were based upon the history of redemption. In this system, as in any philosophical system, everything is somehow detached from its historical basis, becomes 'abstract', and so it is presented to us today: everything fits into its correct logical place so that all can be surveyed more or less at a glance. Piety, too, has more and more followed this course, and has condensed into a single timeless image, in a single point, we might say, things which were widely separated in history: the revelation of divine love which assumed human form and a human heart, giving itself up in agony without reserve. And now, this seeks a responsive love, again using the image of a heart.

The Church's liturgy too, in harmony with its origin in those centuries, follows at first this redemptive-historical line. This is already evident in the pattern of the celebration of the Eucharist. What is supposed to be celebrated in the Eucharist is nothing other than the memory of the Redemption, i.e. the revelation of divine love. But even where only few words can be spared, this memory is described as the memory 'of the blessed Passion, the Resurrection from the dead, and the glorious Ascension into heaven'; and where the theme can be treated more expansively in the lessons prefixed to the celebration, we are given, not meditations on divine love, but passages from books of the Bible, chiefly the narratives of the evangelists. In those places, however, where the subject can be treated in full detail, in the feasts and celebrations of the Christian Year, it is again the historical course of the redemptive events which is presented: in the Easter celebration, the triduum of the Passion, the resting in the tomb, the Resurrection and its extension into Pentecost with its thought of the Ascension and the descent of the Spirit; and in the Christmas cycle, the coming of our Lord into the world and His manifestation to the peoples of the earth.

This attachment to historical narrative does not at all imply limitation to a purely psychological calling to mind of facts which once happened. It is rather, that all the time we are aware of the timeless redemptive significance and effectiveness of those redemptive events whose story we hear told. Within the Church, which is here and now assembled, in her word and in her sacrament in grace and in sanctification, in faith and in the love of the faithful, that which appeared once upon a time is made immediately present; and therefore on feast days the Church's prayer regularly begins: 'O God, who on this day . . .' And at this we realize instantly that as the Lord Himself blessed His disciples and ascended into heaven He was not viewing His work as completed and handing over a treasure of grace for His Church to guard: He is much more, 'living and ruling' eternally as the Head of His Church in the glory of His Father; and our prayers are always offered 'through Him', ennobled and consecrated by His mediation and so reaching the Father. What thankfulness, what trust and love are contained in this constant upward glance! How must the men, whose piety devised such a scheme of prayer, have been imbued with the mystery of divine mercy which was perfected in Christ! Today many prayers are written and printed which do not lack fervour and eloquence; but hardly ever does the thought emerge that we are so close to divine love in the person of the God-man who desires to be our advocate and High Priest, and that it is only through Him that we have access to God (Rom. 5, 12).

This applies to the Church's prayer of petition. But, arising from the same thought of the overwhelming greatness of divine mercy surges, for the first time at all adequately, the prayer of thanksgiving, the full import of which we perhaps miss because we are so used to the sound of it: 'It is truly meet and just, right and available to salvation to give thanks, to thank Thee always and in all places' so that our whole life ought to be a single act of thanksgiving. And this puny thanksgiving, which cannot find proper words and which on each feast day can but touch on one or other of the *magnalia Dei*, becomes praise and thanksgiving and then adoration; and this adoration strives to be joined with the adoration which the angel-choirs present to the divine Majesty; and the prayer and hymn of the priest carries the whole throng with it on high in the hymn of the thrice-holy to be joined with the praise and thanksgiving of Him who comes and comes ever and again, and who is amongst us again this day in the name of the Lord.

Someone may say: All this is certainly thanksgiving and adoration but all the same, simply an act of the virtue of religion, not of the theological virtue of love as we have in the veneration of the Sacred Heart through which we honour divine and divine-human love in the heart of our Lord and desire to respond to this with our love. To this we can reply in the words of Heinrich Kahlefeld: "Love declares itself, and dedication is perfected in the word of worship. All who love know this. And because those who love are accepted by God through grace their language appears in holy Scripture. The Bridegroom says: 'Beautiful art thou my beloved' (Cant. 6, 15), and the singer says, in the Bride's name: 'Thou art the fairest among the sons of men' (Ps. 44)."[1] Even in the liturgy, protestations of love are of this sort. Love expresses itself—theology calls this an *actus imperatus* of that virtue—in admiration, praise and thanksgiving. It is right, however, that the word of love with which we seek to respond to the divine mercy is used but sparingly and with reticence (as in the petition: Increase our faith, hope and love); but not only so: the mercies of God themselves are left as a rule in the many sidedness in which they appear in the redemptive history without our attempting to focus them narrowly as they appear in picture and in word in our usual Sacred Heart devotion.

Nonetheless the attempt is not absent entirely. At the point where the celebration of the mystery of Redemption is brought to an end with the octave of Easter, there follows Good Shepherd

1. H. Kahlefeld, *Das Eucharistie-Gebet: Geist und Leben* 30 (1957) 166.—A theoretical elucidation of the relation between the virtues of religion and of love, in prayer. V. LThK IV² (1960) 543.

Sunday. For the Mass of this day one of those rituals has been composed which expresses a unified idea within a self-contained scheme. It is that pictorial idea which the early centuries, from the Shepherd of Hermas to the artless mural paintings of the catacombs to the sarcophagus ceramics of the age of Constantine, loved to use as an expression of their total profession of faith: the picture of the Good Shepherd. This is the picture in which the Fathers see the mystery of the redemption of the world expressed. For the Lord is the Shepherd who left the hosts of angels to seek the lost sheep—mankind. He looked for them, following the way of His Passion and Cross: and now He has found him and brought him back rejoicing, whether one sheep or many. In the spring landscape of heaven they crowd round their shepherd, full of gratitude and trust.[2]

The closeness to the Sacred Heart motif is striking when we look at the Mass for Good Shepherd Sunday more closely. It begins with Psalm 32, the same psalm with which the present-day Mass for the Sacred Heart begins,[3] and it stresses the word of mercy in the *Misericordia Domini plena est terra*. Both lessons are about the Good Shepherd motif itself. In the reticent language of the liturgy the Communion verse expressed the basic theme of love and responsive love, which forms the heart and soul of devotion to the Sacred Heart: 'I am the Good Shepherd, I *know* my sheep and my own *know* me'.

And in the end, the liturgy has accepted the language about the heart of Jesus—in the feast of the Sacred Heart which was first of all allowed in separate churches in 1765 and prescribed for the universal Church in 1856. It is significant that this feast falls exactly at the end of the movable Christian Year, thus forming the concluding point of all the *offices de tempore* in which the year of feasts runs out. When Pentecost season, the feast of Pentecost and its octave and the (now diminished) octave of Corpus Christi are over, on the following Friday, as if to sum up all the foregoing festive thoughts and mysteries, our Redeemer's Heart is to glow

2. Cf. Th. K. Kempf, *Christus der Hirt. Ursprung und Deutung einer altchristlichen Symbolgestalt*, Rome 1942, esp. 160-166.
3. As we know, the present-day ritual for the Feast of the Sacred Heart is not the first which has been drawn up. In N. Nilles, *De rationibus festorum ss. Cordis Jesus et purissimi Cordis Mariae* II*, Innsbruck 1885, 1-42, thirteen others which preceded the present one are cited.

and we are to turn our eyes to the ultimate source of all mysteries. This is in line with Karl Rahner's penetrating remark about the word 'heart': 'We have to use it with reserve. We must first possess what is to be collected and unified'.4 At no other place in the Christian Year could that which is spread through the whole year be so fittingly 'collected and unified' as at the point where now stands the feast of the Sacred Heart of Jesus. Undoubtedly, all that is 'collected and unified' in devotion to the Sacred Heart especially amongst its great representatives, was there in isolated . pieces before. It was there in the whole doctrine of faith, in the catechisms, in theology, in sermons, in spiritual writings, in meditation on the life and Passion of Christ; but it was perhaps not present there so strikingly or so ostensibly. In part, it was there only as a subject of knowledge, having little connection with the life of piety. In the catechisms, theological analysis was too much to the fore. At the edges we could see defence against heresy pushing its way out at several points. There were times when, even in religion, cold reason set the linguistic tone. Holy Scripture, even the New Testament, was a far less popular book than the Missal. Then devotion to the Sacred Heart stepped into the wide breach and spoke to the feelings of the faithful. It instructed thousands—millions, so that they were able 'to comprehend . . . the breadth and length, and height and depth; to know the charity of Christ, which surpresseth all knowledge'. (Eph. 3, 18f). In its many-sided variations, in its expansion into a doctrine of virtue, orientated upon meditation on the Heart of Jesus, with its call to absolute self-dedication to redemptive love it could have become the glowing hearth of a heroic Christianity, even without the valuable foundation of those elements which must have been present beforehand waiting to be 'collected and unified'. It did become just this. Only God knows the number of those who through it have attained to the highest sanctity.

On the other hand we will not be astonished if, as a result of the opening up of the sources which flow in Scripture and the liturgy, and of the newly aroused preference for the redemptive-historical

4. Karl Rahner, *Der theologische Sinn der Verehrung des Herzans Jesu: Festschrift zur Hundertjahrfeier des Theologischen Konvikts Innsbruck* 1858-1958, 106 (now also in *Sundung und Gnade*, Innsbruck 1959, 547). Cf. same author, *Schriften zur Theologie* III², Einsidedeln 1959, 379-390.

perspective, for the primitive and dynamic in piety, we do not find speech about the Sacred Heart coming so directly and so readily from our lips in the course of everyday religion. The mysteries of the story of Redemption which follow upon one another in a splendid sweep in the course of the Church's year have become much more luminous for us. That which the language of the Sacred Heart wishes to sing out all at once in a single mighty chord has already been heard by us in the quieter melody of the spaced out sequence of prayers of the Church's liturgy and in the language of Biblical images and parables.

Certainly no one will deny that the separate factors, in which the greatness of the divine work of salvation is revealed, emerge more clearly in this. The forms of the Sacred Heart devotion, handed down from the 17th century, show, for all their richness, a certain limitation of their own time, corresponding to its theological and religious situation: it has been said with good reason, therefore, that these forms do not give enough place to individual perspectives. In this sense attention has been drawn to the lack of Trinitarian context and of a lively realization of the dogma of Christ's meditorial office. 'But these "temporal limitations" are not of the essence of the feast of the Sacred Heart and are easily overcome'.[5]

They have already been essentially overcome in the liturgical formation of the devotion. We learn this from a glance at the Mass for the feast with its appropriate Preface of the Sacred Heart, or at the Breviary hymns with their wide horizon taking in both Church and sacrament; and there is nothing to hinder these temporal limitations gradually being overcome in other public forms of the devotion (private devotion is indeed tied to no form), so that the last objections, which may still be raised against a less happy style of prayer belonging to this devotion, shall vanish.

In that day, worship of the Sacred Heart will become even more the crowning climax of Christian piety. Then it will show itself to be the sum of all previous experience. Then it will become the absolute standard against which we can measure over and over

5. Karl Rahner, *Schriften zur Theologie* III, 402.—Cf. also R. Gutzwiller, *Widerstände: Cor Salvatoris*, ed. by J. Stierli. Freiburg 1954, p. 18, and also other essays in this volume.

again how far we have risen towards the heights of that gratitude and love which we owe to the love of God. And then, for the priest at least, it will become, as well, that resting-place to which his prayer and his priestly care and zeal evermore return.

PART III

THE FUNDAMENTALS OF LITURGY AND KERYGMA

1. Christianity—Conscious or Unconscious?

THE high Middle Ages, and in many respects the late Middle Ages too, must always be accounted the flowering period of the Christian way of life. Far into the secular sphere, life was permeated and nourished by concepts and views which derived from the Christian revelation and the activity of the Church. We can speak of a highly developed religious culture in this period. This continues and in many respects grows in the later Baroque period.[1] Its effects are still felt today, especially in the structure of rural life.

The characteristic of this kind of Christian moulding of life was the practice of religion. This practice determined the way in which a man began his day's work and how he kept Sunday, how children were carried to baptism and the dead to the grave. Religious practice regulated the days for receiving the sacraments and provided rites of prayer through which men turned to God and His saints: it produced the pious phrase with which men greeted one another. In a way religious practice is a tortoise-shell protecting religious life. Itself it is a store-house of religious life. It has arisen out of an intense religious life and experience, as the protective bark grows from the life of the tree. Beneath it life goes on, carefree and assured, perhaps still young and fresh as in the days when the protective and supporting bark began to grow. For this bark of custom is as inseparable from true religious life as is the bark or the firm stock from the vegetable life of the plant. Where it is not present in some strength, it must be formed anew. The labouring families, torn from the land and settled in industrial areas, must re-fashion for themselves a daily routine consecrated by religion and a way of life which is enobled by religion. Without such a strong husk, religious life could not long survive the

1. Cf. above Liturgical Life in the Baroque Period.

325

raw atmosphere of everyday secular life. But it may also be true—
and herein lies the tragedy of traditional custom—that beneath
the bark the long-preserved life has now died away or become
narrowed down into a few starved vessels—and the stem still
holds aloft the mighty branches as in former days.

Under cover of custom, Christianity can endure through
centuries without being illumined by the bright light of reflexion
and without thinking on its origins. An unconscious Christianity
can be handed on beneath its shell from generation to generation,
from a Christianity which fulfils the requirements of Christian
life and leads men to salvation, but which in a deeper sense, in its
inner structure and its power to overcome the world, is no longer
comprehended by those who profess it.

Presuming certain circumstances, such a Christianity is
capable of theological justification. We receive the grace of God
as a gift from on high; it is given us in Baptism and in Penance.
To ensure the salvation of our souls we must only keep it. We
must stand ready, our lamps burning in our hands, if we desire
to be allowed to enter when the Bridegroom comes. More than
this is not demanded. It is not necessary for us to have a more
precise knowledge of the nature of grace, of where it comes from,
of the conditions of its increase, of its value which can far more
than supply all human needs, of its final unfolding in the vision of
God. The condition of the adult is not essentially any different
from that of the child who has not yet reached an age of reason.
The child has no notion of what has been given to him in Baptism,
yet it is received into heavenly glory if it dies in baptismal in-
nocence. Even the adult does not require to be completely aware
of the magnitude of what faith brings to him. He is only asked to
know a few elementary things: about the one God, and eternal
judgement and something of the outline of the Christian story of
Redemption, besides what is required for the reception of the
sacraments. It is so little that, as St. Thomas says, it can be gained
from assisting at the Church's festivals themselves; so little, that
it does not at all include a grasp of the ineffable worth of the
Christian faith and of the riches of grace which it contains. The
Christian must only possess grace in fact: he does not have to know
what it is or that he must possess it, still less why he must possess it.

Such a state of Christian awareness is only tolerable, it is true, when men are living without serious disturbance in the full security of simple conditions where not only the family but also the whole community is imbued with Christian tradition and where all the requirements of the business of salvation are guaranteed by Christian customs and fixed usage.

In such conditions, too, a programme of pastoral care is possible which is based upon minimum services and which can rest content with preserving what is already in existence. On average, the pastor or parish priest of the medieval parish did not go beyond this. It was enough if he said Mass and sang the Hours with his scholars, if he baptized the children, cared for the sick and buried the dead. Before Easter and perhaps also before the several greater festivals he had to be ready to hear confessions. On Sunday he had to preach and expound Christian doctrine; but this usually went no further than reading out a homily from the Fathers and occasionally commenting on basic dogmas. What the pastor provided remained as much within the narrow framework of custom and usage as did that which was demanded of the faithful.[2] People lived as Christians: but it was an unconscious Christianity they lived.

Towards the close of the Middle Ages, what was designated as pastoral care was concerned more with moral instruction and admonition, and less with introduction to the mysteries of faith. Sins which men must avoid were defined in an increasing number of formulae, and so too the good works which they should pursue. At that time, besides the commandments of God and the cardinal sins there were introduced into the catechisms, for example, the enumeration of the carnal sins, the sins against the Holy Spirit, the sins crying to heaven, and over against these, the works of corporal and spiritual mercy and other lists drawn up out of holy Scripture. The first precursor of the catechism, the confession booklet, as its name suggests, covers almost exclusively the sphere of moral instruction.

An exact parallel to this exists today when, imagining that he is able to confine himself purely to pastoral care, the preacher allows the moral sermon in contrast to the dogmatic sermon always to

2. Cf. A. Schrott, *Seelsorge im Wandel der Zeiten*, Graz 1959, 50.

stand in the foreground. The pastor, a zealous shepherd of his flock, wages war on the old ineradicable sins and vices, against the frivolity of youth, the vanity of women, the carelessness of mothers and the harshness of men, against intemperance and love of pleasure; he exhorts to love one's neighbour and to fulfil the Christian duties; even the sermon on a feast-day suddenly takes on a moralistic slant. Where the conditions are right, such a way of going on is appropriate. Its justification lies in what has been said about an unconscious form of Christianity. Grace has merely to be protected and defended against the assault of sin. When the wolf breaks into the flock the sheep must be gone after and brought back to the flock.

But in what has been said, the limits of such pastoral care and such a Christianity have been indicated. When these peaceful conditions have been broken down such a Christianity will fail. This is what can so clearly be seen in the eruption of the Reformation at the beginning of modern times. The people and the clergy too, stood helpless in the face of the passionate criticism which the innovators launched against the structure of the Church and its ancient traditional doctrine. The majority of the clergy, even, do not seem to have noticed when the battle against abuses over-reached itself and began to affect the inviolable basic content of Christian doctrine and when pearl after pearl was being torn from the crown of Christian doctrine. What until then had been piety, somersaulted: the Mass now became idolatry the images of the saints were thrown out of the churches, mass apostasy set in. The rule of tradition was overthrown by a few boldly uttered slogans and by an immoderate criticism of the *status quo*. At last all was sacrificed: what was ephemeral and what was immutable, the husk and the kernel—because they had not learned to understand what it was that they possessed within Catholic Christianity and within the Church.

This case is instructive for our own day. Today it is obvious that we are in the middle of a great crisis. It may not be as acute as the crisis of the Reformation storm, but it is chronic and none the less dangerous. Today it is not a matter of defection from the Catholic Church but of defection from Christianity in general. Since the 18th century, and especially since the emergence of idealist philosophy on the one hand and then materialistic Marxism on the other, a heathen atmosphere has come into being by which the Christian air in both Protestant and Catholic countries has become progressively rarified and by which it will become more rarified still. For this heathen atmosphere which opposes Christianity, not indeed by active hostility but usually by superciliously ignoring it, and which desires a purely this-wordly, secular way of life, is always on the attack—and in various ways: through the printed word and through the radio, through the cinema and places of amusement, through mechanisation and industrialization, and, not least, through experiences such as the war and its aftermath have brought, with their mixing up of all types of people and the destruction of all human relationships.

The defection itself has taken chronic forms this time. It has not been an avalanche but a gradual erosion of ancient rock. But even this erosion can lead to complete collapse in a Catholic land. Most of the people affected still remain outwardly attached to the Church; they remain on the fringe of the Christian community but the sap of sacramental life reaches them no longer. We are not here concerned with the question how these Christians on the fringe, estranged from the life of the Church, could be won back again. We ask, rather about the still faithful church-going people, the faithful who still attend Mass on Sundays and observe Easter. Will a pastoral care, aiming at the preservation of purity, suffice in the same measure as a pragmatic, habitual, un-conscious or half-conscious Christianity suffices. Where it has not already done so, pastoral care will have to throw off its stiffness, become dynamic and go out to win victory—not in the first place to win the assent of new believers or merely to reclaim the lost and the luke-warm, but to conquer the faithful spiritually. These must be startled out of their dream of supposed safe possession and brought once more into contact with the swelling springs of Christian life and thought—even when they feel no need of it, even when to begin with they feel any alteration in the manner of celebrating Mass or any delving into the books of holy Scripture as unnecessary innovations. The wise pastor—this is the first step—will know how to raise the sense of this need; he will direct his labour, his preaching, his arrangement of public worship

systematically towards the fostering of a conscious Christianity.[3]
And what is conscious Christianity? Conscious Christianity is
not necessarily there already as soon as it can be said of someone
that he is a conscious, convinced Catholic Christian. This very
simply means that the person in question consciously asserts that
he is a Catholic Christian and openly declares himself to be one.
This is part of conscious Christianity, but there is more to it than
that. Conscious Christianity exists when a person knows also *why*
he is a Catholic Christian—not simply in the sense of a purely
intellectual apologetic argument, but in the sense of having
grasped the unique value of Christianity. Conscious Christianity
is present, then, when a person does not merely possess the treasure
in the field in fact, but also knows that he possesses it and would
be prepared to give his whole inheritance to win it or to keep it.

What does this mean in greater detail? Above all, conscious
Christianity contains the knowledge that Christianity is more than
believing in a God. How widespread is this awareness? Is it not
so, that many, when they remark that someone believes in God,
assume that he is a good Christian? For them, Christianity consists
in believing in God and in eternal reward. Conversely, how often
does it happen that young people ask: Why do I have to go to
church on Sunday? Surely I can pray at home or out in the open.
Up in the hills I feel much more devout than in a stuffy church.
In another situation the question might run: Why must I belong
to the Catholic Church even? Without any Church I can be a
decent person, an honest man, maybe even a good Christian.

The minds of such people are already in the realm of what in
the Third Reich was lauded as 'Belief in God'. In theological
language they lacked awareness, complete awareness at any rate,
of the supernatural character of Christianity—leaving aside the
question whether we are in fact dealing with faith at all. And the
second, the positive mark of conscious Christianity is that we
firmly realize that through Christianity—or better, through
Christ—we are raised up into a new and higher order of being;
that we are no longer in the *status naturae purae* in which we
met God only at the level of natural reason, and had to serve
Him according to the dictates of conscience. This *status naturae*

3. Cf. Bishop Paul Rusch, *Kirche im Gebirge und anderswo*, Innsbruck 1959, 237 seq.,
where the required new type of Christian is described as an adult, missionary Christian.

purae is not, however, transcended by our believing in the Person of Christ; for in this way the notion could still persist that Christ only came to teach us a higher morality, to preach the ideals of the Sermon on The Mount. The liberal Christianity of Harnack—and not that alone—remains on this plane. But even where—unlike the case mentioned—there is belief in Christ's divinity, this idea is still possible and sometimes it can govern Catholic thought: In Christ, God is appearing upon earth in human form, in order to bring the light of divine Wisdom into the darkness of our earthly existence, through the word and example. The various Gnostic systems which have appeared since the 2nd century thought of Christianity in this way, as a better philosophy, an enlightment, a gnosis. In all this man's condition was not changed: for new birth to a life in God does not take place or does so only in a figurative sense by the way of illumination or knowledge. In this way the supernatural character of Christianity was utterly ignored. Clearly, one can cast off such a Christianity when one thinks that one has discovered other ways of solving life's riddle, and has found the required moral attitude (if both have not been abandoned altogether, that is). Such a Christianity too, would be nothing but an embroidered 'Belief in God'.

If we seek a conscious Christianity and desire to foster it amongst the faithful then we come to the decisive point when we must arouse an awareness of its supernatural quality. This does not mean at all that we must expect the faithful to have a comprehensive grasp of all the intellectual distinctions by means of which we clarify the essence of the supernatural in the course of theological study. The word 'supernatural' itself, can perfectly well be done without. But it must be made abundantly clear that in Christianity God has given us very much more than we could have claimed; that in Christ He has restored in a still more marvellous manner that human nature which originally He created most wonderfully; that in the God-man has shone out brightly the dignity to which God has called us, for we are to share in His Sonship of God and so in His closeness to God and in His divine glory; that the name 'Christian' means nothing else than a man who belongs in this fashion to Christ, that the Church is the community of those who have found this link with Christ and follow His trail to the eternal home; that there is no other way by which

we can find God than this highway which Christ has opened up
for us; that for this reason, the kingdom of God is a treasure
hidden in a field for which a man would have to give up everything—it is the pearl of great price to buy which a man would
have to sell all his possessions. Whoever has grasped this and made
it the plumb-line of his life possesses a conscious Christianity. The
pastor who, by attachment to the language of Scripture and
through the shape of the liturgical celebration, arouses and keeps
alive these insights, always striving to elevate to holy joy and
enthusiasm, is fostering a conscious Christianity. It is obvious that
the dogmatic sermon—in the sense indicated—takes on a fresh
importance.

Did the Church of old foster a conscious Christianity or was it
satisfied with pragmatic Christianity? Did the apostles encourage
conscious Christianity? Only listen to St. Paul who rejoices over
the Corinthians (I, 1, 5) because they can understand the hope to
which they are called, how rich and magnificent is the inheritance
of the saints. Christ the Lord said Himself in His High Priestly
prayer: 'Now this is eternal life: That they may know thee, the
only true God, and Jesus Christ whom thou hast sent.' (Jn. 17, 3).
If the ancient Church and the primitive Church had not made
men aware of the essence and value of Christianity, if it had not .
fostered a conscious Christianity, the heathen would never have
become Christian, still less would there ever have been a flowering
of Christian life.

For the same reasons we are compelled to say today as well: If
now, in an age when there is a resurgence of heathendom, we do
not once more foster a conscious Christianity, as we have described it, if we do not find conscious Christians everywhere as
leaders amongst the mass of the people,4 then Christians will not
remain Christian for long: they will be swallowed up in heathendom. A pure habitual Christianity, a pure Christianity living by
tradition and conservation cannot last much longer or it must sink
into insignificance, into a paganism which ekes out its life on the
mere crumbs of a past age.

Conscious or unconscious Christianity—or instead we could
say: original or conventional and habitual Christianity. Here we

4. Cf. the line of thought of V. Schnurr, *Seelsorge in einer neuen Welt*, Salzburg 1957,
63 seq.

find an instructive parallel from the periphery of the Church's life, from Church architecture. In the 19th and early 20th centuries the historical style was still in vogue in Church architecture. We built Romanesque and then, for preference, Gothic buildings. We said to ourselves: Gothic architecture is the expression of the medieval age of faith, therefore we follow it as a model; and we revived most carefully all the forms of the architecture of that time, pointed arches and high windows, altars with side wings, and all the ornamentation of the Gothic masters. All of a sudden about 1910 the course was altered. In Vienna a first attempt at a new style was made with the churches in the central square and in the Steinhof. Since that time we do not find in these lands any architect who will build us a Gothic Church, nor any artist in general (or craftsman) who will make anything in the traditional style. Is this all capricious fancy? Not by any means. Art had felt first the change in intellectual climate, the inadequacy and redundancy of sheer convention, the need of building and shaping out of one's own conviction and by one's own power. People did not want any longer to ask: How did people build until now, how did the Middle Ages conceive a church? They ask instead: What is a church? What is an altar? What is a pulpit? What is a candlestick? And thereupon they fashioned a style out of their own perception of what was a genuine expression of a true thought, just as the men of olden days had done. For example, they said: An altar is a table upon which one can celebrate the holy Sacrifice in front of the faithful who join in the celebration; a holy table, a precious table, a table which stands brightly in the sight of all, upon which the light of heaven gleams, and above all, a table. And so we have to do away with all merely traditional ornaments, adjuncts and images, which we can indeed treasure as the original expression of the piety of an earlier age, but which would only disguise with cheap imitation the nature of the altar as we have come to understand it once more. At first the result of such a style of architecture may be somewhat austere. But to those Christians and priests likewise who wish to cultivate a conscious Christianity it will seem right that it should be so. A greater wealth of decoration will come in due time; but it must grow up organically from within.

The basic elements in Christian Church building are always the same: sanctuary and nave, altar and communion-rail, pulpit, baptistry and confessionals. But from time to time it can become necessary to stress energetically something which for centuries of quiet and sure acceptance has remained in the background; to declaim once more in all its primitive power and clarity and with all the language which is at the disposal of Christian preaching, the message of the Redemption which has become ours in Christ; to preach this through sermons and catechizing, through the form of public worship and festival celebration, in word and writing, in sound and in colour, so that men may know again who is the Light of the World.

2. *The Liturgy, a School of Faith*

My task[1] is to develop a few lines of thought which could form a guide in our attempt to see the liturgy as a means of leading youth into a Christian way of thinking and into a Christian attitude. From a theoretician who knows the rough and tumble of every-day instruction of the young only from a distance, all that can be expected is a picture of ultimate aims, a pointer to the possibilities presented by the liturgical life of the Church, but which could only be realized through laborious detailed work.

From the very start this much is clear, that in the liturgy of the Church there is deposited a mighty potential for human guidance, the Christian orientation of life and for the mastering of life; but it is a potential which up till now has been only partially utilized. Since the Council of Trent we have indeed learned how to value the inner heart of the Mass and the Sacrament, the *opus operatum* of the consecration and the reception of Communion, but the

1. Address at the yearly conference of the German and Austrian diocesan youth-pastors in Vienna April 29-May 4, 1957. The form of a lecture has been preserved.—On the same occasion the object was developed in another direction by Fr. Karl Rahner in a lecture: *Messopfer und Jugendaszese*, now printed in a volume entitled *Sendung und Gnade*, Innsbruck 1959, 151-186.

Church's elaboration of the sacramental sign, the liturgical un-folding of prayer and ceremony has habitually been regarded as something to be carefully performed by the priest according to the rubrics, but which has scarcely any importance for our religious life. The liturgy has been an affair for the priest, and the faithful felt it as their prime duty to assist at Mass on Sundays until everything had been completed conscientiously. In this way the minimum conditions of a Christian way of life were assured. In an age threatened by heresy, this was how the essentials were safeguarded. But a mere trickle ran where a mighty stream should have been flowing. Now we can no longer be content with the mere trickle. The land is thirsty, the youth who are to remain faithful to Christ are hungry and thirsty for more solid food. The well-stocked larder must be opened up: it is at hand in the liturgy of the Church.

We are thinking of that edifice of word and ceremony which in early times the Church raised up around the sacred mysteries. This has been reverently carried along through the centuries. People have scarcely dared to alter it here and there even a little, to enlarge this feature or to modify that symbol. But for us this edifice is all the more precious because we can thus rediscover in the Church's liturgy the deep thoughts and the great prayer of the primitive Church. For us, the forms of expression are preserved which belonged to that period when an inspired Christianity faced and defeated ancient heathenism, and in which are contained its ever-effective world-conquering powers. The liturgy gives us a concise picture of the Christian world of faith in strong simple lines. We see a cosmos within which our life can fit into every-thing which pertains to it. Youth, especially youth coming to maturity requires this concise picture, this cosmos. We must disclose it to them. And this is only saying what everyone feels. All the same it must be made articulate in order to become a foundation for practical considerations which must be built upon it. There are three factors to which I wish to draw attention: to the clear oreientation of life as a whole, to the Christian picture of the world, and to the experience of the Church.

The first great blessing of the liturgy is that it always helps us to relate our life as a whole to God and to confess Him. First and foremost the liturgy is adoration and glorification of God, committal of the whole of life to God. This calculation is not obvious to modern youth. They are always sorely in need of having the twisted and battered lines of life straightened out and brought into harmony with a greater plan, at least in the public worship of Sunday; for the powers of disintegration have acquired great strength. It is not simply the tendency to degenerate which afflicts our human nature from the very start, and the increased allurements of the world of sense in this age of comfortable prosperity. In addition to all this, technology today has built up what might be described as a wall of human works which obstructs the modern city-dweller's and industrial man's unrestricted and direct vision of God. Even all the Sunday and holiday trekking through the country with all its majesty and wonder does not speak clearly to them any longer of Him who created them. We have learned only too well how to see secondary causes. Nature appears to us as a self-contained system, into which no hand reaches from outside, in which man alone rules as lord of creation —as lord indeed of the creation (and at this point the liturgy interrupts him) because the Creator 'who made heaven and earth' is still there, even greater and more all-embracing and more powerful than the lord of *this* universe.

From another angle, too, this feature of adoration which the liturgy teaches is important for youth. In the religious sense we have been born late. It is not merely that for two thousand years men have been strengthened by the redemptive facts of the mysteries of faith. Although they have been faithfully guarded by the Church as the *depositum fidei*, as the material of devotion they have been elaborated in many ways, developed, examined and analysed. The mystics have conceived them in ever fresh images in the course of their visions and have fashioned their fervent prayers. The choirs of angels and saints in the course of the centuries, in constantly growing number have themselves become objects of devotion. They are not only models of virtue but its protectors and patrons in this or that situation. Often youth has been confronted with a confusing wealth of forms at the service of religious life, within an old Christian family or in some prayer book or other. We have only to look at one of the printed morning prayers. Wealth is a good thing: a wealth of holy things is doubly good. We need, and youth needs the warmth of Marian devotion. In our devotional life we need all the bright colours of the rainbow in which the pure light of God's nature and action is made visible to us. We need the full volume of sound. But in all this the dominant tune must not be lost: it must stand out strongly.

In the liturgy of the Church this theme does stand out with great distinctness. Here, prayer is real raising up of the mind to God: 'Almighty, eternal God'—in this way the prayers begin, and the Canon which begins with the Preface, reaches its peak in the *Sanctus* which we present in song in unison with the choir of angels. And the first time the priest raises his voice at Sunday Mass is when he sings the *Gloria in excelsis Deo*.

The *Gloria Dei* is truly a pedagogic phrase of colossal importance. To seek the glory of God, to praise God is more than simply submitting to the sovereignty of God. It is joyful service, enthusiastic homage, it is an exultation in which all of one's life is caught up. Youthful life with its tumult and its weaknesses gradually merges into the right order when it is illuminated by the ideal of the *Gloria Dei*. And a well arranged service of worship can make this ideal a real experience. A Hungarian priest who was looking after refugee students said recently that he had now seen that to undo the effects of Communist education with its experiences and attractions it was not enough to give rational instruction: a counter-experience is required, a celebration, experience of the Christian community. Something the same could be said about the experience of the materialistic world which presses upon our young people daily. Here we require the counter-experience of the divine world, of the holy order which has its climax in the glorification of God, and is realized in the liturgy.

A bare half-hour tucked in somewhere within the Sunday will scarcely suffice to accomplish this. Some time ago the question arose whether there were not a place within canon law for a late evening Mass at about nine o'clock when people were returning home from outings. For my own part I should hate to have to give an answer. Of course such a thing is possible: but such iron rations are not enough for the true nourishment of religion. Worship, especially public community worship must be a creation of love. The simple, dignified place, the fine vestments and furnishings, all the movement and ceremonies should be an adoration in themselves; the praying and the singing in choice and performance should breathe the same spirit of adoration from start to finish. Even a devotion or holy hour appointed on some special occasion must show an orderly arrangement. There must not be a confused jumble of ideas. The great outline of the Christian cosmos must be presented for all to see: the message of God which has come to us, perhaps in a Bible reading, then the response of communal singing which in turn is summed up and offered to God in the prayer of the priest. This would be something like real worship: the leading of life towards God.

Besides this, through worship the Christian shape of our picture of the universe can and should be made effective—our Christian consciousness. We might say too: awareness of Christ must be formed through worship. We must not underestimate the danger in which we stand in the free West. People do not want to be Godless, they even want to be Christians; but Christ—the personal Christ, the God-man scarcely counts. That God has come down to us in Him, has spoken to us through Him, that His coming was the turning point in the world's history and that since then He has continued to be a decisive factor in the course of the world and its order, is more or less overlooked. We have only to think of how Christmas is celebrated publicly; to look at the average Christmas card (Easter cards are no better) to detect how unreal Christ has become, how little He is taken in earnest. Perhaps He is still accepted as the teacher of a noble morality. People are enthusiastic over the Sermon on the Mount, they treasure this or that work of art which depicts Him in some scene or other; but it all remains in an ineffectual world of ideas, a poetic glorification of life. That He is the keystone and remains in the structure of our very existence, that He alone is the bridge linking us with God, is no longer a living thought. Only this makes sense of faith, sacraments, grace, and the Church.

In grasping this and bringing it to the mind of youth we are helped by properly arranged and actively and communally celebrated public worship, above all by the holy Mass. The Mass is a sacrifice, but not only sacrifice. Perhaps we ought to be a little more reticent about the notion of sacrifice than we have been since the Council of Trent under pressure of defence of the doctrine against heresy. The Mass is a sacrifice, but antecedently is a memorial of the Lord, memorial of His person of His life and work, of His Passion and self-oblation for us in sacrifice. It is itself a sacrifice which even we are permitted to carry out and present along with Him. 'Do this for a memorial of me'—and these are the words with which our Lord presented us the Sacrament. With gracious condescension He had valued our remembering Him. But He knew also what it would mean to us if we did not forget Him, if we did not lose contact with Him through all the centuries until His coming again. This is reflected in the structure which the Church has in fact given to the Mass. First there are the readings which ultimately speak only about Him, culminating in the Gospel, the account of His words and deeds. Then after the necessary technical preparation follows the great prayer of thanksgiving and remembrance in which, in changing pictures corresponding to the festival of the time, we commemorate the work of Redemption which He has performed for us, and through which we thank God for it, knowing that we must always and everywhere give thanks, never able to thank Him enough. Only then is a sacrificial gift put into our hands which we are able to offer along with Him.

The constancy with which, in the sphere of prayer, our Roman liturgy expresses this structure of our relationship with God, is significant. Prayer is offered to God while we look up to Him who is our mediator, who has gained access for us and keeps it open for ever to the Father's throne. The very first cry is turned to Him in the Kyrie eleison. It is like a calling down of Him who must lead us in our sacred work. And as soon as we have finished praising God in the Gloria the song of praise changes and becomes once again a cry to Him: *Domine Fili... qui sedes ad dexteram Patris.* Then comes the collect which sums everything up, always ending in the solemn words: *Per Dominum nostrum,* through Him we make our request to Thee—and then, in succinct, forceful words, there emerges a praise of His regal splendour: through Him who lives and reigns with Thee . . . and whose reign knows no end *in saecula saeculorum.* This language of prayer comes from the very early days of the Church, from the period of its youthful impulse and heroic fight for Christ and His right. It is not as though all prayer has stuck to this stylistic law. Alongside liturgical prayer there has always been personal prayer bound to no fixed form. But it is in the formal prayer of the Christian community that the structure of our relationship to God is directly expressed.

Only when we realize how the average prayer, which is appointed to be used publicly with the congregation in church, is designed, do we become aware of this astonishing fact about the prayer language of early Christian times, that language to which we have become so accustomed since our childhood in the liturgy of the Church, the fact namely that we never turn to God at all without mentioning Christ, without entertaining the thought: It is only through Him that we are children of the Father and so near to God. We have to admit that these men must still have been permeated with the Christ-event, with the experience of Christ, indeed; obsessed with the fact that He has set Himself at the apex of our lost human race, making a way for us out of sin and guilt through the pain and darkness of this world to the glory of the Resurrection; full of the knowledge that He still stands at the Head of our race, the Head of redeemed humanity; in short, that He is our hope. Christ our hope as St. Paul says. But this view of the Christian mystery is valid for all ages. It is specially needed in our age of hollowed-out Christianity as a synthesis of what has been torn apart, a compendium of a heritage of faith which has been attenuated in diverse abstract concepts, now scarcely comprehensible. Above all it is required as a guide for youth. Youth requires a concrete image, above all a personal ideal; and here is the finest ideal in personal form. The idea is already common property amongst all Catholic youth-leaders: no more need be said.

There are, however, two things which I would still like to mention: first, the fundamental theological importance of such a viewpoint. Christianity is a matter of faith, and faith is demanded of us for many dogmas and for many dark mysteries. If I consider various mysteries: the Immaculate Conception; the Real Presence in the Eucharist; the Infallibility of the Pope, I feel in the dark, and obstacles rise up, all the more as the separate dogmas are isolated and examined on their own. But it is quite different when I turn my eyes to the person of Christ. Faith is by no means dispensed with: but here it is demanded once and for all. Here in Christ I embrace the sum total of all mystery. The separate dogmas which all seem so dark are but radiations from the one mystery which is contained in His person, emanating from the one mysterious decree that in Him God desired to draw all men to Himself in grace, through Him, through His sacraments, within the Church and by her authority. And it is here that I comprehend in a single glance the whole foundation of faith. For in the end Christ Himself is the great miracle in which God manifests Himself. He is God's eruption into human history, visible from afar, real as lightning which lights up the sky from East to West: it is an eruption which reverberates to this day and all can feel it if they heed the existence and activity of the Church. We do not refrain from demanding faith of our youth and we would not wish to, but we make it easier and demand it in a form which at once inspires and strengthens.

And the second point in this: we must turn our gaze first and foremost upon the Christ of Easter, who is risen and lives on, the glorified Head of His Church. There can be no doubt that we need the picture of His earthly life and work because we ourselves are pilgrims upon this earth; we need His example and His fortifying word. But we do not want to tarry beside what has been. Christ is not a past but also a present being. That is why the representation of Easter night has such a mighty significance—Easter night, the climax of the whole Christian year, Easter night with its symbol of the Christ-Light which penetrates and fills the whole Church step by step, Easter-night with its echo through all the Easter season. Not for nothing is the constant theme repeated every Sunday in these words: 'for I go to my Father'. The thought is always present: if you love me you would rejoice that I am going to the Father, to be as one of you beside Him, your representative and the preparer of your path, one who has gone before you and has already reached the goal. From this Easter centre where the revival of the liturgy has begun, the revival of religious life, too, must take its rise. We have rather forgotten (in the new

German Catechism, however, it finds expression once more) that Sunday is the Lord's Day, that is, the day of Christ, the day of the completion of Redemption in the victory of Easter, the day which reminds us that as Christians we are the redeemed and favoured ones, and that therefore on Sunday we must celebrate together the sacrifice of Redemption, the *memoria passionis*. This knowledge may well be more compelling to youth than the mere heightening of the sense of their Sunday duty. On Sunday the youth will want to go off into the country. It is true that God, too, is present in the woods; but those who seek Him only in the woods will not find Him. We must worship God as Christians, and if we want to do this then we will have to seek Him where Christ is, where His memory is being kept and where along with Him we are permitted to present His sacrifice to God.

The liturgy teaches us to glorify God. It teaches us to do this in union with Christ the Lord; and a third factor is also involved, one in which the liturgy is safeguarded as the pre-eminent school of faith: this Christian worship of God is performed in the liturgy *as a Church*. In spite of all spiritual awakening we have still not cast off everywhere that too narrow conception of the Church according to which the Pope, the bishops and the clergy make up the Church in which the faithful are merely looked after and led, the object merely of pastoral care, but not really themselves the Church. This notion, the origins of which lie far in the past, has become even more entrenched as a result of heretical movements during recent centuries. The hierarchical structure of the Church must be vindicated, and in doing this its social structure, its character as the community of the faithful has been left somewhat in the dark. The obvious consequence has been the remoteness of the faithful from the Church so understood and a lack of interest in their tasks. The Church was the concern of the clergy. The corrective to this misconception is at hand in the liturgy. The liturgy can indeed be celebrated in such a way, and has been celebrated far too long in such a way, that it exactly corresponds to that hieratical conception of the Church: the priest at the altar does everything, he alone says the prayers, acts, offers, assisted as far as is required, by an altar-boy. The people need only be present, must only *assist* at Mass and so fulfil their Sunday obligation.

Half a century ago the liturgical movement made its onslaught on such a manner of celebrating the liturgy. It stood for an enlivening of the liturgy and consequently for an enlivening of the notion of the Church. Then the liturgical movement began to draw attention to the actual text of the liturgy, to the plural form of the prayers, to the greetings and their responses, to the persistent Amen, and finally to all of the elements which, as history had proved, represented the part played by the people. Nor did it hesitate to draw the conclusions from the knowledge it possessed. In the foundation of the people's Mass and within the framework of what was already possible, a new way of celebrating the liturgy came into use. The liturgy came alive. Finally, the hierarchy themselves, especially in the encyclical *Mediator Dei* of Pope Pius XII, confirmed and underlined this view of the liturgy, so that even the most sacred part of the whole liturgy, the presentation of the sacrifice, is a matter for the faithful along with the priest.

It is not an exaggeration to say that this change of affairs is of immense significance. Without polemics, without harsh criticism, simply through doing things the right way, the full conception of what the Church is is once again being built up. The Church, that is the totality of all the faithful, the community of those who belong to Christ—the people of God who have emerged from the waters of Baptism. And this does not point to some ideal Church or other which exists somewhere beyond this earthly world. Yes, the liturgy helps us on even one step more: 'Church' in the liturgy is not only the Church universal—*per totum orbem terrarum*—but is also and primarily the congregation here and now, the assembly in this house of God, led by the duly appointed and ordained bearers of the priestly office who represent the link with the *Ecclesia universalis: Ecclesia tua, populus tuus, familia tua, plebs tua sancta*—that is the faithful who are gathered around the altar in this place. If Leo the Great makes the appeal in his Christmas homily: 'O Christian, know your dignity'—this is the place where the Christian—the young Christian—becomes aware of his dignity, his dignity as a member of the holy people of God.

2. Account is taken of this aspect alone in the historical study of R. Schulte, *Die Messe als Opfer der Kirche*. Münster 1959. But cf. the collection of the theological faculty of Lucerne entitled, *Das Opfer der Kirche*, Lucerne 1954.

When all together alternate with the priest, raising their voices around the altar, when they sing the *Sanctus una voce* with the choir of angels, when together, perhaps through some external symbolic act, they present the sacrifice and share together in the common meal, there the Church is visible.

But there is still another thing which is important, especially in the leadership of youth. If the Church comes to life in the participants in the actively celebrated liturgy, then a new relationship to the surrounding world comes into being; a new relationship to the material world itself, to the world of trades and professions. For it is real men of flesh and blood who are caught up in the process of the liturgy. It is their voices, their goings and comings which have become part of the sacred action. It is the bread from the work-a-day world which is carried to the altar. It is the work of the tradesman's hand which appears in the sacred furnishings and decorations, in the building which encloses everything. It is the every-day world which is drawn into the sacred action, joined with the sacrifice which Christ presents with His Church assembled here.

In guiding youth, we must awaken and foster awareness of this. We are the Church. But the Church is the world, the real world in which we live, redeemed by Christ and brought back home to God. This awareness is aroused when the words and actions of the liturgy are properly carried out, when the forms are again filled with spirit, when the sacred signs (as Guardini understands them) are taken seriously: in short: when the symbolism of the liturgy, which through its sensuous elements reaches out into all the world and then draws the world back into itself again, constantly comes into its own. Thus the liturgy will avoid the danger of falling into a spirituality out of touch with the world, in which the hour of celebration with its spiritual uplift would be but a lost island in a world without God, having no influence, no effect on the conduct of life; thus men will come to see that worship—divine service—must be nothing but the distillation of a way of life in which men serve God, that divine service, in the sense of worship, and the service of God must merge into one another. In the liturgy we must only see what is always present in a latent form. Above all, the Church must be visible in the liturgy. It is true that the Church is visible in her authority which guides her, and in the many institutions she has created, but most of all she must become visible in the public worship for which she assembles in church as the Church.

A notion of pastoral care has arisen and may possibly still be current in some places according to which all that is involved is the rescuing of souls, making sure that the individual is kept on the straight and narrow path or at least finds his way back to God in his dying hour. In that case, the *ars moriendi*, the ensuring of a good death would be the supreme concern of pastoral care. We would not despise such a concern by any means. But we have to set against such an outlook the words of the Psalmist: *Non mortui laudabunt te Domine*. God desires our praise while we are still upon this earth, and above all He desires to be praised by His Church: *Te per orbem terrarum sancta confitetur Ecclesia*. And it is the youth who are chiefly called upon to realize this ideal and put it into practice wherever possible, with pride and joy. Our whole life shall be a glorifying of God—in the calmness of labour, in the selfless fulfilment of duty; often it will be through a lonely and unnoticed life of devotion to duty. But on Sundays above all it should all flow together in the holy assembly. There its interior splendour should shine forth in the public worship of the Church; there the full harmony should be heard within the congregation: in the unity of the Holy Spirit, through Him and with Him, for the glory of the triune God. In this way the liturgy becomes revelation, and at the same time an enduring school of Christian faith.

3. *Liturgy and Congregational Singing**

When we compare the magnificent achievements of ancient and modern Church music with popular Church music, it is like seeing the undergrowth beneath the mighty trunks of forest trees—bushes and shrubs upon which one is inclined to set little value. On the other hand it is obvious that in recent decades, the value of popular Church music has been recognized, not only by priests and people who are fond of singing, but also by the hierarchy, most of all by local bishops. New and improved diocesan hymn-books are appearing everywhere; congregational singing is being encouraged in dioceses where it was never known before. In Austria as in Germany in recent years, for the first time, unison songs have been appointed which are sung everywhere with the same text and melody.

This is no accidental phenomenon: rather it must be considered as part of that religious revival affecting, not the bulk of the people, but a very important section of the Christian people. It began with Pius X who led the way, on the one hand, towards a strengthening of sacramental and liturgical life, and on the other towards a deepened understanding of the Church—to the 'awakening of the Church in the soul'.

It is plain to see that awareness of the nature of the Church has known a revival in our time; and the experience goes on. For all too long, even amongst the clergy, there has been a wide-spread tendency to think of the Church only in terms of the ecclesiastical hierarchy: Pope, Bishops and priests, and to some extent it has been forgotten that the faithful do not merely come to Church, are not merely looked after by the Church, but are themselves the Church. The Church, ἐκκλησία, from the very beginning has been the assembly of the faithful, the community of those who belong to Christ, who have been baptized into His death and Resurrection and have a share in His life. It is true that within this community certain organs have to emerge and must be given authority to exercise their various functions for the good of the whole community, but the whole organism must be alive.

This more complete concept of the Church as the holy community of the faithful was already operative at the beginning of this century. It was behind the Communion decrees of Pius X. It was behind Pius XI's cry for Catholic Action. It has been proclaimed formally and in its full extent in the encyclical *Mystici corporis* of Pius XII; and in this the ancient thought of St. Paul and

* Lecture at the 2nd International Congress for Church Music in Wien-Klosterneuburg, October 1954.

1. Balth. Fischer, *Das Deutsche Hochamt: Liturgisches Jahrbuch* 3 (1953) 41-53, esp. 44.

the Fathers that the Church is the Mystical Body of Christ is re-awakened. Above all it lies behind the liturgical movement, which is commonly said to have begun at the congress of Catholic societies in Mecheln in 1909, but which had its preparation in the Communion decrees and the *Motu proprio* concerning Church music of Pius X.

In this *Motu proprio* the active participation of the faithful in the mysteries and in the prayer of the Church is mentioned for the first time. But once mentioned it has been stressed repeatedly by succeeding Popes. Pius X was thinking primarily of the people singing during worship. In general he was thinking first of all of the sung Mass in which the people were to take part, and he expressly stressed the fact that within the Mass (i.e., the *Missa cantata*) and the Office, hymns in the vernacular were forbidden. In the early days of the liturgical revival this was an understandable limitation. It was the confirmation of a settled practice which had been first prescribed universally, at least from Rome, by a decree of 1894. This adherence to the exclusive use of Latin did, it is true, place an obstacle in the way of the progress of congregational singing; at any rate a perceptible tension was created between the demands made by a popular Latin form of hymn-singing, and the demands made by the active participation of the people in the service—a tension which would have to be resolved sooner or later.

The liturgical movement thereupon sought to mend things by changing course. It improved the situation by choosing the Low Mass (*Missa lecta*) as its basic form; from this is advanced to the community Mass and then developed the prayer-song Mass. For, as the Low Mass for centuries had been capable of association with various prayers in the vernacular—the Rosary, for example—so it could have joined with it prayers and hymns which were part of an active participation in it.

On the other hand it was proved by history that hymns in the vernacular had originally been linked, not with the Low Mass, but with the public High Mass. The Jesuit missionaries who went to the Canadian Indians in the 17th century found it perfectly natural to allow their Iroquois Christians to sing the Ordinary of the Mass—Kyrie, Gloria, etc.—in their own tongué, and the same

348   PASTORAL LITURGY

thing was done at that time by missionaries to China.² But most important, within the Latin Mass, hymns in the vernacular had long been customary in Germany. As early as the Middle Ages they appear as interpolations in the Latin Sequence, and as hymns before the sermon.³ These beginnings grew in the succeeding centuries, and in the 18th century were elaborated into complete Mass hymns which took the place of the Latin Ordinary and Proper, trying in a more or less free manner to follow the course of the Mass. This style—the Latin Office with German hymns, besides the responses to the celebrant—has become well-known and common since that time in most north and west German dioceses, and is known as the 'German High Mass'. Until this century it was maintained as by right of custom, but many attacks were made against it. In 1943 Cardinal Bertram applied, therefore, to the Sacred Congregation of Rites to have the permission for this type of celebration of the Mass explicitly declared. The cardinal received a formal reply on December 24, 1943 granting permission for the whole of Germany as it then was. The cardinal's request was granted in this statement: *ita ut hic tertius modus* (i.e. the German High Mass) *benignissime toleretur.*⁴

Nor is it unknown to find texts and hymns in the vernacular inserted into the Latin service itself. Liturgy and the vernacular are no longer mutually exclusive. The encyclical on the liturgy of 1947 contains an indication in the same direction when it says: 'Admittedly the adaption of the vernacular in quite a number of functions may prove of great benefit to the faithful'.⁵ This is a fundamental statement of great significance. It is applied today mostly to the administration the sacraments (Baptism, Marriage, Extreme Unction, Burial), and not only in Germany, but also in the French, English and Indian speaking world as well as in Negro African Churches. Corresponding to this, attempts have been

2. N. Kowalsky, *Römische Entscheidungen uber den Gebrauch der Landessprache bei der heiligen Messe in den Missionen: Neue Zeitschrift fur Missionswissenschaft* 9 (1953) 241-251.
3. Jungmann, *Missarum Sollemnia* I, 194 seq. 563.
4. For the complete text of the reply v. *Liturgisches Jahrbuch* 3 (1953) 108-110. The privileges granted here for the regions named remain in force despite the restrictive new order of 1958; v. *Instructio de musica sacra.* Besides this they are confirmed by the letter to Cardinal Frings dated Dec. 23, 1958; v. *Liturgisches Jahrbuch* 9 (1959) 119.—Cf. also J. Wagner, *Gestaltung des deutschen Hochamts: Die Messe der Glaubensverkündigung,* Freiburg 1953, 321-328.
5. *Acta Ap. Sed.* 39 (1947) 545.

made to copy the idea of the German High Mass and to extend that regional ruling to the world in general. This is remarkable on account of the fact that in many countries—France for example—hymns were as good as unknown until quite recently, not only at Mass, but even at evening benediction: they were permitted only on the very fringe of worship, before and after the sermon, at processions and things like that.6

At the International Liturgical Congress in Lugano in September 1953, in which seventeen bishops and one representative from the Congregation of Rites took part, two of the four resolutions concerned the position of the vernacular in the liturgy.7 One of these made the petition: As Pius X made the Eucharistic Bread freely available for the Christian people, might not the Bread of God's Word be made more readily available by letting the people hear the readings at Mass in their own tongues, directly from the lips of the priest. This motion was only summing up what no less a person that Cardinal Lercaro, Bishop of Bologna had expressed to the congress in an extensive referendum. The other resolution concerned the hymns in the Latin Mass. It ran: The congress requests: so that the people may more easily and with more benefit take part in the liturgy, may bishops have authority to allow the people, not only to hear the Word of God in their own language, but to pray and sing in that language even in the Mass (*Missa cantata*), and so make some sort of response. As well as by Bishop Weskaman of Berlin, the matter was specially represented by the former missionary to China, P. Hofinger.7a The report in the Liturgical Year Book adds the comment: in this it would be a case of relaxing the prohibitions of 1894 and 1903 (which demanded the exclusive use of Latin hymns); and goes on to observe: 'Heed would have to be paid to the sacral character of the vernacular hymns'8 All this leads on to further extension of the possibilities of congregational singing in the various languages, and that for the sake of vitalizing the concept of the Church.

Beside the awakening of the Church in the soul and the desire for active participation in the life of the Church, in public

6. Cf. Ch. Grimaud, *La Liturgie dans la vie chrétienne* (*Liturgia*, Paris 1935, 955-984) 974.
7. The proceedings are published in German in the *Liturgisches Jahrbuch* 3 (1953) 125-322.
7a. Cf. also J. Hofinger-J. Kellner, *Liturgische Erneuerung in der Weltmission*, Innsbruck 1957, 131, 422 seq.
8. *Liturgisches Jahrbuch* 3 (1953) 142-144.

worship, we must mention also a second factor, which concerns the singing of the people within the Mass, that is the better understanding of the meaning of the liturgy, especially of the Mass.

Understanding of the Mass has not been of a very high order since the Middle Ages. People, for the most part, were satisfied if they were simply present at Mass and knew about the sacred mystery which was being celebrated here: and at the same time they emphasized the memory of Christ's Passion, and especially in the later Middle Ages, the adoration of the sacred Body and Blood. In the Mass, therefore, the aspect of Christ's coming to us was stressed. The Mass was seen and described primarily as an epiphany of Christ, an appearance of Christ, or, more vaguely, as God's appearance before the congregation. Corresponding to this aspect was the interpretation of the external action of the rite of the Mass in an allegorical way. The Gloria represented the Christmas mystery, the Epistle was the preaching of the Baptist, the Sanctus the entry into Jerusalem, the last blessing was the Ascension. In the external action people wanted to make visible the whole work of Redemption. And this was consistently in line with the fact that the people felt no need to be active themselves. They only wanted to look on, laying hold of the mystery reverently with eye and ear.

This was not a false, but was an inadequate conception of the Mass. For in truth the Mass is more than an epiphany of Christ; it is thanksgiving, sacrificial devotion. 'Eucharistia' is one of the oldest names for the Mass, and the idea of thanksgiving determines its essential structure to this day. Eucharistia means thanksgiving. The authentic action of the Mass begins with the invitation: Let us give thanks, Gratia agamus, Εὐχαριστῶμεν. In essence the Mass is a mighty prayer of thanks which moves on into the thank-offering. It is not just a God-manward happening, a descent of God to man, but, based upon that, is an activity from man's side, a reaching up towards God. It is observance before God, led by Christ who acts through the celebrating priest at the moment of consecration; it is obeisance before God indeed, which is fulfilled not by Christ alone, but precisely so that it is offered to God by Him in the midst of His Church and along with His Church. And so this movement upwards is present in the prayers and hymns of the Mass, not in the sense that a solitary individual makes this movement as representative of the rest, but in the sense that the whole congregation is assembled for the very purpose of entering into Christ's sacrifice, into His thanksgiving, homage and devotion, and so of being raised up to God. Hence the 'we' of the prayers of the Mass; hence all along the line (if we look at the older textual material) the situation was such that the attending people were called upon to answer and confirm the prayers with their Amen—and also to join in the singing.

First and foremost, and according to the oldest tradition, this applies to the hymn which formed the first climax to the prayer of thanksgiving, the Sanctus. For centuries, and in our northern lands, until the height of the Middle Ages, the Sanctus was a song of the people. By the entire congregation taking up the song, there was a simple fulfilment of what was announced by the concluding words of the Preface: *Cum quibus et nostras voces* . . . This is indeed a climax in the liturgical action, and the dignity of the Church on earth should be manifest by its being raised up through the priest's prayer of thanksgiving to join with the Church in heaven to sing the one hymn of praise to God's triune Majesty, thus sharing, while still on this earth, in the praise of the celestial spirits. Obviously the other Mass hymns will be influenced too by this active conception of the liturgy which invites the people to join in, a conception now beginning to take hold and which we are gradually winning back. It would be specially easy to accomplish the active participation of the faithful in the Kyrie because it is the reiterated, litany-like cry of petition which rises to the *Kyrios* from His people; and likewise with the *Credo*, the profession of faith which ought to be spoken by all present.

These are all conclusions drawn predominantly from the history of the liturgy, and yet they are at the same time fundamental and therefore claim general application. Concerning the people singing at Mass, we are not interested in reviving a custom simply because it once prevailed: we wish rather to reinstate something which was more clearly appreciated in early times for the very reason that it is in harmony with the timeless meaning of the Mass and its liturgy.

In all of this we must bear in mind the well-known fact that the hymns of the Ordinary of the Mass, strictly speaking, were not originally songs in the musical sense of the word: they were spoken chorally with slight intonation, at most in a dignified recitative like that of the chant of the celebrant at the altar. This is obvious of the Sanctus, which was but the extension of the Preface, and of the Credo, which is only a profession of faith, said in unison. The fact applies least of all, perhaps, to the Gloria which has always had something of the style of a hymn. It is significant that the Carolingian composer, Aurelian of Reaumé was still treating only the following as chants of the Mass: the Kyrie and the Gloria, and besides these, only the Proper chants—Introit, Gradual, Alleluia, Offertory and Communion. By contrast, the Credo, Sanctus and Agnus Dei are not included.[9]

The Ordinary was the people's portion: but this did not remain so. In festal celebration when richer melody was desired, and then later in general, this became the preserve of the clergy who now formed the choir. Clergy and chorus meant the same thing, and even the sanctuary took from this its name of 'choir' which it keeps to this day. The liturgical recitative, the song of the Church, became the chorale. Within this choir with its chorales there was always the *schola cantorum* as a special group who took over the more elaborate melodies of the antiphonary or the Gradual. The people began to lose their voice.

At the same time the musicianship of the choir progressed and polyphony arose. Having first been tried out on the Proper, this spread to the Ordinary, and to develop its potentialities to the limit, it enlisted the help of the laity. Polyphony now flourished and displayed all of its wonderful richness. Church music had filled up the vacuum created by the silence of the people. Two forces, one positive and the other negative, both worked towards the same end: the positive power of the mightily progressing development of Church music and the negative tendencies which led to the silence of the people. Awareness of the Church vanished, as did understanding of the Mass in its complete sense as Eucharistia and sacrifice of the Church. It is significant that in the Middle Ages the word 'Eucharistia' was no longer translated by 'thanksgiving,' but by *bona gratia*: the Mass was understood to be an actual gift

9. *Musica disciplina* c. 20 (Gerbert, *Scriptores de musica sacra* I, 60 seq.).

from on high—which it is; but that it was also the upsurge of the Christian people to God, was forgotten.

Today we are again beginning to overcome the people's silence. Does this mean that church choirs and polyphonic High Masses must fall into decay? In the heat of the battle such things have been said.[10] These must be seen in the context of the battle of a young struggling movement which is important for the life of the Church, and which can only prevail after much labour. On other points too, and with complete deliberation, Pius Parsch has confronted the thesis of the status quo with the antithesis of his ideals in a somewhat abrupt manner. But, as elsewhere, thesis and antithesis must be followed here by a synthesis which will unite in a higher unity what is valuable in both position—not as in a sheer compromise, but truly in a higher unity, such as can arise from the fundamental evaluation of both sides of the case.

The liturgical movement has fittingly been called a renaissance which the Church has experienced in our own day, a re-birth in which a formerly attained happy condition has been brought back. In the liturgical movement the life of worship of the young Church is revived as a model, as a model for the active participation of the faithful in public worship. But no true renaissance can ignore the years that lie between; it must always try to understand the value of the immediate tradition, and to bring into harmony with the re-discovered values of the ancient model.

The liturgy is the public worship of the Church. Therefore it is and remains an ideal that the whole Church, the congregation here assembled, present its praise to God as a living organism. But the liturgy is the Church's service to God: it is God, infinite, eternal and almighty, who is to be given honour. In all ages and amongst all peoples it has always been accepted as obvious that for the glorification of God only the best is good enough, that to show homage to Him the very highest of which man is capable must be offered. Thus religion and its cult has always been that central point around which the arts have gathered: architecture, plastic and pictorial arts, and music.

The actual assembly of the faithful who are here and now united to worship God, made up of city-folk and country-folk,

10. P. Parsch, *Volksliturgie. Ihr Sinn und Umfang*, Klosterneuburg 1940, 331.

officials, businessmen and housewives, of parents and their children, can never provide, on their own, what advanced musical art can offer to God's honour. Often they will have to retire into passivity before it. They will not therefore refrain from praising God out of their own mouths also; but at the same time, where it is fitting, they will sometimes ask great music to offer in their name what they cannot themselves perform. And so ever and again all will resound in harmony with the splendour and beauty of the festally decorated house of God, with the richness of the vestments, the gold of the sacred vessels; and in God's house all of creation will join together to sound the praise of the Creator.

Against all this it could be argued that the Church of early times possessed the possibility of taking artistic song and musical instruments into its worship, and that it did not do this; more than this, that through the mouths of its most prominent men it constantly declined emphatically to have such accessories in its spiritual worship.

This shows us that they were unwilling to adopt forms which were current amongst the heathen cults. They did not want to use the lyres, tympani, and symbols of Greek sacrifice, or the flutes of the Roman. They did not want to become confused with the cults of the gods or with the orgies of the mystery religions with their highly developed music.[11] They had to stress the inner spiritual nature of their own worship in contrast to the external heathenish cults. A more serious consideration, however, is this: the early Church also declined to follow the example of Old Testament reference according to which the Word of God declared that God was supposed to be worshipped *in psalterio et cithara, in tympano et choro, in chordis et organo*. Even Chrysostom considered the instrumental music of Jewish worship to be but a concession to the weakness of the Jews, something to keep them back from worse things.[12] And for a long time even vocal choirs were unheard of.

What should we think of the attitude of the early Church? Besides the contrast to heathendom there is another factor which

11. J. Quasten, *Music und Gesang in den Kulten der heidnischen Antike und christliche Frühzeit*, Münster 1930, 12 seq.
12. Quasten 87 seq.

must be considered. This was the extraordinary mistrust of the world of sense which arose, not from Christian revelation but from Platonic and neo-Platonic philosophy which constituted the intellectual habitat of the early Fathers. For Plato, the body with its senses is but a prison in which the soul is confined during this earthly life. Consequently, the formation of the soul necessitates the rejection of this prison as much as possible. The faculties of sense must be suppressed and weakened, certainly they must not be cultivated. St. Augustine is still deprecating the fact that he finds pleasure in harmonious sound and that the words of the holy Scripture move him more deeply when they are sung than when merely spoken.[13] Ambrose took a different view, and Augustine began, as he admits, to change his. Nevertheless the feeling persisted right up to the flowering of scholasticism in the 13th century. Not till then did that pessimistic outlook give way, and the philosophy of Aristotle propounded the principle that all spiritual life must follow the path of the sense, and that even sensuous passions are not evil but necessary, only requiring to be controlled and kept in due proportion.

The negative appraisal of musical art by the Fathers and their refusal to use it in worship need not be normative for us, quite apart from the fact that Church music of recent centuries, especially vocal music, is something quite different from the noisy instrumental music of heathendom with its reliance mainly on rhythm.

Congregational singing will once again take its place in the liturgy, but it will no longer reign alone. This arises from our conception of the liturgy. Congregational singing must be admitted because the liturgy is the *Church's* worship; but the potentialities of Church musical art must also be admitted because the liturgy is *God's* service. The question now is how to achieve the right balance. I would like to suggest a few lines of thought, confining myself to the heart of the liturgy, the celebration of the Mass.

On great feast-days congregational singing will not be absent, but Church music will predominate. On these festal occasions the great settings of the Ordinary of the Mass which have been written

13. *Confessiones* X, 33.

during recent centuries will always come into their own. The same sort of thing will take place apart from great festivals in representative Churches in large cities—in cathedrals and the like.

On ordinary Sundays in the average parish, congregational singing according to the prescribed rules, must always have preference. Certain latitude and compromise will, of course, always be possible. There remains the Proper, containing those chants which have more the character of decorative interludes and to execute which the declining Middle Ages created the *Schola cantorum*.

We know that many serious obstacles stand in the way of the polyphonic intonation of the Proper. The chants of the Proper change Sunday by Sunday and can indeed be used but once in the year. In the traditional Latin form their texts are not understood by the faithful, less understood than the text of the Ordinary. Very often the texts are not particularly apposite, bearing a particular reference neither to the rest of the Mass formula nor to the relevant part of the action of the Mass. In short, they need reforming. Several ways of reform are possible, all of which present tasks to the Church music of the future. One line of reform would consist in fixing more appropriate and more easily understood texts for each sequence of Sundays. A radical reform has already been suggested: that even in a Latin High Mass, the Latin chants of the Proper should be replaced with the spirit of the liturgy. And there seems to be no reason why such chants could not be adopted by church choirs just as they were adopted in their older Latin form by the *Schola cantorum*.

With regard to the Ordinary too, the solution can be envisaged in the average parish, whereby congregational singing of the choir would be combined just as a soli and choir have been combined elsewhere, or in such a way that there is an alternation from verse to verse. Such a solution has already been tried—in St. Stephen's in Vienna for example. Only the people's part must remain genuine congregational singing.

Today moreover, congregational singing and Church music are in a position to draw much closer together than they could formerly. All can read, many can read music, and everyone can get a hold of a book. Singing is of a higher standard—at least it is more widespread than it used to be. Congregational singing is no longer felt to be something foreign to worship. Whereas in Pius X's time we were only speaking about Gregorian Chant in Latin, Pius XII speaks in *Mediator Dei* of the fostering of religious congregational singing without reservation, of appropriate hymns which the people should sing within the Mass.14 Congregational singing in Church has re-awakened. Even Church music will not shrink from recognizing the people's singing as her true, if plainer, sister.

4. Liturgy and Church Art*

From time immemorial liturgy—and not the Christian liturgy only—has been bound up with art. Especially where it has assumed a festal style, it has been thrown at every step upon the good services of art.

As can been seen even by the uninitiated, in recent decades the history of art has considerably altered its approach to its subject. It is no longer content to point out and describe isolated works, nor yet to classify definite periods according to attitudes of style and form, but now it inquires rather into the intellectual forces behind the appearances, into social, political, philosophical and religious ideas and ideals of which they are the expression. The history of art is becoming the history of the mind.

This approach is particularly forceful in the realm of Christian art; more precisely, of Church art, that art which not only deals with Christian material as a kind of house-decoration or adornment of books and which consequently is affected by extraneous factors, but which is at the service of the Christian community and is part of the furnishing of the holy place of worship—and which is somehow a mirror of the liturgy, is itself liturgy.

It is of Christian art in this sense only that we speak here. Obviously, consideration of the content, of the thought expressed

14. *Acta Ap. Sed.* 39 (1947) 560-590.

358   PASTORAL LITURGY

is of paramount importance. It is not simply that we are to know something about the history of revelation in order to understand the separate works: it is rather that the various forms which religious thought has assumed in the different epochs, the various manners in which it has been expressed through the liturgy is the only thing which makes it possible to understand more deeply the changing face of Church art or the variations in preference over theme and range of subject.

The shape of the church building which could be a purely functional building is determined in its finer details by the contemporary form of religious thought. In this sense architecture has been called 'representational' art.[1]

In the days of Christianity's freedom, when it could justifiably indulge in a sense of triumph, the front part of the church building—the basilica—was designed as God's throne-room into which the Christian people were allowed to enter, into which they streamed, guided by the row of pillars of the nave.[2] In the precarious conditions of the early Middle ages and again in the Romanesque period the church was conceived as a strong city, built up out of massive walls and guarded by strong towers. Inside the people of God were safe. In the flourishing, joyously sensuous Gothic culture, the cathedral—as Hans Sedlmayr has recently shown[3]—was seen as the heavenly city, come down upon this earth, as described in the Apocalypse. Underneath were the massive foundations; above, like the arch of heaven, was the aetherial baldachino of the vault, on light supports which did not reach the ground; the walls were relieved by colourful windows, so that the whole space was filled with unearthly light—by the light of the heavenly Jerusalem.

We could also mention the rule of eastern orientation. This was at one time a living law, proceeding from the thought that when praying—especially when taking part in liturgical prayer—one should turn towards the light, to the rising sun. In early centuries Christians were accustomed to describe Christ as their Sun who had set in the underworld, but in the Resurrection had risen in

* Rectoiral address in Innsbruck, November 14, 1953.
1. H. Sedlmayr, *Architectur als abbildende Kunst (Sitzungsberichte d. Osterr. Akad. d. Wiss., Phil.-hist. Kl.*, 225, 3), Vienna 1948.
2. A. Stange, *Das frühchristliche Kirchengebäude als Bild des Himmels*, Cologne 1950.
3. H. Sedmayerl, *Die Entstehung der Kathedrale*, Zürich 1950.—The idea which Sedmayerl presents admittedly became a matter for controversy.

brightness, the *Sol salutis* or *Sol iustitiae*.4 Therefore when at prayer, one looked towards Him who would one day come again: one faced the East. The dead, too, were buried facing east, and churches were similarly orientated.

If all this is true of church architecture, then the same sort of thing must be true of pictorial art, but in a higher degree.

The great theme of Church art of all time is the history of redemption, especially the more decisive section of this history: the foundation of redemption in the appearance of Christ and His work. In the sacred books, a wealth of separate themes lies ready to hand in which the general theme could be depicted variously and magnificently: raising of the dead, healing of the sick, sovereignty over nature, the triumphal entry into Jerusalem. It has long been realized, however, that medieval art in particular and also modern religious art have only made use of a very small selection from this rich store of material. Almost the only things to be portrayed are the beginning and the end of the life of Jesus: the Annunciation, the birth of Christ, the infancy story on the one hand, the Passion, the Cross, the Resurrection on the other. It is not only art within the Church building which confines its attention to those themes: all through the Middle Ages even the miniatures in the manuscripts—in the Gospel manuscripts themselves—know only of these themes. How do we explain this?

The answer is very simply: they chose these scenes which were in the forefront of liturgical life, i.e. chiefly those marked by a feast.

This is an ancient Christian and general principle of choice. It is told of the painter-monks of the monastery of Mount Athos that they have painted and still paint only the 'fifteen great feasts of the Church'. And of Church art in the West we can say that it really knows but two sets of subjects: the Christmas series and the Easter series: that is to say: the infancy group extended to include the life of Mary, and the Passion—Resurrection story. In high medieval painting only a few themes concerning our Lord's public life are heeded. There are scarcely more than four themes: the Baptism, the Marriage at Cana, the Temptation, and the Transfiguration. These are moreover the events described in the

4. F. J. Dölger, *Sol salutis. Gebet und Gesang im christlichen Altertum mit besonderer Rücksicht auf die Ostung in Gebet und Liturgie,*² Münster 1925.

Gospels of the Sundays between Christmas and Easter: Baptism and Cana, attached to epiphany; Temptation and Transfiguration, at the beginning of Lent. These themes too, are dictated by the liturgy.[5]

Church art is a profession of faith, just as public worship itself is profession and proclamation. Church art proclaims first of all, therefore, those facts which lie at the base of the Christian world-order; thus they are the same as those which are accentuated in the Apostles' Creed, the same as are observed in the feasts of the Church. Hence: the fact that Christ has come, 'conceived by the Holy Ghost, born of the Virgin Mary'—gives us the Easter motif.

To sum up shortly what has so far emerged, we could say: in the first century the Easter motif carried the emphasis notably; in the second century the Christmas motif had it. As could not be otherwise, in both cases Christ was in the centre; but in the first century He was seen as He had entered the other world in His glorified Body: in the second century, however, He was seen as He had entered our earthly World, to suffer and die.

To a certain extent the Easter motif still had its place in the late Middle Ages, as in the second century. No period in Christian history can leave out the redemptive Passion of Christ. To some extent, however, it had become limited to this—its wordly component: the redemptive Passion and death, the tears of Christ, the Piétà, the laying in the tomb, and perhaps even the Resurrection too, as a singular occurrence, but still in this world.

Over against this, during the first century the Easter motif was treated in quite a different way. It was constantly in the foreground: but not so much as a representation of the unique event of the Resurrection of Christ on Easter morning; not so much in the style of Matthias Grünewald's portrayal, with the figure of our Lord rising up in a pillar of light while the guards fall back in terror. It was more in the manner of the liturgy: the risen Christ is the principle of new life, the risen Christ and the Church, the new creation which has begun in His Resurrection and which is to re-mould the old creation. It is not the Resurrection as an event so much as the Risen One and the world of the Risen One as a condition, a new order.

5. E. Mâle, *L'art religieux du XIIIe siecle en France*,[1] Paris 1931, 180 seq.

This idea lies behind the art of the catacombs. By far the commonest picture here is the Good Shepherd, but the Shepherd with His flock, or the Shepherd carrying the rescued sheep on His shoulders—Christ, who has saved mankind.

The other pictures in the catacombs which recur with some regularity, all say the same thing: by far the bulk are taken from the Old Testament and at first sight might appear as enigmatic as they are naive and primitive in execution. They tell of the deliverance which is at hand, of the Redemption which is already accomplished, of the hope of the Christian. This is contained in the various pictures: Noe and Jonas who were rescued; the thirsty people in the wilderness, who were given water from the rock; the young men in the fiery furnace who were not touched by the flame. These are disguised representations of the Easter mystery.

With less disguise the art of the basilicas from the 4th century on speaks of the reality of Easter: certainly they speak of the Christ of Easter. In many examples the image of Christ is surrounded by the four living creatures of the Prophet Ezechiel—a man, an ox, a lion and an eagle. We usually understand these figures as symbols of the four evangelists—and this meaning is in fact given them in Christian antiquity—but this is their secondary meaning. The original meaning, as it appears in the older Fathers, thus supplying an adequate reason for these symbols appearing in the apse along with the image of Christ, is found in the thought that in these our Lord's work, especially its Easter consummation, is summed up: He became man—the image of a man; He became a sacrifice—the image of an ox; He remains victorious in His Resurrection—the image of a lion; He ascended into heaven—the image of an eagle.[6]

This all corresponds with the fact that in the older Church art at least the enthroned Christ is seldom represented alone. In however abbreviated a form, His completed work is shown beside Him: after His Resurrection victory our Lord gathered His people—the Church—around Him. The Church is represented by the apostles who gaze up at Him in homage—or who receive the scroll of the law from the hand of the law-giver (*Dominus legem dat*)—or by a line of sheep who press towards their Shepherd, or

6. Künstle, *Ikonographie der christlichen Kunst* I, 611 seq.

by deer who drink from the streams of paradise, or in some other similar fashion. Sometimes it is the Church triumphant which is shown, as when the twenty-four elders are depicted on the triumphal arch or it may be, laying down their crowns in homage before the Lamb.

There are no representations of the Crucifixion in the ancient churches—as we know. The Cross—yes, but in a stylized form as the Cross of Glory, as τροπαῖον as a victory sign erected after the victory. But when later they began to represent the Crucified Christ Himself they did so to a certain extent only in the light of Easter—as they still do in Roman art. The Cross is the King's throne; instead of the thorns there is a kingly crown upon His head; the linen cloth has become a regal robe; at His feet the Church looks up, full of trust, while the synagogue turns away in shame.

A glance at these hastily indicated facts is enough to show that we have here a unified and thorough viewpoint and idiom of representation. Ildefons Herwegen, the great abbot of Maria Laach has suggested the title of 'Mysterium' for this[7]: the thought of the Mysterium lay at the foundation of the piety of that early Christianity: people regarded the basic redemptive fact (the Passion and Resurrection of Christ) as continuously becoming present, above all in the worship which the Church performed and through which she shared in salvation.

However we like to define 'Mysterium' more narrowly, it suffices to maintain the core of the idea: viz. that in those very ancient times, the basic redemptive fact—the Easter-fact: Christ's Passion and Resurrection—was present to the Christian mind in a different, much more intense way, and this arose out of the liturgy. In those days they did not see the Resurrection and glorification of Christ as a single point (even if the climatic point) in a chain of events, but as the finale of the work which now lay complete, the consummation of the Christian universe in which men lived and breathed. In this sense they set the Risen One at the centre of their religious life. This receives pungent expression in the liturgy.

For centuries Easter was not only the highest but the only feast

7. I. Herwegen, *Kirche und Seele, Die Seelenhaltung des Mysterienkultes und ihr Wandel im Mittelalter* (*Aschendorffs zeitgemässe Schriften* 9), Münster 1926.

celebrated throughout all of Christendom. It was felt to be, we might say, the annual feast of the institution of Christianity and the Church. For this reason it had added to it a long period of preparation, and a still longer subsequent celebration.

The way in which Easter was—and is—celebrated is instructive. The mind dwells not solely on the thought of the Risen One and His triumph, on His glorification, but always embraces the thought of His people as well—those who have risen together with Him. Since the 2nd century Easter, moreover, had always been the first baptismal festival. Today the baptismal water is still blessed within the Easter liturgy, and the liturgy of Easter week speaks constantly of those who have been led into the land flowing with milk and honey, those whom He has called as the blessed who will possess the kingdom of His Father. To this day the liturgy for the second Sunday after Easter is still dominated purely and simply by the image of the Good Shepherd who has gathered His flock around Him—just as we proclaimed in the ancient Christian representations of the catacombs and sarcophagi.

But this Easter motif which runs through the Christian pictorial art of the first century was not restricted within the liturgy to the Easter season. Easter was celebrated every week—indeed Sunday was the ἀναστάσιμος ἡμέρα, the day of the Resurrection; this was its name for centuries in the Greek Orient, and its manner of celebration brought this out more clearly than is now done.

Still, however, the liturgy reveals Easter features at various points throughout the year, displays, indeed, an Easter attitude. Every prayer which is offered to God is ended with a reference to Him, *qui tecum vivit et regnat.*

This way of thinking, which is still preserved in the official texts of the Church's liturgy, suffered a widespread decline in the mind of the Christian community in later times. In general we could say that in the 2nd century the Christmas motif took its place alongside that of Easter.

Certainly, Christmas came into the liturgy at a very early date; it has been observed since the 4th century. In this way, the beginning of the work as well as its completion is now being marked by a festival, but as a festival of the Church it always remained in second place. In the Christian mind, however, it began more and more to take precedence over Easter and, as we all know, it has maintained its position until the present day.

This is a symptom behind which must lie an important process in spiritual history, stretching over several centuries. The change-over began in the Carolingian period and was an accomplished fact soon after the turn of the millennium (11th-12th century). First of all it established itself in the realm of theology and then spread slowly into the realm of Church art.

In the end it became a matter of viewing the person of Christ in a new light. Arianism had questioned the true divinity of Christ. On the Catholic side this necessitated the defence and consequent emphasis of all which expressed the divine power and dignity of our Lord. This involved the Christmas and Epiphany series of ideas. On the other side it meant a certain suppression of those lines of thought which allowed of Arian misunderstanding. This involved the Lord's mediatorial office in His transfigured humanity of Easter.[8]

This manner of thought had spread throughout the whole Carolingian realm from the battle-grounds of Western Arianism; and it had increasingly overlaid the more ancient Roman tradition. The great advocates of this new religious attitude are St. Bernard of Clairvaux in the 12th century with his Marian lyrics and mysticism of the Cross, and St. Francis of Assisi at the beginning of the 13th century, who constructed the first crib and received the stigmata.

Other forces may also have contributed to this development, especially the racial temperament of the now dominant Teutonic peoples who were appealed to more by what was sensibly perceptible and ostentatious, by what touched the feelings. There was also a certain primitive quality in medieval man, showing itself not least in his religious formation, which may have tended in the same direction. They liked to hold onto the earthly mani-festation of God.

In common speech people no longer distinguished between God and Christ, the God-man. The well-known opening sentence of the *Lex Salica* runs: 'Long live Christ whom the Franks love'. In late medival language people spoke of God's corpse, of God's

8. Cf. above Pt. I, Chap. 6.

agony, of God's hands and feet, and by that they meant the Body of Christ, the Passion of Christ, His hands and feet. The expressions still survive in popular speech when we hear of God-carvers and God's niche. Such a manner of speech is not incorrect, but is most inexact.

This historical background makes sense of various phenomena in the sphere of Church art. There is, for example, the Biblical portrayal of God, i.e., in this context, of God the Father. All through the first century, Church art never knew of any representation of God the Father. If they wanted to represent God in some Old Testament scene, showing His almighty power, saving men and so on, He was represented simply by a hand emerging from the clouds. They did not dare to depict the invisible God; and, indeed, He cannot be depicted. Only in the 13th century, on account of the religious development we have indicated, did they begin to depict God as a venerable old man holding the orb of the world in His hand. Then followed representations of the Blessed Trinity as well—in the form of the Mercy-Seat or in the crowning of Mary or other ways.

The following process of thought clearly lies behind this development. If from time immemorial men have been representing the God-man in human form—as is obviously the case—and, if to some degree we allow ourselves to look beyond His humanity and to use such expressions as God's birth, God's Passion, and so on, then the converse, too, has to be allowed; when we speak directly of God—God the Father—we must be permitted to apply the anthropomorphic form. Clearly it is permitted: whether it is a gain for religion, for a worthy conception of God, is another matter. Pastoral theology inclines to disfavour this tendency.

Church art of this later medieval period is thus chiefly characterized by the love and devotion with which it portrays the Christmas theme and the Passion of Christ, those great mysteries of faith which are set within the earthly scene—the Annunciation, the Nativity, the Adoration of the Magi, the Flight into Egypt, the life of Mary and then the separate scenes of the Passion story from Gethsemani, with the sleeping disciples, until the laying in the tomb and the Resurrection.

Here we might observe that from the point of view of skilful execution, lively expression, and psychological penetration of forms, this is the point in time when we first begin to be able to speak of a high quality of artistic performance. Now for the first time men are learning to represent, with growing mastery, pain and joy and amazement, all the states of the human soul, and finally, dramatic scenes involving large groups. The incident, which formerly had been confined to a general scheme surrounded by the aura of transfiguration, is now portrayed in every detail of historic happening and with growing realism. But as earthly beauty becomes taken into Church art and extended, in the same measure, the proclamation of supernatural reality loses clarity and power, loses it sacral character.

The Last Supper of Leonardo da Vinci is a marvel of psychological penetration and dramatic form. But no longer has the artist set the mystery itself in the centre, but has taken a subsidiary scene—'One of you will betray me'—and made that the central interest. The Gothic winged altars and the Baroque altar super-structures are superb creations, in their own way: but the fundamental lituricgal idea from which the whole development derived and which was all-controlling in the first century, the idea namely of making the altar-table, the place of the sacramental action, stand out against a decorated rear wall, has almost become lost. It has become overwhelmed by the exaggeration of the incidental construction.

To turn to another sphere: polyphonic Church music of recent centuries, when judged purely musically, leaves far behind anything that the Middle Ages ever produced. In its greatest achievement, however. it has lost touch with true liturgy, fallen away from the all-embracing plan of divine worship, and become an autonomous work of art.

There seems to be a hestiant attitude, a certain puzzlement in the Church in the face of this problem. This arises from the nature of the case. It is almost impossible to preserve the perfect connexion between the aesthetic and the religious ideal over a long period of time. Perfect artistic workmanship within the Church lies for ever in an unsure balance. On one hand, the very best of which human capacity and art are capable must be offered for the service of God: on the other, this offering only makes sense when it is inspired by the spirit of adoration—'in Spirit and in truth'—when it comes truly from the heart, a grateful acknowledgment of what has been given to men through Christ and in the Church.

For this reason we hear warning voices raised even in the time of early Christianity, especially after Constantine's time when the Church's cultural advance began. In those days, the introduction of artistic singing and a special choir into the Church was met in many places with serious resistance.9 In the 12th century when the late Romanticism of the Cluniacs began to supercede the simple forms of an earlier age, St. Bernard of Clairvaux took up a bitter polemic against them, and in the 13th and in the 16th centuries, when Gothic was unfolding its richness, the Franciscan Order, and then the Capuchins in particular, raised a silent but inescapable protest in their poverty and in the poverty of their very churches.

It would seem that whenever the church building and Church worship become overloaded with a wealth of decoration, the Church has to rid itself of this superfluity, just as a tree gets rid of its withered leaves every autumn in order to begin fresh blossoming again. Thus it happened as the Middle Ages declined; as the Baroque period declined; and so it seems to be happening once more today.

In those places where Christian life is genuine and begins to burst forth in fresh young life, its forms are consciously simple. Today in Church architecture no one asks: how did people, living in the great periods of artistic achievement, design a church or an altar? They ask: What is a church? What is an altar? A great orchestra is no longer an absolute necessity in the divine service on festal occasions, and on Sundays, at least, the unison song of the assembled people is of more account than an artistic performance. This does not imply the rejection of art in Church. It means, however, that it must fit into the over-all plan of the liturgy and remain firmly rooted in a religious conception, not only in the personal religious experience of the artist but in a religious experience which has become part and parcel of the common spiritual possession of the whole congregation. It is true that genuine art must always be the self-expression of the subject: but Church art is communal art and can only be the self-expression of

9. J. Quasten, *Musik und Gesang in den Kulten der heidnischen Antike und der christlichen Frühzeit (Liturgiegesch. Quellen u. Forschungen 25)*, Münster 1930.

the Church as community, the Church as *plebs sancta*, the expression of those who know that they have been redeemed and raised to a new life through Christ.

To say this implies that before Church art can blossom Christians in their thinking must once more give the proper stress to the basic essentials—to the thoughts which centre on Easter.

When Christian art has thus assimilated the spirit of the liturgy, i.e., the spirit of Easter, and proceeds to use it as material for its creativity, then it is contributing to that communal work of art to which the rest of our people have constantly turned their eyes, and in which building and pictures, word and song, vestment and movement blend together in one mighty creation—in Christian public worship.10

5. *Pastoral Care—Key to the History of the Liturgy**

Christ the Lord taught His Church how to pray, and He gave her the sacraments, above all the Eucharist—a priceless treasure which she has carried with her down the centuries. Not only has the Church preserved and guarded this treasure: she has developed it. In the course of the centuries she has created what we call the liturgy of the Church.

The liturgy has a long history, a history almost as eventful as that of the Church herself. In recent centuries this history has become material for all sorts of studies, beginning with early attempts, in the time of the Council of Trent, to examine the folios of the Maurines down to the learned work of our own time. To begin with these studies had to be content with establishing data, with elucidating connexions and developments, with analysing the factors operating in these developments, factors which were bound up in external, cultural and political circumstances, and in man's spiritual history in general.

10. The thing with which this lecture is concerned has now been taken up by Th. Filthaut, *Die Auferstehungsbotschaft und die kirchliche Kunst der Gegenwart: Paschatis Sollemnia*, ed. by Balth. Fischer and J. Wagner, Freiburg 1959, 337-344.

But the more such labours yield fruit, the more we are able to trace the effects of the unseen powers which have been active from within. The liturgy is like a tree which had, indeed, raised itself in the changing climate of world history, knowing its seasons of storm and of blossoming, but whose growth has nevertheless been from within, from the divine powers in which it originated. The liturgy is the life of the Church as it is turned towards God, of the Church which is the community of all who are joined to Christ in Baptism, and who, led by its priesthood, assemble Sunday by Sunday to keep the memory of their Lord.

Led by its official priesthood. In all ages the priesthood has seen its most sublime function to be the carrying out of public worship at the head of their assembled people. But in the times when the form of the liturgy was in a state of flux they had another special task as well. It had to create these forms and regulate them. What attitudes of mind lay behind the creation of these forms? Where do we find the key to the mystery of these varied and often enigmatic forms of words, to this alteration of reading, hymns, and prayers, to this wealth of movement and ceremony? Why, in general, this multiplicity of forms?

The answer lies in the care of the hierarchy for the Church as the community of the faithful, for the Church as the *plebs sancta* who, led by its pastors and even during its sojourn on this earth, are to offer worthy service to God and so to become sanctified. This care was decisive in the shaping of public worship. It accounts for everything.

The first thing we find actualized in the liturgy, and which we must look for is this: the Church had to be brought together in the liturgy. The Lord's institution bore the marks of a community meal. And thus in the first generation we see the faithful holding the Breaking of Bread *per domos*—in little groups from house to house. The community grew, churches were built, then basilicas, then mighty cathedrals. But the fact was never lost sight of, that the Church through which God must be glorified did not consist of the stones which human hands had erected, no matter how good the building might be, but first and foremost in that dwelling place which God desired to build for Himself *ex vivis et electis lapidibus*. And this meant not merely His ordained servants who stood at the altar but the whole number of the faithful whom these were called to serve. We see therefore how the liturgy tried to gather this community of the faithful within an earthly space and make them visible. The people of God must be visible. In thousands upon thousands of places it is to be seen and heard. The faithful gather about their ordained officials and their common prayer rises up to God.

This can be detected even in the oldest forms of the liturgy. They did not want a liturgy wherein the bishop or the priest spoke mysterious formulae under his breath, the faithful meanwhile only requiring to be present as silent witnesses. They desired that they should say the prayers loudly, audibly, in their name and in the plural form: *we* pray, *we* offer, *we* praise and give thanks. At the beginning of the prayer, in fact, he invites them to join with him: *Gratias agamus*—let us present our sacrifice of thanksgiving; *oremus*—let us pray.

To make his invitation more pressing, first of all he greets the assembled company: *Dominus vobiscum*. And this greeting demands an answer: *Et cum spiritu tuo*. Only then does he say the prayer—the prayer of the assembled people of God: *populus tuus, Ecclesia tua, plebs tua sancta*. When the prayer is finished he expects the people to respond once more with their Amen. As St. Augustine puts it: this might be called the people's signature to the prayer: *Amen dicere subscribere est*.[1]

In the early days this Amen, especially the Amen at the end of the Eucharistic prayer, was thought most important. Justin Martyr, whose Apology contains our first account of the Church's Eucharistic celebration—a double account indeed—described the presentation of gifts and the prayer of thanksgiving very briefly, saying merely that the president offers everything up to the Father; but on both occasions he mentions the Amen, emphasizing with obvious pride—he himself was a layman—that all the people were asked to say it; and he specially explains this Hebrew word to his heathen audience. It means, 'so let it happen'.

In all Christian liturgical orders of prayer—not only in the Roman—we hear this sound of the language of the primitive Church, the speech of the first generation. Here, in the realm of

* Address at the Pastoral-Liturgical congress in Assisi, September 19, 1956.
1. *Serm.* Denis 6, 3.

worship we stand before the Church's oldest and most venerable tradition. It is not only in the Amen that we still hear the language of the apostles and of our Lord: greeting and answer, too, still reveal clearly the characteristic idiom of that time. There could be no plainer indication that the young Church liked to think of its worship as a matter for the whole community.

The infant Church spread beyond the bounds of the land of the Bible out into the world of Hellenistic culture and Greek-speaking peoples. She took her tradition with her—the tradition of which we have just been speaking. And she took along with her also the basic principle that worship should be an affair of the whole community. The liturgy kept a colour from its land of origin, it is true, but in its reading and prayer we see that the Church did not stick to Hebrew or Aramaic but assumed the linguistic dress of new peoples: it did not make use of the dialects of the separate races of Asia Minor or Illyria but the language of literature and business correspondence—Greek, which was universally understood more or less. As in Rome the Christian community stretched more and more beyond the limits of the Greek colony and the indigenous Latin population came to have a majority, so there took place in the third century yet another change of language in public worship, this time from Greek to Latin. And so the use of the Latin tongue was maintained, the tongue which since that time remained far more than a thousand years the language not only of literature but also of common speech amongst educated people in the West, and hence, naturally, the language of all ecclesiastical assemblies. For this very reason it was able to become the language of the liturgy.

Finally, a law of Constantine was put into practice and Latin became, as it were, a sacred language: then we can observe also in Rome itself, right down to the beginning of the Middle Ages, an amazing flexibility at work within liturgical forms. In a very special sense we can speak here of a liturgical pastoral care. We see, in fact, how the liturgy does not concern itself merely with the people at large but links up with the local feelings of the faithful in this or that place, in this very corner of the city. Chosen so as to harmonize with the shrine in question or its surroundings. On Sexagesima the station is at St. Paul's: this is made the occasion of reading the life-history of that apostle. Another time the station is at St. Cosmas' and St. Damian's, the much frequented pilgrimage—church: the reading alluded to the eagerness of the faithful to go on pilgrimages and in the words of the Prophet warned against saying presumptuously: *templum Domini, templum Domini.* Conversely: the celebration was once transferred to a cemetery church, St. Eusebius', because they wanted to refer to Baptism in terms of the judgement at the Resurrection of the dead.

It is true that this penetration of the liturgy, in the time of its formation, by national and local elements must have given rise to strain when these forms were handed on to other places and other peoples. For the liturgy cannot always be freshly created: it must be conserved at least in substance, and handed on. It requires not only adaptation but also, as far as possible, pious conservation and faithful tradition. For the liturgy is sacred speech; liturgy avoids restless change; liturgy in some measure shares in the rest of God, and thus mediates something of the peace of God to the faithful.

But in handing on liturgical forms, how far should adaptation from land to land, and how far should adherence to tradition be normative? How far should the particular nationality and the needs of the here and now call the tune? According to circumstances, various solutions are possible.

One element in public worship—the sermon—has always addressed itself to the particular nationality, to the needs of those who are here and now assembled in this place, and the Church has fought to keep this right, even when minorities and small groups are concerned. And when, frustrated by difficult circumstances, preaching and catechizing have not been able to thrive, as was the case for centuries amongst many Oriental people, then the Church, if it has not completely adopted the vernacular, has used it for those parts of public worship at least which touch the people most nearly. For the readings and for the litanies at least, which the deacon had to say along with the people she has adopted the new languages—especially Arabic.

There are other times, as today, when at least for the administration of the sacraments, for the Offices of the *Rituale*, the vernacular speech is allowed. The rites at weddings, the prayers at burials are so to be performed that those taking part understand the meaning of the hour in terms of the great truths and are able to raise their hearts to God in common prayer. For Sunday worship, too, at least in so far as it is carried out in the basis of the *Missa lecta*, a wider field is left open for common prayer and singing in connexion with the forms of the liturgy.

At all times it is the desire of the liturgy to bring the faithful together so that, as the Church, as the people of God, they can appear before God. But the liturgy would take them further, it would lead the faithful to full consciousness of their Christianity.

In the course of the history of the liturgy an abundance of forms have been created, above all, forms of prayer of which only a small selection is current amongst us today. The Church has never been content merely to take up the sacramental actions with which she was commissioned by her founder. She has not been content merely to pour water upon the head of the candidate for Baptism —as early as the 3rd century she blessed the water with solemn prayer and led the candidate step by step towards the sacrament of re-birth. She has never been content to pass on priestly power with a mere imposition of hands—at an early date she surrounded the proceedings with meaningful ceremonies and prayers. Nor is she content to pronounce the sacred words over bread and wine— a reverent gradation leads up to this climax of the sacramental action.

What is the meaning of this prodigal wealth of forms, especially of forms of words? Why this definite structure of prayer, this expression of the concepts of faith in the course of the festal year? In the encyclical *Mediator Dei*, Pius XII, set the well-known saying: *Lex orandi est lex credendi* over against its converse: *Lex crendedi est lex orandi*. There can be no doubt that the Church has always been at pains to express her knowledge of faith in association with the sacred actions through prayer—directed in all simplicity to God, but also in the hearing of the faithful people. The spiritual world in which we stand as the redeemed people is to be brought alive every time the Church is assembled. In this way the faithful are to be led to a conscious Christianity and preserved in it. And as the mosaics in the apses of the Roman basilicas lighted up the heavenly Jerusalem to which we are invited before the eyes of all who entered, and revealed the enthroned

Christ who is our hope, and the rivers of paradise, so should the words of prayer and reading bring the awareness of the great truths of faith fresh into our minds.

Rightly it has been said that the oldest formulations of the Canon of the Mass, of the Eucharistic prayer, are related in the closest possible way to the creeds. The Preface, indeed, was often called by a name which would have suited a creed just as well. Thus when it is called, on occasion, *praedicatio* or quite simply a profession—*exhomologesis*. In this profession of faith through prayer we find over and over again, especially in the oldest formulae, that those concepts of faith are stressed which were fundamental for the Christian. Liturgical prayer was at the same time a catechism of Christian doctrine; not a catechism, it is true, of separate details of doctrine with fine distinctions and numerous headings, but a catechism nonetheless which impressively declared the decisive concepts of faith, those beliefs above all which make the Christian glad.

From the start, the Canon of the Mass had been conceived as a prayer of thanksgiving. The people were summoned to join in it with the words: *Gratias agamus!* What has happened is that God 'hath delivered us from the powers of darkness and hath translated us into the Kingdom of the Son of his love' (Col. I, 13), and so what else can we do but thank God, *semper et ubique gratias agere*, because God's action to us is the result of unmerited, overflowing grace? It is very significant that this knowledge increasingly becomes the basic mood of the believing Christian: Christianity is not a torment and a burdensome duty, it is supreme grace. And the liturgy leads us into a fully conscious Christianity.

In the prayer-language of the oldest Christian liturgies and in that of the contemporary Roman liturgy we find the notable characteristic that almost every prayer, every collect, every Preface and, in particular, the ending to the Eucharistic prayer is so constructed that the ascent to God is accomplished *per Christum Dominum nostrum, per Dominum nostrum Jesum Christum, per ipsum et cum ipso*. And this, too, is a tradition going back to the earliest liturgical period. Hearing these words over and over again and always adding our own Amen to them we can only approach God with confidence because Christ has gone before us, as our

Head and our Lord, the Risen One who has passed through death and won life for us. The recurrence of this phrase alone must have made plain to the faithful that Christianity is not some collection or other of doctrines and commandments, but is the good news of Christ who desires to lead us home to the Father, that in its essence it is a joining with Christ and is life with Him. But from the beginning this declaration about the One in whom we can find redemption was explained and expanded. It was expounded in the readings. And even in primitive Christian times the last reading was always the one in which Christ Himself appeared as speaker and actor—the Gospel. And so, to this day, when this lesson is announced, the cry resounds with which we greet the Lord as though present: *Gloria tibi Domini*. These readings were designed for the people to hear. They were read from the Ambo, the reader facing the people, and, more often than not, they were preceded by a special call to attention: Πρόσχωμεν—take heed! Again, the declaration was further expanded and explained in the sequence of feast days which the Church observed from earliest times. The great feasts which we keep in the course of the Christian year are all, so to speak, feasts of our Lord, the feast of His Nativity and of His Easter triumph, of His Ascension and the descent of His Holy Spirit; and then there are feasts of His mother, His apostles, and His evangelists. Finally there is His weekly commemoration day—Sunday, *Dominica:* the day of the *Dominus noster*, or, as the Greek has it: Κυριακὴ the day of our Κύριος because it is the day on which He completed the work of Redemption through His Easter victory.

If in this way the figure of our Lord appeared before the mind's eye of the faithful week by week and year by year, it must have been borne in upon them what it meant to be a Christian. As long as the faithful understood this language and were impressed by it they could not go astray, even if in other ways their knowledge of the content of faith was modest, even if they were not familar with the finer distinctions of theology. We can understand, therefore, how for centuries a Christian pastoral care was possible which followed no systematic catechism, in which sermons were few and then given only by the bishop, in which varied instruction through the printed word played no part, and which yet allowed a flourishing Christianity to live—because the great truths of

Christianity were kept alive in and through the liturgy.

If thus the Church never tired of placing the figure and work of our Lord before the eyes of the faithful in a lively fashion, then she was fundamentally doing only what the Lord Himself had commissioned her to do in His last hours when He said: 'Do this in memory of me'. In these words the primary commission was to carry out the sacramental mystery; but they also continued the admonition to His Church to do it in such a way that His faithful could never forget what He meant to them, viz., that He is for them the Way, the Truth, and the Life. Liturgy: a guide to conscious Christianity.

Still we must ask: Why all this liturgical wealth of forms? Why has the Church not been content to keep the memory of the Lord alive in the minds of the faithful simply in a didatic fashion through readings and sermons, or in poetic expression through hymns and songs? Why the multifarious forms of prayer and why the predominance of prayer and of praying aloud, when prayer is an affair of the heart, of the secret devotion of the soul? Or why has not the Mass at least, this holiest of all mysteries, been designed from the beginning as a silent celebration, as a series of prayers which the priest has to say and the people follow from a distance in holy awe? Eight centuries had to pass, after all, before the central core of the Mass, the Canon, was hidden away in such a manner, and, then because of the special conditions prevailing in the Frankish Church at that time. The answer must plainly be: the liturgy was designed to be a guide of the faithful—ultimately a guide to Christian prayer and sacrifice.

Everywhere faith appears, there also is prayer—prayer as the spontaneous response of the creature to the Creator. But the prayer of the individual is always in danger of confining itself within the restricted horizon of his own interests and to rest content with petition. For this reason the Church has always placed praise and thanksgiving and adoration in the foreground of her liturgy. She has always kept in mind what the Lord said to the woman at the well of Sychar: God seeks worshippers, and those who worship Him must worship Him in Spirit and in truth. Where else shall He find them if not in His holy Church? Just as the Lord's Prayer begins with the *Sanctificetur*, so the prayer of the Church's public worship reaches its climax in the threefold Sanctus, in the Sanctus which emerges from the great prayer of thanksgiving. The Sanctus is the oldest song in the liturgy of the Mass, and it is a song which the faithful all sang together for nearly a thousand years. It was taken for granted that they sang it *una voce*, joining with the angels in heaven to give homage to God. What exultation the faithful must have felt, knowing in what company they were raising their voices.

The Sanctus was not the only song in early times. At the end of the readings especially, and chiefly the readings at Mass, the song of the people had its place. The psalmist—frequently a young lector with a clear voice—had to sing the psalm but after every verse the people sang a refrain, an Alleluja or cry of joy, or the verse of the psalm which had been given out at the beginning. St. Augustine reveals his quality as a true pastor of souls, as a master of liturgical pastoral care when, in his *Enarrationes in psalmos*, he very obviously picks out those verses which all had just sung together. "We have heard the psalm" he says, "and we have mutually cheered one another up by singing the response with one heart and voice: 'Come let us adore.'[2]" Such a verse was bound to make a lasting impression on the hearts of the faithful: it became a priceless treasure of prayer and a holy joy.

The liturgy was designed to be a guide of the faithful to Christian prayer. Petition forms part of Christian prayer. On various occasions petition even takes up great space within the liturgy; so much so that certain days have been named *Rogationes, Litania*. Within the regular Sunday Mass, too, for centuries after Justin Martyr's time it was the custom, and it still is the custom in the East today, to follow up the readings with prayer—prayer for the general needs of Christendom, for all sorts of conditions of men, and for the faithful themselves. This is a prayer, in fact, which normally was said responsorially and was summed up by the priest in a collect.

In other cases—and from of old this was a custom chiefly in the Roman liturgy—people were only called to prayer and there followed a short silence for private prayer. To emphasize the fervour of this they were asked to kneel: *Flectamus genua*. In the

2. *Serm.* 176, 1.

silence of his own heart each was supposed to dwell on the words of the lesson he had just read or to commend the particular concerns to God which touched him personally or which had been mentioned in the invitation to prayer. They were to rise up again only when the signal was given: *Levate*, and the priest began his summing-up prayer. This form of prayer has been given back to us once again by the Holy Father through the reform of the Easter liturgy: a guide to Christian prayer.

A guide to Christian prayer. No matter how much the liturgy acknowledges veneration of saints—and the oldest sacramentaries of the Roman liturgy display a great number of feast of martyrs— it never permits prayer to become dissipated, never permits us to make God and His servants interchangeable, never permits us to talk as though our heavenly helpers could help us by their own power, or to lose sight of Him who, as St. Paul says, is the only mediator between God and man. Liturgical prayer does know the *Ora pro nobis*, knows, in hymns especially, many bold expressions in praise of the might of the saints, but ever and again the cry flows back into the main stream: we bow down before the majesty of God and ask to be heard *intercedentibus Sanctis tuis per Dominum nostrum Jesum Christum*. It is instructive to note that here for many centuries the rule was observed of facing east during such prayers, towards the rising sun—even today, most of our churches are orientated—for in the rising sun men see a figure of Him who is the Light of the world, and our advocate with the Father. Even bodily posture was made to show who it was through whom we hoped to be heard—a guide to Christian prayer. Without doing any violence to the freedom with which the faithful prayed in his own heart, he was bound to be made aware, simply by hearing such prayer of the Church—to which he assented with his Amen— of the relation in which we stand to God: the Christian view of the universe must repeatedly have come to his mind and he must have learned the right attitude which it is fitting for Christian prayer to adopt.

A guide to Christian prayer. The supreme thing in which the Church has to instruct her faithful was and is the sacrifice of the new Covenant. It is a tremendous thing that since the Church's very first origins, wherever there have been Catholic Christians,

Sunday after Sunday thousands and millions have congregated in churches in order to be present at the holy sacrifice. At all times there may have been many amongst them who wanted to fulfil their duty merely by being present, and pastoral care may, at times, have sought to encourage little more than that the faithful remained there in holy reverence until the sacred action was over. But if we go to the liturgy of the Church, observing it in those places where its forms were still infused with some traces of life, we find that the Church's liturgy aims much higher. It desires the faithful, as *circumstantes*, to gather around the altar, if not geometrically, at least in spirit. It would have them bring bread or wine or some sort of gift to the altar. The faithful are to respond to the priests invitation and in the prayer spoken by the priest it is they who are named as the people who present the sacrifice: *nos servi tui sed et plebs tua sancta*, and they are required to answer this prayer of sacrifice, too, with their Amen.

Wherever the faithful have entered into what the liturgy disclosed to them they have become aware that they were called upon to be no mere witnesses of that which Christ through this priest was performing in mysterious prayers and ceremonies at the altar, that here it was not only Christ's sacrifice as High Priest which was offered but the sacrifice which Christ desires to offer at the head of His priestly people and into which He desires to involve all of His faithful with their labours and sorrows, their struggles and suffering—the sacrifice which presents the world to the heavenly Father, until the day breaks when God is all in all (I. Cor. 15, 28).

The faithful who follow the Church's lead in this way cannot fail to be filled with holy pride, with the joyful knowledge that they have already entered the kingdom of God. Such knowledge is bound to strengthen their faith much more than a multitude of intellectual instructions because it is holy joy—a foretaste of our heavenly inheritance.

The crucial test of pastoral care is certainly its success in saving souls, in leading men into the right path and so to reach their goal, at least in the hour of death. But a greater thing and more worthy of the Christian calling, the true task of the Church, indeed, is to lead the Christian people so that, while still on earth, it can assemble in holy joy to give glory to God—as St. Peter described the Christian calling—to 'declare his virtues who hath called you out of darkness into his marvellous light' (I. Pet. 2, 9). In every age this is the very thing which the liturgy has sought to do.

For centuries, the liturgy, actively celebrated, has been the most important form of pastoral care. This was especially true of those centuries in which the liturgy was being created. Unfavourable conditions brought it about that in the late Middle Ages, in spite of the liturgy being celebrated and developed in numerous churches with great fervour and magnificence by collegiate clergy and monastic communities, a veil became drawn between the liturgy and the people, a veil through which the faithful could only dimly see what was happening at the altar. Even in all this we can still see how pastoral concern led to development and adaptation of the liturgy. In that time when the language of the liturgy had become strange to the people the want was made good by the introduction of dramatic elements. All through the Middle Ages the only form of the Mass for the people on Sundays was the solemn form with singing, and, if possible, the *ministri sacri*. In this way the senses received a strong and many-sided stimulus. The solemnity was intensified even more. Candles and incense were no longer carried only on entering the church: the altar was once more incensed—and then a second time—with definite movements—and the incensing was extended to choir and people. The candles were raised up on to the altar. The Gospel procession was built up into a triumphal march of Christ. The Sanctus-candle announced the approaching mystery. Finally, in the elevation of both species at the Consecration, a visible climax was provided.

Nevertheless, the veil was still there. The greatest of all vehicles of the soul's ascent to God, the words of the liturgy became inaccessible to the people. The prayers and chants through which the sacred action worked itself out became but sounds which touched only the outward ear. The liturgy became a mere sequence of mysterious words and ceremonies which had to be performed in accordance with set rules, while the people followed in holy awe. In the end the liturgy itself became rigid. This rigidity may possibly have been necessary as a protection against the attacks which heresy was levelling against the sacrifice of the

Church, necessary, too, in order to preserve the sacred inheritance for later generations living in times of greater distress and more pressing decisions such as we are passing through today, times when once more the faithful will be specially in need of that guidance of the liturgy which the Christians of early centuries enjoyed.

Today the numbness is beginning to thaw out. Forms which seemed to have ossified are coming to life again. The Church feels that she no longer requires the protection of rigidity. And as the Church under Pius XI through the Lateran treaties gave up that outward protection which the crude Middle Ages had thought necessary in the form of secular power, so under Pius XII she began to shake off that protective armour which hitherto had enclosed the hallowed forms of the liturgy. As of old, pastoral concern begins to utter the decisive word, that care for the flock from which the forms of the liturgy emerged in the early days of the Church.

How the faithful in many places have been amazed in our time at the way in which they have been able to follow with understanding the mighty action of the liturgy in Holy Week and Easter night! Once again we realize that this is *our* service.

The mist begins to disperse: a brighter day dawns. The Church assembles with fresh vigour. Bravely she faces the future—the people of God at prayer.

6. *Pastoral Care and Parish Worship*

There can be no doubt whatever that the liturgy, especially Sunday worship, represents an important point in the circle of parish activities. We might be justified in asking however, what more precisely the place of the liturgy is in parochial life. Is it but one activity amongst others, is it a solitary peak above everything else, or is it perhaps destined to form the unifying centre of all parochial work? Parochial work today is many-sided. Different

age-groups, different classes, the sick, the poor, all require particular attention; those in remote places must not be forgotten, and
further away still the missions call to us. Public worship on
Sunday appears thus as a small item on an overloaded agenda.

Such a notion is not only true to fact but would seem to be
theologically unobjectionable. But if we ask about the task of
Church, the catechism is ready with the answer: she was instituted
to lead men to everlasting bliss. Ecclesiastical, priestly, pastoral
work must be motivated solely by the desire to lead men to this
other—worldly goal—by all the available means. This happens
when children are baptized and young people are guided along
the right path, when the wavering are strengthened and the erring
are retrieved, when grace of the sacraments is dispensed to all, in
short, when God's law is proclaimed and followed by the faithful;
and one of these laws which must be obeyed is the command to
take part in public worship on Sundays and holidays of obligation.

The pastor who is guided by such a mode of thought wears
himself out caring for his sheep. He has to be all things to all men
and the need to save souls often drags him to the limits of what is
possible. He sows the Word of God diligently, he is tireless in the
confessional, at the side of the sick, and the greatest joy of his
priestly heart is when the numbers at Communion go on increasing. We might think that no nobler or more perfect conception was possible of the performance of the priestly task.

And yet we must raise an objection. In all this attention is
directed almost exclusively upon individuals. The parish, the congregation, is but an external framework—little more than a
geographical demarcation—within which such pastoral care is
carried on, just as the parish hall and the kindergarten are the
framework for others of the pastor's tasks. Pastoral work carried
out in this fashion never brings the faithful together in the here
and now as a community. Each individual makes his own way
through the manifold darkness of earthly life until he comes to the
point where time turns into eternity. Perhaps it is only then,
beyond the frontier of time, that the elect will find themselves
united in the eternal praise of God. So this conception would
suggest.

It is not unfair to look back and say that in those centuries when the sense of the Church was universally weak, it was the type of pastoral care which at least helped to encourage this weakness. These were the centuries when the prime aim of the spiritual life and of pastoral work was to ensure a good death. The faithful prepared for the hour of death, and this seemed to be the sum total of pastoral concern. The thought of death was never supposed to be absent throughout life, and the faithful were kept from sin by the thought that they might suffer sudden, unprovided death. For long a favourite subject in art had been the Dance of Death, the figure of the Reaper who tore away the King from his throne, the peasant from his plough, the child from its mother's breast and the bride from the bridegroom's arms. In the same period one of the favourite forms of spiritual literature had been the 'Ars moriendi'?[1] And amongst the many confraternities which flourished since the end of the Middle Ages, that which has kept in the front rank for centuries is the Confraternity of the Good Death.

It would be foolish to deny that endless good has been achieved in this way. In the circumstances perhaps nothing better could have been devised. It would be equally foolish to suggest that the *memento mori* is superfluous in any age. But at the same time, such over-emphasis on these thoughts can lead to the overlooking of an important aspect of pastoral care, an aspect which is only caught sight of when awareness is re-aroused that, in the work of Redemption, the Church is the primary thing—and then the individual. First comes the visible society of the redeemed upon earth —then, within her, the individual Christian, reborn out of the womb of Mother Church and from that time onwards a member of the family of God, a freeman of the sanctuary set as a living stone into the spiritual building, into the priestly people of God who are called 'to offer up spiritual sacrifices, acceptable to God by Jesus Christ' (I. Pet, 2, 5).

Christ the Lord intended His Church to be a social structure even in this world. A whole series of parables show that this is so. Even though the kingdom of God can only be completed at the end of time, yet it must be inaugurated in this temporal world. It is here that the true vine must spread its branches and let the sap

1. Cf. R. Rudolf, *Ars moriendi* (*Forschungen zur Volkskunde* 39), Cologne 1957.

flow through them; here that the grain of mustard seed must grow into a tree; here that the yeast must leaven the lump. And here, too, God must be adored by His true worshippers who worship Him in Spirit and in truth. This adoration is not to be offered only by individuals praying to their heavenly Father in the privacy of their own rooms, but at the common table established for this very purpose. Round this table the family of God are meant to gather and to continue for all time that thanksgiving which the Lord Himself began at the Last Supper.

For all time the Eucharist is the special gathering-place for the people of God. It is here that the Church as Church becomes visible. In the prayers of the Mass we speak of 'Thy people', 'Thy holy people', 'Thy family', 'Thy Church', and such phrases do not merely denote some sort of ideal image of the Church hovering above earthly reality. First and foremost they denote the congregation of the faithful who are assembled here and now, enfolded, it is true, within the whole Church which, under its lawful pastors, is spread throughout the whole world. Communion is the closest bond which binds this congregation together: in this all approach the same table and eat the same Bread which is the Body of the Lord.

Nicolas Afanasiev, a Russian theologian of the dissident Eastern Church recently emphasized the way in which the Eucharist moulds the Church to such an extent that he simply identified Eucharist and Church: 'Where the Eucharist is there is the Church, and *vice versa*'. He arrived at the extreme position: the Church was fully formed only at the first celebration of the Eucharist after Pentecost, and it is a decline from the primitive ideal, a perversion of the concept of the Church, if the group of people gathered under one bishop no longer coincides with the group gathered around the one celebration of the Eucharist.[1a] This would overlook the fact that as well as the Sacrament of the Eucharist there is also the hierarchial authority to govern which is a force in the formation of the Church. Of its nature the latter must extend beyond the limits of an area served by a simple Eucharistic centre which since the beginning has been adapted to a more or less expanded table-fellowship. A piece of bread, a cup

1a. Cf. B. Schultze, *Eucharistie und Kirche in der russischen Theologie der Gegenwart:* Zk Th 77 (1955) 257-300.

of wine, the praying voices of those who can hear and answer one another, sharing the holy food from a single table: these are the factors in the institution which give it what Karl Rahner has called 'neighbourhood'. This neighbourhood is of the essence of the Eucharist, and it results in an intense but specially limited actualization of the Church.2 Thus the parish, the assembled neighbourhood-congregation under their pastor, is the ideal framework in which the Eucharist can be celebrated and the Church made real.

Conversely, the Sunday liturgical celebration is the climax which gathers up all the life of the parish and which in the end is what makes sense of it all. This idea has come alive once more in our own time—a happy sign of true religous revival. In no less important a document than the new German Catechism we read: 'Public worship is the Church's most sacred task . . . the faithful are to co-operate in celebrating public worship by joining in the prayer and in the sacrifice; through Baptism they have been called to this task and equipped for it.'3

To say this is only to say what St. Thomas wrote about from another angle in the Summa Theologica4: The power conferred through the Sacrament of Order is directed either to the consecration of the Eucharist itself (as in the ordination of priests) or to a ministry which is related to the Sacrament of the Eucharist (as in the grades of orders which lead up to the priesthood).

The Christian people who are committed to the care of their pastor join with him on Sundays and feast-days to celebrate worthily and with joyful hearts the sacrifice of the new Covenant. In this all its activity, all its labours and struggles, are led back in Christ to their ultimate source, and the creation comes home to its Creator; and this is the final blossoming and the greatest glory of all pastoral efforts. Care for the dying does not become superfluous thereby; but it becomes obvious that our life on earth should not be a chancy game which wavers all the time between sin and grace, wherein the individual oscillates between good and bad, between love of God and hatred of God, always hoping to be caught up at the last moment by the love of God. The true

2. K. Rahner, Zur Theologie der Pfarre: Die Pfarre, ed. by Hugo Rahner, Freiburg im Br, 1956, 27-39.
3. 53. Section.
4. Summa Theol. III q. 37 a. 2.

picture is rather that we are called as children of holy Church to walk in the light, and, as a priestly people, to bring acceptable sacrifices to God through Christ—as St. Peter says—sacrifices which are not provided solely by the Eucharist, it is true, but which find their complete expression therein.

It is of great significance for the programme of pastoral care that St. Thomas, in the passage quoted, expresses the meaning of all future pastoral care, to which the grades of orders lead up, by saying that it ought to prepare the Christian people for the celebration of the Eucharist. That is a bold statement, but it holds good even for the most highly organized pastoral scheme in a modern city parish. The statement does not mean the sort of thing that for a century past it has been so often thought to mean: that, for example, the chaplain of the youth group must play football and arrange excursions to encourage them all to make a general Communion. It means rather that all catechesis and all preaching, all child-welfare and youth work, all charity and all care of particular classes and conditions of people, all work for Catholic education and all religious journalism, can only be seen as a preparation which will lead the faithful to that outlook on life, that disposition of faith, hope and love, that attitude of thankfulness to the revealing and redeeming God, which breaks forth on Sunday like a mighty stream in the corporate celebration of the Eucharist, and presents to God 'all honour and glory'.

The dispensing of the Sacrament itself, this in particular, must fit into this plan. The Eucharist is not only the Blessed Sacrament which surpasses all others by its holiness: it is also the end and consummation of all sacramental life. If we usually place it third in the series of sacraments this is because reception of the sacrament—Communion—is the dominant thought, and in ancient Christian practice this was at first the conclusion of initiation which went through the stages of Baptism then Confirmation. As late as the high Middle Ages not only were adults but infants too given Communion immediately after Baptism. But Baptism and Confirmation serve as the first introduction to the 'initiation' into Christian life which is consummated in the celebration of the Eucharist, the rest of the sacraments, too, serve to edify the people of God, that is, they make more secure those foundations which were laid in Baptism and Confirmation. The Sacrament of Penance, expanded at life's end to become Extreme Unction repairs the broken structure, cleanses us from sin, reincorporates once more into that *plebs sancta* which is called to present the Sacrifice. The Sacrament of Holy Order transmits the power necessary for ruling and guiding the Church and for celebrating the Eucharist. The Sacrament of Matrimony sanctifies the soil from which the Church must raise up new members to adore the divine Majesty.

In the actual Christian community, whose normal expression is the parish, the liturgy does not form one group of activities amongst others, even if the most sacred of all. In the form of Sunday and feast-day worship it is much more the goal and, in this world, the ultimate raison d'etre of all pastoral work. It is a prelude to and the soft beginnings of that worship of the heavenly hosts in which, from afar and with longing, we pilgrims are called upon to share whenever, as the climax of the Eucharist approaches we join with 'angels and archangels, with principalities and powers' in the sublime hymn of the threefold Sanctus.

7. A 'Feast of the Church'

The Church performs its task of proclaiming the faith in many ways, not least through the celebration of her feast-days. We might go so far as to say that in those places where the faith is deeply rooted the first and basic way in which she proclaims it is through her feast-days. It is the method which alone remains in troubled times, and when properly observed can suffice in time of necessity. For centuries oriental Christian communities enjoyed neither catechisms nor sermons, but the faith was maintained through the celebration of the liturgy at Church festivals. In the West there were times when the same thing happened.

It is all the more important, therefore, that we have the right notion of what a Christian feast-day is, and that it should be realized without travesty. Today it is threatened on all sides. There

388   PASTORAL LITURGY

is the competition with secular festivals and the temptation to confuse these with Christian festivals. How to use the festival gatherings
or, for example, holidays of obligation, is a pastoral-practical
question, a question affecting mission, diaspora, charity. And not
least there is the analysis of the idea of the Christian feast-day itself
which seems to become enriched through constant expansion into
ever new forms, but which in fact is becoming impoverished.

What exactly is a feast-day? Just as one can say that an altar is a
piece of earth raised a little towards heaven, so one can say of a
feast-day that it is a piece of time which touches eternity.

On a feast-day, time stands still for a moment, restlessness and
the stir of business fall back, people 'take their time'. A feast which
is hurried is no longer a feast. A feast implies an exaltation of
human existence. Festive clothes and games, above all music and
song, characterize a feast-day. On a feast-day the important things
in life come to the fore, the deeper levels of life, the ultimate
values or what are taken to be the ultimate values. On a feast-day
people give themselves up to these things, seek to become aware of
them in a higher degree.¹ In the process the values which go to
make up the structure of their society are revealed. Conversely, a
society is always an assembly around values, an assembly which
culminates in festival.

In the concept of the feast-day, therefore, we must distinguish
the primitive form of the feast from the recurrent feast which has
become an institution. The primitive form of the feast arises
where a significant event is its object. Someone has reached a high
point of his life—a festive group gather around him. Thus we
celebrate a wedding or a priest's first Mass or the return home of
one thought to be dead. In this way the return of the Prodigal
Son gave rise to a feast. The close of life, too, a funeral can take on
a more or less festive character; for here a life is surveyed on the
border between time and eternity. Another occasion for a feast in
its original sense is the start or the finish of a great undertaking.
Thus the laying of the foundation of a public building or the
opening of a bridge or railway or a school becomes a feast-
day. The dedication of a church becomes a feast-day for the

1. Cf. the definition of the feast by K. Kerenyi, *Die antike Religion*, Amsterdam 1952,
66: the feast is characterized by 'Rest, intensity of life and contemplation blended together'. Cf. J. Pieper, *Leisure the Basis of Culture*, Faber, London, 1952.

congregation concerned. It may be that someone takes up office
as head of the community: a coronation becomes a festival. The
consecration or enthronement of a bishop is the same sort of
thing. Or, to return to secular things at a lower level altogether, in
a village the ingathering of the harvest or the home-coming
from the mountain pastures is an occasion for a rural feast.

The rank of a feast is decided by its level in the scale of values
and by the size of the community by which it is observed. Every
feast of any importance is forced to take account of ultimate
values and so becomes a cult.[2]

As a deviation from this primitive type we find the type of
feast which has grown into an institution and which now becomes
observed at regular intervals according to the calendar without
further occasion. A constant, ever-present value is forcing its way
into consciousness from time to time. This may be a value in the
natural order like the fertility of the earth, celebrated in the yearly
cycle of seasons, in spring and the solstice. In the primitive cultures
of people tied to nature this lead to the seasonal festive customs
in which a strong dash of magic is infused. By festive ritual
practices, such peoples tried to force nature to be kind and to ward
off calamities. The harvest festival, in as much as it is a recurring
festival, belongs here: primitive type and institution meet in it.
To the periodic nature festivals have always belonged those
at the end and the beginning of the year—the New Year which
we mark by our mutual well-wishing. Even that perfectly rational
idea—Mother's Day belongs to this group.

But cultural values, too, can become material for periodically
repeated festivity. State festivals are of this sort. Finally, every
society celebrates periodically its feast of institution so that it will
keep in mind the foundation upon which it rests. In such cases,
however, it must concern a value of some importance if there is
to be a genuine feast-day. The feasts of the Christian year fall into
this category but they are of quite a special kind. Let us begin
with their outward appearance.

To begin with we have the weekly feast-day—Sunday.[3] At an

2. J. Pieper, *Leisure the Basis of Culture* 71: 'There is no such thing as a feast "without
Gods"—whether it be a carnival or a marriage.'
3. The apostolic origin of Sunday appears from Acts 20, 7; I Cor. 16, 2; Acts 1, 10.—
Cf. the fact that the celebration of the Sunday is older than that of Easter, C. Callewaert,
Sacris erudiri, Steenbrugge 1940, 300 seq.

early date—in apostolic times—this was associated with the yearly feast of Easter. Easter, for centuries the only yearly Christian feast (setting aside the early developments in Asia Minor), is but a special Sunday, strongly stressed once in the course of the year and given an increased value. And it is from Sunday and from Easter that we must learn how to think about a Christian feast. This is not to say that later development could not also provide valid concepts.

From the beginning Sunday was the day upon which the Church fulfilled the Lord's command: 'Do this for a memorial of me.' In a mystical meal when the Body and Blood of the Lord are separated, His death is presented before our eyes. In the chalice is the Blood of the new Covenant by which God has graciously drawn men to Himself. But the celebration takes place on Sunday, the day of the week upon which our Lord conquered death and completed His work.[4] The subject here is the work of the world's redemption which is to be kept alive in the mind of the faithful and to become operative afresh in them as the source of new life, the main-spring of their unceasing praise of God.

It is precisely this consonance of the first, original feast-day of Christianity—Sunday—with the basic meaning of the Eucharist which helps us to understand what a Christian feast-day is. The Eucharist is celebrated in order to declare the Lord's death or, as the oldest Mass ritual we know—that of Hyppolitas of Rome—has it: *Memores igitur mortis et resurrectionis eius.* But Sunday is quite plainly the setting for this memorial celebration. Sunday is nothing other than the memorial day of the Lord, the 'Lord's day' (Κυριακή *dominica*), or, as it was called later on in the Greek-speaking world: ἀναστάσιμος ἡμέρα the day of His Resurrection, a name which persists to this day in the normal Russian term for Sunday: *wosskressenige.*

Right from the start Easter has been simply an accentuated Sunday, a Sunday preceded by a fast, which exceeds the usual weekly Friday fast but is not any more precisely regulated, and by a full vigil. The festive 50 days of Pentecost which follow this full

4. This original meaning of Sunday has now been brought out emphatically by J. Gaillard, Art. *Dimanche: Dictionaire de spiritualité* III (1955) 948-982, esp. 967 seq. Cf. also J. A. Jungmann, *Die sonntägliche Messfeier und ihre Bedeutung für das kirchliche und religiöse Leben geschichtlich gesehen: Eucharistiefeier am Sonntag. Reden und Verhandlungen des I. Deutschen Liturgischen Kongresses,* Trier 1951, 81-96.

vigil is 'something like an extended and specially solemn Lord's Day'.5 As on Sunday, the subject of the solemnity is the work of the Redemption: 'The ancient Christian Easter celebration as a whole is the feast of our Redemption through the death and Resurrection of the Lord.'6 To speak in greater detail: the Pasch, which suggests the idea of the fulfilment of the Old Testament pre-figuring, was thought of in early times as predominantly a commemoration of our Lord's death; but the death was seen as the pathway through to the Resurrection,7 and, as a result, the thought of the Resurrection received the chief emphasis, though it contained the remembrance of the Passion struggle which went before it. The essence of the Christian feast day lies quite clearly, therefore, in its memorial character, in the *Anamnesis*. On its feast-day the people of God are supposed to look back to the foundations of their existence. That which is for ever with us— the fact that we have been redeemed from the fate of the God-estranged world and raised up into, 'the kingdom of the Son of his love' (Col. 1, 13)—is meant to be kept always in the forefront of the minds of the faithful so that it will burst into a fervour of thanksgiving and adoration in pious hymns and festive pageantry, in celebrations which are already shot through with the light of their final consummation. And because this thought is more than a human reverie, because it is εὐχαριστία and sacrament it represents first and foremost, whenever it takes place, an act of God. The work of Redemption itself is made present and effective afresh: *opus redemptionis exerceter;* it becomes effective as we try to comprehend in terms of the deep concept of the mystery.8

The Redemption is the motif of Sunday and of Easter. This motif has persisted, unabridged since the 4th century when Easter appeared as a triduum, each day of which had its own separate sub-motif. In the *triduum crucifixi, sepultu, suscitati* (Augustine) it is the work of Redemption which is the more clearly being celebrated.

5. O. Casel, *Art und Sinn der ältesten christlichen Osterfeier*: JL 14 (1938, 1-78) 17. In connection with sayings of Tertullian.
6. Ibid. 46.
7. Ibid. 19.
8. Thus the definition of a feast which Sigisbert Kraft gives in *Was ist ein christliches Fest?: Katech. Blätter* 81 (1956, 3-7) 6, is acceptable: 'A Christian feast is the glad commemoration of a redemptive act of God, through which we renew our gracious participation in that act.'

Anyway, with this the dividing up of the total theme into parts begins. The Ascension and Pentecost Sunday emerge as feast-days in their own right. But these are only partial aspects of the single great action of God which formerly was viewed only in its totality and which continued to be celebrated as present in the Eucharist in its full substance.

The same thing is true of the evolution of the Christian year. In this we are shown ever and again new partial aspects: now it is the entry of the Redeemer into the world, the rising of the new Sun at Christmas, the ἐπιράνια before all nations. In still greater detail it is His birth of the Virgin; then in the Marian feasts it becomes the life of the Blessed Virgin herself in which once again the life of her divine Son is mirrored. But all of these feasts have an Easter component.[9] The endings of the prayers are enough to show that the liturgy, even at Christmas or on Good Friday, never loses sight of Him who has risen from the dead and rules at the Father's right hand—King of His people. In the Marian feasts too, the mind is led from the mother to her Son who is the world's Redemption. For instance, on the feast of Mary's nativity the song of praise runs: *quia ex te ortus est sol justitiae Christus Deus noster.* In this way, the thought that the Redemption is the core of a Christian feast may have been more distinctly acknowledged in earlier days, because until well into the Middle Ages people regarded the Mass primarily as a commemorative celebration, as *memoria passionis* (cf. also the allegorical interpretation of the Mass), and, only arising from this, as a sacrifice as well.

This basic substance of a Christian feast was kept vigorously in mind in early Christian times, even in those feasts which had apparently become quite independent of this motif viz. in feasts of saints. The saints' feast-days—we know—began as days when the martyrs were commemorated. First of all the burial of the martyr took place, and this fixed in a manner, the primitive form of the feast-day. It had of necessity to take place within a small circle of people, and in a very modest fashion. Then, as with other deceased persons a yearly commemoration took place at the grave, but on these occasions the ceremony increased and the number of

9. The *Capitular eccl. ord.* of the 8th century (=OR XV Andrieu) expresses the idea of Sunday and feast day by the phrase *dominici vel paschales dies*; Andrieu, *Les Ordines Romani* III, 97.

participants increased. Soon, it is not merely a group of mourners, who gather to celebrate, but the local congregation. And, because it is the Church which celebrates, and, it may well be, by the public offering of the Eucharistic sacrifice which implies the commemoration of the work of Redemption, the connexion with the basic motif will be consciously expressed. Many of the numerous traditional Prefaces in the Leonine Sacramentary draw some sort of parallel between the fate of the martyr and the work of our Redeemer.10 And it is significant how the feast of all the holy martyrs, which occurs in several liturgies, is related in a striking way to the Easter feast.11 Where the custom of such commemorative festivity is extended beyond the circle of martyrs to include the confessors, the term itself provides the justification for holding these people in equal regard with *martyrs*. Confessor means the same as μάρτυς and it is only a linguistic convention which uses it only to denote those confessors who have remained alive after confessing Christ. Finally it became applied to those who have confessed Christ by a holy life.12

As long as such celebrations remained fundamentally associated with the grave of the martyr or confessor it was indeed a true feast—a feast with a celebrating congregation. The Roman calendar of saints was at first nothing but an index to the separate local yearly feasts of the various Roman cemetery churches. This was transplanted onto Frankish soil and became a liturgical calendar for every church, and so when these days were kept they had, in general, to do without their celebrating congregation. Only at this stage can we speak of a feast in the broader sense. As long as a further title such as *Patrocinum* is not added, saints' days in the main form a limiting case of a feast of the Church. We have a second border-line case in a yearly feast whose subject is an event from the history of the Church. A typical example of this is

10. Cf. Casel, *Mysterium und Martyrium in den römischen Sacramentarien:* JL 2 (1922, 18-38) 28 seq.
11. J. A. Jungmann, *Public Worship,* Challoner London 1957, p. 219.
12. The fact that finally the commemoration day of a saint was commonly called his *dies natalis* has no significance for our understanding of the saints' feast days. For dies natalis (γενέθλια) means birthday, it is true, but in antiquity it possessed also the connotation of a day of commemoration; cf. natalis Urbis. That the appropriate day for commemorating the saint was his heavenly birthday is a retrospective interpretation. W. Durig, *Die Geburtstagsmesse des Cod. Reg. 316: Münchener Theol. Zeitschr.* 54 (1953, 46-64) 54 seq.

the observance since 842 by the Byzantine Rite Orthodox Church of the first Sunday in Lent as a commemoration of the final victory in the iconoclastic heresy.13 The climax of this comes in a mighty procession of icons and a solemn homage to the Orthodox Fathers, and an equally solemn anathematizing of the heresy and its representatives before the Eucharistic worship. The Western Church, too, has this sort of feast: the feast which was introduced as a memorial of the victory over the Turks; the feast of the Transfiguration; of Mary, Queen of the Rosary; of the Name of Mary.14 But here the historical factor is little more than the occasion, and, apart from the mention in the martyrology and perhaps also in the Breviary lesson, the event itself has no influence on the shape of the liturgy of the day. This is in harmony with the inner law of the liturgy. For, even if the event were important in advancing the kingdom of God, it still could not become the subject of the liturigcal *anamnesis*.

When the event before us is not only an apparent divine intervention but contains the appearance of a figure from Redemptive history, as, for example, the apparition of the Blessed Virgin at Lourdes, the case is somewhat different. Even when it is the stigmatization of St. Francis of Assisi that is being celebrated, we may count it a memorial day in this way. In this the event has affected the form of the liturgy—even the liturgy of the Mass.

In such cases we are presented with some facet of the history of Redemption, a patch of colour of more or less intensity from that spectrum into which the white light of the whole Christ-event is broken up. In the end, however, all saints' day could be listed under this heading. In all the saints the life of Christ has become re-embodied in the course of the history of the Church. In them the history of Redemption has continued. And yet in all this we are still on the fringe of a feast of the Church. This is confirmed by the way in which such feasts are celebrated. They are no longer feast-days in the fullest sense: the celebrating people are absent for the most part. They are no longer *festa fori* but rather *festa chori*. And very often the chorus has long since dwindled to a solitary person

13. Cf. N. Nilles, *Kalendarium manuale utriusque Ecclesiae II*,² Innsbruck 1897, 101-118.
14. It was clearly an extreme border-line case when Pius XI instituted the Feast of the Maternity of the Blessed Virgin Mary in commemoration of the 1500th anniversary of the Council of Ephesus.

at prayer (or solitary celebrant). They are memorial days which impart a certain colouring to the ordinary daily Mass which has become more or less dissociated from the celebrating congregation. In this connexion, the Western liturgy is distinguished from all forms of the Eastern liturgy which never permits the calendar of saints to affect the rite of the Mass in any way, with the exception of isolated chants like the *Apolytikion* of the Byzantine liturgy. In the main, however, such colouration remains on the fringe of the Roman rite of the Mass—in the collects before and after the central core of the liturgy, and in the choice of readings. The commemoration of martyrs and saints is allowed to affect the Eucharistic prayer only in passing. Such forms, moreover, apart from some more or less well-established exceptions,15 have once more been pruned out as superfluous growth.

This basic principle remains: the feasts of the Christian year all have to do with the Christ-event, that fundamental fact of history upon which rests the existence of the Church and hence the spiritual existence of all her children. It has to do either with this event in its entirety or with some aspect of it. And here we must say something about the question of the *idea* feast. In his energetic way Anton Baumstark affirms as an absolute, general, and obvious fact, revealed by comparative liturgical study, that 'the great feasts of ancient Christian times, are not essentially historical commemorations (commemoraisons historiques) of this or that episode from redemptive history' but rather represent means of expressing great religious ideas.16 Bernard Botte, to whom we owe the revised edition of Baumstark's view.17 Easter, Epiphany, and Christmas he maintains, are no 'fêtes d'idée'. They have to do with facts of the history of Redemption, not with 'eternal truths'.

These two conceptions do not stand in irreconcileable opposition. The great feasts are concerned with the fundamental redemptive events; but precisely because these are not just any events but are redemptive events, forming the basis in all ages of the salvation which the Church mediates, we can say of them that their subject is Redemption, or Salvation, the Redemption itself

15. Cf. B. Opfermann, *Die heutigen liturgischen Sonderpräfationen: Theologie und Glaube* 46 (1956) 204-215.
16. Baumstark, *Liturgie comparée*¹ 173.
17. Thus in *Maison-Dieu* 30 (1952) 69. seq.

(Easter) or the beginning of Redemption (the Christmas feasts)17a. In this context it is worth noting that St. Ambrose was able to transfer the name of the old Roman civic festival the *Salus publica* on the 30th March, to the Christian festival of Easter.18 But salvation and redemption are abstract ideas which become suitably expressed on the occasion of the appropriate feasts. And this shows that in these ancient feasts the chief interest was directed not to the making present of historical details but to the redemptive meaning, to the continuing Christ-mystery.

In this matter we are constantly meeting a distinction between points of view, a distinction which has become of some importance in the life of the Church. The great liturgies of the East, like the Roman liturgy, follow the line we have described, preferring to dwell on the full depth of the redemptive significance of the events celebrated: not until the 4th century in Jerusalem do we meet the manner of celebration which picks out and reproduces details, a method which made sense in the places where those events once actually happened.19 It is met again, in various examples, in liturgies of Gallican provenance. Thus, on Palm Sunday, following the Jerusalem pattern, our Lord's entry into the Holy City is enacted; or the octave day of Christmas becomes the Feast of the Circumcision. It is met too in the popular devotion which, since the time of Bernard of Clairvaux and Francis of Assisi, has developed in an ever-widening stream, ending in the tendency to think and speak—even in the catechisms as though the various feasts of our Lord were but memories of events now lost in the past—the Birth, the Resurrection, the Ascension of the Lord.20

Besides the great feasts which carry a great weight of redemptive meaning there are, however, 'fêtes d'idée' in the sense given them by Botte. Such an *idea* feast, which can be subsumed under the general notion of *anamnesis* only with difficulty, is the Feast of

17a. Cf. J. Gaillard, *Noel mémoire ou mystere: Maison-Dieu* 59 (1959) 37-59, and in the same book the contributions of G. Hudon (60-84) and Y. Congar (132-161), also concerning Christmas.
18. Ambrose, *Ep.* 23, n. 22 (PL 16, 1035): He calls Easter *festum publicae salutis.* Cf. H. Franke: *Liturgische Zeitschrift* 5 (1932-33, 145-160) 154.—The Sundays after Epiphany too, conform to the type of the idea-feast.
19. *Perigrination Aetheriae* c. 29 seq.—And Baumstark op. cit. refers to this.
20. Cf. Fr. X. Arnold, *Dienst am Glauben*, Freiburg 1948, 40 seq. 77 seq. In the sphere of art, too, this development has had a profound effect. To rouse us to the danger inherent in this was no doubt the purpose of Abbot Ild. Herwegen's *Kirche und Seele. Die Seelenhaltung des Mysterienkultes und ihr Wandel im Mittelalter*, Münster 1926.

the Blessed Trinity. This is a belated fruit of the doctrinal warfare of declining Christian antiquity. In the Roman Church it was only able to spread at a late date after initial opposition.21 The only justification we can give of such a feast is that God has desired to crown this love which calls us children by granting us a glimpse into the mystery of His own inner essence. It would be more exact to say that the feast is a summing up of the whole scheme of salvation in which God the Father has desired to send us the Holy Spirit through His Son. This sort of reasoning was what led Clement XIII in 1759 to prescribe the Preface of the Trinity as the Sunday Preface.22 And yet there is no trace of such a thought in the Preface itself,22a nor yet in the antiphons23 and readings for the Feast of the Blessed Trinity. The Feast of the Trinity is a true *idea*—feast. Here we have one of the 'eternal truths' which are valid independently of any redemptive event. It was no accident therefore that people began subsequently to misunderstand the Feast of Pentecost as the feast of the Holy Spirit, and that people in the 18th century were asking for a Feast of the Heavenly Father.24

The feasts which Botte names in the same context—Corpus Christi, the Sacred Heart, Christ the King—are much more firmly rooted in redemptive events. It is true that in these it is no longer a redemptive event as such which forms the subject-matter, but it is redemption itself—redemption expressed in concrete form. And the connexion with the great feast of Easter is obvious. Corpus Christi—as the choice of the first Thursday after the Easter cycle shows—is nothing but the resumption of that theme which could only be touched on in passing on Holy Thursday:25 the Lord's gift of His body and Blood to His Church, to be a memorial of Himself—even if the liturgical expression and observance of the feast sets the gift itself in the foreground. Similarly, on the first

21. A. Klaus, *Ursprung und Verbreitung der Dreifaltigkeitsmesse*, Werl 1938 108-129.
22. Decree of the Congregation of Rites dated 3:1:1759 (*Decreta auth.* SRC II, 118).
22a. Cf. Jungmann, *Um die Herkunft der Dreifaltigkeits präfation:* Zk Th 81 (1959) 461-465.
23. The striking expressions which, in the antiphons produced by the Trinitarian theology in question, end with *o beata Trinitas*, are already present for the greater part in Victorinus After (about 350), *De Trinitate hymni* III (PL 8, 1143-1146).
24. Cardinal J. M. Thomasius and later Benedict XIV referred to the opposition to the idea of the Christian feast which inheres in such desires. Cf. *Questions liturgiques et paroissiales* 17 (1922) 225-227.
25. Thus St. Thomas, who certainly is an appropriate historical witness on this point. *Opusc.* 53 (former Breviary lesson on Friday in the octave).

Friday after the octave of Corpus Christi the theme of Good Friday is taken up once again, and the memory of the redeeming ·Passion, joined with meditation on the interior source thereof, is marked by the feast of the Sacred Heart. The feast of Christ the King, however, is but a Sunday made to stand out in the language of this century, with the accent on the social and political factors, stressing these things which have always been signified by the names Κυριακή and *dominica*. Christ as Κύριος is king, the divinely appointed ruler. In this sense we would have to describe Sunday itself as a 'fetê d'idée.' Indeed, rightly understood, it is the weekly feast of the Redemption and the redeemed.

Feasts of the same sort, even if today they incline to be *festa chori*, are the two days dedicated to the memory of the holy Cross. The relevant events in Church history are in this case only the occasion of the celebration. Like the feast of the Sacred Heart, the subject is the work of Redemption seen from the angle of Good Friday, but including the Easter note of triumph.

In other ways attempts have been made to express the mystery of Christ: in the feast of the Name of Jesus in which Spiritual patrimony from the declining Middle Ages was built up into a liturgical celebration or in the feast of the Precious Blood in which the piety of a St. Caspar del Bufalo (d. 1851) came into its own. These, too, are *idea*-feasts, and we gain the impression that in them the degree of abstraction has been further increased. Thus they have not really taken hold in the popular imagination.

It can always be said of all of these themes of Christian feasts, that it is not merely an·abstract idea that is being celebrated. It is not mercy or justice that is being made the subject of a feast. Still less is it a virtue or a moral ideal as was attempted by secular thought in the days of the enlightenment.26 It is always a living person, the person of the God-man who is being surveyed from different angles. This means that in all these Church feasts the basic theme of the *Anamnesis*, the work of Redemption, remains present—the work which was a free, historical activity of the triune God in Jesus Christ. This prevents the gift of salvation from

26. Individual representatives of the Protestant Enlightenment have followed this course to its extreme limits. Thus it has been proposed to celebrate Christmas as the festival of birth, Easter as that of immortality, and to introduce other feasts of the Fatherland, Sanctity, Friendship and so on. G. Kunze, *Die gottesdienstliche Zeit: Liturgia* I, Kassel 1954, 478 seq.

being presented in the feast in an abstract form, be it faith or grace or sanctity or heaven: the mind is always turned in the celebration upon a personal figure.

In the feasts of saints, too, this fashion of person and idea is present. As separate feast days, independent of the burial-place, They are meant to portray types of heroic Christian life; thanks are offered to God and the Christian people are spurred on. They represent types of vocation as we find them distinguished in the *Commune Sanctorum*, types of renunciation of the world through various forms of 'confession', types of apostolic activity as we see it on the scale of Church history in the founders of the great religious orders, types, too, representing the various nations and races in whom the Church is able to work out its effect.[27]

Representation of peoples especially leads to the idea of the patron. The patronage idea, more or less accentuated is further developed in the figures of other saints. This happens quite consciously with the feast of St. Joseph the worker. It was a happy decision which made the highest ecclesiastical authority resist pressure for a feast of Christ the worker. Had this request been granted, the fundamental facts of the story of Redemption would have been dangerously scaled down to the proclamation of a moral ideal. This would have meant going a step further than has been gone in the feast of the Holy Family[28] or than what has been aimed at since 1937 by an American 'crusade' for a feast of 'Christ the Divine Teacher.'[29]

The feast of St. Joseph the worker is the Church's attempt to Christianize the secular festival of work. In this we touch on a vital contemporary problem. The Church and the world: Christian feast-day and wordly celebration. Should or can the Church raise secular festivity to the dignity of a Christian festival, and that not merely by attaching a specifically religious feast to an already present occasion, as the ancient Church did with the *dies*

27. Concerning the latter we may refer to an important observation by M. Pfiegler (published in a lost passage) in the Vienna *Furche* of January 7, 1956, p. 8: in the calendar which formed the basis of the Missal and the Breviary of Pius V, it was provided that the then sovereign states each received a representative of at least princely rank: thus the following found a place in it: Casimir (Poland), Hermengild (Spain), Elisabeth (Portugal), Henry (Germany), St. Louis (France), Stephen (Hungary), Wenceslaus (Bohemia), Edward (England), Margaret (Scotland), Cnut (Denmark).
28. It is symptomatic in this regard, that pictorial representations of Christ as worker are permitted only as part of the representation of the Holy Family.
29. Helene E. Fröhlicher, *A Preaching Crusade: Lumen Vitae* I (1946) 260-268.

Solis Invicti; for example? Already sharp controversies have arisen on this point. Notable amongst these was the discussion amongst French liturgists and pastoral theologians which was reported some years ago.[30]

At all events it would be a good thing if we always bear in mind that such *idea*-feasts belong to the fringe of what is possible for Christian feasts; and that the warning, with which the Roman organ for liturgical questions accompanies its report of a pertinent controversy, is not ill-founded, the warning, viz., that such innovation ought not to be the result of 'd'un calcolo burocratio e propagandistico'.[31] On the one hand we have the Church's task to sanctify the world in every age, nation, and condition, to sanctify every form of social life and business, every sort of work and all human joy. The leaven of the Christian message should permeate every corner of this world. On the other hand, the festivals of the Church stand traditionally firm, almost to the point of rigidity, in all their jealously guarded sacred forms and with a depth of meaning which nevertheless scarcely shines through these forms any longer and which seems to resist all change— leaving out of account the confusion with secular festivities.

Do these two entities have to remain completely estranged? How far can, not only the Church, but also the Christian festival be brought into line with the values of the secular world?

Again we must begin at the heart of the Christian feast—the celebration of the Eucharist. Is this, of its essence, so self-contained, so impervious to outside influence, that there is no possibility of any connexion? For a time the French discussion seemed to suggest that there was none. Pastoral theologians, who wished to emphasize the fact that the world of work can be presented to God and sanctified in the Mass, were opposed sharply by technical liturgists who maintained that in the Mass we offer Christ alone, for 'the sacrifice which redeems the world is Christ's sacrifice alone'.[32] The Mass is not our own self-offering: this must be accomplished through our lives as a whole. Here we come to a

30. Under the title: *Fetes humaines et liturgie sacrée*, in a special book about the congress of Vannes 1950: *Maison-Dieu* 30 (1952) 79–100.
31. *Eph. liturg.* 61 (1947) 389. This is concerned with the controversy between Fr. Thiry O.S.B., who opposes the multiplication of 'feste votive' in *Scuola catt.* 74 (1946) 49 seq. and Fr. Roschini O.S.M., who defends their introduction. Ibid. 74 (1946) 320–324.
32. H. Chirat: *Maison-Dieu*, op. cit. 91 seq.

parting of the ways, to a misunderstanding which reaches right into the realms of advanced theology. Is the Mass as Mass truly the sacrifice which redeemed the world? May we so exaggerate the identity of the sacrifice on the Cross with the Mass, that—contrary to all appearance—all which is said of the former can be applied to the latter, only distinguishing the former as a bloody sacrifice and the latter as unbloody? At this point we must make another fundamental distinction. The world has been redeemed by the once-for-all sacrifice of Christ upon the Cross. The sacrifice of the Cross is the sacrifice upon which Redemption rests. But the Mass is the continuing, cultic sacrifice of the redeemed. Granted, as Trent teaches, in both, Christ is not only victim but priest as well; but in such a way that on the Cross He was sacrificing alone while in the Mass He sacrifices along with His Church, drawing it to Him as co-operating in His sacrifice. The Mass was essentially like this from the very beginning,[33] and He framed His commission so that it originated in bread and wine—things taken from this world. In two ways, therefore, the Mass opens out onto the world.

Because bread and wine stand at the beginning of our sacrifice, not only is the created world from which come these gifts but our life too, our life of work and weariness, caught up into Christ's sacrifice and presented to God. It is true that the whole of life ought to be lived in obedience to God. But this self-surrender is expressed in that sacrifice which is *in genere signi*, and that in a sublime and sanctifying manner by being joined to Christ's sacrifice. If this expression is intensified and made even plainer at the Offertory and finally in the Offertory procession of the faithful, this is a legitimate expansion of the symbolic character immanent in the sacrifice. This expansion must indeed accept certain limitations. It is a legitimate extension of sacramental symbolism, acknowledged by liturgical history, for representatives of the faithful to bring not only gifts of bread and wine to the altar on specially festive occasions, but also objects used in the liturgy—candles, altar-linen or offerings for a charitable use. And even when, on an extraordinary occasion, the celebration begins with the erection of the altar and sanctuary by workmen

33. *Conc. Trid.*, Sess. XXII, c. 1.

from the congregation, this, too is an illuminating intensification of the symbolism inherent in the nature of the thing. A further development along this direction lies in the increasing desire that the altar-breads should be less unlike common, every-day bread, and that Consecration should take place and Communion given with such bread which has been presented at the Offertory.

Against this we have to agree with the critics who dislike the idea of an Offertory procession wherein tools of trade or photographs of children are carried to the altar—things which are brought back again.[34] On the other hand it is not impossible to bring into relation with the Eucharistic sacrifice things which afterwards are to be taken home. In this it is a matter not of sacrifice but of receiving a blessing. In the rite of the Mass there still is a formula which has to do with this: *Per quem haec omnia.* The blessing of food on Easter Sunday, which today takes place before or after the service, for long occurred at this place in the Canon and was often provided in the text of the Missal. This blessing was often a blessing of fresh-fruits of the harvest as well. The blessing of fresh-grapes on the feast of St. Sixtus (August 6)— a custom which endured for centuries—was of this sort. This clearly gives a historic precedent which could be taken up in relation to Church harvest festivals.

This brings us already to the second line of approach by which the secular world can enter into the Eucharistic sacrifice and the Christian feast. It is we men who, as the Church, must present a sacrifice along with Christ—we men with our joys and suffering, with our work and fears, with our cares and sorrows. The holy Sacrifice is the very place where we must ever and again renew our thanksgiving and adoration, seeking to enter into God's plan with contrition, supplication, trust and devotion.

In as much as it is one of the demands upon our way of life, such entering into God's plan can be prepared by the word of preaching which is a normal component of a liturgical festival. It is the function of the sermon constantly to form a bridge out of the everyday world into the world of divine mystery. In so far as this entry into the divine order has to do with confident petition, in which we lay bare our human poverty before God, it finds this

34. Cf. the critical remarks of A. N. Roguet: *Maison-Dieu,* op. cit. 95.

expression in intercession, which the ancient Church formed a bridge between the readings and the service of sacrifice, and which today in the *Missa cantata* can follow the sermon—in the vernacular.[35] Properly constructed in litany form and in some phrase or other made to suit the occasion, the pertinent petitions can be made to fit happily into the public service without destroying any of its dignity.

We could go even further. Many of the interests and occasions arising from this world's life which demand a celebration and which will not be denied that religious culmination with which they have been crowned from time immemorial, could give their stamp to the formula of a Mass in its less central aspects. For long enough we have known this in the conditions of an agrarian economy: the quarterly Ember days have always been primarily fast days, but they were always marked by a celebration of the Mass, they possessed, that is, a liturgical character; and this celebration of the Mass, was so vividly affected by the thought of seed time and harvest, that no less an authority than Germain Morin believed that these days were relics of ancient harvests festivals—*feriae sementinae, feriae messis* and *feriae vindemiales*.[36] The same is true of the major and minor litanies: in the Roman Church, at any rate, they were never kept as fast days.

If we grant that this is a genuine liturgical development and do not limit further development to the same sort of thing, then we must ask whether the working life of this mechanical age has not a claim on similar consideration. Factory and office are no more profane than field and stall. And if it is Catholic Christians who inhabit the factories and offices they have as much right to have their work transfigured through worship as peasants have. In every case, vocation is a religious concept and points to Him who calls us. An American liturgist has, in fact, already given us a bold picture of the rich development of the liturgy of the future along

35. These intercessions, as now regulated in liturgical books, display a most truncated condition, and in the prayers of Leo XIII they have found a most inadequate substitute. They represent, therefore, a matter of great concern for liturgical renewal. V. the expositions of J. Gülden, *Das allgemeine Kirchenbeget in der Sicht der Seelsorge: Die Messe in der Glaubensverkündigung,*² Freiburg 1953, 337-353. In several diocesan prayerbooks there are already some very acceptable formulae of such inccessions. V., for example, the *Gottesdienst* of the Diocese of Münster 1955, 522 seq. 604, and the *Gesang-und Gebetbuch fur das Bistum Trier,* Trier 1955, 502 seq.
36. G. Morin, *L'origine des Quatre-temps: Revue Bénéd.* 14 (1897) 336 seq.

these lines.37 In the Missal of the future he sees a Mass for every calling listed in the American index of trades—motorists, bank-clerks, insurance-agents, chemists and doctors. Every vocational group has its own votive Mass.

The idea is not so novel as it seems. Each medieval guild had its own patron and its patronal feast which was kept with public worship on the feast-day. Thus the cartwrights kept the feast of St. Catherine, the tailors that of St. Martin; and in many places the people in the mountains still celebrate the feast of St. Barbara. Such feast-day celebrations were regularly accompanied by an Offertory procession led by the master of the guild. These were genuine festivals when earthly values were celebrated, but were at the same time traced to their heavenly home and overshadowed by a feast of the Church. The new feast of St. Joseph the Worker which does not distinguish between different kinds of work appears as the beginnings of the resuscitation of the older order.

Along these lines we must seek the solution of what have been called 'topical Sundays'.38 There are interests within the religious-secular order which cannot, indeed, become the theme of a service, but which must be mentioned. The congregation must call to mind the diaspora and the foreign missions; they must consider the work and the needs of Caritas; sometimes Catholic Action must be brought into prominence; some great event has to be concluded with a solemn act of worship. It would be most unnatural if on a Sunday the sermon were full of an appeal on some topical concern but in the course of the liturgy no mention whatsoever were made of the subject. We do not know how such concerns were built into worship in the early days of the Church.39 At any rate, such important concerns ought to be reflected in the liturgy, whether by choosing a day which will provide an appropriate background to the concern,40 or by mentioning the matter

37. G. Ellard S.J., *The Mass of the Future*, Milwaukee 1948, 297-307: *Occupational Worship*.
38. A. Beil, *Einheig in der Liebe*,² Freiburg 1955, 153, n. 109.
39. At Rome in the time of Leo the Great there used to be an ancient feast of collections between July 5 and 15; it was the day of the *ludi Appollinares*, for which contributions were collected. The Christians collected for the poor. On the previous Sunday there was a sermon on the subject. Leo the Great, *Serm.* 6-11 (PL 54, 158-168). Cf. V. Monachino, *La cura pastorale a Milano, Cartagine e Roma (Analecta Gregoriana 41)*, Rome 1947, 375 seq.
40. Thus there was a movement to choose Pentecost and the Feast of Christ the King as the most suitable days for Catholic Action Sunday; R. Graber, *Die dogmatischen Grundlage der Katholischen Aktion*, Augsburg 1932, 55.

in one of the ways suggested above—as is done when the school year is opened by celebrating a votive Mass of the Holy Spirit.41

Certainly we do not say that every consecration of a secular festival should be exalted to the highest level of sacredness into a celebration of the holy Eucharist. The celebration may be purely local as at the blessing of a bridge or a blast-furnace. For these the formulae of the Rituale are appropriate. Again, those who desire the Church's blessing may indeed be Christians and ought not to be refused, yet their faith is weak and imperfect; or the celebration may attract both believers and unbelievers so that it would not be fitting to incorporate the most sacred possession of the Church in the celebration. On such occasions slighter and more peripheral forms would be more suitable. In this connexion the French discussions mentioned a 'liturgie catechumenale'.42 This is the proper title. In such circumstances it is the Mass of the Catechumens, so to speak, which must suffice. By this we mean the outline of the Mass of Catechumens in its original shape: a service of readings which correspond to the circumstances, leading on to hymns and responsorial prayer which is rounded off by the priest's prayer. This is to some extent the plan behind the proposals for the solemn form of blessings in the Rituale in the second part of the German Collectio rituum.43

In her solicitude for the proper celebration of a feast the Church faces a double task: first she must preserve the purity of the Christian feast, and second, she must not ignore the world.

Easter must always remain—as the ancients had it—a feast ἡ ἑορτή ; and it is about to become this once more in the fullest

41. A unique case is the 'Crusade' which has originated in Brazil in the past few years and which requires a yearly solemn Te Deum on the fourth Thursday of November—ad dandas Deo gratias pro omnibus beneficiis ab eo ubique largiter effusis, and having as a further aim a 'jour de Dieu' on which the rulers of the state in particular, shall recognize the hand of Providence. The same sort of thing would seem to be the idea behind the American Thanksgiving Day. That this particular Thursday should have been chosen can be understood only in terms of American tradition arising after 1863. Cf. F. X. Weiser, Handbook of Christian Feasts and Customs, New York 1958, 271 seq.—Perhaps this could also become an occasion for a much wider circle to be reminded that every Mass is indeed a thanksgiving (semper et ubique).

42. A. Maurice: Maison-Dieu, loc. cit. 89.—Similar ideas were expressed at an earlier French congress. Cf. the volume, La messe et sa catéchese (Le x orandi 7), Paris 1947, 294-298. The idea of such a 'liturgie catéchuménale' is certainly a happier one than that of the 'paraliturgie', which is often seen in French publications.

43. For the fundamentals of such a structure cf. J. A. Jungmann, Die liturgische Feier, Regensburg 1939.

sense. The revival of the Easter liturgy from 1951-55 with its marked stress on fundamental soteriological ideas was a mighty achievement in this respect. But the idea of Sunday as the weekly Easter must more and more take possession of the popular mind.44 Something of that mentality would have to be revived, of which St. Paul spoke when he said that we Christians should be celebrating a perpetual Easter (ὥστε ἑορτάξωμεν I. Cor. 5, 8), because our Paschal Lamb has been slain and Christ has completed His redeeming Passion. This then is the real reason which makes it possible for the Church to celebrate her feasts out of a spiritual wealth such as the world does not know. It was truly said that we could change 'See how they love one another' into 'See how they know how to celebrate their feasts'.45

To give effect to this inner wealth of a Christian feast it is only necessary for the Eucharist to be able to disclose its hidden splendour more and more. This is already happening, for the majority of the faithful are taking a more conscious part in the memorial of the Lord; no longer do they merely assist in faith at the celebration, but share in it actively. Eucharistic piety has for long concentrated somewhat one-sidedly on reverence for the real presence of our Lord: now it can do nothing but good if it develops as the thanksgiving of the people of grace in the direction of the Christian festival. The wealth which is contained in this precious legacy of the Lord will then be able to display itself in various ways: in the low Mass attended by small groups; in the parochial Mass; in the solemn pontifical Mass of the bishop, who as the chief pastor, gathers his people around him; in the great closing celebrations of Mass at Catholic conferences and international congresses. And so the rhythm of Christian festivity will permeate everything, whatever its size, whatever its grade: the regular Morning Hour of a religious community: the weekly Sunday celebration in which the Christian community renews its youth; the yearly recurring feasts of our Lord which lift up our hearts in the course of the Christian year and reach a climax in Easter; the world Eucharistic congress—which we may scarcely

44. We are already speaking of gains achieved since the time of Pius X; J. Gaillard, art. *Dimanche: Dict. de Spiritualité* III, 966 seq. This can only mean that the beginnings of such regaining is apparent. The liturgy itself would have to show a much greater emphasis on Easter once again, not least by its re-adoption of the once plentiful Sunday Prefaces.
45. Cf. A. Gundlach, *Verklärung des Herrn*, Munich 1957, 86.

ignore—in which the entire Church has once more made itself visible, and by which it moves from one city to another throughout the world, just as the Papal worship used to be carried out at the stational churches of the Eternal City in turn.

By such variety of measure and rhythm the accommodation to the special and temporal values of the world is already being affirmed and realized. The 'coefficient of realism'[46] which has been inherent in the Eucharist from the start has only to be applied to the actual circumstances, as we have suggested. For the Sacrament and the feast which gathers round it is designed to hallow this earthly world and advance that work which was begun by the advent of the Son of God in the fullness of time, as the martyrology for Christmas Eve puts it: *volens piissimo suo adventu mundum consecrare*. Thus the mighty vision must be fulfilled, in which the great cardinal, Nicolas of Cusa, once expressed the meaning of the sacrifice of the Mass. The world of sense is a great temple which God has built; and Christ is the altar in it. He is also the sacrifice which testifies to the greatest glory of God. But we have all been made members of Christ, and as God the Father accepts that sacrifice, so He grants us fellowship with Himself and strengthens us with eternal life.[47]

8. *Easter Christianity*

Anyone who has spent a few moments meditating on one of the mosaics which decorate the apse or the chancel-vault in a Roman basilica like that of St. Clement or St. Pudenziana or the Lateran will have experienced a sense of serene calm and solemn exaltation coming from the venerable work of art. What is the secret of this atmosphere? It is not the magic of the bright coloured stones; nor is it the harmony in the lines of these creations of early Christianity; principally it is the subject which speaks to us. Here

46. H. Jenny: *Maison-Dieu*, loc. cit. 97.
47. Nicolas of Cusa, *Excitationum* I. IV; quoted by a. Gaudel: DThCX, 1072 seq.

we do not find the narration of dramatic events from the past—even if they be concerned with the history of Redemption: here there is a plain statement of *what is*. Here we see a universe, the Christian order of all those things that the Church knows and which she declares proudly and joyfully to all who enter these places. The Christian faith is confessed there in an exultation of glittering colour. These representations well earn the name of confessional pictures.

Closer study reveals the law which governs these pictures. The fixed centre is always the image of Christ, whether under the symbol of the radiant Cross, or the Lamb of God or Mount Sion, or in the straightforward representation of the enthroned Christ. He is always cast in the same part: the Redeemer, the bringer of salvation, the Lord of His people. The extension of the material makes this even clearer; for the space all around this radiant centre is filled with symbolic representations of the redeemed: lambs coming from both sides—from Jerusalem and from Bethlehem, from Jewry and from heathendom—all converging on the one centre. Rivers of paradise are there too, flowing from the holy mountain and quenching the thirst of the harts; and the mystic vine sending out its branches in all directions; and there are the figures of the apostles or of specially venerated martyrs arranged on each side as the principal representatives of the redeemed people of God. Every time it is the completed work of Redemption, the Easter theme, which is portrayed; and this is what strikes everyone who enters the house of God. All through the year Easter is being celebrated in this place.

We have not exaggerated in the slightest. What has been said is true not only in the realm of Church art but also in that of the Church calendar. Until the 4th century Easter was *the* feast, the only feast of all Christendom, and Sunday was regarded as the weekly resumption of the feast of Easter.

Such a conception is much less current with average Christians today. For us, Easter is one feast in a series of feasts. It is true that we do not hesitate to follow the tradition of placing Easter first and highest amongst feasts. But we have a feeling that Christmas comes very close to it; and Easter cannot compare in festive splendour with Corpus Christi as it is celebrated in Catholic countries. Many indeed, may be inclined to confer equal rank upon the feast of the Most Holy Trinity because of its theological depth, and the feast of the Sacred Heart because of its spiritual richness.

Setting aside these reasons of sentiment which colour our conception of the relative rank of Church festivals, we still find the thought that Easter is of overwhelming importance strange to our minds. We are accustomed to regard progress through the Church's year as an up and down oscillation, a journey now through the gloomy valley of penance, now upon the highway of holy joy; now through the abyss of separation from God, now into the fellowship of the saints. Easter is just one of the points of intersection. Or we may see in the Christian year the yearly re-enactment of the Life of Jesus, beginning with the expectation of His coming by the fathers of the old dispensation, having a first climax in the contemplation of the Infant in the crib, continuing with the events of the childhood narrative, gathering intensity in the way of the Passion and Cross, triumphing in the Resurrection and Ascension and the extension of the kingdom of God. We try to re-discover the supreme model, which is the life of Jesus, in the Church's year, and zealously we study the readings and meditations to this end. From this angle we wish to derive stimulus and encouragement for our Christian life which must ever be an imitation of Christ. We seek the moral impulse we need so badly; but in the same measure we openly depart from the Easter-piety of the ancient Church, of which we have just been speaking. We would ask first of all, therefore, whether this constitutes a loss, or, on the whole, a gain.

There is another thing, however, of which account must be taken in describing exactly the contrast between the older and the more modern evaluation of Easter. Precisely because we tend to re-discover the historical course of the life of Jesus in the Church's year instead of using it simply as a means of venerating the fundamental mysteries of the kingdom of God, the theme of the feast takes on a certain historical remoteness; the sequence of festival mysteries becomes a series of pictures—a play, indeed, which we are able to observe from a certain neutral distance. The annunciation by the angel Gabriel, the Presentation in the temple, the entry of Jesus on Palm Sunday, His Resurrection from the dead and Ascension into heaven, all of these stand to some extent in an even sequence, all equally remote—or equally near.

Our Lord's life is once more brought near to us by historical study and enumeration of the various separate mysteries of the story of Redemption. Is it not this absorption in the historical accounts which has been initially responsible for our familiarization with the details of the life of Jesus? Is it not responsible for that familiarity in which the historical setting has faded away and the past event has become present, as, for example, in the thousand upon thousand cribs which have been erected since the days of the Poverello of Assisi? Is it not responsible, too, for enkindling out of this that kind of devotion, which finds itself in the presence of the divine Persons? 'We will rock you' they sang in olden days, and today we sing: 'Sleep holy Babe.'

At bottom it is not surprising that in song and poem people directly address the persons they have in mind. And in all ages inspired preachers have addressed the divine Persons when in the full flight of their eloquence: they have greeted the Virgin-Mother as though she were still holding the divine Child upon her knee; they have spoken to the Lord on the Cross as though He were hanging upon it at that very moment. It is not self-evident, however, that this way of thinking should have become the everyday speech of religious life, as it has very generally become in the devotional literature of the last few centuries.

Until the 12th century there were only isolated places where space and time receded and the past became viewed as present. But this style of devotion widened to a flood. It was not simply that art began to depict the mysteries of Jesus' infancy and the scenes of His Passion in endless variations and with a fervour hitherto unknown; devotional literature as well, found it quite natural to follow in meditation not only the Way of the Cross, but to call upon Him at each stage as if He were going through His sufferings at that very moment. And here Easter is no longer an exception. It is attached to the preceding redemptive events and takes on the same remoteness or nearness which they have.

In saying this, no criticism at all is intended of such a style of piety. It would indeed be plainly irreverent and unseemly to measure the stream of devotion and sanctity which has been nourished from these sources, by any literary or stylistic standard. In her journey down the centuries the Church traverses regions with the most varied spiritual climates, some of which encourage an exuberant growth, some a very bare harvest. We do not claim that our own era belongs to the former type. But for this very reason we must ask which plants are most suited to the stony soil of our age. The age of natural science and technology is sober and realistic. It likes best to stick to tangible facts, certainly to demonstrable realities. This sobriety has long since taken hold of religion and religious life, and we must take account of it if we wish to practise something more than an impotent religion of sentiment. We can detect this in Church architecture and in the sphere of lesser Church art where it is the utilitarian, the functional, the simply designed and mechanically perfect which receives our acclaim. We see it in the confusion which prevails in Church and art where the master of colour, still unaware of the realities of revelation, falls back on the attempt to create something out of subjective experience.

Once again we must become settled on firm ground. First of all we must look for the immovable realities which do not have to be conjured up from the past out of our imaginations, but which are simply there. We must bring into the foreground once more that which is, and allow that which has been to recede into the background. It is right that we should be egocentric to this extent, that we enquire about the order in which we are placed, into which we must set our activity, and which tells us what we may hope for and what we must fear.

The answer can quite simply be given. As Christians—and it will be profitable if we stress this honourable title which we would not wish to relinquish—as Christians, that is, as those who are baptized into the mystery of Christ, we stand within that order which Christ established through His death and sealed by His Resurrection. We are not faced with God and His judgement directly—left to our own resources; but we are incorporated in the holy community of the Church whose Head is Christ, the Risen One, who sits at the right hand of the Father. Many are the ties which bind us to Him: we look up to Him in faith; in the

Eucharist He comes amongst us and gathers us into His own prayer and sacrifice. We are to become conformed to His likeness —by our moral striving, as much as our human weakness can accomplish on this earth, until we appear completely like Him at the Last Day.

The picture before us is one of confident hope. In the Resurrection and Ascension we are not looking merely at past events which are linked in sequence with other events in the life of Jesus and which, like them, remain as things of the past: we recognize rather the Easter mystery as the pivot of our Christian existence and think of ourselves as received into the 'kingdom of His beloved Son' (Col. 1, 13). The former manner of thinking easily leads to a view of the world which sees only a grey sky overhead with streaks of light only in the horizon. Thus we would live like men who felt themselves to be helpless victims of this enigmatic existence, swinging at random between heaven and hell, even if the Christian still clung to the thought that a hand was always stretched out ready to take hold of him at the critical moment: but the Christian realities are hidden behind a thick veil of mist. According to the other way of thinking, the new creation has already come into being: it is irradiated by the streaming light from Easter morning: it is the new world of God in which Christ is the eldest brother who is already exalted on high; and we are His brothers and sisters, even if still only in the roadway of life.

There is undoubtedly another way of conceiving the Christian realities of grace: a more abstract way, in which they are detached from their basis in the history of Redemption and seen as homage to God, the adornment of the soul, justification before God. But the human soul being what it is, such a manner of thinking cannot easily take possession of the whole being of a man and give him that sense of security and safety which is a prerequisite of unreserved devotion to the demands and tasks of the kingdom of God.

The ancient Church knew full well why she had placed the Easter Christ and His Easter work in the apses of her basilicas, why she had proclaimed Easter so loudly, providing it with a forty-day preparatory celebration and a fifty-day aftermath, and had given the stamp of Easter to every Sunday. This played a great part in educating the Christian in the knowledge of His Christian dignity and in confirming his confidence. And in the peaceful days after Constantine, the Church only developed the inheritance which she had received from the previous centuries. For even the art of the catacombs—and this was a graveyard—art encompassed by the seriousness of death—had a completely Easter character. No mourning angels decorate the surfaces of the walls, never once do we see the sorrowful Mother of God with her Son in her arms, portrayed as a comfort to those who are left behind: it is the Good Shepherd feeding His flocks in the meadows of paradise which we see; or there are mystical pictures from the Old Testament which symbolize new the life which Christ has won by the Resurrection and which His people gain through Him: Jonas cast up on the shore, Noe and his family saved by the ark; Daniel in the lions' den, etc.

The prayer of the Church was in line with this. As a rule, prayer was offered standing, facing the rising sun. The Council of Nicea (325) thought it worth-while to stress in Canon 20 that people should pray on Sundays and at Easter only in a standing position. Like the practice of facing the rising sun, this may have been an ancient custom but very early on it had assumed a definitely Christian significance. It is quite plain: we have risen with Christ, therefore we stand. And if we face the rising sun as we pray, then we think of Christ the true Sun who rose victorious on Easter morning.

The content of the Church's prayer too, was inspired by this same spirit. It still is. In its manner of prayer the Roman liturgy has preserved an unbroken continuity of the Easter tradition of the ancient Church, not only by having a thanksgiving as the chief prayer—as in every liturgy: *Gratias agamus Domino Deo nostro;* nor yet only by having the content of the celebration marked by a memorial of the Passion, Resurrection and Ascension of the Lord—again like every liturgy—but by concluding every prayer (with a few late exceptions) with a reference to Him who, in His glorified humanity, is our Head and our advocate with the Father. We offer our prayers at the throne of God 'through Jesus Christ Thy Son who lives and reigns with Thee'. This 'through Christ' persists, from the beginning to the end of liturgical prayer, and the law holds not only after Easter or Ascension, but throughout the whole year. Easter remains the dominant theme in the Church's prayer. The Office for Christmas expresses the same thought. He whose gracious birth we celebrate is the King, the King of Peace, the Bridegroom who comes forth in splendour from the bridal chamber; at Epiphany the prophetic vision is recalled of the ruler upon whose shoulders the government vests: in Advent we look forward to the Lord's coming again; and on Good Friday itself the triumph of the Resurrection is not forgotten.

The Easter note is introduced into various prayers of the daily liturgy also. The *Gloria in excelsis* appeals to Him who takes away the sins of the world and now sits at the Father's right hand and in its concluding acclamation it calls Him '*holy . . . Lord . . . most high* in the glory of God the Father'. The Eucharist itself is to some extent illuminated with reference to the glorified Christ in heaven. Even very late prayers such as those in the *Ordo Missae* before the priest's Communion, which are said with the sacred Host in mind, turn to Christ not as He is present in the Sacrament, but look beyond to His heavenly existence. For all that the Sacrament contains the entire Christ, yet it is looked upon and used primarily as a holy thing, the greatest of all gifts, which points beyond itself to an even greater thing (*beneficia potiora*), and which is a pledge of coming glory; for it grants us union with the glorified Body of the Lord, with the exalted Christ in heaven who desires to draw us into His own glorious Sonship.

To day the Church spurs us on to yield our minds to such a manner of thinking. Pius XII wrote a special encyclical on the Mystical Body of the Lord; and by so doing he indicated that we are to learn to see the Church as that holy organism whose Head is the glorified Christ: we are not to think of the sacraments apart from Him, but as holy signs through which He imparts the power of His own life to us. No one will deny that there are a few things here which we must re-learn.

At the close of the ancient Christian era, when the world was already Christian, the denial by Arius that the Son was equal in substance to the Father evoked a violent reaction. As a result, in order to safeguard the tradition of the Church, the divinity of the

Son was so strongly emphasized, even in liturgical prayer, that the glory of divinity swamped all humanity, and prayer to the Father 'through Christ' was kept as little more than a form of words. The figure of the glorified God-man became somewhat obscured in the popular mind. Thus our Lord's earthly appearance assumed a correspondingly greater importance, until we reach the realism of the late Gothic Passion and Crucifixion scenes, and the wounds of our Lord. In the popular mind the other heavenly helpers became more and more important, and the number of devotions multiplied which had in some degree lost track with their central point. The Christian heart was nourished from many sources. But did the knowledge of the faith gain in clarity and assurance?

In our own day, when secularism threatens, we see religion forced to concentrate upon essentials. Our people now seek of necessity the clear outlines of the Christian universe, seek the unity and compactness of the Christian picture of the world. We do not have to destroy anything which former ages have asked of the Church, either in the realm of belief itself, where truth can never become error, or in that of devotional life. But it would be a good thing if we were to pay careful attention to arranging things in the right order. The apostles preached the Risen Christ; and it was around Him that the congregations of the faithful gathered. The Risen One, the Easter Christ will always stand at the centre of the Christian cosmos.

This is not to say that we shall overlook the historical Christ, that we have any right to lose sight of Him. As long as we are pilgrims here on earth it is His earthly footsteps which must guide us upon our own way. His every word is our light and direction, and His example in poverty and labour, in intercourse with men, and above all, in suffering and death, are an indispensable teaching for us. His Cross is the world's salvation: that remains the start and the finish of Christian preaching. But in the Cross we do not have to see *only* the Good Friday scene—the scene as it appeared to the impudent eyes of the mocking high-priests and scribes. No matter how much we venerate the wounds, the pains, and the death-agony of our Lord, the believing heart cannot fail to see that the wounds radiate the glory of victory, and that the agony of death is swallowed up in the jubilant cry: 'It is consummated'. The masters of Romanesque art set the kingly crown upon the head of the Crucified and turned the linen cloth into a billowing cloak; they made of the Cross a regal throne, following the saying which the early Christians developed from the verse of the Psalmist (Ps. 95, 10): The Lord shall rule from the tree.

Truly this is the triumph of Christianity: in suffering it is victorious; man gains his life by giving it up. But our assurance that we do not follow Him in vain first comes when we look up at our Redeemer who has conquered death and blazed the trail into the bright world of divine grace and love: it is this which gives us courage to offer our own lives for His work and for His Kingdom. We must be inflamed with something of the mood of those partisans who met the enemy step by step even on his own ground, fearing him no more because they knew that his front had already been breached. Our kind of Christianity must once more become Easter Christianity.[1]

---

1. This cause has meanwhile been greatly advanced through the publication in Freiburg, 1959, of the volume, *Paschatis Sollemnia. Studien zur Osterfeier und Osterfrömmigkeit*, ed. by Balth. Fischer and J. Wagner.

INDEX

417

Historia Lausica, 158, 173
History of redemption, 88, 314, 320, 359
Hoeber, K., 76
Hofinger, J., 349
Holstenius, L., 301
Holweg, F. G., 275
Holy Family, Feast of, 399
Holy Name, Feast of, 398
Holy Saturday, 226, 228, 235, 275, 289
Holy Sepulchre, 223, 227, 236
Holy Spirit, 23, 76, 239, 242, 252, 255, 257, 264, 265, 397
Holy Thursday, 224, 234, 235, 246, 249, 289
Homilies, 167, 171
ὅμοιος 23
ὁμοούσιος 16, 24, 25
Honorius Augustodunensis, 238, 265, 273, 279
Hörmann, W., 175, 183
Hortulus Marianus, 304, 307
Hösl, J., 36
Hospitallers, 76
Host, Fraction of, 289; Elevation of, 279, 285; See *fermentum*
Hours of Prayer, 105. Cf. Choir-prayer; Breviary
Hucke, H., 134
Hudon, 9, 396
Huguccio, 199
Hum, J. M., 100
Hunerich, 17, 25, 26
Hungary, 97, 254
Hupperts, J. M., 311, 313
Huysmans, K. J., 90
Hymni matutini, 130, 132, 134, 144, 148, 149
Hymns, 135, 136, 143, 149, 151, 203
Hyppolitus of Rome, 14, 106, 108, 129, 163, 225, 281, 286

Ignatius of Antioch, 4, 206, 209, 284
Ignatius of Loyala, 262, 269, 270, 302
Illumination, 121
Ildefons of Toledo, 49, 127
Incensing, 380
Individualism, 6, 88
Indulgencies, 262
Inn names, 76
Innocent I, 247, 249, 253, 288
Innocent III, 37
Innsbruck-Feldkirchen, 230, 233
Institution, account of, 277
Instructio eccl. ordinis, 167, 227
Instructio, of 1958, 96, 348
Intercession, 70, 100, 377, 403
International liturgical study-congress, 95
Investiture dispute, 67

Ireland, 20, 173, 310
Irenaeus, 324
Iserloh, E., 31
Isidore of Seville, 17, 24, 31, 34, 141, 150, 170, 173

James-*anaphora*, 277
James of Vitry, 179, 265
Janssen, J., 74
Japan, 56
Jecker, G., 20
Jenner, J., 141
Jenny, H., 407
Jerome, 33, 106, 109, 114, 235, 247
Jesuits, 15, 205, 233, 270, 302, 347
'Jesus-worship,' 57
John the Baptist, 260, 276
John Berchmans, 86
John IV of Portugal, 305
John VIII, 61
John XXII, 35
John the deacon, 191
John Eudes, 310
John the Evangelist, 315
John of Gorze, 168
Jorden of Saxony, 179
Jörgensen, J., 90
Joseph, St., 262, 264, 270, 274, 297, 298, 399, 404
Joseph of Ferno, 223
Judgment, 244, 269, 270, 272, 359
Julian of Toledo, 40, 46, 127
Jungbauar, G., 300
Justin, 282, 370, 377

Kahlefeld, H., 317
Kahles, W., 55
Kattenbusch, F., 49, 227
Kempf, Th., 5
Kerenyi, K., 388
Kerygma, 1, 36. Cf. Preaching the faith
Kettel, J., 237
Kings, the Three, 76
Kirch, K., 107
Kirsch, J. P., 4, 245
Kirschbaum, E., 4
Klaus, A., 35, 256, 397
Klauser, Th., 5, 19, 22, 162, 215, 218, 240, 290
Knees and kneeling, 147, 176, 194, 247
Kolde, D., 65
Kolping, A., 72
Konen, W., 37
Korolevsky, C., 96
Kowalsky, N., 348
Kraft, S., 391
Kriemhilde, 133

Joseph A. Jungmann, S.J. (1889–1975), an Austrian Roman Catholic priest and scholar, was ordained to the priesthood in 1913 and entered the Society of Jesus (the Jesuits) four years later. He spent most of his career as professor of pastoral theology at the University of Innsbruck, where he taught both catechetics and liturgy. With the exception of the years during which Hitler closed down the theological faculty (1939–1945), Jungmann's entire teaching career was spent at Innsbruck, where for a time he also served as rector of the community of Jesuits.

Jungmann is best known for his contributions to Catholic catechetics and liturgical studies. In particular, he is associated with the renewal of the Eucharistic liturgy and served on the Second Vatican Council's commission that produced *Sacrosanctum Concilium*, a document on liturgy and worship, in 1964. He authored many books, including *Liturgical Worship, Christian Prayer through the Centuries, Pastoral Liturgy*, and *The Mass of the Roman Rite*.

Founded in 1865, Ave Maria Press,
a ministry of the Congregation of
Holy Cross, is a Catholic publishing
company that serves the spiritual and
formative needs of the Church and its
schools, institutions, and ministers;
Christian individuals and families; and
others seeking spiritual nourishment.

For a complete listing of titles from

Ave Maria Press

Sorin Books

Forest of Peace

Christian Classics

visit www.avemariapress.com

ave maria press® / Notre Dame, IN 46556
A Ministry of the United States Province of Holy Cross